Dreamweaver™ 2
Bible

Dreamweaver™ 2
Bible

Joseph W. Lowery

IDG Books Worldwide, Inc.
An International Data Group Company

Foster City, CA ✦ Chicago, IL ✦ Indianapolis, IN ✦ New York, NY

Dreamweaver™ 2 Bible

Published by
IDG Books Worldwide, Inc.
An International Data Group Company
919 E. Hillsdale Blvd., Suite 400
Foster City, CA 94404
www.idgbooks.com (IDG Books Worldwide Web site)

ISBN: 0-7645-3322-3

Printed in the United States of America

10 9 8 7 6 5 4 3

1B/RZ/QU/ZZ/FC

Distributed in the United States by IDG Books Worldwide, Inc.

Distributed by CDG Books Canada Inc. for Canada; by Transworld Publishers Limited in the United Kingdom; by IDG Norge Books for Norway; by IDG Sweden Books for Sweden; by Woodslane Pty. Ltd. for Australia; by Woodslane (NZ) Ltd. for New Zealand; by TransQuest Publishers Pte Ltd. for Singapore, Malaysia, Thailand, Indonesia, and Hong Kong; by ICG Muse, Inc. for Japan; by Norma Comunicaciones S.A. for Colombia; by Intersoft for South Africa; by Le Monde en Tique for France; by International Thomson Publishing for Germany, Austria and Switzerland; by Distribuidora Cuspide for Argentina; by Livraria Cultura for Brazil; by Ediciones ZETA S.C.R. Ltda. for Peru; by WS Computer Publishing Corporation, Inc., for the Philippines; by Contemporanea de Ediciones for Venezuela; by Express Computer Distributors for the Caribbean and West Indies; by Micronesia Media Distributor, Inc. for Micronesia; by Grupo Editorial Norma S.A. for Guatemala; by Chips Computadoras S.A. de C.V. for Mexico; by Editorial Norma de Panama S.A. for Panama; by American Bookshops for Finland. Authorized Sales Agent: Anthony Rudkin Associates for the Middle East and North Africa.

For general information on IDG Books Worldwide's books in the U.S., please call our Consumer Customer Service department at 800-762-2974. For reseller information, including discounts and premium sales, please call our Reseller Customer Service department at 800-434-3422.

For information on where to purchase IDG Books Worldwide's books outside the U.S., please contact our International Sales department at 317-596-5530 or fax 317-596-5692.

For consumer information on foreign language translations, please contact our Customer Service department at 800-434-3422, fax 317-596-5692, or e-mail rights@idgbooks.com.

For information on licensing foreign or domestic rights, please phone +1-650-655-3109.

For sales inquiries and special prices for bulk quantities, please contact our Sales department at 650-655-3200 or write to the address above.

For information on using IDG Books Worldwide's books in the classroom or for ordering examination copies, please contact our Educational Sales department at 800-434-2086 or fax 317-596-5499.

For press review copies, author interviews, or other publicity information, please contact our Public Relations department at 650-655-3000 or fax 650-655-3299.

For authorization to photocopy items for corporate, personal, or educational use, please contact Copyright Clearance Center, 222 Rosewood Drive, Danvers, MA 01923, or fax 978-750-4470.

Library of Congress Cataloging-in-Publication Data

Lowery, Joseph (Joseph W.)
   Dreamweaver 2 Bible / Joseph W. Lowery
      p.   cm.
   Includes Index.
   ISBN 0-7645-3322-3 (alk. paper)
    1. Dreamweaver (Computer file) 2. Web sites --
Authoring 3. Web publishing.   I. Title.
TK5105.8885.D74L68   1999
005.7'2 -- dc21
                                     99-19199
                                           CIP

ABOUT IDG BOOKS WORLDWIDE

Welcome to the world of IDG Books Worldwide.

IDG Books Worldwide, Inc., is a subsidiary of International Data Group, the world's largest publisher of computer-related information and the leading global provider of information services on information technology. IDG was founded more than 30 years ago by Patrick J. McGovern and now employs more than 9,000 people worldwide. IDG publishes more than 290 computer publications in over 75 countries. More than 90 million people read one or more IDG publications each month.

Launched in 1990, IDG Books Worldwide is today the #1 publisher of best-selling computer books in the United States. We are proud to have received eight awards from the Computer Press Association in recognition of editorial excellence and three from Computer Currents' First Annual Readers' Choice Awards. Our best-selling ...For Dummies® series has more than 50 million copies in print with translations in 31 languages. IDG Books Worldwide, through a joint venture with IDG's Hi-Tech Beijing, became the first U.S. publisher to publish a computer book in the People's Republic of China. In record time, IDG Books Worldwide has become the first choice for millions of readers around the world who want to learn how to better manage their businesses.

Our mission is simple: Every one of our books is designed to bring extra value and skill-building instructions to the reader. Our books are written by experts who understand and care about our readers. The knowledge base of our editorial staff comes from years of experience in publishing, education, and journalism — experience we use to produce books to carry us into the new millennium. In short, we care about books, so we attract the best people. We devote special attention to details such as audience, interior design, use of icons, and illustrations. And because we use an efficient process of authoring, editing, and desktop publishing our books electronically, we can spend more time ensuring superior content and less time on the technicalities of making books.

You can count on our commitment to deliver high-quality books at competitive prices on topics you want to read about. At IDG Books Worldwide, we continue in the IDG tradition of delivering quality for more than 30 years. You'll find no better book on a subject than one from IDG Books Worldwide.

John Kilcullen
Chairman and CEO
IDG Books Worldwide, Inc.

Steven Berkowitz
President and Publisher
IDG Books Worldwide, Inc.

Eighth Annual Computer Press Awards ≥1992

Ninth Annual Computer Press Awards ≥1993

Tenth Annual Computer Press Awards ≥1994

Eleventh Annual Computer Press Awards ≥1995

Credits

Acquisitions Editor
Debra Williams Cauley

Development Editors
Kathryn J. Duggan
Tracy Brown
Philip Wescott

Technical Editor
Simon White

Copy Editors
Luann Rouff
Michael D. Welch
Victoria Lee

Production
Foster City Production Department

Proofreading and Indexing
York Graphic Services

Cover Design
Murder By Design

About the Author

Joseph W. Lowery has been writing about computers and new technology since 1981. He is the author of the *Dreamweaver Bible* and *Buying Online For Dummies* (IDG Books Worldwide). He has also written books on using the Internet for business and HTML, and has contributed to several books on Microsoft Office. Joseph is currently Webmaster for a variety of sites, including the MCP Office 97 Resource Center; a managed health care organization; an international public relations school; and a bar. Joseph and his wife, dancer/choreographer Debra Wanner, have a daughter, Margot.

For my extended family in appreciation of all their expansive love and concern—Nelee, Gavin, Paul, Louis, Jennifer, Al, and, of course, Cara.

Foreword

I can tell it's been a busy year for all of us. I spend a good chunk of time each week surfing the Web (just ask my wife), and you Web authors have been amazingly busy creating new sites and redesigning existing ones. The Dreamweaver team has been working hard to keep pace with you, releasing 1.0, 1.2, and 2.0 within a year. This means Joseph Lowery has been busy too, having just finished the first version of *Dreamweaver Bible*, only to turn around and begin the next.

Joseph has done his homework thoroughly. To write the most up-to-date and accurate volume, he was a very active participant in our earliest 2.0 beta programs. There he had access to the Dreamweaver engineers, and he made good use of the resource — asking insightful questions and making useful observations. His feedback certainly improved the product, while at the same time making him an expert in the details of Dreamweaver.

As part of his research, he once asked me why we chose the features we did; how did 2.0 come to be? While some of the features seem obvious in retrospect, I never know exactly what a release is going to contain before we all go out and talk with our customers, and read the newsgroups and e-mailed suggestions (if this were HTML, those last two items would be links: `news://forums.macromedia.com` and `mail://wish-dreamweaver@macromedia.com`).

So that's exactly what we did after 1.0 and during the development of 1.2. We went out and visited Web designers and watched them in action. Some used Dreamweaver and we watched what worked and what was still slowing them down. Some didn't use Dreamweaver and we would find out why. We read the notes, both the pleasantly worded and the flames. All the while we would group together similar requests into what would be the feature themes for the release.

For example, it became apparent that many Web pages start out as bitmap images created by graphic artists in tools other than HTML editors. These are then handed off to HTML authors who try to cast the image in terms of bandwidth-efficient HTML. We noticed that as authors tried to accomplish this translation, they had to rapidly switch between viewing the bitmap and working in Dreamweaver — sometimes using two monitors to go faster. Watching this time-consuming task generated the "from comps to pages" theme, a mission to greatly reduce the amount of time it takes to accomplish this sometimes tedious task.

Each theme can generate multiple features. One specific feature for the "from comps to pages" theme is the tracing layer, which enables you to see a semi-transparent image as a background guide when laying out your Web page. Turning a bitmap into a Web page has never been faster.

Choosing which themes and which features to implement is also done in conjunction with Web developers. While we visited customers, we recruited some of them into our Advisory Council. Just as in 1.0, this group helped us prioritize the feature themes and features, making certain we chose those that would help them the most. The group also acted as a touchstone throughout development, making certain the features as coded were actually useful.

Every time we do a release we also like adding in a few features that aren't yet mainstream, but give you room to grow. In 1.0 we added Cascading Style Sheets (CSS) support that allowed for absolutely positioned page elements as well as styled text. While CSS is not currently in use on many Web sites, there was a lot of interest on the part of Web developers in finding out what exactly it was and how to use it.

For 2.0 we decided to greatly expand the extensibility of Dreamweaver. Among other things, you can now do all of the following:

- Create new menu items anywhere in the menu structure using only HTML and JavaScript
- Create new property inspectors, again using HTML and JavaScript
- Add knowledge of new tags to Dreamweaver and specify how they'll be treated
- Add new character encodings to support Web pages in more languages
- Add support for third-party database servers to accurately visualize dynamically created Web pages by having the page bounced off the server prior to rendering in Dreamweaver

While these features are not apparent on the surface, they actually generated the most excitement and e-mail on the beta list. It was fun to watch as our beta testers found out exactly how much was possible to add to the product externally, and began extending it. I hope you agree that it's nice to have something to explore after hours.

But that is all in the past; the future of the Web still beckons and technology questions still abound. Will XML replace HTML? Will the 5.0 browsers really allow for in-depth use of CSS? How will teams work together to create dynamic Web sites? The answers to these questions will come from you, and as they do we hope to work with you on the tools that you need to get your job done faster. Our job is to take out the tedium of yours, to allow more time for creativity. So if you have any ideas about how we can better do that for you, please don't hesitate to send them along, and we'll keep Joseph busy on the next edition of *Dreamweaver Bible*.

Paul Madar
Vice President of Engineering
Dreamweaver Macromedia, Inc.

Preface

Among other accolades, Macromedia's Dreamweaver has one of the most appropriate product names in recent memory. Web page design is a blend of art and craft; whether you're a deadline-driven professional or a vision-filled amateur, Dreamweaver is the perfect tool for many Web designers. Dreamweaver is not only the first Web authoring tool to bring the ease of visual editing to an HTML code-oriented world, it also brings a point-and-click interface to complex JavaScript coding.

To use this book, you only need two items: the Dreamweaver software and a desire to make cutting-edge Web pages. (Actually, you don't even need Dreamweaver to begin; the CD-ROM contains a fully functional demo.) From quick design prototyping to ongoing Web site management, Dreamweaver automates and simplifies much of a Webmaster's workload. Unfortunately, even Dynamic HTML, which Dreamweaver handles elegantly, cannot accomplish all the tasks of a modern Web page. As a result, this book contains step-by-step instructions on how to handle every Web design task — through Dreamweaver's visual interface or its integrated HTML code editors.

Underneath its simple, intuitive interface, Dreamweaver is a complex program that makes high-end Web concepts (Dynamic HTML, Cascading Style Sheets, and JavaScript behaviors) accessible for the first time. The *Dreamweaver 2 Bible* is designed to help you master every nuance of the program. Are you creating a straightforward layout with the visual editor? Do you need to extend Dreamweaver's capabilities by building your own custom objects? With Dreamweaver and this book, you can weave your dreams into reality for the entire world to experience.

What's New in This Edition

If I had to sum up the differences between the earlier versions of Dreamweaver and Dreamweaver 2 in one word, that word would be *productivity*. Major features, such as Dream Templates, Roundtrip XML, and enhanced server connectivity, have been added; and are aimed at increasing a Web designer's total productivity. With Dreamweaver 2, you can simply do more, faster. The *Dreamweaver 2 Bible* has full chapters on the new features dedicated to covering them in detail.

Productivity is the name of the game in e-commerce and database-driven sites as well, and you'll find both areas given an increased focus in Dreamweaver 2. A new part of the book, "Connectivity Through Dreamweaver," explains the why and the how of active content Web pages that form such a growing segment of the Internet today. Need to connect to a database or build an e-commerce site? I'll show you how and explain why one approach is better than another, depending on your situation.

One of Dreamweaver's major advances has been its extensibility. Much of Web creation is a custom, almost personal affair — the more your Web authoring tool can work the way you do, the more productive you'll become. *Dreamweaver 2 Bible* details all of the new and enhanced expansion possibilities: objects, behaviors, commands, Property Inspectors, translators, custom tags, and even C-level Extensions. If you're more interested in using Dreamweaver extensions than building them, I've included a huge range of them on the CD-ROM, courtesy of the leading Dreamweaver developers working today.

Who Should Read This Book?

Dreamweaver attracts a wide range of Web developers. Because it's the first Web authoring tool that doesn't rewrite original code, veteran designers are drawn to using Dreamweaver as their first visual editor. Because it also automates complicated effects, beginning Web designers are interested in Dreamweaver's power and performance. *Dreamweaver 2 Bible* addresses the full spectrum of Web professionals, providing basic information on HTML if you're just starting, as well as advanced tips and tricks for seasoned pros. Moreover, this book is a complete reference for everyone working with Dreamweaver on a daily basis.

What Hardware and Software Do You Need?

Dreamweaver 2 Bible includes coverage of Dreamweaver 2. If you don't own a copy of the program, the CD-ROM contains a demo version for your trial use. Written to be platform-independent, this book covers both Macintosh and Windows 95/98/NT versions of Dreamweaver 2.

Macromedia recommends the following minimum requirements for running Dreamweaver on a Macintosh:

- ✦ Power Macintosh
- ✦ MacOS 7.5 or later
- ✦ 24MB of available RAM
- ✦ 20MB of available disk space
- ✦ Color monitor capable of 800 × 600 resolution
- ✦ CD-ROM drive

Macromedia recommends the following minimum requirements for running Dreamweaver on a Windows system:

- ✦ Intel Pentium processor, 90MHz or equivalent
- ✦ Windows 95/98, NT 4.0 or later
- ✦ 32MB of available RAM
- ✦ 20MB of available disk space
- ✦ 256-color monitor capable of 800 × 600 resolution
- ✦ CD-ROM drive

Please note that these are the minimum requirements. As with all graphics-based design tools, more capability is definitely better for using Dreamweaver, especially in terms of memory and processor speed.

How This Book Is Organized

Dreamweaver 2 Bible can take you from raw beginner to full-fledged professional if read cover-to-cover. However, you're more likely to read each section as needed, taking the necessary information and coming back later. To facilitate this approach, *Dreamweaver 2 Bible* is divided into nine major task-oriented parts. Once you're familiar with Dreamweaver, feel free to skip around the book, using it as a reference guide as you build up your own knowledge base.

The early chapters present the basics, and all chapters contain clearly written steps for the tasks you need to perform. In later chapters, you encounter boxed sections labeled "Dreamweaver Techniques." Dreamweaver Techniques are step-by-step instructions for accomplishing specific Web designer tasks; for example, building an image map that uses rollovers, or eliminating underlines from hyperlinks through Cascading Style Sheets. Naturally, you can also use the Dreamweaver Techniques as stepping-stones for your own explorations into Web page creation.

If you're running Dreamweaver while reading this book, don't forget to use the CD-ROM. An integral element of the book, the CD-ROM offers a vast number of additional Dreamweaver behaviors, objects, commands, browser profiles, and other extensions in addition to relevant code from the book.

Part I: Getting Started with Dreamweaver

Part I begins with an overview of Dreamweaver's philosophy and design. To get the most out of the program, you need to understand the key advantages it offers and the deficiencies it addresses. Part I takes you all the way to setting up your first site.

The opening chapters give you a full reference to the Dreamweaver interface and all of its customizable features. You also learn how you can access Dreamweaver's full-bodied online Help and find additional resources on the Web. Chapter 5 takes you from the consideration of various Web site design models to publishing your finished site on the Internet.

Part II: Using Basic HTML in Dreamweaver

Although Dreamweaver is partly a visual design tool, its roots derive from the language of the Web: HTML. Part II gives you a solid foundation in the basics of HTML, even if you've never seen code. Chapter 6 covers HTML theory, describing how a Web page is constructed and alerting you to some potential pitfalls to look out for.

The three fundamentals of Web pages are text, images, and links. You explore how to incorporate these elements to their fullest extent in Chapters 7, 8, and 9, respectively. Chapter 8, "Inserting Images," also includes a special section on the new integration possibilities with Fireworks 2, as well as one on using animated GIFs. Chapter 10 examines another fundamental HTML option: lists. You study the list in all of its forms: numbered lists, bulleted lists, definition lists, nested lists, and more.

Part III: Incorporating Advanced HTML

Part III begins to investigate some of the more advanced structural elements of HTML as implemented in Dreamweaver. Chapter 11 examines the various uses of tables — from a clear presentation of data to organizing entire Web pages. Here you learn how to use Dreamweaver 2's greatly enhanced visual table editing capabilities to resize and reshape your HTML tables quickly.

Chapter 12 is devoted to image maps and shows how to use Dreamweaver's built-in Image Map Editor to create client-side image maps. The chapter also explains how you can build server-side image maps and demonstrates a technique for creating image map rollovers. Forms are the focus of Chapter 13, where you find all you need to know about gathering information from your Web page visitors. Chapter 14 investigates the somewhat complex world of frames — and shows how Dreamweaver has greatly simplified the task of building and managing these multifile creations. You also learn how to handle more advanced design tasks such as updating multiple frames with just one click.

Part IV: Extending HTML Through Dreamweaver

HTML is a language with extensive capabilities for expanding its own power. Part IV begins with Chapter 15, which introduces you to the world of CGI programs, external plug-ins, Java applets, ActiveX controls, and scripting with JavaScript and VBScript. You also find techniques for ensuring a secure middle ground of cross-browser compatibility in the ongoing browser wars.

With its own set of objects and behaviors, Dreamweaver complements HTML's extensibility. Chapter 16 shows you how you can use the built-in objects to accomplish most of your Web page-layout chores quickly and efficiently — and when you're ready for increased automation, the chapter explains how to build your own custom objects. Chapter 17 offers an in-depth look at the capabilities of Dreamweaver behaviors. Each standard behavior is covered in detail with step-by-step instructions. If you're JavaScript-savvy, then Chapter 18 gives you the material you need to construct your own behaviors and reduce your day-to-day workload. Finally, Chapter 19 explores the brave new world of Dreamweaver extensibility, with complete coverage of using and building commands as well as custom tags, translators, and C-level Extensions.

Part V: Adding Multimedia Elements

In recent years, the Web has moved from a relatively static display of text and simple images to a full-blown multimedia circus with streaming video, background music, and interactive animations. Part V contains the power tools for incorporating various media files into your Web site.

Chapter 20 covers digital video in its many forms: downloadable AVI files, streaming RealVideo displays, and panoramic QuickTime movies. Chapter 21 focuses on digital audio, with coverage of standard WAV and MIDI sound files as well as the newer streaming audio formats. A special section covers the exciting possibilities offered by Beatnik and the new Rich Music Format, with new coverage of the Beatnik ActionSet.

In addition to Dreamweaver, Macromedia is perhaps best known for one other contribution to Web multimedia: Shockwave. Chapter 22 explores the possibilities offered by incorporating Shockwave and Flash movies into Dreamweaver-designed Web pages, and includes everything you need to know about configuring MIME types. You also find step-by-step instructions for building Shockwave inline controls and playing Shockwave movies in frame-based Web pages.

Part VI: Dynamic HTML and Dreamweaver

Dynamic HTML brought a new world of promises to Web designers — promises that went largely unfulfilled until Dreamweaver was released. Part VI of *Dreamweaver 2 Bible* examines this brave new world of pixel-perfect positioning, layers that fly in and then disappear as if by magic, and Web sites that can change their look and feel at the click of the mouse.

Chapter 23 provides an overview of Dynamic HTML and explores the different implementations by the major browsers — with new information on how to embed cross-platform, cross-browser fonts in your Web pages. Chapter 24 takes a detailed look at the elegance of Cascading Style Sheets and offers techniques for accomplishing the most frequently requested tasks, such as creating an external style sheet. Much of the advantages of Dynamic HTML come from the use of layers, which enable absolute positioning of page elements, visibility control, and a sense of depth. You discover how to handle all of these layer capabilities and more in Chapter 25. Chapter 26 focuses on timelines, which have the potential to take your Web page into the fourth dimension. The chapter concludes with a blow-by-blow description of how to create a multiscreen slide show, complete with layers that fly in and out on command.

Part VII: Creating Next-Generation Code with Dreamweaver

The Web is one fast-moving train, and if you're not running when you try to board, you're going to get left behind. Keeping up with the latest technological developments is essential for working Web designers. Sooner or later, your clients are going to demand the cutting-edge, and Part VII is here to help you create the sharpest sites online.

I can't think of any new technology on the Web that has so quickly gained the widespread acceptance that XML has. In a nutshell, XML (short for Extensible Markup Language) enables you to create your own custom tags that make the most sense for your business or profession. While XML doesn't enjoy full browser support as of this writing, it's only a matter of time — and little time at that. Chapter 27 shows you how to apply this fast-approaching technology of tomorrow in Dreamweaver today.

Virtually every day another breakthrough in Web multimedia is announced — and through it's open-ended architecture, Dreamweaver 2 is ready to support them all. Macromedia has partnered with several leaders in this ever-growing field: Real Networks, IBM, and Hewlett-Packard, to name a few. Chapter 28 delves into their contributions and demonstrates how you can use their technology to enhance your site's interactivity and razzmatazz.

Part VIII: Connectivity through Dreamweaver

The Web has become one vast information junkie: the more data you put online now, the more information required tomorrow. Part of this tremendous growth is due to the explosion of electronic commerce (e-commerce) — the Internet is almost at the point where if you can buy it, you can buy it online. To manage this overwhelming flood of info, Web designers are turning to database-driven pages and sites. Dreamweaver 2 now offers numerous connectivity and e-commerce solutions, covered in Part VIII, to help Web designers create such active content.

Databases are simple — if you're a database programmer. Most Web designer's aren't, however, and Chapter 29 takes special care to explain database basics as well as detail-specific Dreamweaver solutions now in place. In Chapter 30, you'll learn how you can use Dreamweaver to establish an e-commerce site — whether you're selling fewer than 10 items or more than 3,000.

Part IX: Web Site Management under Dreamweaver

Although Web page design gets all the glory, Web site management pays the bills. In Part IX, you see how Dreamweaver makes this essential part of any Webmaster's day easier to handle. Chapter 31 describes Dreamweaver's built-in tools for maintaining cross- and backward-browser compatibility. A Dreamweaver Technique demonstrates a browser-checking Web page that automatically directs users to appropriate links.

Chapter 32 covers the Library, which can significantly reduce any Webmaster's workload. Chapter 33 explains all you need to know about managing your working Web site through Dreamweaver's primary management tool, the Site Window — including such innovative features as file check-in/check-out and Dreamweaver 2's new Site Map. Chapter 34 rounds out Part IX with a look at the new Dream Templates and how they can speed up production while ensuring a unified look and feel across your Web site.

Appendixes

Appendix A describes the contents of the CD-ROM that accompanies this book.

Dreamweaver comes with a fully functional internal HTML editor, and the full version of the program is bundled with two industrial-strength external HTML editors: BBEdit for the Macintosh and HomeSite for Windows. Although both editors offer extensive online help, an abbreviated user's manual for both programs appears in Appendixes B and C. Each appendix also has detailed information on integrating the external editors with Dreamweaver.

One special area of the Web — online learning — has experienced so much explosive growth that it has been granted its own special version of Dreamweaver: Dreamweaver 2 Attain. Appendix D dives into this unique application and provides an overview of its most vital features.

Conventions Used in This Book

The following conventions are used throughout this book.

Windows and Macintosh conventions

Because *Dreamweaver 2 Bible* is a cross-platform book, it gives instructions for both Windows and Macintosh users when keystrokes for a particular task differ.

Throughout this book, the Windows keystrokes are given first; the Macintosh are given second in parentheses, as follows:

To undo an action, press Ctrl-Z (Command-Z).

The first action instructs Windows users to press the Ctrl and Z keys in combination, and the second action (in parentheses) instructs Macintosh users to press the Command and Z keys together.

Key combinations

When you are instructed to press two or more keys simultaneously, each key in the combination is separated by a hyphen. For example:

Ctrl-Alt-T (Command-Option-T)

The preceding tells you to press the three listed keys for your system at the same time. You can also hold down one or more keys and then press the final key. Release all the keys at the same time.

Mouse instructions

When instructed to click an item, you must move the mouse pointer to the specified item and click the mouse button once. Windows users use the left mouse button unless otherwise instructed. Double-click means clicking the mouse button twice in rapid succession.

When instructed to select an item, you may click it once as previously described. If you are selecting text or multiple objects, you must click the mouse button once, hold it down, and then move the mouse to a new location. The item or items selected invert color. To clear the selection, click once anywhere on the Web page.

Menu commands

When instructed to select a command from a menu, you see the menu and the command separated by an arrow symbol. For example, when instructed to execute the Open command from the File menu, you see the notation File ⇨ Open. Some menus use submenus, in which case you see an arrow for each submenu, as follows: Insert ⇨ Form Object ⇨ Text Field.

Typographical conventions

Italic type is used for new terms and for emphasis. **Boldface** type is used for text that you need to type directly from the computer keyboard.

Code

A special typeface indicates HTML or other code, as demonstrated in the following example:

```
<html>
<head>
<title>Untitled Document</title>
</head>
<body bgcolor="#FFFFFF">
</body>
</html>
```

This code font is also used within paragraphs to designate HTML tags, attributes, and values such as <body>, bgcolor, and #FFFFFF. All HTML tags are presented in lowercase, as written by Dreamweaver, although browsers are not generally case-sensitive in terms of HTML.

The (¬) character at the end of a code line means you should type the next line of code before pressing the Enter (Return) key.

Navigating Through This Book

Various signposts and icons are located throughout *Dreamweaver 2 Bible* for your assistance. Each chapter begins with an overview of its information, and ends with a quick summary.

Icons are placed in the text to indicate important or especially helpful items. Here's a list of the icons and their functions:

 Tip Tips provide you with extra knowledge that separates the novice from the pro.

 Note Notes provide additional or critical information and technical data on the current topic.

 New Feature Sections marked with a New Feature icon detail an innovation introduced in Dreamweaver 2.

 Cross-Reference Cross-Reference icons indicate places where you can find more information on a particular topic.

 Caution The Caution icon is your warning of a potential problem or pitfall.

The On the CD-ROM icon indicates that the CD-ROM contains a related file in the given folder.

Further Information

You can find more help for specific problems and questions by investigating several Web sites. Macromedia's own Dreamweaver Web site is the best place to start:

```
http://www.dreamweaver.com
```

I heartily recommend that you visit and participate in the official Dreamweaver newsgroup:

```
news://forums.macromedia.com/macromedia.dreamweaver
```

You're also invited to visit my Web site for book updates and new developments:

```
http://www.idest.com/dreamweaver
```

You can also e-mail me:

```
jlowery@idest.com
```

I can't promise instantaneous turnaround, but I answer all my mail to the best of my abilities.

Acknowledgments

Whoever said "writing is a lonely business" never wrote a computer book. Sometimes I feel like the point man of a large swing band filled with seasoned pros. All the folks in this group can both play their parts exceedingly well, supporting the main theme, and are ready to solo at the drop of a hat. And now it's time to introduce, and applaud, the band. . . .

If this book feels richer, more dense in detail (not to mention a pound or two heavier) than the previous edition, a great deal of the credit goes to my technical editor, Simon White. Simon has been absolutely top-notch in providing insightful background comments, on-the-money tips, and real-world work experience. Simon is a Macromedia evangelist and routinely offers some of the best Web authoring advice around via the Dreamweaver newsgroup. A special thank-you goes out to his ace Web design shop in San Francisco, MediaFear, for letting me borrow him for a few days . . . oh, all right, months.

You can always tell someone who has only read about the Internet when they despair about how the Internet increases our isolation. Baloney. I've got more colleagues and friends around the world now than I ever did. The Dreamweaver community has been especially gracious and giving of their time and expertise to further the goals of this book. I'd like to express my gratitude to the slowly growing pool of developers who have taken their valuable time to create Dreamweaver extensions and offer them freely to the public. If you've spent any time haunting the Dreamweaver newsgroups, you know their names: Andrew Wooldridge, Massimo Foti, Jaro von Flocken, Brendan Dawes, Taylor, and Nadav. I'm particularly grateful because all of these authors (and many others) have kindly permitted their work to be included in this book's CD-ROM. I now owe a good 40 percent of the user base a drink.

Macromedia has been wonderfully supportive of my efforts to bring out the most detailed Bible possible. I can only imagine the collective groan that goes up when yet another e-mailed question from me — with a deadline, no less — arrives. Warm thanks and heartfelt appreciation to Dave George, Sho Kuwamoto, Hava Edelstein, Heidi Bauer, Darrick Brown, and all the other Dreamweaver engineers and techs who opened up their brains for me to pick. A special "Gawd, what would I have done without you?" award goes to Lori Hylan for help above and beyond the call of duty. I'd also like to single out the Dreamweaver Technical Support staff — and particularly Calvin Kwan — whose answers to users' queries have been a tremendous source of information. And who's that in the back of the room? Macromedia management — in the form of David Mendels, Beth Davis, Matt Brown, and others — has opened many, many doors to me and should stand up and take a bow. And finally, I and the rest of the Dreamweaver community are beholden to

Kevin Lynch and Paul Madar for their vision and hard work in bringing this dream home.

I owe another tip of the hat to Macromedia for partnering with such great companies — and then giving me their direct telephone numbers. Larry Concannon from Allaire has been extremely supportive of this book since the first edition was just a gleam in my eyes, and as his HomeSite and Cold Fusion continue to evolve and grow, I hope our friendship will as well. I owe Michael Senechal and Renata Rubinsztajn of Pervasive Software a debt of gratitude also; I greatly appreciate the insider's viewpoint they allowed me to have. And to an old partner of mine, Tom Holaday, a heartfelt thanks for helping me to explore the murkier depths of C-level Extensions.

To me, there's no higher compliment than to be told that I know my business. Well, the folks I work with at IDG Books Worldwide sure know their business: acquisitions editor Debra Williams Cauley; development editors Tracy Brown and Chip Wescott; copy editors Luann Rouff and Michael Welch, and all the additional support staff. I'd like to particularly thank my pick-up-the-ball-and-run-with-it development editor, Kathi Duggan, who has done an excellent job of shaping this work and making it better than it was before. I also greatly appreciate the work contributed by Debbie Stoller for its professionalism and clarity. And to someone whose business is to know my business, a double thank-you with a cherry on top for my agent, Laura Belt of Adler & Robin Books.

One last note of appreciation — for all the people who took a chance with some of their hard-earned money and bought the first edition of this book. That small sound you hear in the background is me applauding you as thanks for your support. I hope my efforts continue to be worthy.

Contents at a Glance

Contents

Part IV: Extending HTML Through Dreamweaver   393

Chapter 15: Accessing External Programs 395

Chapter 16: Creating and Using Objects 419

Part V: Adding Multimedia Elements   559

Part IX: Web Site Management Under Dreamweaver 825

Chapter 31: Maximizing Browser Targeting 827

Chapter 32: Using the Repeating Elements Library 849

Chapter 33: Publishing Via Site FTP 867

Getting Started with Dreamweaver

◆ ◆ ◆ ◆

◆ ◆ ◆ ◆

What Is Dreamweaver?

Dreamweaver, by Macromedia, is a professional Web site development program. Among its many distinctions, Dreamweaver is the first Web development program to take advantage of the capabilities of the latest generation of browsers, making it easy for developers to use advanced features such as Cascading Style Sheets and Dynamic HTML.

Dreamweaver is truly a tool designed by Web developers for Web developers. Designed from the ground up to work the way professional Web designers do, Dreamweaver speeds site construction and streamlines site maintenance. Throughout this chapter you'll see the philosophical underpinnings of the program and get a better sense of how Dreamweaver blends traditional HTML with cutting-edge techniques. You'll also learn some of the advanced features that Dreamweaver offers to help you manage a Web site.

The Real World of Dreamweaver

Dreamweaver is a program very much rooted in the real world. For example, Dreamweaver recognizes the problem of incompatible browser commands and addresses it by producing cross-browser compatible code. Dreamweaver even includes browser-specific HTML validation so you can see how your existing or new code works in a particular browser.

Dreamweaver 2 extends the real-world concept to the workplace. Additions such as Dream templates streamline the production and maintenance process on large Web sites. Dreamweaver's advanced layers-to-tables features make it possible to quickly position content during the design stage, while keeping your pages backwardly browser-compatible when published. Dreamweaver 2's new Commands capability enables Web designers to automate their most difficult Web creations.

Integrated visual and text editors

In the early days of the World Wide Web, most developers "hand-coded" their Web pages using simple text editors such as Notepad and SimpleText. The second generation of Web authoring tools brought visual design or WYSIWYG ("what you see is what you get") editors to market. What these products furnished in ease of layout they lacked in completeness of code. Professional Web developers found they still needed to hand-code their Web pages, even with the most sophisticated WYSIWYG editor.

Dreamweaver acknowledges this reality and has integrated a superb visual editor with a number of text editors. You can work with Dreamweaver's internal HTML Inspector or a dedicated external editor. Figure 1-1 shows Dreamweaver's visual editor and text editor working together. Any change made in the visual editor is instantly reflected into the text editor and vice versa. While Dreamweaver lets you work with any text editor you like, it includes both BBEdit for Macintosh developers and HomeSite for Microsoft Windows developers. Dreamweaver enables a natural, dynamic flow between the visual and text editors.

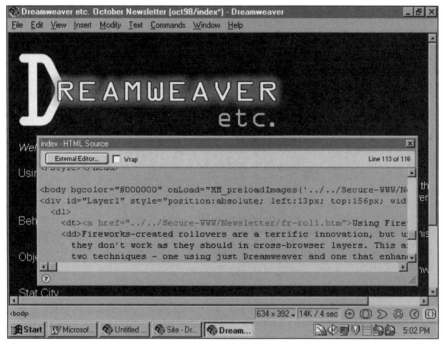

Figure 1-1: Dreamweaver lets you work with both a visual WYSIWYG editor and an HTML text editor simultaneously.

Roundtrip HTML

Most Web authoring programs modify any code that passes through their system — inserting returns, removing indents, adding <meta> tags, uppercasing commands, and so forth. Dreamweaver's programmers understand and respect that Web developers all have their own particular coding styles. An underlying concept, Roundtrip HTML, ensures that you can move back and forth between the visual editor and any HTML text editor without your code being rewritten.

Web site maintenance tools

The Dreamweaver creators also understand that creating a site is only a part of the Webmaster's job. Maintaining the Web site can be an ongoing, time-consuming chore. Dreamweaver simplifies the job with a group of site management tools, including a library of repeating elements and a file-locking capability for easy team updates.

New Feature

In Dreamweaver 2, Web site maintenance has improved dramatically — and most graphically. Take note of the new Site Map feature that enables you to view your Web site structure at a glance, and to access any file for modification. Links are now updated automatically, or are under user control, if a file moves from one directory to another. And now, not only can you access a library of repeating elements to be inserted in the page, you can define templates to control the entire look and feel of a Web site — and modify a single template to update all the pages, sitewide.

The Dreamweaver Interface

When creating a Web page, Webmasters do two things over and over: they insert an element — whether text, image, or layer — and then they modify it. Dreamweaver excels at such Web page creation. The Dreamweaver workspace combines a series of windows, palettes, and inspectors to make the process as fluid as possible, thereby speeding up the Webmaster's work.

Easy text entry

Although much of the World Wide Web's glitz comes from multimedia elements such as images and sound, Web pages are primarily a text-based medium. Dreamweaver recognizes this and makes the text cursor the default tool. To add text, just click in Dreamweaver's main workspace — the document window — and start typing. As shown in Figure 1-2, the Text Property Inspector lets you change characteristics of the text such as the size, font, position, or color.

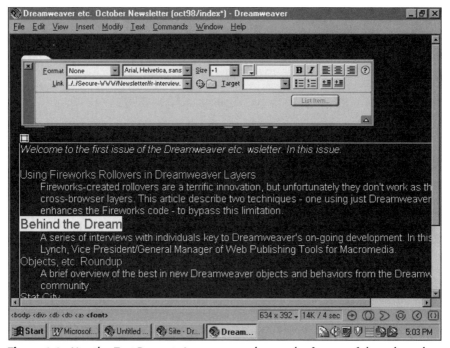

Figure 1-2: Use the Text Property Inspector to change the format of the selected text.

One-stop object modification

You can select Web page elements other than text from the Objects Palette. Adding a picture to a Web page is as easy as clicking the Insert Image button from the Objects Palette. Dreamweaver asks you to select the file for the image, and a placeholder appears in your current cursor position. Once your graphic is on screen, selecting it brings up the appropriate Property Inspector to enable you to make modifications. The same technique holds true for any other inserted element — from horizontal rules to Shockwave Flash movies.

Complete custom environment

Dreamweaver lets you customize your workspace to suit you best. A handy Launcher opens and closes various windows, palettes, and inspectors, all of which are movable. Just drag them wherever you want them on screen. Want to see your page by itself? You can hide all windows at the touch of a function button; press it again and your controls are revealed.

Dreamweaver's customization capabilities extend even further. If you find that you are inserting something over and over, such as a QuickTime video or .wav sound file, you can add that element to your Objects Palette. Dreamweaver even lets you add a specific element, a "Home" button for example, to the Objects Palette. In fact, you can add entire categories of objects if you like.

Cross-Reference For more information on customizing your Objects Palette, see Chapter 16, "Creating and Using Objects."

Simple selection process

As with most modern layout programs, in order to modify anything in Dreamweaver you must select it first. The usual process for this is to click an object to highlight it, or to click and drag over a block of text to select it. Dreamweaver adds another option for this process with the Tag Selector feature. Click anywhere on a Web page under construction and then look at Dreamweaver's status bar. The applicable HTML tags appear on the left side of the status bar.

In the example shown in Figure 1-3, the Tag Selector shows

```
<body> <div> <table> <tr> <td> <p>
```

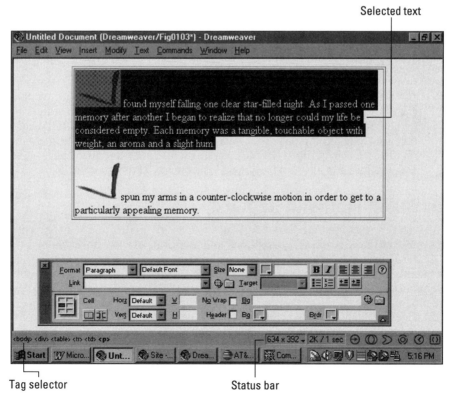

Figure 1-3: Choosing the `<p>` tag in Dreamweaver's Tag Selector is a quick and easy way to highlight the current paragraph on your Web page.

Click one of these tags and the corresponding elements are selected on your page, ready for modification. The Tag Selector is a terrific timesaver; throughout this book I'll point out how you can use it under various circumstances.

Enhanced layout options

Dreamweaver works much more like a desktop publishing program than do other visual HTML editors. Today's browser capabilities permit images and text to be placed in specific locations on the Web page—a concept known as *absolute positioning*. To enable you to take full advantage of this new power, Dreamweaver includes both rulers and grids. You can specify the type of measurement to be used (inches, pixels, or centimeters), as well as the spacing and appearance of the grid lines. You can even have objects snap to the grid for easy alignment.

Cross-Reference   To find out more about absolute positioning, see Chapter 25, "Working with Layers."

Active Content Preview

In order for a browser to display anything beyond standard format graphics, a plug-in is generally required. Plug-ins extend the capability of most browsers to show animations, play music, or even explore 3D worlds. Dreamweaver 2 is one of the first Web authoring tools to enable you to design your Web page with an active plug-in playing the extended file; with all other systems you have to preview your page in a browser to see the active content.

New Feature   The active content feature in Dreamweaver 2 enables the playback of plug-ins such as Macromedia Flash, Shockwave, and others. However, this feature extends far beyond that. Many Web pages are coded with *Server-Side Includes*, which traditionally required the page to be viewed through a Web server. Dreamweaver 2 translates much of the server-side information so that the entire page—Server-Side Includes and all—can be viewed in its entirety at design time.

Extended Find and Replace

The Web is a very fluid medium. Pages are constantly in flux and because changes are relatively easy to effect, corrections and additions are the norm. Quite often a Web designer needs to update or alter an existing page—or series of pages. Dreamweaver 2's new enhanced Find and Replace feature is a real power tool when it comes to making modifications.

New Feature   Find and Replace now works in the Document Window as well as the HTML Inspector to alter code and regular content. Moreover, changes are applicable to the current page, the working site, selected Web pages, or an entire folder of pages, regardless of the number. Complex find and replace queries can be stored and retrieved later to further automate your work.

Up-to-Date HTML Standards

Most Web pages are created in HyperText Markup Language (HTML). This programming language — really a series of tags that modify a text file — is standardized by an organization known as the World Wide Web Consortium (http://www.w3.org). Each new release of HTML incorporates an enhanced set of commands and features. The current version, HTML 4, is recognized by the majority of browsers in use today. Dreamweaver writes clear, easy-to-follow, real-world HTML 4 code whenever you insert or modify an element in the visual editor.

Straightforward text and graphics support

Text is a basic building block of any Web page, and Dreamweaver makes formatting your text a snap. Once you've inserted your text, either by typing it in directly or pasting it in from another program, you can change its appearance. You can use the generic HTML formats, such as the H1 through H6 headings and their relative sizes, or you can use font families and exact point sizes.

Chapter 7, "Adding Text to Your Web Page," shows you how to work with text in Dreamweaver.

Additional text support in Dreamweaver enables you to add both numbered and bulleted lists to your Web page. The Text Property Inspector gives you buttons for both kinds of lists as well as easy alignment control. Some elements, including lists, offer extended options. In Dreamweaver, clicking the Property Inspector's expander arrow opens a section in which you can access additional controls.

Graphics are handled in much the same easy-to-use manner. Select the image or its placeholder to enable the Image Property Inspector. From there, you can modify any available attributes, including the image's source, its width or height, and its alignment on the page. Need to touch up your image? Send it to your favorite graphics program with just a click of the Edit Image button.

You'll learn all about adding and modifying Dreamweaver images — including Dreamweaver 2's new integration capabilities with Macromedia's Fireworks 2 — in Chapter 8, "Inserting Images."

Enhanced table capabilities

Other features — standard, yet more advanced — are similarly straightforward in Dreamweaver. Tables are a key component in today's Web pages, and Dreamweaver gives you full control over all their functionality. Dreamweaver changes the work of resizing the column or row of a table, previously a tedious hand-coding task, into an easy click-and-drag motion. Likewise, you can delete all the width and height values from a table with the click of a button. Figure 1-4 shows the Table Property Inspector, which centralizes many of these options in Dreamweaver 2.

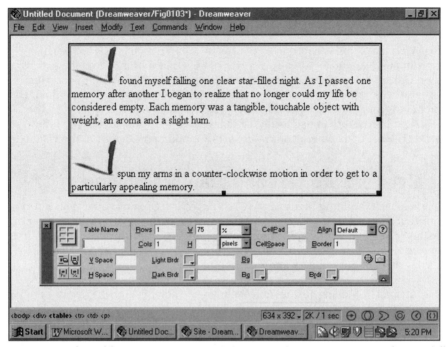

Figure 1-4: The Table Property Inspector is just one of Dreamweaver's paths to a full range of control over the appearance of your table.

New Feature   Tables are greatly enhanced in Dreamweaver 2. Now, font changes can be applied to any number of selected cells, rows, or columns. New commands enable you to automatically format or sort a table as well.

Easy form entry

Forms, the basic vehicle for Web page data exchange, are just as easy to implement as tables in Dreamweaver. Switch to the Forms panel of the Objects Palette and insert any of the available elements: text boxes, radio buttons, check boxes, and even pop-up menus or scrolling lists. With the Validate Form behavior, you can easily specify any field as a required field and even check to ensure that the requested type of information has been entered.

Click-and-drag frame setup

Frames, which enable separate Web pages to be viewed on a single screen, are often considered one of the most difficult HTML techniques to master. Dreamweaver employs a click-and-drag method for establishing your frame outlines. After you've set up your frame structure, open the Frame Inspector (see Figure 1-5) to select any frame and modify it with the Property Inspector. Dreamweaver writes the necessary code for linking all the HTML files in a frameset, no matter how many Web pages are used.

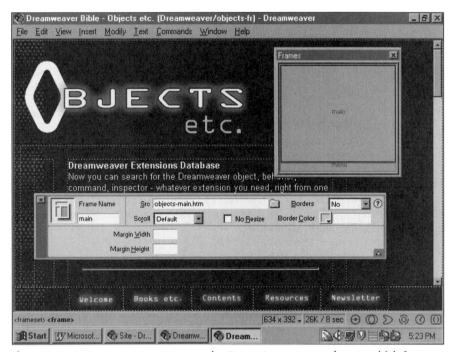

Figure 1-5: In Dreamweaver you use the Frame Inspector to choose which frame you want to modify through the Property Inspector.

Cross-Reference For more information on creating frame-based Web pages, see Chapter 14, "Using Frames and Framesets."

Multimedia enhancements

Dreamweaver enables you to drop in any number of multimedia extensions, plug-ins, applets, or controls. Just click the appropriate button on the Objects Palette and modify with the Property Inspector. Two multimedia elements, Shockwave movies and Flash files — both from Macromedia — warrant special consideration in Macromedia's Dreamweaver. When you insert either of these objects, Dreamweaver automatically includes the necessary HTML code to ensure the widest browser acceptance, and you can edit all the respective properties.

New Feature Macromedia has formed partnerships with numerous cutting-edge multimedia companies such as RealNetworks, IBM, and Headspace. Dreamweaver 2 introduces some of the fruits of those partnerships: custom objects that enable complex images, audio, and presentations to be easily inserted and displayed in Web pages.

Next-Generation Features

Dreamweaver was among the first Web authoring tools to work with the capabilities brought in by the 4.0 generation of browsers. Both Netscape Communicator 4.0 and Microsoft Internet Explorer 4.0 include variations of Dynamic HTML (DHTML). Moreover, both of these browsers adhere to the Cascading Style Sheet (CSS) standards, with support for absolute and relative positioning. Dreamweaver gives Web developers an interface that takes these advanced possibilities and makes them realities.

3D layers

One particular Dynamic HTML feature enables Dreamweaver to be called "the first 3D Web authoring tool." Until now, Web pages existed on a two-dimensional plane — images and text could only be placed side-by-side. Dreamweaver supports control of Dynamic HTML *layers*, meaning that objects can be placed in front of or behind other objects. Layers can contain text, graphics, links, controls — you can even nest one layer inside another.

You create a layer in Dreamweaver by clicking the Layer button on the Objects Palette. Once created, layers can be positioned anywhere on the page by clicking and dragging the selection handle. As with other Dreamweaver objects, you can modify a layer through the Property Inspector.

Cross-Reference   Detailed information on using Dynamic HTML in Dreamweaver starts in Chapter 23, "What's Dynamic HTML?"

Animated objects

Not only can objects in layers be positioned anywhere on the Web page during its creation, they can also be moved when the page is viewed. Dreamweaver takes this capability and, with the addition of its Timeline Inspector, becomes the first *4D* Web authoring tool! The Timeline Inspector, shown in Figure 1-6, is designed along the lines of Macromedia's world-class multimedia creation program, Director. With timelines, you can control a layer's position, size, 3D placement, and even visibility on a frame-by-frame basis.

New Feature   With Dreamweaver 2, you no longer have to plot a layer's path on a timeline — now you can just draw it using the Record Path of Layer feature.

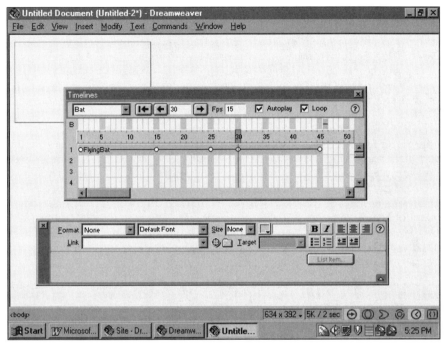

Figure 1-6: Use the Timeline Inspector to animate objects in layers using Dreamweaver's advanced Dynamic HTML features.

Dynamic style updates

Dreamweaver completely supports the Cascading Style Sheets (CSS) specification agreed upon by the World Wide Web Consortium. CSS gives Web designers more flexible control over almost every element on their Web pages. Dreamweaver applies CSS abilities as if they were styles in a word processor. For example, you can make all the ⟨h1⟩ tags blue, italic, and in small caps. If your site's color scheme changes, you can make all the ⟨h1⟩ tags red — and you can do this throughout your Web site with one command. Dreamweaver gives you style control over type, background, blocks, boxes, borders, lists, and positioning.

Dreamweaver enables you to change styles online as well as offline. By linking a CSS change to a user-driven event such as moving the mouse, text can be highlighted or de-emphasized, screen areas can light up, and figures can even be animated. And it can all be done without repeated trips to the server or huge file downloads.

Cross-Reference   Details on using CSS begin in Chapter 24, "Building Style Sheet Web Pages."

JavaScript behaviors

Through the development of JavaScript behaviors, Dreamweaver combines the power of JavaScript with the ease of a drag-and-drop interface. A *behavior* is defined as a combination of an event and an action—whenever your Web page user does something and then something else happens, that's a behavior. What makes behaviors extremely useful is that they require no programming whatsoever.

Behaviors are JavaScript-based, and this is significant because JavaScript is supported to varying degrees by existing browsers. Dreamweaver has simplified the task of identifying which JavaScript command works with a particular browser. You simply select the Web page element that you want to use to control the action, and open the Behavior Inspector from the Launcher. As shown in Figure 1-7, Dreamweaver lets you pick a JavaScript command that works with all browsers or a subset of browsers or one browser in particular. Next, you choose from a full list of available actions, such as go to a URL, play a sound, pop up a message, or start an animation. You can assign multiple actions and even determine when they occur.

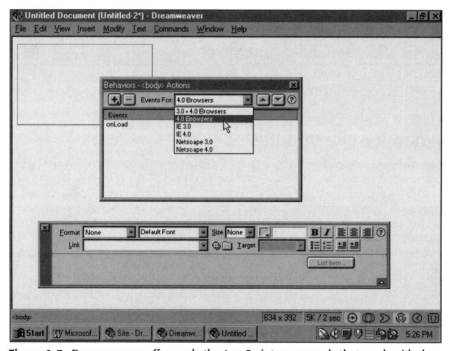

Figure 1-7: Dreamweaver offers only the JavaScript commands that work with the browser you specify.

Cross-Reference

For complete details on working with JavaScript behaviors, see Chapter 17, "Using Behaviors."

Roundtrip XML

A new type of markup language has excited a wide cross-section of Web designers, intranet developers, and corporate users. XML, which stands for *Extensible Markup Language*, has piqued the interest of many because of its underlying customizable nature. With XML, tags are created to describe the *use* of the information, rather than its appearance.

New Feature

Dreamweaver 2 is capable of exporting and importing XML tags, no matter what the tag definition. As XML grows in popularity, Dreamweaver is ready to handle the work. To learn more about XML and its use in Dreamweaver, see Chapter 27, "Extending with XML."

Program Extensibility

One of Dreamweaver's primary strengths is its extensibility. Virtually no two Web sites are alike, either in their design or execution. With such a tremendous variety of end results, the more flexible a Web authoring tool, the more useful it is to a wider group of designers. When it was introduced, Dreamweaver broke new ground with objects and behaviors that were easily customizable. Now, Dreamweaver 2 lengthens its lead with custom Commands, Translators, and Property Inspectors. The basic underpinnings of Dreamweaver can even be extended with the C-Level Extensibilty options.

Objects and behaviors

In Dreamweaver parlance, an object is a bit of HTML code that represents a specific image or HTML tag such as a `<table>` or a `<form>`. Dreamweaver's objects are completely open to user customization, or even out-and-out creation. If you'd rather your tables open at 100% width instead of the standard 75%, you can easily make that modification to the Table object file — right from within Dreamweaver — and every subsequent table is inserted as you'd prefer.

Objects are a terrific timesaving device, essentially enabling you to drop in significant blocks of HTML code at the click of a mouse. Likewise, Dreamweaver behaviors enable even the most novice Web designer to insert complex JavaScript functions designed to propel the pages to the cutting edge. Dreamweaver ships with a full array of standard behaviors — but that's only the tip of the behavior iceberg. Because behaviors, too, are customizable and can be built by anyone with a working knowledge of JavaScript, many Dreamweaver designers have created custom behaviors and made them publicly available.

On the CD-ROM

You'll find a large assortment of custom objects, behaviors, and commands included on the CD-ROM that accompanies this book.

Commands

Objects and behaviors are great ways to help build the final result of a Web page, but what about automating the work of producing that page? Dreamweaver 2 introduces Commands, which are generally used to modify the existing page and streamline production. A great example is the Sort Table command, standard with Dreamweaver 2. If you've ever had to sort a large table by hand—meticulously moving data, one row at a time—you'll appreciate the power of commands the first time you alphabetize or otherwise re-sort a table using this option.

New Feature

Commands hold a great promise—they are, in effect, more powerful than either objects or behaviors combined. In fact, some of the more complex objects, such as the new Rollover Image object, are actually commands. Commands can also extract information sitewide and offer a very powerful programmable language within Dreamweaver.

Custom Tags, Translators, and Property Inspectors

In Dreamweaver 2, almost every part of the user interface can now be customized—including the tags themselves. Once you've developed your custom, third-party tags, you can display and modify their current properties with a custom Property Inspector. Moreover, if your custom tags include content not typically shown in Dreamweaver's Document Window, a custom Translator can be built, enabling the content to be displayed.

New Feature

Programs like Dreamweaver are generally built in the programming language called C or C++, which must be compiled before it is used. Generally, the basic functions of a C program are frozen solid; there's no way you can extend them. This is not the case with Dreamweaver 2, however. The most current version of Dreamweaver offers a C-Level Extensibility that permits programmers to create libraries to install new functionality into the program. Translators, for example, generally rely on new C libraries to enable content to be displayed in Dreamweaver that could not be shown otherwise. Companies can use the C-Level Extensibility feature to integrate Dreamweaver into their existing workflow and maximize productivity.

Site Management Tools

Long after your killer Web site is launched, you'll find yourself continually updating and revising it. For this reason, site *management* tools are as important as site creation tools are to a Web authoring program. Dreamweaver delivers on both counts.

Object Libraries

In addition to site management functions that have become traditional, such as FTP publishing, Dreamweaver adds a whole new class of functionality called *Libraries*.

One of the truisms of Web page development is that if you repeat an element across your site, you're sure to have to change it — on every page. Dreamweaver Libraries eliminate that drudgery.

You can define almost anything as a Library element: a paragraph of text, an image, a link, a table, a form, a Java applet, an ActiveX control, and so on. Just choose the item and open the Library palette (see Figure 1-8). Once you've created the Library entry, you can reuse it throughout your Web site. Each Web site can have its own Library, and you can copy entries from one Library to another.

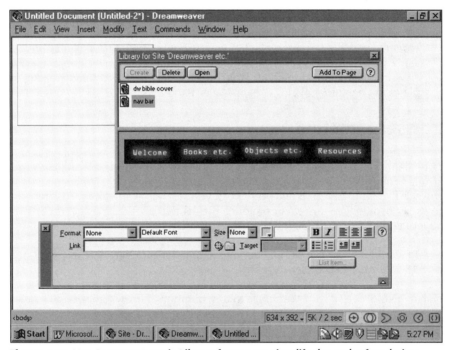

Figure 1-8: Use Dreamweaver's Library feature to simplify the task of updating elements repeated across many Web pages.

Being able to include "boilerplate" Web elements is one thing, being able to update them across the site simultaneously is quite another! You can easily change a Library entry through the Library Palette. Once the change is complete, Dreamweaver detects the modification and asks if you want to update your site. Imagine updating copyright information across a 400+ page Web site in the wink of an eye, and you'll start to understand the power of Dreamweaver Libraries.

Cross-Reference To find out more about making sitewide changes, see Chapter 32, "Using the Repeating Elements Library."

Templates

The more your Web site grows, the more you'll find yourself using the same basic format for different pages. Dreamweaver enables the use of Web page templates to standardize the look and feel of a Web site and to cut down on the repetitive work of creating new pages. A Dreamweaver template can hold the basic structure for the page — an image embedded in the background, a navigation bar along the left side, or a set-width table in the center for holding the main text, for example — with as many elements predefined as possible.

New Feature

Templates have become even more powerful in Dreamweaver 2. Now, templates work with a series of locked and editable regions. To update an entire site based on a template, all you have to do is alter one or more of the template's locked regions. Naturally, Dreamweaver lets you save any template that you create in the same folder, so that your own templates, too, are accessible through the File ⇨ New from Template command. (You'll find more about using and creating templates in Chapter 34, "Using Dreamweaver Templates.")

Browser targeting

Browser targeting is another site management innovation from Dreamweaver. One of the major steps in any site development project is to test the Web pages in various browsers to look for inconsistencies and invalid code. Dreamweaver's Browser Targeting function lets you check your HTML against any existing browser's profile. Dreamweaver includes predefined profiles for several browsers and lets you create a profile for any browser you'd like to check.

Cross-Reference

To learn how you can set up your own profile for Browser Targeting, see Chapter 31, "Maximizing Browser Targeting."

You can also preview your Web page in any number of browsers. Dreamweaver lets you specify primary and secondary browsers that can display your page at the press of a function key. You can install up to 18 other browsers for previewing your Web page. The entire list of browsers is available through the Preview in Browser command under the File menu.

Converting Web pages

Although Web site designers may have access to the latest HTML tools and browsers, much of the public uses older, more limited versions of browsers. Dreamweaver gives you the power to build Web pages with the high-end capabilities of fourth-generation browsers — and then convert those pages so that older browsers can also read what you've created. Moreover, you can take previously designed Web pages that use tables and "upgrade" them to take advantage of the latest HTML features with the Tables to Layers command. Dreamweaver goes a long way toward helping you bridge the gap between browser versions.

Verifying links

Web sites are ever-evolving entities. Maintaining valid connections and links amid all that diversity is a constant challenge. Dreamweaver includes a built-in link checker so you can verify the links on a page, in a directory, or across your entire site. The link checker quickly shows you which files have broken links, which files have links to external sites, and which files may have been "orphaned" (so that no other file connects with them).

FTP publishing

The final step in Web page creation is publishing your page on the Internet. As any Webmaster knows, this "final step" is one that happens over and over again, as the site is continually updated and maintained. Dreamweaver includes an FTP publisher that simplifies the work of posting your site (FTP stands for *file transfer protocol*).

You can work with sites originating from a local folder, such as one on your own hard drive. Or, in a collaborative team environment, you can work with sites being developed on a remote server. Dreamweaver lets you set up an unlimited number of sites to include the source and destination directories, FTP user names and passwords, and more.

The Dreamweaver FTP Site window, shown in Figure 1-9, is a visual interface in which you can click and drag files, or select a number of files and transfer them with the Get and Put buttons. You can even set the preferences so the system automatically disconnects after remaining idle for a user-definable period of time.

Site Map

Web sites can quickly outgrow the stage in which the designer can keep all the linked pages in mind. Dreamweaver 2 adds a new visual aid to the Web site management toolbox: the Site Map. With the Site Map, the Web designer can see how the entire Web site is structured. However, you can use the Site Map to do far more than just visualize the Web.

New Feature   The new Site Map, shown in Figure 1-10, can be used to establish the structure of the Web site in addition to viewing it. New pages can be created, and links can be added, modified, or deleted. In fact, the Site Map is so powerful, it becomes a site manager as well.

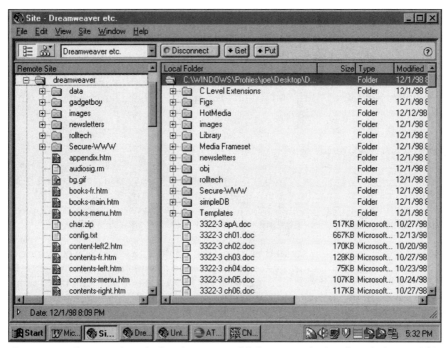

Figure 1-9: The FTP Site window lets you publish your Web site directly from within Dreamweaver.

File check-out/check-in

On larger Web projects, more than one person is usually responsible for creation and daily upkeep of the site. An editor may need to include the latest company press release, or a graphic artist may have to upload a photo of the newest product—all on the same page. To avoid conflicts with overlapping updates, Dreamweaver has devised a system under which Web pages can be marked as "checked out" and locked to prevent any other corrections until the file is once again "checked in."

Dreamweaver places a green check mark over a file's icon in the FTP Site window when it has been checked out by you, and a red mark if it has been checked out by another member of your team. And, so you won't have to guess who that team member is, Dreamweaver displays the name of the person next to the filename. You can also keep track of who last checked out a particular Web page (or image)— Dreamweaver keeps an ongoing log listing the file, person, and date and time of the check-out.

Cross-Reference You can learn all about Dreamweaver's Web publishing capabilities in Chapter 33, "Publishing Via Site FTP."

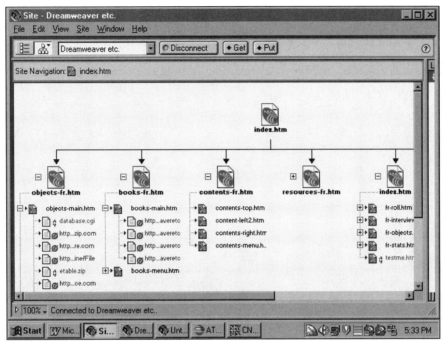

Figure 1-10: Use the Site Map to get an overall picture of your site — and then add new pages or links, right on the Map.

Summary

Building a Web site is half craft and half art, and Dreamweaver is the perfect tool for blending these often dueling disciplines. Dreamweaver's visual editor enables quick and artful page creation and, at the same time, its integrated text editors offer the detail-oriented focus required by programmers. Dreamweaver's key features include the following:

✦ Dreamweaver works the way professional Web developers do, with integrated visual and text editors. Dreamweaver won't convert your HTML code when it's used with pre-existing Web pages.

✦ Dreamweaver supports HTML standard commands with easy entry and editing of text, graphics, tables, and multimedia elements.

✦ Dreamweaver makes cutting-edge features, such as Dynamic HTML and Cascading Style Sheets, easy to use.

✦ Dreamweaver offers you a variety of reusable JavaScript behaviors, object libraries, commands, and templates to streamline your Web page creation.

✦ Dreamweaver's wide range of site management tools include FTP Publishing with a file-locking capability that encourages team creation and maintenance, as well as a built-in link checker and visual Site Map.

In the next chapter, you'll receive a full tour of the Dreamweaver workspace.

✦   ✦   ✦

Touring Dreamweaver

Dreamweaver's user interface is very clean, very efficient, and very powerful. By offering streamlined tools and controls, Dreamweaver helps you focus on the most important area of the screen: your Web page design. This chapter provides a detailed overview of the Dreamweaver workspace so you'll know where all the tools are when you need to use them.

Many other Web authoring programs surround your page-in-progress with numerous menu strips, icons, and other interface paraphernalia. Dreamweaver takes a more streamlined approach, however, which enables you to keep the focus on your workspace as your page develops. Dreamweaver 2 enhances this approach by introducing dockable windows and palettes to further reduce on-screen clutter.

Viewing the Document Window

Dreamweaver's primary workspace is the Document Window. When you first start Dreamweaver, you'll see what is essentially an empty canvas, as shown in Figure 2-1. This is where you create your Web pages by typing in headlines and paragraphs, inserting images and links, and creating tables, forms, and other HTML elements.

The Web design process consists of creating your page in Dreamweaver and then previewing the results in one or more browsers. As your Web page begins to take shape, Dreamweaver shows you a close representation of how the page will look when viewed through a browser such as Netscape Communicator or Internet Explorer. You can do this as often as you like — Dreamweaver displays the page in your favorite browser with the press of a button. Moreover, in Dreamweaver 2 you can even view active elements, such as QuickTime movies or Shockwave Director and Flash files, in your Web page as you're building it.

Menus   Document Window   Objects Palette

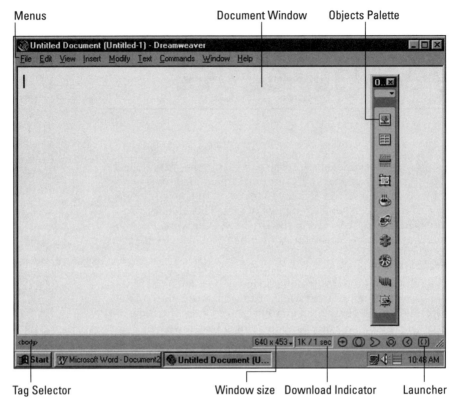

Tag Selector   Window size   Download Indicator   Launcher

Figure 2-1: Dreamweaver's opening screen is designed to maximize your workspace with a minimum of distracting tools and windows.

Dreamweaver surrounds your "empty canvas" with the tools you'll need to create your Web masterpiece. We'll start our tour with the first of these: the status bar.

Working with the Status Bar

The status bar is found at the bottom of the Document Window. Embedded here are four important tools: the Tag Selector, the Window Size pop-up menu, the Download Indicator, and the Launcher. Beyond displaying useful information such as which windows are open, these status bar tools are extremely helpful and provide the Web designer with several timesaving utilities.

Tip If you don't see the status bar at the bottom of your screen, check the View menu. Make sure there's a check mark next to the status bar item; if not, select it with your mouse to enable it.

Tag Selector

The Tag Selector is an excellent example of Dreamweaver's elegant design approach. On the left side of the status bar you'll see a listing of the current HTML tags. When you first open a blank page in Dreamweaver, you'll see only the `<body>` tag. If you type a line of text and then press Enter (Return), the paragraph tag `<p>` appears. Your cursor's position in the document determines which tags are displayed in the Tag Selector. The Tag Selector constantly keeps track of where you are in the HTML document by displaying the tags surrounding your current cursor position. This becomes especially important when you are building complex Web pages that use such features as nested tables.

As its name implies, the Tag Selector does more than just indicate a position in a document. Using the Tag Selector, you can quickly choose any of the elements surrounding your current cursor. Once an element is selected, you can quickly modify or delete it. If you have the Property Inspector (described later in this chapter) on screen, choosing a different code from the Tag Selector makes the corresponding options available in the Property Inspector.

Tip If you want to quickly clear most of your HTML page, choose the `<body>` tag and press Delete. All graphics, text, and other elements you have inserted through the Document Window will be erased. Left intact is any HTML code in the `<head>` section, including your title, `<meta>` tags, and any preliminary JavaScript.

In a more complex Web page section such as the one shown in Figure 2-2, the Tag Selector shows a wider variety of HTML tags. As you move your pointer over individual codes in the Tag Selector, they are highlighted; click one and the code becomes bold. Tags are displayed from left to right in the Tag Selector, starting on the far left with the most inclusive (in this case the `<body>` tag) and proceeding to the narrowest selection (here, the underline `<u>` tag) on the far right.

As a Web page developer, you're constantly selecting elements in order to modify them. Rather than relying on the clicking-and-dragging method to highlight an area—which often grabs unwanted sections of your code—use the Tag Selector to unerringly pick just the code you want. Dreamweaver's Tag Selector is a subtle but extremely useful tool that can speed up your work significantly.

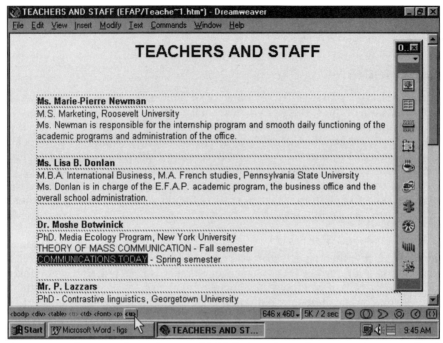

Figure 2-2: The Tag Selector lets you highlight just the code you want. Here, selecting the ⟨u⟩ tag chooses only the underlined portion of the text.

Window Size pop-up menu

The universality of the Internet enables virtually any type of computer system from anywhere in the world to access publicly available Web pages. While this accessibility is a boon to global communication, it forces Web designers to be aware of how their creations look under various circumstances — especially different screen sizes.

New Feature   Dreamweaver 2 introduces a new feature — the Window Size pop-up menu — to give designers a sense of how their pages look on different monitors. Located just right of center on the status bar, the Window Size pop-up menu indicates the screen size of the current Document Window, in pixels, in *width* x *height* format. If you resize your Document Window, the Window Size indicator updates instantly. This indicator gives you an immediate check on the view dimensions of the current page.

But the Window Size pop-up menu goes beyond just telling you the size of your screen — it also enables you to quickly view your page through a wide variety of monitor sizes. Naturally, your monitor must be capable of displaying the larger screen dimensions before they can be selected. To select a different screen size, follow these steps:

1. Click once on the expander arrow to the right of the displayed dimensions.

   A menu listing the standard sizes, shown in Figure 2-3, will pop up.

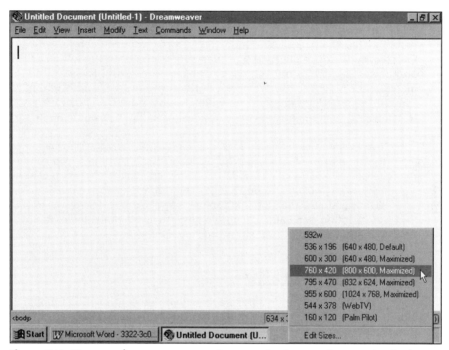

Figure 2-3: You can change your current screen size to any of seven standard sizes — or add your own custom sizes — with the new Window Size pop-up menu.

2. Holding down the mouse button, move your mouse over a desired screen size.

3. To select a size, release the mouse button.

The standard sizes, and the machines most commonly using them, are as follows:

   ✦ 536 × 196 (640 × 480, Default)

   ✦ 600 × 300 (640 × 480, Maximized)

   ✦ 760 × 420 (800 × 600, Maximized)

   ✦ 795 × 470 (832 × 624, Maximized)

   ✦ 955 × 600 (1024 × 768, Maximized)

   ✦ 544 × 378 (WebTV)

   ✦ 160 × 120 (PalmPilot)

Cross-Reference You can set up your own custom screen settings by choosing Edit Sizes from the Window Size pop-up menu. This option opens the Status Bar panel of the Preferences dialog box. How you modify the pop-up list is described in Chapter 3, "Setting Your Preferences."

The dimensions offered by the Window Size pop-up menu describe the entire editable area of a page. The Document Window has been carefully designed to match specifications set by the primary browsers. Both the left and right margins are the same width as both the Netscape and Microsoft browsers and the status bar matches the height of the browser's bottom row as well. The height of any given browser environment depends on which toolbars are being used; however, Dreamweaver's menu strip is the same height as the browsers' menu strips.

Tip If you want to compensate for the other browser user interface elements, like the Toolbar and the Address bar (collectively called "chrome"), you can increase the height of your Document Window by approximately 72 pixels. Combined, Navigator's Toolbar (44 pixels high) and Address bar (24 pixels) at 68 pixels are slightly narrower than Internet Explorer's total chrome. Microsoft includes an additional bottom separator that adds 6 pixels to its other elements (Toolbar, 42 pixels; and Address bar, 24) for a total of 72 pixels.

Download Indicator

So you've built your Web masterpiece and you've just finished uploading the HTML, along with the 23 JPEGs, eight audio files and three QuickTime movies that make up the page. You open the page over the Net and — surprise! — it takes five minutes to download. Okay, this example is a tad extreme, but every Web developer knows that opening a page from your hard drive and opening a page over the Internet are two vastly different experiences. Dreamweaver has taken the guesswork out of loading a page from the Web by providing the Download Indicator.

The Download Indicator is located to the right of the Window Size pop-up menu on the status bar. As illustrated in Figure 2-4, Dreamweaver gives you two values, separated by a slash character:

✦ The cumulative size of the page, including all the associated graphics, plug-ins, and multimedia files, measured in kilobytes (K).

✦ The time it takes to download at a particular modem connection speed, measured in seconds (sec).

Tip You can check the download size of any individual graphic by selecting it and looking at the Property Inspector — you'll find the file size in kilobytes next to the thumbnail image on the left.

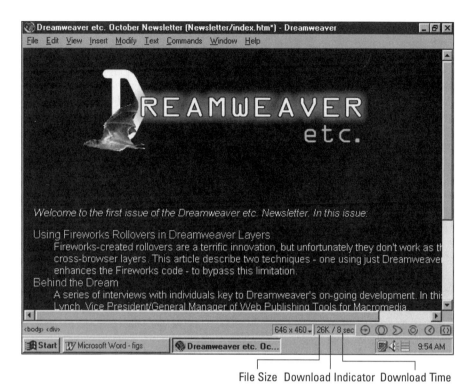

File Size Download Indicator Download Time

Figure 2-4: Take notice of the Download Indicator whenever you lay out a page with extensive graphics or other large multimedia files.

The Download Indicator is a very handy real-world check. As you build your Web pages, it's a good practice to keep an eye on your file's download size — both in kilobytes and seconds. Ultimately, as a Web designer you have to decide what your audience will deem is worth the wait and what will have them reaching for that Stop button. For example, the graphic shown in Figure 2-4 is very pretty, but at 56K it's on the borderline of an acceptable size. The graphic should probably either be resized or the colors reduced to lower the overall "weight" of the page.

Cross-Reference

Not everybody has a standard 28.8 modem connection. If you are working with an intranet, you can set your connection speed far higher. Likewise, if your site gets a lot of traffic, you can lower the connection speed. You change the anticipated download speed through the Dreamweaver Preferences, as explained in Chapter 3, "Setting Your Preferences."

Launcher

On the far right of the status bar, you'll find the Launcher — or, rather, one of the Launchers. In addition to the one on the status bar (known as the Mini-Launcher), Dreamweaver offers an independent, draggable palette with larger, named buttons that is also known as the Launcher. Both Launchers open and close the same windows: Site, Library, Styles, Behavior, Timeline, and HTML windows and Inspectors.

As with the Tag Selector, each one of the buttons in the Mini-Launcher lights up when the pointer passes over it and stays lit when selected. You can also use the Launcher to close the windows it has opened — just click the highlighted button. Dreamweaver lets you keep open any or all of the six different windows at the same time.

Clicking a Launcher or Mini-Launcher button when a window is already open has one of two effects. If the window for the button is on top, the window closes. If the window is hidden behind another floating window, the window corresponding to the button is brought forward.

Tip   If you don't want to have the Mini-Launcher appear in the status bar, you can turn it off. Choose Edit ➪ Preferences and then select the Status Bar category. Click Show Mini-Launcher in Status Bar to remove its check mark and then click OK. Naturally, you can turn the Mini-Launcher back on by rechecking its box.

The features of the various windows controlled through the Mini-Launcher are discussed in "Using the Launcher" later in this chapter.

Selecting from the Objects Palette

The Objects Palette holds the items most often used — the primary colors, as it were — when designing Web pages. Everything from images to ActiveX plug-ins to HTML comments can be selected from the Objects Palette. Moreover, the Objects Palette is completely customizable — you can add your own favorite items and even set up how the Objects Palette is organized.

Cross-Reference   To see how you can build your own Dreamweaver objects and modify the Objects Palette, turn to Chapter 16, "Creating and Using Objects."

The Objects Palette is divided into four separate panels of objects: Common, Forms, Head, and Invisibles. The initial view is of the Common panel. To switch from one panel to another, select the small expander arrow at the top of the Objects Palette (see Figure 2-5) and then choose an option from the resulting pop-up menu. Each panel is described in detail in the following sections.

If the Objects Palette is not available when you first start Dreamweaver, you can enable it by choosing Window ➪ Objects or the keyboard shortcut, Ctrl-F2 (Command-F2). Likewise, choosing Window ➪ Objects (or the shortcut) again deselects it and closes the Objects Palette. You can also remove the Objects Palette from your screen by clicking its Close button.

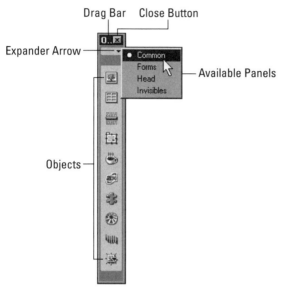

Figure 2-5: The Objects Palette acts as a toolbox for holding your most commonly used Web page elements.

To reposition the Objects Palette — or any of the Dreamweaver windows or floating toolbars — just position your cursor over the drag bar at the top of the window and drag it to a new place. The Objects Palette can be placed anywhere on the screen, not just inside the Document Window. Some Web designers like to size their Document Window to a standard width that renders well across a variety of platforms and resolutions, and then place the Objects Palette outside of that window so they have a clear canvas with which to work.

Tip   You can reshape the Objects Palette by positioning your pointer over the Palette's border so that a double-headed arrow appears. Click and drag the rectangle into a new size or shape, and the icons within the Objects Palette will rearrange themselves to fit. If your resized Objects Palette is too small to contain all the objects, a small scroll arrow is displayed. Select the arrow, and the Objects Palette scrolls to show additional objects; at the same time, another arrow appears at the opposite side of the window to indicate more hidden objects.

Common objects

The most often-used HTML elements, aside from text, are accessible through the Common Objects panel of the Objects Palette. Table 2-1 explains what each of the Common Objects Panel icons represents.

Table 2-1
Common Objects Panel

Icon	Name	Description	Detailed Info
	Insert Image	Use for including any graphic or picture, including animated GIFs, at the cursor position	Chapter 8, "Inserting Images"
	Insert Table	Opens a dialog box for creating a table at the cursor position	Chapter 11, "Setting Up Tables"
	Insert Horizontal Rule.	Draws a line across the page at the cursor position	See "Dividing the Web Page with Horizontal Rules" in Chapter 8
	Draw Layer	Enables you to drag out a layer of specific size and shape at a specific location	Chapter 25, "Working with Layers"
	Insert Applet	Includes a Java applet at the cursor position	See "Adding Java Applets" in Chapter 15
	Insert ActiveX	Puts a placeholder for an ActiveX control at the cursor position, using the `<object>` tag	See "Working with ActiveX Components" in Chapter 15
	Insert Plug-in	Use for including a file that requires a plug-in	See "Incorporating Plug-ins" in Chapter 15
	Insert Flash	Use to include a Shockwave Flash movie	Chapter 22, "Inserting Shockwave Movies"
	Insert Shockwave	Use to include a Shockwave Director movie	Chapt31er 22, "Inserting Shockwave Movies"
	Insert Rollover Image	Inserts an image that changes into another image when the user's mouse moves over it	Chapter 8, "Inserting Images"

All of the Common objects except for Insert Horizontal Rule and Draw Layer open a dialog box that enables you to specify or browse for a file.

Tip   If you'd prefer to enter all your information, including the necessary file names, through the Property Inspector, you can turn off the automatic appearance of the file requester when you insert any object through the Objects Palette or the menus. Choose Edit ⇨ Preferences and, from the General Category, select Show Dialog When Inserting Objects to uncheck it.

Form objects

The form is the primary method for implementing HTML interactivity. The Forms panel of the Objects Palette gives you nine basic building blocks for creating your Web-based form. Table 2-2 describes each of the elements found in the Forms panel.

Table 2-2
Forms Panel

Icon	Name	Description	Detailed Info
	Insert Form	Creates the overall HTML form structure at the cursor position	Chapter 13, "Interactive Forms"
	Insert Text Field	Places a text box or a text area at the cursor position	See "Using Text Boxes" in Chapter 13
	Insert Button position	Inserts a Submit, Reset, or user-definable button at the cursor	See "Activating Your Form with Buttons" in Chapter 13
	Insert Check Box	Inserts a check box for selecting any number of options at the cursor position	See "Providing Check Boxes and Radio Buttons" in Chapter 13
	Insert Radio Button	Inserts a radio button for making a single selection from a set of options at the cursor position	See "Providing Check Boxes and Radio Buttons" in Chapter 13
	Insert List/ Menu	Enables either a drop-down menu or a scrolling list at the cursor position	See "Creating Form Lists and Menus" in Chapter 13
	Insert File Field	Inserts a text box and Browse button for selecting a file to submit	See "Using the Hidden Field and the File Field" in Chapter 13
	Insert Image Field	Includes an image that can be used as a button	See "Activating Your Form with Buttons" in Chapter 13
	Insert Hidden Field	Inserts an invisible field used for passing variables to a CGI or JavaScript program	See "Using the Hidden Field and the File Field" in Chapter 13

As demonstrated in Figure 2-6, you can use a table inside a form to get objects to line up properly. All forms return user input via a CGI or JavaScript program. See Chapter 13, "Interactive Forms," for more detailed information.

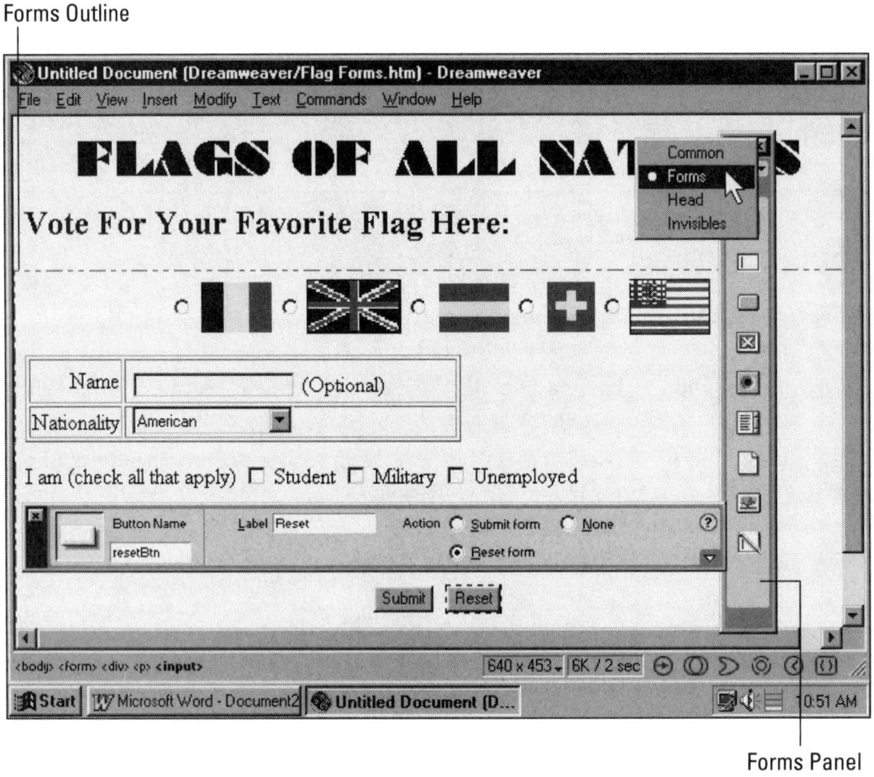

Forms Outline

Forms Panel

Figure 2-6: Dreamweaver puts a distinctive dashed line around any form.

Head objects

Before Dreamweaver 2, almost all of the general document information written into the <head> section of an HTML document had to be hand-coded. The new release adds a full range of functionality that enables Web designers to drop in <meta> tags with keywords for search engines, specify refresh times, and do many more tasks that impact a Web site's overall performance.

New Feature While Dreamweaver 2 lets you see the <head> objects on screen via the View ⇨ Head Content menu option, you don't have to have the <head> window open to drop in the objects. Simply click on any of the nine objects detailed in Table 2-3, and a dialog box will open prompting you for the needed information.

Table 2-3
Head Objects Panel

Icon	Name	Description	Detailed Info
	Insert Meta	Includes document information usable by servers and browsers	See "Understanding <meta> and other <head> tags" in Chapter 6
	Insert Keywords	Inserts keywords used by search engines to catalog the Web page	See " Understanding <meta> and other <head> tags" in Chapter 6
	Insert Description	Provides a description of the current page	See "Understanding <meta> and other <head> tags" in Chapter 6
	Insert Refresh	Sets a *e to refresh the current page or redirect the browser to another URL	See "Refreshing the page and redirecting users" in Chapter 6
	Insert Base	Specifies the base address of the current document	See "Understanding <meta> and other <head> tags" in Chapter 6
	Insert Link	Declares a relationship between the current document and another object or file	See "Linking to Other Files" in Chapter 6

Invisible objects

As any experienced Web designer knows, what you see on screen is, increasingly, a small part of the code necessary for the page's generation. Often you need to include an element that Dreamweaver categorizes as an Invisible. The fourth panel of the Objects Palette gives you quick access to the most commonly inserted behind-the-scenes tags, as described in Table 2-4.

Table 2-4
Invisible Objects

Icon	Name	Description	Detailed Info
	Insert Named Anchor	Puts a hyperlink at a particular place on a Web page	See "Navigating with Anchors" in Chapter 9

Continued

Table 2-4 (continued)			
Icon	*Name*	*Description*	*Detailed Info*
	Insert Comment	Places HTML comment tags inside your script; these comments are ignored by the browser	See "Commenting Your Code" in Chapter 7
	Insert Script	Inserts JavaScript or VBScript either directly or from a file	See "Adding JavaScript and VBScript" in Chapter 15
	Insert Line Break	Puts in a ⟨br⟩ tag that causes the line to wrap at the cursor position	See "Working with Paragraphs" in Chapter 7
	Insert Non-Break-ing Space	Inserts a hard space in the current cursor position	See "Inserting Symbols and Special Characters" in Chapter 6
	Insert Server-Side Include	Includes code that causes the server to process the page	See "Applying Server-Side Includes" in Chapter 32

Tip   Other invisible elements can be turned on or off through the Preferences dialog box. Choose Edit ⇨ Preferences and then select the Invisible Elements category. You'll see a list of 13 options (including the first four listed in the Invisibles panel). To turn off an option, click once to remove the check mark from the option's check box. For a complete description of all the Invisible elements and other preferences, see Chapter 3, "Setting Your Preferences."

Getting the Most Out of the Property Inspector

Dreamweaver's Property Inspector is your primary tool for specifying an object's particulars. What exactly those particulars are — in HTML, these are known as *attributes* — depends on the object itself. The contents of the Property Inspector change depending on which object is selected. For example, click anywhere on a blank Web page and the Property Inspector shows text attributes for format, font name and size, and so on. If you click an image, the Property Inspector displays a small thumbnail of the picture, and the image's attributes for height and width, image source, link, and alternative text. Figure 2-7 shows a Property Inspector for a line of text with an attached hyperlink.

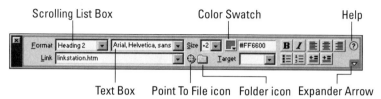

Scrolling List Box   Color Swatch   Help

Text Box   Point To File icon   Folder icon   Expander Arrow

Figure 2-7: The Property Inspector takes many forms, depending on which HTML element you select.

Manipulating the Property Inspector

The Property Inspector is enabled by choosing Window ➪ Properties or selecting the keyboard shortcut, Ctrl-F3. As with the Objects Palette, the Property Inspector can be closed by selecting the Close button, unchecking Window ➪ Properties, or choosing the keyboard shortcut again.

You can reposition the Property Inspector in one of two ways. You can click and drag the title bar of the window and move it to a new location, or — unlike the Objects Palette — you can click and drag any open gray area in the Inspector itself. This is very handy for quickly moving the Inspector aside, out of your way.

Tip
In addition to using the expander arrow, you can reveal (or hide) the expanded attributes by double-clicking any open gray area of the Property Inspector.

The Property Inspector initially displays the most typical attributes for a given element. To see additional properties, click the expander arrow in the lower-right corner of the Property Inspector. Virtually all the inserted objects have additional parameters that can be modified. Unless you're tight on screen real estate, it's a good idea to keep the Property Inspector expanded so you can see all your options.

Property Inspector elements

Many of the attributes in the Property Inspector are text boxes; just click in any one and enter the desired value. If a value already appears in the text box, whether number or name, double-click it (or click and drag over it) to highlight the information and then enter your new data — the old value is immediately replaced. You can see the effect your modification has had by pressing the Tab key to move to the next attribute or by clicking outside of the Property Inspector.

The Property Inspector also uses scrolling list boxes for several attributes that provide a limited number of responses for you to choose. To open the drop-down list of available options, click the arrow button to the right of the list box. Then choose an option by highlighting it.

Tip

Some options on the Property Inspector are a combination drop-down list and text box—you can select from available options or type in your own values. For example, when text is selected, the font name, size, and color options are all combination list/text boxes.

If you see a folder icon next to a text box (see the List item in the Inspector shown in Figure 2-7), you have the option of browsing for a filename on your local or networked drive, or manually inputting a name. Clicking the folder opens a standard Open File dialog box; after you've chosen your file and clicked Open, Dreamweaver inputs the name and any necessary path information in the correct attribute.

New Feature

Dreamweaver 2 enables you to quickly select an on-screen file in either a Document Window or a Site Window as a link, with its new Point to File icon, found next to the Folder icon. Just click and drag the Point to File icon until it touches the file (or filename from the Site Window) you want to reference. The path is automatically written into the Link text box.

Cross-Reference

Dreamweaver can handle all forms of absolute and relative addressing. For more information on specifying HTML pages, be sure to see "Understanding Relative and Absolute Paths" in Chapter 5.

Certain objects such as text, layers, and tables enable you to specify a color attribute. The Property Inspector alerts you to these options with a small color swatch next to the text box. You can type in a color's name (such as "blue") or its six-figure hexadecimal value ("#3366FF"), or select the color swatch. Choosing the color swatch displays a color picker, shown in Figure 2-8, with the 212 colors common to both the Netscape and Microsoft browsers — the so-called *browser-safe* colors. (Some of the 212 Web-safe colors are duplicated to create a more user-friendly interface.) You can go outside of this range by clicking the small painter's palette in the lower-right corner of the color picker. This opens a full-range Color dialog box in which you can choose a color visually or enter its red, green, and blue values or its hue, saturation, and luminance values.

New Feature

The color picker in Dreamweaver 2 (see Figure 2-8) is greatly enhanced. Not only can you choose from a newly reorganized palette, but you can also select any color on screen with Dreamweaver's Eyedropper tool. There's also an Eraser tool, located in the lower-right corner, that deletes any color choice previously inserted.

One final aspect of the Property Inspector is worth noting: The encircled question mark in the upper-right corner of the Property Inspector is the Help button. Selecting this button invokes online help and displays specific information about the particular Property Inspector you're using.

The Help button is also available throughout all of the windows opened by the Launcher, as described in the next section.

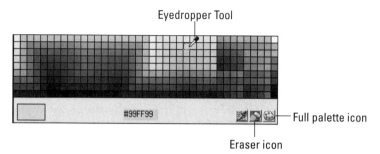

Figure 2-8: Dreamweaver 2's new color picker lets you choose from a wider selection of colors, right from the palette or right off the desktop with the Eyedropper tool.

Using the Launcher

Dreamweaver's third main control panel, along with the Objects Palette and the Property Inspector, is called the *Launcher*, shown in Figure 2-9.

Figure 2-9: The Launcher gives you access to six different Dreamweaver functions.

The Launcher opens and closes six windows, each of which handles a different aspect of the program:

> ✦ **The Site Window** handles all elements of publishing to the Web, as well as basic file maintenance such as moving and deleting folders.
>
> ✦ **The Library Palette** is used to manage the repeating elements feature, which enables Dreamweaver to simultaneously update any number of Web pages on a site.
>
> ✦ **The Styles Palette** coordinates the Cascading Style Sheet modifications on each Web page and, if used in conjunction with an external style sheet, throughout your entire Web site.
>
> ✦ **The Behavior Inspector** assigns one or more JavaScript actions to a JavaScript event selected from a browser-targeted list.
>
> ✦ **The Timeline Inspector** controls the animations of images or layers over time.
>
> ✦ **The HTML Inspector** is Dreamweaver's internal HTML editor, integrated with the Document Window's visual editor.

Similarly to the other control panels, the Launcher can be started by choosing Window ⇨ Launcher, and closed by either selecting the Close button or choosing Window ⇨ Launcher again. A standard title bar is available on the Launcher for dragging the palette into a new position. The Launcher also includes a small button in the lower-right corner (see Figure 2-9) that serves to change the panel's orientation from a horizontal shape to a vertical one, and vice versa.

The free-floating Launcher Palette functions identically to the status bar Launcher. Each one of the Launcher buttons is highlighted when the pointer passes over it, and remains highlighted when chosen. As noted, the Launcher can be used to close the windows or bring them to the front as well as open them—just click the highlighted button. Any or all of the windows can be "launched" simultaneously.

Site Window

The Site Window is your gateway to the Web. Through it, you can transfer files from the development folder on your local drive to your online Web server. Any member of your development team can check out a file to work on with no fear that another member is making changes at the same time. The team leader can even check Dreamweaver's log to see who is working on what.

New Feature   Web sites can become quite complex very quickly and it's often difficult to remember how pages are linked together. Dreamweaver 2 now offers a visual representation of your Web site through its Site Map Window. The Site Map Window not only enables you to quickly review the structure of a site, you can also use it to add, move, or modify links. You can learn all the details about the new Site Map feature in Chapter 33, "Publishing Via Site FTP."

Open the Site Window by choosing the Site button, on either the Launcher Palette or the status bar Launcher, by selecting Window ⇨ Site Files or by pressing F5. As you can see in Figure 2-10, the Site Window is two-paned: Local files are shown on the right side and remote files are displayed on the left. The headings across the top of each pane and the panes themselves can be resized. Position your pointer over a border until a double-headed arrow appears and then click and drag the border to a new position.

 Tip   The files of both local and remote folders can be sorted by name, file size, file type, date modified, or checkout status—all the options corresponding to the headings across each pane. For example, to display your files in A-to-Z alphabetical order, click the Name button once. To show them in descending (Z-to-A) order, click the Name button again. If you're constantly updating your site, it's good practice to have your folders sorted in descending date order so that your most recently modified files appear at the top of each pane.

Site Map Button   Local Pane

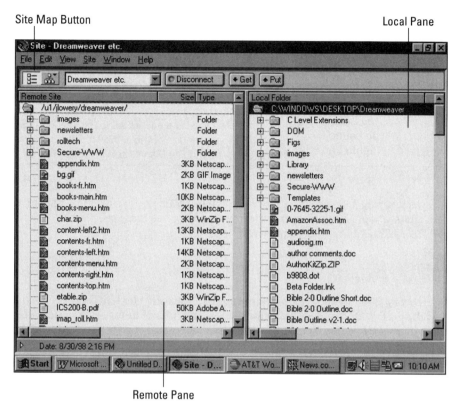

Remote Pane

Figure 2-10: Dreamweaver's Site Window handles the Webmaster's site management chores.

The major operations performed in the Site Window include the following:

Site Window Function	Site Window Actions
Connecting to the site	When your site is properly configured, the Connect button automatically calls your remote site and uses whatever log-in and password are necessary to get you online. After the connection is confirmed, the button changes into a Disconnect button.
Transferring files	To move files between your local drive and the remote server, use the Get and Put buttons. The Get button copies whatever files are highlighted in the Remote pane to the local folder, and the Put button copies files highlighted in the Local pane to the remote directory. To stop a transfer, select the Stop Current Task button — the stop sign in the lower-right corner of the window.

Continued

Site Window Function	Site Window Actions
Locking files	When a team of Web designers is working on a site, you have to be able to prevent two people from working on the same file simultaneously. The Checked In/Checked Out indicator not only shows that a file is in use, but who has the file.
Site Map representation	As a site grows in complexity, it is often helpful to get an overview of a site's structure and its links. The Site Map feature gives a visual representation of the complete site and can be chosen by selecting the Site Map button.

Cross-Reference

Maintaining a Web site is a major portion of a Webmaster's responsibility. To learn more about Dreamweaver's site management features, see Part 9, "Web Site Management Under Dreamweaver."

Library Palette

The Library Palette manages Dreamweaver's repeating element feature. Through the Library Palette you can turn any item — or series of items — on your Web page into a kind of "linked boilerplate." Not only can you drop your "boilerplate" text or images into any page of your site, but you can update them all by just modifying one item. The Library feature can save a Web development team many, many hours of work in both the creation and maintenance phases.

You can open the Library Palette by selecting the Library button from the Launcher, by choosing Window ➪ Library, or by pressing F6. As you can see from Figure 2-11, the Library Palette is a draggable, resizable window divided horizontally into two panes. The upper portion of the window displays the list of Library items for the current Web site. When one of these items is selected, the lower portion of the Library Palette, the Preview pane, illustrates the item. You can resize the two panes by positioning your pointer over the separating border and then clicking and dragging the border to a new place.

Cross-Reference

You'll notice a new window grouped with the Library Palette — Templates. You can find out more about this powerful new Dreamweaver 2 feature in Chapter 34, "Using Dreamweaver Templates."

Figure 2-11: The Library Palette manages the
repeating elements throughout your Web site.

The primary features of the Library Palette are listed in the following table:

Library Palette Function	*Document Window Actions*
Creating new entries	You define a Library item by first selecting it, either in the Document Window or the HTML Inspector, and then clicking the Create button.
Deleting old entries	Remove an item from the Library by selecting the Delete button.
Editing entries	To alter a defined Library item, select it and press the Open button. This opens another Dreamweaver window containing your Library item. After you've made your modifications, closing the window alerts Dreamweaver to your changes, and the item is updated.
Inserting entries	After you've built and defined your Library items, use the Add to Page button to insert it into your pages at the current cursor position.

Cross-Reference   To find out more about the powerful Library feature, turn to Chapter 32, "Using the Repeating Elements Library."

Styles Palette

Through the Styles Palette, Dreamweaver makes creating and applying Cascading Style Sheets (CSS) easy. CSS give the Web designer a terrific degree of control over the appearance of text and other elements, throughout the creation stage and when the Web site is live. Styles can be used in conjunction with a single Web page or an entire site.

The Styles Palette, shown in Figure 2-12, is accessed by clicking the Styles button from either the Launcher Palette or the status bar Launcher. You can also open the Styles Palette by choosing Window ⇨ Styles or by pressing F7. You can drag or resize the Styles Palette with the mouse.

Figure 2-12: The Styles Palette displays custom styles and gives you access to Dreamweaver's point-and-click CSS editing capabilities.

The Styles Palette has three key uses:

Styles Palette Function	Document Window Actions
Defining styles	Through the Style Sheet button on the Styles Palette you can create, modify, and remove CSS formats. CSS either redefine existing HTML tags or create new user-defined classes.
Applying styles	Once your styles are defined, you can easily apply them to any selected text throughout your Web page. Just click the desired style in the Styles Palette list.
Viewing styled tags	It can be difficult to tell which style has already been applied to which tag. With the Styles Palette, pick any text or item on the screen and the applied style (if any) is highlighted.

Cross-
Reference

For more detailed information on how to use the Styles Palette, see Chapter 24, "Building Style Sheet Web Pages."

Behavior Inspector

The Behavior Inspector enables nonprogrammers to build cutting-edge Web pages through prebuilt JavaScript actions. Briefly, behaviors are composed of two parts: an action and an event that triggers the action. Dreamweaver includes 19 standard behaviors and, because behaviors can be custom built, hundreds more are available on the Web — and of course, on the CD-ROM that accompanies this book.

The Behavior Inspector is browser-savvy and won't let you assign a JavaScript event that only works on 4.0 browsers when you need 3.0 compatibility. With the Behavior Inspector, not only can you link several actions to a single event, but you can also specify the order of the actions.

New Feature

The Behavior Inspector has been reorganized in Dreamweaver 2. Now, you only have to choose the action of your behavior and the most frequently used event is automatically assigned. Naturally, you can specify another event if you like by selecting the Event button that appears when you select the behavior.

Use the Behavior button on either Launcher (Palette or status bar) to open the Behavior Inspector. You can also press F8 or choose Window ➪ Behaviors. Like the other windows, you can resize or reposition the Behavior Inspector with the mouse using the click-and-drag technique. As shown in Figure 2-13, the Behavior Inspector displays the events on the left side and the actions on the right.

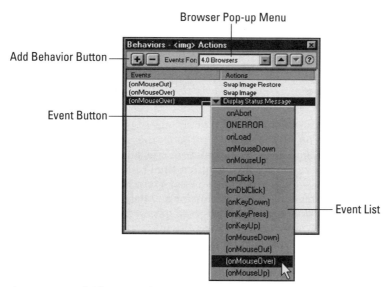

Figure 2-13: Linking an action to an event creates a JavaScript behavior in the Behavior Inspector.

Use the Behavior Inspector to perform the functions outlined in the following table:

Behavior Inspector Function	Document Window Actions
Specifying a browser	The various browsers and browser versions understand specific JavaScript commands. You can target individual browsers by manufacturer or version number, or a combination of the two, by using the Browser pop-up menu.
Picking an action	Behaviors are linked to specific HTML tags; not all HTML tags have behaviors associated with them. Selecting the Behavior pop-up menu (the + button) displays a list of available actions. Remove an action by highlighting it and clicking the – button.
Changing an event	The events listed under the Events pop-up menu (the arrow button in-between the action and the event) are determined by what's selected in the Browser pop-up menu.
Order the actions	Because you can assign more than one action to an event, Dreamweaver enables you to rearrange the order of the actions. Use the Up/Down arrows to rearrange the order of your action list for each event.

Behaviors are user-definable. In Chapter 18, "Creating Behaviors," you'll learn how to create your own actions.

On the CD-ROM Be sure to check out the Behaviors section of the CD-ROM to add to your list of Dreamweaver action capabilities.

Timeline Inspector

Dreamweaver controls the potential of built-in Dynamic HTML animation through its Timeline Inspector. The Timeline Inspector plots the position of a selected image or layer on a frame-by-frame basis. In your new role as animator in addition to Web designer, you select one keyframe after another; then Dreamweaver interpolates — or, as animators say, "tweens" — the frames in between. The Timeline Inspector can handle any number of objects on the timeline for any length of time, limited only by system resources such as memory and processing power.

Open the Timeline Inspector through one of the usual methods: Select its button from either Launcher, press F9, or choose Window ➪ Timelines. As shown in Figure 2-14, the Timeline Inspector is grid-based — the numbers running horizontally denote frames, and the vertical numbers indicate the object in the timeline.

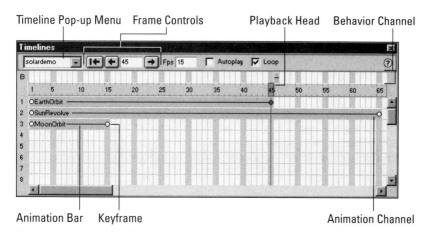

Figure 2-14: The Timeline Inspector can animate layers or images, which can be previewed in Dreamweaver or in any 4.0 or higher browser.

Use the Timeline Inspector for the functions in the following table:

Timeline Inspector Function	Document Window Actions
Drag and drop objects	To link an object to a timeline, just drag and drop it onto the Timeline Inspector's next available Animation Channel. At present, only layers and images can be animated.
Set the run length	The Animation Bar determines how many frames each object plays. You can extend the length of the animation by dragging out the Animation Bar's endpoint.
Make the keyframes	Keyframes indicate moments of change — in position, size, or visibility. You can set a keyframe on the Timeline Inspector in a number of ways, including choosing Modify ⇨ Timeline ⇨ Add Keyframe.
Add a behavior	The simplest way to add a behavior to a timeline is by selecting the Loop option. This creates an event in the Behavior Channel that causes the timeline to run itself again at the end of the animation. You can add numerous actions to specific frames.
View the frames	By dragging the Playback Head or selecting one of the Frame Controls, you can view any frame of your animation.
Use multiple timelines	Your Dreamweaver-built Web page can employ multiple timelines for your animation. Use the Timeline pop-up menu to choose which timeline is displayed in the Timeline Inspector.

Cross-Reference   To better understand how you can manipulate timelines, see Chapter 26, "Working with Timelines."

HTML Inspector

The final window controlled by the Launcher is the HTML Inspector (shown in Figure 2-15) — the internal editor designed to complement Dreamweaver's visual layout facility. Although you can opt to use an external editor such as the bundled BBEdit or HomeSite for extensive coding, the HTML Inspector is great for making spot edits or quickly checking your code. The tight integration between the Dreamweaver's text and visual editors allows for simultaneous input and instant updating.

Tip   You can see the tight integration between the visual editor and the HTML Inspector when you have both windows open and you select an object in the Document Window. The corresponding code is instantly displayed in the HTML Inspector. This feature is very useful for quickly finding a specific HTML element for alteration.

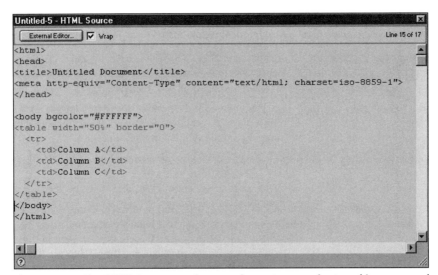

Figure 2-15: The HTML Inspector gives you instant access for tweaking your code — or adding entirely new elements by hand.

Clicking the HTML button on either Launcher opens and closes the HTML Inspector, as does choosing Window ➪ HTML or pressing F10. Once the HTML Inspector is open, changes made in the Document Window are incorporated in real-time. However, in order to properly check the code, any changes made in the HTML

Inspector are not updated in the Document Window until the Document Window is activated. You can alternate between the two windows by pressing Ctrl-Tab (Command-Tab).

Note

Note to MS Office for Mac 4 users: The Command-Tab hot switch in Dreamweaver conflicts with Office's QuickSwitch feature. To turn off the QuickSwitch in MS Office, go to the Office Manager drop-down menu, select Customize, and then deselect the QuickSwitch check box.

By design, the HTML Inspector's layout is simple, to give maximum emphasis to your code. There are really only two buttons, aside from Help and Close, in the HTML Inspector. First, you can turn on or off the line wrap function by selecting the Wrap button. This is useful if you encounter an error message that displays a line number; temporarily turn off the wrap feature to locate the line. Second, if you decide you need to do more extensive coding, you can select the External Editor button (or the Launch BBEdit button on the Macintosh) to open your full-featured editor.

Tip

You might notice that the code in the HTML Inspector is colored. The color-coding (no pun intended) is set by the HTML Colors panel of the Preferences dialog box — you can even modify the background color of the Inspector.

Template Palette

Increasingly, Web sites require a common look and feel across all pages in which only specific content changes from page to page. To aid this type of production effort — and when we're talking about 300 or more pages to maintain, we're definitely talking "effort" — Dreamweaver 2 introduces an expanded Templates feature.

New Feature

Dreamweaver 2 templates now enable you to create master pages in which certain elements (whether they are images, text, or plug-ins) are locked and cannot be normally modified, while other areas can be inserted or changed at will. Moreover, if an alteration is made to a Dreamweaver 2 template, all the pages based upon that template can be updated automatically. Templates are an extremely powerful and timesaving addition for the Web designer.

In Dreamweaver 2, templates are managed through the Template Palette. Grouped with the Library Palette — which, as can be seen in Figure 2-16, it resembles — the Template Palette allows for the easy creation, editing, and deletion of any template. Open the Template Palette by choosing Window ➪ Templates or by pressing Ctrl-F11. Like the Library Palette, the window is divided into a List pane and a Preview pane. The upper portion of the Template Palette shows the list of templates for the current site, and when one of these is selected, the lower portion of the window shows a preview of the template. If you've enabled the highlighting of a template's locked and editable regions, you can see these in the Preview pane. The two panes can be resized by clicking and dragging the border separating them.

Locked Region

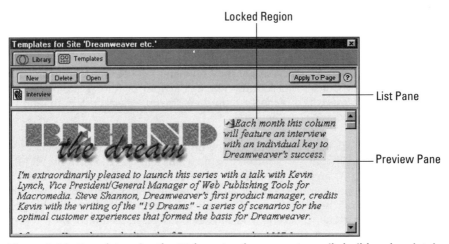

List Pane

Preview Pane

Figure 2-16: Templates give the Webmaster the power to easily build and maintain sites with a common look and feel.

The Template Palette is used for the following major operations:

Template Palette Function	Document Window Actions
Creating new templates	Selecting the New button opens a blank page for you to build a Dreamweaver template from scratch. If this is the first template you've made in the site, Dreamweaver creates a Templates folder in the site directory.
Removing templates	Deletes a template from the Templates folder
Editing templates	To alter a defined template, select its name in the List pane and press the Open button. This opens another Dreamweaver window containing your template. After you've made your modifications, Dreamweaver asks if you'd like to update pages based upon this template.
Applying templates	When you want to add a template's contents to an existing page, choose the Apply to Page button. This technique can also be used for updating a page with a previously applied template.

The more work you do on the Web, the more value you'll find in Dreamweaver templates. To find out how to get the most out of this new feature, see Chapter 34, "Using Dreamweaver Templates."

Customizing Your Workspace with Dockable Windows and Palettes

Dreamweaver is known for its powerful set of tools: Objects, Behaviors, Layers, Timelines, and so much more. To be truly useful, each tool needs its own palette or window; but the more tools you use, the more cluttered your workspace can become.

New Feature
To reduce the amount of screen real estate taken up by the individual windows, but still keep their power, Dreamweaver 2 introduces dockable windows and palettes. Almost all of Dreamweaver's 11 floating palettes can now be grouped into a single window (see Figure 2-17) — or several windows, if you like. The dockable window system is completely customizable to give you optimum control over your workflow.

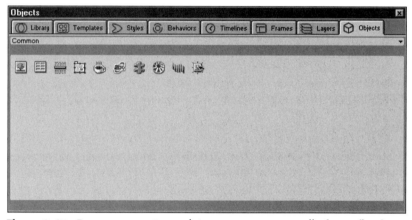

Figure 2-17: Dreamweaver 2 now lets you group any or all of your floating windows and palettes into a docking window.

As you may have noticed, the Library Palette and the Template Palette are already grouped together in the standard Dreamweaver 2 setting. Whenever one window is docked with another, each becomes accessible by clicking the representative tab. Selecting the tab brings the window or palette to the front of the docked window. Grouping windows and palettes together is very straightforward. Simply drag one window by its title bar on top of another window. When you see a border appear inside the stationary window, release your mouse button. A new tab is created to the right of the existing tabs, if any. To remove a palette from a docked window, click the tab and drag the window clear. When you release the mouse button, the palette returns to being an independent object, but retains the size and shape of the previously docked window.

Note   Three Dreamweaver floating palettes cannot be docked: the Property Inspector, the HTML Inspector, and the Launcher.

As you group more palettes together, Dreamweaver displays a symbol for the window and its name on each tab. When too many palettes are combined to fit within the docking window, Dreamweaver shows just the symbol to make room for more. If you add an additional palette to a docking window that is too small, Dreamweaver automatically expands the docking window.

Tip   As noted earlier, when you move a palette from a docking window, the palette keeps the size and shape of the docking window. To resize any window, click and drag its borders.

Accessing the Menus

Like many programs, Dreamweaver's menus duplicate most of the features accessible through windows and palettes. Certain features, however, are only available through the menus or through a corresponding keyboard shortcut. This section offers a reference guide to the menus when you need a particular feature or command. (*Note to Windows users:* The menus referred to here are those for the Document Window and not the Site Window; those menu options particular to the Site Window are covered in Chapter 33, "Publishing Via Site FTP.")

New Feature   Dreamweaver greatly expands its shortcut menus in its new version. To access a shortcut menu, right-click (Control-click) any area or object. The new shortcut menus are context-sensitive and change according to which object or area is selected. Using the shortcut menus can enhance your productivity tremendously.

The File menu

The File menu contains commands for file handling and overall site management. Table 2-5 describes the commands and their keyboard shortcuts.

Note   Macintosh users: The site-related commands listed here — New Site, Open Site ⇨ Your Site List and Open Site ⇨ Define Sites — are described in more detail in "The Site menu (Macintosh only)" section later in this chapter.

Table 2-5
File Menu Commands

Command	Description	Windows	Macintosh
New	Adds a new Document Window	Ctrl-N	n/a
New from Template	Creates a document based on an existing template	n/a	n/a
New Site (Windows only)	Displays the Site Definition dialog box for creating a new site	n/a	n/a
Open	Displays the Open dialog box for opening an existing file	Ctrl-O	Command-O
Open in Frame	Opens an existing file in the selected frame	Ctrl-Shift-O	Command-Shift-O
Open Site ⇨ Your Site List (Windows only)	Displays user-definable list of.sites; when one is selected, the Site Window opens pointing to the selected site.	n/a	n/a
Open Site ⇨ Define Sites (Windows only)	Displays the Site Information dialog box for setting up a new site, or for modifying or deleting an existing site	n/a	n/a
Close	Closes the current window	Ctrl-W or Ctrl-F4	Command-W or Command-F4
Save	Saves the current document, or displays the Save As dialog box for an unnamed document	Ctrl-S	Command-S
Save As	Displays the Save As dialog box before saving the document	n/a	n/a
Save As Template	Stores the current document as a template in the Templates folder	n/a	n/a
Save Frameset	Saves a file describing the current frameset, or displays the Save As dialog box for an unnamed document	n/a	n/a

Continued

	Table 2-5 *(continued)*		
Command	**Description**	**Windows**	**Macintosh**
Save Frameset As	Displays the Save As Frameset before saving the current frameset	n/a	n/a
Save All	Saves all open documents (including framesets, if applicable)	Ctrl-Shift-S	Command-Shift-S
Revert	Loads the previously saved version of the current page	n/a	n/a
Import ⇨ Import XML into Template	Creates a new document by inserting an XML file into the current template	n/a	n/a
Export ⇨ Editable Regions as XML	Saves the current template's editable regions as an XML file	n/a	n/a
Export ⇨ CSS Styles	Creates an external style sheet based on CSS styles in the current document	n/a	n/a
Convert ⇨ 3.0 Browser Compatible	Creates a new Web page, converting all layers to tables	n/a	n/a
Convert ⇨ Tables to Layers	Creates a new Web page, converting all tables to layers	n/a	n/a
Preview in Browser ⇨ Your Browser List	Displays list of browsers established in Preferences; choose one to preview the current page using that browser	F12 (Primary) Shift-F12 (Secondary)	F12 (Primary) Shift-F12 (Secondary)
Preview in Browser ⇨ Edit Browser List	Displays the Preview in Browser category of Preferences, where the user can add, edit, or delete additional preview browsers	n/a	n/a
Check Links ⇨ This Document	Verifies hypertext links for the current document	Ctrl-F7	Command-F7
Check Links ⇨ Entire Site	Verifies hypertext links for the current site	Ctrl-F8	Command-F8

Command	Description	Windows	Macintosh
Check Target Browsers	Displays the Check Target Browsers dialog box, where the user can validate the current file against installed browser profiles	n/a	n/a
Your Last Opened Files	Displays the last four opened files; select any name to reopen the file	n/a	n/a
Exit (Quit)	Closes all open files and quits	Ctrl-Q or Alt-F4	Command-Q

Tip   Although the menu option for replacing the current window with a new, blank document is no longer available in Dreamweaver 2, the keyboard shortcut still works: Ctrl-Shift-N (Command-Shift-N).

The Edit menu

The Edit menu gives you the commands necessary to quickly modify your page — or recover from a devastating accident. Many of the commands (Cut, Copy, and Paste) are standard on other programs; others, such as Paste As Text, are unique to Dreamweaver. Table 2-6 details all of the features found under the Edit menu.

Table 2-6 Edit Menu Commands			
Command	**Description**	**Windows**	**Macintosh**
Undo	Reverses the last action; the number of times you can Undo is determined by system resources	Ctrl-Z	Command-Z
Redo	Reverses the last Undo; the number of times you can Redo is determined by system resources	Ctrl-Y	Command-Y
Cut	Places a copy of the current selection on the clipboard and removes the selection from the current document	Ctrl-X	Command-X
Copy	Places a copy of the current selection on the clipboard and leaves the selection in the current document	Ctrl-C	Command-C

Continued

Table 2-6 *(continued)*

Command	Description	Windows	Macintosh
Paste	Copies the clipboard to the current cursor position	Ctrl-V	Command-V
Clear	Removes the current selection from the document	Delete	Delete
Select All	Highlights all the elements in the current document or frame	Ctrl-A	Command-A
Invert Selection (Macintosh only)	Highlights everything in the current document or frame except the current selection	n/a	n/a
Copy Text Only	Copies the current selection onto the clipboard with the HTML codes	Ctrl-Shift-C	Command-Shift-C
Paste As Text	Pastes the current selection from the clipboard without any HTML codes rendered as text	Ctrl-Shift-V	Command-Shift-V
Find	Displays the Find dialog box for searching the current document	Ctrl-F	Command-F
Find Next (Find Again)	Repeats the previous Find operation	F3	Command-G
Replace	Displays the Replace dialog box	Ctrl-H	Command-H
Launch External Editor (Launch BBEdit)	Opens the External HTML Editor as defined in Preferences ⇨ External Editors	Ctrl-E	Command-E
Preferences	Displays the Preferences dialog box	Ctrl-U	Command-U or Command-K

The View menu

As you build your Web pages, you'll find that it's helpful to be able to turn certain features on and off. The View menu centralizes all these commands. Certain capabilities, such as rulers and grids, are only useful when combined with layers. Table 2-7 describes each command under the View menu.

Table 2-7
View Menu Commands

Command	Description	Windows	Macintosh
Head Contents	Displays symbols for elements inserted in the <head> section of the current document	Ctrl-Shift-W	Command-Shift-W
Invisible Elements	Controls whether the symbols for certain HTML tags are shown	Ctrl-Shift-I	Command-Shift-I
Rulers ⇨ Show	Displays the horizontal and vertical rulers	Ctrl-Alt-Shift-R	Command-Option-Shift-R
Rulers ⇨ Reset Origin	Resets the ruler's 0,0 coordinates to the upper-left corner of the window	n/a	n/a
Rulers ⇨ Pixels/Inches /Centimeters	Sets the rulers to a selected measurement system	n/a	n/a
Grid ⇨ Show	Displays a background grid using the current settings	Ctrl-Alt-Shift-G	Command-Option-Shift-G
Grid ⇨ Snap To	Forces inserted objects to align with the nearest snap setting	Ctrl-Alt-G	Command-Option-G
Grid ⇨ Settings	Displays the Grid Settings dialog box	n/a	n/a
Tracing Image ⇨ Show	Displays the image chosen as the Tracing Image according to the Page Properties settings	n/a	n/a
Tracing Image ⇨ Align with Selection	Aligns the top left corner of the Tracing Image with the top left corner of the selected object	n/a	n/a
Tracing Image ⇨ Adjust Position	Enables the Tracing Image to be moved using the cursor keys or numerically	n/a	n/a
Tracing Image ⇨ Reset Position	Resets the position of the Tracing Image to the upper-left corner of the document	n/a	n/a

Continued

	Table 2-7 *(continued)*		
Command	**Description**	**Windows**	**Macintosh**
Tracing Image ⇨ Load	Displays the Open File dialog box for inserting the Tracing Image	n/a	n/a
Plug-ins ⇨ Play	Plays the selected plug-in	Ctrl-P	Command-P
Plug-ins ⇨ Stop	Stops the selected plug-in from playing	Ctrl-. (period)	Command-. (period)
Plug-ins ⇨ Play All	Plays all plug-ins on the current page	Ctrl-Shift-P	Command-Shift-P
Plug-ins ⇨ Stop All	Stops all plug-ins from playing on the current page	Ctrl-Shift-. (period)	Command-Shift-. (period)
Status Bar	Enables the status bar to be shown	n/a	n/a
Layer Borders	Makes a border visible outlining an unselected layer	n/a	n/a
Table Borders	Makes a border visible outlining an unselected table	n/a	n/a
Frame Borders	Enables borders necessary for drag-and-drop frame creation	n/a	n/a
Prevent Layer Overlaps	Stops newly created layers from overlapping	n/a	n/a

The Insert menu

The Insert menu contains the same items available through the Objects Palette. In fact, if you add additional objects (as discussed in Chapter 16, "Creating and Using Objects") the next time you start Dreamweaver you'll see your objects listed on the Insert menu. All objects are inserted at the current cursor position.

Table 2-8 details the items available to be inserted in the standard Dreamweaver.

Table 2-8			
Insert Menu Commands			
Command	**Description**	**Windows**	**Macintosh**
Image	Opens the Insert Image dialog box that lets you input or browse for a graphics file	Ctrl-Alt-I	Command-Option-I

Command	Description	Windows	Macintosh
Table	Opens the Insert Table dialog box for establishing a table layout	Ctrl-Alt-T	Command-Option-T
Horizontal Rule	Inserts a horizontal line the width of the current window	n/a	n/a
Layer	Inserts a layer of a preset size	n/a	n/a
Applet	Opens the Insert Applet dialog box that permits you to input or browse for a Java Class source	n/a	n/a
ActiveX	Inserts an ActiveX place-holder	n/a	n/a
Plug-in	Opens the Insert Plug-in you can either input or browse for a plug-in	n/a	n/adialog box so
Flash	Opens the Insert Flash Movie dialog box so you can either type in or browse for a movie file	Ctrl-Alt-F	Command-Option-F
Shockwave	Opens the Insert Shockwave Director dialog box for you to input or browse for a Director file	Ctrl-Alt-D	Command-Option-D
Rollover Image	Opens the Rollover dialog box for inserting a rollover button	n/a	n/a
Form	Creates the form structure on your Web page	n/a	n/a
Form Object ⇨ Text Field/Button/Check Box/Radio Button/List /Menu/File Field/Image Field/Hidden Field	Inserts the selected form object at the current cursor position	n/a	n/a
Named Anchor	Displays the Insert Named Anchor dialog box	Ctrl-Alt-A	Command-Option-A
Comment	Displays the Insert Comment dialog box	n/a	n/a
Script	Displays the Insert Script dialog box	n/a	n/a

Continued

Table 2-8 *(continued)*

Command	Description	Windows	Macintosh
Line Break	Inserts a line break tag	Shift-Enter	Shift-Enter
Non-breaking Space	Inserts a hard space Space	Ctrl-Shift-	Option-Space
Server-Side Include	Opens the dialog box for inserting a server-side include	n/a	n/a
Head ⇨ Meta/Keywords /Description/Refresh /Base/Link	Displays the appropriate dialog box for inserting the selected HTML tag in the <head> section	n/a	n/a

The Modify menu

Inserting objects is less than half the battle of creating a Web page. Most Web designers spend most of their time adjusting, experimenting with, and tweaking the various elements. The Modify menu lists all the commands for altering existing selections. Table 2-9 details all the Modify options.

Table 2-9
Modify Menu Commands

Command	Description	Windows	Macintosh
Page Properties	Opens the Page Properties dialog box	Ctrl-J	Command-J
Selection Properties	Displays and hides the Property Inspector	n/a	n/a
Hyperlink ⇨ Make Link	Presents the Select HTML File dialog box for picking a linking file	Ctrl-L	Command-L
Hyperlink ⇨ Remove Link	Deletes the current link	Ctrl-Shift-L	Command-Shift-L
Hyperlink ⇨ Open Linked Page	Opens the linked page in Dreamweaver	n/a	n/a

Command	Description	Windows	Macintosh
Hyperlink ⇨ Target Frame ⇨ Default/_blank /_parent/_self/_top	Selects the target for the current link	n/a	n/a
Hyperlink ⇨ Target Frame ⇨ Set	Enables you to name a target for the link		
Table ⇨ Select Table	Highlights the entire table surrounding the current cursor position	Ctrl-A	Command-A
Table ⇨ Merge Cells	Merges selected cells using spans	M	M
Table ⇨ Split Cell	Splits cells into rows or columns	Ctrl-Alt-S	Command-Option-S
Table ⇨ Insert Row	Adds a new row above the current row	Ctrl-M	Command-M
Table ⇨ Insert Column	Adds a new column before the current column	Ctrl-Shift-A	Command-Shift-A
Table ⇨ Insert Rows or Columns	Opens the Insert Rows /Columns dialog box that enables multiple rows or columns to be inserted relative to the cursor position	n/a	n/a
Table ⇨ Delete Row	Removes the current row	Ctrl-Shift-M	Command-Shift-M
Table ⇨ Delete Column	Removes the current column	n/a	n/a
Table ⇨ Increase Row Span / Decrease Row Span	Increases or decreases by one row the span of the current cell	n/a	n/a
Table ⇨ Increase Column Span / Decrease Column Span	Increases or decreases the column span of the current cell by one column	Ctrl-Shift-] (Increase Column Span) Ctrl-Shift-[(Decrease Column Span)	Command-Shift-] (Increase Column Span) Command-Shift-[(Decrease Column Span)
Table ⇨ Clear Cell Heights	Removes specified row height values for the entire selected table	n/a	n/a
Table ⇨ Clear Cell Widths	Removes specified column width values for the entire selected table	n/a	n/a

Continued

Table 2-9 *(continued)*

Command	Description	Windows	Macintosh
Table ➪ Convert Widths to Pixels	Changes column widths from percents to pixels for the entire selected table	n/a	n/a
Table ➪ Convert Widths to Percent	Changes column widths from pixels to percents for the entire selected table	n/a	n/a
Layers ➪ Align Left	Aligns grouped layers on the left edge	Ctrl-Left Arrow	Command-Left Arrow
Layers ➪ Align Right	Aligns grouped layers on the right edge	Ctrl-Right Arrow	Command-Right Arrow
Layers ➪ Align Top	Aligns grouped layers on the top edge	Ctrl-Up Arrow	Command-Up Arrow
Layers ➪ Align Bottom	Aligns grouped layers on the bottom edge	Ctrl-Down Arrow	Command-Down Arrow
Layers ➪ Make Same Width	Changes the width of grouped layers to that of the last selected layer	Ctrl-Shift-[	Command-Shift-[
Layers ➪ Make Same Height	Changes the height of grouped layers to that of the last selected layer	Ctrl-Shift-]	Command-Shift-]
Frameset ➪ Edit No Frames Content	Opens a new window for content to be seen by browsers that do not support frames	n/a	n/a
Frameset ➪ Split Frame Left/Split Frame Right/ Split Frame Up/Split Frame Down	Moves the current frame in the specified direction and adds a new frame opposite	n/a	n/a
Alignment ➪ Left	Aligns the selected object or the current line to the left	Ctrl-Alt-L	Command-Option-L
Alignment ➪ Center	Centers the selected object or the current line on the page	Ctrl-Alt-C	Command-Option-C
Alignment ➪ Right	Aligns the selected object or the current line to the right	Ctrl-Alt-R	Command-Option-R
Layout ➪ Reposition Content Using Layers	Places all content on the page in layers	Ctrl-F6	Command-F6

Continued

Command	Description	Windows	Macintosh
Layout ⇨ Convert Layers to Table	Places all content in layers in tables	Ctrl-Shift-F6	Command-Shift-F6
Library ⇨ Add Object to Library	Opens the Library Palette and adds the selected object	n/a	n/a
Library ⇨ Update Current Page/Update Pages	Replaces any modified Library items in the current page or current site	n/a	n/a
Templates ⇨ Apply Template to Page	Enables the selection of a template to be overlaid on the current page	n/a	n/a
Templates ⇨ Detach from Template	Breaks the link between the template and the current page	n/a	n/a
Templates ⇨ Open Attached Template	Opens the current template for editing	n/a	n/a
Templates ⇨ Update Current Page	Automatically updates the page with template changes	n/a	n/a
Templates ⇨ Update Pages	Enables the updating of an entire site or of all pages using a particular template	n/a	n/a
Templates ⇨ New Editable Region	Inserts the placeholder for a new editable region	Ctrl-Alt-V Option-V	Command-Option-V
Templates ⇨ Mark Selection as Editable	Converts the selected text or objects from locked to editable	Ctrl-Alt-W	Command-Option-W
Templates ⇨ Unmark Editable Region	Converts the selected region from editable to locked	n/a	n/a
Add Object to Timeline	Opens the Timeline Inspector and inserts the current image or layer	n/a	n/a
Add Behavior to Timeline	Opens the Timeline Inspector and inserts an onFrame event using the current frame	n/a	n/a
Record Path of Timeline	Plots the path of a dragged layer onto a timeline	n/a	n/a
Timeline ⇨ Add Keyframe	Inserts a keyframe at the current Playback Head position	Shift-F9	Shift-F9
Timeline ⇨ Remove Keyframe	Deletes the currently selected keyframe	Delete	Delete (above cursor keys)

Continued

Table 2-9 *(continued)*			
Command	*Description*	*Windows*	*Macintosh*
Timeline ⇨ Change Object	Applies a timeline path to another object	n/a	n/a
Timeline ⇨ Remove Object / Remove Behavior	Deletes the currently selected Object or behavior	n/a	n/a
Timeline ⇨ Add Frame/Remove Frame	Inserts or deletes a frame at the current Playback Head position	n/a	n/a
Timeline ⇨ Add Timeline/Remove Timeline/Rename Timeline	Inserts an additional timeline, deletes the current timeline, or renames the current timeline	n/a	n/a
Translate ⇨ Server-side Includes	*Makes nonconditional server-side includes visible in the current document*	n/a	n/a

The Text menu

The Internet was initially an all-text medium and, despite all the multimedia development, the World Wide Web hasn't traveled far from these beginnings. The Text menu, as described in Table 2-10, covers overall formatting as well as text-oriented functions such as spell-checking.

Table 2-10 Text Menu Commands			
Command	*Description*	*Windows*	*Macintosh*
Indent	Marks the selected text or the current paragraph with the `<blockquote>` tag toindent it	Ctrl-]	Command-]
Outdent	Removes a `<dir>` or `<blockquote>` surrounding the selected text or current indented paragraph	Ctrl-[	Command-[
Format ⇨ None	Removes all HTML formatting tags surrounding the current selection	Ctrl-0 (zero)	Command-0 (zero)
Format ⇨ Paragraph	Converts the selected text to paragraph format	Ctrl-T	Command-T

Command	Description	Windows	Macintosh
Format ⇨ Heading 1–6	Changes the selected text to the specified heading format	Ctrl-1–6	Command-1–6
Format ⇨ Preformatted Text	Formats the selected text with a monospaced font	n/a	n/a
List ⇨ None	Changes a list item into a paragraph	n/a	n/a
List ⇨ Unordered List	Makes the selected text into a bulleted list	n/a	n/a
List ⇨ Ordered List	Makes the selected text into a numbered list	n/a	n/a
List ⇨ Definition List	Converts the selected text into alternating definition terms and items	n/a	n/a
List ⇨ Properties	Opens the List Properties dialog box	n/a	n/a
Alignment ⇨ Left	Aligns the selected text to the left of the page, table, or layer	Ctrl-Alt-L	Command-Option-L
Alignment ⇨ Center	Aligns the selected text to the center of the current page, table, or layer	Ctrl-Alt-C	Command-Option-C
Alignment ⇨ Right	Aligns the selected text to the right of the page, table, or layer	Ctrl-Alt-R	Command-Option-R
Font ⇨ Default	Changes the current selection to the default font	n/a	n/a
Font ⇨ Your Font List	Displays fonts in your current font list	n/a	n/a
Font ⇨ Edit Font List	Opens the Font List dialog box for adding or deleting fonts from the current list	n/a	n/a
Style ⇨ Bold	Makes the selected text bold	Ctrl-B	Command-B
Style ⇨ Italic	Makes the selected text italic	Ctrl-I	Command-I
Style ⇨ Underline	Underlines the selected text	n/a	n/a
Style ⇨ Strikethrough	Surrounds the selected text with the `<s>`...`</s>` tags for text with a line through it	n/a	n/a
Style ⇨ Teletype	Surrounds the selected text with the `<tt>`...`</tt>` tags for a monospaced font	n/a	n/a
Style ⇨ Emphasis	Surrounds the selected text with the `<emp>`...`</emp>` tags for slightly emphasized, usually italic, text	n/a	n/a

Continued

Table 2-10 *(continued)*			
Command	**Description**	**Windows**	**Macintosh**
Style ➪ Strong	Surrounds the selected text with the `<strong>...</strong>` tags for more emphasized, usually bold, text	n/a	n/a
Style ➪ Code	Surrounds the selected text with HTML code for depicting programming code	n/a	n/a
Style ➪ Variable	Surrounds the selected text with HTML code for depicting a variable in programming, typically in italic	n/a	n/a
Style ➪ Sample ➪ Keyboard	Surrounds the selected text with HTML code for depicting monospaced fonts	n/a	n/a
Style ➪ Citation	Surrounds the selected text with HTML code for depicting cited text, usually in italic	n/a	n/a
Style ➪ Definition	Surrounds the selected text with HTML code for depicting a definition, usually in italic	n/a	n/a
Custom Style (selection) ➪ None/Your Style List	Applies a user-defined style to selected text. The None selection removes previously applied styles.	n/a	n/a
Custom Style (selection) ➪ Edit Style Sheet	Opens the Edit Style Sheet dialog box for adding, deleting, or modifying custom styles	Ctrl-Shift-E	Command-Shift-E
Size ➪ Default ➪ 1–7	Converts the selected text to the chosen font size	n/a	n/a
Size Increase ➪ +1–+7	Increases the size of the selected text relative to the defined basefont size (default is 3)	n/a	n/a
Size Decrease ➪ –1 through –7	Decreases the size of the selected text relative to the defined basefont size (default is 3)	n/a	n/a
Color	Opens the Color dialog box to alter the color of selected or following text	n/a	n/a
Check Spelling	Opens the Spell Check dialog box	Shift-F7	Shift-F7

The Commands menu

Dreamweaver 2 now offers a further enhancement to its already impressive extensibility palette: commands. Commands are user-definable code capable of affecting almost any tag, attribute, or item on the current page—or even the current site. Commands increase your productivity by automating many of the mundane, repetitive tasks in Web page creation.

New Feature Dreamweaver 2 comes with several very handy Commands, but they are truly just the tip of the iceberg. Commands, like Objects and Behaviors, are written in HTML and JavaScript and can be created and modified by any capable programmer.

Table 2-11 describes the standard Dreamweaver 2 Commands.

<table>
<tr><td colspan="4" align="center">Table 2-11
Commands Menu</td></tr>
<tr><td>*Command*</td><td>*Description*</td><td>*Windows*</td><td>*Macintosh*</td></tr>
<tr><td>Clean Up HTML</td><td>Processes the current page according to various options to remove extraneous HTML</td><td>n/a</td><td>n/a</td></tr>
<tr><td>Apply Source Formatting</td><td>Structures the current page according to the Source Format Profile</td><td>n/a</td><td>n/a</td></tr>
<tr><td>Set Color Scheme</td><td>Selects a color scheme for the current page affecting background color, text color, and the link colors</td><td>n/a</td><td>n/a</td></tr>
<tr><td>Sort Table</td><td>Sorts the current table alphabetically or numerically</td><td>n/a</td><td>n/a</td></tr>
<tr><td>Format Table</td><td>Enables a predesigned format to be set on the current table</td><td>n/a</td><td>n/a</td></tr>
</table>

Cross-Reference You'll find a number of new commands on the CD-ROM, as well as information on how to build your own in Chapter 19, "Customizing Dreamweaver."

The Site menu (Macintosh only)

By design, any program running under the Macintosh operating system uses one central menu regardless of the number of windows opened. For this reason, the Macintosh implementation of Dreamweaver contains a separate menu, Site, that Windows systems display on the Site Window. All the commands found in the Site menu, as detailed in Table 2-12, are naturally concerned with Dreamweaver's Site FTP functions.

Note Because the Site menu is Macintosh only, the column listing Windows shortcuts has been left out.

Table 2-12
Site Menu Commands

Command	Description	Macintosh
New Site	Presents the Site Definition dialog box for creating a new site	n/a
Open Site ⇨ Your Site List	Displays a user-definable list of sites; when one is selected, the Site Window opens pointing to the selected site	n/a
Define Sites	Displays the Site Information dialog box for setting up a new site, or for modifying or deleting an existing site	n/a
Site Files View ⇨ New Folder	Creates a new folder in the current site	Command-Shift-Option-N
Site Files View ⇨ New File	Creates a new HTML file in the current site	Command-Shift-N
Site Files View ⇨ Refresh Local	Rereads and displays the current local folder	Command-F5
Site Files View ⇨ Refresh Remote	Rereads and displays the current remote folder	Option F5
Site Files View ⇨ Select Newer Local	Highlights files that have been modified locally but not transferred to the remote site	n/a
Site Map View ⇨ Select Newer Remote	Highlights files with a later file modification date on the remote site than the same file on the local site	n/a
Site Map View ⇨ View as Root	Makes the selected file the starting point for the map	Command-Shift-R
Site Map View ⇨ Link to New File	Creates a new file and adds a link to the selected page	Command-Shift-N
Site Map View ⇨ Link to Existing File	Adds a text link to an existing file to the selected page	Command-Shift-K
Site Map View ⇨ Change Link	Selects a new page to use as a link instead of the selected file and updates the link	Command-L
Site Map View ⇨ Remove Link	Deletes the selected link	Command-Shift-L
Site Map View ⇨ Show/Hide Link	Marks a file and all its dependent files as hidden or displayable	Command-Shift-Y
Site Map View ⇨ Open Source of Link	Opens the HTML file containing the selected link in Dreamweaver	n/a

Command	*Description*	*Macintosh*
Site Map View ⇨ Save Site Map as PICT	Stores the current site map as a graphic file	n/a
Site Map View ⇨ New Home Page	Makes the selected file the starting point for the Site Map	n/a
Site Map View ⇨ Select Home Page	Presents a Select File dialog box to choose a file that becomes the new starting point for the Site Map	n/a
Site Map View ⇨ Show Files Marked as Hidden	Displays all hidden files with the filename in italics	n/a
Site Map View ⇨ Show Dependent Files	Shows all the graphic and other additional files associated with the HTML pages	n/a
Site Map View ⇨ Show Page Titles	Displays icons identified by page titles instead of by filenames.	Command-Shift-T
Site Map View ⇨ Layout	Opens the Layout dialog box that determines the structure of the Site Map	n/a
Site Map View ⇨ Refresh	Redraws the Site Map	Command-F5
Change Links Sitewide	Updates links from one pointing to one page to point to another	n/a
Recreate Site Cache	Rebuilds the Site Cache to allow for quicker updates	n/a
Open	Loads a selected file into Dreamweaver	Command-Shift-Option-O
Rename	Renames the selected file	n/a
Unlock	Makes selected read-only files accessible	n/a
Disconnect	Severs the FTP connection	Command-Shift-Option-F5
Get	Transfers the selected files from the remote site to the local folder	Command-Shift-D
Check Out	Marks selected files on the remote site as checked out	Command-Shift-Option-D
Put	Transfers the selected files from the local folder to the remote site	Command-Shift-U
Check In	Marks selected files as checked in	Command-Shift-Option-U

Continued

	Table 2-12 *(continued)*		
Command	**Description**		**Macintosh**
Undo Check Out	Removes the Check Out designation on selected files		n/a
Check Links ⇨ Selected	Verifies hypertext links for the current or selected documents		Command-F7
Check Links ⇨ Entire	Verifies hypertext links for the current site		Command-F8
FTP Log	Opens the FTP Log window		n/a
Tool Tips	Enables long filenames or page titles to be displayed when passed over by the pointer		n/a

The Window menu

The Window menu manages both program and user-opened windows. Through this menu, detailed in Table 2-13, you can open, close, arrange, bring to the front, or hide all of the additional Dreamweaver screens. There's even a command to open one additional window — that of Dreamweaver.com.

Tip   All the commands for Dreamweaver's various windows, palettes, and inspectors are toggles. Select it once to open the window; select again to close it.

	Table 2-13 **Window Menu Commands**		
Command	**Description**	**Windows**	**Macintosh**
Objects	Opens the Objects Palette	Ctrl-F2	Command-F2
Properties	Shows the Property Inspector for the currently selected item	Ctrl-F3	Command-F3
Launcher	Opens the Launcher Palette	n/a	n/a
Sites Files	Displays the Sites Window	F5	F5
Site Map	Displays the current site map	Shift-F5	Shift-F5
Library	Opens the Library Palette	F6	F6
Styles	Opens the Styles Inspector	F7	F7
Behaviors	Shows the Behaviors Inspector	F8	F8
Timelines	Shows the Timelines Inspector	F9	F9
HTML	Displays the HTML Inspector	F10	F10

Command	Description	Windows	Macintosh
Layers	Opens the Layers Inspector	F11	F11
Frames	Opens the Frames Inspector	Ctrl-F10	Command-F10
Templates	Opens the Template Palette	Ctrl-F11	Command-F11
Arrange Floating Palettes	Moves all open windows to preset positions	n/a	n/a
Show/Hide Floating Palettes	Displays/hides all open windows	F4	F4
Dreamweaver Online	Goes online to the Dreamweaver Developer's Center Support Web site	Ctrl-F1	Command-F1
Your Open Windows	Displays a list of the currently open Dreamweaver windows	n/a	n/a

The Help menu

The final menu, the Help menu, offers access to Dreamweaver's excellent online Help, as well as special examples and templates. Table 2-14 explains each of these useful options.

Table 2-14 Help Menu Commands			
Command	Description	Windows	Macintosh
Dreamweaver Help Pages	Opens the Dreamweaver online Help system in your primary browser	F1	n/a
Register Dreamweaver	Goes online to register your copy of Dreamweaver	n/a	n/a
About Dreamweaver	Shows the opening Dreamweaver splash screen with credits, registration, and version information	n/a	n/a

Summary

In this chapter, you've observed Dreamweaver's power and had a look at its well-designed layout. From the Objects Palette to the various tools controlled through the Launcher, Dreamweaver offers you an elegant, flexible workspace for creating next-generation Web sites.

✦ The Document Window is your main canvas for visually designing your Dreamweaver Web pages. This workspace includes simple, powerful tools such as the Tag Selector and the status bar Launcher.

✦ The Objects Palette is Dreamweaver's toolbox. Completely customizable, the Objects Palette holds the elements you'll need most often, in four initial categories: Common, Forms, Head, and Invisibles.

✦ Dreamweaver's mechanism for assigning details and attributes to an HTML object is the Property Inspector. The Property Inspector is context-sensitive and its options vary according to the object selected.

✦ The Launcher is the control center for Dreamweaver's specialized functions: the Site Window, the Library Palette, the Styles Palette, the Behavior Inspector, the Timeline Inspector, and the HTML Inspector. You have two Launchers to choose from: one free-floating palette and the one accessible through the status bar, the Mini-Launcher.

✦ Dreamweaver 2's new dockable palettes enable you to group your most commonly accessed tools together — and minimize on-screen clutter.

✦ Dreamweaver's full-featured menus offer complete file manipulation, a wide range of insertable objects, the tools to modify them, and extensive online — and on-the-Web — help. Many menu items can be invoked through keyboard shortcuts.

In the next chapter, you'll learn how to customize Dreamweaver to work the way you work by establishing your own preferences for the program and its interface.

✦   ✦   ✦

Setting Your Preferences

Everyone works differently. Whether you need to conform to a corporate style sheet handed down from the powers that be or you think "it just looks better that way," Dreamweaver offers you the flexibility to shape your Web page tools and your code output. This chapter describes the options available to you in Dreamweaver's Preferences and then details how you can tell Dreamweaver to format your source code *your* way.

Customizing Your Environment

The vast majority of Dreamweaver's settings are controlled through the Preferences dialog box. You can open Preferences by choosing Edit ➪ Preferences, or by using the keyboard shortcuts Ctrl-U (Command-U). Within Preferences, you'll find 15 different subjects listed on the left side of the screen. As you switch from one category to another by selecting its name from this Category list, the options available for that category appear in the main area of the dialog box. Although this chapter covers all the options available to you in each category, the categories are grouped by function, rather than examined in the same order as in the Category list.

Most changes to Preferences take effect immediately after you close the window by clicking OK or the Close button. Only two preferences are not updated instantly:

✦ First, the Show Only Site Window on Startup option goes into effect on the next running of Dreamweaver.

✦ Second, if you elect to modify the source format profile, as described in "Source Format Preferences," you should complete this modification outside of Dreamweaver (in a text editor), save your work, and then start the program.

General Preferences

Dreamweaver's General Preferences, as seen in Figure 3-1, cover program appearance, user operation, and external editor integration. The appearance of the program's interface may seem to be a trivial matter, but Dreamweaver is a program for designers — to whom appearance is extremely important. These user-operation options are based purely on how you, the user, work best.

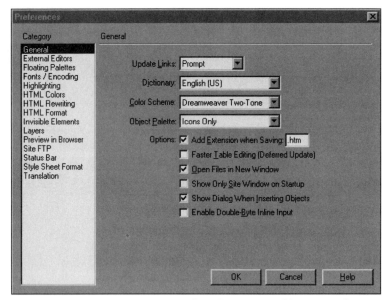

Figure 3-1: Dreamweaver's General Preferences enable you to change your program's appearance and certain overall operations.

Tip   In choosing all the preferences, including the General ones, you can work in two ways. If you are a seasoned Web designer, you'll probably want Dreamweaver to work in your established manner to minimize your learning curve. If you're just starting out as a Web page creator, work with the default options for a while, and then go back and try other options. You'll know right away which style works for you.

Update Links

As your site grows in complexity, you'll find that keeping track of the various links is an increasingly difficult task. Dreamweaver 2 has several enhanced features to help you manage links, and the Update Links option is one of them. Dreamweaver can check each link on a page when a file is moved — whether it is the Web page you're working on or one of the support files, such as image, that goes on the page. The Update Links option determines how Dreamweaver reacts when it notes an altered link.

By default, the Update Links option is set to Prompt, which causes Dreamweaver 2 to alert you to any link changes and requires you to "OK" the code alterations by selecting the Update button. To leave the files as they are, you choose the Don't Update button. You can elect to have Dreamweaver automatically keep your pages up-to-date by selecting the Always option from the Update Links drop-down list. Finally, you can select the Never option and Dreamweaver will ignore the link changes necessary when you move, rename, or delete a file.

As a general rule, I keep my Update Links option set to Always. It is a very rare circumstance when I intentionally want to maintain a bad link on my Web page. Likewise, I would recommend using the Never option with extreme caution.

The Update Links option replaces the Correct Relative Links on Save As option found in earlier versions of Dreamweaver.

Dictionary

The Dictionary option lets you select a spell-checking dictionary from any of those installed. In addition to the standard English language version which has three options — English (US), English (UK -ise), and English (UK -ize) — as of this writing, there are also German and French dictionaries available. You can download these dictionaries from Macromedia's Dreamweaver Object Exchange at http://www.macromedia/support/dreamweaver/upndown/objects. Once downloaded, save the .dat file in the Configuration\Dictionaries folder and restart Dreamweaver.

To select a different dictionary for spell-checking, select the Dictionary option button and choose an item from the drop-down list. Although not visible on the list, Dreamweaver also maintains a Personal dictionary to hold those words you wish Dreamweaver to learn during the spell-checking process.

Color Scheme

The first option is purely a cosmetic one: the color scheme of the screens presented to you as you work with the program. Dreamweaver offers three different color combinations. Click the arrow button next to Color Scheme to open the drop-down list and choose from the following options:

Color Scheme Options	Description
Dreamweaver Two-Tone	The default color scheme; uses two shades of gray
Desktop Two-Tone	Picks up your desktop primary color and one contrasting color to define window borders and other areas
Desktop Standard	Uses the system default colors for a monochromatic approach

Tip   On the Launcher Palette, the icon text is anti-aliased to appear smooth against the default background, which is a light gray. If your desktop or system color is much darker in tone, you'll probably notice some distracting artifacts (miscolored pixels) around the letters. To fix this problem, switch to a lighter desktop color or choose the Dreamweaver Two-Tone color scheme.

Objects Palette

Learning a new software program can be tough — just memorizing which icon means what can increase your learning curve. With Dreamweaver 2, you don't have to try to remember all the Object symbols right off the bat. If you like, you can opt to have the names of the Objects next to their icons — or even just the names themselves. You make this choice in the Objects Palette option.

New Feature   By default, the Objects Palette is composed only of icons. When you pass your mouse over each one, a tooltip appears that names the Object. However, if you don't want to hunt for your Object, you can select Icons and Text from the Objects Palette option, or Text Only. Whichever option you select, when you exit from Preferences, the Objects Palette changes size and shape to accommodate the new format, as shown in Figure 3-2.

Figure 3-2: In Dreamweaver 2, the Objects Palette can display each Object's name along with its icon.

General options

The second main section of the General Preferences screen consists of numerous check-box options you can turn on or off. Overall, these options fall into the user-interaction category or "What's good for you?" Take the Show Dialog When Inserting Objects option, for example. Some Web creators prefer to enter all their attributes at one time through the Property Inspector and would rather not have the dialog boxes appear for every inserted object. Others want to get their file sources in immediately and modify the rest later. Your selection depends on how you want to work.

The following paragraphs describe the listed options.

Add Extension When Saving

HTML files originally were identified — cleverly enough — by their .html filename extension. When Windows jumped on the Internet bandwagon, they reduced the extension to three letters, .htm, to fit their pre-Windows 95 format. But now there is an explosion of different Web file formats and extensions to match: .asp, .shtml, .stm, and .phtml to name just a few. In previous versions of Dreamweaver, the .htm extension was the default — and a difficult one to change at that. Dreamweaver 2 now includes the capability to save your files using any filename extension you specify.

New Feature
The Add Extension When Saving option is very straightforward. Just enter the extension of your choosing in a text box and make sure the option is selected. For example, if you are building nothing but Active Server Pages for a particular Web site, you would change the Add Extension When Saving text box to .asp and select Okay in the Preferences dialog box. Now, to save a file you only have to enter the initial part of the file name and the appropriate extension is automatically appended.

Faster Table Editing (Deferred Update)

When you enter text into a table, the current column width automatically expands while the other columns shrink correspondingly. If you're working with very large tables, this updating process can slow down your editing. Dreamweaver gives you the choice between faster input or instantaneous feedback.

When the Faster Table Editing preference is turned on, Dreamweaver updates the entire table only when you click outside the table, or if you press Ctrl-spacebar (Command-spacebar). If you prefer to see the table form as you type, turn this option off.

Tip
Two other ways to update tables: Select any tag in the Tag Selector (a useful approach when working with a very large table) or resize the Document Window.

Open Files in New Window (Windows Only)

Select the Open Files in New Window option when you need to have several Web pages open simultaneously. Alternately, if you want to free up some of your system resources (such as memory) and you only need one Dreamweaver window, you can deselect this option.

Note
If this option is not selected and changes are made to the current file, Dreamweaver asks if you'd like to save the current page when you attempt to load a new file.

Show Only Site Window on Startup (Windows Only)

Some Web designers prefer to use the Site Window as their "base of operations," rather than the Document Window. For them, it's easier — particularly with many of Dreamweaver 2's new features — to construct and maintain their Web pages from the sitewide perspective offered through the Site Window. Dreamweaver 2 now offers you the option to begin a Web authoring session with just the Site Window.

New Feature   Selecting the Show Only Site Window on Startup option displays just the Site Window the next time you open Dreamweaver. The Site Window is shown in the configuration used the last time you had it open — with or without the Site Map enabled and with the various columns positioned in the same manner. To bring up the Document Window, choose File ➪ New Window from the Site Window menu. This feature also enables you to close all the Document Windows and keep just the Site Window open — a combination not possible before Dreamweaver 2.

Show Dialog When Inserting Objects

By default, almost all the objects that Dreamweaver inserts — via either the Objects Palette or the Insert menu — open an initial dialog box to gather needed information. In most cases, the dialog box enables you to input an URL or browse for a source file. Turning off the Show Dialog option causes Dreamweaver to insert a default-sized object, or a placeholder, for the object. You must then enter all attributes through the Property Inspector.

Enable Double-Byte Inline Input

Some computer representations of languages, primarily those from Asia, require more raw descriptive power than others. The ideogram for "snow," for example, is far more complex than a four-letter word. These languages need twice the number of bytes per character and are known as *double-byte languages*. In previous versions of Dreamweaver, all double-byte characters had to go through a separate text input window instead of directly into the Document Window.

New Feature   Dreamweaver 2 simplifies the page creation process for double-byte languages with the Enable Double-Byte Inline Input option. Once selected, this option enables double-byte characters to be entered directly into the Document Window. To use the old method of inserting such characters, deselect this option.

Preferences for Invisible Elements

By their nature, all HTML markup tags remain unseen to one degree or another when presented for viewing through the browser. You may want to see certain elements while designing a page, however. For example, adjusting line spacing is a common task, and turning on the visibility of the line break tag `<BR>` can help you understand the layout.

Dreamweaver enables you to control the visibility of 13 different codes — or rather their symbols, as shown in Figure 3-3. When, for example, a named anchor is inserted, Dreamweaver shows you a small gold shield with an anchor emblem. Not only does this shield indicate the anchor's position, but you can also manipulate the code with cut-and-paste or drag-and-drop techniques. Moreover, double-clicking a symbol opens the pertinent Property Inspector and enables quick changes to the tag's attributes.

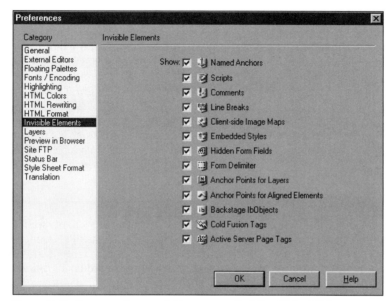

Figure 3-3: You can show or hide any or all of the 13 invisible elements listed in the Preferences dialog box.

Tip   You can temporarily hide all invisible elements by deselecting View ➪ Invisible Elements.

The 13 items controlled through the Invisible Elements panel are as follows:

✦ Named Anchors

✦ Scripts

✦ Comments

✦ Line Breaks

✦ Client-Side Image Maps

✦ Embedded Styles

✦ Hidden Form Fields

✦ Form Delimiter

✦ Anchor Points for Layers

✦ Anchor Points for Aligned Elements

   ✦ Backstage lbObjects

   ✦ Cold Fusion Tags

   ✦ Active Server Page Tags

Most of the Invisible Elements options display or hide small symbols in Dreamweaver's visual Document Window. Several options, however, show an outline or another type of highlight. Turning off Form Delimiter, for example, removes the dashed line that surrounds a form in the Document Window. Similarly, deselecting the Library Item highlight removes the yellow highlighting automatically applied to any portion of the page created from a library item.

New Feature   You may have noticed the two new Invisible Elements included in Dreamweaver 2: Cold Fusion Tags and Active Server Page Tags. Dreamweaver 2's ability to handle dynamic pages generated by databases makes these new Invisible Elements essential.

Floating Palettes

Although the various windows, palettes, and inspectors are convenient, sometimes you just want a clear view of your document. The Floating Palettes Preferences panel enables you to choose which of Dreamweaver's accessory screens stay on top of the Document Window. As shown in Figure 3-4, you can adjust 11 different elements. By default, they are all set to float above the Document Window.

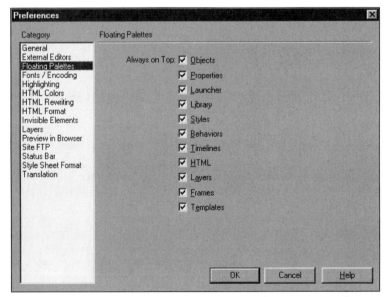

Figure 3-4: If you deselect any of the Floating Palettes screens, they move behind the Document Window.

If you use the HTML Inspector often, you might consider taking it off the "always on top" list. Then, after you've made your HTML code edits, click in the Document Window. This sequence updates the visual document, incorporating any changes, and simultaneously pushes the HTML Inspector behind the document window. You can switch between the two views of your Web page by using the Ctrl-Tab (Command-Tab) key combination.

Tip You can use the Show/Hide Floating Palettes key to bring back any screen element that has gone behind the Document Window. Just press F4 twice.

Highlighting preferences

Dreamweaver 2 is far more extensible than previous versions — library items are more prevalent, templates are more powerful, and more third-party tags are supported. Many of these features depend on "hidden" abilities that are not noticeable in the final HTML page, but the Web designer must take them into account. Dreamweaver 2 uses user-selectable highlighting to mark areas on a Web page under construction.

New Feature The Highlighting panel of the Preferences dialog box, shown in Figure 3-5, enables you to choose the highlight color for four different types of extended objects: Editable and Locked Regions, both used in templates; Library items; and Third-Party Tags. In each case, to choose a highlight color, select the color swatch to open Dreamweaver's color picker. Then use the Eyedropper to pick a color from the Web-safe palette or from your desktop. After you've chosen an appropriate color, make sure to select the related Show check-box so that the highlighting will be displayed.

Status Bar preferences

The status bar is a handy collection of four different tool sets: the Tag Selector, the Window Size pop-up menu, the Connection Speed Indicator, and the Mini-Launcher. The Status Bar panel of the Preferences dialog box, shown in Figure 3-6, controls options for three of the four tools.

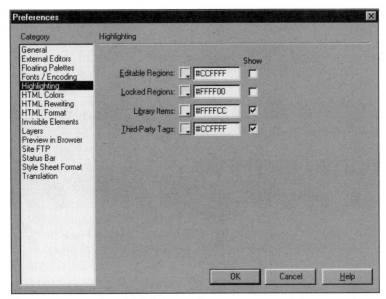

Figure 3-5: Use the Highlighting preferences to control how template regions, Library Items, and Third-Party Tags appear in the Document Window.

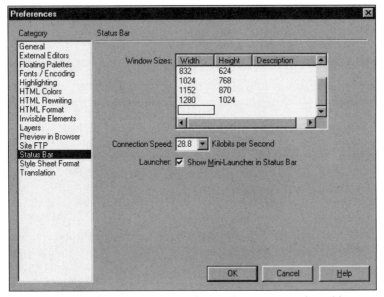

Figure 3-6: Use the Status Bar panel to evaluate your real-world download times.

Window Sizes

The Window Sizes list at the top of the Status Bar panel shows the current options for the Window Sizes pop-up menu. This list is completely user-editable and enables you to add new window sizes, modify existing dimensions, add descriptions, or delete little-used measurements.

New
Feature

As discussed in Chapter 2, "Touring Dreamweaver," the Window Sizes pop-up is a new feature in Dreamweaver 2 that enables you to instantly change your screen size so that you may view and build your page under different monitor conditions. To change any of the current dimensions, simply click on the measurement you wish to alter and enter a new value. You can also change any description of the existing widths and heights by clicking in the Description column and entering your text. While you can enter as much text as you like, it's not practical to enter more than about 15–20 characters.

To enter a new set of dimensions in the Window Sizes list box, follow these steps:

1. From the Status Bar panel of the Preferences dialog box, locate the last entry in the current list.

   If the last entry is not immediately available, use the vertical scroll bar to move to the end.

2. Click once in the Width column on the line below the last entry.

3. Enter the desired width of the new window size in pixels.

4. Press Tab to move to the Height column.

5. Enter the desired height for the new window size. Press Tab again.

6. Optionally, you can enter a short descriptive text in the Description column. Press Tab when you're done.

7. To continue adding new sizes, repeat Steps 2–6. Select OK when you finish.

Caution

You don't have to enter the word "pixels" or the abbreviation "px" after your values in the Width and Height columns of the Window Sizes list box, but you can. Any other type of dimension entered, such as "inches" or "in," is automatically converted to pixels. Finally, if you enter any dimensions under 20, Dreamweaver converts the measurement to its smallest possible window size, 20 pixels.

Connection Speed

Dreamweaver understands that not all access speeds are created equal, so the Connection Speed option enables you to check the download time for your page (or the individual images) at a variety of rates. The Connection Speed setting evaluates the download statistics in the status bar. You can choose from seven preset connection speeds, all in kilobits per second: 14.4, 28.8, 33.6, 56, 64, 128, and 1,500. The lower speeds (14.4 through 33.6) represent common dial-up modem connection rates — if you are building a page for the mass market, you should select one of these slower rates. Although 56K modems are widespread on the market today, the true 56K connection is a rare occurrence. Use the 128 setting if your audience connects through an ISDN line. If everyone will be viewing your page through a direct LAN connection, change the connection speed to 1,500.

You are not limited to these preset settings. You can type any desired speed directly into the Connection Speed text box. You could, for example, specify a connection speed more often experienced in the real world, such as 23.3. If you find yourself designing for an audience using cable modems in the near future, you could change the Connection Speed to 500.

Show Mini-Launcher in Status Bar

The default setting enables the status bar Mini-Launcher. When this option is disabled, you always have to access the Launcher by choosing Window ⇨ Launcher from the menus.

External Editor preferences

Refinement is often the name of the game in Web design, and giving you quick access to your favorite modification tools — whether you're modifying code or graphics — is one of Dreamweaver's key features. The External Editors panel, shown in Figure 3-7, is where you specify the program you want Dreamweaver to call for you.

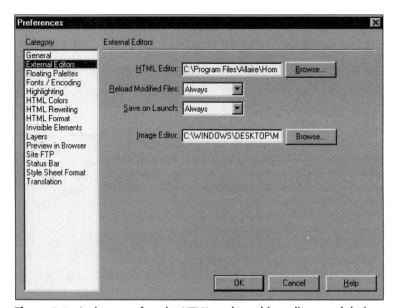

Figure 3-7: Assign your favorite HTML and graphics editors and their associated options through the External Editors panel of the Preferences dialog box.

Dreamweaver recognizes the importance of your choice of a text editor. Although Dreamweaver ships with two extremely robust HTML editors, you can opt to use any other program. To select your editor, enter the path in the HTML text box, or select the Browse (Choose) button to choose the appropriate executable file.

The two included editors, BBEdit for Macintosh and HomeSite for Windows, are integrated with Dreamweaver to varying degrees. Both of the editors can be called from within Dreamweaver and both have "Dreamweaver" buttons for returning to the main program — switching between the editor and Dreamweaver automatically updates the page. Like Dreamweaver's internal HTML editor, BBEdit highlights the corresponding code to a selection made in Dreamweaver; this property does not, however, extend to HomeSite.

You specify and control your external editor selection with the following options.

Enable BBEdit Integration (Macintosh only)

Dreamweaver for Macintosh ships with this option activated. If you prefer to use another editor or an older version of BBEdit that lacks the integration capabilities, deselect this option.

Reload Modified Files

The drop-down list for this setting offers three options for working with an external editor:

✦ **Prompt** detects when files are updated by another program and enables you to decide whether to update them within Dreamweaver.

✦ **Always** updates the file in Dreamweaver automatically when the file is changed in an outside program.

✦ **Never** assumes that you want to make all updates from within Dreamweaver yourself.

Personally, I prefer to have Dreamweaver always update my files. I find it saves a couple of mouse clicks — not to mention time.

Save on Launch

Any external HTML editor — even the integrated HomeSite or BBEdit — opens and reads a previously saved file. Therefore, if you make any changes in Dreamweaver's visual editor and switch to your editor without saving, the editor will only show the most recently saved version. To control this function, you have three options:

✦ **Prompt** determines that unsaved changes have been made and asks you to save the file. If you do not, the external editor reverts to the last saved version.

✦ **Always** saves the file automatically before opening it in the external editor.

✦ **Never** disregards any changes made since the last save, and the external editor opens the previously saved file.

Here again, as with Reload Modified Files, I prefer to always save my files when switching back and forth. Keep in mind, however, that saving a file clears Dreamweaver's Undo memory and the changes cannot be undone.

Tip   If you try to open a file that has never been saved in an external editor, Dreamweaver prompts you to save it regardless of your preference settings. If you opt not to save the file, the external editor is not opened because it has no saved file to display.

Image Editor preferences

Dreamweaver has the ability to call an image editor at the touch of a button. When you import a graphic, you often need to modify its color, size, shape, transparency, or another feature to make it work correctly on the Web page. Rather than force you to start your graphics program independently, load the image, make the changes, and resave the image, Dreamweaver lets you send any selected image directly to your editor. After you've made your modifications and saved the file, the altered image appears automatically in Dreamweaver.

Select your favorite graphics program as your Dreamweaver image editor by entering the program's path and filename in the Images text box. You can also use the Browse button to locate and select the executable file.

Cross-Reference   Be sure that your graphics program is adept at handling the three graphic formats used on the Web: GIFs, JPEGs, and PNG images. Macromedia makes Fireworks 2, a graphics editor designed for the Web that integrates nicely with Dreamweaver. In fact, it integrates so nicely, there's an entire section on it in Chapter 8, "Inserting Images."

Adjusting Advanced Features

Evolution of the Web and its language, HTML, never ends. New features emerge often from leading browser developers. A competing developer can introduce a similar feature that works in a slightly different way. The HTML standards organization — the World Wide Web Consortium, also known as the W3C — can then endorse one approach or introduce an entirely new method of reaching a similar goal. Eventually, one method usually wins the approval of the marketplace and becomes the accepted coding technique.

To permit the widest range of features, Dreamweaver enables you to designate how your code is written to accommodate the latest HTML features: layers and style sheets. The default preferences for these elements offer the highest degree of cross-browser and backward compatibility. If your Web pages are intended for a more specific audience, such as a Netscape Navigator-only intranet, Dreamweaver lets you take advantage of a more specific feature set.

Layers preferences

Aside from helping you control the underlying coding method for producing layers, Dreamweaver lets you define the default layer. This capability is especially useful during a major production effort in which the Web development team must produce hundreds of layers spread over a Web site. Being able to specify in advance the initial size, color, background, and visibility saves numerous steps — each of which would have to be repeated for every layer. Figure 3-8 shows the layout of the Layers panel of the Preferences dialog box.

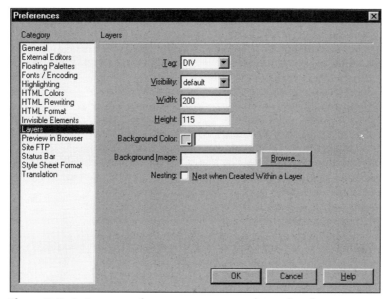

Figure 3-8: In Layers preferences, you can predetermine the structure of the default Dreamweaver layer.

The controls accessible through the Layers panel include the following.

Tag

Select the arrow button to see the tags for the four HTML code methods for implementing layers: `<div>`, `<span>`, `<layer>`, and `<ilayer>`. The first two, `<div>` and `<span>`, were developed by the W3C as part of their Cascading Style Sheets recommendation and are supported by both the Netscape and Microsoft 4.0 browsers. Netscape developed the latter two HTML commands, `<layer>` and `<ilayer>`; currently only Communicator 4.0 supports these tags.

Dreamweaver uses the `<div>` tag for its default. Supported by both major 4.0 browsers, the `<div>` element offers the widest cross-browser compatibility. You should only use one of the other Tag options if you are building a Web site intended for a specific browser.

Cross-Reference To learn more about the uses of the various positioning tags, see Chapter 25, "Working with Layers."

Visibility

Layers can be either visible or hidden when the Web page is first loaded. A layer created using the default visibility option is always displayed initially; however, no specific information is written into the code. Selecting Visible forces Dreamweaver to include a `visibility:visible` line in your layer code. Likewise, if you select Hidden from the Visibility options, the layer is initially hidden.

Use the Inherit option when creating nested layers. Creating one layer inside another makes the outer layer the parent, and the inner layer the child. If the parent layer is visible and the child layer is set to `visibility:inherit`, then the child is also visible. This option makes it possible to affect the visibility of many layers with one command — hide the parent layer, and all the inheriting child layers disappear as well.

Width and Height

When you choose Draw Layer from the Objects Palette, you drag out the size and shape of your layer. Choosing Insert ⇨ Layer puts a layer of a default size and shape at your current cursor position. The Width and Height options enable you to set these defaults. Select the text boxes and type your new values. Dreamweaver's default is a layer 200 pixels wide by 115 pixels high.

Background Color

Layers can have their own background color independent of the Web page's overall background color (which is set as a `<body>` attribute). You can define the default background color of any inserted layer through either the Insert menu or the Objects Palette. For this preference setting, type a color, either by its standard name or as a hexadecimal triplet, directly into the text box. You can also click on the color swatch to display the Dreamweaver browser-safe color picker.

Caution Note that while you can specify a different background color for the layer, you can't alter the layer's default text and link colors (except on a layer-by-layer basis) as you can with a page. If your page and layer background colors are highly contrasting, be sure your text and links are readable in both environments. A similar caveat applies to the use of a layer's background image, as explained in the next section.

Background Image

Just as you can pick a specific background color for layers, you can select a different background image for layers. You can type a file source directly into the Background Image text box or select your file from a dialog box by choosing the Browse button. The layer's background image supersedes the layer background color, just as it does with the HTML page. Also, just as the page's background image tiles to fill the page, so does the layer's background image.

Nesting

The two best options about layers seem to be directly opposed: overlapping and nesting layers. You can design layers to appear one on top of another, and you can code layers so that they are within one another. Both techniques are valuable options, and Dreamweaver lets you decide which one should be the overriding method.

If you are working primarily with nested layers and plan on using the inheritance facility, check the Nest when Created Within a Layer option. If your design entails a number of overlapping but independent layers, make sure this option is turned off. Regardless of your preference, you can reverse it on an individual basis by pressing the Ctrl (Command) key when drawing out your layers.

Style Sheet Format preferences

The Style Sheet Format panel (see Figure 3-9) is entirely devoted to how your code is written. As specified by the W3C, Cascading Style Sheets (CSS) declarations — the specifications of a style — can be written in several ways. One method displays a series of items, separated by semicolons:

```
H1 { font-family: helvetica; font-size: 12pt; line-height:
14pt; font-weight: bold;}
```

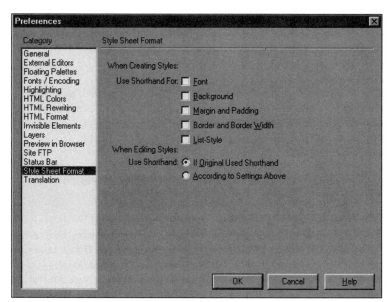

Figure 3-9: The Style Sheet Format panel lets you code the style sheet sections of your Web pages in a graphics designer–friendly manner.

Certain properties (such as font) have their own grouping shorthand, developed to be more readable to designers coming from a traditional print background. A second, "shorthand" method of rendering the preceding declaration follows:

```
H1 { font: helvetica 12pt/14pt bold  }
```

The Style Sheet Format panel lets you enable the shorthand method for any or all of the five different properties that permit it. Select any of the check-boxes under Use Shorthand For to have Dreamweaver write your style code in this fashion.

The second option on the Style Sheet Format panel determines how Dreamweaver edits styles in previously coded pages. If you want to retain the format of the original page, click Use Shorthand If Original Used Shorthand. If you want Dreamweaver to write new code in the manner that you specify, select Use Shorthand According to Settings Above.

Caution   Although the leading varieties of the 4.0 browsers can read the style's shorthand with no difficulty, Internet Explorer 3.0 does not have this capability. IE3 is the only other mainstream browser that can claim support for Cascading Style Sheets, but it doesn't understand the shorthand form. If you want to maintain browser back-ward-compatibility, don't enable any of the shorthand options.

Translation Preference

In order to properly view server-generated content for server-side includes or database-linked pages in Dreamweaver's Document Window, the information has to be *translated*. Code in server-side includes looks something like the following:

```
<!--#include file="footer.inc" -->
```

New Feature   Before Dreamweaver 2, you had to send all your files to the Web server and look at them online to view the complete content on the page. Dreamweaver 2 gives you the power to translate the server-side information so that you can design your page in context. The Translation panel, shown in Figure 3-10, specifies how trans-lations are to be handled.

Features of the Translation panel are detailed in the following sections.

Translators

The Translators list box displays the currently available translators. Dreamweaver 2 ships with one included translator: server-side includes (SSI). Other translators can be custom written or purchased from third-party companies. When you add additional translators to the system—by copying their files to the Configuration\ Translators folder—their names appear in the Translators list box, and the Up and Down buttons become active. The Up/Down buttons are used to specify the order in which the translations occur.

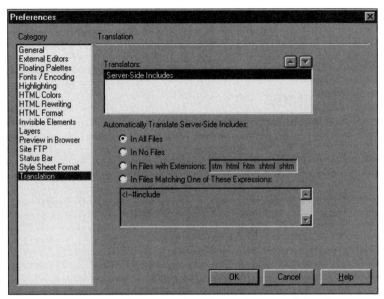

Figure 3-10: The Translation panel of the Preferences dialog box determines when your server-side content is capable of being viewed in the Document Window.

Translation options

The translation options in the lower portion of the Translation panel are specific to each translator. For server-side includes, the options are to automatically translate SSI under the following conditions:

✦ **In All Files.** Displays server-side includes unconditionally (default).

✦ **In No Files.** Never translates SSIs in the Document Window.

✦ **In Files with Extensions.** Only files with the listed extensions are translated.

✦ **In Files Matching One of These Expressions.** If this option is selected, Dreamweaver scans the code of the entire page. If one or more of the listed expressions are found, all SSIs included on the page are translated.

To learn more about translators and server-side includes, see Chapter 15, "Accessing External Programs."

Making Online Connections

Dreamweaver's visual layout editor offers an approximation of your Web page's appearance in the real world of browsers — offline or online. After you've created the initial draft of your Web page, you should preview it through one or more browsers. And when your project nears completion, you should transfer the files to a server for online, real-time viewing and further testing through a File Transfer Protocol program (FTP). Dreamweaver gives you control over all these stages of Web page development, through the Site FTP and Preview in Browser panels.

Site FTP preferences

As your Web site takes shape, you'll spend more time with the Site FTP portion of Dreamweaver. The Site FTP panel, seen in Figure 3-11, enables you to customize the look and feel of your site, as well as enter essential connection information.

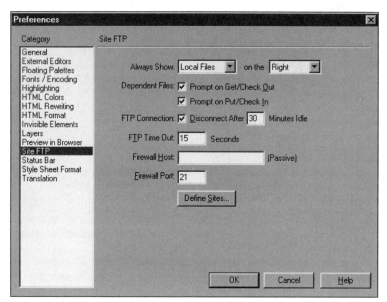

Figure 3-11: Options for Dreamweaver's Site Window are handled through the Site FTP panel.

The available Site FTP preferences are described in the following sections.

Always Show Local/Remote Files on the Right/Left

The Site Window is divided into two panes: one showing local files and one showing remote files on the server. By default, Dreamweaver puts the Local pane on the right and the Remote pane on the left. However, version 2 enables you to customize that option. Like many designers, I'm used to using other FTP programs in which the Remote files are on the right and the Local files on the left; Dreamweaver 2 now lets me work the way I'm used to working.

To switch the layout of your Site Window, select the file type you want to change to (Local Files or Remote Files) from the Always Show drop-down list *or* select the panel you want to change to (Right or Left) from the "on the" drop-down list. Be careful not to switch both options or you'll end up where you started!

Dependent files

Web pages are very seldom just single HTML files. Any graphic — whether it's in the background, part of your main logo, or used on a navigational button — is uploaded as a separate file. The same is true for any additional multimedia add-ons such as audio or video files. If you've enabled File Check In/Check Out when defining your site, Dreamweaver can also track these so-called *dependent files*.

Enabling the Prompt check-boxes causes Dreamweaver to ask you if you'd like to move the dependent files when you transfer an HTML file. You can opt to show the dialog box for Get/Check Out, Put/Check In, or both.

You're not stuck with your Dependent Files choice. If you turn off the Dependent Files prompt, you can make it appear by pressing the Alt key while clicking the Get or Put button.

FTP Connection: Disconnect After __ Minutes Idle

You can easily forget you're online when you are busy modifying a page. You can set Dreamweaver to automatically disconnect you from an FTP site after a specified interval. The default is 30 minutes; if you want to set a different interval, you can select the FTP Connection value in the Disconnect After text box. Dreamweaver now asks if you want to continue to wait or to disconnect when the time limit is reached, but you can maintain your FTP connection regardless by deselecting this option.

FTP Time Out

Client-server communication is very prone to glitches. Rather than hanging up your machine while trying to reach a server that is down, Dreamweaver alerts you to an apparent problem after a set period. You can determine the number of seconds you want Dreamweaver to wait by altering the FTP Time Out value. The default is 30 seconds.

Firewall information

Dreamweaver enables users to access remote FTP servers outside their network firewall. A *firewall* is a security component that protects the internal network from unauthorized outsiders, while enabling Internet access. To enable firewall access, enter the Firewall Host and External Port numbers in the appropriate text boxes; if you do not know these values, contact your network administrator.

If you're having trouble transferring files via FTP through the firewall, make sure the Use Firewall (in Preferences) option is enabled in the Site Definition dialog box. You'll find the option on the Web Server Info panel.

Preview in Browser preferences

Browser testing is an essential stage of Web page development. Previewing your Web page within the environment of a particular browser gives you a more exact representation of how it looks when viewed online. Because each browser renders the HTML slightly differently, you should preview your work in several browsers. Dreamweaver lets you select both a primary and secondary browser, which can both be called by pressing a function key. You can name up to 18 additional browsers through the Preview in Browser panel shown in Figure 3-12. This list of preferences is also called when you choose File ➪ Preview in Browser ➪ Edit Browser List.

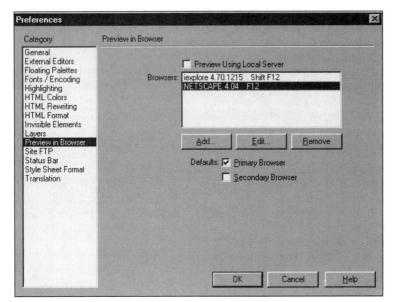

Figure 3-12: The Preview in Browser panel lists browsers currently available for preview and lets you modify the list.

If you are developing on Windows, your Web page is using site root relative paths for links, *and* you have a local server setup, enable the Preview Using Local Server option. This capability ensures that your previews link correctly. The other method to preview sites using site root relative paths places the files on a remote server.

Adding a browser to the preview list

To add a browser to your preview list, follow these steps:

1. Choose Edit ➪ Preferences or press the keyboard shortcut: Ctrl-U (Command-U).

2. Select the Preview in Browser category.

3. Select the Add button.

4. In the Add Browser dialog box, type the browser name you want listed into the Name text box.

5. Enter the path to the browser file in the Path text box, or click the Browse (Choose) button to pick the file from the Select Browser dialog box.

6. If you want to designate this browser as your Primary or Secondary browser, select one of those check-boxes in the Defaults section.

7. Click OK when you have finished.

8. You can continue to add browsers (up to a total of 20) by following Steps 3 through 7. Click OK when you have finished.

Once you've added a browser to your list, you can modify your selection by following these steps:

1. Open the Preview in Browser panel and highlight the browser you want to alter.

2. Select the Edit button to get the Edit Browser dialog box.

3. After you've made your modifications, click OK to close the dialog box.

Tip   You can quickly make a browser your Primary or Secondary previewing choice without going through the Edit screen. From the Preview in Browser panel, select the desired browser and click either Primary Browser or Secondary Browser. Note that if you already have a primary or secondary browser defined, this action overrides your previous choice.

You can also easily remove a browser from your Preview list:

1. Open the Preview in Browser panel and choose the browser you want to delete from the list.

2. Select the Remove button and click OK.

Customizing Your Code

For all its multimedia flash and visual interactivity, the Web is based on code. The more you code, the more particular about your code you are likely to become. Achieving a consistent look and feel to your code enhances its readability and, thus, your productivity. In Dreamweaver, you can even design the HTML code that underlies a Web page's structure.

Every time you open a new document, the default Web page already has several key elements in place, such as the language the page is to be rendered in. Dreamweaver also enables you to customize your work environment by selecting default fonts and even the colors of your HTML code.

Fonts/Encoding preferences

In the Fonts/Encoding panel, shown in Figure 3-13, you can control the fonts as seen by a user's browser and the fonts that you see when programming. The Default Encoding section lets you choose either Western style fonts for Web pages to be rendered in English, one of the Asian languages (Japanese, Traditional Chinese, Simplified Chinese, or Korean) or another language such as Cyrillic, Greek, or Icelandic Mac.

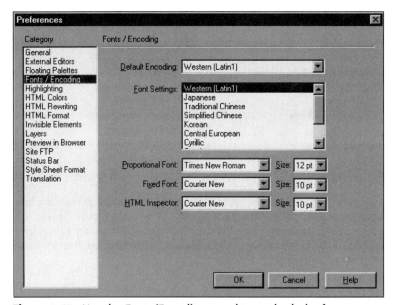

Figure 3-13: Use the Fonts/Encoding panel to set both the font encoding for each Web page and the fonts you use when programming.

In the bottom portion of the Fonts/Encoding panel, you can alter the default font and size for three different fonts:

✦ **Proportional Font.** This font option sets the default font used in Dreamweaver's Document Window to depict paragraphs, headings, and lists.

✦ **Fixed Font.** In a fixed font, every character is allocated the same width. Dreamweaver uses your chosen fixed font to depict preformatted styled text.

✦ **HTML Inspector.** The HTML Inspector font is used by Dreamweaver's built-in text editor. You should probably use a monospaced font like Courier or Monaco. A monospaced font makes it easy to count characters, which is often necessary when debugging your code.

For all three font options, select your font by clicking the list and highlighting your choice of font. Change the font size by selecting the value in the Size text box or by typing in a new number.

Caution   Don't be misled into thinking that by changing your Proportional Font preference to Arial or another font, all of your Web pages are automatically viewed in that typeface. Changing these font preferences only affects the default fonts that you see when developing the Web page; the default font that the user sees is controlled by the user's browser. To ensure that a different font is used, you have to specify it for any selected text through the Text Properties Inspector.

HTML Rewriting preferences

The exception to Dreamweaver's policy of not altering imported code occurs when HTML is incorrectly structured. Dreamweaver automatically fixes tags that are nested in the wrong order or have additional, unnecessary closing tags — unless you tell Dreamweaver otherwise by setting up the HTML Rewriting preferences accordingly (see Figure 3-14).

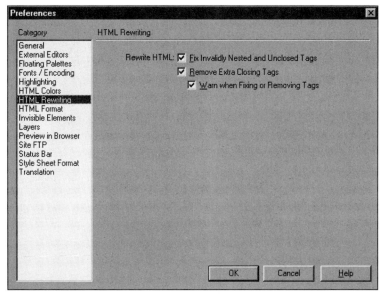

Figure 3-14: The HTML Rewriting panel can be used to protect nonstandard HTML from being automatically changed by Dreamweaver.

Following are descriptions of the particular controls of the HTML Rewriting preferences.

Fix Invalidly Nested and Unclosed Tags

When enabled, this option repairs incorrectly placed HTML tags. For example, if a file contained the following line:

```
<h3><b>Welcome to the Monkey House!</h3></b>
```

Dreamweaver rewrites it as follows:

```
<h3><b>Welcome to the Monkey House!</b></h3>
```

Open that same file while the Fix option is turned off, and Dreamweaver highlights the misplaced code in the Document Window. Double-clicking the code brings up a window with a brief explanation.

Caution   If a browser encounters nonstandard HTML, the code will probably be ignored. Dreamweaver does not follow this protocol, however. Unless Dreamweaver is familiar with the type of code you are using, your code could be altered when the page is opened. If you are using specially formatted database tags or other nonstandard HTML programming, be sure to open a test page first.

Remove Extra Closing Tags

When you're editing your code by hand, it's fairly easy to miss a closing tag. Dreamweaver cleans up such code if you enable the Remove Extra Closing Tags option. You may, for example, have the following line in a previously edited file:

```
<p>And now back to our show...</p></i>
```

Notice that the closing italic tag, `</i>`, has no matching opening partner. If you open this file into Dreamweaver with the Remove option enabled, Dreamweaver plucks out the offending `</i>`.

Tip   In some circumstances, you want to make sure your pages remain as originally formatted. If you edit pages in Dreamweaver that are preprocessed by a server unknown to Dreamweaver prior to the display of the pages, make sure to disable both the Fix Invalidly Nested and Unclosed Tags option where possible and the Remove Extra Closing Tags option.

Warn when Fixing or Removing Tags

If you're editing a lot of Web pages created on another system, you should enable the Warn when Fixing or Removing Tags option. If this setting is turned on, Dreamweaver displays a list of changes that have been made to your code in the HTML Corrections dialog box. As you can see from Figure 3-15, the changes can be quite extensive when Dreamweaver opens what it regards as a poorly formatted page.

Caution   Remember that once you've enabled these Rewrite HTML options, the fixes occur automatically. If this sequence happens to you by mistake, immediately close the file (without saving it!), disable the HTML Rewriting preferences options, and reopen the document.

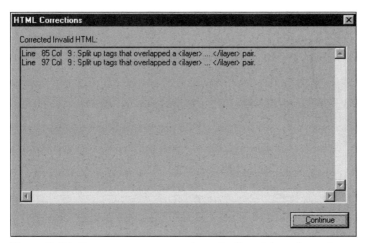

Figure 3-15: Dreamweaver can automatically catch and repair certain HTML errors. You can set Dreamweaver to send a report to the screen in the HTML Corrections dialog box.

HTML Colors preferences

HTML code is a combination of the tags that structure the language and the text that provides the content. Often a Web page designer has difficulty distinguishing swiftly between the two — and finding the right code to modify. Dreamweaver enables you to set color preferences for the code as it appears in the HTML Inspector. Not only can you alter colors for the background, default tags, and text and general comments, but you can also specify certain tags to get certain colors.

To modify any of the basic elements (Background, Text, Comments, or Tag Default), select the color swatch next to the corresponding name, as illustrated in Figure 3-16. Select a color from any of the 216 displayed in the color picker or choose the small palette icon to select from the full range of colors available to your system. You can also use the Eyedropper tool to pick a color from the Document Window.

To select a different color for a specific tag, first select the tag from the Tag Specific list box. Then choose either the Default option (which assigns the same color as specified for the Tag Default) or a custom color by clicking the color swatch and choosing the color. If you want to set all of the code and text enclosed by the selected tag to the same color, choose the Apply Color to Tag Contents option. This option is useful for setting off large blocks of code, such as the code included in the `<script>` section.

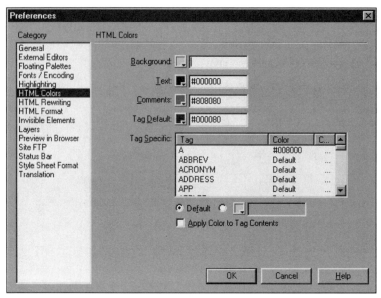

Figure 3-16: Use the HTML Colors panel to custom color-code the HTML Inspector.

HTML Format preferences

Dreamweaver includes two other tools for customizing your HTML. The first is an easy-to-use, point-and-click preferences panel called HTML Format. The second is a text file called the Source Format Profile (SourceFormat.profile), which must be modified by hand and controls the output of every HTML tag. You can modify your HTML using either or both techniques. All of the options controlled by the HTML Format panel are written out to the text file.

Most of your HTML code parameters can be controlled through the HTML Format panel. The only reason to alter the SourceFormat.profile text file by hand is if you want to control the appearance of your HTML code at the tag level.

In the preferences panel, you can decide whether to use indentations — if so, whether to use spaces or tabs and how many of each — or to turn off indents for major elements such as tables and frames. You can also globally control the case of your HTML tags and their attributes. As you can see in Figure 3-17, the HTML Format panel is full-featured.

To examine the available options in the HTML Format panel, let's separate them into four areas: indent control, line control, case control, and centering.

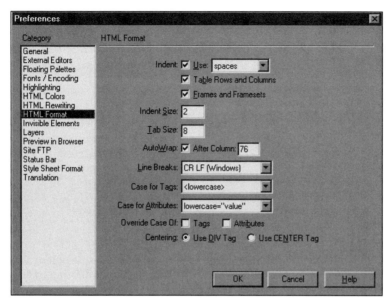

Figure 3-17: The HTML Format panel enables you to shape your HTML to your own specifications.

Indent control

Indenting your code generally makes it more readable. Dreamweaver defaults to indenting most HTML tags with two spaces, giving extra indentation grouping to tables and frames. All of these parameters can be altered through the HTML Format panel of the Preferences dialog box.

The first indent option enables indenting and lets you switch from spaces to tabs. To permit indenting, make sure a check mark is displayed in the Indent check-box. Of the 52 separate HTML tags Dreamweaver identifies in its Source Format Profile, 29 tags are designed to be indented. If you prefer your code to be displayed flush left, turn off the Indent option altogether.

To use tabs instead of the default spaces, click the Use arrow button and select tabs from the drop-down list. If you anticipate transferring your code to a word-processing program for formatting and print out, you should use tabs; otherwise, stay with the default spaces.

Dreamweaver formats both tables and frames as special indentation groups. Within each of these structural elements, the related tags are indented (or nested) more than the initial two spaces. As you can see in Listing 3-1, each table row (<tr>) is indented within the table tag, and the table data tags (<td>) are nested within the table row.

Listing 3-1: **An indented code sample**

```
<table border="1" width="75%">
  <tr>
    <td>Row 1, Column 1</td>
    <td>Row 1, Column 2</td>
    <td>Row 1, Column 3</td>
  </tr>
  <tr>
    <td>Row 2, Column 1</td>
    <td>Row 2, Column 2 </td>
    <td>Row 2, Column 3</td>
  </tr>
</table>
```

If you want to disable the special indentation grouping for tables, deselect Table Rows and Columns in the HTML Format panel. Turn off frame indenting by unchecking Frames and Framesets (this option is selected by default).

The other two items in the indent control section of HTML Format preferences are Indent Size and Tab Size. Change the value in Indent Size to establish the size of indents using spaces. To alter the size of tab indents, change the Tab Size value.

Line control

The browser is responsible for ultimately formatting an HTML page for viewing. This formatting includes wrapping text according to each user's screen size and the placement of the paragraph ($<p>...</p>$) tags. Therefore, you control how your code wraps in your HTML editor. You can turn off the automatic wrapping feature or set it for a particular column through the line control options of the HTML Format panel.

To turn off the automatic word-wrapping capability, deselect AutoWrap. When you are trying to debug your code and looking for specific line numbers and character positions, enable this option. You can also set the specific column for the word wrap to take effect. Be sure AutoWrap is enabled, and then type your new value in the After Column text box.

Tip   If you're using the HTML Inspector, selecting its Wrap option overrides the AutoWrap setting in HTML Format.

The Line Breaks setting determines which line break character is appended to each line of the page. Each of the major operating systems employs a different ending character: Macintosh uses a carriage return (CR), UNIX uses a line feed (LF), and Windows uses both (CR LF). If you know the operating system for your remote server, choosing the corresponding line break character helps the file to appear correctly when viewed online. Click the arrow button next to Line Breaks and select your system.

Caution

The operating system for your local development machine may be different from the operating system of your remote server. If so, using the Line Breaks option may cause your HTML to appear incorrectly when viewed through a simple text editor (like Notepad or vi). The Dreamweaver HTML Inspector, however, does render the code correctly.

Case control

Whether an HTML tag or attribute is in uppercase or lowercase doesn't matter to most browsers—the command is rendered regardless of case. Case is only a personal preference among Web designers. That said, some Webmasters take case consideration as a serious preference and insist on their codes being all uppercase, all lowercase, or a combination. Dreamweaver gives you control over the tags and attributes it creates, as well as over case conversion for files that Dreamweaver imports.

The Dreamweaver default for both tags and attributes is lowercase. Click the arrow button next to Case for Tags and/or Case for Attributes to alter the selection. After you have selected OK from the HTML Format panel, Dreamweaver changes all the tags in any currently open file. Choose File ➪ Save to write the changes to disk.

You can also use Dreamweaver to standardize the letter case in tags of previously saved files. To alter imported files, select the Override Case Of Tags and/or the Override Case Of Attributes options. When enabled, these options enforce your choices made in the Case for Tags and Case for Attributes option boxes in any file Dreamweaver loads. Again, be sure to save your file to keep the changes.

Centering

When an object—whether it's an image or text—is centered on a page, HTML tags are placed around the object (or objects) to indicate the alignment. Since the release of HTML 3.2, the `<center>` tag has been deprecated by the W3C in favor of the using a `<div>` tag with an align="center" attribute. By default, Dreamweaver uses the officially preferred method of `<div align="center">`.

New Feature

Many Web designers are partial to the older `<center>` tag and prefer to use it to align their objects. Dreamweaver 2 now offers a choice with the Centering option in the HTML Format panel. To use the new method, select the Use DIV Tag option (the default). To switch to the older `<center>` method, select the Use CENTER Tag option. Although use of `<center>` has been officially discouraged, it is so widespread that all browsers continue to support it.

Understanding the Source Format Profile

As noted earlier, Dreamweaver pulls its code configuration guidelines from a text file named SourceFormat.profile. When Dreamweaver is installed, this file is put in the Dreamweaver\Configuration folder along with the file, SourceFormat.original. When you make a modification to the HTML Format panel, the initial profile is renamed as SourceFormat.backup and then Dreamweaver writes a new SourceFormat.profile.

Tip   You can restore the default Source Profile settings at any time. When Dreamweaver is closed, delete SourceFormat.profile and then make a copy of the SourceFormat.original file. Finally, rename the copy as SourceFormat.profile.

Dreamweaver uses a specialized HTML format to create a SourceFormat.profile that can be viewed and edited in any text editor. Three main sections exist, each denoted with a `<?keyword>` format: `<?options>`, `<?elements>`, and `<?attributes>`. Prior to each section, Dreamweaver uses the HTML comment tags to describe them. The file closes with the `<?end>` keyword.

The Source Format Profile (see Listing 3-2) starts with two HTML comments. The first describes the overall document (`Dreamweaver source formatting profile`), followed by the Options section.

Listing 3-2: **The Source Format Profile**

```
<!-- Dreamweaver source formatting profile -->

<!-- options

    INDENTION  : indention options
      ENABLE   - allows indention
      INDENT   - columns per indention
      TABS     - columns per tab character
      USE      - TABS or SPACES for indention
      ACTIVE   - active indention groups (IGROUP)

    LINES  : end-of-line options
      AUTOWRAP - enable automatic line wrapping
      BREAK    - CRLF, CR, LF
      COLUMN   - auto wrap lines after column

    OMIT  : element omission options
      OPTIONS  - options

    ELEMENT  : element options
      CASE   - "UPPER" or "lower" case
      ALWAYS - always use preferred element case (instead of
original case)

    ATTRIBUTE  : attribute options
      CASE   - "UPPER" or "lower" case
      ALWAYS - always use preferred attribute case (instead of
original case)
```

```
-->
<?options>
<indention enable indent="2" tabs="8" use="spaces"
active="1,2">
<lines autowrap column="76">
<omit options="0">
<element case="lower">
<attribute case="lower">

<!-- element information
  line breaks          : BREAK  = "before, inside start, inside
end, after"
  indent contents      : INDENT
  indent group         : IGROUP = "indention group number" (1
through 8)
  specific name case   : NAMECASE = "CustomName"
  prevent formatting   : NOFORMAT
-->
<?elements>
<address break="1,0,0,1">
<applet break="0,1,1,0" indent>
<area break="1,0,0,1">
<base break="1,0,0,1">
<blockquote break="1,0,0,1" indent>
<body break="1,1,1,1">
<br break="0,0,0,1">
<caption break="1,0,0,1">
<center break="1,1,1,1" indent>
<dd break="1,0,0,1" indent>
<dir break="1,0,0,1" indent>
<div break="1,0,0,1" indent>
<dl break="1,0,0,1" indent>
<dt break="1,0,0,1" indent>
<embed break="1,0,0,1" indent>
<form break="1,1,1,1" indent>
<frame break="1,0,0,1">
<frameset break="1,0,0,1" indent igroup="2">
<h1 break="1,0,0,1" indent>
<h2 break="1,0,0,1" indent>
<h3 break="1,0,0,1" indent>
<h4 break="1,0,0,1" indent>
<h5 break="1,0,0,1" indent>
<h6 break="1,0,0,1" indent>
<head break="1,1,1,1">
<hr break="1,0,0,1">
<html break="1,1,1,1">
<ilayer break="1,0,0,1">
<input break="1,0,0,1">
<isindex break="1,0,0,1">
<layer break="1,0,0,1">
<li break="1,0,0,1" indent>
<link break="1,0,0,1">
<map break="0,1,1,0" indent>
<menu break="1,0,0,1" indent>
```

```
<meta break="1,0,0,1">
<object break="0,1,1,0" indent>
<ol break="1,1,1,1" indent>
<option break="1,0,0,1">
<p break="1,0,0,1" indent>
<param break="1,0,0,1">
<pre break="1,0,0,1" noformat>
<script break="1,0,0,1" noformat>
<select break="1,1,1,1" indent>
<style break="1,0,0,1" noformat>
<table break="1,1,1,1" indent igroup="1">
<td break="1,0,0,1" indent igroup="1">
<textarea break="1,0,0,1" noformat>
<th break="1,0,0,1" indent igroup="1">
<title break="1,0,0,1">
<tr break="1,0,0,1" indent igroup="1">
<ul break="1,1,1,1" indent>

<!-- attribute information
  specific name case      : NAMECASE = "CustomName"
  values follow attr case  : SAMECASE
-->
<?attributes>
<onAbort namecase="onAbort">
<onBlur namecase="onBlur">
<onChange namecase="onChange">
<onClick namecase="onClick">
<onDragDrop namecase="onDragDrop">
<onError namecase="onError">
<onFocus namecase="onFocus">
<onKeyDown namecase="onKeyDown">
<onKeyPress namecase="onKeyPress">
<onKeyUp namecase="onKeyUp">
<onLoad namecase="onLoad">
<onMouseDown namecase="onMouseDown">
<onMouseMove namecase="onMouseMove">
<onMouseOut namecase="onMouseOut">
<onMouseOver namecase="onMouseOver">
<onMouseUp namecase="onMouseUp">
<onMove namecase="onMove">
<onReset namecase="onReset">
<onResize namecase="onResize">
<onSelect namecase="onSelect">
<onSubmit namecase="onSubmit">
<onUnload namecase="onUnload">
<onDblClick namecase="onDblClick">
<onAfterUpdate namecase="onAfterUpdate">
<onBeforeUpdate namecase="onBeforeUpdate">
<onHelp namecase="onHelp">
<onReadyStateChange namecase="onReadyStateChange">
<onScroll namecase="onScroll">
<onRowEnter namecase="onRowEnter">
<onRowExit namecase="onRowExit">
<align samecase>
```

```
<checked samecase>
<codetype samecase>
<compact samecase>
<ismap samecase>
<frame samecase>
<method samecase>
<multiple samecase>
<noresize samecase>
<noshade samecase>
<nowrap samecase>
<selected samecase>
<shape samecase>
<type samecase>
<valign samecase>
<visibility samecase>
<?end>
```

Options

The Options section parallels the options set in the HTML Format panel. You can either use Dreamweaver's point-and-click interface by choosing Edit ⇨ Preferences and then selecting the HTML Format category; or you can edit the `<?options>` section of the SourceFormat.profile file. In the Options description, five parameters are outlined: indention, lines, omit, element, and attribute.

The indention item denotes the indent options:

```
ENABLE   - allows indention
INDENT   - columns per indention
TABS     - columns per tab character
USE      - TABS or SPACES for indention
ACTIVE   - active indention groups (IGROUP)
```

The final indention option, `ACTIVE`, relates to the special grouping function that Dreamweaver calls `IGROUPS`. By default, Dreamweaver assigns `IGROUP #1` to Table Rows and Columns, and `IGROUP #2` to Frames and Framesets.

The line options are detailed as follows:

```
AUTOWRAP - enable automatic line wrapping
BREAK    - CRLF, CR, LF
COLUMN   - auto wrap lines after column
```

As mentioned earlier, the `BREAK` options are used to insert the type of line break character recognized by your Web server's operating system. Use CRLF for Windows, CR for Macintosh, and LF for Unix.

The next Options section, `OMIT`, is reserved by Dreamweaver for further expansion and is not currently used.

The Element and Attribute sections control the case of HTML elements (or tags) and attributes:

```
CASE    - "UPPER" or "lower" case
ALWAYS  - always use preferred element case (instead of
original case)
```

If the ALWAYS keyword is used, Dreamweaver alters the case of tags and/or attributes when you import a previously saved file.

The following section of the Source Format Profile that starts with <?options> contains the actual options read by Dreamweaver at startup. This listing shows the default options from the SourceFormat.original file for Dreamweaver 2:

```
<?options>
<indention enable indent="2" tabs="8" use="spaces"
active="1,2">
<lines autowrap column="76">
<omit options="0">
<element case="lower">
<attribute case="lower">
```

Elements

The Element information in the next section of the Source Format Profile describes the syntax and options for individually controlling each HTML tag.

```
line breaks      : BREAK  = "before, inside start, inside end,
after"
indent contents  : INDENT
indent group     : IGROUP = "indention group number" (1 through
8)
specific name case   : NAMECASE = "CustomName"
prevent formatting   : NOFORMAT
```

break

The syntax for break refers to the number of line breaks surrounding the opening and closing HTML tags. For example, the default syntax for the <h1> tag follows:

```
<h1 break="1,0,0,1" indent>
```

The preceding produces code that looks like the following:

```
<h1>Welcome!</h1>
```

If you want to display the opening and closing tags on their own lines, you could change the break value as follows:

```
<h1 break="1,1,1,1" indent>
```

The preceding gives you the following result:

```
<h1>
 Welcome!
</h1>
```

Use zero in the "before" and "after" positions when you want a tag to appear in line with the other code, as in this map tag:

```
<map break="0,1,1,0" indent>
```

The Elements list only contains tags that have opening and closing elements, which are also known as *container tags*. Any single-element tags, such as the image tag, `<img>`, are presented in line with other elements.

You're not restricted to using 1 and 0 values for `break`. If you want to isolate a tag so that it really stands out, use 2 in the "before" and "after" positions. For example:

```
<p break="2,1,1,2" indent>
```

The preceding produces completely separated paragraphs like the following:

```
<p>
Synapse Advertising is your first choice for the best in
subliminal advertising.
</p>

<p>
Call Synapse when you want your clients to come a-knockin' at
your door -- and have no idea why!
</p>
```

indent

The `indent` keyword ensures that the text contained between the opening and closing tags wraps to the same text column as the tag, rather than appearing flush left. The difference is apparent when you compare almost any text format tag, from paragraph `<p>`, to any heading `<h1>` through `<h6>` tag, to the preformatted tag `<pre>`.

```
    <p>Four score and seven years ago our fathers brought forth
    on this continent, a new nation, conceived in liberty, and
    dedicated to the proposition that all men are created
    equal.</p>

<pre>The above speech was offered by President Abraham Lincoln
and is known as the Gettysburg Address. Now recognized by many
as the leading speech of the Lincoln presidency, the Gettysburg
Address was initially received to mixed reviews...</pre>
```

igroup

The igroup keyword is used only when applied to special indentation groups such as tables and frames. For example, all the elements contained in a table have igroup="1" as part of their source profile, as shown in the following:

```
<table break="1,1,1,1" indent igroup="1">
<td break="1,0,0,1" indent igroup="1">
<th break="1,0,0,1" indent igroup="1">
<tr break="1,0,0,1" indent igroup="1">
```

The igroup attribute in the indention option activates the indentation set for all the tags in that group. For example, if the indention option read as follows:

```
<indention enable indent="2" tabs="8" use="spaces" active="2">
```

then indenting would be turned off for igroup number 1, tables.

The active igroup causes each element to use the indentation level of the outermost group member as its left margin — and indent from there. Thus, with the indented <table>...</table> pair as the outer igroup member, the <tr>...</tr> pair is indented two more spaces and the <td>...</td> pair is indented another two spaces, so it looks like the following:

```
<table border="2" width="50%">
  <tr>
    <td>Symbol</td>
    <td>Element</td>
  </tr>
  <tr>
    <td>H</td>
    <td>Hydrogen</td>
  </tr>
</table>
```

You can currently define up to six igroups, in addition to the preset tables and frames.

namecase

You can override the general case conventions for any element with the namecase keyword. If you want to use a title case or mixed case for certain tags, you would define them in the following way:

```
<applet break="0,1,1,0" indent namecase="Applet">
<blockquote break="1,0,0,1" indent namecase="BlockQuote">
```

You may also use the namecase keyword when defining a custom tag for use in conjunction with a new object. Let's say you've created a series of objects for use with Cold Fusion and you want them to stand out in the code. To accentuate your new tag pair, <cfif>...</cfif>, you could add the following line to your Source Format Profile:

```
<cfif break="1,1,1,1" indent namecase="CFIf">
```

This line ensures that a Cold Fusion "if" tag is always inserted in the specified mixed case.

noformat

As the name implies, the `noformat` keyword presents the tag-surrounded text without any additional formatting. This keyword is primarily used when the tag is used to reproduce verbatim information, such as when using the preformatted tag `<pre>`. The `noformat` keyword is also used when the element requires attributes and values in a specific format, such as with `<style>` or `<script>`.

Attributes

The Attributes section has only two options: `namecase`, which works as previously described for the Elements section, and `samecase`. The `namecase` option is used to maintain a consistent mixed case approach to JavaScript events, such as `onKeyDown`. The `samecase` option ensures that an attribute and its value use the same case as its tag. If the `<input>` tag is uppercase, then the named attribute and the value will be uppercase.

Caution   Never use the `samecase` option with any attribute that requires a case-sensitive value. The most common instance of this situation is an attribute like src that takes a filename as its value — which in most cases is case-sensitive.

Case is generally determined for all attributes by the following line found in the Objects section:

```
<attribute case="lower">
```

As with the Elements, you can alter the case of attributes individually by specifying them in this section. For example, if you always want the source attribute of the image tag to be uppercase, you can include the following line in the Attributes section:

```
<src namecase="SRC">
```

The preceding produces code like the following:

```
<img SRC="logo.gif>
```

This capability is handy when you are scanning your code and quickly want to find all the source files.

Modifying the Source Format Profile

Because you have to restart Dreamweaver in order for any Source Format Profile modifications to take effect, you should edit the file with Dreamweaver closed. You can use any editor capable of saving an ASCII or regular text file. If you want to preserve the previous profile, you can use the Save As feature of your editor to save the file under a different name, such as SourceFormat.backup, prior to making any changes. Then, after you complete your alterations, use Save As again and name it SourceFormat.profile.

Make your changes only to those sections marked with the <?keyword>, such as <?options> or <?elements>. Remember that Dreamweaver is not case-sensitive when it comes to changing commands — other than with the namecase keyword — so you can write lines like the following:

```
<element case="LOWER">
```

In the preceding, all of your tags are still created, as specified, in lowercase.

Dreamweaver is fairly protective of its Source Format Profile. If you accidentally misspell a keyword (for example, "ident" instead of "indent"), Dreamweaver ignores and then deletes the misspelled keyword. Likewise, misplaced keywords — for instance, using the enable keyword when defining an element instead of an option — are removed from the file when Dreamweaver loads.

New Feature

One of the new Dreamweaver 2 Commands enables you to apply the Source Format to an existing page — typically one created outside of Dreamweaver. To use this capability, you first make changes to the Source Format Profile and save it. Then restart Dreamweaver and open the page you want to affect. Finally, choose Command ➪ Apply Source Formatting. Whatever modifications you made to the Source Format Profile are written to the existing code.

The Source Format Profile is an HTML tinker's paradise. You can shape your code as precisely as necessary and Dreamweaver outputs it for you. Feel free to experiment and try different code arrangements. Just be sure to have a copy of the original Source Format Profile available as a reference.

Summary

Creating Web pages, like any design job, is easier when the tools fit your hands. Through Preferences and the Source Format Profile, you can make Dreamweaver work the way you work.

✦ Dreamweaver lets you customize your Web page design and HTML coding environment through a series of easy-to-use point-and-click panels.

✦ You can decide how best to use cutting-edge features, such as layers and style sheets, depending on the degree of cross-browser and backward compatibility you need.

✦ Dreamweaver gives you plenty of elbow room for previewing and testing by providing for 20 selections on your browser list.

✦ The Source Format Profile can be modified. You can make alterations, from across-the-board case changes to tag-by-tag presentation, to define the way Dreamweaver writes your HTML code.

In the next chapter, you'll learn how to get online and offline help from Dreamweaver.

✦   ✦   ✦

Using the Help System

◆   ◆   ◆   ◆

In This Chapter

Browsing for Help

Step-by-step
techniques

Online assistance

◆   ◆   ◆   ◆

Dreamweaver includes a multifaceted Help system that you can rely on in any number of situations:

✦ To provide quick context-sensitive answers to questions about how to use specific Dreamweaver features.

✦ To learn the program using step-by-step instructions presented in a tutorial format.

✦ To explain various concepts and capabilities through the hyperlinked Help Pages and their embedded Show Me movies.

✦ To seek specific programming assistance from the peer-to-peer network of the online newsgroups or the Dreamweaver technical support team at Macromedia.

Navigating the Help Screen

To assist your understanding of Dreamweaver — in both the short term and the long term — Macromedia includes a full electronic manual with the program.

✦ For Windows system users, choose Help ➪ Help Pages or press the keyboard shortcut, F1, to open the Dreamweaver HTML Help Pages.

✦ To access Dreamweaver Help on the Macintosh, select Help ➪ Dreamweaver Help Pages.

If you have defined a primary browser in Dreamweaver through the Preferences, or with File ➪ Preview in Browser ➪ Edit Browser List, that browser opens and the Help Pages are loaded. Otherwise, Dreamweaver uses your system's default browser to display the Help Pages.

The Dreamweaver Help Pages are presented within an HTML frameset as shown in Figure 4-1. Navigational buttons — Back, Forward, Previous, Next, and What's New — are positioned along the top frame. At the top of the frame on the left side of the screen, you'll find the main control buttons for switching between the Help Contents, Index, and Search facilities. The main portion of the frame is reserved for showing the Help Pages themselves.

Controls   Navigational buttons

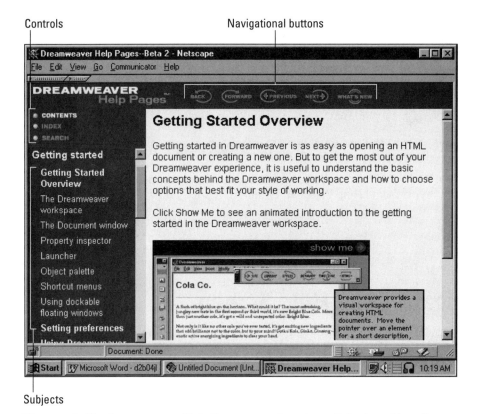

Subjects

Figure 4-1: The Dreamweaver Help Pages comprise a hyperlinked, multimedia manual that is displayed in your primary or default browser.

Browsing the Help Contents

To get the most benefit from the Help Pages, maximize your browser window. You can alternate between the Contents and Index by selecting one or the other control button. When you choose Contents, the frame immediately below the control buttons provides a list of Dreamweaver main subjects and a handy scroll bar for moving through the list.

Selecting any main topic in the Help Contents reveals another list of subtopics. You can collapse the main topic by selecting it again or by choosing another main topic.

Note that you must click a subtopic to load the information into the main viewing frame. If there is too much information to be displayed on a single screen, another scroll bar appears on the far-right side of the frame. To see the additional text, you can drag the scroll bar or select the frame and use your Page Up and Page Down keys.

Note   Dreamweaver takes advantage of your browser's HTML capabilities, and many Help Pages contain hyperlinks to other Help screens. However, if you follow a hyperlink from the main screen, the Contents listing does not update to reflect your new position.

Using the navigational controls

As you browse through the Help Pages, you'll find you can use your browser's Back and Forward buttons to revisit pages you have already viewed. You can also use the Help Pages' own navigational system to move back and forth or from topic to topic. The Help Pages navigational controls are described in Table 4-1.

Table 4-1
Help Pages Navigational Buttons

Button	Name	Purpose
BACK	**Back**	Moves to the last page viewed
FORWA	**Forward**	Returns to the most recent page viewed, if you have clicked the Back button
PRE	**Previous**	Displays the prior subtopic in the current subject
NEXT	**Next**	Shows the subtopic following the current one in the present subject
WHAT'S	**What's New**	Goes online to visit the Dreamweaver Developers Center

The Help Pages' Back and Forward buttons function identically to those of your browser's — although without some of the functionality of the 4.0 browser's buttons. The Next and Previous buttons, however, are somewhat different. Next and Previous are tied to the Help Pages' content structure and only display current subtopics within each major subject. If you reach the last subtopic and attempt to use the Next button, you'll get a JavaScript alert telling you are at the end of a section. A similar event occurs when you are looking at the first subtopic and try to view the Previous one. To go to another major subject, you have to select it from the Contents listing and then select one of the subtopics.

The final navigational button, What's New, is a direct link to the Dreamweaver Web site. This button takes you to a special section of the Dreamweaver Support Center, also called What's New. There you'll find the most recently published articles for beginners, which are also helpful to advanced users interested in getting the most out of Dreamweaver. The What's New page opens within the Help Pages frameset, so you still have access to your Contents listing or the Index. For a complete description of the What's New page, see "Getting Help Online" later in this chapter.

Playing the Show Me movies

Dreamweaver incorporates a number of multimedia feature demonstrations called Show Me movies. Each Show Me movie is a separate Shockwave animation that graphically illustrates the workings of the interface or one of the more advanced Dreamweaver capabilities.

Caution   To run the Show Me movies, you must have the Shockwave (for Director) plug-in for your browser installed. If you installed Dreamweaver through its CD-ROM, the appropriate plug-in was included in the installation. If you downloaded Dreamweaver from the Macromedia or another Web site, you can get the plug-in by visiting www.macromedia.com/shockwave/download/

The Guided Tour of Dreamweaver contains a Show Me movie that plays all of the animations in sequence, or you can pick your topic. You start the entire tour by clicking the Show Me All button. This loads the first movie, an introduction to the Dreamweaver workspace.

There are a few simple controls for viewing any of the Show Me movies:

1. When you are ready to view the movie, select the flashing Show Me button.
2. At the end of each screen's presentation, the Next button begins to flash. Click the Next button to proceed.
3. To review a previous step, select the Back button, shown in Figure 4-2.
4. When you have finished viewing the movie, select the Exit button.
5. If you are taking the Guided Tour, the next movie starts immediately after you exit from the previous one. To stop the Guided Tour completely, press the Exit button from the Guided Tour main screen.

Tip   Be sure the sound is turned up on your system when running the Show Me movies. All the movies punctuate their actions with sound, and audio is especially integral to the Show Me movie on Behaviors.

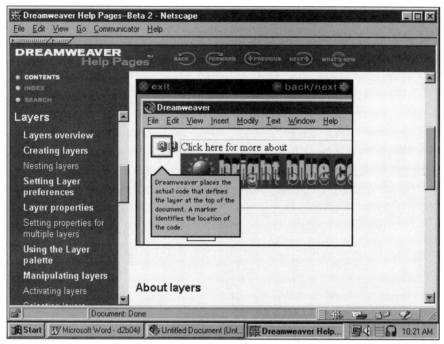

Figure 4-2: All the Show Me movies, like this one about working with layers, provide excellent introductions to the subjects.

Using the Help Index

Selecting the Index control button loads an alphabetical listing of topics covered in the Dreamweaver Help Pages. To find the subject you need, scroll down the list by dragging the scroll bar at the near-right. You can also click anywhere in the frame and use your system's Page Up and Page Down keys to navigate through the Index.

When you find your subject, select it from the list. The corresponding Help Page appears in the main frame. Note that when an index listing is divided into a topic and related subtopics, you must choose one of the subtopics to get the related Help Page. In this case, the topics themselves are not linked to any specific Help Page.

Searching the Help Files

Dreamweaver has included a search function with the Help Pages. As designed by Macromedia, the search engine is actually a Java applet that runs within your browser displaying the Help Pages. There is one major advantage to this approach: it lets you keep the search window available as you look for the material you need.

To search the Help Pages for a particular topic, follow these steps:

1. Select the Search button found on the left side of the Help Pages frame.

   The contents listing below the command buttons are replaced by a Launch button and a note regarding the search applet. As the note states, after selecting the Launch button, you may receive a warning from your system advising you that the Java applet is trying to read the files on your hard drive. If you receive the warning, click OK to permit the search engine to proceed. The message further states that nothing is written to the hard drive and only the Dreamweaver Help Pages are searched.

2. Select the Launch button to start the Java applet.

3. In the Search window (see Figure 4-3), enter keywords in the upper text box.

   - To search for a phrase, enter the words as you would normally, for example, "shockwave director" (without the quotes).

   - To search for several related keywords that do not have to appear next to each other, enter the words with a plus sign between them, like this:

     ```
     shockwave + director
     ```

   - By default the search is case-sensitive. To turn off this feature, deselect the Case sensitive check-box.

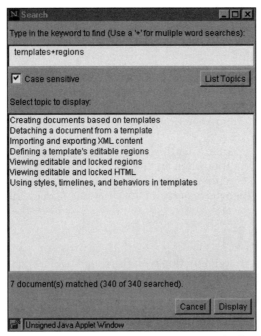

Figure 4-3: Quickly find the topics you're looking for with Dreamweaver's new Help Pages search engine.

4. After you've entered your search criteria, select the List Topics button.

   As each page is searched, pages matching your search criteria are displayed in the results window.

5. To see an individual page, double-click its title in the results window. You can also select the title of the page and click the Display button.

   The page linked to the title is displayed in the main frame of the Help Pages.

6. Repeat Steps 3–5 to continue searching.

7. Click the Cancel button to close the Search window.

To return to either the Contents or the Index listing, select the Contents or Index command buttons, respectively.

Stepping Through the Tutorial

The Dreamweaver Help Pages include a step-by-step tutorial that demonstrates how to use the latest Dynamic HTML features to create a Web page. To access the tutorial, first select the Index control button and then scroll down to first choose Tutorial and then select Tutorial Overview.

The Dreamweaver 2 Tutorial takes the form of a complete sample Web site for a fictitious company, Olivebranch Gourmet Foods. In the process of building up its Web pages, you get to try your hand at defining a local site, editing existing pages, working with templates, formatting complex page layouts, attaching behaviors, and even inserting a Flash movie.

To see the sample Web site, choose File ⇨ Open and browse to the Dreamweaver 2\Tutorial\Olivebranch_site. Then, select the index.htm file to open it. The example home page, shown in Figure 4-4, should be previewed in a 4.0 or later browser to understand how the various pages link together.

Tip

Be sure to try out the Flash movie hidden underneath the graphic on the bottom of the page by choosing View ⇨ Plugins ⇨ Play All. Even though the Flash movie is placed beneath a layer with a graphic, it becomes visible when played because all active content "rises to the top" of any layers. Stop the movie by choosing View ⇨ Plugins ⇨ Stop All.

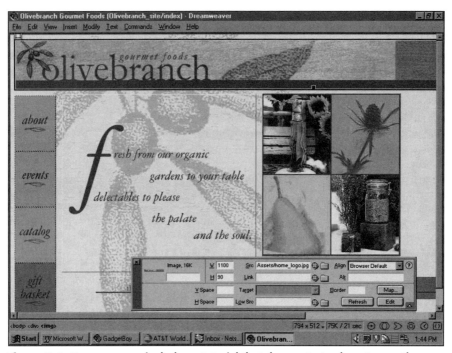

Figure 4-4: Dreamweaver includes a tutorial that demonstrates how to use the program to build an advanced Web page, step by step.

Getting Help Online

I think one of the factors helping the Web to grow so rapidly is the fact that it is largely self-documenting. Want to learn more about developing Web pages? Find out on the Web! The same holds true for Dreamweaver. There is an extensive array of information about Dreamweaver available online—and more coming every day.

Macromedia has done—and continues to do—an excellent job of supporting Dreamweaver on the Web. To that end, Macromedia has developed and sponsored two Web sites. One, the Dynamic HTML Zone, is dedicated to an extensive discussion of issues related to implementing DHTML. The other Web source is a part of the general Macromedia site and focuses exclusively on providing support for Dreamweaver. Let's take a look at this one first.

Note   As with many popular Web sites, the Macromedia sites are constantly in a state of revision. The following information was current when written but some of the content or structure may have changed by the time you read it. If all else fails, you should always be able to find assistance by starting at www.macromedia.com and looking for the Dreamweaver support area.

Dreamweaver support site

Macromedia's primary help center on the Web for Dreamweaver is a terrific resource. Visit the Dreamweaver Support Center at:

```
www.macromedia.com/support/dreamweaver/contents.html
```

to find the latest technical data, free downloads, and peer-to-peer connections—and it's all specific to Dreamweaver, naturally. One of the most impressive aspects of the site is its multilevel approach; there's material here for everyone, from rank beginner to the savviest code jockey.

When you visit the Dreamweaver Support Center, you'll find various areas of help as well as a search facility. Macromedia generally updates the site, shown in Figure 4-5, on a monthly or better basis. It's definitely worth bookmarking in your browser and visiting often.

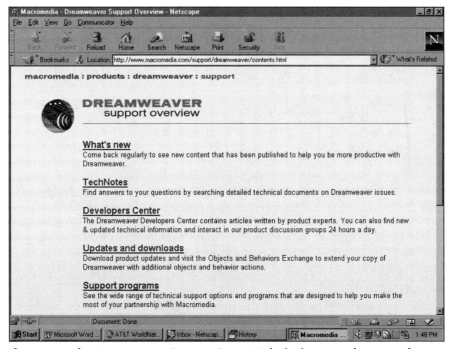

Figure 4-5: The Dreamweaver Support Center Web site is a central resource for gathering the newest information and software related to Dreamweaver.

What's New

As mentioned earlier in the chapter, the What's New page is a launching point for the latest in Dreamweaver technology. Each of the different areas of the

Dreamweaver Developers Center contributes an article or two that is listed on the What's New page each month. Here, you'll find links to

✦ Articles in the Dreamweaver for Beginners series

✦ Tutorials on intermediate techniques such as creating a slideshow with layers

✦ Interviews with Webmasters on how they work their magic with Dreamweaver

✦ Expert-level information such as the Behavior Development Kit and Tutorial

Select any of the links to reach the desired article.

TechNotes

TechNotes are straightforward answers from the Dreamweaver development team to specific questions from users. Each TechNote addresses a single issue. Here are some samples:

✦ **12761.** How can I edit the name of the Title property of the Frameset HTML page without using the HTML Inspector?

✦ **12787.** How can I use Dreamweaver to Create Documents in non-Latin Encoding?

✦ **12786.** Why aren't my WAVE audios playing back from Navigator on my MAC?

Tip

The numbers that appear at the beginning of each TechNote title are identification numbers. Often you'll encounter a response in the Dreamweaver newsgroup to a question that includes a TechNote ID number — and it's a lot easier to jot down than the URL.

You can jump to two of the TechNotes areas right from the Dreamweaver Support Center: Top TechNotes and New & Updated TechNotes. Go to Top TechNotes to find links to the most common troubleshooting problems and answers. From there you can also search the TechNotes by keyword or ID number, or you can gain access to the full list of Dreamweaver TechNotes. New & Updated TechNotes brings you to a list of the TechNotes added or revised in the last month.

Developers Center

Where do you go when you need an expert? To the Dreamweaver Developers Center, of course. Macromedia posts key articles written by Dreamweaver masters, both in-house and from the developer community. Many of the listings are organized by skill level to make it easy to find the information you need. There are presently four major sections of the Dreamweaver Developers Center:

✦ How Do I?

✦ DocStuff

✦ Resources

✦ Discussion Groups

How Do I?

You can directly access the skill area you're most interested in through the How Do I? sections: Dreamweaver for New Users, Show Me, Advanced Techniques, Experts Speak, and Extending Dreamweaver. These sections contain all the articles posted to date to the Dreamweaver Developers Center — use them to quickly find just the expertise you want.

DocStuff

Look to DocStuff for official supplementary documentation. In recent months, DocStuff has held a Quick Reference Guide that details all the keyboard shortcuts in one very handy printable guide. You can expect DocStuff to be the place to go for documentation on advanced features.

Resources

Another area in the Dreamweaver Developers Center is a disparate but valuable collection of resources for the Web designer. The Resources area includes links to the following:

✦ **User Groups.** Macromedia has a list of official user groups around the world. These grassroots organizations provide excellent connections to other developers, business contacts, and Macromedia itself. Check the list for the group nearest you.

✦ **Web Sites.** On this page you'll find links to specific technical resources such as the W3C's Positioning HTML Elements with Cascading Style Sheets spec, as well as general resources such as the DHTML Zone (covered in the next section).

✦ **Events.** Keep in touch with Macromedia on the road by visiting this Events page. Highlights of past events and dates for upcoming shows and seminars are listed.

✦ **Made with Macromedia Program.** If you wish to distribute your applications made with Director or Authorware, visit this page to learn how to participate in Macromedia's royalty-free licensing program.

Discussion Groups

To pose a technical question or to offer the Dreamweaver Development Team some feedback, visit the Discussion Groups area of the support site. There you'll find links to newsgroups hosted by Macromedia, including the Dreamweaver and Dynamic.HTML forums. Newsgroups are extraordinarily useful for getting help from other users or the Dreamweaver support team. It's likely that, quite often, other users will have encountered the same or similar problems to the ones you are facing. Or you may have unearthed a unique situation that reveals an undiscovered bug in the program — which the Dreamweaver staff needs to know about. Participating in the newsgroup is an especially rewarding way to broaden your connection to the Dreamweaver community.

If you'd like to make some program suggestions to the Dreamweaver Development Team, select the Feedback link in the Discussion Groups area. You'll be lead to a page explaining your options for communicating with Macromedia. If you don't find a suitable resource, click the Feedback link at the bottom of the page. The next page displays a full list of e-mail addresses for sending feedback directly to the various areas at Macromedia. The Dreamweaver address is wish-dreamweaver@ macromedia.com. Feel free to send the Dreamweaver Team a list of the items on your wish list.

Updates and downloads

Being able to extend Dreamweaver's power with additional objects and behaviors offers great creative potential. But where do you find such new tools? The Object & Behaviors Exchange is the online center for Dreamweaver developers to submit and download program extensions. Anyone can enter an object or behavior action for posting. Once an item is accepted by the Dreamweaver development team, it is free to download and freely distributable.

After you enter the Object & Behaviors Exchange area, select either the Download Objects Or Behavior Actions link or the Submit Objects Or Behavior Actions link. Both selections take you to a Macromedia licensing agreement, to which you must agree before proceeding. Be sure to read the agreement carefully. Select the Accept button if you wish to continue.

The Download area is divided into two areas: objects and behavior actions. If you find an item that provides you with a new, needed functionality, select the correct file for your platform (Windows or Macintosh). The Save As dialog box appears; enter the appropriate path and filename and press the Save button. After the file has downloaded to your computer, decompress it and move the expanded files to their proper folder. New objects consist of two files — an HTML file and a GIF file — and are stored in the Dreamweaver\Configuration\Objects\panel folder (where panel represents either the Common, Forms, or Invisibles folder). New behaviors are contained in a single HTML file and should be moved to the Dreamweaver\ Configuration\Behaviors\Actions folder. Dreamweaver must be restarted before it will recognize new behavior actions or objects.

If you wish to upload a new object or behavior action, you'll be asked to submit your Dreamweaver tool via e-mail. Follow the instructions from the Submit page; they ask you to include your personal information as well as information about the item you are submitting. Attach the necessary files to the e-mail and send it to the posted address. If approved, the object or behavior action is posted within a month. (The item might not be approved because it duplicates an already existing element or doesn't meet Macromedia's quality standards.)

Support Programs

The Support Programs area details the wide range of assistance options offered by Macromedia to help you in your Web building. In addition to details on the free help available to registered customers, you'll also find links to information on charged support possibilities.

The Support Programs area is also a gateway into other Macromedia programs such as Macromedia's Authorized Training Program with personal assistance available world-wide, the Beta Program for testing new software, the Developer Support Network with discounts and referrals, and more.

Dynamic HTML Zone

The Dynamic HTML Zone, at www.dhtmlzone.com is another extremely valuable online resource center. This site is also hosted by Macromedia, but here the focus is less on Dreamweaver than on implementing Dynamic HTML features in your Web pages. The Dynamic HTML Zone, shown in Figure 4-6, is a great jumping off place for learning about DHTML through a variety of methods. The following is just some of what you'll find at "the Dzone."

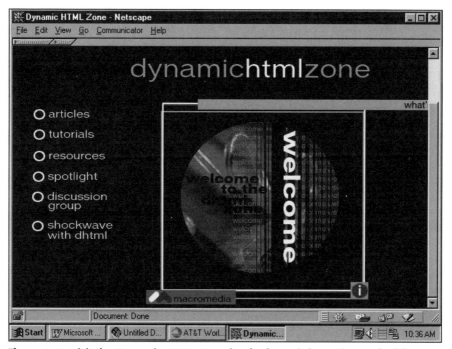

Figure 4-6: Visit the Dynamic HTML Zone for the latest information on building your Web pages with cutting-edge DHTML capabilities.

Articles

The Dynamic HTML Zone contains a collection of some of the finest technical papers about creating DHTML pages on the Web. Both browser-specific and cross-browser features are explained by experts in the field. Sample articles include "Creating Multimedia with Dynamic HTML: An Overview," "Cross-Browser Dynamic HTML," and "Techniques for Building Backward Compatible DHTML."

Tutorials

Learning from tutorials can be dry and tedious — but not at the DZone! Visit SuperFly Fashions and learn helpful general techniques, such as working with CSS layers and Initializations. You also find more advanced methods, such as pull-down menus and scrolling text. The tutorials come with an overview as well as a line-by-line analysis of the JavaScript subroutines and other needed HTML code.

Resources

The Resources area is a collection of links to articles, reference guides, demos, various tutorials, and browser data — all related to DHTML. Pulling equally from the Microsoft and Netscape camps, as well as independent organizations such as C I Net and the W3C, these links are a great jumping-off place for all things DHTML.

Spotlight

Want to see what else is being accomplished with Dynamic HTML? Check out the Spotlight area. In addition to the site that's currently "in the spotlight," this page maintains an archive of past sites so honored.

Shockwave in DHTML

Combining the interactivity of Shockwave with the flexibility of Dynamic HTML is an exciting concept, and this area of the DZone gives you all the tools you need to make this marriage happen. You'll find both technical white papers and full-featured demos you can learn from.

Summary

Dreamweaver is a full-featured program incorporating many new technologies. This chapter describes the substantial alternatives available to you for shortening your learning curve. Key methods include the following:

✦ The expansive electronic manual, Dreamweaver Help Pages, which explains how to accomplish specific Web page building tasks through hyperlinked text and embedded multimedia.

✦ Built-in tutorials for learning how to get started with Dreamweaver, by making a Web page with some of the latest effects.

✦ Examples of the most popular HTML features as created in Dreamweaver. You can also use the Examples as templates, by substituting your own objects and text for Macromedia's.

✦ A wealth of information, online. Constantly updated, always available, Dreamweaver's online resources are a tremendous benefit to any Web designer or developer, no matter what your level of skills.

In the next chapter, you'll see how to set up your first Dreamweaver site, step by step.

✦   ✦   ✦

Setting Up Your First Site

◆ ◆ ◆ ◆

In This Chapter

Web site design and structure

Making a local site

All about paths and addresses

Previewing your Web site

Publishing online

◆ ◆ ◆ ◆

Web sites are far more than collections of HTML documents. Every image — from the smallest navigational button to the largest image map — is a separate file that must be uploaded with your HTML page. And if you add any additional elements, such as a background sound, digital video, or Java applet, their files must be transferred as well. To preview the Web site locally and view it properly on the Internet, you have to organize your material in a specific manner.

Each time you begin developing a new site, you can follow the straightforward procedure described in this chapter. These steps lay the groundwork for Dreamweaver to properly link your local development site with your remote online site. For those who are just starting to create Web sites, this chapter begins with a brief discussion of approaches to online design. The remainder of the chapter is devoted to the mechanics of setting up your site — which type of Internet addressing to use, file management in Dreamweaver, and publishing to the Web with Dreamweaver's Site FTP facility.

Planning Your Site

Planning in Web design, just as in any other design process, is essential. Not only will careful planning cut your development time considerably, but it makes it far easier to achieve a uniform look and feel for your Web site — and thus make it friendlier and easier to use. This first section briefly covers some of the basics of Web site design: what to focus on, what options to consider, and what pitfalls to avoid. If you are an established Web site developer who has covered this ground before, feel free to skip this section.

Primary considerations

Even before you choose from various models to design your site, you'll need to address the all-important issues of message, audience, and budget.

What do you want to say?

If I had to pick one overriding concern for Web site design, it would be to answer the following question: "What are you trying to say?" The clearer your idea of your message, the more focused your Web site will be. To this end, I find it useful to try to state the purpose of a Web site in one sentence. "Creating the coolest Web site on the planet" doesn't count. Though it could be regarded as a goal, it's so open-ended that it's almost no concept at all.

Here are some examples of clearly stated Web site concepts:

✦ "To provide the best small-business resource center focused on Microsoft's Office software."

✦ "To chronicle the world's first voyage around the world by hot air balloon."

✦ "To advertise music lessons offered by a collective of keyboard teachers in New York City."

Who is your audience?

Right behind a site's concept—some would say neck-and-neck with it—is the site's audience. Who are you trying to reach? Quite often a site's style is heavily influenced by a clear vision of the site's intended audience. Take, for example, Macromedia's Dynamic HTML Zone (www.dhtmlzone.com) discussed in Chapter 4, "Using the Help System." This is an excellent example of a site that is perfectly pitched toward its target; in this case, the intended audience is composed of professional developers and designers. Hence, you'll find the site snazzy but informative and filled with exciting examples of cutting-edge programming techniques.

In contrast, a site that is devoted to mass-market e-commerce must work with a very different group in mind: shoppers. Everyone at one time or another falls into this category, so we're really talking about a state of mind, rather than a profession. Many shopping sites use a very straightforward page design—one that is easily maneuverable, comforting in its repetition, and where visitors can quickly find what they are looking for and—with as few impediments as possible—buy it.

What are your resources?

Unfortunately, Web sites aren't created in a vacuum. Virtually all development work happens under real-world constraints of some kind. A professional Web designer is accustomed to working within a budget. In fact, the term *budget* can apply to several concepts.

First, you have a monetary budget—how much is the client willing to spend? This translates into a combination of development time (for designers and programmers), materials (custom graphics, stock photos, and the like), and ongoing maintenance. You can build a large site with many pages that pulls dynamically from an internal database and requires very little hands-on upkeep. Or you can construct a small, graphics-intensive site that must be updated by hand weekly. Yet it's entirely possible that both sites will end up costing the same.

Second, *budget* also applies to the amount of time you can afford to spend on any given project. The professional Web designer is quick to realize that time is an essential commodity. The resources needed when undertaking a showcase for yourself with no deadline are very different from contracting on June 30th for a job that must be ready to launch on July 4th.

The third real-world budgetary item to consider is bandwidth. The Web, with faster modems and an improved infrastructure, is slowly shedding its image as the "World Wide Wait." That means today's Webmaster must keep a steady eye on a page's weight—how long it takes to download under the most typical modem rates. Of course, you can always decide to include that animated video masterpiece that takes 33 minutes to download on a 28.8 modem—you just can't expect anyone to wait to see it.

In conclusion, when you are trying to define your Web page, filter it through these three ideas: message, audience, and the various faces of the budget. The time spent visualizing your Web page in these terms will be time decidedly well-spent.

Design options

Many Web professionals borrow a technique used extensively in developing other mass-marketing forms: storyboarding. *Storyboarding* for the Web entails first diagramming the various pages in your site—much like the more traditional storyboarding in videos or filmmaking—and then detailing connections for the separate pages to form the overall site. How you connect the disparate pages determines how your visitors will navigate the completed Web site.

There are several basic navigational models; the modern Web designer should be familiar with them all because each one serves a different purpose and they can be mixed and matched as needed.

The linear approach

Prior to the World Wide Web, most media formats were linear—that is, one image or page followed another in an unalterable sequence. In contrast, the Web and its interactive personality enable the user to jump from topic to topic. Nevertheless, you can still use a linear approach to a Web site and have one page appear after another, like a multimedia book.

The linear navigational model, shown in Figure 5-1, works well for computer-based training applications and other expository scenarios in which you want to tightly control the viewer's experience. Some Web designers use a linear-style entrance or exit from their main site, connected to a multilevel navigational model. One advantage that Dynamic HTML brings is that you can achieve the effects of moving through several pages in a single page through layering.

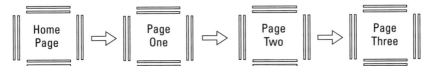

Figure 5-1: The linear navigational model takes the visitor through a series of Web pages.

Keep in mind that Web search engines can index the content of every page of your site separately. Each page of your site—not just your home page—then becomes a potential independent entrance point. So be sure to include, on every page, navigation buttons back to your home page, especially if you use a linear navigational model.

The hierarchical model

Hierarchical navigational models emerge from top-down designs. These start with one key concept that becomes your home page. From the home page, users branch off to several main pages; if needed, these main pages can, in turn, branch off into many separate pages. Everything flows from the home page; it's very much like a company's organization chart, with the CEO on top followed by the various company divisions.

The hierarchical Web site, shown in Figure 5-2, is best known for maintaining a visitor's sense of place in the site. Some Web designers even depict the treelike structure as a navigation device and include each branch traveled as a link. This enables visitors to quickly retrace their steps, branch by branch, to investigate different routes.

The spoke-and-hub model

Given the Web's flexible hyperlink structure, the spoke-and-hub navigational model works extremely well. The hub is, naturally, the site's home page. The spokes projecting out from the center connect to all the major pages in the site. This layout permits fairly immediate access to any key page in just two jumps—one jump always leading back to the hub/home page and one jump leading off to a new direction. Figure 5-3 shows a typical spoke-and-hub structure for a Web site.

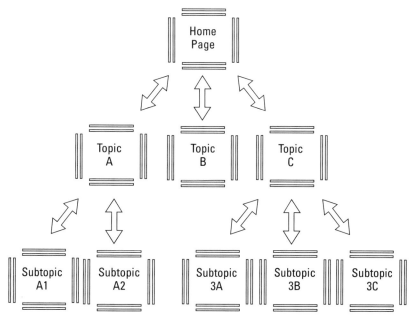

Figure 5-2: A hierarchical Web layout enables the main topics to branch into their own subtopics.

The main drawback to the spoke-and-hub structure is the constant return to the home page. Many Web designers get around this limitation by making the first jump off the hub into a Web page using frames, in which the navigation bars are always available. This design also enables visitors using nonframes-capable browsers to take a different path.

The full Web design

The seemingly least structured approach for a Web site — FullWeb — takes the most advantage of the Web's hyperlink capabilities. This design enables virtually every page to connect to every other page. The full Web design, shown in Figure 5-4, works well for sites that are explorations of a particular topic, because the approach encourages visitors to experience the site according to their own needs, not based on the notions of any one designer. The danger in using full Web for your site design is that the visitor can literally get lost. As an escape hatch, many Web designers include a link to a clickable site map, especially for large-scale sites of this design.

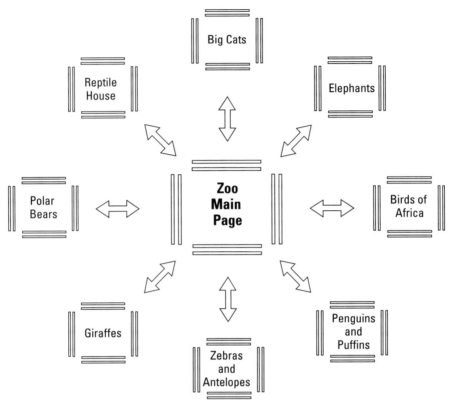

Figure 5-3: This storyboard diagram for a zoo's Web site shows how a spoke-and-hub model might work.

Tip   A common rule of thumb for Web-site navigation is to make sure that none of your content is more than three jumps away from the home page. You want to avoid making it difficult for your visitors to find the material they want on your site; otherwise, they'll look elsewhere.

Defining a Local Site

Now that you've decided on a design and mapped your site, you're ready to set it up in Dreamweaver. Once your site is on your Web server and fully operational, it consists of many files — HTML, graphics, and others — that make up the individual Web pages. All of these associated files are kept on the server in one main folder, which may use one or more subfolders. This main folder is called the *remote site root*. In order for Dreamweaver to properly display your linked pages and embedded images — just as they are displayed online — the program creates a mirror of your remote site on your local development system. This primary mirror folder on your system is known as the *local site root*.

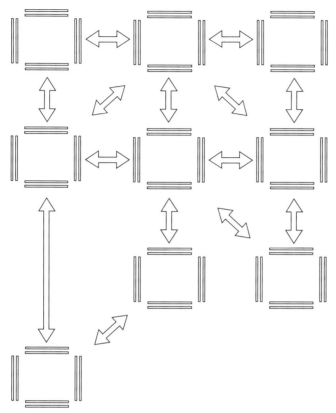

Figure 5-4: In a full Web design, each page can have multiple links to other pages.

Although you can establish the local site root at any time, it's best to do it at the beginning of a project. This ensures that Dreamweaver duplicates the complete structure of the Web development site when it comes time to publish your pages to the Web. One of Dreamweaver's key site-management features enables you to select just the HTML pages for publication; Dreamweaver then automatically transfers all the associated files, creating any needed folders in the process. The mirror images of your local and remote site roots are critical to Dreamweaver's ability to expedite your workload in this way.

Tip   If you do decide to transfer an existing Web site to a new Dreamweaver local site root, run Dreamweaver's Link Checker after you've consolidated all your files. Choose File ➪ Check Links ➪ Entire Site or press the keyboard shortcut, Ctrl-F8 (Command-F8). The Link Checker tells you of broken links and orphan files as well. For more information on the Link Checker, see Chapter 33, "Publishing Via Site FTP."

To set up a local site root folder in Dreamweaver, follow these steps:

1. Select File ➪ New Site (Site ➪ New Site) from the main Dreamweaver menu.

Tip   In Window systems, you can also choose Site ➪ New Site from the Site Window menu. Macintosh systems use a single menu for both the Document Window and the Site Window and you'll find all the site functions under the Site Window.

The Site Window opens, followed shortly by the Site Definition dialog box, as shown in Figure 5-5. The Site Definition dialog box has four different categories: Local Info, Web Server Info, Check In/Out, and Site Map Layout.

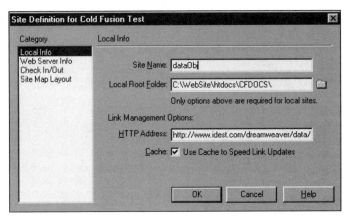

Figure 5-5: Set up your local site root through the Site Definition dialog box.

2. From the Local Info category, type a name for your Site in the Site Name text box.

   This name appears in the user-defined site list displayed when you select File ➪ Open Site.

3. Specify the folder to serve as the local site root, by either typing the path name directly into the Local Root Folder text box or clicking the Browse button. The Browse button opens the Choose Local Directory dialog box. When you've made your choice there, click the Select button.

   If you're just working on the site locally with no intention of uploading it to a server, you don't have to enter any additional information.

4. Enter the full URL for your site in the HTTP Address text box.

Note   When checking links for your Web site, Dreamweaver uses the HTTP Address to determine whether absolute links, such as `http://www.idest/dreamweaver /index.htm`, reference external files or files on your site.

5. Select the Web Server Info category from the Site Definition dialog box.

6. From the Server Access options in the Web Server Info category, choose the Web server description that applies to your site:

- **None**—Choose this option if your site is being developed locally and will not be uploaded to a Web server.

   If you selected None for Server Access, click OK to close the dialog box.

- **Local/Network**—Select this option if you are running a local Web server or if your Web server is mounted as a network drive (on Windows systems) or as an NFS drive (on Macintosh systems).

   If you selected Local/Network for Server Access, enter the name of the remote folder in the Remote Folder text box or click the Browse button to locate the folder. Then click OK to close the dialog box.

- **FTP**—Select this option if you connect to your Web server via File Transfer Protocol (FTP).

   If FTP is selected, the following options appear:

FTP Host	The host name of the FTP connection for your Web server, usually in the form `www.sitename.com`. Do not include the full URL, such as `ftp://www.sitename.com/index.html`.
Host Directory	The directory in which publicly accessible documents are stored on the server. Typical Host Directory names are `www/public/docs/` and `public_html/htdoc/`. Your remote site root folder will be a subfolder of the Host Directory. If you are unsure of the exact name of the Host Directory, check with your Web server administrator for the proper directory path.
Login	The login name you have been assigned for access to the Web server.
Password	The password necessary for you to gain access to the Web server. Many servers are case-sensitive when it comes to logins and passwords.
Save	Dreamweaver automatically selects this option after you enter a password. Deselect this box only if you and others access the server from the current system.
Use Firewall	This option will be selected for you if you've set the Preferences with the correct host and port information.

7. Click OK when you finish entering your FTP information.

Turning on the Check In/Out System

When the Web site is being developed or maintained by a team of designers and programmers, Dreamweaver's file Check In/Out is especially useful. In a typical session, a graphic designer may get the current version of a page off the Web site, in order to revise a logo. If Check In/Out is enabled, Dreamweaver places a check mark next to the file in the remote directory pane of the Site Window for all team members to see. Moreover, Dreamweaver displays the name of the person checking out the file and records the file transfer in a log.

To enable this file control feature, select the Check In/Out category, shown in Figure 5-6, in the Site Definition dialog box. Click the Enable File Check In and Check Out option. Once the overall capability is selected, the Check Out Files when Opening option is available. When this option is turned on, Dreamweaver marks your files as checked out automatically when you open them. This feature works when opening files from either the remote or the local directories of the Site Window.

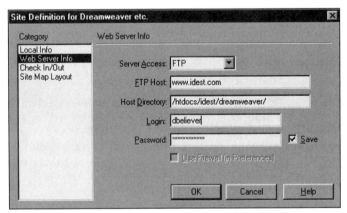

Figure 5-6: You can keep track of who's got what file with Dreamweaver's Check In/Out capability.

The final option on the Check In/Out panel of the Site Definition dialog box is to enter a Check Out Name. When a file is checked out, this name is posted next to the file in the Site Window in the Checked Out By column. The naming facility is helpful in several ways. First, you can identify yourself and your department, as in "Margot L. - Graphic Design." Or, if you are working on the same site from multiple machines, you can keep track of where the latest version of a particular file is stored by using labels such as "Home - Mac" and "Office - Win98-03."

Managing Site Info

You can change any of the information associated with your local site roots by selecting File ➪ Open Site ➪ Define Sites (Site ➪ Open Site ➪ Define Sites) from either the main Dreamweaver menu or from the Site Window menu. Choose the site you want to modify from the Site list box at the top of the Site Information dialog box; you'll see the corresponding information for you to edit.

After your participation in a project has ended, you can remove the site from your list. Select File ⇨ Open Site ⇨ Define Sites (Site ⇨ Open Site ⇨ Define Sites) to open the Site Information dialog box, choose the site you want to remove in the Site list box, and click the Delete Site button. Note that this action removes the site only from Dreamweaver's internal list; it does not delete any files or folders from your hard drive.

With the local site root folder established, Dreamweaver can properly manage links no matter which address format is used. The various address formats are explained in the following section.

Relative and Absolute Addresses

In Dreamweaver, you can specify the type of link as well as the link itself. There are three formats for HTML links or URLs: absolute addresses, document relative addresses, and site root relative addresses.

Before you begin coding your Web pages with one form of addressing or another, it's best to understand the differences between them so that you can pick the best format for your Web site. Otherwise, you might find that you have to recode most if not all of the links on your site — a time-consuming, tedious task.

Absolute addresses

An *absolute address* is the *full uniform resource locator* (URL), specifying the type of protocol, the domain name or ID, the path, and the filename. Most often, the absolute address takes a form similar to the following:

```
http://www.idest.com/dreamweaver/index.htm
```

Absolute addresses are generally used when you are linking to a Web page on another server. Although you could code all the links on your Dreamweaver pages with absolute addresses, this approach has two drawbacks. First, it takes a lot more typing than using relative addresses; second — and much more significantly — you have to redo every single link if your linked files get moved.

As an example of a worst-case scenario, let's assume the Dreamweaver site listed just above (currently in a subfolder on my own domain) becomes so popular that I decide to move it to its own domain. With absolute addressing in effect, I will have to go and change every link that points to my home page, to something like this:

```
http://www.dreamweaver-etc.com/index.html
```

The best policy is to avoid using an absolute address except when you have no other choice—specifically, when the file is on another server out of your control.

Tip   Should you ever need to rename every link in your Web site, Dreamweaver 2 offers extensive automated help through the enhanced Find and Replace features, where you can establish substitutes for multiple files in one operation. For more information on these features, see Chapter 7, "Adding Text to Your Web Page."

Document relative addresses

Whereas an absolute address includes every part of the URL, a relative address omits one or more elements. As its name implies, a *document relative address* assumes that the current HTML page is the point of departure, and all elements leading up to the document name are left out of the address. For example, if I were using absolute addresses to establish a link between a button on my home page (index.html) and another page (say, objects.html) stored in the same folder, I would set the link to:

```
http://www.idest.com/dreamweaver/objects.html
```

However, because they are in the same folder, I could use document relative addressing and shorten the link to:

```
objects.html
```

This is possible because the linked page is, relative to the current document (index.html), in the same location. More importantly, if the site changes servers or domains, all the links will still be valid.

Caution   To use document relative addresses in Dreamweaver, you must first save your file, preferably in an established local site root. If you attempt to link anything on the current page without first saving it, Dreamweaver suggests that you save it first. If you don't save the file, the link will be inserted with a `file://path` prefix, where *path* is the location of the object on your local drive. For example:

```
file://C|/Dreamweaver/Dev/images/button04.gif
```

The `file://` references will not work properly if posted to a remote server.

You can specify a link to a subfolder using document relative addressing. It's a relatively common practice for Web designers to store their graphics in a separate folder from their HTML pages. To insert a logo kept in a subfolder called images, for instance, you would use the following syntax in the link:

```
images/logo.gif
```

The slash character indicates a subfolder contained in the same directory as the current document. You can also nest folders, like this:

```
images/flags/states/ny/cities/nyc.gif
```

which links to a graphic located five subfolders deep, relative to the current page.

It is also possible to use relative document addressing to link to an object located in a folder above the current one in the directory structure. The symbol indicating a higher folder is two dots and a slash (../) and looks like this:

```
../../resume.html
```

Such a link would move up the directory tree two folders from the current document, and then call a document found there.

Document relative addressing is a good all-around solution for small-to-medium Web sites. If you are working on a large-scale Web site that employs multiple servers, site root relative addresses (explained next) are a better choice.

Site root relative addresses

Just as a document relative address omits the protocol, server, and path portion of an URL, a *site root relative address* leaves off the protocol and server segments, but retains the path. Why is this difference important? The answer lies in the capability of Web servers to host more than one site at a time — or to enable one site to be spread across multiple servers.

All Web site folders are stored on a Web server in a special directory that has been designated as being publicly accessible — unlike other, administrator-only areas of the system. This special directory is known as the *Host Directory*; you'll recall that it is noted in one of the fields of Dreamweaver's Site Information dialog box when the local root folder is established. A site root relative address uses the Host Directory as its base, much as a document relative address uses the current HTML page.

The format for a site root relative address calls for the link to start with a slash, followed by the folder name. Let's again use my Dreamweaver site as an example. Suppose I'm keeping it in the root directory of my domain. I could use the following form of site root relative addressing:

```
/dreamweaver-etc/objects.html
```

Note the beginning forward-slash character in the preceding line of code. Site root relative addressing is used on larger sites that require multiple servers to handle the substantial number of hits received. The same material can be mirrored onto several Web servers that the system administrator has set up as aliases of one another. Site root relative addressing also enables a site to be easily moved from one server to another.

The primary drawback to using site root relative addressing is that browsers cannot recognize a site root when it is used locally. In other words, if you attempt to call a graphic with a link such as this:

```
/dreamweaver-etc/images/logo.gif
```

when previewed on your system with your primary or alternate browser, the image would not display, although you can still see it within the Dreamweaver Document Window. To preview content that is site root relative addressed, you must make one of the following arrangements:

✦ (Windows only) Set up a local server and enable the Preview Using Local Server option found in the Preview in Browser panel of Preferences.

✦ Move the file to a remote server to view the page in your browser.

For these reasons, you'll want to use the site root relative addressing format only when you are working on a large-scale Web site and your in-process pages are stored on a local (or remote) server.

Building Placeholder Pages

One technique that I've found helpful over the years—and especially so with the use of document relative addressing in Dreamweaver Web projects—is what I call *placeholder pages*. These placeholder pages can fill the need to include links as you create each Web page, in as effortless a manner as possible.

Let's say, for example, you've just finished laying out most of the text and graphics for your home page and you want to put in some navigational buttons. You drop in your button images and align them just so. All that's missing is the link. If you're using document relative addressing, the best way to handle assigning the link would be to click the Browse for File button in the Property Inspector and select your file. But what do you do if you haven't created any other pages yet and there aren't any files to select? That's when you can put placeholder pages to work.

After you've designed the basics of your site and created your local site root, as described elsewhere in this chapter, start with a blank Dreamweaver page. Type a single identifying word on the page and save it in the local site root. Do this for all the Web pages in your plan. When it comes time to make your links, all you have to do is point and click to the appropriate placeholder page. This arrangement also gives you an immediate framework for link testing. When it comes time to work on the next page, just open up the correct placeholder page and start to work.

Another style of working involves using the Site Window as your base of operations, rather than the Document Window. It's very easy in Dreamweaver 2 to choose File ⇨ New File from the Site Window menu several times and create the basic files of your site. You can also create any needed subfolders, such as ones for images or other media, by selecting File ⇨ New Folder.

Creating and Saving New Pages

You've considered message, audience, and budget issues. You've chosen a design. You've set up your site and its address. All the preliminary planning is completed, and now you're ready to really rev up Dreamweaver and begin creating pages. This section covers the basic mechanics of opening and saving Web pages in development.

Starting Dreamweaver

Start Dreamweaver as you would any other program. Double-click the Dreamweaver program icon, or single-click if you are using Internet Explorer 4.0's Desktop Integration feature in Windows.

After the splash screen, Dreamweaver opens with a new blank page. This page is created from the Default.html file found in the Dreamweaver/Configuration/ Templates folder. Of course, it's likely that you'll want to replace the original Default.html file with one of your own — perhaps with your copyright information. All of your blank pages will then be created from a template that you've created.

Tip If you do decide to create your own Default template, it's probably a good idea to rename the Dreamweaver Default template — as Original-Default.html or something similar — prior to creating your new, personalized Default template.

Opening an existing file

If you're looking to work on a Web page in Dreamweaver that was created in another application, choose File ➪ Open, or the keyboard shortcut Ctrl-Ctrl-O (Command-O). From the standard Open File dialog box, you can browse to your file's location and select it.

If you have just started Dreamweaver or if your current document is blank, your selected file will load into the current window. If, however, you have another Web page open or have begun creating a new one, Dreamweaver opens your file in a new window.

When you first open an existing Web page, Dreamweaver checks the HTML syntax. If it finds any errors, Dreamweaver corrects them and then informs you of the corrections through the HTML Parser Results dialog box. As discussed in Chapter 3, "Setting Your Preferences," you can turn off this HTML syntax-checking feature. Select Edit ➪ Preferences and then, from the HTML pane of the Preferences dialog box, deselect one or more of the check-box options for HTML syntax-checking.

Opening Other Types of Files

Dreamweaver defaults to searching for HTML files with an extension of either .html or .htm. To look for other types of files, select the Files of Type arrow button. Dreamweaver allows several other file types, including server-side includes (.shtml, .shtm, or .stm), Active server pages (.asp), and Cold Fusion (.cfm or .cfml). If you need to load a valid HTML file with a different extension, select the All Files option.

If you are working consistently with a different file format, you can add your own extensions and file types to the Dreamweaver Open File dialog box. In the Configuration folder, there is an editable text file called Extensions.txt. Open this file in your favorite text editor to make any additions. If you use Dreamweaver, be sure to edit the file in the HTML Inspector to see the correct format.

The syntax must follow this format:

```
HTM,HTML:HTML Documents
SHTM,SHTML,STM:Server-Side Includes
LBI:Library Files
DWT:Template Files
CSS:Style Sheets
ASP:Active Server Pages
CFM,CFML:Cold Fusion Templates
TXT:Text Files
```

To add an entry, place your cursor at the end of the line above where you want your new file format to be placed, and press Enter (Return). Type in your file extension(s) in capital letters, followed by a colon and then the text description. Save the Extensions.txt file and restart Dreamweaver to see your modifications.

Opening a new window

You can work on as many Dreamweaver documents as your system memory can sustain. When you choose File ➪ New or one of the keyboard shortcuts (Ctrl-N or Command-N), Dreamweaver opens a new blank page in a separate window. Once the window is open, you can switch among the various windows. To do this in Windows, you select the appropriate icon in the taskbar or use the Alt-Tab method. To switch between Dreamweaver windows on a Macintosh, click on the individual window or use the Window menu.

Opening a new page

After working for a while on a design, you sometimes need to start over or switch entirely to a new project. In either case, choose File ➪ New or one of the keyboard shortcuts, Ctrl-Shift-N (Command-Shift-N). This closes the current document and opens a new blank page in the same window.

> **Tip** You can also drag and drop an HTML file onto the Dreamweaver Document Window or — if you're just starting a session — onto the Dreamweaver icon on your desktop.

If you've made any modifications to your page, Dreamweaver asks if you would like to save the page. Click the Yes button to save the file or the No button to continue without saving it. To abort the new page opening, click Cancel.

Each time you open a new page, whether in the existing window or in a new window, Dreamweaver temporarily names the file "Untitled-n," where n is the next number in sequence. This prevents you from accidentally overwriting a new file opened in the same session.

Saving your page

Saving your work is very important in any computer-related task, and Dreamweaver is no exception. To initially save the current page, choose File ➪ Save or the keyboard shortcut Ctrl-S (Command-S). The Save dialog box opens; you can enter a filename and, if desired, a different path.

By default, all files are saved with an .htm file name extension for Windows and .html for Macintosh. To save your file with another extension, such as .shtml, change the Files of Type option to the specific file type and then enter your full filename, without the extension.

> **Caution** It seems kind of backward in this day and age of long filenames, but it's still a good idea to choose names for your files without spaces or punctuation other than an underscore or hyphen. Otherwise, not all servers will read the filename correctly and you'll have problems linking your pages.

Closing the page

When you're finished with a page — or if your system is running low on resources — you can close a file without quitting Dreamweaver. To close a page, select File ➪ Close or the keyboard shortcuts, Ctrl-W (Command-W). If you made any changes to the page since you saved it last, Dreamweaver prompts you to save it.

If you only have one Dreamweaver window open and you close the current page, Dreamweaver asks you if you'd like to quit the program.

Quitting the program

Once you're done for the day—or, more often, the late, late night—you can close Dreamweaver by choosing File ⇨ Exit (File ⇨ Quit) or one of the standard keyboard shortcuts, Ctrl-Q (Command-Q).

In Windows systems, to make sure you're really ready to shut down the program, Dreamweaver 2 asks you to confirm your desire to quit. If you're confident that you won't quit the program accidentally, select the Don't Warn Me Again option to stop this dialog box from reappearing.

 Caution

You won't receive an opportunity to confirm your choice if you quit from the Site Window in Windows or in Macintosh systems.

Previewing Your Web Pages

When using Dreamweaver or any other Web authoring tool, it's important to constantly check your progress in one or more browsers. Dreamweaver's Document Window offers a near-browser view of your Web page, but because of the variations among the different browsers, it's imperative that you preview your page early and often. Dreamweaver offers you easy access to a maximum of 20 browsers—and they're just a function key away.

You add a browser to your preview list by selecting File ⇨ Preview in Browser ⇨ Edit Browser List or by choosing the Preview in Browser category from the Preferences dialog box. Both actions open the Preview in Browser Preferences panel. The steps for editing your browser list are described in detail in Chapter 3, "Setting Your Preferences." Here's a brief recap:

1. Select File ⇨ Preview in Browser ⇨ Edit Browser List.

2. To add a browser (up to 20), click the Add button and fill out the following fields:

Name	How you want the browser listed.
Application	Type in the path to the browser program or click the Browse button to locate the browser executable (.EXE) file.
Primary Browser/Secondary Browser	If desired, select one of these checkboxes to designate the current browser as such.

3. After you've added a browser to your list, you can easily edit or delete it. Choose File ⇨ Preview in Browser ⇨ Edit Browser List as before, and highlight the browser you want to modify or delete.

4. To alter your selection, click the Edit button. To delete your selection, click the Remove button.

5. After you've completed your modifications, click OK to close the dialog box.

Once you've added one or more browsers to your list, you can preview the current page in these browsers. Select File ➪ Preview in Browser ➪ *BrowserName,* where *BrowserName* indicates the particular program. Dreamweaver saves the page to a temporary file, starts the browser, and loads the page.

Note that in order to view any changes you've made to your Web page under construction, you must select the Preview in Browser menu option again (or press one of the function keys for primary/secondary browser previewing, described in the following paragraph). Clicking the Refresh/Reload button in your browser will not load in any modifications. The temporary preview files are deleted when you quit Dreamweaver.

You can also use keyboard shortcuts to preview two different browsers, by pressing a function key: Press F12 to preview the current Dreamweaver page in your primary browser, and Shift-F12 to preview the same page in your secondary browser. These are the Primary and Secondary Browser settings you establish in the Preferences /Preview in Browser dialog box, explained in Chapter 3, "Setting Your Preferences."

In fact, with Dreamweaver's Preview in Browser Preferences you can so easily switch the designations of Primary and Secondary browser that you can use that setup for "debugging" a Web page in any browser, simply by changing the preferences. Go to the Preview in Browser Preferences pane, select the browser you want to use for debugging, and check the appropriate check-box to designate the browser as Primary or Secondary. In the list of browsers in this Preferences pane, you'll see the indicator of F12 or Shift-F12 appear next to the browser's name.

Tip

In addition to checking your Web page output on a variety of browsers on your system, it's also a good idea to preview the page on other platforms. If you're designing on a Macintosh, try to view your pages on a Windows system, and vice versa. Watch out for some not-so-subtle differences between the two environments, in terms of color rendering (colors in Macs tend to be brighter than in PCs) and screen resolution.

Putting Your Pages Online

The final phase of setting up your Dreamweaver site is publishing your pages to the Web. When you begin this publishing process is up to you. Some Web designers wait until everything is absolutely perfect on the local development site and then upload everything at once. Others like to establish an early connection to the remote site and extend the transfer of files over a longer period of time.

I fall into the latter camp. When I start transferring files at the beginning of the process, I find that I catch my mistakes earlier and avoid having to effect massive changes to the site after everything is up. For example, in developing one large site I started out using filenames with mixed case, as in `ELFhome.html`. After publishing some early drafts of a few Web pages, however, I discovered that the host had switched servers; on the new server, filenames had to be all lowercase. Had I waited until the last moment to upload everything, I would have been faced with an unexpected and gigantic search-and-replace job.

Once you've established your local site root — and you've included your remote site's FTP information in the setup — the actual publishing of your files to the Web is a very straightforward process. To transfer your local Web pages to an online site, follow these steps:

1. Choose File ➪ Open Site ➪ *Site Name* (Site ➪ Open Site ➪ *Site Name*), where *Site Name* is the current site.

   The Site Window opens, displaying the current site.

2. From the Site Window, click the Connect button. (You may need to complete your connection to the Internet prior to choosing the Connect button.)

   Dreamweaver displays a message box showing the progress of the connection.

3. If you didn't enter a Password in the Site Information dialog box, or if you entered a password but didn't opt to save it, Dreamweaver asks you to type in your password.

   Once the connection is complete, the directory listing of the remote site appears in the Remote (left-hand by default) pane of the Site Window.

4. In the Local (right-hand by default) pane, highlight the HTML files you would like to transfer.

5. Click the Put button at the top of the Site Window.

6. Dreamweaver asks if you would like to move the dependent files as well. Select Yes to transfer all embedded graphics and other objects, or No if you'd prefer to move these yourself. You can also select the Don't Ask Me Again box to make transfers of dependent files automatic in the future.

   Dreamweaver displays the progress of the file transfer in the Site Window's status bar.

7. When each file transfer is finished, Dreamweaver places a green check mark next to each file (if File Check In/Out has been enabled in the Site FTP Preferences pane).

8. When you've finished transferring your files, click the Disconnect button.

Remember, the only files you have to highlight for transfer to the remote site are the HTML files. As noted previously, Dreamweaver automatically transfers any dependent file (if you allow it), which means that you'll never forget to move a GIF again! (Nor will you ever move an unnecessary file, such as an earlier version of an image, by mistake.) Moreover, Dreamweaver automatically creates any subfolders necessary to maintain the site's integrity. These two features combined will save you substantial time and worry.

 Some files, especially CGI programs, require that you set the file permissions before they can be used. For information about setting file permissions from within Dreamweaver, see Chapter 15, "Accessing External Programs."

So now your site has been prepped from the planning stages, through the local site root and onto the Web. Congratulations — all that's left is to fill those pages with insightful content, amazing graphics, and wondrous code. Let's get to it!

Summary

In this chapter, you studied some options for planning your Web site and what you need to do in Dreamweaver to initialize the site. This planning and initialization process is not a detailed one, but there are particular steps to take that can greatly smooth your development path down the road.

✦ Put as much time into planning your site as possible. The more clearly conceived the site, the cleaner the execution.

✦ Set up your local site root in Dreamweaver right away. The local site root is essential for Dreamweaver to properly publish your files to the remote site later.

✦ If you're working in a team environment, enable the Check In/Out features to prevent two or more team members from editing the same file at the same time.

✦ Decide on the type of addressing to use in your links. Document relative addressing is good for most small-to-medium Web sites, and site root relative addressing is best for most large sites. Use absolute addressing only when linking to an outside server.

✦ Preview early, often, and with various browsers. Dreamweaver gives you quick function-key access to a primary and secondary browser. Check your pages frequently in these browsers, and then spend some time checking your pages against other available browsers and browser versions.

✦ Establish an early connection to the Web and use it frequently. You can begin publishing your local site through Dreamweaver's Site Window almost immediately.

In the next chapter, you'll see how to use Dreamweaver to begin coding your Web pages.

✦　　✦　　✦

Using Basic HTML in Dreamweaver

Understanding How HTML Works

✦   ✦   ✦   ✦

In This Chapter

Laying the HTML foundation

Working with the `<head>` section

Developing the `<body>` section

Adding special characters

✦   ✦   ✦   ✦

In a perfect world, you could lay out the most complex Web site with a visual authoring tool and never have to see the HTML, much less code in it. Dreamweaver takes you a long way toward this goal — in fact, you can create many types of Web pages using only Dreamweaver's Document Window. As your pages become more complex, however, you will probably need to tweak your HTML just a tad.

This chapter gives you a basic understanding of how HTML works in general, and the specific building blocks you need to begin creating Web pages. Also, in this chapter you'll get your first look at a Dreamweaver 2 innovation: visual layout for HTML that previously had to be hand-coded. The other Dreamweaver-specific material in this chapter — primarily describing how Dreamweaver sets and modifies a page's properties — is suitable for even the most accomplished Web designers. Armed with these fundamentals, you'll be ready to begin your exploration of Web page creation.

The Structure of an HTML Page

The simplest explanation of how HTML works derives from the full expansion of its acronym: HyperText Markup Language. *HyperText* refers to one of the World Wide Web's main properties — the capability to jump from one page to another, no matter where the pages are located on the Web. *Markup Language* means that a Web page is really just a heavily annotated text file. The basic building blocks of HTML, such as `<strong>` and `<p>`, are known as *markup elements*, or *tags*. The terms *element* and *tag* are used interchangeably.

An HTML page, then, is a set of instructions (the tags) suggesting to your browser how to display the enclosed text and images. The browser knows what kind of page it is handling based on the tag that opens the page, `<html>`, and the tag that closes the page, `</html>`. The great majority of HTML tags come in such pairs, in which the closing tag always has a forward slash before the keyword. Two examples of tag pairs are: `<p>...</p>` and `<title>...</title>`. A few important tags are represented by a single element; the image tag `<img>`, for example.

The HTML page is divided into two primary sections: the `<head>` and the `<body>`. Information relating to the entire document goes in the `<head>` section: the title, description, keywords, and any language subroutines that may be called from within the `<body>`. The content of the Web page is found in the `<body>` section. All the text, graphics, embedded animations, Java applets, and other elements of the page are found between the opening `<body>` and the closing `</body>` tags.

When you start a new document in Dreamweaver, the basic format is already laid out for you. Listing 6-1 shows the code from a Dreamweaver blank Web page.

Listing 6-1: **The HTML for a new Dreamweaver page**

```
<html>
<head>
<title>Untitled Document</title>
<meta http-equiv="Content-Type" content="text/html;
charset=iso-8859-1">
</head>

<body bgcolor="#FFFFFF">

</body>
</html>
```

Notice how the `<head>...</head>` pair is separate from the `<body>...</body>` pair, and that both are contained within the `<html>...</html>` tags.

Also notice that the `<body>` tag has an additional element:

```
bgcolor="#FFFFFF"
```

This type of element is known as an attribute. *Attributes* modify the basic tag and can either be equal to a value or can stand alone; in this example, the attribute, `bgcolor`, is set to a hexadecimal number that represents the color white. Thus, this attribute sets the background color of the body — the page — to white. Not every tag has attributes, but when it does, the attributes are specific.

Tip
If you're using the PC version of Dreamweaver, you have access to an excellent HTML guide through the HomeSite editor. From the HomeSite window, select Help ⇨ Help Topics and then open the HTML Reference from the Help pane.

One last note about an HTML page: You are free to use carriage returns, spaces, and tabs as needed to make your code more readable. The interpreting browser ignores all but the included tags and text to create your page. There are some minor, browser-specific differences in interpretation of these elements that will be pointed out through the book, but by and large, you can indent or space your code as you desire.

Defining \<head> Elements

Information pertaining to the Web page overall is contained in the \<head> section of an HTML page. Browsers read the \<head> to find out how to render the page — for example, is the page to be displayed using the Western, Chinese, or some other character set? This section is also read by search engine spiders to glean a summary of the page quickly.

When you begin inserting JavaScript (or code from another scripting language like VBScript) into your Web page, all of the subroutines and document-wide declarations go into the \<head> area. Dreamweaver uses this format by default when you insert a JavaScript behavior.

New Feature
Dreamweaver now lets you insert, view, and modify \<head> content without opening an HTML editor. Dreamweaver 2's new View Head Content capability enables you to work with \<meta> tags and other \<head> HTML code as you do with the regular content in the visual editor.

Establishing page properties

When you first start Dreamweaver, your default Web page is untitled, with no background image but a plain white background. You can change all of these properties and more through Dreamweaver's Page Properties dialog box.

As usual, Dreamweaver gives you more than one method for accessing the Page Properties dialog box. You can select Modify ⇨ Page Properties, or you can use the keyboard shortcut, Ctrl-J (Command-J).

Tip
Here's the other way to open the Page Properties. Right-click (Command-click) any open area in the Document Window — that is, any part of the screen not occupied by an image, table, or other object (text outside of tables is okay to click, however). From the bottom of the Shortcut menu, select Page Properties.

The Page Properties dialog box, shown in Figure 6-1, gives you easy control of your HTML page's overall look and feel.

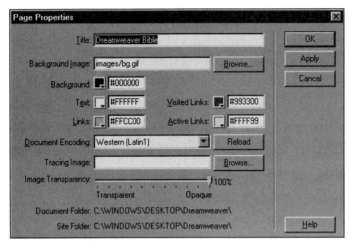

Figure 6-1: Change your Web page's overall appearance through the Page Properties dialog box.

Note   Technically, some of the values you assign through the Page Properties dialog box are applied to the `<body>` tag; because they affect the overall appearance of a page, however, they are covered in this `<head>` section.

The key areas of the Page Properties dialog box are as follows:

Page Property	Description
Title	The title of your Web page. The name you enter here appears in the browser's title bar when your page is viewed and is also regarded as one of the important indexing clues by search engine spiders.
Background Image	The file name of the graphic you want in the page background. Either type in the path directly or pick a file by clicking the Browse button. You can embed any graphic of your choice in the background of your page; if the image is smaller than your content requires, the browser tiles the image to fill out the page. Specifying a background image overrides any selection in the Background color field.
Background	Click this color swatch to change the background color of the Web page. Select one of the browser-safe colors from the pop-up menu, or enter its name or hexadecimal representation (for example, "#FFFFFF") directly into the text box.

Page Property	Description
Text	Click this color swatch to control the color of default text.
Links	Click this color swatch to modify the color of any text designated as a link, or the border around an image link.
Visited Links	Click this color swatch to select the color to which linked text will change after a visitor to your Web page has selected that link and then returns to the page.
Active Links	Click this color swatch to choose the color to which linked text changes briefly when a user selects the link.
Document Encoding	The character set in which you want your Web page to be displayed. Choose one from the drop-down list. The default is Western (Latin 1).
Tracing Image	Selects an image to use as a layout guide.
Image Transparency	Sets the degree of transparency for the tracing image.

The Page Properties dialog box also displays the document folder if the page has been saved, and the current site root folder if one has been selected.

 New Feature The Tracing Image option is a powerful layering feature new to Dreamweaver 2. For details about this feature and how to use it, see "Tracing Your Design with Layers" in Chapter 25.

Choosing Colors from an Onscreen Image

One of the new features found throughout Dreamweaver 2, the Eyedropper tool, is especially useful in the Page Properties options. The Eyedropper tool appears whenever you open any of Dreamweaver's color swatches, such as those attached to the Background, Text, and Links colors. Not only can you pick a color from the Web-safe palette that appears, but you can also use the Eyedropper to select any color on any Dreamweaver page — including system colors like those found in dialog boxes and menu strips.

To use the Eyedropper tool to choose a color for the background (or any of the other options) from an on-screen image, follow these steps:

1. Insert your image on the page and, using the vertical scroll bar, position the Document Window so that the image and the Page Properties dialog box can be viewed simultaneously.

Continued

(continued)

If your image is too big to fit both it and the Page Properties dialog box on the same screen, temporarily resize your image by dragging its sizing handles. You can restore the original image size when you're done by selecting the Refresh button on the Image Property Inspector.

2. Open the Page Properties dialog box by choosing Modify ⇨ Page Properties or using the keyboard shortcut, Ctrl-J (Command-J).

3. Drag the Page Properties dialog box to a place where the image can be seen.

4. Select the Background color swatch (or whichever one you wish to change).

    The Dreamweaver color picker opens and the pointer becomes an eyedropper.

5. Move the Eyedropper tool over the image until you find the correct color. As you move the Eyedropper over an image, its colors are reflected in the color well and its hex value is shown on the color picker. Click once when you've found the appropriate color.

    The color picker closes.

6. Repeat Steps 4 and 5 to grab other colors from the screen for other color swatches. Click OK when you've finished modifying the page properties.

You don't have to keep the image on your page to get its color. Just insert it temporarily and then delete it after you've used the Eyedropper to grab the shade you want.

Choosing a Page Palette

Until now, getting the right text and link colors to match your background color has been largely a trial-and-error process. Generally, you'd set the background color, add a contrasting text color, and then add some variations of different colors for the three different link colors — all the while clicking the Apply button and checking your results until you found a satisfactory combination. This is a time-intensive chore, to say the least.

New Feature

Now, however, Dreamweaver 2 ships with a new command that enables you to quickly pick an entire palette for your page in one fell swoop. The Set Color Scheme command, shown in Figure 6-2, features palette combinations from noted Web designers Lynda Weinman and Bruce Heavin. The colors available in the command are all Web-safe — which means that they will appear the same in the major browsers on all Macintosh and Windows systems without dithering.

Figure 6-2: Get a Web-safe page palette with one click by using the Set Color Scheme command.

To use the Set Color Scheme command, follow these steps:

1. Choose Command ⇨ Set Color Scheme

   The Set Color Scheme dialog box opens.

2. Select the background color from the Background column on the left.

   The Text and Links column is updated to show available combinations for the selected background color.

3. Select a color set from the Text and Links column to see various combinations in the Preview pane.

   The color names — such as White, Pink, Brown — refer to the Text, Link, and Visited Link colors, generally. If only one color name is offered, the entire color scheme uses shades of that color. Note that the background color changes slightly for various color combinations to work better with the foreground colors choices.

4. Click Apply to see the effect on your current page. Click OK when you finish.

Cross-Reference To learn more about Commands in general — including how to build your own — check out Chapter 19, "Customizing Dreamweaver."

Understanding <meta> and other <head> tags

Summary information about the content of a page — and a lot more — is conveyed through <meta> tags used within the <head> section. The <meta> tag can be read by the server to create a header file, which makes it easier for indexing software used by search engines to catalog sites. Numerous different types of <meta> tags exist. And, with the introduction of Dreamweaver 2, you can insert them in your document just like other objects.

One `<meta>` tag is included by default in every Dreamweaver page. The Document Encoding option of the Page Properties dialog box determines the character set used by the current Web page and is displayed in the `<head>` section as follows:

```
<meta http-equiv="Content-Type" content="text/html;
charset=iso-8859-1">
```

The preceding `<meta>` tag tells the browser that this page is, in fact, an HTML page and that the page should be rendered using the specified character set (the `charset` attribute). The key attribute here is `http-equiv`, which is responsible for generating a server response header.

Tip   Once you've determined your `<meta>` tags for a Web site, the same basic `<meta>` information can go on every Web page. Dreamweaver gives you a way to avoid inserting the same lines again and again: templates. Once you've set up the `<head>` elements the way you'd like them, choose File ➪ Save As Template. If you want to add `<meta>` or any other `<head>` tags to an existing template, you can edit the template and then update the affected pages. For more on templates, turn to Chapter 34, "Utilizing Dreamweaver Templates."

New Feature   In Dreamweaver 2, you can insert a `<meta>` tag or any other tag using the new `<head>` tag objects, which you access via the Head panel in the Objects palette or the Insert ➪ Head menu option. The new `<head>` tag objects are described in Table 6-1 and subsequent subsections.

Table 6-1 Head Tag Objects	
Head Tag Object	**Description**
Meta	Inserts information that describes or affects the entire document.
Keywords	Includes a series of words used by the search engine to index the current Web page and/or site.
Description	Includes a text description of the current Web page and/or site.
Refresh	Reloads the current document or loads a new URL within a specified number of seconds.
Base	Establishes a reference for all other URLs in the current Web page.
Link	Inserts a link to an external document, such as a style sheet.

Inserting tags with the Meta object

The Meta object is used to insert tags that provide information for the Web server through the `HTTP-equiv` attribute and other overall data that you want to include in your Web page, but not make visible to the casual browser. Some Web pages, for example, have built-in expiration dates after which the content is to be considered outmoded. In Dreamweaver, you can use the Meta object to insert a wide range of descriptive data.

You can access the Meta object on the Head panel of the Objects palette or via the Insert menu by choosing Insert ➪ Head ➪ Meta. Like all the Head objects, you don't have to have the Head Content visible to insert the Meta object; although you will have to choose View ➪ Head Content if you wish to edit the object. To insert a Meta object, follow these steps:

1. Select Insert ➪ Head ➪ Meta or the Meta object from the Head panel of the Objects palette. Your current cursor position is irrelevant.

The Insert Meta dialog box opens, as shown in Figure 6-3.

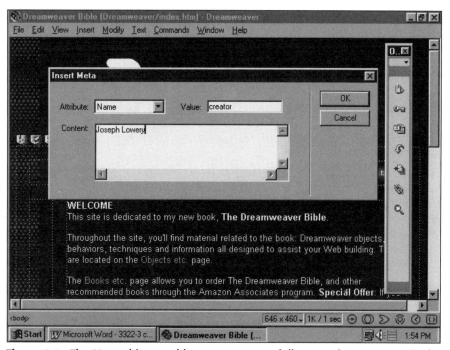

Figure 6-3: The Meta object enables you to enter a full range of `<meta>` tags in the `<head>` section of your Web page.

2. Choose the desired attribute: Name or an HTTP-equivalent from the Attribute list box. Press Tab.

3. Enter the value for the selected attribute in the Value text box. Press Tab.

4. Enter the value for the content attribute in the Content text box.

5. Click OK when you're done.

To edit an existing Meta object, you must first choose View ➪ Head Content to reveal the `<head>` code, indicated by the various icons. Select the Meta tag icon and make your changes in the Property Inspector.

Built-In Meta Commands

Although Dreamweaver presents six different Head objects, `<meta>` tags form the basis of four of them: Meta, Description, Keywords, and Refresh. By specifying different `name` attributes, the purpose of the `<meta>` tags changes. For example, a Keywords object uses this format:

```
<meta name="keywords" content="dreamweaver, web, authoring, HTML,
DHTML, CSS, Macromedia">
```

whereas a Description object inserts this type of code:

```
<meta name="description" content="This site is devoted to
extensions made possible by Macromedia's Dreamweaver, the premier
Web authoring tool.">
```

It is possible to create all your `<meta>` tags with the Meta object by specifying the name attribute and giving it the pertinent value, but it's easier to just use the standard Dreamweaver 2 Head objects.

Aiding search engines with the Keywords and Description objects

Let's take a closer look at the tags responsible for conveying indexing and descriptive information to search engine spiders. In Dreamweaver 2, these chores are handled by the Keywords and Description objects. As noted in the sidebar, "Built-In Meta Commands," the Keywords and Description objects output specialized `<meta>` tags.

Both objects are very straightforward to use. Choose Insert ➪ Head ➪ Keywords or Insert ➪ Head ➪ Description. You can also choose the corresponding objects from the Head panel of the Objects palette. Once selected, these objects open a dialog box with a single entry area, a large text box, as shown in Figure 6-4. Enter the values — whether keywords or a description — in the text box and click OK when you're done. Like the Meta object, you can edit the Keywords and Description objects by selecting their icons in the Head area of the Document Window, revealed by choosing View ➪ Head Contents.

Caution Although you can enter paragraph returns in your Keywords and Description objects, there's no reason to. Browsers ignore all such formatting when processing your code.

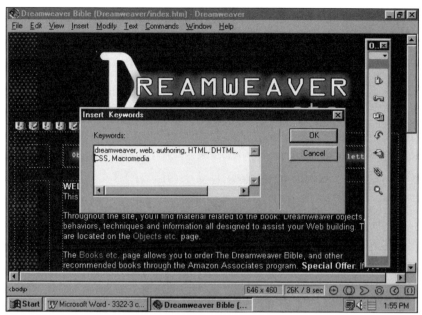

Figure 6-4: Entering information through the Keywords object helps search engines correctly index your Web page.

What you place in the Keywords and Description objects can have a big impact on your Web page's accessibility. If, for example, you want to categorize your Web page as an homage to the music of the early seventies, you could enter the following in the Content area of the Keywords object:

```
music, 70s, 70's, eagles, ronstadt, bee gees, pop, rock
```

In the preceding case, the content list is composed of words or phrases, separated by commas. Use sentences in the Description object, like this:

```
The definitive look back to the power pop rock stylings of
early 1970s music, with special sections devoted to the Eagles,
Linda Ronstadt, and the Bee Gees.
```

Keep in mind that the content in the Description should complement and extend both the Keywords and the Web page title. You have more room in both the Description and Keywords objects — really, an unlimited amount — than in the page title, which should be on the short side in order to fit into the browser's title bar.

Caution

When using `<meta>` tags with the Keywords or Description attributes, don't stuff the `<meta>` tags with the same word repeated over and over again. The search engines are engineered to reject multiple words and your description will not get the attention it deserves.

Refreshing the page and redirecting users

The Refresh object forces a browser to reload the current page or to load a new page after a user-set interval. Refreshing a page is generally something controlled by the Web page visitor; if, for some reason, the display has become garbled, the user can choose Reload from the menu to redraw the screen. Impatient Web surfer that I am, I often stop a page from loading to see what text links are available and — if I don't see what I need — hit Reload to bring in the full page. The code inserted by the Refresh object, on the other hand, tells the *server* to reload the page, not the browser. This can be a powerful tool, and one that will lead to trouble if used improperly.

To insert a Refresh object, follow these steps:

1. Choose Insert ➪ Head ➪ Refresh or select the Insert Refresh object from the Head panel of the Objects palette.

   The Insert Refresh dialog box, as shown in Figure 6-5, opens.

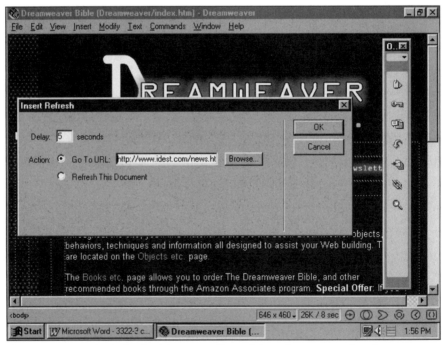

Figure 6-5: Use the Refresh object to redirect visitors from an outdated page.

2. Enter the number of seconds you want to wait before the Refresh command takes effect in the Delay text box.

   The Delay value is calculated from the time the page finishes loading.

3. Select the desired Action:

- Go to URL

- Refresh This Document

4. If you selected Go to URL, enter a path to another page in the text box or select the Browse button to select a file.

5. Click OK when you're done.

The Refresh object is most often used to redirect a visitor to another Web page. The Web is a very fluid place and sites often move from one address to another. Typically, a page at the old address contains the Refresh code that automatically takes the user to the new address. It's good practice to include a link to your new URL on the "change-of-address" page because not all browsers support the Refresh option. One other tip: Keep the number of seconds to a minimum — there's no point in waiting for something to happen automatically when you could click a link sooner.

Caution

If you elect to choose the Refresh This Document option, use extreme caution. You can easily set up an endless loop for your visitors in which the same page is constantly being refreshed. If you are working with a page that updates often, enter a longer Refresh value such as 300–500. Also, you should be sure to include a link to another page to enable them to exit from the continually refreshed page.

Changing bases

Through the Base object, the `<head>` section enables you to exert fundamental control over the basic HTML element: the link. The code inserted by this object specifies the base URL for the current page. If you use relative addressing (covered in Chapter 5, "Setting Up Your First Site"), you can switch all of your links to another directory — even another Web site — with one command. The Base object takes two attributes: `Href`, which redirects all the other relative links on your page; and `target`, which specifies where the links will be rendered.

To insert a Base object in your page, follow these steps:

1. Choose Insert ⇨ Head ⇨ Refresh or select the Insert Base object from the Head panel of the Objects palette.

   The Insert Base dialog box opens.

2. Input the path that you want all other relative links to be based on in the Href text box or choose the Browse button to pick the path.

3. If desired, enter a default target for all links without a specific target to be rendered in the Target text box.

4. Click OK when you're done.

How does a `<base>` tag affect your page? Let's say you define one link as follows:

```
images/backgnd.gif
```

Normally, the browser looks in the same folder as the current page for a subfolder named images. A different sequence occurs, however, if you set the `<base>` tag to another URL in the following way:

```
<base href="http://www.testsite.com/client-demo01/">
```

With this `<base>` tag, when the same images/backgnd.gif link is activated, the browser looks for its file in the following location:

```
http://www.testsite.com/client-demo01/images/backgnd.gif
```

Caution Because of the all-or-nothing capability of `<base>` tags, many Webmasters use them cautiously, if at all.

Linking to other files

The Link object is used to indicate a relationship between the current page and another page or file. Although there are many other intended uses, the `<link>` tag is most commonly used to apply an external Cascading Style Sheet (CSS) to the current page. This code is entered automatically in Dreamweaver when you create a new linked style sheet (as described in Chapter 24, "Building Style Sheet Web Pages"), but to apply an existing style sheet, you need to use the Link object. The Link tag is also used to include TrueDoc dynamic fonts.

To insert a Link object, first choose Insert ➪ Head ➪ Link or select the Insert Link object from the Head panel of the Objects palette. This opens the Insert Link dialog box, shown in Figure 6-6.

Next, enter the necessary attributes:

Attribute	Description
Href	The path to the file being linked. Use the Browse button to open the Select File dialog box.
ID	The ID attribute can be used by scripts to identify this particular object and affect it if need be.
Title	The Title attribute is displayed as a tooltip by Internet Explorer browsers.
Rel	A keyword that describes the relationship of the linked document to the current page. For example, an external style sheet uses the keyword `stylesheet`.
Rev	Rev, like Rel, also describes a relationship, but in the reverse. For example, if home.html contained a link tag with a Rel attribute set to intro.html, intro.html could contain a link tag with a Rev attribute set to home.html.

Figure 6-6: The Link object is primarily used to include external style sheets.

Note   Aside from the style sheet use, there's little browser support for the other link functions. However, the W3C supports an initiative to use the `<link>` tag to address other media, such as speech synthesis and Braille devices, and it's entirely possible that the Link object will be used for this purpose in the future.

Adding to the `<body>`

The content of a Web page — the text, images, links, and plug-ins — is all contained in the `<body>` section of an HTML document. The great majority of `<body>` tags can be inserted through Dreamweaver's visual layout interface.

To use the `<body>` tags efficiently, you need to understand the distinction between *logical styles* and *physical styles* used in HTML. An underlying philosophy of HTML is to keep the Web as universally accessible as possible. Web content is not only intended to be platform- and resolution-independent, but the content itself is designed to be styled by its intent as well. This philosophy is supported by the existence of logical `<body>` tags (such as `<code>` and `<cite>`), with which a block of text can be rendered according to its meaning, as well as physical style tags for directly italicizing or underlining text. HTML lets you choose between logical styles, which are relative to the text, or physical styles, which can be regarded as absolute.

Logical styles

Logical styles are contextual rather than explicit. Choose a logical style when you want to ensure that the meaning, rather than a specific look, is conveyed. Table 6-2 shows a listing of logical style tags and their most common usage. Tags not supported through Dreamweaver's visual interface are noted.

Table 6-2 HTML Logical Style Tags	
Tag	**Usage**
`<big>`	Increases the size of the selected text relative to the surrounding text. Not currently supported by Dreamweaver.
`<cite>`	Citations, titles, and references; usually shown in italic.
`<code>`	Code; for showing programming code, usually displayed in a monospaced font.
`<dfn>`	Defining instance; used to mark the introduction of a new term.
`<em>`	Emphasis; usually depicted as underlined or italicized text.
`<kbd>`	Keyboard; used to render text to be entered exactly.
`<s>`	Strikethrough text; used for showing text that has been deleted.
`<samp>`	Sample; a sequence of literal characters.
`<small>`	Decreases the size of the selected text relative to the surrounding text. Not currently supported by Dreamweaver.
`<strong>`	Strong emphasis; usually rendered as bold text.
`<sub>`	Subscript; the text is shown slightly lowered below the baseline. Not currently supported by Dreamweaver.
`<sup>`	Superscript; the text is shown slightly raised above the baseline. Not currently supported by Dreamweaver.
`<tt>`	Teletype; displayed with a monospaced font such as Courier.
`<var>`	Variable; used to distinguish variables from other programming code.

Logical styles are going to become increasingly important as more browsers accept Cascading Style Sheets. Style sheets make it possible to combine the best elements of both logical and physical styles. With style sheets, you can easily make the text within your `<code>` tags blue, and the variables, denoted with the `<var>` tag, green.

Caution If a tag is not currently supported by Dreamweaver, you must enter the tag by hand and preview the result in a browser. For example, you can use the `<sub>` tag to create a formula for water (H_2O), but you don't see the subscripted 2 in the formula until you view the page through a browser.

Physical styles

HTML picked up the use of physical styles from modern typography and word-processing programs. Use a physical style when you want something to be bold, italic, or underlined (or, as we say in HTML, `<b>`, `<i>`, and `<u>`, respectively) absolutely. You can apply the bold and the italic tags to selected text through the Property Inspector or by selecting Text ➪ Style; the underline style is only available through the Text menu.

With HTML Version 3.2, a fourth physical style tag was added: `<font>`. Most browsers recognize the size attribute, which enables you to make the selected text larger or smaller, relatively or directly. To change a font size absolutely, select your text and then select Text ➪ Size; Dreamweaver inserts a

```
<font size=n>
```

tag, where *n* is a number from 1 to 7. To make text larger than the default text, select Text ➪ Size Increase and then choose the value you want. Here Dreamweaver inserts the

```
<font size=+n>
```

The plus sign indicates the relative nature of the font. Make text smaller than the default text by selecting Text ➪ Size Decrease; Dreamweaver inserts

```
<font size=-n>
```

You can also expressly change the type of font used and its color through the face and color attributes. Because you can't be sure what fonts will be on a user's system, common practice and good form dictates that you should list alternatives for a selected font. For instance, rather than just specifying Arial — a sans serif font common on PCs but relatively unknown on the Mac — you could insert a tag like the following:

```
<font face="Arial, Helvetica, sans-serif">
```

In the preceding case, if the browser doesn't find the first font, it looks for the second one (and so forth, as specified). Dreamweaver handles the font face attribute through its Font List dialog box, which is explained fully in Chapter 7, "Adding Text to Your Web Page."

Inserting Symbols and Special Characters

When working with Dreamweaver, you're usually entering text directly from your keyboard, one keystroke at a time, with each representing a letter, number, or other keyboard character. Some situations, however, require special letters that have diacritics or common symbols such as the copyright mark, which are outside of the regular, standard character set represented on your keyboard. HTML enables you to insert a full range of such *character entities* through two systems. The more familiar special characters have been assigned a mnemonic code-name to make them easy to remember; these are called *named characters*. Less typical characters must be inserted by entering a numeric code; these are known as *decimal characters*. For the sake of completeness, named characters also have a corresponding decimal character code.

Both named and decimal characters codes begin with an ampersand (&) symbol and end with a semicolon. For example, the HTML code for an ampersand symbol follows:

&

Its decimal character equivalent follows:

&

Caution

If, during the browser-testing phase of your Web page, you suddenly see an HTML code on screen rather than a symbol, double-check your HTML. The code could be just a typo; you may have left off the closing semicolon, for instance. If the code is correct and you're using a named character, however, switch to its decimal equivalent. Some of the earlier browser versions are not perfect in rendering named characters.

Named characters

HTML coding conventions require that certain characters, including the angle brackets that surround tags, be entered as character entities. Table 6-3 lists the most common named characters.

Table 6-3
Common Named Characters

Named Entity	Symbol	Description
&lt;	<	A left-hand angle bracket or the less-than symbol
&gt;	>	A right-hand angle bracket or the greater-than symbol
&amp;	&	An ampersand

Named Entity	Symbol	Description
&quot;	"	A double quotation mark
	°	A nonbreaking space
&copy;	©	A copyright symbol
&reg;	®	A registered mark
&trade;	™	A trademark symbol. Cannot be previewed in Dreamweaver, but is supported in Internet Explorer

Tip Those characters that you can type directly into Dreamweaver's Document Window, including the brackets and the ampersand, are automatically translated into the correct named characters in HTML. Try this with the HTML Inspector open. Also, you can enter a nonbreaking space in Dreamweaver by typing Shift-Ctrl-spacebar (Shift-Command-spacebar) or by choosing the Non-breaking Space object.

Decimal characters

To enter almost any character that has a diacritic — such as á, ñ, or â — in Dreamweaver, you must explicitly enter the corresponding decimal character into your HTML page. As mentioned in the preceding section, decimal characters take the form of &#*number*, where the *number* can range from 00 to 255. Not all numbers have matching symbols; the sequence from 14 through 31 is currently unused, while the upper range 127 through 159 is only partially supported by Internet Explorer and Netscape Navigator.

On the CD-ROM To make your life — or at least the part concerned with decimal characters — a little simpler, the CD-ROM includes a Characters object. Copy both the char_entities.htm and char_entities.gif files into one of your Object folders (Common, Invisibles, or Forms) and then start Dreamweaver. You'll find a new item, Character Entities, on the Objects palette. Position your cursor where you want to insert the decimal character, and select the Character Entities object. Choose your symbol from the table that opens on the screen and click OK. If you have the HTML Inspector open, you see the decimal character inserted into your code. With the Character Entities object, you can enter a single decimal character or a series of them at one time.

To enter a decimal code by hand, look up the symbol in Table 6-4 and type its code on your page in the HTML Inspector. Dreamweaver previews the code correctly in its document window.

Tip There are a couple of additional methods for inserting high ASCII characters into your document. On Windows systems, you can enter the characters directly by holding down Alt and typing the four-digit decimal number on the numeric keypad in the Document Window. For example, for copyright, hold down Alt and type **0169** on the numeric keypad — the copyright symbol appears. You can also use the Character Map utility found under Start/Programs/Accessories. On Macintosh systems, the Key Caps utility under the Apple menu details which key inserts which high ASCII character when pressed along with the Option key.

Table 6-4
Decimal Character Codes

Decimal Code	Character Produced	Description
&#00; – &#08;		Unused
&#09;		Horizontal tab
&#10;		Line feed
&#13;		Carriage return
&#11; – 		Unused
&#32;		Space
&#33;	!	Exclamation mark
&#34;	"	Quotation mark
&#35;	#	Number sign
&#36;	$	Dollar sign
&#37;	%	Percent sign
&#38;	&	Ampersand
&#39;	'	Apostrophe
&#40;	(	Left parenthesis
&#41;	)	Right parenthesis
&#42;	*	Asterisk
&#43;	+	Plus sign
&#44;	,	Comma
&#14; – &#31;		Unused
&#45;	-	Hyphen
&#46;	.	Period (full stop)
&#47;	/	Solidus (slash)
0 – 9	0 – 9	Decimal digits

Decimal Code	Character Produced	Description
&#58;	:	Colon
&#59;	;	Semicolon
&#60;	<	Less than
&#61;	=	Equals sign
&#62;	>	Greater than
&#63;	?	Question mark
&#64;	@	Commercial at
A – Z	A – Z	Uppercase letters
&#91;	[	Left square bracket
&#92;	\	Reverse solidus (backslash)
&#93;	]	Right square bracket
&#94;	^	Caret
&#95;	_	Horizontal bar
&#96;	`	Grave accent
a – z	a – z	Lowercase letters
&#123;	{	Left curly brace
|	|	Vertical bar
&#125;	}	Right curly brace
&#126;	~	Tilde
&#127; – 		Unused
&#130;	,	Comma
&#131;	ƒ	Mathematical function f
&#132;	„	Low quotation mark
&#133;	…	Triple dots (ellipsis)
&#134;	†	Footnote mark
&#135;	‡	Double footnote mark
&#136;	ˆ	Circumflex accent
&#137;	‰	Per thousandth
&#138;	Š	Capital S, inverted circumflex
&#139;	‹	Small less than
&#140;	Œ	Capital OE diphthong

Continued

Table 6-4 *(continued)*

Decimal Code	Character Produced	Description
 – 		Unused
&#145;	'	Single quote, opening
&#146;	'	Single quote, closing
&#147;	"	Double quote, opening
&#148;	"	Double quote, closing
&#149;	•	Large middle dot
&#150;	–	Middle dash
&#151;	—	Double middle dash
&#152;	~	Tilde
&#153;	™	Trademark (IE and NS 4 only)
&#154;	š	Small s, inverted circumflex
&#155;	›	Small greater than
&#156;	œ	Small oe diphthong
 – ž		Unused
&#159;	Ÿ	Capital Y with umlaut
		Nonbreaking space
&#161;	¡	Inverted exclamation
&#162;	¢	Cent sign
&#163;	£	Pound sterling
&#164;	¤	General currency sign
&#165;	¥	Yen sign
&#166;	¦	Broken vertical bar
&#167;	§	Section sign
&#168;	¨	Umlaut
&#169;	©	Copyright
&#170;	ª	Feminine ordinal
&#171;	«	Left angle bracket
&#172;	¬	Not sign
&#173;		Soft hyphen
&#174;	®	Registered trademark
&#175;	¯	Macron accent

Decimal Code	Character Produced	Description
&#176;	°	Degree sign
&#177;	±	Plus or minus
&#178;	²	Superscript 2
&#179;	³	Superscript 3
&#180;	´	Acute accent
&#181;	µ	Micro sign
&#182;	¶	Paragraph sign
&#183;	·	Middle dot
&#184;	¸	Cedilla
&#185;	¹	Superscript 1
&#186;	º	Masculine ordinal
&#187;	»	Right angle quote
&#188;	¼	Fraction one-fourth
&#189;	½	Fraction one-half
&#190;	¾	Fraction three-fourths
&#191;	¿	Inverted question mark
&#192;	À	Capital A, grave accent
&#193;	Á	Capital A, acute accent
&#194;	Â	Capital A, circumflex accent
&#195;	Ã	Capital A, tilde
&#196;	Ä	Capital A, dieresis or umlaut mark
&#197;	Å	Capital A, ring
&#198;	Æ	Capital AE diphthong (ligature)
&#199;	Ç	Capital C, cedilla
&#200;	È	Capital E, grave accent
&#201;	É	Capital E, acute accent
&#202;	Ê	Capital E, circumflex accent
&#203;	Ë	Capital E, dieresis or umlaut mark
&#204;	Ì	Capital I, grave accent
&#205;	Í	Capital I, acute accent
&#206;	Î	Capital I, circumflex accent

Continued

Table 6-4 (continued)		
Decimal Code	**Character Produced**	**Description**
&#207;	Ï	Capital I, dieresis or umlaut mark
&#208;	Ð	Capital Eth, Icelandic
&#209;	Ñ	Capital N, tilde
&#210;	Ò	Capital O, grave accent
&#211;	Ó	Capital O, acute accent
&#212;	Ô	Capital O, circumflex accent
&#213;	Õ	Capital O, tilde
&#214;	Ö	Capital O, dieresis or umlaut mark
&#215;	x	Multiplication sign
&#216;	Ø	Capital O, slash
&#217;	Ù	Capital U, grave accent
&#218;	Ú	Capital U, acute accent
&#219;	Û	Capital U, circumflex accent
&#220;	Ü	Capital U, dieresis or umlaut mark
&#221;	Ý	Capital Y, acute accent
&#222;	Þ	Capital THORN, Icelandic
&#223;	ß	Small sharp s, German (sz ligature)
&#224;	à	Small a, grave accent
&#225;	á	Small a, acute accent
&#226;	â	Small a, circumflex accent
&#227;	ã	Small a, tilde
&#228;	ä	Small a, dieresis or umlaut mark
&#229;	å	Small a, ring
&#230;	æ	Small ae diphthong (ligature)
&#231;	ç	Small c, cedilla
&#232;	è	Small e, grave accent
&#233;	é	Small e, acute accent
&#234;	ê	Small e, circumflex accent
&#235;	ë	Small e, dieresis or umlaut mark
&#236;	ì	Small i, grave accent
&#237;	í	Small i, acute accent

Decimal Code	Character Produced	Description
&#238;	î	Small i, circumflex accent
&#239;	ï	Small i, dieresis or umlaut mark
&#240;	ð	Small eth, Icelandic
&#241;	ñ	Small n, tilde
&#242;	ò	Small o, grave accent
&#243;	ó	Small o, acute accent
&#244;	ô	Small o, circumflex accent
&#245;	õ	Small o, tilde
&#246;	ö	Small o, dieresis or umlaut mark
&#247;	÷	Division sign
&#248;	ø	Small o, slash
&#249;	ù	Small u, grave accent
&#250;	ú	Small u, acute accent
&#251;	û	Small u, circumflex accent
&#252;	ü	Small u, dieresis or umlaut mark
&#253;	ý	Small y, acute accent
&#254;	þ	Small thorn, Icelandic
&#255;	ÿ	Small y, dieresis or umlaut mark

Summary

Creating Web pages with Dreamweaver is a special blend of using visual layout tools and HTML coding. Regardless, you need to understand the basics of HTML so that you'll have the knowledge and the tools to modify your code when necessary. This chapter covered these key areas:

✦ An HTML page is divided into two main sections: the `<head>` and the `<body>`. Information pertaining to the entire page is kept in the `<head>` section; all the actual content of the Web page goes in the `<body>` section.

✦ You can change the color and background of your entire page, as well as set its title, through the Page Properties dialog box.

✦ Use `<meta>` tags to summarize your Web page so that search engines can properly catalog it. In Dreamweaver 2, you can use the View Head Contents feature to easily alter these and other `<head>` tags.

✦ When possible, use logical style tags, such as `<strong>` and `<cite>`, rather than hard-coding your page with physical style tags. Style sheets bring a great deal of control and flexibility to logical style tags.

✦ Special extended characters such as symbols and accented letters require the use of HTML character entities, which can either be named (as in ") or in decimal format (as in ").

In the next chapter, you'll see how to insert and format text in Dreamweaver.

✦   ✦   ✦

Adding Text to Your Web Page

If content is king on the Web, then certainly style is queen — together they rule hand in hand. Entering, editing, and formatting text on a Web page is a major part of a Webmaster's job. Dreamweaver gives you the tools to make the task as clear-cut as possible. From headlines to comments, this chapter covers the essentials of working with basic text.

Until relatively recently, Web designers didn't have many options for manipulating text. The majority of browsers can now understand a limited number of text-related commands, and the designer can specify the font as well as its color and size. Dreamweaver 2 adds a range of text manipulation tools, highlighted by its enhanced Find and Replace capabilities. These topics are covered in this chapter, along with an important discussion of manipulating whitespace on the Web page.

Starting with Headings

Text in HTML is primarily composed of headings and paragraphs. Headings separate and introduce major sections of the document, just as a newspaper uses headlines to announce a story and subheads to provide essential details. HTML has six levels of headings; the syntax for the heading tags is ⟨hn⟩, where n is a number from 1 to 6. The largest heading is ⟨h1⟩ and the smallest is ⟨h6⟩.

Remember that HTML headings are not linked to any specific point size, unlike type produced in a page layout or word-processing program. Headings in an HTML document are sized relative to one another, and their final, exact size depends on the browser used. The sample headlines in Figure 7-1 depict the basic headings as rendered through Internet Explorer 4.0, and as compared to the default paragraph font size. As you can see, some headings are rendered in type smaller than that used for the default paragraph. Headings are usually displayed with a boldface attribute.

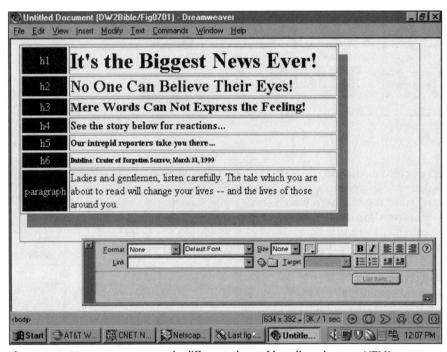

Figure 7-1: You can use up to six different sizes of headings in your HTML page.

Two methods set text as a particular heading size in Dreamweaver. In both cases, you first need to select the text you want to affect. If you are styling a single line or paragraph as a heading, just position the cursor anywhere in the paragraph to select it. If you want to convert more than one paragraph, click and drag out your selection.

Tip   You can't mix heading levels in a single paragraph. That is, you can't have a word with an `<h1>` heading in a line next to a word styled with an `<h4>` heading. Furthermore, headings belong to a group of HTML text tags called *block elements*. All block elements are rendered with a paragraph return both above and below, which isolates ("blocks") the text. To work around both of these restrictions, you can use `<font size=n>` tags to achieve the effect of varying sizes for words within the same line, or for lines of different sizes close to one another. The `<font size=n>` tag is covered later in this chapter in "Styling Your Text."

Once the text for the heading is selected, you can choose your heading level by selecting Text ➪ Format and then one of the Headings 1 through 6 from the submenu. Alternately, you can make your selection from the Text Property Inspector. (If it's not already open, display the Property Inspector by selecting Window ➪ Properties.) In the Text Property Inspector, open the Format drop-down list (see Figure 7-2) and choose one of the six headings.

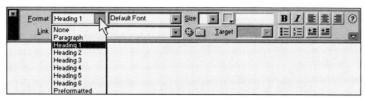

Figure 7-2: You can convert any paragraph or line into a heading through the Format options in the Text Property Inspector.

Headings are often used in a hierarchical fashion, largest to smallest — but you don't have to do it that way. You can have an ⟨h4⟩ line followed by an ⟨h1⟩ paragraph, if that's what your design needs. Be careful using the smallest heading, ⟨h6⟩; it's likely to be difficult to read on any resolution higher than 800 × 600.

Working with Paragraphs

Usually the bulk of text on any Web page is composed of paragraphs. Paragraphs in HTML are denoted by the ⟨p⟩ and ⟨/p⟩ pair of tags. When your Web page is processed, the browser formats everything between those two tags as one paragraph and renders it to fit the user's screen, word wrapping as needed at the margins. Any additional line breaks and unnecessary whitespace (beyond one space between words and between sentences) in the HTML code are ignored.

Tip In the early version of HTML, paragraphs used just the opening ⟨p⟩ tag, and browsers rendered everything between ⟨p⟩ tags as one paragraph; the closing tag was optional. As of HTML 3.2, however, an optional closing ⟨/p⟩ tag was added. Because so many Web pages have been created with just the opening paragraph tag, most browsers still recognize the single-tag format. To be on the safe side in terms of future compatibility, you should enclose your paragraphs with both the opening and closing tags if you do any hand-coding, as Dreamweaver does.

Dreamweaver starts a new paragraph every time you press Enter (Return) when composing text in the Document Window. If you have the HTML Inspector open when you work, you can see that Dreamweaver inserts the following code with each new paragraph:

```
<p> </p>
```

The code between the tags creates a nonbreaking space that allows the new line to be visible. You won't see the new line if you have just the paragraph tags with nothing (neither a character nor a character entity, such as) in between:

```
<p></p>
```

When you continue typing, Dreamweaver replaces the nonbreaking space with your input, unless you press Enter (Return) again. Figure 7-3 illustrates two paragraphs with text and a third paragraph with the nonbreaking space still in place.

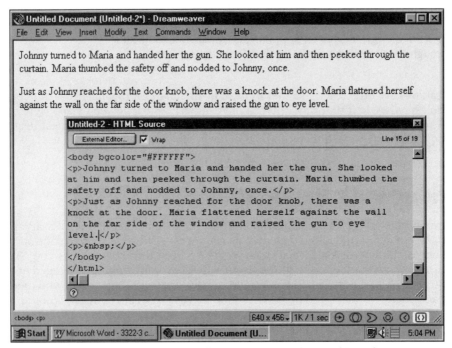

Figure 7-3: Dreamweaver automatically wraps any text inserted into the Document Window. If you press Enter (Return) without entering text, Dreamweaver enters paragraph tags surrounding a nonbreaking space.

You can easily change text from most other formats, such as a heading, to paragraph format. First, select the text you want to alter. Then, in the Property Inspector, open the Format options drop-down list and choose Paragraph. You can also choose Text ➪ Format ➪ Paragraph from the menu or use the keyboard shortcut, Ctrl-T (Command-T). Hint: Think *T* for *text*.

All paragraphs are initially rendered on the page in the default font at the default size. The user can designate these defaults through the browser preferences, although most people don't bother to alter them. If you want to change the font name or the font size for selected paragraphs explicitly, use the techniques described in the upcoming section, "Styling Your Text."

Tip

Remember, you can always use the Tag Selector on the status bar to select and highlight any tag surrounding your current cursor position. This method makes it easy to see what exactly is being affected by a particular tag.

Editing paragraphs

By and large, the editing features of Dreamweaver are similar to other modern word-processing programs — with one or two Web-oriented twists. Dreamweaver has cut, copy, and paste options, as well as Undo and Redo commands. You can search for and replace any text on your Web page under construction and even check its spelling.

The "twists" come from the relationship between the Document Window and the HTML Inspector. Dreamweaver has some special functionality for copying and pasting text. Let's see how that works.

Inserting text

You've already seen how you can position the cursor on the page and directly enter text. In this sense, Dreamweaver acts like a word-processing program, rather than a page layout program. On a blank page, the cursor starts at the top-left corner of the page. Words automatically wrap to the next line when the text exceeds the right margin. Press Enter (Return) to end the current paragraph and start the next one.

Indenting text

In Dreamweaver, you cannot indent text as in a word processor. Tabs normally have no effect in HTML. To indent a paragraph's first line, one method uses nonbreaking spaces, which can be inserted with the keyboard shortcut: Ctrl-Shift-Space (Command-Shift-Space). Nonbreaking spaces are an essential part of any Web designer's palette because they provide single-character spacing — often necessary to nudge an image or other object into alignment. You've already seen the code for a nonbreaking space — the   — that Dreamweaver inserts between the <p>...</p> tag pair to make the line visible.

Aside from the keyboard shortcut, two other methods insert a nonbreaking space. You can enter its character code —   — directly into the HTML code. You can also style your text as preformatted; this technique is discussed later in this chapter.

Tip   Another method exists for indenting the first line of a paragraph: Cascading Style Sheets. You can set an existing HTML tag, such as <p>, to any indent amount using the Text Indent option found on the Box panel of the Style Sheet dialog box. Be aware, however, that style sheets have only recently been fully implemented in browsers. In fact, text indent won't appear in Dreamweaver; you have to use Internet Explorer 3.0 or either primary 4.0 browser. You'll find a full discussion of text indent and other style sheet controls in Chapter 24, "Building Style Sheet Web Pages."

Cutting, copying, and pasting

Text can be moved from one place to another — or from one Web document to another — by using the standard cut-and-paste techniques. No surprises here: before you can cut or copy anything, you must select it. Select by clicking the mouse at the beginning of the text you want to cut or copy, drag the highlight to the end of your selection, and then release the mouse button.

Here are some other selection methods:

✦ Double-click a word to select it.

✦ Move the pointer to the left margin of the text until the pointer changes to an arrow. Click once to highlight a single line. Click and drag down the margin to select a group of lines.

✦ Position the cursor at the beginning of your selection. Hold down the Shift key and then click once at the end of the selection.

✦ You can select everything in the body of your document by using Edit ➪ Select All or the keyboard shortcut Ctrl-A (Command-A).

✦ Use the Tag Selector to select text or other objects contained within specific tags.

When you want to move a block of text, first select it and then use Edit ➪ Cut or the keyboard shortcut, Ctrl-X (Command-X). This sequence places the text on your system's Clipboard. To paste the text, move the pointer to the new location and click once to place the cursor. Then select Edit ➪ Paste or the keyboard shortcut, Ctrl-V (Command-V). The text is copied from the Clipboard to its new location. You can continue pasting this same text from the Clipboard until another block of text is copied or cut.

To copy text, the procedure is much the same. Select the text using one of the preceding methods, and then use Edit ➪ Copy or Ctrl-C (Command-C). The selected text is copied to the Clipboard and the original text is left in place. Then position the cursor in a new location and select Edit ➪ Paste (or use the keyboard shortcut).

Using Drag-and-Drop: The other, quicker method for moving or copying text is the drag-and-drop technique. Once you've selected your text, release the mouse button and move the cursor over the highlighted area. The cursor changes from an I-beam to an arrow. To move the text, click the selected area with the arrow cursor and drag your mouse to a new location. The arrow cursor now has a small box attached to it, indicating that it is carrying something. As you move your cursor, a bar (the insertion point) moves with you, indicating where the text will be positioned. Release the mouse button to drop the text. You can copy text in the same manner by holding down the Ctrl (Command) key as you drag-and-drop your selected text. When copying this way, the box attached to the cursor is marked with a plus sign.

To completely remove text, select it and then choose Edit ➪ Clear or press Delete. The only way to recover deleted text is to use the Undo feature described in the following section.

Inserting Text from Other Applications

The Paste command can also insert text from another program into Dreamweaver. If you cut or copy text from a file in any other program—whether it is a word processor, spreadsheet, or a database program—Dreamweaver inserts it at the cursor position. The results of this paste operation vary, however.

Dreamweaver can only paste plain, unformatted text. In addition, all the text on the Clipboard is inserted as a single paragraph, no matter how many returns are in the original text, if you use the regular Paste command. To retain text in separate paragraphs coming from a file in another program, you must copy and then paste them into Dreamweaver using the Paste As Text command, covered in detail later in this chapter.

If you need to import a great deal of text and want to retain as much formatting as possible, you can use another application, such as the latest version of Microsoft Word, to save your text as an HTML file. Then open that file in Dreamweaver.

Undo and Redo

The Undo command has to be one of the greatest inventions of the twentieth century. Make a mistake? Undo! Want to experiment with two different options? Undo! Change your mind again? Redo! The Undo command reverses your last action, whether you changed a link, added a graphic, or deleted the entire page. The Redo command lets you reverse your Undo actions.

Dreamweaver's implementation of the Undo command enables you to back up as many steps as your system's memory allows. To use the Undo command, simply choose Edit ➪ Undo or press the keyboard shortcut, Ctrl-Z (Command-Z).

The complement to Undo is the Redo command. To reverse an Undo command, choose Edit ➪ Redo or Ctrl-Y (Command-Y). Like Undo, the number of Redo steps available to you is limited only by memory.

Tip

The best use I've found for the Redo command is in concert with Undo. When I'm trying to decide between two alternatives, such as two different images, I'll replace one choice with another and then use the Undo/Redo combination to go back and forth between them. Because Dreamweaver replaces any selected object with the current object from the Clipboard—even if one is a block of text and the other is a layer—you can easily view two separate options with this trick.

The Undo and Redo "memories" are maintained until you save your file, at which point the memories are cleared. You can't undo or redo an operation after you've saved your file. If this approach seems limiting to you, remember that saving your file also has the effect of speeding up an increasingly sluggish system by releasing whatever amount of memory has been set aside for the Undo/Redo commands. You should save your file after every major change.

Copy Text Only and Paste As Text

A preceding section mentioned that Dreamweaver includes a couple of "twists" to the standard cut, copy, and paste options. You've seen how regular text entered into the Document Window is converted to text marked up by HTML tags, visible in the HTML Inspector. Dreamweaver includes two functions that let you translate text and corresponding codes back and forth from one form to the other.

To understand these two features, Copy Text Only and Paste As Text (both on the Edit menu), let's examine how they are used. Table 7-1 explains each command.

<table>
<tr><td colspan="5" align="center"><strong>Table 7-1
Results of Copy/Paste Compared to
Copy/Paste as Text Commands</strong></td></tr>
<tr><td><em>Selected Text</em></td><td><em>Copy From</em></td><td><em>Command Used</em></td><td><em>Paste To</em></td><td><em>Result</em></td></tr>
<tr><td><strong>Example Text</strong></td><td>Document Window</td><td>Copy</td><td>Other program</td><td><code><b></code>Example Text<code></b></code></td></tr>
<tr><td><strong>Example Text</strong></td><td>Document Window</td><td>Copy Text Only</td><td>Other program</td><td>Example Text</td></tr>
<tr><td><code><b></code>Example Text<code></b></code></td><td>HTML Inspector or other program</td><td>Paste</td><td>Document Window</td><td><strong>Example Text</strong></td></tr>
<tr><td><code><b></code>Example Text<code></b></code></td><td>HTML Inspector or other program</td><td>Paste As Text</td><td>Document Window</td><td><code><b></code>Example Text<code></b></code></td></tr>
<tr><td><strong>Example Text</strong></td><td>Document Window</td><td>Paste As Text</td><td>HTML Inspector</td><td>&lt;b&gt; Example Text&lt;/b &gt;</td></tr>
</table>

Notice that in the final row of Table 7-1, if you copy formatted text like the boldface "Example Text" sample and use the Paste As Text command to insert it in the HTML Inspector, you get the following:

```
&lt;b&gt;Example Text&lt;/b&gt;
```

If you remember the section on named character entities in Chapter 6, you may recognize < as the code for the less-than symbol (<), and > as the code for the greater-than symbol (>). These symbols are used to represent tags such as <b> and </b> to prevent a browser from interpreting them as tag delimiters.

So what possible real-life uses could there be for the Copy/Paste As Text command and Dreamweaver's implementation of the regular Copy/Paste commands? First, these commands are a major benefit for programmers, teachers, and writers who constantly have to communicate in both HTML code and regular text. If an instructor is attempting to demonstrate a coding technique on a Web page, for example, she can just copy the code in the HTML Inspector (or the Document Window) and use Paste As Text to put it into the Document Window — instantly transforming the code into something readable online. Previously, this task required a tedious hand-coding process to convert the angle brackets to character entities.

Another use of this approach transfers code from another text editor directly into the Dreamweaver Document Window. You copy the code in the other window normally, position the cursor in Dreamweaver, and then paste in the Document Window. No need to open the HTML Inspector and hunt for the right place in the code — another troublesome task eliminated.

I find these commands to be a major boost to my productivity and an excellent example of how Dreamweaver is firmly rooted in the real world of the Webmaster.

Checking your spelling

A typo can make a significant impression. Not much is more embarrassing than showing a new Web site to a client and having that client point out a spelling error. Dreamweaver includes an easy-to-use Spell Checker to avoid such awkward moments. I make it a practice to spell-check every Web page before it's posted online.

You start the process by choosing Text ➪ Check Spelling, or you can press the keyboard shortcut, Shift-F7. This sequence opens the Check Spelling dialog box, as seen in Figure 7-4.

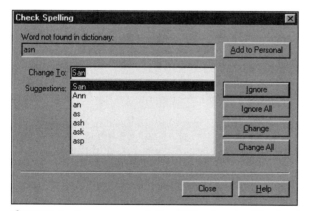

Figure 7-4: Dreamweaver's Spell Checker double-checks your spelling and can find the typos on any Web page.

Once you've opened the Check Spelling dialog box, Dreamweaver begins searching your text for errors. As a general rule, position your cursor at the top of the Web page before you begin spell-checking. When you reach the bottom of the page, Dreamweaver asks if you want to continue checking from the top of the document. By beginning at the top, you know that you've already checked the full document.

Spell-Checking in Non-English Languages

Macromedia has made additional language dictionaries available. As of this writing, you can find French and German dictionaries — for both Windows and Macintosh — on their Web site at `http://www.macromedia.com/support/dreamweaver/upndown/dictionary/contents.html`.

To use the dictionaries, download the compressed file to your system. After uncompressing them, store the file with the .dat extension in the Configuration\Dictionaries folder and restart Dreamweaver. Finally, open Preferences (Edit ⇨ Preferences) and from the General panel select the Dictionary option button. Choose the new language from the drop-down list and you're ready to spell correctly in another tongue.

Dreamweaver checks your Web page text against two dictionaries: a standard English dictionary and a personal dictionary to which you can add words. If the Spell Checker finds any text not in either of the program's dictionaries, the text is highlighted in the Document Window and appears in the Word Not Found In Dictionary field of the dialog box. A list of suggested corrections appears in the Suggestions list box, with the topmost one highlighted and also displayed in the Change To box. If Dreamweaver cannot find any suggestions, the Change To box is left blank. At this point, you have the following options:

✦ **Add to Personal.** Select this button to include the highlighted word in your personal dictionary and prevent Dreamweaver from tagging it as an error in the future.

✦ **Ignore.** Select this button when you want Dreamweaver to leave the currently highlighted word alone and continue searching the text.

✦ **Ignore All.** Select this button when you want Dreamweaver to disregard all occurrences of this word in the current document.

✦ **Change.** If you see the correct replacement among the list of suggestions, highlight it and select the Change button. If no suggestion is appropriate, you can type the correct word into the Change To text box and then select this button.

✦ **Change All.** Choosing this button causes all instances of the current word to be replaced with the word in the Change To text box.

Tip

Have you ever accidentally added a misspelled word to your personal dictionary and then been stuck with the error for all eternity? Dreamweaver lets you recover from your mistake by giving you access to the dictionary itself. The personal dictionary, stored in the Dreamweaver/Configuration/Dictionaries/personal.dat file, can be opened and modified in any text editor.

Using Find and Replace

Dreamweaver 2's greatly enhanced Find and Replace features are both timesaving and lifesaving (well, almost). You can use Find and Replace to cut your input time substantially by searching for abbreviations and expanding them to their full state. You can also find a client's incorrectly spelled name and replace it with the correctly spelled version — that's a lifesaver! However, that's just the tip of the iceberg when it comes to what Find and Replace can really do.

New Feature The Find and Replace engine has been completely redesigned for Dreamweaver 2 and should be considered a key power tool for any Web developer. Not only can multiple files be searched, but you can also easily check the code separately from the content.

Here's a short list of what the enhanced Find and Replace feature makes possible:

✦ Search the Document Window to find any type of text.

✦ Search the underlying HTML to find tags, attributes, or text within tags.

✦ Look for text within specific tags with specific attributes — or look for text that's *outside* of a specific tag with specific attributes.

✦ Find and replace patterns of text, using wildcard characters called *Regular Expressions.*

✦ Apply any of the above Find and Replace operations to the current document, the current site, any folder, or any group of selected files.

As in earlier Dreamweaver versions, three basic commands make up the Find and Replace set: Find, Find Next (Find Again, on the Macintosh), and Replace. Now, however, you can use all three commands in Dreamweaver's Document Window, the HTML Inspector, and, in Windows systems, the Site Window. In every situation, you can use Find independently or in conjunction with Replace.

Where your find and replace operations can be applied depends on whether you launch the Find/Replace command from the Document Window or the Site Window. Table 7-2 details the differences:

Table 7-2 Find/Replace Selection Options	
To Find/Replace In	**Launch From**
Current Document	Document Window
Current Site	Document Window or Site Window
All files in a specific folder	Document Window or Site Window
Selected file or files	Site Window

Finding on the visual page

The most basic method of using the Find and Replace takes place in the Document Window. Whenever you need to search for any text that can be seen by the public on your Web page — whether it's to correct a spelling or change a name — Dreamweaver makes it fast and simple.

Tip   The Find and Replace dialog box, unlike most of Dreamweaver's dialog boxes, is actually a *nonmodal window*. This technical terms just means that you can easily move back and forth between your Document Window and the Find and Replace dialog box without having to close the dialog box first, as you do with the other Dreamweaver windows.

To find some text on your Web page, follow these steps:

1. From the Document Window, choose Edit ⇨ Find or use the keyboard shortcut, Ctrl-F (Command-F).

2. In the Find dialog box, shown in Figure 7-5, make sure that "text" is the selected Find What option.

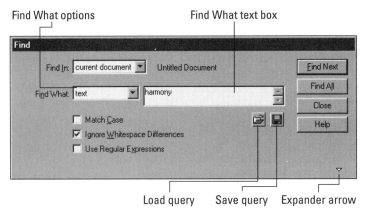

Find What options   Find What text box

Load query   Save query   Expander arrow

Figure 7-5: The Find dialog box has been completely redesigned with many new features for Dreamweaver 2.

3. In the text box next to the Find What option, type the word or phrase you're looking for.

Tip   If you select your text *before* launching the Find dialog box, it automatically appears in the Find What text box. If the text is even moderately lengthy, you might notice the lines wrapping differently than they do on the screen. This is because Dreamweaver is actually using the text as it appears in the HTML Inspector. For this reason, it's best to keep the Ignore Whitespace Differences option (described in the next step) selected.

4. Select the appropriate search options, if any:

- If you want to find an exact replica of the word as you entered it, select the Match Case check box; otherwise, Dreamweaver searches for all variations of your text, regardless of case.

- To force Dreamweaver to disregard any whitespace variations, such as additional spaces, hardspaces or tabs, select the Ignore Whitespace Differences option.

- Selecting Use Regular Expressions lets you work with Dreamweaver's wildcard characters (discussed later in this section). Use Regular Expressions and Ignore Whitespace Differences are mutually exclusive options.

5. Select the Find Next button to begin the search from the cursor's current position.

- If Dreamweaver finds the desired text, it highlights the text in the Document Window.

- If Dreamweaver doesn't find the text in the remaining portion of the document, it asks if you want to continue searching from the beginning. Select Yes to continue or No to exit.

6. If you want to look for the next occurrence of your selected text, click the Find Next button again.

7. To look for all occurrences of your text, choose Find All.

The Find dialog box expands to display the List Window. Dreamweaver lists each found occurrence on a separate line in the List Window.

Tip You can quickly move from one found selection to another by double-clicking the line in the List Window. Dreamweaver highlights the selection, scrolling the Document Window, if necessary.

After searching the page, Dreamweaver tells you how many occurrences of your selection, if any, were found.

8. You can enter other text for which to search, or exit the Find dialog box by clicking the Close button.

The text you enter in the Find dialog box is kept in memory until it's replaced by your next use of the Find feature. After you have executed the Find command once, you can continue to search for your text without redisplaying the Find dialog box, by selecting Edit ➪ Find Next (Find Again) or the keyboard shortcut, F3 (Command-G). If Dreamweaver finds your text, it is highlighted — in fact, Dreamweaver acts exactly the same as when the Find dialog box is open. The Find Next (Find Again) command gives you a quick way to search through a long document — especially when you put the F3 (Command-G) key to work.

Caution   The preceding tip about redoing a search is unfortunately not uniform across all of Dreamweaver's search capabilities. Using F3 (Command-G) to avoid redisplaying the dialog box only works if you redo a text, tag, or text (advanced) search from the Document Window—not for an HTML Source search. For example, if you search for HTML Source - <font face="Arial">, and it is found, the HTML Inspector opens with the tag highlighted. Now if you close the HTML Inspector and the Find dialog box and press F3 (Command-G), Dreamweaver will search for Text - <font face="Arial"> instead because Dreamweaver only remembers if it last did a tag or text (advanced). Similarly, (on Windows only) if opened from the Site Window, it defaults to HTML Source. There is no Find Next command in the Site Window, though, so if you're working there exclusively, there is no way to repeat an HTML Source find except to open it from the menus.

When you add the Replace command to a Find operation, you can search your text for a word or phrase and, if it's found, replace it with a word or phrase of your choice. As mentioned earlier, the Replace feature is a handy way to correct mistakes and expand abbreviations. Figure 7-6 shows an example of the latter operation. This example intentionally uses the abbreviation DW throughout the input text of a Web page article. Then the example uses the Replace All function to expand all the *DW*s to *Dreamweaver*—in one fell swoop. This technique is much faster than typing "Dreamweaver" 14 times.

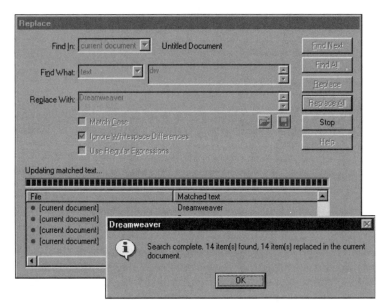

Figure 7-6: Use the Edit ⇨ Replace command to correct your text, one item at a time or all at once.

When you replace text in the Document Window, it is replaced regardless of its formatting. For example, suppose you had the following paragraph:

Mary's accusation reminded Jon of studying synchrones in high school. *Synchrones*, he recalled, were graphs in which the lines constantly approached zero, but never made it. "Yeah," he thought, "That's me, all right. I'm one big **synchrone**."

Upon discovering that "synchrone" should actually be "asymptote" you could use the Find and Replace feature to replace all the plain, italic, and bold versions of the "synchrone" text simultaneously.

Tip It's possible to alter formatting as well — to change all the formatting to just underlining for example — but for that, you need to perform your Find and Replace operations in the HTML Inspector, as discussed in the following section.

Follow these steps to use Dreamweaver's Replace feature in the Document Window:

1. Choose Edit ➪ Replace, or the keyboard shortcut Ctrl-H (Command-H), to open the Replace dialog box.

2. In the Replace dialog box, make sure that "text" is the selected Find What option; and then in the text box next to the Find What option, type the word or phrase you're looking for.

3. In the Replace With text box, type the substitute word.

4. Click the Find Next button. Dreamweaver begins searching from the current cursor position. If Dreamweaver finds the text, it is highlighted.

   If the text is not found, Dreamweaver asks if you want to continue searching from the top of the document. Select Yes to continue or No to exit.

5. To replace the highlighted occurrence of your text, select the Replace button. Dreamweaver replaces the found text with the substitute text and then automatically searches for the next occurrence.

6. If you want to replace all instances of the Find text, select the Replace All button.

   When Dreamweaver has found all the occurrences of your Find text, it displays the number of replacement operations and a line for each in the List Window.

   Double-clicking a line in the List Window highlights the changed text in the Document Window.

7. When you've finished using the Replace dialog box, click the Close button to exit.

Storing and Retrieving Queries

Dreamweaver now offers significantly more powerful Find and Replace features that allow extremely complex queries to be developed. Rather than forcing you to reenter queries used over and over again, Dreamweaver 2 allows you to save and load them when needed. You can store and retrieve both Find and Find/Replace queries; Dreamweaver saves them with .dwq and .dwr file extensions, respectively.

To save a query, select the Disk icon on the Find or Replace dialog box. The standard Save As dialog box appears for you to enter a filename; the appropriate file extension is appended automatically. To load a previously saved query, select the Folder icon on the Find or Replace dialog box to open the Load Query dialog box. From the Find dialog box, you can only open .dwq files, but you can load both .dwq and .dwr files from the Replace dialog box.

While saving and opening queries is an obvious advantage when working with complex wildcard operations, you can also make it work for you in an everyday situation. If, for example, you have a set series of acronyms or abbreviations that you must convert repeatedly, you can save your simple text queries and use them as needed without having to remember all the details.

A note for advanced users: Dreamweaver queries are actually XML files. For sufficiently complex operations, you could open the query file in a text editor (or Dreamweaver), and modify the code by hand. To learn more about XML, see Chapter 27, "Extending with XML."

Searching the code

The power curve ramps up significantly when you start to explore Dreamweaver 2's HTML Find and Replace capabilities. Should your client decide that he wants the company's name to appear bold, blue, and in 18-point type throughout the 300-page site, you can accommodate him with a few keystrokes — instead of hours of mind-numbing grunt work.

You can perform three different types of searches that use the HTML in your Web page:

✦ **You can search for text anywhere in the HTML code.** With this capability you can look for text within `alt` or any other attribute — and change it.

✦ **You can search for text relative to specific tags.** Sometimes you need to change just the text contained within the `<b>` tag and leave all other matching text alone.

✦ **You can search for specific HTML tags and/or their attributes.** Dreamweaver 2's Find and Replace feature gives you the ability to insert, delete, or modify tags and attributes.

Looking for text in the HTML Inspector

Text that appears onscreen is often replicated in various sections of your offscreen HTML code. It's not uncommon, for example, to use the `alt` attribute in an `<img>` tag that repeats the caption under the picture. What do you think would happen if, under those circumstances, you replaced the wording with the standard find-and-replace features in the Document Window? You're still left with the task of tracking down the `alt` attribute and making that change as well. Dreamweaver 2 allows you to act on both content and programming text in one operation — a major savings in time and effort, not to mention aggravation.

To find and replace text in both the content and the code, follow these steps:

1. Choose Edit ➪ Find or Edit ➪ Replace to open the Find and Replace dialog box.

2. Select the parameters of your search from the Find In option: Current Page, Current Site, or Folder.

   Remember, you can also search specific files, if you launch the Find and Replace dialog box from the Site Window.

3. Choose the Find What option button and select the "HTML source" option from the drop-down list.

4. Enter the text you're searching for in the text box next to the Find What option.

5. If you are replacing, enter the new text in the Replace With text box.

6. Select any options desired: Match Case, Ignore Whitespace Differences, or Use Regular Expressions.

7. Choose your Find/Replace option: Find Next, Find All, Replace, or Replace All

   If you don't have the HTML Inspector open, it appears with the text selected when you use the Find Next option.

8. Select Close when finished.

Caution

As with all Find and Replace operations — especially those in which you decide to Replace All — you need to exercise extreme caution when replacing text throughout your code. If you're unsure about what's going to be affected, choose Find All first and, with your HTML Inspector open, step through all the selections to be positive there are no unwanted surprises. Should you replace some code in error, you can always Undo the operation.

Using advanced text options in Find and Replace

In Find and Replace operations, the global Replace All isn't appropriate for every situation; sometimes you need a more precise approach. Dreamweaver 2 allows you to fine-tune your searches to pinpoint accuracy. You can look for text within particular tags — and even within particular tags with specific attributes. Moreover, you can find (and replace) text that is outside of particular tags with specific attributes.

Dreamweaver assists you by providing a drop-down list of every standard HTML tag, as well as numerous special function tags like those used for Cold Fusion applications. You can also search for your own custom tags. You don't have to try to remember which attributes go with which tag, either. Dreamweaver also supplies you with a context-sensitive list of attributes that changes according to the tag selected.

In addition to using the tag's attributes as a search filter, Dreamweaver 2 can also search within the tag for text or another tag. Most HTML tags are so-called container tags that consist of an opening tag and a closing tag, like <b> and </b>. You can set up a filter to look for text within a tag that contains (or explicitly doesn't contain) specific text or another tag. For example, if you were searching the following code:

```
The <b>big, red</b> boat was a <b>big</b> waste of money.
```

you could build a find and replace operation that changed the one phrase (<b>big, red</b>) but not the other (<b>big</b>)—or vice versa.

To look for text in or out of specific tags and attributes, follow these steps:

1. Choose Edit ➪ Find or Edit ➪ Replace to open the Find and Replace dialog box.

2. Select the parameters of your search from the Find In option: Current Page, Current Site, or Folder.

3. Choose the Find What option button and select the "text (advanced)" option from the drop-down list.

   The Add and Delete (+ and -) tag options are made available, as shown in Figure 7-7.

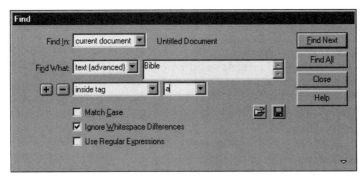

Figure 7-7: The advanced text features of Find and Replace allow you to manipulate text and code simultaneously.

4. Enter the text you're searching for in the text box next to the Find What option.

5. Select either "inside tag" or "not inside tag" from the option list.

6. Select the tag to include or exclude from the adjacent option list.

7. To add a further restriction on the search, click the Add button (the plus sign).

   Another line of search options is added to the dialog box.

8. Select the additional search filter. The available options include the following:

Filter	Description
With Attribute	Allows you to select any attribute from the adjacent option list. You can set this attribute to be equal to, less than, greater than, or not equal to any given value by choosing from the available drop-down lists.
Without Attribute	Finds text within a particular tag that does not include a specific attribute. Choose the attribute to be equal to, less than, greater than, or not equal to any given value by choosing from the available drop-down lists.
Containing	Searches the tag for either specified text or another user-selectable tag found within the initial tag pair.
Not Containing	Searches the tag for either text or a tag not found within the initial tag pair.
Inside Tag	Allows you to look for text that is within two (or more) sets of specific tags.
Not Inside Tag	Allows you to look for text that is in one tag, but not in another tag, or vice versa.

9. To continue adding filter conditions, select the Add button (the plus sign) and repeat Steps 7–8.

10. To remove a filter condition, select the Delete button (the minus sign).

11. If you are replacing, enter the new text in the Replace With text box.

12. Select any options desired: Match Case, Ignore Whitespace Differences, or Use Regular Expressions.

13. Choose your Find/Replace option: Find Next, Find All, Replace, or Replace All.

14. Select Close when finished.

Tip   You can continue to add conditions by clicking the Add (+) button. In fact, I was able to add so many conditions, the Find/Replace dialog box began to disappear off the screen! To erase all conditions, change the Find What option to "text" or "HTML source" and then change it back to "text (advanced)."

Replacing HTML tags and attributes

Let's say a new edict has come down from the HTML gurus of your company: No longer is the <b> tag to be used to indicate emphasis; from now on, use only the <strong> tag. Oh, and by the way, change all the existing pages — all 3,000+ Web and intranet pages — so that they're compliant. Dreamweaver 2 makes short work out of nightmare situations such as these by giving you the power to search and replace HTML tags and their attributes.

But Dreamweaver 2 doesn't stop there. Not only can you replace one tag with another, you can also perform the following:

✦ Change or delete the tag (with or without its contents)

✦ Set an attribute in the tag to another value

✦ Remove any or all attributes

✦ Add text and/or code before or after the starting or the ending tag

To alter your code using Dreamweaver's Find and Replace feature, follow these steps:

1. As with other find and replace operations, choose Edit ➪ Find or Edit ➪ Replace to open the Find and Replace dialog box.

2. Select the parameters of your search from the Find In option: Current Page, Current Site, or Folder.

3. Choose the Find What option button and select the tag option from the drop-down list.

   The dialog box changes to include the tag functions.

4. Select the desired tag from the option list next to the Find What option.

Tip   You can either scroll down the list box to find the tag or you can type the first letter of the tag in the box. Dreamweaver scrolls to the group of tags that begin with
that letter when the list is visible.

5. If desired, you can limit the search by specifying an attribute and value or with other conditions, as discussed in detail in the previous section.

Note   If you want to search for just a tag, select the Remove button (the minus key) to
eliminate the additional condition.

6. Make a selection from the Action list, shown in Figure 7-8. The options are as follows:

Action	Description
Replace Tag & Contents	Substitutes the selected tag and all included content with a text string. The text string can include HTML code.
Replace Contents Only	Changes the content between the specified tag to a given text string, which can also include HTML code.
Remove Tag & Contents	Deletes the tag and all contents.

Action	Description
Strip Tag	Removes the tag but leaves the previously enclosed content.
Change Tag	Substitutes one tag for another.
Set Attribute	Sets an existing attribute to a new value or inserts a new attribute set to a specific value.
Remove Attribute	Deletes a specified attribute.
Add Before Start Tag	Inserts a text string (with or without HTML) before the opening tag.
Add After End Tag	Inserts a text string (with or without HTML) after the end tag.
Add After Start Tag	Inserts a text string (with or without HTML) after the opening tag.
Add Before End Tag	Inserts a text string (with or without HTML) before the end tag.

Note Not all the options listed in the preceding table are available for all tags. Some so-called empty tags, such as <img> consist of a single tag and not tag pairs. Empty tags have only Add Before and Add After options instead of Add Before Start Tag, Add After Start Tag, Add Before End Tag, and Add After End Tag.

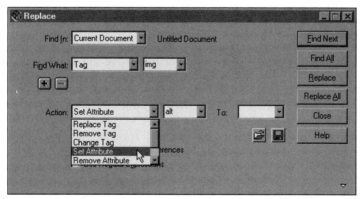

Figure 7-8: The Action list lets you replace tags or modify them by setting the existing attributes or adding new ones.

7. Select any options desired: Match Case, Ignore Whitespace Differences, or Use Regular Expressions.

8. Choose your Find/Replace option: Find Next, Find All, Replace, or Replace All.

9. Select Close when finished.

Tip   You don't have to apply a single action to all the instances Dreamweaver locates if you choose Find All. In the list of found expressions, select a single item and then choose Replace. Dreamweaver makes the revision and places a green dot next to the item so you can tell it's been altered. If you want, you can now select another item from the list, choose a different action, and then select Replace.

Concentrating your search with Regular Expressions

As powerful as all the other new Find and Replace features are, they are boosted to a new level of flexibility with the addition of Regular Expressions. I've referred to Regular Expressions as being similar to wildcards in other programs, but their capabilities are really far more extensive.

Regular Expressions are best described as a text pattern matching system. If you can identify any pattern in your text, you can manipulate it with Regular Expressions. What kind of pattern? Let's say you have a spreadsheet-like table with lots of numbers, showing both dollars and cents, mixed with explanatory text. With Regular Expressions, you can match the pattern formed by the dollar sign and the decimal point and reformat the entire table, turning all the figures deep blue with a new font — all in one Find and Replace operation.

Note   If you're into Unix, you'll recognize Regular Expressions as being very close to the grep utility — *grep*, by the way, stands for Get Regular Expressions and Print. The Find and Replace feature in BBEdit also features a grep-like syntax.

You can apply Regular Expressions to any of the types of Find and Replace operations previously discussed, with just a click of the check box labeled "Using Regular Expressions." You'll note that when you select Using Regular Expressions, the Ignore Unnecessary Whitespace option is deselected. This is because the two options are mutually exclusive and cannot be used together.

The most basic Regular Expression is the text itself. If you enable the feature and then enter **th** in the Find What text box, Dreamweaver will locate every example of "th" in the text and/or source. Although this capability by itself has little use, it's important to remember this functionality as you begin to build your patterns.

Wildcard characters

Initially, it's helpful to be able to use what traditionally are know as *wildcards* — characters that match different types of characters. The wildcards in Regular Expressions represent single characters and are described in Table 7-3. In other words, there is no single Regular Expression to represent all the characters, as the asterisk does when used in PC file searches (such as *.*). However such a condition can be represented with a slightly more complex Regular Expression (described later in this section).

Table 7-3
Regular Expression Wildcard Characters

Character	Matches	Example
.	Any single character	**w.d** matches **wid**e but not world
\w	Any alphanumeric character, including the underscore	**w\wd** matches **wid**e and **world**
\W	Any nonalphanumeric character	**jboy\Widest.com** matches **jboy@idest.com**
\d	Any numeric character, 0–9	**y\dk** matches **Y2K**
\D	Any nonnumeric character	**\D2\D** matches **Y2K** and H_2O
\s	Any whitespace character, including space, tab, form feed, or line feed	**\smedia** matches **media** but not Macromedia
\S	Any nonwhitespace character	**\Smedia** matches Macro**media** but not media
\t	A tab	Matches any single tab character in the HTML source
\f	Form feed	Matches any single form-feed character in the HTML source
\n	Line feed	Matches any single line-feed character in the HTML source
\r	Carriage return	Matches any single carriage-return character in the HTML source

Tip The backslash character, "\", is used to escape special characters so that they can be included in a search. For example, if you want to look for an asterisk, you need to specify it like this: *. Likewise, when trying to find the backslash character, precede it with another backslash character: \\.

Matching character positions and repeating characters

With Regular Expressions, not only can you match the type of character, but you can also match its position in the text. This feature allows you to perform operations on characters at the beginning, end, or middle of the word or line. Regular Expressions also allows you to find instances in which a character is repeated an unspecified number of times or a specific number of times. Combined, these features broaden the scope of the patterns that can be found.

Table 7-4 details the options available for matching by text placement and character repetition.

Table 7-4
Regular Expression Character Positions and Repeating Characters

Character	Matches	Example
^	Beginning of a line	^c matches "Call me Ishmael"
$	End of a line	d$ matches the final "d" in "Be afraid. Be very afraid"
\b	A word boundary, like a space or carriage return	\btext matches textbook but not SimpleText
\B	A nonword boundary inside a word	\Btext matches SimpleText but not textbook
*	The preceding character zero or more times	b*c matches BBC and cold
+	The preceding character one or more times	b+c matches BBC but not cold
?	The preceding character zero or one time	st?un matches stun and sun but not strung
{n}	Exactly n instances of the preceding character	e{2} matches reed and each pair of two e's in "Aieeeeeee! but nothing in Dreamweaver
{n,m}	At least n and m instances of the preceding character	C{2,4} matches #CC00FF and #CCCC00 but not the full string #CCCCCC

Matching character ranges

Beyond single characters, or repetitions of single characters, Regular Expressions incorporate the ability to find or exclude ranges of characters. This feature is particularly useful when you're working with groups of names or titles. Ranges are specified in *set brackets*. A match is made when any one of the characters within the set brackets is found, not necessarily all of the characters.

Descriptions of how to match character ranges with Regular Expressions can be found in Table 7-5.

Table 7-5
Regular Expression Character Ranges

Character	Matches	Example
[abc]	Any one of the characters a, b, or c	**[lmrt]** matches the l and m's in **lemm**ings and the r and t in **r**oad**t**rip
[^abc]	Any character except a, b, or c	**[^etc]** matches **GIFs**, but not etc in the phrase "GIFs etc"
[a-z]	Any character in the range from a to z	**[l-p]** matches l and o in **lo**wery and m, n, o an p in **p**oint**m**an
x|y	Either x or y	**boy|girl** matches both **boy** and **girl**

Using grouping with Regular Expressions

Grouping is perhaps the single most powerful concept in Regular Expressions. With it, any matched text pattern is easily manipulated — for example, the following list of names:

```
John Jacob Jingleheimer Schmidt
James T. Kirk
Cara Fishman
```

could be rearranged so that the last name is first, separated by a comma, like this:

```
Schmidt, John Jacob Jingleheimer
Kirk, James T.
Fishman, Cara
```

Grouping is handled primarily with parentheses. To indicate a group, enclose it in parentheses in the Find text field. Regular Expressions can manage up to nine grouped patterns. Each grouped patterned is designated by a dollar sign ($) in front of a number, (1–9) in the Replace text field, like this: $3.

Caution   Remember that the dollar sign is also used after a character or pattern to indicate the last character in a line.

Table 7-6 shows how Regular Expressions uses grouping.

	Table 7-6	
	Regular Expressions Grouping	
Character	*Matches*	*Example*
(p)	Any pattern p	`(\d).(\d)` matches two patterns, the first before a period and the second, after; such as in a filename with an extension
$1, $2 . . . $9	The nth pattern noted with parentheses	The replacement pattern **$1's extension is ".$2"** would manipulate the above described pattern so that Chapter07.txt and Image12.gif would become **Chapter07's extension is ".txt"** and **Image12's extension is ".gif"**

The <br> tag

The paragraph tag falls among the class of HTML objects called *block elements,* just like headings. As such, any text marked with the `<p></p>` tag pair is always rendered with an extra line above and below the text. To have a series of blank lines appear one after the other, use the break tag `<br>`.

Break tags are used within block elements, such as headings and paragraphs, to provide a line break where the `<br>` is inserted. Dreamweaver provides two ways to insert a `<br>` tag: You can choose the Enter Line Break button from the Invisibles panel of the Objects Palette, or you can use the keyboard shortcut Shift-Enter (Shift-Return).

Figure 7-9 clearly demonstrates the effect of the `<br>` tag. The menu items in Column A on the left are the result of using the `<br>` tag within a paragraph. In Column B on the right, paragraph tags alone are used. The `<h1>` heading is also split at the top (modified through style sheet selections) with a break tag to avoid the insertion of an unwanted line.

By default, Dreamweaver marks `<br>` tags with a symbol: a gold shield with the letters BR and the standard Enter/Return symbol. You can turn off this display feature by choosing Preferences ⇨ Invisible Elements and deselecting the Line Breaks check-box.

Insert Line Break button   Line break <br> symbol

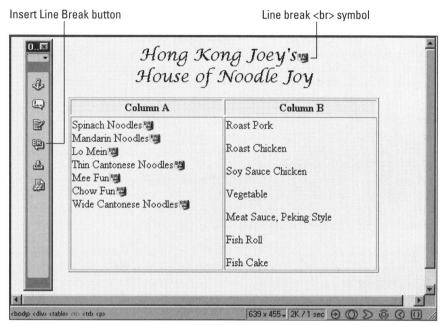

Figure 7-9: Use break tags to have your lines wrap without the additional line spacing brought about by <p> tags.

Overcoming Line-Spacing Difficulties

Line spacing is a major issue and a common problem for Web designers. Often a design calls for lines to be tightly spaced, but also of various sizes. If you use the break tag to separate your lines, you'll get the tight spacing required, but you won't be able to make each line a different heading size. As far as HTML and your browser are concerned, the text is still one block element, no matter how many line breaks are inserted. If, on the other hand, you make each line a separate paragraph or heading, the line spacing will be unattractively "open."

You can use one of several workarounds for this problem. First, if you're using line breaks, you can alter the size of each line by selecting it and choosing a different font size, either from the Property Inspector or the Text ⇨ Size menu. The only drawback to this approach is that the attribute you insert with this action — <font size=n> — is not recognized by older browsers.

A second option renders all the text as a graphics object and inserts it as an image. This gives you total control over the font's appearance and line spacing, as well as across-the-board browser compliance at the cost of added download time.

For a third possible solution, take a look at the section on preformatted text later in this chapter. Because you can apply styles to a preformatted text block (which can include line breaks and extra white space), you can alter the size, color, and font of each line, if necessary.

Other whitespace tags

If you can't get the alignment effect you want through the regular text options available in Dreamweaver, two other HTML tags can affect whitespace: <nobr> and <wbr>. Although a tad on the obscure side, these tags can be just the ticket in certain circumstances. Let's see how they work.

The <nobr> tag

Most of the time, you want the user's browser to handle word-wrapping chores automatically. Occasionally, however, you may need to make sure that a particular string of text is rendered in one piece. For these situations, you can use the no break tag <nobr>. Any text that comes in between the opening and closing tag pair — <nobr>...</nobr> — is displayed in one continuous line. If the line of text is wider than the current browser window, a horizontal scroll bar automatically appears along the bottom of the browser.

The <nobr> tag is only supported through the Netscape and Microsoft browsers and must be entered by hand into your HTML code. Use the <nobr> tag under very special circumstances.

The <wbr> tag

The companion to the <nobr> tag is the word break tag <wbr>. Similar to a soft hyphen in a word-processing program, the <wbr> tag tells the browser where to break a word, if necessary. When used within <nobr> tags, <wbr> is the equivalent of telling a browser, "Keep all this text in one line, but if you have to break it, break it here."

Like the <nobr> tag, <wbr> is only supported by Netscape and Microsoft browsers and must be entered by hand in either the HTML Inspector or your external editor.

Styling Your Text

When the Internet was founded, its intended focus was to make scientific data widely accessible. Soon it became apparent that even raw data could benefit from being styled contextually without detracting from the Internet's openness and universality. Over the short history of HTML, text styles have become increasingly important and the W3C has sought to keep a balance between substance and style.

Dreamweaver enables the Web designer to apply the most popular HTML styles directly through the program's menus and Property Inspector. Less prevalent styles can be inserted through the integrated text editors or by hand.

Working with preformatted text

Browsers ignore formatting niceties considered irrelevant to page content: tabs, extra line-feeds, indents, and added whitespace. You can force browsers to read all the text, including whitespace, exactly as you have entered it. By applying the preformatted tag, <pre>, you tell the browser that it should keep any additional whitespace encountered within the text. By default, the <pre> tag also renders its content with a monospace font such as Courier. For these reasons, in the early days of HTML, the <pre> tag was used to lay out text in columns, before tables were widely available.

You can apply the preformatted tag either through the Property Inspector or the menus. Before you use either technique, however, be sure to select the text or position the cursor where you want the preformatted text to begin. To use the Property Inspector, open the Format list box and choose Preformatted. To use the menus, choose Text ➪ Format ➪ Preformatted.

The <pre> tag is a block element format, like the paragraph or the headings tags, rather than a style. This designation as a block element format has two important implications: First, you can't apply the <pre> tag to part of a line; when you use this tag, the entire paragraph is altered. Second, you can apply styles to preformatted text — this lets you increase the size or alter the font, but at the same time maintain the whitespace feature made possible with the <pre> tag. All text in Figure 7-10 uses the <pre> tag; the column on the left is the standard output with monospaced font; the column on the right uses a different font in a larger size.

Figure 7-10: Preformatted text gives you full control over the line breaks, tabs, and other whitespace in your Web page.

Depicting various styles

As explained in Chapter 6, "Understanding How HTML Works," HTML's logical styles are used to mark text relatively or within a particular context, rather than with a specific look. The eventual displayed appearance of logical styles is completely up to the viewer's browser. This is very useful when you are working with documents from different sources — reports from different research laboratories around the country, for instance — and you want a certain conformity of style. Logical styles are very utilitarian; physical styles like boldface and italic are decorative. Both types of styles have their uses in material published on today's Web.

All of Dreamweaver's styles are accessed by choosing Text ⇨ Style and selecting from the 13 available style name options. A check mark appears next to the selected tags. Style tags can be nested (put inside one another), and you can mix logical and physical tags within a word, line, or document. You can have a bold, strikethrough, *variable* style; or you can have an underlined *cited* style. (Both *variable* and *cite* are particular logical styles covered later in this section.) If, however, you are trying to achieve a particular look using logical styles, you should probably use the Cascading Style Sheets feature.

Cross-Reference

The styles that can be applied through regular HTML are just the tip of the iceberg compared to the possibilities with Cascading Style Sheets. For details on using this feature, see Chapter 24, "Building Style Sheet Web Pages."

Take a look at Figure 7-11 for a comparison of how the styles are rendered in Dreamweaver, Internet Explorer 4.0, and Netscape Communicator 4.0. While the various renderings are mostly the same, notice the browser differences in the Definition styles, and the difference in how the Keyboard style is rendered in Dreamweaver and either browser.

Two of the three physical style tags — bold and italic — are both available from the Text Property Inspector and through keyboard shortcuts (Ctrl-B or Command-B, and Ctrl-I or Command-I, respectively). The Underline tag, <u>, is only available through the Text ⇨ Style menu. Underlining text on a Web page is generally discouraged, to avoid confusion with links, which are typically displayed underlined.

Both physical and logical style tags are described, with example uses, in Table 7-7.

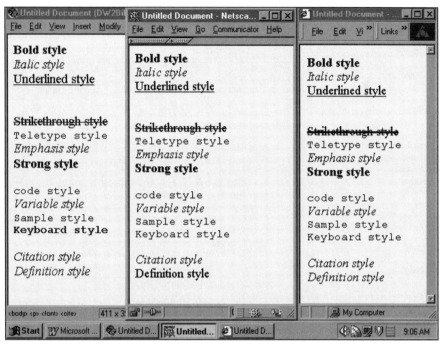

Figure 7-11: In this comparison chart, the various renderings of Dreamweaver style tags are, from left to right, from Dreamweaver, Internet Explorer 4.0, and Netscape Communicator 4.0.

	Table 7-7	
	Dreamweaver Style Tags	
Style	**Tag**	**Description**
Bold	`<b>`	Text is rendered with a bold style.
Italic	`<i>`	Text is rendered with an italic style.
Underline	`<u>`	Text is rendered underlined.
Strikethrough	`<s>`	Used primarily in edited documents to depict edited text. Usually rendered with a line through the text.
Teletype	`<tt>`	Used to represent an old-style typewriter. Rendered in a monospace font such as Courier.
Emphasis	`<em>`	Used to accentuate certain words relative to the surrounding text. Most often rendered in italic.

Continued

	Table 7-7 *(continued)*	
Style	**Tag**	**Description**
Strong Emphasis	`<strong>`	Used to strongly accentuate certain words relative to the surrounding text. Most often rendered in boldface.
Code	`<code>`	Used to depict programming code, usually in a monospaced font.
Sample	`<samp>`	Used to display characters in a literal sequence, usually in a monospaced font.
Variable	`<var>`	Used to mark variables in programming code. Most often displayed in italics.
Keyboard	`<kbd>`	Used to indicate what should be typed in by a user. Often shown in a monospaced font, sometimes in boldface.
Citation	`<cite>`	Used to mark citations, references, and titles. Most often displayed in italic.
Definition	`<dfn>`	Used to denote the first, defining instance of a term. Usually displayed in italic.

Using the <address> tag

One useful style tag is not currently supported by Dreamweaver: the `<address>` tag. Rendered as italic text by browsers, the `<address>`...`</address>` tag pair often marks the signature and e-mail address of a Web page's creator. The `<address>` tags should go around a paragraph tag pair; otherwise, Dreamweaver flags the closing `</p>` as invalid. Also, you should use `<br>` tags to form line breaks. The following example shows the proper use of the `<address>` tags:

```
<address><p>The President<br>
   1600 Pennsylvania Avenue<br>
   Washington, DC 20001</p></address>
```

This preceding code will be shown on a Web browser as follows:

The President
1600 Pennsylvania Avenue
Washington, DC 20001

Tip

To remove a style, highlight the styled text, choose Text ➪ Style, and select the name of the style you want to remove. The check mark disappears from the style name.

Modifying Text Format

As a Web designer, you easily spend at least as much time adjusting your text as you do getting it into your Web pages. Luckily, Dreamweaver puts most of the tools you need for this task right at your fingertips. All the text-formatting options are available through the Text Property Inspector. Instead of hand-coding `<font>`, `<blockquote>`, and alignment tags, just select your text and click a button.

Note   The general move in HTML text formatting today is toward using Cascading Style Sheets and away from hard-coding text with `<font>` and other tags. Both 4.0 versions of the major Web browsers support Cascading Style Sheets more than ever, and Internet Explorer has had some support since the 3.0 version. The current realities of browser competition, however, dictate that to take advantage of the widest support range, Web designers must continue to use the character-specific tags for now. Even after Cascading Style Sheets gain widespread acceptance, you'll probably still need to apply tags on the "local level" occasionally.

Adjusting font size

The six HTML heading types enable you to assign relative sizes to a line or to an entire paragraph. In addition, HTML gives you a finer degree of control through the size attribute of the font tag. In contrast to publishing environments, both traditional and desktop, font size is not specified in HTML with points. Rather, the `<font>` tag enables you to choose one of seven different explicit sizes that the browser can render (absolute sizing), or you can select one relative to the page's basic font. Figure 7-12 shows the default absolute and relative sizes, compared to a more page-designer-friendly point chart (accomplished with Dreamweaver's Cascading Style Sheets features).

Which way should you go — absolute or relative? Some designers think that relative sizing gives them more options. As you can see by the chart in Figure 7-12, browsers are limited to displaying seven different sizes no matter what — unless you're using Cascading Style Sheets. Relative sizing does give you additional flexibility, though, because you can resize all the fonts in an entire Web page with one command. Absolute sizes, on the other hand, are more straightforward to use and can be coded in Dreamweaver without any additional HTML programming. Once again, it's the designer's choice.

Point Sizes	Absolute Sizes	Relative Sizes Base Font (Default = 3)	
8 pt.	Size 1	Size +1	Size -1
10 pt.	Size 2	Size +2	Size -2
12 pt.	Size 3	Size +3	Size -3
14 pt.	Size 4	Size +4	Size -4
18 pt.	Size 5	Size +5	Size -5
24 pt.	Size 6	Size +6	Size -6
36 pt.	Size 7	Size +7	Size -7

`<body> <div> <table> <tr> <td> <font>` 639 x 455 ▾ 3K / 1 sec

Figure 7-12: In this chart, you can see the relationships between the various font sizes in an HTML browser and as compared to "real-world" point sizes.

Absolute size

You can assign an absolute font size either through the Property Inspector or through the menus. In both cases you choose a value, 1 (smallest) through 7 (largest), to which you want to resize your text; you might note that this order is the reverse of the heading sizes, which range from H1 to H6, largest to smallest.

To use the Property Inspector to pick an absolute font size, follow these steps:

1. Select your text.

2. In the Property Inspector, open the Font Size drop-down list of options.

3. Choose a value from 1 to 7.

To pick an absolute font size from the menu, follow these steps:

1. Select your text.

2. Choose Text ➪ Size and pick a value from 1 to 7, or Default (which is 3).

Tip
You can also use the keyboard shortcuts for changing absolute font sizes. Headings 1 through 6 correspond to Ctrl-1 through Ctrl-6 (Command-1 through Command-6). The Paragraph option is rendered with a Ctrl-T (Command-T); you can remove all formatting with Ctrl-0 (Command-0).

Relative size

To what exactly are relative font sizes relative? The default font size, of course. The advantage of relative font sizes is that you can alter a Web page's default font size with one command, the `<basefont>` tag. The tag takes the following form:

```
<basefont size=value>
```

where *value* is a number from 1 to 7. The `<basefont>` tag is usually placed immediately following the opening `<body>` tag. Dreamweaver does not support the previewing of results of altering the `<basefont>` tag, and the tag has to be entered by hand or through the external editor.

You can distinguish a relative font size from an absolute font size by the plus or minus sign that precedes the value. The relative sizes are plus or minus the current `<basefont>` size. Thus a `<font size=+1>` is normally rendered with a size 4 font, because the default `<basefont>` is 3. If you include the following line in your Web page:

```
<basefont size=5>
```

text marked with a `<font size=+1>` is displayed with a size 6 font. Because browsers only display seven different size fonts with a `<basefont size=5>` setting — unless you're using Cascading Style Sheets — any relative size over `<font size=+2>` won't display differently when previewed in a browser.

Relative font sizes can also be selected from either the Property Inspector or the menus. To use the Property Inspector to pick a relative font size, follow these steps:

1. Select your text or position the cursor where you want the new text size to begin.

2. In the Property Inspector, open the Font Size drop-down list of options.

3. To increase the size of your text, choose a value from +1 through +7.

   To decrease the size of your text, choose a value from –1 to –7.

To pick a relative font size from the menus, follow these steps:

1. Select your text or position the cursor where you want the new text size to begin.

2. To increase the size of your text, choose Text ⇨ Size Increase and pick a value from +1 to +7.

   To reduce the size of your text, choose Text ⇨ Size Decrease and pick a value from –1 to –7.

Dreamweaver's Color Pickers

Dreamweaver includes a color picker that includes the 212 colors common to the Macintosh and Windows palette—you already know these as the browser-safe colors. While it's generally believed that there are 216 common colors, the Macromedia engineers found that Internet Explorer on Windows systems renders four incorrectly: colors #0033FF (0,51,255), #3300FF (51,0,255), #00FF33 (0,255,51), and #33FF00 (51,255,0).

If you choose a color outside of the "safe" range, you have no assurances of how the color is rendered on a viewer's browser. Some systems select the closest color in RGB values; some use dithering (positioning two or more colors next to each other to simulate another color) to try to overcome the limitations of the current screen color depth. So be forewarned: If at all possible, stick with the browser-safe colors, especially when coloring text.

Mac Users: The color picker for Macintosh systems is far more elaborate than the one available for Window users. The Mac version has several color schemes to use: CMYK (for print-related colors), RGB (for screen-based colors), and HTML (for Web-based colors). The CMYK, HTML, and RGB systems offer you color swatches and three or four sliders with text entry boxes, and accept percentage values for RGB and CMYK and hex values for HTML. Both RGB and HTML also have a "snap-to-Web color" option for matching your chosen color to the closest browser-safe color. The Hue, Saturation, and Value (or Lightness) sliders also have color wheels.

Adding font color

Unless you assign a color to text on your Web page, the browser uses its own default, typically black. As noted in "Establishing Page Properties" in Chapter 6, you can change the font color for the entire page by choosing Modify ➪ Page Properties and selecting a new color from the Text Color swatch. You can also color any specific headings, words, or paragraphs that you have selected in Dreamweaver.

Tip   When adding a new font color, size, or name to text that already has one <font> tag applied to it, it's best to use the Tag Selector to highlight the text by selecting that <font> tag. If you select your text by clicking-and-dragging, you're likely to not select the entire contents of the tag, which results in multiple <font> tags being applied.

The <font> tag goes to work again when you add color to selected elements of the page—this time, with the color attribute set to a particular value. HTML color is expressed in either a hexadecimal color number or a color name. The hexadecimal color number is based on the color's red-green-blue value and is written as follows:

```
#FFFFFF
```

The preceding represents the color white. You can also use standard color names instead of the hexadecimal color numbers. A sample color code line follows:

```
I'm <font color="green">GREEN</font> with envy.
```

Dreamweaver understands both color names and hexadecimal color numbers, but its HTML code output is in hexadecimal color numbers only.

Again, you have two ways to add color to your text in Dreamweaver. The Property Inspector displays a drop-down list of the browser-safe colors, and also gives you an option to choose from a full-spectrum Color dialog box. If you approach your coloring task via the menus, the Text ⇨ Color command takes you immediately to the Color dialog box.

To use the Property Inspector to color a range of text in Dreamweaver, follow these steps:

1. Select the text you want to color, or position the cursor where you want the new text color to begin.

2. From the Property Inspector, you can

   • type a hexadecimal color number directly into the Font Color text box.

   • type a color name directly into the Font Color text box.

   • select the Font Color swatch to open the browser-safe color picker.

3. If you chose to type a color name or number directly into the Font Color text box, press Tab or click on the Document Window to see the color applied.

4. If you clicked the Font Color swatch, select your color from the browser-safe colors available. As you move your pointer over the color swatches, Dreamweaver displays the color in the corner and the color's hexadecimal number below.

5. For a wider color selection from the Color dialog box, select the Palette icon in the lower-right corner of the color swatch.

To access the full-spectrum color picker in Windows, follow these steps:

1. Select your text or position your cursor where you want the new text color to begin.

2. Choose Text ⇨ Color to open the Color dialog box, as shown in Figure 7-13.

Standard colors   Hue/Saturation pointer

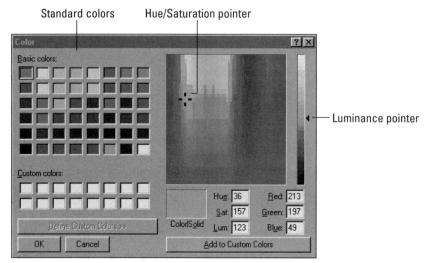

Luminance pointer

Figure 7-13: Use the Color dialog box in Windows to choose a color for your font outside of the browser-safe palette.

3. Select one of the 48 preset standard colors from the color swatches on the left of the Color dialog box, or use either of the following methods:

- Select a color by moving the Hue/Saturation pointer and the Luminance pointer.

- Enter decimal values directly into either the Red, Green, and Blue boxes or the Hue, Saturation, and Luminance boxes.

4. If you create a custom color, you can add it to your palette by selecting Add to Custom Colors. You can add up to 16 custom colors.

5. Click OK when you are finished.

When you add a custom color to your palette in Windows, the new color swatch goes into the currently selected swatch or, if no swatch is selected, the next available swatch. Make sure you have selected an empty or replaceable swatch before selecting the Add to Custom Color button. To clear the custom colors, first set the palette to white by bringing the Luminance slider all the way to the top. Then, select the Add to Custom Color button until all the color swatch text boxes are empty.

To access the full-spectrum color picker in Macintosh systems, follow these steps:

1. Select the text or position your cursor where you want the new text color to begin.

2. Choose Text ➪ Color to open the Color dialog box.

3. From the Color dialog box, select the Color Palette icon.

    The Macintosh color picker opens.

4. In the Macintosh color picker, the list of available pickers is displayed in the left pane and each particular interface is shown in the right. Choose the specific color picker icon from the left pane and create the color desired in the right.

    The number and type of color pickers varies from system to system, depending on the version of the operating system and the software installed.

5. When you've found the desired color, click OK.

Assigning a specific font

Along with size and color, you can also specify the typeface in which you want particular text to be rendered. Dreamweaver uses a special method for choosing font names for a range of selected text, due to HTML's unique way of handling fonts. Before you learn how to change a typeface in Dreamweaver, let's further examine how fonts in HTML work.

About HTML fonts

Page layout designers can incorporate as many different fonts as available to their own systems. Web layout designers, on the other hand, can use only those fonts on their viewers' systems. If you designate a paragraph to be in Bodoni Bold Condensed, for instance, and put it on the Web, the paragraph will be displayed with that font only if that exact font name is on the user's system. Otherwise, the browser uses the default system font, which is often Times or Times New Roman.

Fonts are specified with the `<font>` tag, aided by the `name` attribute. Because a designer can never be certain of which fonts are on visitors' computers, HTML enables you to offer a number of options to the browser, as follows:

```
<font name="Arial, Helvetica, sans-serif">Swiss Maid
Foundry</font>
```

The browser encountering the preceding tag first looks for the Arial font to render the enclosed text. If Arial isn't there, the browser looks for the next font in the list, which in this case is Helvetica. Failing to find any of the specified fonts listed, the browser uses whichever font has been assigned to the category for the font — sans-serif in this case.

Five main categories of fonts are recognized by the W3C and some Web browsers: serif, sans-serif, monospace, cursive, and fantasy. Internet Explorer has a higher compliance rating on this issue than Netscape Communicator.

Selecting a font

The process for assigning a font name to a range of text is similar to that of assigning a font size or color. Instead of selecting one font name, however, you're usually selecting one font series. That series could contain three or more fonts, as previously explained. Font series are chosen from the Property Inspector or through a menu item.

Tip Dreamweaver lets you assign any font on your system — or even any font you can name — to a font series, as covered in "Editing the Font List" later in this chapter.

To assign a specific font series to your text, follow these steps:

1. Select the text or position your cursor where you want the new text font to begin.

2. From the Property Inspector, open the drop-down list of font names. You can also choose Text ⇨ Font from the menu bar. Your Font List is displayed.

3. Select a font from the Font List. To return to the system font, choose Default Font from the list.

It's also possible to enter the font name or font series directly in the Property Inspector's Font drop-down list box.

Tip Font peculiarities are one of the key reasons to always test your Web pages on several platforms. Not only do Macintosh and Windows have different names for the same basic fonts (Arial in Windows is almost identical to Helvetica in Macintosh, for instance), but even the standard font sizes vary between the platforms. Overall, PC fonts are larger than fonts on a Macintosh. Be sure to check out your page on as many systems as possible before finalizing your design.

Editing the Font List

With the Edit Font List dialog box, Dreamweaver gives you a point-and-click interface for building your font lists. Once the Edit Font List dialog box is open, you can delete an existing font series, add a new one, or change the order of the list so your favorite ones are on top. Take a look at Figure 7-14 to see the sections of the Edit Font List dialog box: the current Font List, the Available Fonts on your system, and the Chosen Fonts. The Chosen Fonts are the individual fonts that you've selected to be incorporated into a font series.

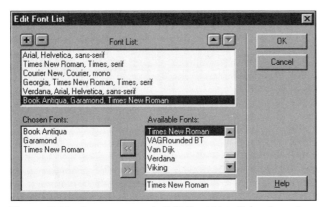

Figure 7-14: Dreamweaver's Edit Font List dialog box gives you considerable control over the fonts that you can add to your Web page.

Let's step through the process of constructing a new font series and adding it to the Font List:

1. To open the Edit Font List dialog box, either choose Edit Font List through the Font Name option arrow in the Property Inspector, or select Text ➪ Font ➪ Edit Font List.

2. If the Chosen Font box is not empty, clear the Chosen Font box by selecting the plus (+) button at the top of the dialog box. You can also scroll down to the bottom of the current Font List and select "(Add fonts in list below)".

3. Select a font from the Available Fonts list.

4. Click the << button to transfer the selected font to the Chosen Fonts list.

5. To remove a font you no longer want or have chosen in error, highlight it in the Chosen Fonts list and select the > button.

6. Repeat Steps 3 through 5 until the Chosen Fonts list contains the alternative fonts desired.

7. If you want to add another, separate font series, repeat Steps 2 through 5.

8. Click OK when you are finished adding fonts.

To change the order in which font series are listed in the Font List, follow these steps:

1. In the Font List dialog box, select the font series that you want to move.

2. If you want to move the series higher up the list, select the up arrow button at the top-right of the Font List. If you want to move the series lower down the list, select the down arrow button.

To remove a font series from the current Font List, highlight it and select the minus (–) button at the top-left of the list.

Remember, you need to have the fonts on your system to make them a part of your font list. To add a font unavailable on your computer, type the name of the font into the text box below the Available Fonts list and press Enter (Return).

Aligning text

You can easily align text in Dreamweaver as in a traditional word-processing program. HTML supports the alignment of text to the left or right margin, or in the center of the browser window. Like a word-processing program, Dreamweaver aligns text one paragraph at a time. You can't left-align one word, center the next, and then right-align the third word in the same paragraph.

To align text, you can use one of three methods: a menu command, the Property Inspector, or a keyboard shortcut. To use the menus, choose Text ➪ Alignment and then pick the alignment you prefer (Left, Right, or Center). Table 7-8 explains the Text Property Inspector's Alignment buttons and the associated keyboard shortcuts.

Note

There is actually a fourth way to align text: Cascading Style Sheets. Any style can be set to align your text. Moreover, not only Left, Right, and Center are supported; so is Justify, which causes text to be flush against both left and right margins, creating a block-like appearance. The Justify value is supported in browsers 4.0 and higher.

	Table 7-8	
	Text Alignment Options in the Property Inspector	
Button	*Alignment*	*Keyboard Shortcut*
▤	Left	Ctrl-Alt-L (Command-Option-L)
▤	Center	Ctrl-Alt-C (Command-Option-C)
▤	Right	Ctrl-Alt-R (Command-Option-R)

Cross-Reference

Traditional HTML alignment options are limited. For a finer degree of control, be sure to investigate precise positioning with layers in Chapter 25, "Working with Layers."

Indenting entire paragraphs

HTML offers a tag that enables you to indent whole paragraphs, such as inset quotations or name-and-address blocks. Not too surprisingly, the tag used is called the <blockquote> tag. Dreamweaver gives you instant access to the <blockquote> tag through the Indent and Outdent buttons located on the Text Property Inspector, as shown in Figure 7-15.

Outdent Button

Indent Button

Figure 7-15: Indent paragraphs and blocks of text with the Indent and the Outdent buttons.

To indent one or more paragraphs, select them and click the Indent button in the Property Inspector. Paragraphs can be indented multiple times; each time you click the Indent button, another <blockquote>...</blockquote> tag pair is added.

Note that you can't control how much space by which a single <blockquote> indents a paragraph — that characteristic is determined by the browser.

If you find that you have over-indented, you can use the Outdent button, which is also located on the Property Inspector. The Outdent button has no effect if your text is already at the left edge.

You also have the option of indenting your paragraphs through the menus; choose Text ➪ Indent or Text ➪ Outdent.

Tip   You can tell how many <blockquote> tags are being used to create a particular look by placing your cursor in the text and looking at the Tag Selector.

Commenting Your Code

When will you know to start inserting comments into your HTML code? The first time you go back to an earlier Web page, look at the code and say, "What on earth was I thinking?" You should plan ahead and develop the habit of commenting your code now.

Browsers run fine without your comments, but for any continued development — of the Web page or of yourself as a Webmaster — commenting your code is extremely beneficial. Sometimes, as in a corporate setting, Web pages are codeveloped by teams of designers and programmers. In this situation, commenting your code may not just be a good idea; it may be required.

An HTML comment looks like the following:

```
<!-- Created by Hummer Associates, Inc. -->
```

You're not restricted to any particular line length or number of lines for comments. The text included between the opening of the comment, ⟨!--, and the closing, --⟩, can span regular paragraphs or HTML code. In fact, one of the most common uses for comments during the testing and debugging phase of page design is to "comment out" sections of code as a means of tracking down an elusive bug.

To insert a comment in Dreamweaver, first place your cursor in either the Document Window or the HTML Inspector where you want the comment to appear. Then select the Insert Comment button from the Invisibles panel of the Objects Palette. This sequence opens the Insert Comment dialog box, where you can insert the desired text; click OK when you've finished. Figure 7-16 shows the Insert Comment dialog box, with the corresponding completed comment in the HTML Inspector.

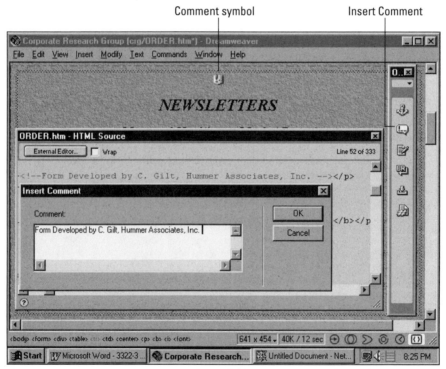

Figure 7-16: Comments are extremely useful for inserting into the code information not visible on the rendered Web page.

By default, Dreamweaver inserts a Comment symbol in the Document Window. As with the other Invisibles, you can hide the Comment symbol by choosing Edit ⇨ Preferences and then deselecting the Comments check-box in the Invisible Elements panel. You can also hide any displayed Invisibles by selecting View ⇨ Invisible Elements or using the keyboard shortcut, Ctrl-Shift-I (Command-Shift-I).

When you need to edit a comment, double-click the Comment symbol to display the current comment in an editable window. After you've finished making your changes to the comment, select the Close button of the Comment window. A comment can be moved or duplicated by selecting its symbol and using the Cut, Copy, and Paste commands under the Edit menu. You can also right-click (Command-click) the Comment symbol to bring up the shortcut menu. Finally, you can click and drag Comment symbols to move the corresponding comment to a new location.

Summary

Learning to manipulate text is an essential design skill for creating Web pages. Dreamweaver gives you all the tools you need to insert and modify the full range of HTML text quickly and easily.

✦ HTML headings are available in six different sizes: <h1> through <h6>. Headings are used primarily as headlines and subheads to separate divisions of the Web page.

✦ Blocks of text are formatted with the paragraph tag, <p>. Each paragraph is separated from the other paragraphs by a line of whitespace above and below. Use the line break tag, <br>, to make lines appear directly above or below one another.

✦ Dreamweaver offers a full complement of text-editing tools — everything from cut-and-paste to find-and-replace. Two commands, Copy Text Only and Paste As Text, are unique to Dreamweaver and make short work of switching between text and code.

✦ Dreamweaver 2's enhanced Find and Replace feature goes a long way toward automating your work on the current page as well as throughout the Web site. Both content and code can be searched in a basic or very advanced fashion.

✦ Where possible, text in HTML is formatted according to its meaning. Dreamweaver applies the styles selected through the Text ⇨ Style menu. For most styles, the browser determines what the user views.

✦ You can format Web page text much as you can text in a word-processing program. Within certain limitations, you can select a font's size and color, as well as the font itself.

✦ HTML comments are a useful (and often requisite) vehicle for embedding information into a Web page that remains unseen by the casual viewer. Comments can annotate program code or insert copyright information.

In the next chapter, you learn how to insert and work with graphics.

✦   ✦   ✦

Inserting Images

The Internet started as a text-based medium primarily used for sharing data among research scientists and the U.S. military. Today, the Web is as visually appealing as any mass medium. Dreamweaver's power becomes even more apparent as you use its visual layout tools to incorporate background and foreground images into your Web page designs.

Completely baffled by all the various image formats out there? This chapter opens with an overview of the key Web-oriented graphics formats, including PNG. Also, this chapter covers techniques for incorporating both background and foreground images — and modifying them using new methods available in Dreamweaver 2. Animation graphics and how you can use them in your Web pages are also covered here, as are techniques for creating rollover buttons. Finally, this chapter delves into integration with Fireworks, Macromedia's award-winning Web graphics tool; you'll see how Dreamweaver and Fireworks make a potent team for creating and publishing Web graphics.

Web Graphic Formats

If you've worked in the computer graphics field, you know that virtually every platform — as well as every paint and graphics program — has its own proprietary file format for images. One of the critical factors in the Web's rapid, expansive growth is the use of cross-platform graphics. Regardless of the system you use to create your images, these versatile files ensure that the graphics can be viewed by all platforms.

The trade-off for universal acceptance of image files is a restricted field: just two file formats, with a possible third just coming into view. Currently, only GIF and JPEG formats are fully supported by browsers. A third alternative, the PNG graphics format, is experiencing a limited but growing acceptance.

You need to understand the uses and limitations of each of the formats so you can apply them successfully in Dreamweaver. Let's look at the fundamentals.

GIF

GIF, the Graphics Interchange Format, was developed by CompuServe in the late 1980s to address the problem of cross-platform compatibility. With GIF viewers available for every system from PC and Macintosh to Amiga and NeXT, the format became a natural choice for an inline (adjacent to text) image graphic. GIFs are *bitmapped* images, which means that each pixel is given or *mapped* to a specific color. You can have up to 256 colors for a GIF graphic. These images are generally used for illustrations, logos, or cartoons — anything that doesn't require thousands of colors for a smooth color blend, such as a photograph. With a proper graphics tool, you can reduce the number of colors in a GIF image to a minimum, thereby compressing the file and reducing download time.

The GIF format has two varieties: "regular" (technically, GIF87a) and an enhanced version known as GIF89a. This improved GIF file brings three important attributes to the format. First, GIF89a supports *transparency*, where one or more of the colors can become invisible. This property is necessary for creating nonrectangular-appearing images. Whenever you see a round or irregularly-shaped logo or illustration on the Web, a rectangular frame is displayed as the image is loading — this is the actual size and shape of the graphic. The colors surrounding the irregularly shaped central image are set to transparent in a graphics editing program (such as Fireworks or Adobe Photoshop) before the image is saved in GIF89a format.

Note Most of the latest versions of the popular graphic tools default to using GIF89a, so you're not too likely to encounter the less flexible GIF87a format.

Although the outer area of a graphic seems to disappear with GIF89a, you won't be able to overlap your Web images using this format without using layers. Figure 8-1 demonstrates this situation. In this figure, the same image is presented twice — one lacks transparency and one has transparency applied. The image on the left is saved as a standard GIF without transparency, and you can plainly see the shape of the full image. The image on the right was saved with the white background color made transparent, so the central figure seems to float on the background.

Tip You may also notice a bit of a problem in Figure 8-1. In the transparent image on the right, the man's shadow doesn't blend well with the contrasting background. This image was constructed to work with an off-white background. Any images using blends or drop shadows should use a background close to the final Web page background. Otherwise, you get *artifacting* similar to this image.

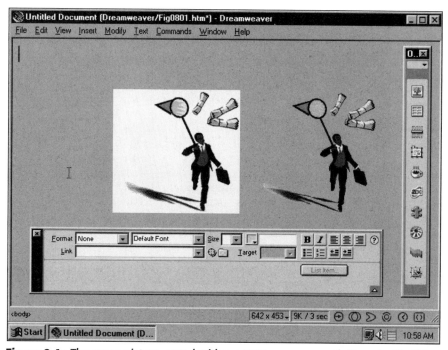

Figure 8-1: The same picture, saved without GIF transparency (left) and with GIF transparency (right).

The second valuable attribute contributed by GIF89a format is *interlacing.* One of the most common complaints about graphics on the Web is lengthy download times. Interlacing won't speed up your GIF downloads, but it gives your Web page visitors something to view other than a blank screen. A graphic saved with the interlace turned on gives the appearance of "developing," like an instant picture, as the file is downloading. Use of this design option is up to you and your clients. Some folks swear by it; others can't abide it.

Animation is the final advantage offered by the GIF89a format. Certain software programs enable you to group your GIF files together into one large, page-flipping file. With this capability, you can bring simple animation to your page without additional plug-ins or helper applications. Unfortunately, the trade-off is that the files get very big, very fast.

Cross-Reference   For more on animated GIFs in Dreamweaver, see "Applying Simple Web Animation," later in this chapter.

JPEG

The JPEG format was developed by the Joint Photographic Experts Groups specifically to handle photographic images. JPEGs offer millions of colors at 24 bits of color information available per pixel, as opposed to the GIF format's 8-bit and 256 colors. To make JPEGs usable, the large amount of color information must be compressed, which is accomplished by removing what the algorithm considers redundant information.

The more compressed your JPEG file, the more degraded the image. When you first save a JPEG image, your graphics program asks you for the desired level of compression. As an example, take a look at the three pictures in Figure 8-2. Here you can compare the effects of JPEG compression ratios and resulting file sizes to the original image itself. As you can probably tell, JPEG does an excellent job of compression, with even the highest degree of compression having only a little visible impact. Keep in mind that each picture has its own reaction to compression.

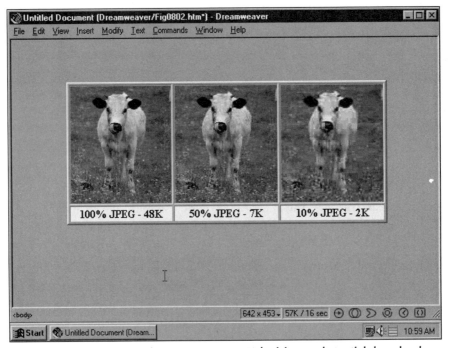

Figure 8-2: JPEG compression can save your Web visitors substantial download time, with little loss of image quality.

Tip With the JPEG image-compression algorithm, the initial elements of an image "compressed away" are least noticeable. Subtle variations in brightness and hue are the first to disappear. When possible, preview your image in your graphics program while adjusting the compression level to observe the changes. With additional compression, the image grows darker and less varied in its color range.

With JPEGs, what is compressed for storage must be uncompressed for viewing. When a JPEG picture on your Web page is accessed by a visitor's browser, the image must first be downloaded to the browser and then uncompressed before it can be viewed. This dual process adds additional time to the Web browsing process, but it is time well-spent for photographic images.

JPEGs, unlike GIFs, have neither transparency nor animation features. A new strand of JPEG called Progressive JPEG gives you the interlace option of the GIF format, however. Although not all browsers support the interlace feature of Progressive JPEG, they render the image regardless.

PNG

The latest entry into the Web graphics arena is the Portable Network Graphics format, or PNG. Combining the best of both worlds, PNG has lossless compression, like GIF, and is capable of millions of colors, like JPEG. Moreover, PNG offers an interlace scheme that appears much more quickly than either GIF or JPEG, as well as transparency support that is far superior to both the other formats.

One valuable aspect of the PNG format allows the display of PNG pictures to appear more uniform across various computer platforms. Generally, graphics made on a PC look brighter on a Macintosh, and Mac-made images seem darker on a PC. PNG includes gamma correction capabilities that alter the image depending on the computer used by the viewer.

Until recently, the various browsers supported PNG only through plug-ins. After PNG was endorsed as a new Web graphic format by the W3C, both 4.0 versions of Netscape and Microsoft browsers added native, inline support of the new format. Perhaps most important, however, Dreamweaver was among the first Web authoring tools to offer native PNG support. Inserted PNG images preview in the Document Window just like GIFs and JPEGs. Browser support is currently not widespread enough to warrant a total switch to the PNG format, but its growing acceptance certainly bears watching.

Tip If you're really excited about the potential of PNG, check out Macromedia's Fireworks, the first Web graphics tool to use PNG as its native format. Fireworks takes full advantage of PNG's alpha transparency features and enhanced palette.

Two excellent resources for more on the PNG format is the PNG home page at `http://www.cdrom.com/pub/png` and the W3C's PNG page at `http://www.w3.org/Graphics/PNG/`

Using Inline Images

An *inline image* can appear directly next to text — literally in the same line. The ability to render inline images is one of the major innovations of the World Wide Web's transition from the Internet. This section covers all the basics of inserting inline images into Dreamweaver and modifying their attributes.

Inserting images

Dreamweaver can open and preview any graphic in a GIF, JPEG, or PNG format. With Dreamweaver 2, there are now five methods for placing a graphic on your Web page.

✦ From the Objects Palette, select the Insert Image button.

✦ From the menu bar, choose Insert ➪ Image.

✦ From the keyboard, press Ctrl-Alt-I (Command-Option-I).

✦ Point to an image file in the Site Window using Dreamweaver 2's new Point to File feature.

✦ Drag either the Insert Image button or an icon from your file manager to your page.

The first four methods require that you first position the cursor at the point where you want the image to appear on the page; only the drag-and-drop method allows you to place the image inline with any existing element or in a layer.

After you've used one of the preceding methods, Dreamweaver opens the Select Image Source dialog box (shown in Figure 8-3) and asks you for the path or address to your image file. Remember that in HTML, all graphics are stored in separate files linked from your Web page. The image's address can be just a filename, a directory path and filename on your system, a directory path and filename on your remote system, or a full URL to a graphic on a completely separate Web server. You don't have to have the file immediately available to insert the code into your HTML. If you cancel the dialog box, Dreamweaver inserts a placeholder depicting a broken image. The placeholder is also inserted when you include your image via the keyboard shortcut, Ctrl-Alt-I (Command-Option-I) without opening the Select Image Source dialog box.

New Feature   From the Select Image Source dialog box, you can browse to the folder to select your images. You'll notice a major enhancement here — you can now preview images before you load them. To enable this feature, make sure the Preview Images option is selected. Dreamweaver can preview GIF, JPEG, or PNG files.

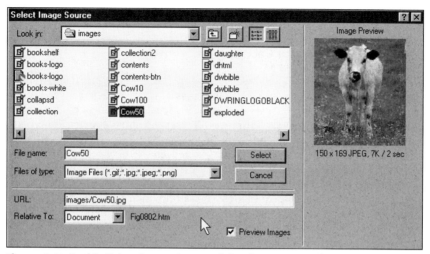

Figure 8-3: In this Select Image Source dialog box, you can keep track of your image's location relative to your current Web page.

In the lower portion of the dialog box, the URL text box displays the format of the address Dreamweaver inserts into your code. Below the URL text box is the Relative To option list box. Here you can choose to declare an image to be relative to the document you're working on (the default), or relative to the Site Root. (After you've saved your document, you'll see its name beside the Relative To box.)

Cross-Reference

To take full advantage of Dreamweaver's site management features, you must open a site, establish a local site root, and save the current Web page before beginning to insert images. For more on how to begin a Dreamweaver project, and about document-relative and site root-relative addressing, see Chapter 5, "Setting Up Your First Site."

Relative to Document

Once you've saved your Web page and have chosen Relative to Document, Dreamweaver displays the address in the URL text box. If the image is located in a folder on the same level as, or within, your current site root folder, the address is formatted with just a path and filename. For instance, if you're inserting a graphic from the subfolder named images, Dreamweaver inserts an address like the following:

```
images/men10.jpg
```

If you try to insert an image currently stored outside of the local site root folder, Dreamweaver temporarily appends a prefix that tells the browser to look on your local system for the file. For instance, the file would look like the following in Windows:

```
file:///C|/Dreamweaver/Figs/men10.jpg
```

while on the Macintosh, the same file is listed as follows:

```
file:///Dreamweaver/Figs/men10.jpg
```

Caution

Dreamweaver also appends the `file:///C|` prefix (or just `file:///` in Macintosh) if you haven't yet saved your document. It is strongly recommended that you save your file before you begin developing the Web page. You can easily upload Web pages with this `file:///C|` (`file:///`) prefix in place—and miss the error completely. Because your local browser can find the referenced image on your system, even when you are browsing the remote site, the Web page appears perfect. However, anyone else browsing your Web site only sees placeholders for broken links. Saving your page before you begin allows Dreamweaver to help you avoid these errors. To this end, do not check the "Don't show me this message again" check-box that appears when you're reminded to save your file the first time. This message will save you an enormous amount of grief!

After you select your image file, you'll see the prompt window shown in Figure 8-4. Dreamweaver asks if you want to copy this image to your local site root folder. Whenever possible, keep all of your images within the local site root folder so that Dreamweaver can handle site management most efficiently. Click Yes, and you next see a Save Copy As dialog box, which points to the local site root folder. If you select No, the file is inserted with the src attribute pointing to the path of the file.

Figure 8-4: Dreamweaver reminds you to keep all of your graphics in the local site root folder for easy site management.

Relative to Site Root

Should you select Site Root in the Relative To field of the Select Image Source dialog box, and you are within your site root folder, Dreamweaver appends a leading forward slash to the directory in the path so the browser can correctly read the address. Thus, the same men10.jpg file appears in both the URL box and the HTML code as follows:

```
/images/men10.jpg
```

When you use site-root relative addressing and you select a file outside of the site root, you get the same reminder from Dreamweaver about copying the file into your local site root folder—just as with document relative addressing.

Modifying images

When you insert an image in Dreamweaver, the image tag, `<img>`, is inserted into your HTML code. The `<img>` tag takes several attributes, all of which can be entered through the Property Inspector. Code for a basic image looks like the following:

```
<img src="images/Collection01.gif" width="172" height="180">
```

Dreamweaver centralizes all of its image functions in the Property Inspector. The Image Property Inspector, shown in Figure 8-5, displays a small thumbnail of the image as well as its file size. Dreamweaver automatically inserts the image filename in the Src text box (as the `src` attribute). To replace a currently selected image with another, click the Folder icon next to the Src text box, or double-click the image itself. This sequence opens the Select Image Source dialog box. When you've selected the desired file, Dreamweaver automatically refreshes the page and corrects the code.

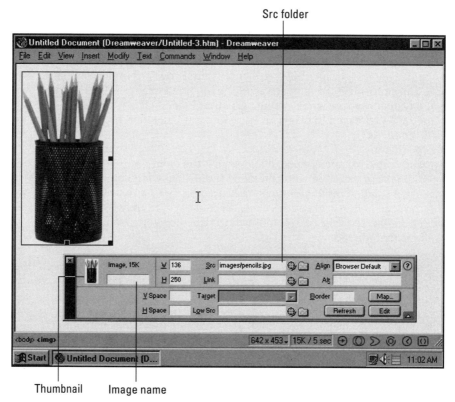

Figure 8-5: The Image Property Inspector gives you total control over the HTML code for every image.

With the Property Inspector open when you insert your image, you can begin to modify it immediately.

Editing the image

Dreamweaver is a terrific Web authoring tool, but it's not a graphics editor. Quite often, after you've inserted an image into your Web page, you'll find that the picture needs to be altered in some way. Perhaps you need to crop part of the image or make the background transparent. Dreamweaver lets you specify your primary graphics editor in the External Editors panel of Preferences.

Once you've picked an image editor, clicking the Edit Image button in the Property Inspector opens the application with the current image. After you've made the modifications, just save the file in your image editor and switch back to Dreamweaver. You'll see that the new, modified graphic has already been included in the Web page.

Note   Dreamweaver seamlessly refreshed the images being edited in all the image editors I tested. However, there have been reports of images not reappearing in their modified form. If this happens, click the Refresh button in the Property Inspector after you select your image.

Adjusting height and width

The width and height attributes are important: Browsers build Web pages faster when they know the size and shape of the included images. These attributes are read by Dreamweaver when the image is first loaded. The width and height values are initially expressed in pixels and are automatically inserted as attributes in the HTML code.

Browsers can dynamically resize an image if the height and width are different than the original. For example, you can load your primary logo on the home page and then use a smaller version of it on subsequent pages by inserting the same image with reduced height and width values. Because you're only loading the image once and letting the browser resize it, download time for your Web page can be significantly reduced.

Note   Resizing an image just means you're changing its appearance on screen; the file size stays exactly the same. To reduce a file size for an image, you need to scale it down in a graphics program like Fireworks 2.

You don't have to use pixels to enter your resizing measurements into Dreamweaver's Property Inspector. You can also use inches (in), picas (pc), points (pt), millimeters (mm), or centimeters (cm). The values must be entered without spaces between the number and the measurement abbreviation, as follows:

72pt

You can also combine measurement systems. Suppose, for example, you want to resize a picture's height to 2 inches and 5 centimeters. In the Property Inspector, you enter the following value in the H text box:

```
2in+5cm
```

When you use values with a combined measurement system, you can only add values — you can't subtract them. When you press the Tab key or click outside of the height and width boxes, Dreamweaver converts your value to pixels.

Tip With Dreamweaver, you can visually resize your graphics by using the click-and-drag method. A selected image has three sizing handles located on the right, bottom, and lower-right corners of its bounding box. Click any of these handles and drag it out to a new location — when you release the mouse, Dreamweaver resizes the image. You can hold down the Shift key while dragging the corner sizing handle, and Dreamweaver maintains the current height/width aspect ratio.

If you alter either the height or the width of an image in the Property Inspector, Dreamweaver displays the values in bold in their respective fields. You can restore an image's default measurements by selecting the H or the W independently — or you can choose the Refresh button to restore both values.

Caution If you elect to allow your viewer's browser to resize your image on-the-fly using the height/width values you specify, keep in mind that the browser is not a graphics editing program and that its resizing algorithms are not sophisticated. View your resized images through several browsers to make sure that the results are acceptable.

Using margins

You can offset images with surrounding whitespace by using the margin attributes. The amount of whitespace around your image can be designated both vertically and horizontally through the vspace and hspace attributes, respectively. These margin values are entered, in pixels, into the V Space and H Space text boxes in the Image Property Inspector.

The V Space value adds the same amount of whitespace along the top and bottom of your image; the H Space value increases the whitespace along the left and right sides of the image. These values must be positive; HTML doesn't allow images to overlap text or other images (outside of layers); unlike in page layout, "negative whitespace" does not exist.

Titling your image

When you first insert a graphic into the page, the Image Property Inspector displays a blank text box next to the thumbnail and file size. Fill in this box with a unique name for the image, to be used in JavaScript and other applications.

As a page is loading over the Web, the image is first displayed as an empty rectangle if the <img> tag contains the width and height information. Sometimes these rectangles include a brief title to describe the coming image. You can enter this alternative text in the Alt text box of the Image Property Inspector.

Tip

Good coding practice associates an Alt title with all of your graphics. Aside from giving the user some clue as to what's coming, these mini-titles are also used to display the screen tips that pop up when the user's pointer passes over the graphic by some browsers. The real benefit of mini-titles, however, is providing input for browsers not displaying graphics. Text-only browsers are still in use and some users, interested only in content, turn off the graphics to speed up the text display. Moreover, the W3C is working toward standards for browsers for the visually impaired, and the Alt text can be used to describe the page.

Bordering a graphic

When you're working with *thumbnails* (a series of small versions of images) on your Web page, you may need a quick way to distinguish one from another. The border attribute allows you to place a one-color rectangular border around any graphic. The width of the border is measured in pixels and the color is the same as the default for the page's text color as specified in the Page Properties dialog box. To turn on the border, enter a value in the Border text box located on the lower half of the Image Property Inspector. Entering a value of 0 (zero) explicitly turns off the border.

New Feature

One of the most frequent cries for help among Dreamweaver (and other) beginning Web designers results from the sudden appearance of a bright blue border around their image. Whenever you assign a link to an image, HTML automatically places a border around that image; the color is determined by the Page Properties' Link color, where the default is bright blue. Now, Dreamweaver 2 intelligently assigns a "0" to the Border attribute whenever you enter a URL in the Link text box. If you've already declared a border value and enter a link, Dreamweaver won't zero-out the border. You can, of course, override the no-border option by entering a value in the Border text box.

Specifying a lowsrc

Another option for loading Web page images, the lowsrc attribute, displays a smaller version of a large graphic file while the larger file is loading. The lowsrc file can be a grayscale version of the original, or a version that is physically smaller or reduced in color or resolution. This option is designed to reduce the file size significantly for quick loading.

Select your lowsrc file by choosing the File icon next to the Low text box in the Image Property Inspector. The same criteria that applies to inserting your original image also applies to the lowsrc picture.

One handy `lowsrc` technique first proportionately scales down a large file in a graphics processing program. This file becomes your `lowsrc` file. Because browsers use the final image's height and width information for both the `lowsrc` and the final image, your visitors immediately see a "blocky" version of your graphic, which is replaced by the final version when the picture is fully loaded.

Working with alignment options

Images can be aligned to the left, right, or center, just like text. In fact, images have much more flexibility than text in terms of alignment. In addition to the same horizontal alignment options, you can align your images vertically in nine different ways. You can even turn a picture into a floating image type, allowing text to wrap around it.

Horizontal alignment

When you change the horizontal alignment of a line—from left to center or from center to right—the entire paragraph moves. Any inline images that are part of that paragraph also move. Likewise, selecting one of a series of inline images in a row and realigning it horizontally causes all the images in the row to shift.

In Dreamweaver, the horizontal alignment of an inline image is changed in exactly the same way you realign text. Select Text ➪ Alignment and then choose your option: Left, Right, or Center. You can also click the Left, Center, and Right buttons from the Text Property Inspector or use the following keyboard shortcuts:

✦ Ctrl-Alt-L (Command-Option-L) for Left

✦ Ctrl-Alt-C (Command-Option-C) for Center

✦ Ctrl-Alt-R (Command-Option-R) for Right

Vertical alignment

Because you can place text next to an image—and images vary so greatly in size— HTML includes a variety of options for specifying just how image and text line up. As you can see from the chart in Figure 8-6, a wide range of possibilities are available.

To change the vertical alignment of any graphic in Dreamweaver, open the Align drop-down list in the Image Property Inspector and choose one of the options. Dreamweaver writes your choice into the `align` attribute of the `<img>` tag.

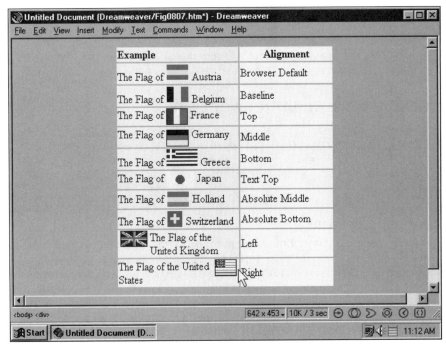

Figure 8-6: You can align text and images in one of nine different ways using the Align option box on the Image Property Inspector.

The various vertical alignment options are listed in the following table, and you can see examples of each type of alignment in Figure 8-6.

Vertical Alignment Option	Results
Browser Default	No alignment attribute is included in the <img> tag. Most browsers use the baseline as an alignment default.
Baseline	The bottom of the image is aligned with the baseline of the surrounding text.
Top	The top of the image is aligned with the top of the tallest object in the current line.
Middle	The middle of the image is aligned with the baseline of the current line.
Text Top	The top of the image is aligned with the tallest letter in the current line.

Vertical Alignment Option	Results
Absolute Middle	The middle of the image is aligned with the middle of the text or object in the current line.
Absolute Bottom	The bottom of the image is aligned with the descenders (as in y, g, p, and so forth) that fall below the current line.
Left	The image is aligned to the left edge of the browser or table cell and all text in the current line flows around the right-hand side of the image.
Right	The image is aligned to the right edge of the browser or table cell and all text in the current line flows around the left-hand side of the image.

The final two alignment options, Left and Right, are special cases; details about how to use their features are covered in the following section.

Wrapping text

Long a popular design option in conventional publishing, wrapping text around an image on a Web page is also supported by most, but not all, browsers. As noted in the preceding section, the Left and Right alignment options turn a picture into a *floating image type*, so called because the image can move depending on the amount of text and the size of the browser window.

Tip

Using both floating image types (Left and Right) in combination, you can actually position images flush-left and flush-right, with text in the middle. Insert both images side-by-side, and then set the leftmost image to align left and the rightmost one to align right. Insert your text immediately following the second image. Unless you place a `<p>` or `<br>` at the top, this arrangement does not render correctly in Dreamweaver (the first line overlaps the left image); but it does display as expected in most browsers.

Your text wraps around the image depending on where the floating image is placed (or anchored). If you have the feature enabled in the Invisibles pane of Preferences, Dreamweaver inserts a Floating Image Anchor symbol to mark the floating image's place. Figure 8-7 shows two examples of text wrapping. In the top case, the Floating Image Anchor symbol is placed at the front of the second paragraph, which causes the three paragraphs to flow around the right-aligned image. In the bottom case, you can't see the Floating Image Anchor because the left-aligned image overlaps the anchor, which is placed at the front of the first paragraph.

Floating image anchor

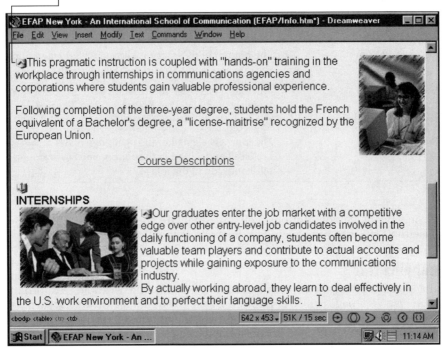

Figure 8-7: Aligning an image left or right allows text to wrap around your images.

The Floating Image Anchor is not just a static symbol. You can click and drag the anchor to a new location and cause the paragraph to wrap in a different fashion. Be careful though — if you delete the Anchor, you also delete the image it represents.

You can also wrap a portion of the text around your left- or right-aligned picture and then force the remaining text to appear below the floating image. However, the HTML necessary to do this task cannot currently be inserted by Dreamweaver, and must be coded by hand. You have to force an opening to appear by inserting a break tag, with a special clear attribute, where you want the text to break. This special `<br>` tag has three forms:

`<br clear=left>`	Causes the line to break, and the following text moves down vertically until there are no floating images on the left.
`<br clear=right>`	Causes the line to break, and the following text moves down vertically until there are no floating images on the right.
`<br clear=all>`	Moves the text following the image down until there are no floating images on either the left or the right.

One of the Dreamweaver objects included on the CD-ROM is an enhanced break tag that enables you to include any version of the `clear` attribute. To access these objects, copy the new_break.htm and new_break.gif files from the Dreamweaver/ Configuration/Objects/Invisibles folder into the same folder on your system; then restart Dreamweaver.

Putting Pictures in the Background

In this chapter, you've learned about working with the surface graphics on a Web page. As seen in Chapter 6, you can also have an image in the background of an HTML page. This section covers some of the basic techniques for incorporating a background image in your Dreamweaver page.

Note

Remember, you add an image to your background in Dreamweaver by modifying the Page Properties. Either choose Modify ➪ Page Properties, or select Page Properties from the shortcut menu that pops up when you right-click (Command-click) any open area on the Web page. In the Page Properties dialog box, select a graphic by choosing the Browse (Choose) button next to the Background Image text box. You can use any file format supported by Dreamweaver — GIF, JPEG, or PNG — although the PNG format is currently not supported in enough browsers to permit widespread distribution.

Two key differences exist between background images and the foreground, inline images discussed in the preceding sections of this chapter. First and most obvious: all other text and graphics on the Web page are superimposed over your chosen background image. This capability can bring extra depth and texture to your work; unfortunately, you have to make sure the foreground text and images work well with the background.

Tip

You can quickly try out a number of professionally designed background and fore-ground color combinations with the Set Color Scheme command. For more infor-mation on how to use this Dreamweaver Command, see Chapter 6, "Understanding How HTML Works."

Basically, you want to ascertain that there is enough contrast between foreground and background. You can set the default text and the various link colors through the Page Properties dialog box. When trying out a new background pattern, you should set up some dummy text and links. Then use the Apply button on the Page Properties dialog box to test different color combinations. See Figure 8-8 for an example of this test at work.

Tiling Images

Web designers use the tiling property of background images to create a variety of effects with very low file-size overhead. The columns typically found on one side of Web pages are a good example of tiling. Columns are popular because they allow the designer to place navigational buttons in a visual context. An easy way to create a column that runs the full length of your Web page uses a long, narrow background image.

Take a look at the following figure. The background image is 45 pixels high, 800 pixels wide, and only 6K in size. When the browser window is set at 640 × 480 or 800 × 600, the image is tiled down the page to create the vertical column effect. You could just as easily create an image 1,000 pixels high by 40 pixels wide to create a horizontal column.

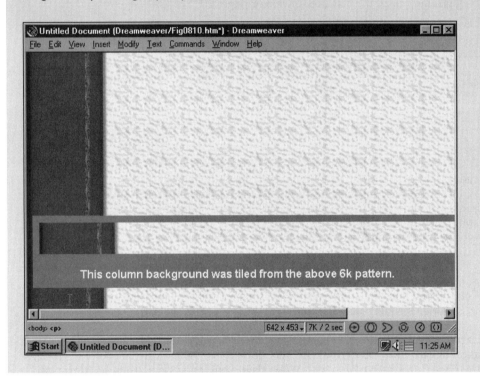

The second distinguishing feature of background images is that the viewing browser completely fills either the browser window or the area behind the content of your Web page, whichever is larger. So, if you've created a splash page with only a 200 × 200 foreground logo, and you've incorporated an amazing 1,024 × 768 background that took you weeks to compose, no one will see the fruits of your labor in the background — unless they resize their browser window to 1,024 × 768. On the other hand, if your background image is smaller than either the browser window or what the Web page content needs to display, the browser and Dreamweaver repeat (or tile) your image to make up the difference.

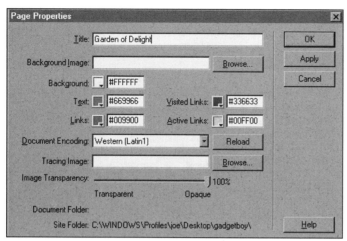

Figure 8-8: If you're using a background image, be sure to check the default colors for text and links to make sure there is enough contrast between background and foreground.

Dividing the Web Page with Horizontal Rules

HTML includes a standard horizontal line that can divide your Web page into specific sections. The horizontal rule tag, <hr>, is a good tool for adding a little diversion to your page without adding download time. You can control the width (either absolutely or relative to the browser window), the height, the alignment, and the shading property of the rule. These horizontal rules appear on a line by themselves; you cannot place text or images on the same line as a horizontal rule.

To insert a horizontal rule in your Web page in Dreamweaver, follow these steps:

1. Place your cursor where you want the horizontal rule to appear.

2. From the Common pane of the Objects Palette, select the Insert Horizontal Rule button or choose the Insert ➪ Horizontal Rule command.

   Dreamweaver inserts the horizontal rule and opens the Horizontal Rule Property Inspector, as shown in Figure 8-9.

3. To change the width of the line, enter a value in the width (W) text box. You can insert either an absolute width in pixels or a relative value as a percentage of the screen.

   • To set a horizontal rule to an exact width, enter the measurement in pixels in the width (W) text box and press the Tab key. Then select pixels in the drop-down list.

   • To set a horizontal rule to a width relative to the browser window, enter the percentage amount in the width (W) text box and press Tab. Then select the percent sign (%) in the drop-down list.

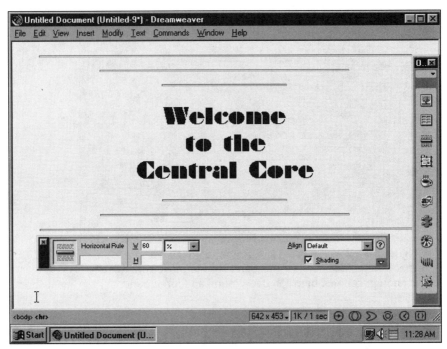

Figure 8-9: The Horizontal Rule Property Inspector controls the width, height, and alignment for these HTML lines.

4. To change the height of the horizontal rule, type a pixel measurement in the height (H) text box.

For both the width and height values, you can also enter a value in inches (in), picas (pc), points (pt), millimeters (mm), or centimeters (cm), just as with images. When you press Tab to leave the text box, Dreamweaver converts your entry to pixels.

5. To change the alignment from the default (centered), open the Align dropdown list and choose another alignment.

6. To disable the default "embossed" look for the rule, deselect the Shading check-box.

7. If you intend to address (call) your horizontal rule in a JavaScript or another application, you can give it a unique name. Type it into the unlabeled name text box located directly to the left of the H text box.

To modify any inserted horizontal rule, simply click it. (If the Property Inspector is not already open, you have to double-click the rule.) As a general practice, size horizontal rules using the percentage option if they are being used to separate items on a full screen. If the horizontal rules are being used to divide items in a specifically sized table column or cell, use the pixel method.

Tip

To use the Shading property of the horizontal rule properly, your background should be a shade of gray. The default shading is black along the top and left, and white along the bottom and right. The center line is generally transparent (although Internet Explorer enables you to assign a color attribute). If you use a different background color or image, be sure to check the appearance of your horizontal rules in that context.

Many designers prefer to create more elaborate horizontal rules; in fact, these rules are an active area of clip-art design. These types of horizontal rules are regular graphics and are inserted and modified as such.

Applying Simple Web Animation

Why include a section on animation in a chapter on inline images? On the Web, animations are, for the most part, inline images that move. Outside of the possibilities offered by Dynamic HTML (covered in Part VI, "Dynamic HTML and Dreamweaver"), Web animations are either animated GIF files or are created with a program such as Flash that requires a plug-in. This section takes a brief look at the capabilities and uses of GIF animations.

A GIF animation is a series of still GIF images flipped rapidly to create the illusion of motion. Because animation-creation programs compress all the frames of your animation into one file, a GIF animation is placed on a Web page in the same manner as a still graphic.

In Dreamweaver, click the Insert Image button in the Objects Palette or choose Insert ➪ Image and then select the file. Dreamweaver shows the first frame of your animation in the Document Window. To play the animation, preview your Web page in any graphics-capable browser.

As you can imagine, GIF animations can quickly grow to be very large. The key to controlling file size is to think small: keep your images as small as possible with a low bit-depth (number of colors), and use as few frames as possible.

To create your animation, use any graphics program to produce the separate frames. One excellent technique uses an image-processing program such as Adobe Photoshop and progressively applies a filter to the same image over a series of frames. Figure 8-10 shows the individual frames created with Photoshop's Lighting Effects filter. When animated, a spotlight appears to move across the word.

You need an animation program to compress the separate frames and build your animated GIF file. GIF Construction Set on the Windows platform and GIFBuilder on the Mac are extremely popular. Both of these programs are shareware; many commercial programs can also handle GIF animation, including Macromedia's new Fireworks. Most animation programs enable you to control the number of times an animation loops, the delay between frames, and how transparency is handled within each frame.

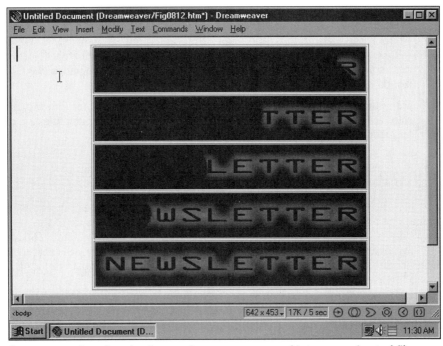

Figure 8-10: Five of twelve frames that are compressed into one animated file.

Tip   If you want to use an advanced animation tool, but still have full backward compatibility, check out Flash and the Aftershock utility, both from Macromedia. Flash
is best known for outputting small vector-based animations that require a plug-in
to view, but it can also save animations as GIFs or AVIs. Aftershock converts vector
animation to GIF animation. Both programs are discussed in Chapter 22, "Inserting
Shockwave Elements."

Inserting Rollover Images

Rollovers are among the most popular of all Web page effects. A *rollover* (also
known as a *mouseover*) occurs when the user's pointer passes over an image and
the image changes in some way. It may appear to glow or change color and/or
shape; when the pointer moves away from the graphic, the image returns to its
original form. The rollover indicates interactivity and attempts to engage the user
with a little bit of flare.

**New
Feature**   Rollovers are usually accomplished with a combination of HTML and JavaScript.
Dreamweaver was among the first Web authoring tools to automate the production of rollovers through the still-available Swap Image and Swap Image Restore
behaviors. Dreamweaver 2 makes rollovers even easier with the new Rollover
Image object. Now, with the Rollover Image object, if you can pick two images,
you can make a rollover.

Technically speaking, a rollover is accomplished by manipulating an ⟨img⟩ tag's src attribute. You'll recall that the src attribute is responsible for providing the actual filename of the graphic to be displayed; it is, quite literally, the source of the image. A rollover changes the value of src from one image file to another. Swapping the src value is analogous to having a picture within a frame and changing the picture while keeping the frame.

Caution
The picture-frame analogy is appropriate on one other level: It serves as a reminder of the size barrier inherent in rollovers. A rollover only changes one property of an ⟨img⟩ tag, the source — it cannot change any other property such as the height or width. For this reason, both your original image and the image that is displayed during the rollover should be the same size. If they are not, the alternate image is resized to match the dimensions of the original image.

Dreamweaver's Rollover Image object automatically changes the image back to its original source when the user moves the pointer off the image. Optionally, you can elect to preload the images with the selection of a check-box. *Preloading* is a Web page technique that reads the intended file or files into the browser's memory before they are displayed. Preloading allows the images to appear on demand, without any download delay.

Rollovers are typically used for buttons that, when clicked, open another Web page. In fact, JavaScript requires that an image include a link before it can detect when a user's pointer moves over it. Dreamweaver automatically includes the minimum link necessary: the #target link. Although JavaScript recognizes this symbol as indicating a link, no action is taken if the image is clicked by the user; the #, by itself, is an empty link. You can, naturally, supply whatever link you want in the Rollover Image object.

To include a Rollover Image object in your Web page, follow these steps:

1. Place your cursor where you want the rollover image to appear and choose Insert ⇨ Rollover Image or select Insert Rollover Image from the Common panel of the Objects Palette. You can also drag the Insert Rollover Image button to any existing location on the Web page.

   Dreamweaver opens the Insert Rollover Image dialog box shown in Figure 8-11.

2. In the Original Image text box, enter the path and name of the graphic you want displayed when the user's mouse is *not* over the graphic. You can also choose the Browse (Choose) button to select the file. Press Tab when you're done.

3. If desired, you can enter a unique name for the image in the Image Name text box or you can leave the name automatically generated by Dreamweaver.

4. In the Rollover Image text box, enter the path and name of the graphic you want displayed when the user's pointer is over the graphic. You can also choose the Browse (Choose) button to select the file.

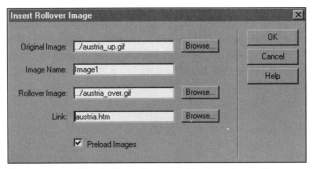

Figure 8-11: The Rollover Image object makes rollover graphics quick and easy.

5. If desired, specify a link for the image by entering it in the Link text box. If you are entering a path and file by hand, be sure to delete the initial target link, #. If you use the Browse (Choose) button to select your file, the target link is deleted for you.

6. To allow images to load only when they are required, deselect the Preload Images option. Generally, it is best to leave this option selected (the default) so that there is no delay in the rollover appearing.

7. Click OK when you're finished.

Tip

Keep in mind that the Rollover Image object inserts both the original image and its alternate, whereas the Swap Image technique is applied to an existing image in the Web page. If you prefer to use the Rollover Image object rather than the Swap Image behavior, there is nothing to prevent you from deleting an existing image from the Web page and inserting it again through the Rollover Image object. Just make sure that you note the path and name of the image before you delete it, so you can find it again.

Integrating Dreamweaver with Fireworks

Imagine demonstrating a newly completed Web site to a client who *didn't* ask for an image to be a little bigger or the text on a button to be reworded or the colors for the background to be revised. In the real world, Web sites — particularly the images — are constantly being tweaked and modified. This fact of Web life explains why Fireworks, Macromedia's premier Web graphics tool, is so popular. One of Firework's main claims to fame is that everything is editable all the time. If that were all that Fireworks did, the program would have already earned a place on every Web designer's shelf just for its sheer expediency. But Fireworks is far more capable a tool — and now, that power can be tapped directly in Dreamweaver.

With the combination of Dreamweaver 2 and Fireworks 2, a whole new level of integration between the two Macromedia products has been achieved. Now you can optimize your images — reduce the file size, crop the graphic, make colors transparent — within Dreamweaver using the Fireworks interface. Moreover, you can edit your image in any fashion in Fireworks and, with one click of the Update command, automatically export the graphic with its original export settings.

A key Fireworks feature is the ability to output HTML and JavaScript for easy creation of rollovers, sliced images, and image maps with behaviors. With Fireworks 2, you can even specify Dreamweaver-style code, so that all your Web pages are consistent. Currently, the official method for combining Fireworks output with Dreamweaver HTML is cut-and-paste, although new commands are quickly emerging to automate the task. Although the integration between the two programs isn't total, the workflow is vastly improved and client modifications are no longer to be feared.

Easy graphics modification

It's not uncommon for graphics to need some alteration before they fully integrate into a Web design. In fact, I'd say it's far more the rule than the exception. The traditional workflow generally goes like this:

1. Create the image in one or more graphics editing programs.

2. Place the new graphic on a Web page via your Web authoring tool.

3. Note where the problems lie — perhaps the image is too big or too small; maybe the drop shadow doesn't blend into the background properly; or maybe the whole image needs to be flipped.

4. Reopen the graphics program, make the modifications, and save the file again.

5. Return to the Web page layout to view the results.

6. Repeat Steps 3–5 ad infinitum until you get it right.

While you're still using two different programs even with Dreamweaver and Fireworks integration, one of the techniques available allows you to open a Fireworks window on the Dreamweaver screen. Now you can make your alterations with the Web page noticeable in the background. I've found that this small advantage cuts the trial-and-error to a bare minimum and streamlines my workflow.

If you're not familiar with Fireworks, you're missing an extremely powerful graphics program made for the Web. Fireworks combines the best of both vector and bitmap technologies and was one of the first graphics programs to use PNG as its native format. You'll also find exceptional export abilities in Fireworks with which images can be optimized for file size, color, and scale. Moreover, Fireworks is terrific at generating GIF animations, rollovers, image maps, and sliced images.

With the latest versions of Dreamweaver and Fireworks, you have two ways to alter your inserted graphics: the Optimize Image in Fireworks command and the Edit button in the Image Property Inspector.

Caution   The full integration described in this section requires that Fireworks 2 be installed after Dreamweaver 2. If you already have Fireworks 2 on your system, but not Dreamweaver, you'll need to uninstall Fireworks 2 and then reinstall it after you've set up Dreamweaver 2.

Optimizing an image in Fireworks

While you can design the most beautiful, compelling image possible in your graphics program, if it's intended for the Internet you need to view it in a Web page. Not only must the graphic work in the context of the entire page, as a Web graphic you have to take the file size into account. All of these factors mean that most, if not all, images need to undergo some degree of modification once they're included in a Web page. Fireworks 2 makes these alterations as straightforward as possible by including a new command for Dreamweaver during its installation.

The Optimize Image in Fireworks command opens the Export module of Fireworks, as shown in Figure 8-12, right in Dreamweaver's Document Window.

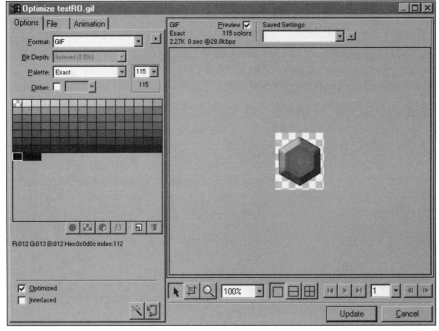

Figure 8-12: With Fireworks 2 installed, you can optimize your images from within Dreamweaver.

The Export module consists of three tabbed panels: Options, File, and Animation. Although a complete description of all of its features is beyond the scope of this book, here's a breakdown of the major uses of each area:

✦ **Options.** The Options panel is primarily used to try different export options and preview them. You can switch file formats from GIF to JPEG (or Animated GIF or PNG) as well as alter the palette, color depth, dithering, and more. Transparency for GIF and PNG images is set in the Options panel. Fireworks 2 has also added an Export to Size wizard that allows you to target a particular file size for your graphic.

✦ **File.** An image's dimensions are defined in the File panel. Images can be rescaled by a selected percentage or pixel size. Moreover, you can crop your image either numerically — by defining the export area — or visually with the Cropping tool.

✦ **Animation.** Frame-by-frame control for animated GIFs is available on the Animation panel. Each frame's delay (how long it is on screen) is capable of being defined independently, and the entire animation can be set to either play once or loop a user-determined number of times.

Tip

If you crop or rescale an inserted image in Fireworks, you'll need to update the height and width in Dreamweaver. The easiest way to accomplish this is to select the Refresh button in the image's Property Inspector.

To use the Optimize Image in Fireworks command, follow these steps:

1. Select the image you'd like to modify in Dreamweaver.

Caution

You must save the current page at least once before running the Optimize Image in Fireworks command. The current state of the page doesn't have to have been saved, but a valid file must exist for the command to work properly. If you haven't saved the file, Dreamweaver alerts you to this fact when you call the command.

2. Choose Commands ⇨ Optimize Image in Fireworks.

3. If the selected image is not in PNG format, you're given the opportunity to select a Fireworks source file. Choose Yes to select the PNG format source file.

The Optimize Images dialog box appears.

4. Make whatever modifications are desired from the Options, File, or Animation tabs of the Optimize Images dialog box.

5. When you're finished, select the Update button.

If you're working with a Fireworks source file, the changes are saved to both your source file and exported file; otherwise, only the exported file is altered.

Editing an image in Fireworks

Optimizing an image is great when all you need to do is tweak the file size or rescale the image. Other images require more detailed modification — as when a client requests that the wording or order of a series of navigation buttons be changed. Dreamweaver allows you to specify Fireworks as your graphics editor; and if you've done so, you can take advantage of Fireworks' ability to keep every element of your graphic always editable. And believe me, this is a major advantage.

You set up Fireworks as your graphics editor in Dreamweaver's Preferences. Choose Edit ➪ Preferences and select the External Editors category from the list on the left. In the External Editors pane, select the Image Editor Browse (Choose) button to locate the main Fireworks program. The default location in Windows systems is in C:\Program Files\Macromedia\Fireworks 2\Fireworks 2.exe; in Macintosh it's /applications/Fireworks 2/Fireworks 2. (The .exe extension may or may not be visible in your Windows system.)

Now, whenever you want to edit a graphic, select the image and click the Edit button in the Property Inspector. (You can also right-click (Command-click) the image and select Edit Image to start editing it.) Fireworks will start up, if it's not already open. As with the Optimize Image in Fireworks command, if the inserted image is a GIF or a JPEG, and not a PNG format, Fireworks asks if you'd like to work with a separate source file. If so, you're given an opportunity to locate the file.

After you've made your alterations to your file in Fireworks, choose File ➪ Update or use the keyboard shortcut, Ctrl-S (Command-S). If you're working with a Fireworks source file, both the source file and the exported file are updated and saved.

Exploring Fireworks Source and Export Files

The separate source file is an important concept in Fireworks and its use is strongly advised. Generally, when working in Fireworks, you'll have a minimum of two files for every image output to the Web: your source file and your exported Web image. Whenever major alterations are made, it's best to make them to the source file and then update the export files. Not only is this an easier method of working, but you'll get a better image this way.

Source files are always Fireworks-style PNG files. Fireworks-style PNG files differ slightly from regular PNG format because they include additional information, such as paths and effects used that can only be read by Fireworks. The exported file is usually in GIF or JPEG format, although it could be in standard PNG format. Many Web designers keep their source files in a separate folder from their exported Web images so the two don't get confused.

Caution Make sure that your source file and exported file are the same dimensions if you choose File ➪ Update. If your exported file is a cropped version of the source file, the complete source file is used as the basis for the export file and any cropping information is discarded. To maintain the cropping, choose File ➪ Export instead of File ➪ Update.

Inserting rollovers

The rollover is a fairly common, but effective, Web technique to indicate interactivity. Named after the user action of "rolling the mouse pointer over" the graphic, this technique uses from two to four different images per button. With Fireworks, you can both create the graphics and output the necessary HTML and JavaScript code from the same program. Moreover, Fireworks 2 has added some new, sophisticated twists to the standard "on/off" rollovers to further easily enhance your Web page.

Rollovers created in Fireworks can be inserted into Dreamweaver using one of two basic methods. First, you can use Fireworks to just build the images; and then export them and attach the behaviors in Dreamweaver. This technique works very well for graphics going into layers or images with other attached behaviors. The second method of integrating Fireworks-created rollovers involves transferring the actual code generated by Fireworks into Dreamweaver. Previously, this technique involved opening the HTML Inspector and copying-and-pasting the code—now, with Dreamweaver 2, you can handle the procedure completely from within the Document Window.

Using Dreamweaver's behaviors

With its full-spectrum editability, Fireworks excels at building consistent rollover graphics simply. The different possible states of an image in a rollover—Up, Over, Down, and Over Down—are handled in Fireworks as separate *frames*. As with an animated GIF, each frame is the same dimensions as the document, but the content is slightly altered to indicate the separate user actions. For example, Figure 8-13 shows the different frames states of a rollover button, side-by-side.

Tip Many Web designers use just the initial two states—Up and Over—in their rollover buttons. The third state, Down, takes place when the user clicks the button, and is useful if you want to indicate that moment to the user. The Down state also indicates which button has been selected (is "down") when a new page appears but the same navigation bar is used. The fourth state, Over Down, is called when the previously selected button is rolled over by the user's pointer.

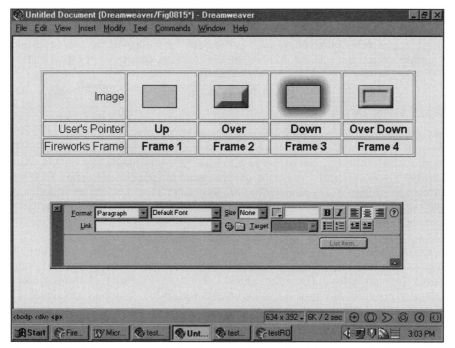

Figure 8-13: A Fireworks-created rollover can be made of four separate frames.

To insert Fireworks-created graphics using Dreamweaver behaviors, follow these steps:

1. Create your graphics in Fireworks, using a different frame for each rollover state.

2. In Fireworks 2, choose File ➪ Export Special ➪ Export as Files.

   The Export Special - Files as dialog box opens (see Figure 18-14).

3. Enter a new Base Name in the text box, if desired.

   The Base Name is used in Fireworks to name multiple images exported from a single file. When exporting frames, the default settings append "_F*n*", where *n* is the number of the frame. Frame numbers 1–10 are listed with a leading zero (for example, `MainButton_F01`).

4. In the `Files From` list box, select Frames.

5. If necessary, change the HTML Style list box option to None.

6. Select the Save button to store your frames as separate files.

Note   You can attach the rollover behaviors to your images in several ways in Dreamweaver. The following technique uses Dreamweaver 2's new Rollover object.

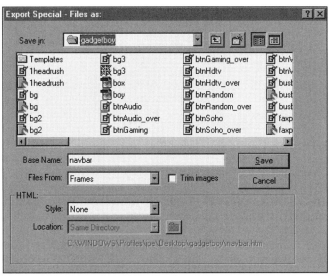

Figure 8-14: From Fireworks, you can export each frame as a separate file to be used in Dreamweaver rollovers.

7. From the Common panel of the Objects Palette, choose the Insert Rollover Image object.

8. In the Insert Rollover Image dialog box, choose the Original Image Browse (Choose) button to locate the image stored with the first frame designation, _F01.

9. If desired, give your image a different unique name than the one automatically assigned in the Image Name text box.

10. Choose the Rollover Image Browse button to locate the image stored with the second frame designation, _F02.

11. Click OK when you're done.

12. If you'd like to use the Down (_F03) and Over Down (_F04) images, attach additional swap image behaviors by opening the Swap Image behavior and following the steps outlined in Chapter 17, "Creating and Using Behaviors."

Tip Many Web designers build their entire navigation bar — complete with rollovers — in Fireworks. Rather than create and export one button at a time, all the navigation buttons are created as one graphic, and slices or hotspots are used to make the different objects or areas interact differently. You'll learn more about slices and hotspots later in this section.

Using Fireworks' code

In some ways, Fireworks is a hybrid program, capable of simultaneously outputting terrific graphics and sophisticated code. You can even select the type of code you want generated in Fireworks 2: Dreamweaver 1.2, 2 or Library compatible; or code compatible with other programs such as CyberStudio and Front Page. You'll also find a more general Generic code option as well as a native Fireworks style from which to choose. All these options are chosen during the Export procedure.

No matter which style of code you select, for rollovers Fireworks always outputs to two different sections of the HTML document, the <head> and the <body>. The <head> section contains the JavaScript code for activating the rollovers and preloading the images; the <body> contains the HTML references to the images themselves, their links, and the event triggers (onClick or onMouseOver) used.

New Feature Currently, code generated by Fireworks must be manually copied and pasted into Dreamweaver. However, with the introduction of the visual Head Elements in Dreamweaver 2, this process is greatly simplified and can be handled completely within the Document Window. The general procedure is to first create your graphics in Fireworks and then export them, simultaneously generating a page of code. Now, the page in progress as well as the just-generated Fireworks HTML page are opened in Dreamweaver. Finally, the proper <head> and <body> sections are copied, one at a time, from the Fireworks document, and pasted in the correct place in your Web page.

Just as an image requires a link to create a rollover in Dreamweaver, Fireworks images need to be designated as either a *slice* or a *hotspot*. The Fireworks program describes slices and hotspots as being part of the graphic's Web layer. The Web layer can be hidden or locked. Figure 8-15 shows the same button with both a slice and a hotspot attached.

Slices are rectangular areas that permit different areas of the same graphic to be saved as separate formats — the entire graphic is formatted as an HTML table. Each slice can also be given its own URL, and is necessary for Fireworks to attach a behavior.

A Fireworks *hotspot* is a region defined for an image map. Hotspots can be rectangular, elliptical, or polygonal — just like those created by Dreamweaver in the Image Map Editor. Because Fireworks is an object-oriented graphics program, any selected image (or part of an image) can be automatically converted to a hotspot. Like slices, hotspots can have both URLs and behaviors assigned to them.

To include Fireworks-generated code in your Dreamweaver document, first follow these steps in Fireworks:

1. Create your graphics in Fireworks 2, placing the image for each interactive state on its own frame.

   The Up state goes on Frame 1, the Over state on Frame 2, the Down state on Frame 3, and the Over Down state on Frame 4. Frames 3 and 4 are optional.

2. When the object is selected, choose Insert ⇨ Hotspot or Insert ⇨ Slice to add the item to your Web layer for attaching behaviors.

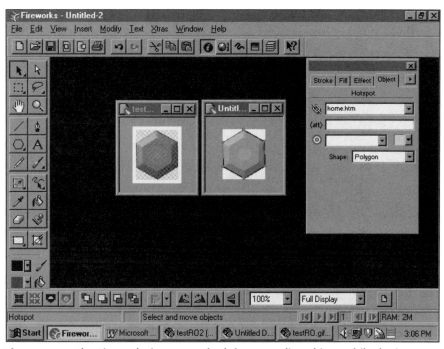

Figure 8-15: The Fireworks image on the left uses a slice object, while the image on the right uses a polygon hotspot.

3. Select the hotspot or slice and use Fireworks' Object Inspector to assign an Internet address to the selected graphic.

4. Open Fireworks' Behavior Inspector, and choose the Add Behavior button (the + sign).

5. Select Simple Rollover.

Note

The Simple Rollover behavior is used create single-button or multiple-button rollovers in which one image is replaced by another image in the same location. Use Swap Image to create more complex rollovers such as those in which the rollover triggers an image change in another location.

6. To include Frame 3 (the Down state) and/or Frame 4 (the Over Down state), select their respective check-boxes in the Simple Rollover dialog box, and click OK when you're done. If you're only using two frames — the Up and Down states — just click OK.

7. Export the object by choosing File ➪ Export. After making any necessary alterations in the Export Preview dialog box, click the Next button.

8. From the Export dialog box, enter a name in the Base Name text box and choose Use Slice Objects or Slice Along Guides from the Slices drop-down list.

9. Select the type of HTML code from the Style drop-down list.

Caution   If your rollovers are going into layers, it's best to export them from Fireworks using either the Fireworks or Generic style. Just as internal Dreamweaver rollovers, once created, cannot be cut-and-pasted into layers, Dreamweaver-style code generated by Fireworks won't work if inserted into a layer.

10. Click Save when you're done.

When Fireworks completes the exporting, you'll have one HTML file and one object file for each frame. Now you're ready to integrate these images and files into your Dreamweaver page. Figure 8-16 shows a page with both a sliced object and a hotspot rollover inserted.

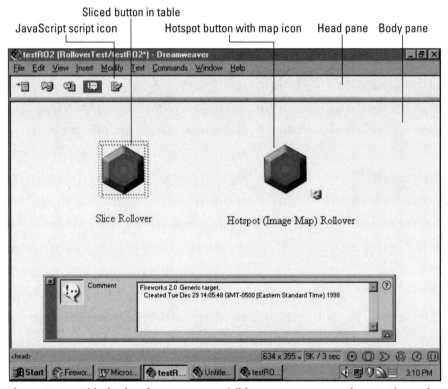

Figure 8-16: With the head content now visible, you can copy-and-paste Fireworks-generated code without opening the HTML Inspector.

To insert the Fireworks code and images into your Dreamweaver page, follow these steps:

1. Open both the Fireworks-created HTML and your current Web page in Dreamweaver.

2. From the Fireworks-created page, choose View ⇨ Head Content.

   The Head pane opens, revealing icons for the various HTML `<head>` tags.

3. Select the last Script icon in the Head pane.

Tip   If you have multiple Script icons, it's a good idea to verify you've got the Fireworks-generated code. Select the Comment icon just before the Script—you should see the Fireworks 2.0 name now in the Property Inspector.

4. Choose Edit ⇨ Copy or use the keyboard shortcut, Ctrl-C (Command-C).

5. Switch to the Dreamweaver window with the Web page in which you want to insert the rollover buttons.

6. Click in the Head pane to activate it.

   The Head pane background turns from gray to white.

7. Choose Edit ⇨ Paste or use the keyboard shortcut, Ctrl-V (Command-V).

   Now that you've copied and pasted the JavaScript code for the buttons, you need to repeat the procedure for the images themselves.

8. Switch to the Dreamweaver window with the Fireworks-generated code.

Note   Be sure that View ⇨ Invisible Elements is enabled so you can see the necessary icons.

9. Select the rollover button to be inserted, in one of two ways:

   • If you're inserting a rollover created with sliced objects, select the entire `<table>` surrounding the graphic.

   • If you're inserting a rollover created with hotspots, select the image and the `<map>` icon next to it.

10. Choose Edit ⇨ Copy or use the keyboard shortcut, Ctrl-C (Command-C).

11. Switch to the Dreamweaver window with the Web page in which you want to insert the rollover buttons.

12. Position your cursor in the Body pane wherever you'd like the button to appear.

13. Choose Edit ⇨ Paste or use the keyboard shortcut, Ctrl-V (Command-V), to insert the button.

While this is a long procedure to follow for a single rollover button, you'll really save time when you build your entire navigation system in Fireworks. Then, you can copy-and-paste the entire navigation bar as a single unit. Moreover, the same copy-and-paste technique can be used for integrating Fireworks-generated graphics that have been sliced or which use image maps without involving rollovers.

Tip   You can also use the HTML Inspector to copy-and-paste the JavaScript and HTML code. If you do, you'll find helpful comments in the Fireworks file such as "Begin copying here" and "Stop copying here."

Summary

In this chapter you learned how to include both foreground and background images in Dreamweaver. Understanding how images are handled in HTML is an absolute necessity for the Web designer. Some of the key points follow:

✦ Web pages are restricted to using specific graphic formats. Virtually all browsers support GIF and JPEG files. A relatively new format, PNG, is rapidly gaining acceptance. Dreamweaver can preview all three image types.

✦ Images are inserted in the foreground in Dreamweaver through the Insert Image command of the Objects Palette. Once the graphic is inserted, almost all modifications can be handled through the Property Inspector.

✦ You can use HTML's background image function to lay a full-frame image or a tiled series of the same image underneath your text and graphics. Tiled images can be employed to create columns and other designs with small files.

✦ The simplest HTML graphic is the built-in horizontal rule. Useful for dividing your Web page into separate sections, you can size the horizontal rule either absolutely or relatively.

✦ Dreamweaver 2 introduces a new object: the Rollover Image. With the Rollover Image, you can easily insert simple rollovers that use two different images. To build a rollover that uses more than two images, you have to use the Swap Image behavior.

✦ Animated images can be inserted alongside, and in the same manner as, still graphics. The individual frames of a GIF animation must be created in a graphics program and then combined in an animation program.

✦ With the release of Fireworks 2, images can now be optimized from within Dreamweaver 2. Moreover, it's easier to integrate code generated from Fireworks — and you can even specify Dreamweaver-style HTML.

In the next chapter, you learn how to use hyperlinks in Dreamweaver.

✦   ✦   ✦

Establishing Web Links

In This Chapter

All about Internet addresses

Linking Web pages

Pointing to a file

Creating anchors within Web pages

URL targeting

To me, links *are* the Web. Everything else about the medium can be replicated in another form, but without links there would be no World Wide Web. As your Web design work becomes more sophisticated, you'll find more enhanced uses for links: sending mail, connecting to an FTP site — even downloading software. In this chapter, you learn how Dreamweaver helps you manage the various types of links, set anchors within documents to get smooth and accurate navigation, and establish targets for your URLs. But first, let's begin with an overview on Internet addresses to give you the full picture of the possibilities.

Understanding URLs

URL stands for Uniform Resource Locator. An awkward phrase, it nonetheless describes itself well — the URL's function is to provide a standard method for finding anything on the Internet. From Web pages to newsgroups to the smallest graphic on the most esoteric of pages, everything can be referenced through the URL system.

The URL can use up to six different parts, although all parts are not necessary for the URL to be read. Each part is separated by some combination of a slash, colon, and hash mark delimiter. When entered as a attribute's value, the entire URL is generally enclosed within quotes to ensure that the address is read as one unit. A generic URL using all the parts looks like the following:

```
method://server:port/path/file#anchor
```

Here's a real-world example that also uses every section:

```
http://www.idest.com:80/dreamweaver/index
.htm#bible
```

In order of appearance in the body of an Internet address, left to right, the parts denote the following:

✦ **The method used to access the resource.** The method to address Web servers is the HyperText Transport Protocol (HTTP). Other methods are discussed later in this section.

✦ **The name of the server providing the resource.** The server can either be a domain name (with or without the "www" prefix) or an Internet Protocol (IP) address such as 199.227.52.143.

✦ **The port number to be used on the server.** Most URLs do not include a port number, which is analogous to a telephone extension number on the server, because most servers use the defaults.

✦ **The directory path to the resource.** Depending on where the resource (for example, the Web page) is located on the server, the following paths can be specified: no path (indicating that the resource is in the public root of the server), a single folder name, or a number of folders and subfolders.

✦ **The file name of the resource.** If the file name is omitted, the Web browser looks for a default page, often named index.html or index.htm. The browser reacts differently depending on the type of file. For example, GIFs and JPEGs are displayed by themselves; executable files are downloaded.

✦ **The named anchor in the HTML document.** This part is another optional section. The named anchor enables the Web designer to send the viewer to a particular section of an HTML page.

Because it is used to communicate with servers, the HTTP access method is far and away the most prevalent method on today's World Wide Web. In addition to the HTTP access method, other methods connect with other types of servers. Table 9-1 discusses some of these options.

<table>
<tr><th colspan="3">Table 9-1
Various Internet Access Methods and Protocols</th></tr>
<tr><th>*Name*</th><th>*Syntax*</th><th>*Usage*</th></tr>
<tr><td>File Transfer Protocol</td><td>ftp://</td><td>Links to an FTP server that is generally used for the uploading and downloading of files. The server can be accessed anonymously, or it may require a user name and password.</td></tr>
<tr><td>Gopher</td><td>gopher://</td><td>Connects to a directory tree structure primarily used for disseminating all-text documents.</td></tr>
<tr><td>HyperText Transfer Protocol</td><td>http://</td><td>Used for connecting to a document available on a World Wide Web server.</td></tr>
</table>

Name	Syntax	Usage
Mailto	mailto:	Opens an e-mail form with the recipient's address already filled in. These links are useful when embedded in your Web pages to provide visitors with an easy feedback method.
News	news:	Connects to the specified Usenet newsgroup. Newsgroups are public, theme-oriented message boards where anyone can post or reply to a message.
Telnet	telnet://	Enables users to log directly on to remote host computers and interact directly with the operating system software.

Part of the richness of today's Web browsers stems from their capability to connect with all the preceding (and additional) services.

Tip

Not only does the mailto: access method enable you to open up a preaddressed e-mail form, you can also specify the topic with a little extra work. For example, if Joe Lowery wants to include a link to his e-mail address with the subject heading "Dreamweaver Bible," he can insert a link like the following:

```
mailto:jlowery@idest.com?subject=Bible Feedback
```

The question mark acts as a delimiter that enables a variable and a value to be passed to the browser. When you're trying to encourage feedback from your Web page visitors, every little bit helps. A note of caution: This method is not standardized HTML and, while it works with most browsers and mail programs, you could get unexpected results with some systems.

Surfing the Web with Hypertext

Most often, you'll be assigning a link to a word or phrase on your page, an image such as a navigation button, or a section of graphic for an image map (a large graphic in which various parts are links). Once you have created the link, you have to preview it in a browser; links are not active in Dreamweaver's document window.

Designate links in HTML through the anchor tag pair: <a> and </a>. The anchor tag generally takes one main attribute—the hypertext reference—which is written as follows:

```
href="link name"
```

When you create a link in Dreamweaver, the anchor pair surrounds the text or object that is being linked. For example, if you link the phrase "Back to Home Page," it may look like the following:

```
<a href="index.html">Back to Home Page</a>
```

When you attach a link to an image, logo.gif, your code looks as follows:

```
<a href="home.html"><img src="images/logo.gif"></a>
```

Creating a basic link in Dreamweaver is easy. Simply follow these steps:

1. Select the text, image, or object you want to establish as a link.

2. In the Property Inspector, enter the URL in the Link text box as shown in Figure 9-1. You can either:

   • Type the URL directly into the Link text box.

   • Select the folder icon next to the Link text box to open the Select HTML File dialog box, where you can browse for the file.

   • Select the Point to File icon and drag your mouse to a existing page or link. This feature, new in Dreamweaver 2.0, is explained later in this section.

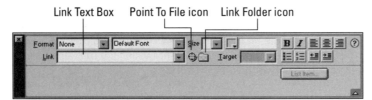

Figure 9-1: You can enter your link directly into the Link text box, select the folder icon to browse for a file or point to it directly in Dreamweaver 2.0.

Only a few restrictions exist for specifying linked URLs. Dreamweaver does not support any letters from the extended character set (also known as High ASCII), such as ¡, à, or ñ. Complete URLs must have fewer than a total of 255 characters. You should be cautious about using spaces in path names and, thus, URLs. Although most browsers can interpret the address, spaces are changed to a %20 symbol for proper UNIX usage, which can make your URLs difficult to read.

Links Without Underscores

To remove the underlined aspect of a link, you can use one of two methods. The classic method — which works for all graphics-capable browsers — uses an image rather than text as the link. You must make sure the border attribute of your image is set to 0, because a linked image usually displays a blue border if a border attribute exists.

The second, newer method uses Cascading Style Sheets. While this is an excellent one-stop solution, bear in mind that these can be read only by the more recent browser versions (generally 4.0 and higher). Refer to the Dreamweaver Technique for eliminating the underlines in links in Chapter 24, "Building Style Sheet Web Pages."

Note

White space in your HTML usually doesn't have an adverse effect. Netscape browsers are sensitive to white space when assigning a link to an image, however. If you isolate your image tag from the anchor tags as in the following example:

```
<a href="index.htm">
<img src="images/Austria.gif" width="34" height="24">
</a>
```

Netscape attaches a small blue underscore — a tail, really — to your image. Because Dreamweaver codes the anchor tag properly, without any additional white space, this odd case only applies to hand-coded or previously coded HTML.

Text links are most often rendered with a blue color and underlined. You can alter the document link color by choosing Modify ⇨ Page Properties and selecting the Link Color swatch. In Page Properties, you can also alter the color to which the links change after being selected (the Visited Link Color) and the color flashed when the link is clicked (the Active Link Color).

Tip

Want to add a little variety to your text links? You can actually change the color of the link on an individual basis. To do this, you have to apply the color before you enter the link in the Property Inspector. Be sure to exercise a little discretion though — you don't want to use so many different colors that your Web page visitors can't figure out the navigation.

Pointing to a file

Dreamweaver 2.0 introduces a new method of identifying a link — pointing to it.

By using the new Point to File icon on the Property Inspector, you can quickly fill in the Link text box by dragging your mouse to any existing named anchor or file visible in the Dreamweaver environment. The Point to File enhancement saves you from having to browse through folder after folder as you search for a file you can clearly see onscreen.

You can point to a file in another open Dreamweaver window or one in another frame in the same window. If your desired link is a named anchor located further down the page, Dreamweaver will automatically scroll to find it. You can even point to a named anchor in another page and Dreamweaver will enter the full syntax correctly. Named anchors are covered in detail later in this chapter.

Perhaps one of the slickest applications of the Point to File icon is when it is used in tandem with the Site FTP Window. The Site FTP Window lists all the existing files in any given Web site, and when both it and the Document Window are onscreen, you can quickly point to any file.

For more details about using the Site FTP Window in this fashion, see Chapter 33, "Publishing Via Site FTP."

Pointing to a file uses what could be called a "drag-and-release" mouse technique, as opposed to the more ordinary point-and-click or drag-and-drop method. To select a new link using the Point to File icon, follow these steps:

1. Select the text or the graphic that you'd like to make into a link.

2. In the Property Inspector, click the Point to File icon located to the right of the Link text box.

3. Holding down the mouse button, drag the mouse until it is over an existing link or named anchor in the Document Window or a file in the Site FTP window.

    As you drag the mouse, a line extends from the Point to File icon and the reminder "Point to a file to make a link" appears in the Link text box.

4. When you locate the file you want to link to, release the mouse button. The file name with the accompanying path information is written into the Link text box as shown in Figure 9.2.

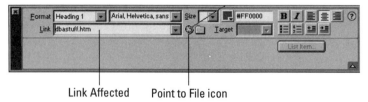

Link Affected   Point to File icon

Figure 9-2: The Point to File capability lets you quickly insert a link to any onscreen page.

Addressing types

As you learned in Chapter 5, "Setting Up Your First Site," three types of URLs are used as links: absolute addresses, document relative addresses, and site root relative addresses. Let's briefly recap these address types.

✦ Absolute addresses require the full URL, as follows:

```
http://www.macromedia.com/software/dreamweaver/
```

This type is most often used for referencing links on another Web server.

✦ Document relative addresses know the method, server, and path aspects of the URL. You only need to include additional path information if the link is outside of the current Web page's folder. Links in the current document's folder can be addressed with their filename only. To reference an item in a subfolder, just name the folder, enter a forward slash, and then enter the item's filename, as follows:

```
images/background.gif
```

✦ Site root relative addresses are indicated with a leading forward slash. For example:

```
/upndown.html
```

The preceding address links to a file named upndown.html stored in the primary directory of the current site. Links using site root relative addresses must be saved on a Web server in order to be previewed.

New Feature
A Webmaster must often perform the tedious but necessary task of verifying the links on all the Web pages in a site. Because of the Web's fluid nature, links can work one day and then be broken the next. Dreamweaver has enhanced its powerful link-checking abilities in 2.0 with link updating features. To find out how to keep your site up-to-date with a minimum of effort, see Chapter 33, "Publishing via Site FTP."

Navigating with Anchors

Whenever you normally link to an HTML page, through absolute or relative addressing, the browser displays the page from the top. Your Web visitors must scroll to any information rendered below the current screen. One HTML technique, however, links to a specific point anywhere on your page regardless of the display window's contents. This technique uses *named anchors*.

Using named anchors is a two-step process. First you place a named anchor somewhere on your Web page. This placement is coded in HTML as an anchor tag using the name attribute, with nothing in between the opening and closing tags. In HTML, named anchors look like the following:

```
<a name="top"></a>
```

The second step includes a link to that named anchor from somewhere else on your Web page. If used, a named anchor is referenced in the final possible portion of an Internet address, designated by the hash mark (#), as follows:

```
<a href="http://www.idest.com/dreamweaver/index.htm#bible>
```

You can include any number of named anchors on the current page or another page. Named anchors are commonly used with a table of contents or index.

To insert a named anchor in Dreamweaver, follow these steps:

1. Place the cursor where you want the named anchor to appear.

2. Choose Insert ⇨ Named Anchor. You can also select the Insert Named Anchor button from the Invisibles panel of the Objects Palette.

3. The Named Anchor dialog box (shown in Figure 9-3) opens. Type the anchor name into the text box.

Caution   Named anchors are case-sensitive and must be unique.

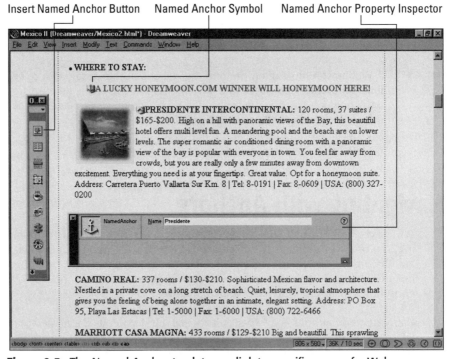

Figure 9-3: The Named Anchor tag lets you link to specific areas of a Web page.

When you press Enter (Return), Dreamweaver places a Named Anchor symbol in the current cursor location and opens the Named Anchor Property Inspector.

4. To change an anchor's name, click the Named Anchor symbol within the page and alter the text in the Property Inspector.

As with other invisible symbols, the Named Anchor symbol can be cut and pasted or moved using the drag-and-drop method.

Moving within the same document

One of the major advantages of using named anchors is the almost instantaneous response the viewer receives when they click them. The browser only needs to scroll to the particular place in the document, because the entire page is loaded. For long text documents, this capability is an invaluable timesaver.

Once you have placed a named anchor in your document — or all of them at once — you can link to these anchors. Follow these steps to create a link to a named anchor in the same document:

1. Select the text or image that you want to designate as a link.

2. In the Link text box of the Property Inspector, type a hash mark, #, followed by the exact anchor name. For example:

`#top`

Remember, anchor names are case-sensitive and must be unique in each document.

 Tip

You should place the named anchor one line above the heading or image to which you want to link the viewer. Browsers tend to be quite literal. If you place the named anchor on the same line, the browser renders it up against the top of the window. Placing your named anchor up one line gives your topic a bit of breathing room in the display.

In Dreamweaver 2.0, you can also use the Point to File icon to choose a named anchor link. If your named anchor is in the same document, just drag the Point to File icon to the named anchor symbol. When you release the mouse, the proper named anchor is inserted into the Link text box. If the named anchor is on the same page but offscreen, Dreamweaver automatically scrolls the Document Window as you approach the edge. In Windows, the closer you move to the edge, the faster Dreamweaver scrolls. Dreamweaver will even return the screen to your original location, with the new link at the top of the screen, after you release the mouse button.

In long documents with a table of contents or index linking to a number of named anchors, it's common practice — and a good idea — to place a link back to the top of the page after every screen or every topic. This technique enables your users to return to the menu quickly and pick another topic without having to scroll all the way back manually.

Using named anchors in a different page

If your table of contents is on a separate page from the topics of your site, you can use named anchors to send the viewer anywhere on a new page. The technique is exactly the same as already explained for placing named anchors, but there is one minor difference when it comes to linking. Instead of placing a hash mark and name to denote the named anchor, you must first include the URL of the linked page.

Let's say you want to call the disclaimer section of a legal page from your table of contents. You could insert something like the following in the Link text box of the Property Inspector:

```
legal.htm#disclaimer
```

This link, when activated, first loads the referenced Web page (legal.htm) and then goes directly to the named anchor place (#disclaimer). Figure 9-4 shows how you would enter this in the Property Inspector. Keep in mind, you can use any form of addressing prior to the hash mark and named anchor.

Figure 9-4: You can also link to any part of a separate Web page using named anchors.

Tip   One of the more obscure uses for named anchors comes into play when you are trying to use Dreamweaver's JavaScript Behavior feature. Because JavaScript needs to work with a particular type of tag to perform `mouseOver` and other events, one trick marks some text or image with a link to #nowhere. You can use any name for the nonexistent named anchor. In fact, you don't even have to use a name — you can just use a hash mark by itself ("#").

Targeting Your Links

Thus far, all of this chapter's links have had a similar effect: they open another Web page or section in your browser's window. What if you want to force the browser to open another window and load that new URL in the new window? HTML lets you specify the target for your links.

Targets are most often used in conjunction with frames — that is, you can make a link in one frame open a file in another. (Chapter 14, "Using Frames and Framesets," covers the subject of frames in depth.) Here, though, let's take a look at one of the HTML predefined targets useful in a situation where you want to load another URL into a new window:

To specify a new browser window as the target for a link in Dreamweaver, follow these steps:

1. Select the text or image you want to designate as your new link.

2. In the Property Inspector, enter the URL into the Link text box.

After you've entered a link, the target option becomes active.

3. Choose the option button next to the Target list box and select "_blank" from the drop-down list. You can also type it in the list box.

Dreamweaver inserts a "_blank" option in the Target list box, as shown in Figure 9-5. Now, when your link is activated, the browser spawns a new window and loads the referenced link into it. The user has both windows available.

Figure 9-5: You can force a user's browser to open a separate window to display a specific link with the Target command.

The _blank target is most often used when the originating Web page is acting as a jump station and has numerous links available. By keeping the original Web page open, the user can check out one site without losing the origin point.

You can even use the _blank target technique on named anchors in the same document, thereby emulating frames to some degree.

Caution   Some key online services, such as America Online and WebTV don't enable their built-in browsers to open new windows. Every link that is accessed is displayed in the same browser window.

Summary

Whether they are links for Web site navigation or jumps to other related sites, hypertext links are an essential part of any Web page. Dreamweaver gives you full control over your inserted anchors.

✦ Through a unique URL, you can access virtually any Web page, graphic, or other item available on the Internet.

✦ The HyperText Transfer Protocol (HTTP) is the most common method of Web connection, but Web pages can link to most other formats, including FTP, e-mail, and newsgroups.

✦ Any of the three basic address formats — absolute, document relative, or site root relative — can be inserted in the Link text box of Dreamweaver's Property Inspector to create a link.

✦ Dreamweaver 2.0 adds a quick linking capability with its Point to File feature.

✦ Named anchors give you the power to jump to specific parts of any Web page, whether the page is the current one or located on another server.

✦ With the _blank target attribute, you can force a link to open in a new browser window, leaving your original window available to the user.

In the next chapter, you'll learn how to use various types of lists in Dreamweaver.

✦   ✦   ✦

Creating Lists

Lists serve several different functions in all publications, including Web pages. A list can itemize a topic's points or catalog the properties of an object. A numbered list is helpful for giving step-by-step instructions. From a page designer's point of view, a list can break up the page and simultaneously draw the viewer's eye to key details.

Lists are an important alternative to the basic textual tools of paragraphs and headings. In this chapter, you study Dreamweaver's tools for designing and working with each of the three basic types of lists available under HTML:

    ✦ Unordered lists

    ✦ Ordered lists

    ✦ Definition lists

The various list types can also be combined to create outlines. Dreamweaver supplies a straightforward method for building these *nested lists*.

Creating Bulleted (Unordered) Lists

What word-processing programs and layout artists refer to as bulleted lists are known in HTML as *unordered lists*. An unordered list is used when the sequence of the listed items is unimportant, as in a recipe's list of ingredients. Each unordered list item is set off by a leading character, and the remainder of the line is indented. By default, the leading character is the bullet; in HTML, you also can specify two other symbols by conventional means, and a custom bullet through Cascading Style Sheets.

You can either create the unordered list from scratch or convert existing text into the bulleted format.

To begin an unordered list from scratch, position the cursor where you want to start the list. Then click the Unordered List button supplied conveniently on the Text Property Inspector (see Figure 10-1), or use the Text ⇨ List ⇨ Unordered List command.

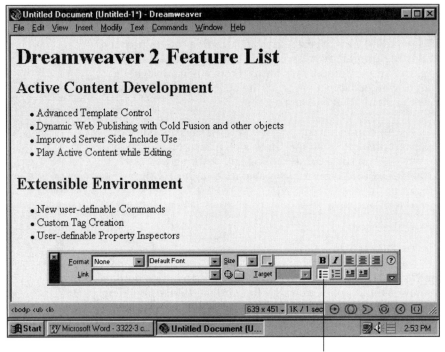

Unordered list button

Figure 10-1: An itemized list that doesn't need to be in any specific order is perfect for formatting as an unordered list.

If you are changing existing text into a list, select the paragraphs first and then execute the Unordered List button or menu command.

Dreamweaver creates one list item for every paragraph. As you can see from Figure 10-1, list items are generally rendered closer together than regular paragraphs. Unlike block elements such as paragraphs or headings, HTML doesn't insert additional lines above and space below each line of a list.

Caution

In terms of lists in Dreamweaver, the word *paragraph* is used literally to mean any text designated with a paragraph tag. Certainly you can apply a heading format to an HTML list, but you probably won't like the results: the heading format reinserts those additional lines below and above each list item—the ones generally not used by the list format. If you want your list items to appear larger in size, you should change the font size through the Property Inspector or with Text ⇨ Size Increase.

Editing unordered lists

Once a series of paragraphs is formatted as an unordered list, you can easily add additional bulleted items. The basic editing techniques are the same for all types of lists:

✦ To continue adding items at the end of a list, simply press Enter (Return) to create each new paragraph. Another bullet is inserted.

✦ To insert an item in an unordered list, place your cursor at the end of the item above the desired position for the added item, and press Enter (Return).

✦ List items can be copied or cut and pasted in a different place on the list. Place your cursor in front of the list item below where you want the repositioned item to appear, and choose Edit ⇨ Paste.

✦ To end a bulleted list, you can press Enter (Return) twice, or deselect the Unordered List button on the Text Property Inspector.

List tags

You may occasionally need to tweak your list code by hand. Two HTML tags are used in creating an unordered list. The first is the outer tag, which defines the type of list; the second is the item delimiter. Unordered lists are designated with the ⟨ul⟩...⟨/ul⟩ tag pair, and the delimiter is the ⟨li⟩...⟨/li⟩ pair. The unordered list code in the HTML Inspector looks like the following:

```
<ul>
   <li>Cascading Style Sheet Support</li>
   <li>Roundtrip HTML</li>
   <li>JavaScript Behaviors</li>
   <li>Repeatable Library Elements</li>
</ul>
```

If a list item is too long to fit in a single line, the browser indents the line when it wraps. By inserting a line break code, you can emulate this behavior even when you're working with lines that aren't long enough to need wrapping. To insert a line break, choose the Insert Line Break button from the Invisibles panel of the Objects Palette, or select Insert ➪ Line Break. Figure 10-2 shows examples of both approaches: the long paragraph that wraps naturally and the inserted line breaks to force the wrapping.

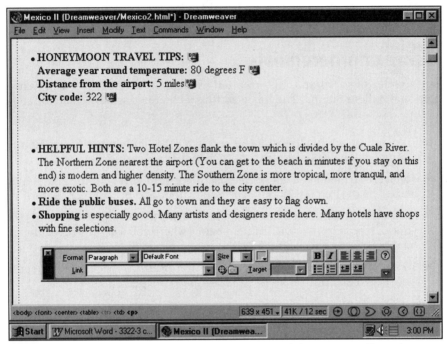

Figure 10-2: A list is indented if the text wraps around the screen or if you insert a line break.

Using other bullet symbols

Although HTML doesn't include a wide range of different symbols to use in an unordered list, you have a few options. Most browsers recognize three different bullet styles: bullet (the default), circle, and square. You can apply the style to the entire unordered list or to one list item at a time.

To change the bullet style of the overall unordered list, follow these steps:

1. Position your cursor anywhere in an existing list.

2. If necessary, click the expander arrow on the Text Property Inspector to display the additional options. Click the List Item button.

3. In the List Properties dialog box that appears (see Figure 10-3), open the Style options list.

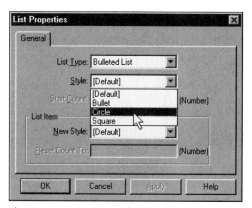

Figure 10-3: You can change the style of the entire list or just one list item through the List Properties dialog box.

4. Select one of the four options:

- **[Default]:** No style is listed and the browser applies its default, usually rendered as a bullet.

- **Bullet:** A solid circle

- **Circle:** An open circle

- **Square:** A solid square

5. Click OK.

Caution If you find the List Item button inactive in your Text Property Inspector, make sure that you have — at most — one list item selected. Selecting more than one list item deactivates the List Item button.

When you try to change the style of just one list item, Dreamweaver alters all the successive list items as well. By default, list items don't specify a bullet style. Therefore, when a new style is inserted, all the following items adopt that style.

When you need to change the bullet style of just one item in a list, follow these steps:

1. Select the list item you wish to change.

2. Make sure the Text Property Inspector is expanded, and select the List Item button.

3. From the List Properties dialog box, in the List Item section, open the New Style drop-down list.

4. Select one of the four bullet options (described in the preceding steps).

You can alter the type of bullet used in two other ways. The time-tested solution substitutes a graphic for the bullet. Just as with graphical horizontal rules, the Web offers a substantial clip art collection of bullets. You have to insert a graphic for each bullet, however. The quickest method is the drag-and-drop copy technique: Hold down the Ctrl (Command) key and then click and drag the bullet graphic — this sequence places a copy of the bullet wherever you release the mouse.

The newer technique for installing bullet styles uses style sheets. Style sheets can switch a list or list item's bullet style just as using the List Properties dialog box can, but with a style sheet you can perform one additional task. You can assign the bullet style type to a specific file — in other words, you can customize your bullet image. The drawback to using this technique is that the list aspect of style sheets is currently only supported by Internet Explorer 4.0. Netscape browsers display the regular bullet symbol.

Cascading Style Sheets are covered in depth in Chapter 24. Here is a brief version of the steps for using a style sheet to assign a new bullet symbol:

1. Select the Style Palette button from the Launcher or choose Window ⇨ Styles.

2. In the Style Inspector, select the Style Sheet button.

3. In the Edit Style Sheet dialog box, select the New button.

4. In the New Style dialog box, choose the Redefine HTML Tag radio button.

5. From the option list, choose the li tag and click OK.

6. In the Style Definition dialog box that appears (see Figure 10-4), choose List in the Category list.

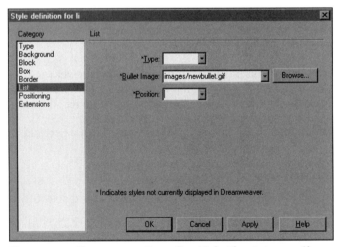

Figure 10-4: You can use Cascading Style Sheets to specify a bullet image for your Web page.

7. Find your graphics file by clicking the Browse button next to the Button Image text box.

8. Click OK, and then click Done in the Edit Style Sheet dialog box.

Note   Your newly defined bullet image doesn't preview in Dreamweaver, but you can view it in Internet Explorer 4.0.

Mastering Numbered (Ordered) Lists

Unlike a bulleted list, in which sequence is not vital, order is important in the numbered list. This relationship translates in HTML as "the opposite of an unordered list is an ordered list." The major advantage of an ordered list is the automatic generation of list item numbers and automatic renumbering when you're editing. If you've ever had to renumber a legal document because paragraph 14.b. became paragraph 2.a., then you recognize the timesaving benefits of this feature.

Ordered lists offer a slightly wider variety of built-in styles than unordered lists, but you cannot customize the leading character further. For instance, you cannot surround a character with parentheses or offset it with a dash. Once again, the browser is the final arbiter of how your list is viewed.

Many of the same techniques used with unordered lists work with ordered lists. To start a new numbered list in Dreamweaver, place your cursor where you want the new list to begin. Then, in the Text Property Inspector, select the Ordered List button or choose Text ➪ List ➪ Ordered List.

As with unordered lists, you can also convert existing paragraphs into a numbered list. First select your text, and then select either the Ordered List button or the Text ➪ List ➪ Ordered List command.

As shown in Figure 10-5, the default numbering system is Arabic numerals: 1, 2, 3, and so forth. In the following section, you learn how to alter this default.

Editing ordered lists

The HTML code for an ordered list is `<ol>`. Both the `<ol>` and the `<ul>` use the list item tag, `<li>`, to mark individual entries, and Dreamweaver handles the formatting identically:

```
<ol>
  <li>Stir in two sets of venetian blinds.</li>
  <li>Add one slowly rotating ceiling fan.</li>
  <li>Combine one flashing neon sign with one dangling light
bulb.</li>
  <li>Toss in 150 cubic yards of fog.</li>
  <li></li>
</ol>
```

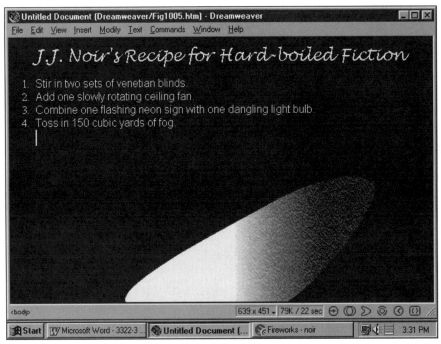

Figure 10-5: Ordered lists are used on this page to create a numbered sequence.

The empty list item pair, `<li></li>`, is displayed on the page as the next number in sequence.

Modifications to an ordered list are handled in the same manner as for an unordered list. The results are far more dramatic, however.

✦ To continue adding to the sequence of numbers, position your cursor at the end of the last item and press Enter (Return). The next number in sequence is generated, and any styles in use (such as font size or name) are carried over.

✦ To insert a new item in the list, put your cursor at the end of the item above where the new item will be positioned, and press Enter (Return). Dreamweaver inserts a new number in sequence and automatically renumbers the following numbers.

✦ To rearrange a numbered list, highlight the entire list item you want to move. Using the drag-and-drop method, release the mouse when your cursor is at the front of the item below the new location for the moved item.

✦ To end an item in a numbered list, press Enter (Return) twice or press Enter (Return) and deselect the Ordered List button.

Using other numbering styles

In all, you can apply five different numbering styles to your numbered lists:

- ✦ **Arabic numerals (the default):** 1, 2, 3, and so forth.
- ✦ **Roman Small:** i, ii, iii, and so forth.
- ✦ **Roman Large:** I, II, III, and so forth.
- ✦ **Alphabet Small:** a, b, c, and so forth.
- ✦ **Alphabet Large:** A, B, C, and so forth.

You can restyle your entire list all at once, or you can just change a single list item. To change the style of the entire ordered list, follow these steps:

1. Position your cursor anywhere in an existing list.

2. If necessary, click the expander arrow on the Text Property Inspector to display the additional options. Select the List Item button.

   The List Properties dialog box opens, with Numbered List showing as the List Type.

3. Open the drop-down list of Style options and choose any of the five preceding numbering types.

4. Click OK.

As with unordered lists, when you modify the style of one ordered list item, all the subsequent items adopt that style. To alter the style of a single and all subsequent items, follow these steps:

1. Select the item you wish to change.

2. In the expanded portion of the Text Property Inspector, select the List Item button.

3. In the List Properties dialog box from the List Item section, open the New Style list of options.

4. Select one of the five numbering options.

Cross-Reference Although you can't automatically generate an outline with a different numbering system for each level, you can simulate this kind of outline with nested lists. See "Using Nested Lists" later in this chapter.

Making Definition Lists

A definition list is another list in HTML that doesn't use leading characters, such as bullets or numbers, in the list items. Definition lists are commonly used in glossaries or other types of documents in which you have a list of terms followed by their description or explanation.

Browsers generally render a definition list with the definition term flush left and the definition data indented, as shown in Figure 10-6. As you can see, no additional styling is added. You can, however, format either the item or the definition with the Text ➪ Style options.

To begin your definition list in Dreamweaver, follow these steps:

1. Choose Text ➪ List ➪ Definition List.

2. Type in the definition term and press Enter (Return) when you are finished. Dreamweaver indents the line.

3. Type in the definition data and press Enter (Return) when you are finished.

4. Repeat Steps 2 and 3 until you have finished your definition list.

5. Press Enter (Return) twice to stop entering definition list items.

Tip If you have an extended definition, you may want to format it in more than one paragraph. Because definition lists are formatted with the terms and their definition data in alternating sequence, you have to use the line break tag, `<br>`, to create blank space under the definition if you want to separate it into paragraphs. Select the Insert Line Break button from the Objects Palette to enter one or two `<br>` tags to separate paragraphs with one or two additional lines.

When you insert a definition list, Dreamweaver denotes it in code using the `<dl>`...`</dl>` tag pair. Definition terms are marked with a `<dt>` tag, and definition data uses the `<dd>` tag. A complete definition list looks like the following in HTML:

```
<dl>
  <dt>Capital</dt>
  <dd>Sum owed by a business to its owners. See Owner's
Equity.</dd>
  <dt>Cash</dt>
  <dd>Total of currency, coins, money orders, checks, bank
drafts, and letters
    of credit the firm has on hand or in bank accounts from
which money can be
    drawn immediately.</dd>
  <dt>Cash Payments Journal</dt>
  <dd>Journal for recording payments made in cash.</dd>
</dl>
```

Definition
data

Definition
term

Figure 10-6: Definition lists are ideal for glossaries or other situations in which you
have a list of terms followed by their definition.

When originally proposed by the World Wide Web Consortium, the `<dt>` column
was intended to take up only one-third of the browser window, but the latest, most
common browsers don't follow this design specification.

Tip   You can vary the structure of a definition list from the standard definition term followed by the definition data format, but you have to code this variation by hand.
For instance, if you want a series of consecutive terms with no definition in
between, you need to insert the `<dt>...</dt>` pairs directly in the HTML
Inspector.

Using Nested Lists

You can combine—*nest*—lists in almost any fashion. For instance, you can mix an
ordered and unordered list to create a numbered list with bulleted points. You can
have one numbered list inside of another numbered list. You can also start with one

numbering style such as Roman Large, switch to another style such as Alphabet Small, and return to Roman Large to continue the sequence (like an outline).

Dreamweaver offers an easy route for making nested lists. The Indent button in the Text Property Inspector — when used within a list — automatically creates a nested list. As an example, the ordered list in Figure 10-7 has a couple of bulleted points (or unordered list items) inserted within it. Notice how the new items are indented one level.

Follow these steps to create a nested list in Dreamweaver:

1. Select the text in an existing list that you want to reformat with a different style.

2. In the Text Property Inspector, choose the Indent button. You can also select the Text ⇨ Indent command. Dreamweaver indents the selected text and creates a separate list in the HTML code with the original list's properties.

3. Go to the List Properties dialog box and select another list type or style, as described in preceding sections.

Caution

You can unnest your list and reverse the effects of the Indent button by selecting the Outdent button in the Text Property Inspector or choosing Text ⇨ Outdent. Be careful, however, when selecting your text for this operation. When you use the mouse to perform a click-and-drag selection, Dreamweaver tends to grab the closing list item tag above your intended selection. A better way to highlight the text in this case uses the Tag Selector on the status bar. Place the cursor in the indented list you want to outdent, and choose the innermost <ol> or <ul> tag from the Tag Selector.

To examine the origins of the term nested list, take a look at the code created for this list type by Dreamweaver:

```
<ol>
  <li>Stir in two sets of venetian blinds.</li>
  <li>Add one slowly rotating ceiling fan.</li>
  <li>Combine one flashing neon sign with one dangling light
bulb.</li>
    <ul>
      <li>Use a bare bulb, preferably swinging.</li>
      <li>The neon sign should throw contrasting shadows.</li>
    </ul>
  <li>Toss in 150 cubic yards of fog.</li>
</ol>
```

Notice how the unordered tag pair, <ul>...</ul>, is completely contained between the ordered list items.

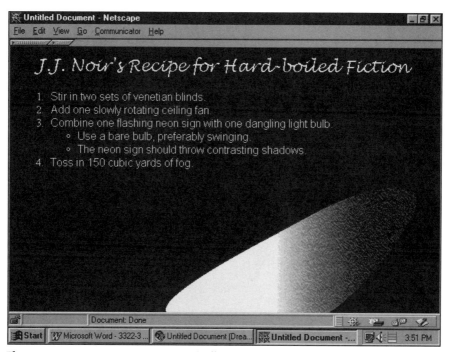

Figure 10-7: Dreamweaver automatically generates the code necessary to build nested lists when you use the Indent button on the Property Inspector.

Caution If you don't indent your list items before you change the list format, Dreamweaver breaks the current list into three separate lists: one for the original list above the selected text, another for the selected text itself, and a third list for the items following the selected text. If you don't want this arrangement, choose the Indent button in the Text Property Inspector, and Dreamweaver nests the list as described previously.

Accessing Special List Types

Dreamweaver gives you access to a couple of special-use list types: *menu lists* and *directory lists*. When the tags for these lists — `<menu>` and `<dir>`, respectively — were included in the HTML 2.0 specification, they were intended to offer several ways to present lists of short items. Unfortunately, browsers tend to render both tags in the same manner: as an unordered list. You can use Cascading Style Sheets to restyle these built-in tags for use in 4.0 and higher browsers.

Menu lists

A menu list generally comprises single items, with each item on its own individual line.

Tip

Because menu lists are rendered as unordered lists with leading bullets, you'll probably want to display the menu list in a more compact manner. Add the attribute `compact` as follows:

```
<menu compact>
```

To apply a menu list style, follow these steps:

1. In an existing list, select one item that you want to convert to a menu list.

2. In the expanded Text Property Inspector, select the List Item button.

3. In the List Properties dialog box, open the List Type drop-down list and choose Menu List, as shown in Figure 10-8.

4. Click OK.

Tip

To apply CSS techniques to either the `<menu>` or the `<dir>` tags in Dreamweaver, you must either hand-code all of the entry, or use a little trick. Here's the trick: Because Dreamweaver doesn't list the menu or directory list tags in its list of HTML tags to redefine in the New Style dialog box, type **menu** or **dir** in the list box, instead of picking it from a list. But be certain you're entering the missing tag names in the text box when Redefine HTML Tag is selected; otherwise, Dreamweaver puts a period in front of your tag name and it won't be recognized.

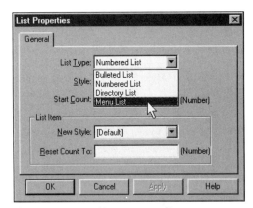

Figure 10-8: Making a menu list

Directory lists

The directory list was originally intended to provide Web designers with an easy way to create multiple-column lists of short items. Unfortunately, the most current browsers present the directory list's items in one long list, rather than in columns.

The directory list format is applied in the same way as the menu list and, here as well, most browsers render the format as an unordered list with bullets.

To apply a directory list style, follow these steps:

1. In the current list, select one item you want to convert to a directory list.
2. In the expanded Text Property Inspector, select the List Item button.
3. In the List Properties dialog box, open the List Type list (previously shown in Figure 10-8) and choose Directory List.
4. Click OK.

Tip

Nested directory lists exhibit a cool feature in most browsers — they automatically change the list style for each level. In many browsers, the outermost level is displayed with a bullet, the second level with a circle, and the third level with a square. Automatic outlining from an unexpected source! One drawback to note: Dreamweaver doesn't preview the changing styles — it only shows the bullets.

Summary

Lists are extremely useful to the Web site designer from the perspectives of both content and layout. Dreamweaver offers point-and-click control over the full range of list capabilities.

✦ The three primary list types in HTML are unordered, ordered, and definition lists.

✦ Use unordered lists when you want to itemize your text in no particular order. Dreamweaver can apply any of the three built-in styles to unordered lists or you can customize your own list style through style sheets.

✦ An ordered list is a numbered list. Items are automatically numbered when added, and the entire list is renumbered when items are rearranged or deleted. Dreamweaver gives you access to five different styles of numbering — everything from regular Arabic to Roman numerals.

✦ Definition lists are designed to display glossaries and other documents in which terms are followed by definitions. A definition list is generally rendered without leading characters such as bullets or numbers; instead, the list terms are displayed flush left, and the definitions are indented.

✦ Dreamweaver gives you the power to nest your lists at the touch of a button — the Indent button on the Text Property Inspector. Nested lists enable you to show different outline levels, and to mix ordered and unordered lists.

✦ Menu and directory lists are also supported by Dreamweaver. Both of these special lists render in a similar fashion, but they can be adapted through style sheets for extensive use.

In the next chapter, you'll learn how to create and use tables in Dreamweaver.

Incorporating Advanced HTML

Setting Up Tables

T ables bring structure to a Web page. Whether used to align numbers in a spreadsheet or to arrange columns of text on a page, an HTML table brings a bit of order to otherwise free-flowing content. Initially, tables were implemented to present raw data in a more readable format. More recently, Web designers have taken up tables as the most capable tool to control page layout.

Dreamweaver's implementation of tables reflects this current trend in Web page design. Drag-and-drop table sizing, easy organization of rows and columns, and instant table reformatting all help get the job done in the shortest time possible. The table editing features have been greatly enhanced in Dreamweaver 2 — now, you can select and modify anything in a table from a single cell to multiple columns. Moreover, Dreamweaver commands let your table be sorted in a variety of ways or completely reformatted.

Although the absolute positioning capabilities offered by Dynamic HTML give Web designers more exact layout control, many Web designers use a combination of tools to get desired effects and maintain wide browser compatibility. In other words, HTML tables are going to be around for a long time.

HTML Table Fundamentals

A table is basically a grid that expands as you add text or images. Tables consist of three main components: rows, columns, and cells. *Rows* go across a table from left to right, and *columns* go up and down. A *cell* is the intersection of a row and a column; it's where you enter your information. Cells expand to fit whatever they hold. If you have enabled the table *border*, your browser shows the outline of the table and all its cells.

In HTML, all the structure and all the data of a table are contained between the table tag pair, `<table>` and `</table>`. The `<table>` tag can take numerous attributes to affect a table's width and height (which can be given in absolute measurement or as a percentage of the screen), as well as the border, alignment on the page, and background color. You can also control the size of the spacing between cells and the amount of padding within cells.

HTML uses a strict hierarchy when describing a table. You can see this very clearly in Listing 11-1, which shows the HTML generated from a default table in Dreamweaver.

Listing 11-1: **Code for an HTML Table**

```
<table border="1" width="75%">
  <tr>
    <td> </td>
    <td> </td>
    <td> </td>
  </tr>
  <tr>
    <td> </td>
    <td> </td>
    <td> </td>
  </tr>
  <tr>
    <td> </td>
    <td> </td>
    <td> </td>
  </tr>
</table>
```

Note   The   seen in the table code is HTML for a nonbreaking space. Dreamweaver inserts the code in each empty table cell because some browsers collapse the cell without it. Enter any text or image in the cell and Dreamweaver automatically removes the   code.

Rows

After the opening `<table>` tag comes the first row tag, `<tr>`. Within the current row, you can specify attributes for horizontal alignment or vertical alignment. In addition, recent browsers recognize row color as an added option.

Cells

Cells are marked in HTML with the `<td>`...`</td>` tag pair. There is no specific code for a column; rather, columns are seen as the number of cells within a row. For example, in Listing 1-1, notice there are three sets of `<td>` tags between each `<tr>` pair. This means the table has three columns. A cell can span more than one row or column—in these cases you'll see a `rowspan=value` or `colspan=value` attribute in the `<td>` tag.

Cells can also be given horizontal or vertical alignment attributes; these attributes override any like attributes specified by the table row. When you give a cell a particular width, all the cells in that column are affected. Width can be specified in either an absolute pixel measurement or as a percentage of the overall table.

Tip

After the initial `<table>` tag, you can place an optional caption for the table. In Dreamweaver, you have to enter the `<caption>` tag by hand or through your text editor. A third option is to use the Enhanced Table Object, included on this book's CD-ROM in the Dreamweaver/Configuration/Objects/Common folder.

Column/row headings

A special type of cell called a *table header* is used for column and row headings. Information in these cells is marked with a `<th>` tag and is generally rendered in boldface, centered within the cell.

Inserting Tables in Dreamweaver

You can control almost all of a table's HTML features through Dreamweaver's point-and-click interface. To insert a Dreamweaver table in the current cursor position, use one of the following three methods:

✦ Select the Insert Table button on the Objects Palette.

✦ Choose Insert ➪ Table from the menus.

✦ Use the keyboard shortcut: Ctrl-Alt-T (Command-Option-T).

The Insert Table dialog box, shown in Figure 11-1, contains the following default values when it is first displayed:

Attribute	Default	Description
Rows	3	The number of horizontal rows
Columns	3	The number of vertical columns
Width	75%	Sets the preset width of the table. Available in a percentage of the containing element (screen, layer, or another table) or an absolute pixel size.

Continued

Attribute	Default	Description
Border	1 pixel	The width of the border around each cell and the entire table
Cell Padding	(Empty)	The space between a cell's border and its contents. Although not shown, Dreamweaver displays 1 pixel of cell padding unless a different value is entered.
Cell Spacing	(Empty)	The number of pixels between each cell. Although not shown, Dreamweaver displays 2 pixels of cell spacing unless a different value is entered.

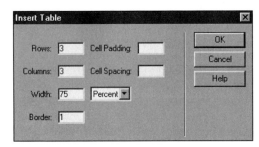

Figure 11-1: The Insert Table dialog box starts out with a default of three columns and three rows; you can adjust as needed.

If you aren't sure of the number of rows and/or columns you'll need, put in your best guess—you can add or delete rows or columns as necessary.

The default table is sized to take up 75 percent of the browser window. You can alter this percentage by changing the value in the Width text box. The table will maintain this proportion as you add text or images, except in two situations:

✦ When an image is larger than the specified percentage

✦ When the nowrap attribute is used for the cell or table row and there is too much text to fit

In either case, the percentage set for the table is ignored and the cell and table expand to accommodate the text or image. (For further information on the nowrap attribute, see "Cell wrap," later in this chapter.)

If you prefer to enter the table width as an absolute pixel value, as opposed to the relative percentage, type the number of pixels in the Width text box and select pixels in the drop-down list of width options.

Figure 11-2 shows three tables: At the top is the default table with the width set to 75 percent. The middle table, set to 100 percent, will take up the full width of the browser window. The third table is fixed at 300 pixels—approximately half of a 640 × 480 window.

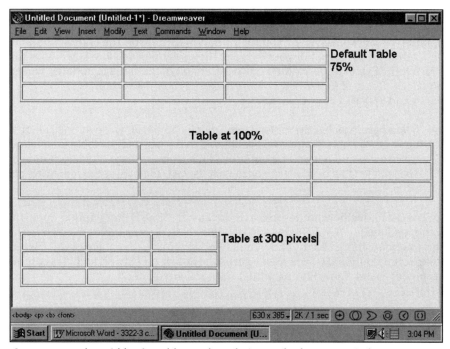

Figure 11-2: The width of a table can be relative to the browser window, or set to an absolute width in pixels.

Tip   You don't have to declare a width for your table at all. If you delete the value in the Width text box of the Insert Table dialog box, your table will start out as small as possible and will only expand to accommodate inserted text or images. However, this can make it difficult to position your cursor inside a cell to enter content. You can always delete any set size — pixel or percentage — later.

Setting Table Preferences

Two preferences directly affect tables. Both can be set by choosing Edit ➪ Preferences and looking in the General category.

The first pertinent option is the Show Dialog when Inserting Objects check box. If this option is turned off, Dreamweaver will always insert a default table (3 rows by 3 columns at 75 percent width of the screen with a 1-pixel border), without displaying a dialog box and asking for your input. Should you wish to change these values, you can adjust them from the Table Property Inspector once the table has been inserted.

Cross-Reference   The Insert Table dialog box is a Dreamweaver object and can be modified to create new default settings. For more information about how to build and alter Dreamweaver objects, see Chapter 16, "Creating and Using Objects."

The second notable preference is the one labeled Faster Table Editing (Deferred Update). Because tables expand and contract dynamically depending on their contents, Dreamweaver gives you the option of turning off the continual updating. (Depending on the speed of your system, the updating can slow down your table input.) If the Faster Table Editing option is enabled, the table is updated whenever you click outside of it or when you press the keyboard shortcut, Ctrl-Space (Command-Space).

Note   If you have enabled the Faster Table Editing and begin typing in one cell of your table, you'll notice that the text wraps within the cell and the table expands vertically. However, when you click outside of the table or press Ctrl-Space (Command-Space), the table cells adjust horizontally as well, completing the redrawing of the table.

You'll want to decide whether to leave the Faster Table Editing option on or turn it off, depending on your system and the complexity of your tables. Nested tables tend to update more slowly, and you may need to take advantage of the Faster Table Editing option if tables aren't getting redrawn quickly enough. I recommend turning off Faster Table Editing until it seems that you need it.

Modifying Tables

Most modifications to tables start in the Property Inspector. Dreamweaver helps you manage the basic table parameters — width, border, and alignment — as well as provides attributes for the other useful but more arcane features of a table, such as converting table width from pixels to percentage of the screen, and vice versa.

Selecting table elements

As with text or images, the first step in altering a table (or any of its elements) is selection.

New Feature   Dreamweaver 2 has simplified the selection process, making it far easier to change both the properties and the contents of entire tables, selected rows or columns, and even non-adjacent cells. Now, you can change the font size and color of a row with a click or two of the mouse — instead of highlighting and modifying each individual cell.

In Dreamweaver 2, you can select the following elements of a table:

- ✦ The entire table
- ✦ A single row
- ✦ Multiple rows, either adjacent or separate
- ✦ A single column

✦ Multiple columns, either adjacent or separate

✦ A single cell

✦ Multiple cells, either adjacent or separate

Once a table element is selected, you can modify its contents. Compared to earlier versions in which you could only select the entire table or a single cell, table editing in Dreamweaver 2 is now far more powerful.

Selecting an entire table

Several methods are available for selecting the entire table, whether you're a menu- or mouse-oriented designer. To select the table via a menu, do one of the following:

✦ Choose Modify ➪ Table ➪ Select Table.

✦ With the cursor positioned in the table, choose Edit ➪ Select All or use the keyboard shortcut, Ctrl-A (Command-A).

✦ Right-click (Control-click) inside a table to display the shortcut menu and choose Table ➪ Select Table.

To select an entire table with the mouse, use one of these techniques:

✦ Click on the bottom or right border of the table. You can also click anywhere along the table border when the pointer becomes a four-sided arrow.

✦ Select the `<table>` tag in the Tag Selector.

✦ Click immediately to one side of the table and drag the mouse over the table.

However you select the table, the selected table is surrounded by a black border with sizing handles along the right, the bottom, and in the right-hand corner (as shown in Figure 11-3), just like a selected graphic.

Selecting a row or column

Altering rows or columns of table text before Dreamweaver 2 was one major time-consuming chore. Previously, each cell had to be individually selected and the changes applied. Dreamweaver 2 has a much more intuitive method for selecting single or multiple columns and rows, comparable — and in some ways, superior — to major word-processing programs.

As with entire tables, you have several methods for selecting columns or rows. None of the techniques, however, use the menus; row and column selection is handled primarily with the mouse. In fact, you can select an entire row or column with one click.

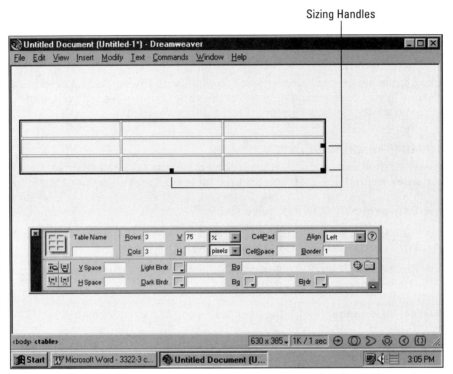

Figure 11-3: A selected table can be identified by the black border outlining the table and the three sizing handles.

The one-click method for selecting a single column or row requires that you position your pointer directly over the column or to the left of the row you want to choose. Move the pointer slowly toward the table—when the pointer becomes a single arrow, with the arrowhead pointing down for columns and to the right for rows, click the mouse. All the cells in the selected column or row are bounded with a black border. Any changes now made in the Property Inspector, such as a change in font size or color, affect the selected column or row.

You can select multiple, contiguous columns or rows by dragging the single arrow pointer across several columns or rows. To select a number of columns or rows that are not next to one another, use the Ctrl (Command) key. Press the Ctrl (Command) key while selecting each individual column, using the one-click method. (Not even Word 97 can handle this degree of complex table selection.)

Tip

If you have trouble positioning the mouse so that the single arrow pointer appears, you can use two other methods for selecting columns or rows. With the first method, you can click and drag across all the cells in a column or row. The second method uses another keyboard modifier, the Shift key. With this technique, click once in the first cell of the column or row. Then, hold down the Shift key while you click in the final cell of the column or row. You can also use this technique to select multiple adjacent columns or rows; just click in another column's or row's last cell.

Selecting cells

Sometimes you need to change the background color of just a few cells in a table, but not the entire row — or you might need to merge several cells to form one wide column span. In these situations, and many others, you can use Dreamweaver 2's new cell selection capabilities. Like columns and rows, you can select multiple cells, whether they are adjacent to one another or separate.

Individual cells are generally selected by dragging the mouse across one or more cell boundaries. To select a single cell, click anywhere in the cell and drag the mouse into another cell. As you pass the border between the two cells, the initial cell is highlighted. If you continue dragging the mouse across another cell boundary, the second cell is selected, and so on. Note that you have to drag the mouse *into* another cell and not cross the table border onto the page; for example, to highlight the lower-right cell of a table, you need to drag the mouse up or to the left.

Tip

You can also select a single cell by pressing the Ctrl (Command) key and clicking once in the cell, or you can select the right-most <td> tag in the Tag Selector.

Extended cell selection is handled identically to extended text selection in Dreamweaver or most word-processing programs. To select adjacent cells, click in the first desired cell, press and hold the Shift key, and click in the final desired cell. Dreamweaver selects all in a rectangular area, using the first cell as the upper-left corner of the rectangle and the last cell as the lower-right. You could, for instance, select an entire table by clicking in the upper-left cell and then Shift-clicking the lower-right cell.

Just as the Shift key is used to make adjacent cell selections, the Ctrl (Command) key is used for all nonadjacent cell selections. You can highlight any number of individual cells — whether they are next to one another or not — by pressing the Ctrl (Command) key while you click in the cell.

Tip

If you Ctrl (Command)-click a cell that is already selected, that cell is deselected — regardless of the method you used to select the cell initially.

Editing a table's contents

Before you learn how to change a table's attributes, let's look at basic editing techniques. Editing text in Dreamweaver tables is slightly different from editing text outside of tables. When you begin to enter text into a table cell, the table borders expand to accommodate your new data. The other cells appear to shrink, but they, too, will expand once you start typing in text or inserting an image. Unless a cell's width is specified, the cell currently being edited expands or contracts, and the other cells are forced to adjust their width. Figure 11-4 shows the same table (with one row and three columns) in three different states. In the top table, only the first cell contains text; notice how the other cells have contracted. In the middle table, text has been entered into the second cell as well, and you can see how the first cell is now smaller. Finally, in the bottom table, all three cells contain text, and the other two cells have adjusted their width to compensate for the expanding third cell.

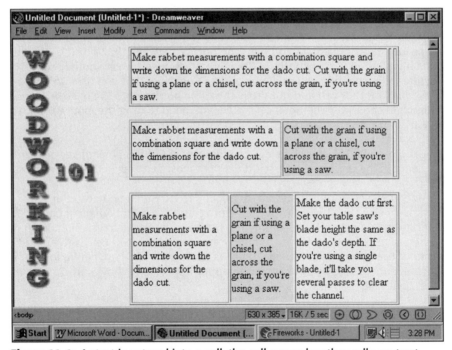

Figure 11-4: As text is entered into a cell, the cell expands; other cells contract, even if they already contain text.

If you look closely at the bottom table in Figure 11-4, you can also see that the text doesn't line up vertically. That's because the default vertical alignment in Dreamweaver, as in most browsers, provides for entries to be positioned in the middle of the cell. (You'll see later in this section how to adjust the vertical alignment.)

Moving through a table

When you've finished entering your text in the first cell, you can move to the next cell in the row by pressing the Tab key. When you reach the end of a row, pressing Tab takes your cursor to the first cell of the next row. To go backward, cell to cell, press Shift-Tab.

Tip   Pressing Tab has a special function when you're in the last cell of a row — it adds a new row, with the same column configuration as the current one.

The Home and End keys take you to the beginning and end, respectively, of the cursor's current line. If a cell's contents is large enough for the text to wrap in the cell, move to the top of the current cell by pressing Ctrl-Home (Command-Home). To get the bottom of the current cell in such a circumstance, press Ctrl-End (Command-End).

When you're at the beginning or end of the contents in a cell, the arrow keys can also be used to navigate from cell to cell. Use the left and right arrows to move from cell to cell in a row, and the up and down arrows to move down a column. When you come to the end of a row or column, the arrow keys move to the first cell in the next row or column. If you're moving left to right horizontally, the cursor goes from the end of one row to the beginning of the next row — and vice-versa, if you move from right to left. When moving from top to bottom vertically, the cursor goes from the end of one column to the start of the next, and vice-versa when moving bottom to top.

Cutting, copying, and pasting in tables

In the early days of Web design (about two years ago), woe if you should accidentally leave out a cell of information. Often, it was almost faster to redo the entire table than to make room by meticulously cutting and pasting everything, one cell at a time. Dreamweaver 2 ends that painstaking work forever with its advanced cutting and pasting features. Now, you can copy a range of cells from one table to another and maintain all the attributes, such as color and alignment as well as the content — text or images — or you can copy just the contents and ignore the attributes.

New Feature   There is one basic restriction to table cut-and-paste operations in Dreamweaver: your selected cells must form a rectangle. In other words, while you can select nonadjacent cells, columns, or rows and modify their properties, you can't cut or copy them. Should you try, you'll get a message from Dreamweaver like the one shown in Figure 11-5; the table above the notification in the figure illustrates an incorrect cell selection.

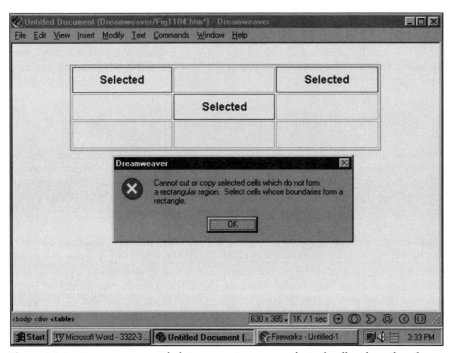

Figure 11-5: Dreamweaver only lets you cut or copy selected cells when they form a rectangle, unlike the table depicted here.

Copying attributes and contents

When you copy or cut a cell using the regular commands, Dreamweaver automatically copies everything — content, formatting, and cell format — in the selected cell. Then, pasting the cell will reproduce it all — however, you can get different results depending on where the cell (or column or row) is pasted.

To cut or copy both the contents and the attributes of any cell, row, or column, follow these steps:

1. Select the cells you wish to cut or copy.

   Remember that to cut or copy a range of cells in Dreamweaver, they must form a solid rectangular region.

2. To copy cells, choose Edit ➪ Copy or use the keyboard shortcut, Ctrl-C (Command-C).

3. To cut cells, choose Edit ➪ Cut or use the keyboard shortcut, Ctrl-X (Command-X).

   If you cut an individual cell, the contents are removed, but the cell remains. If, however, you cut an entire row or column, the cells are removed.

4. Position your cursor to paste the cells in the desired location:

- To replace a cell with a cell on the clipboard, click anywhere in the cell to be replaced. If you cut or copied multiple cells that do not make up a full column or row, click in the upper-left corner of the cells you wish to replace. For example, a range of six cells in a 2 × 3 configuration will replace the same configuration when pasted.

  Dreamweaver alerts you to the differences if you try to paste one configuration of cells into a different cell configuration.

- To insert a new row with the row on the clipboard, click anywhere in the row below where you'd like the new row to appear.

- To insert a new column with the column on the clipboard, click anywhere in the column to the right of where you'd like the new column to appear.

- To replace an existing row or column in a table, select the row or column. If you've cut or copied multiple rows or columns, you must select an equivalent size and shape of cells to replace.

- To insert a new table based on the copied or cut cells, click anywhere outside of the table.

5. Paste the copied or cut cells by choosing Edit ⇨ Paste or pressing Ctrl-V (Command-V).

Tip

To move a row or column that you've cut from the interior of a table to the exterior (the right or bottom), you have to first expand the number of cells in the table. To do this, first select the table by choosing Modify ⇨ Table ⇨ Select Table or using one of the other techniques previously described. Next, in the Table Property Inspector, increase the number of rows or columns by altering the values in the Rows or Cols text boxes. Finally, select the newly added rows or columns and choose Edit ⇨ Paste.

Copying contents only

It's not uncommon to need to move data from one cell to another, while keeping the destination cell's attributes, such as its background color or border, intact. For this, you need to use Dreamweaver's facility for copying just the contents of a cell.

To copy only the contents, you select a cell as previously described and then, instead of choosing Edit ⇨ Copy, choose Edit ⇨ Copy Text Only or use the keyboard shortcut, Ctrl-Shift-C (Command-Shift-C). Instead of selecting the entire cell, you can select a portion of the text and use the Copy Text Only command to avoid pasting in the format of the copied text.

Unlike the copying of both contents and attributes described in the previous section, there are a couple of limitations with content-only copying:

✦ First, you can only copy the contents alone one cell at a time. You can't paste contents only across multiple cells.

✦ Second, you can't replace the entire contents of one cell with another *and* maintain all the text attributes (font, color, and size) of the destination cell. If you select all the text to be replaced, Dreamweaver also selects the ⟨font⟩ tag that holds the attributes and replaces those as well. The workaround is to select all but one letter or word, paste the contents, and then delete the unwanted text.

Caution   Be sure to use the Copy Text Only and Paste combination, rather than the Copy and Paste as Text method. If you copy normally, and then choose Paste as Text, Dreamweaver inserts all the HTML surrounding the contents as well as the contents. Moreover, you'll get special behind-the-scenes Dreamweaver-only codes such as dwcopytype="CopyTableRow".

Working with table properties

The ⟨table⟩ tag has a large number of attributes, and most of them can be modified through Dreamweaver's Property Inspector. As with all objects, the table must be selected before it can be altered. Choose Modify ➪ Table ➪ Select Table or use one of the other selection techniques previously described.

Once you've selected the table, if the Property Inspector is open it will present the table properties as shown in Figure 11-6. Otherwise, you can open the Table Property Inspector by choosing Window ➪ Properties Inspector.

Figure 11-6: The expanded Table Property Inspector gives you control over all the tablewide attributes.

Setting alignment

Aligning a table in Dreamweaver goes beyond the expected left, right, and center options — you can also make a table into a free-floating object around which text can wrap to the left or right.

There are two different HTML methods for aligning a table, and each gives you a different effect. Using the text alignment method (Text ➪ Alignment) results in the conventional positioning (left, right, and center); and using the Table Property Inspector method lets you wrap text around your realigned table. Figure 11-7 compares some of the different results you get from aligning your table with the two methods.

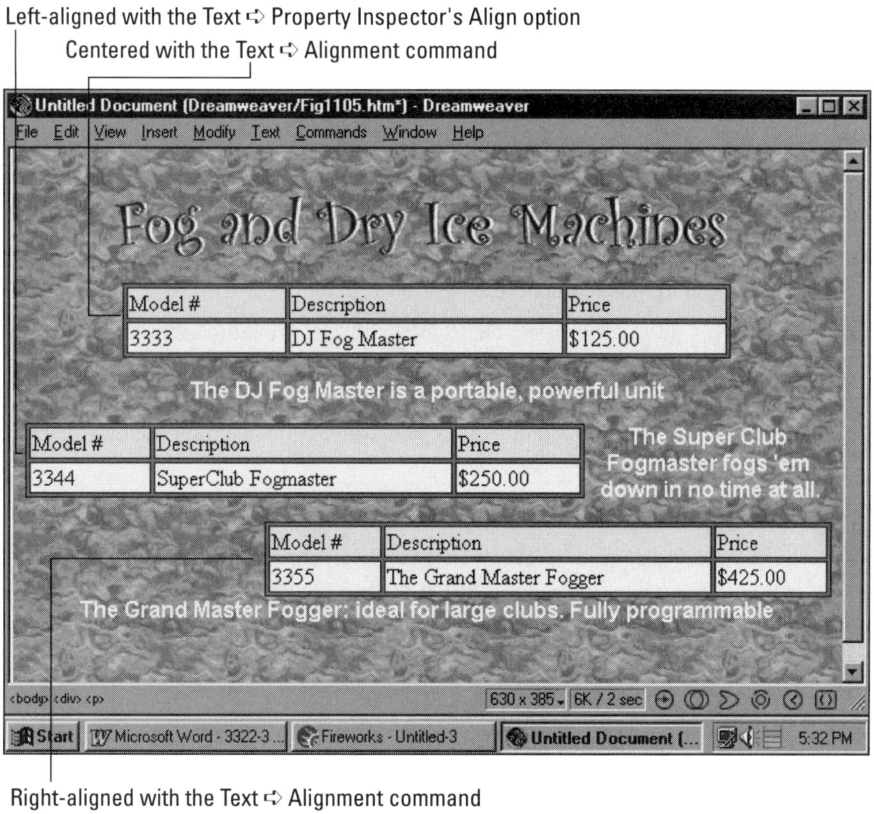

Left-aligned with the Text ⇨ Property Inspector's Align option

Centered with the Text ⇨ Alignment command

Right-aligned with the Text ⇨ Alignment command

Figure 11-7: Tables can be centered, as well as aligned left or right — with or without text wrapping.

To align your table *without* text wrapping, follow these steps:

1. Select your table using one of the methods described earlier.

2. In the Property Inspector, make sure the Align option is set to Default.

3. Select the Text ⇨ Alignment command, and then choose one of the three options: Left, Center, or Right.

   Dreamweaver surrounds your table code with a division tag pair, `<div>...</div>`, with an `align` attribute set to your chosen value.

To align your table with text wrapping, making your table into a floating object, follow these steps:

1. Select the table.

2. In the Table Property Inspector, open the Align drop-down list and choose one of the four options:

Alignment Option	Result
Default	No alignment is written. Table aligns to the browser's default, usually left, with no text wrapping.
Left	Aligns the table to the left side of the browser window and wraps text around the right side.
Right	Aligns the table to the right side of the browser window and wraps text around the left side.
Center	The table aligns to the center of the browser window. Text does not wrap around either side. Note: This alignment option works only with 4.0 browsers.

Dreamweaver codes these alignment attributes in the `<table>` tag. As with floating images, Dreamweaver places an anchor point for floating elements on the Web page. However, unlike most other Invisible symbols, you cannot drag-and-drop or cut-and-paste the anchor point for a floating table.

Caution Bear in mind that choosing Center as the Align option in the Property Inspector is somewhat problematical in terms of browser compatibility. Until more browsers recognize this option, using the Text ⇨ Alignment command for centering tables produces the widest browser compatibility.

Resizing a table

The primary sizing control on the Table Property Inspector is the Width text box. You can enter a new width value for the entire table in either a screen percentage or pixels. Just enter your value in the Width text box, and then select % or pixels in the drop-down list of options.

Dreamweaver also provides a very quick and intuitive way to resize the overall table width, column widths, or row height. Pass your pointer over any of the table's borders, and the pointer becomes a two-headed arrow; this is the *resizing pointer*. When you see the resizing pointer, you can click and drag any border to a new position.

As noted earlier, tables are initially sized according to their contents. Once you move a table border in Dreamweaver, however, the new sizes are written directly into the HTML code and the column width or row height is fixed—unless the contents cannot fit. If, for example, an inserted image is 115 pixels wide and the cell has a width of only 90 pixels, the cell expands to fit the image. The same is true if you try to fit an extremely long, unbroken text string, such as a complex URL, in a cell that's too narrow to hold the string.

New Feature

Dreamweaver 2 now also lets you set the height of a table using the Height text box in much the same way as the Width box. However, the height of a table — whether in pixels or percentages — is maintained only as long as the contents do not require a larger size. A table's width, though, takes precedence over its height, and a table expands vertically before it expands horizontally.

Changes to a cell or column's width are shown in the <td> tags, as are changes to a row's height, using the width and height attribute, respectively. You can see these changes by selecting the table, cell, column, or row affected and looking at the W (Width) and H (Height) text box values.

For an overall view of what happens when you resize a cell, row, or column, it's best to look at the HTML. Here's the HTML for an empty table, resized:

```
<table border="1" width="70%">
  <tr>
    <td width="21%"> </td>
    <td width="34%"> </td>
    <td width="45%"> </td>
  </tr>
  <tr>
    <td width="21%" height="42"> </td>
    <td width="34%" height="42"> </td>
    <td width="45%" height="42"> </td>
  </tr>
  <tr>
    <td width="21%" height="42"> </td>
    <td width="34%" height="42"> </td>
    <td width="45%" height="42"> </td>
  </tr>
</table>
```

Notice how all the widths for the cells and the entire table are expressed as percentages. If the table width were initially set at a pixel value, the cell widths would have been, too. The row height values, on the other hand, are shown as an absolute measurement in pixels.

You can switch from percentages to pixels in all the table measurements, and even clear all the values at once — with the click of a button. There are four measurement controls in the lower-left portion of the expanded Table Property Inspector, as shown in Figure 11-8.

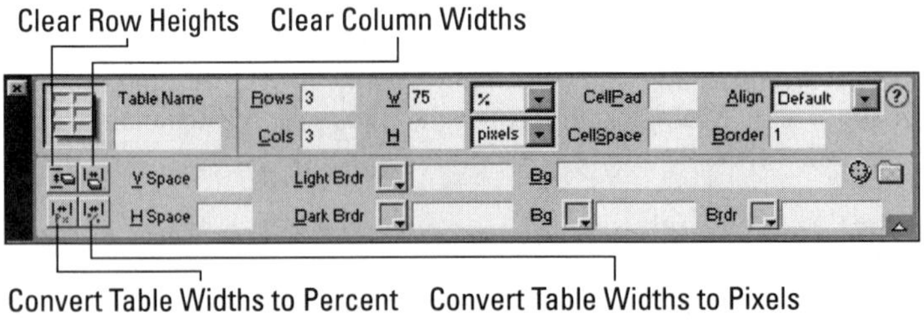

Clear Row Heights   Clear Column Widths

Convert Table Widths to Percent   Convert Table Widths to Pixels

Figure 11-8: You can make tablewide changes with the four control buttons in the Table Property Inspector.

From left to right, the measurement controls are as follows:

Measurement Control Buttons	Description
Clear Row Heights	Erases all the height attributes in the current table
Clear Column Widths	Deletes all the width attributes found in the <td> tags
Convert Table Widths to Pixels	Translates the current widths of all cells and for the full table from percentages to pixels
Convert Table Widths to Percent	Translates the current widths of all cells and for the full table from pixels to percentages

Note   Selecting Clear Row Heights doesn't affect the table height value.

If you clear both row heights and column widths, the table goes back to its "grow as needed" format and, if empty, shrinks to its smallest possible size.

Caution   When converting width percentages to pixels, and vice versa, keep in mind that the percentages are relative to the size of the browser window — and in the development phase that browser window is Dreamweaver. You'll want to expand Dreamweaver's Document Window to the same size as what you expect to be seen in the browser.

Inserting rows and columns

The default Dreamweaver table configuration of three columns and three rows can be changed at any time. You can add rows or columns almost anywhere in a table, using various methods.

There are three methods for adding a single row:

✦ Position the cursor in the last cell of the last row, and press Tab to add a new row below the present one.

✦ Choose Modify ⟳ Table ⟳ Insert Row to insert a new row above the current row.

✦ Right-click (Control-click) to open the shortcut menu, and select Table ⟳ Insert Row. Rows added in this way are inserted above the current row.

There are two ways to add a new column to your table:

✦ Choose Modify ⟳ Table ⟳ Insert Column to insert a new column to the left of the current column.

✦ Right-click (Control-click) to open the shortcut menu, and select Table ⟳ Insert Column from the shortcut menu. The column is inserted to the left of the current column.

You can add multiple rows and columns in one of two different ways:

✦ Increase the number of rows indicated in the Rows text box of the Table Property Inspector. All new rows added in this manner appear below the last table row. Similarly, you can increase the number of columns indicated in the Cols text box of the Table Property Inspector. Columns added in this way appear to the right of the last column.

✦ Use the Insert Rows or Columns dialog box.

New Feature The Insert Rows or Columns feature enables you to include any number of rows or columns anywhere relative to your current cursor position.

To add multiple columns using the Insert Rows or Columns dialog box, follow these steps:

1. Open the Insert Rows or Columns dialog box (shown in Figure 11-9) by selecting Modify ⟳ Table ⟳ Insert Rows or Columns or by choosing Table ⟳ Insert Rows or Columns from the shortcut menu.

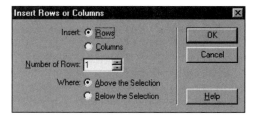

Figure 11-9: Use the Insert Rows or Columns feature to add several columns or rows simultaneously.

2. Select either Rows or Columns.

3. Enter the number of rows or columns you wish to insert — you can either type in a value or use the arrows to increase or decrease the number.

4. Select where you want the rows or columns to be inserted.

   • If you have selected the Rows option, you can insert the rows either Above or Below the Selection (the current row).

   • If you have selected the Columns options, you can insert the columns either Before or After the Current Column.

5. Click OK when you're finished.

Deleting rows and columns

When you want to delete a column or row, you can use either the shortcut menu or the Table Property Inspector. On the shortcut menu, you can remove the current column or row by choosing Delete Column or Delete Row, respectively. Using the Table Property Inspector, you can delete multiple columns and rows by reducing the numbers in the Cols or Rows text boxes. Columns are deleted from the right side of the table, and rows are removed from the bottom.

Caution   Watch out — exercise extreme caution when deleting columns or rows. Dreamweaver does not ask for confirmation and will remove these columns and/or rows whether or not there is data in them.

Setting table borders and backgrounds

Borders are the solid outlines of the table itself. A border's width is measured in pixels; the default width is 1 pixel. This width can be altered in the Border field of the Table Property Inspector.

You can make the border invisible by specifying a border of 0 width. You can still resize your table by clicking and dragging the borders, even when the border is set to 0 (zero). When the View ➪ Table Borders option is selected, Dreamweaver displays a thin dashed line to represent the border.

When the border is visible, you can also see each cell outlined. The width of the outline around the cells stays constant, regardless of the width of the border. However, you can control the amount of space between each cell with the CellSpace value in the Table Property Inspector, covered later in this chapter.

To change the width of a border in Dreamweaver, select your table and enter a new value in the Border text box. With a wider border, you can see the default shading: the top and left side are a lighter shade, and the bottom and right sides are darker. This gives the table border a pseudo-3D appearance. Figure 11-10 shows single-cell tables with borders of various widths.

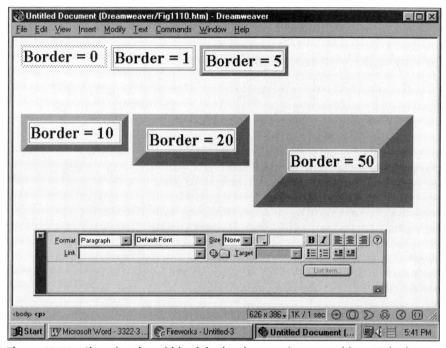

Figure 11-10: Changing the width of the border can give your table a 3D look.

In Dreamweaver, you can assign colors to the border, and to both the light and dark sides of the border. Each of these colors is chosen through the Table Property Inspector, as follows:

✦ To choose a color for the border, select the Border color swatch, or enter a color name in the adjacent text box.

✦ To choose a color for the light (top and left) border, select the Light Brdr color swatch or enter a color name in the adjacent text box.

✦ To choose a color for the dark (bottom and right) border, select the Dark Brdr color swatch or enter a color name in the adjacent text box.

If you assign a border color, it is overridden by any Light Brdr and/or Dark Brdr choices.

Tip   You can change the "light source" of the shadow for your table. To make the light appear to come from the bottom-right instead of the upper-left, choose a dark shade for the Light Brdr color and a light shade for the Dark Brdr color.

In addition to colored borders, a table can also have a colored background. (By default, the table is initially transparent.) Choose the background color in the Table Property Inspector by selecting a color in the Bg Color color swatch or entering a color name in the adjacent text box. As you'll see later in the chapter, you can also assign background colors to rows, columns, and individual cells — if used, these specific colors all override the background color of the overall entire table.

Working with cellspacing and cellpadding

HTML gives you two methods to add white space in tables. *Cellspacing* controls the width between each cell, and *cellpadding* controls the margins within each cell. These values can be set independently through the Table Property Inspector.

Tip   Although not indicated in the Table Property Inspector, the default value is 2 pixels for cellspacing and 1 pixel for cellpadding. Some Web page designs call for a close arrangement of cells and are better served by changing either (or both) the CellSpace or CellPad values to 1 (one) or 0 (zero).

To change the amount of white space *between each cell* in a table, enter a new value in the CellSpace text box of the Table Property Inspector. If you want to adjust the amount of white space *between the borders of the cell and the actual cell data*, alter the value in the CellPad text box of the Table Property Inspector. Figure 11-11 shows an example of a table with wide (10 pixels) cellspacing and cellpadding values.

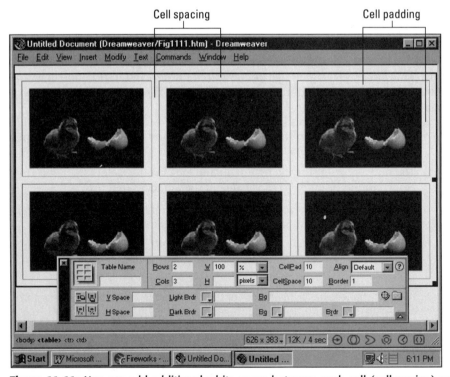

Figure 11-11: You can add additional white space between each cell (cellspacing) or within each cell (cellpadding).

Merging and splitting cells

You have seen how cells in HTML tables can extend across (*span*) multiple columns or rows. By default, a cell spans one column or one row. Increasing a cell's span lets you group any number of topics under one heading. You are effectively *merging* one cell with another to create a larger cell. Likewise, a cell can be *split* into multiple rows or columns.

New Feature

Dreamweaver 2 lets you combine and divide cells in two different ways. If you're more comfortable with the concept of merging and splitting cells, you can use two very handy buttons on the Property Inspector. If, on the other hand, you prefer the older method of increasing and decreasing row or column span, you can still access these commands through the main and shortcut menus.

To combine two or more cells, first select the cells you want to merge. Then, from the Property Inspector, select the Merge Cells button or press the keyboard shortcut, M. If the Merge button is not available, multiple cells have not been selected.

To divide a cell, follow these steps:

1. Position your cursor in the cell to split.

2. From the Property Inspector, select the Split Cell button or press the keyboard shortcut, Ctrl-Alt-S (Command-Option-S).

   The Split Cell dialog box (shown in Figure 11-12) appears.

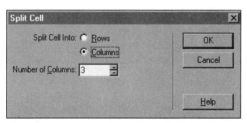

Figure 11-12: Use the Split Cell dialog box to divide cells horizontally or vertically.

3. Select either the Rows or Columns option to decide whether the cell will be split horizontally or vertically.

4. Enter the Number of Rows or Columns in the text box, or use the arrows to change the value.

5. Select OK when you're done.

Prior to Dreamweaver 2, all such cell merging and splitting operations were handled using the Increase/Decrease Row or Column Span commands. Now, these commands are only available through the standard menus. To use them, position the cursor in the cell to be affected and then choose one of the following commands:

Command	Description
Increase Row Span	Joins the current cell with the cell below it
Decrease Row Span	Separates two or more previously spanned cells from the bottom cell
Increase Column Span	Joins the current cell with the cell immediately to its right
Decrease Column Span	Separates two or more previously spanned cells from the right edge.

Existing text or images are put in the same cell if the cells containing them are joined to span rows or columns. Figure 11-13 shows a table containing both row and column spanning.

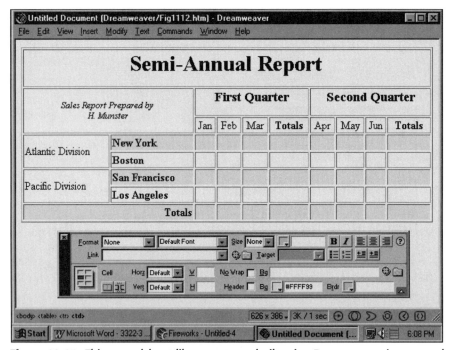

Figure 11-13: This spreadsheet-like report was built using Dreamweaver's row- and column-spanning features.

Tip　　When you need to build a complex table such as this one, it's best to try to map out your table before you begin constructing it, and have it completed prior to entering your data.

Setting cell, column, and row properties

In addition to the overall table controls, Dreamweaver helps you set numerous properties for individual cells one at a time, by the column or by the row. When there are overlapping or conflicting attributes, such as different background colors for a cell in the same row and column, the more specific target wins out. The hierarchy, from most general to most specific, is as follows: tables, rows, columns, and finally cells.

You can call up the specific Property Inspector by selecting the cell, row, or column you want to modify. The Cell, Row, and Column Property Inspectors each affect similar attributes. The following sections explain how the attributes work in general and — if there are any differences — specifically in regards to the cell, column, or row.

Horizontal alignment

You can set the Horizontal Alignment attribute, align, to specify the default alignment, or Left, Right, or Center alignment, for the element in the cell, column, or row. This attribute can be overridden by setting the alignment for the individual line or image. Generally, Left is the default horizontal alignment for cells.

Vertical alignment

The HTML valign attribute determines whether the cell's contents are vertically aligned to the cell's top, middle, bottom, or along the baseline. Typically, browsers align cells vertically in the middle by default. Select the Vertical Alignment option arrow in the Cell, Column, or Row Properties dialog box to specify a different alignment.

Top, Middle, and Bottom vertical alignments work pretty much as you would expect. A Baseline vertical alignment displays text near the top of the cell and positions the text — regardless of font size — so that the baselines of all the text in the affected row, column, or cell are the same. You can see how images and text of various sizes are displayed under the various vertical alignment options in Figure 11-14.

Cell wrap

Normal behavior for any cell is to automatically wrap text or a series of images within the cell's borders. You can turn off this automatic feature by selecting the No Wrap option in the Property Inspector for Cell, Column, or Row.

Note　　I've had occasion to use this option when I absolutely needed three images to appear side-by-side in one cell. In analyzing the results, I found that on some lower-resolution browsers the last image wrapped to the next line.

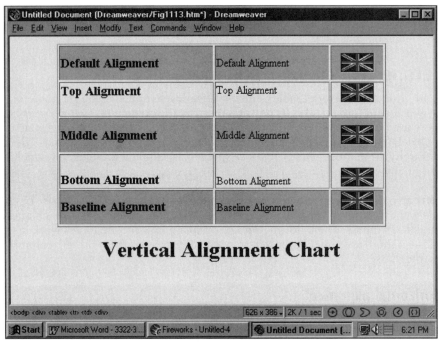

Figure 11-14: You can vertically align text and images in several arrangements in a table cell, row, or column.

Table header cells

Quite often in tables, a column or row functions as the heading for that section of the table, labeling all the information in that particular section. Dreamweaver has an option for designating these cells: the Header option. Table header cells are usually rendered in boldface and centered in each cell. Figure 11-15 shows an example of a table in which both the first row and column are marked as table header cells.

Width and height

The gridlike structure of a table makes it impossible to resize only one cell in a multicolumn table. Therefore, the only way you can enter exact values for a cell's width is through the Width section available only in the Column Properties dialog box. In this section of the dialog box, you can enter values in pixels or as a percentage of the table. The default allows cells to automatically resize with no restrictions outside of the overall dimensions of the table.

Similarly, whenever you change a cell's height, the entire row is altered. If you drag the row to a new height, the value is written into the H (Height) text box for all cells in the row. On the other hand, if you specify a single cell's height, the row will resize, but you can only see the value in the cell you've changed.

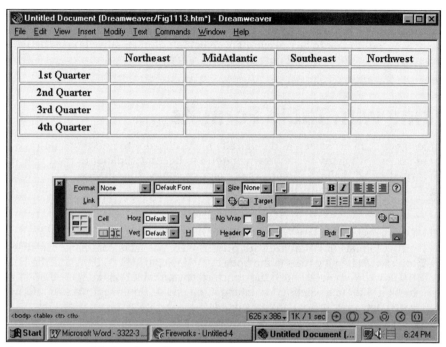

Figure 11-15: Table header cells are a good way to note a category's label — either for a row, a column, or both.

Color elements

Just as you can specify color backgrounds and borders for the overall table, you can do the same for columns, rows, or individual cells. Corresponding color swatches and text boxes are available in all dialog boxes for the following categories:

✦ **Background Color.** Specifies the color for the selected cell, row, or column. Selecting the color swatch opens the standard 216 Web-safe color picker.

✦ **Border Color.** Controls the color of the single-pixel border surrounding each cell.

✦ **Light Border.** Sets the color for the bottom and right borders of each cell.

✦ **Dark Border.** Sets the color for the top and left borders of each cell.

Note Notice that the light and dark shading concept for cell borders is reversed from the light and dark shading for table borders. However, the cell border attributes are just like the table attributes in that, if specified, the light and dark cell borders override any border color that might be chosen.

As with all Dreamweaver 2 color pickers, you can use the Eyedropper tool to select a color from the Web-safe palette or from any item on a page. You can also select the Eraser tool to delete any previously selected color. Finally, choose the Palette tool to open the Color dialog box and select any available color.

Working with Table Formats

Tables keep data organized and generally make it easier to find information quickly. Large tables with many rows, however, tend to become difficult to read unless they are formatted with alternating rows of color or some other device. Formatting a large table is often an afterthought as well as a very time-consuming affair. Unless, of course, you're using Dreamweaver 2's new Format Table command.

New Feature

Dreamweaver 2's new Format Table command permits you to choose from 17 preset formats or customize your own. The Format Table command can style the top row, alternating rows in the body of the table, the left column, and the border. It's best to completely build the structure of your table — although you don't have to fill it with data — before formatting it; otherwise, you might have to reformat it when new rows or columns are added.

To apply one of the preset table formats, follow these steps:

1. Select your table by choosing Modify ➪ Table ➪ Select Table or by using one of the other techniques.

2. Choose Commands ➪ Format Table.

   The Format Table dialog box (shown in Figure 11-16) opens.

3. Select any of the options from the scrolling list box on the left side of the Format Table dialog box.

   As you select an option, a representation of the table appears to the right and the attribute values used are displayed below.

4. When you've found a table format that's appropriate, select OK to close the dialog box and the format is applied.

The preset formats are divided into three groups: Simple, AltRows, and DblRows. The Simple formats maintain the same background color for all rows in the body of the table but change the top row and the left column. The AltRows formats alternate the background color of each row in the body of the table; there are eight different color combinations from which to choose. The final category, DblRows, alternates the background color of every two rows in the body of the table.

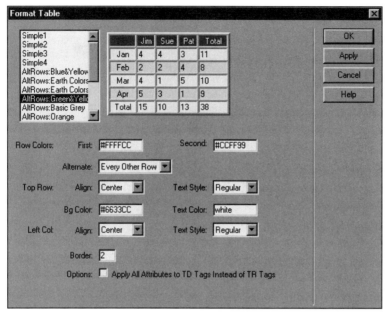

Figure 11-16: Select any one of 17 different preset formats from the Format Table dialog box or customize your own.

While 17 different formats may seem like a lot of choices, it's really just the jumping-off place for what's possible with the Format Table command. Each variable applied to create the preset formats can be customized. Moreover, you don't have to apply the changes to your selected table to see the effect — you can preview the results directly in the Table Format dialog box. Following are the variable attributes in the Table Format dialog box.

Attribute	Description
Row Colors: First	Enter a color (in color name or hexadecimal format) for the background colors of the first row in the body of a table. The Row Colors do not affect the top row of a table.
Row Colors: Second	Enter a color (in color name or hexadecimal format) for the background colors of the second row in the body of a table. The Row Colors do not affect the top row of a table.
Row Colors: Alternate	Establishes the pattern for using the specified Row Colors. Options are: <do not alternate>, Every Other Row, Every Two Rows, Every Three Rows, and Every Four Rows.

Continued

Attribute	Description
Top Row: Align	Sets the alignment of the text in the top row of the table to left, right, or center.
Top Row: Text Style	Sets the style of the text in the top row of the table to Regular, Bold, Italic, or Bold Italic.
Top Row: Bg Color	Sets the background color of the top row of the selected table. Use either color names or hexadecimal values.
Top Row: Text Color	Sets the color of the text in the top row of the selected table. Use either color names or hexadecimal values.
Left Col: Align	Sets the alignment of the text in the left column of the table to Left, Right, or Center.
Left Col: Text Style	Sets the style of the text in the left column of the table to Regular, Bold, Italic, or Bold Italic.
Border	Determines the width of the table's border in pixels.
Options: Apply All Attributes to TD Tags Instead of TR Tags	Writes attribute changes at the cell level, `<td>`, rather than the default, the row level, `<tr>`.

The final option in the Format Table dialog box, Apply All Attributes to TD Tags Instead of TR Tags, should only be used in one of two situations: one, the selected table is nested inside of another table and you want to override the outer table's `<tr>` format; or two, you anticipate moving cells from one table to another and want to maintain the formatting. Generally, the code produced by selecting this option is bulkier and could impact a page's overall download size, if the table is sufficiently large.

 Caution   Currently, there's no way to save your custom format. You need to re-enter the selections each time you apply them.

Sorting Tables

Have you ever painstakingly built a table, alphabetizing every last entry by last name *and* first name, only to have the client call up with a list of 13 additional names that just have to go in? "Oh, and could you sort them by zip code instead of last name?" Dreamweaver 2 adds a new Table Sort command designed to make short work of such requests. All you need to do is select your table and you're ready to do a two-level deep sort, either alphabetically or numerically.

The Table Sort command can rearrange any size table; more important, it's HTML-savvy and gives you the option of keeping the formatting of your table rows. This capability enables you to maintain a table with alternating row colors and still sort the data—something not even the most powerful word processors can handle. The Table Sort command is very useful for generating different views of the same data, without having to use a database.

The Table Sort command is very straightforward to use; just follow these steps:

1. Select your table by choosing Modify ⇨ Table ⇨ Select Table or by using one of the other techniques.

2. Choose Commands ⇨ Sort Table.

   The Sort Table dialog box (shown in Figure 11-17) opens.

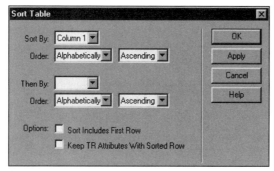

Figure 11-17: Sort your tables numerically or alphabetically with the new Sort Table command.

3. Choose the primary sort column from the Sort By option list.

   Dreamweaver automatically lists the number of columns in the selected table in the option list.

4. Set the type of the primary sort by choosing either Alphabetically or Numerically from the first Order option list.

5. Choose the direction of the sort by selecting either Ascending or Descending from the second Order option list.

6. If you wish to add a second level of sorting, repeat Steps 3 – 5 in the Then By section.

7. If your selected table does not include a header row, select the Sort Includes First Row option.

8. If you have formatted your table with alternating row colors, choose the Keep TR Attributes with Sorted Row option.

9. Click OK when you're finished.

Tip

As with any sorting program, if you leave blank cells in the column you're basing the sort on, those rows will appear as a group on top of the table for an ascending sort and at the end for a descending sort. Be sure that all of the cells in your sort criteria column are filled correctly.

Structuring Your Web Page with Tables

At the beginning of this chapter it was pointed out that experienced Web designers regard tables as one of their primary layout tools. This is because, outside of Dynamic HTML's layers, tables are the only way you can even get close to positioning your page elements the way you want them to appear. Granted, it's a lot of work to do this with tables, but designers are a persistent group — and when you have a vision to impart to the world, you'll do what's necessary.

What often becomes necessary, to get the look you want, is to design your entire Web page with tables — or, at least, the majority of it. And to achieve complete control of the page, you'll frequently put nested tables — tables within tables — to work.

Cross-Reference

Dreamweaver 2 enables what is, for some Web designers, a much more intuitive method of using tables to design your entire page: converting layers to tables. Because it requires an understanding of how layers work, you'll find details about how to use this new feature in Chapter 25, "Working with Layers."

Nesting tables

Dreamweaver has no practical restrictions on nesting tables. You can put as many tables within other tables as you can handle. All you have to do is position your cursor in the cell where you want the new table to appear, and select the Insert Table button on the Objects Palette. Although it's not absolutely faultless, nesting tables give you an increasingly fine degree of control over your Web page layout. One example of a full-page table layout is shown in Figure 11-18.

Following are some pointers to consider when working with nested tables:

✦ **Sketch your work before you begin.** Even just a simple diagram can save you hours of experimentation and rework.

✦ **Work from the outside in.** Create your largest table first and then create the smaller tables within it.

✦ **Don't be afraid to move a table.** No matter how much you plan, you almost never get it right the first time. As long as you select your entire table, all the elements in it will remain intact. Unfortunately, you can't drag and drop a table. So after you've selected the table, choose Edit ➪ Cut, reposition the cursor, and then choose Edit ➪ Paste — or use those fabulous keyboard shortcuts.

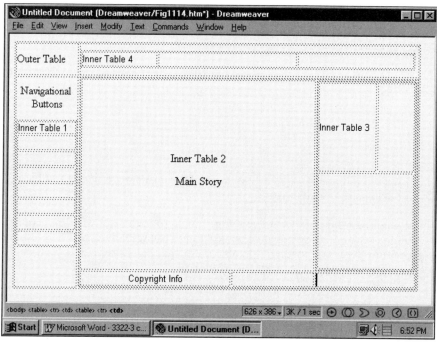

Figure 11-18: Nested tables can give the Web designer tighter command of the Web page elements.

✦ **Let the Tag Selector be your guide.** Because the Tag Selector displays tags in the nesting order (outside-to-inside is shown left-to-right), you can quickly select the table on which you need to work. Then you can switch to either the HTML Inspector or BBEdit, and the table will be highlighted in your code.

✦ **You can't split a cell, so nest a table.** If you've already begun embedding objects in your table and you find you need to split a cell into two or more parts, it's far easier to nest a two-cell table than to add an additional column to the entire table and readjust your column and row spans.

✦ **When resizing row heights, work from the top down.** Dragging a row's border to a new size sets an absolute value in the <td> tag. If you adjust the bottom row first — let's say you set it to about one-fifth of the screen, or 80 pixels high — and then modify a row height above, the table will get larger. That's because Dreamweaver maintains the 80 pixels, not the 20 percent.

✦ **Use absolute measurements on the outside, and relative measurements on the inside.** Though it's not a hard-and-fast rule, it is generally better to lock the outer table into a specific absolute pixel width and then set the inner table to 100 percent widths. Why? It saves the calculation time of trying to figure out the width, and the inner tables blend better this way.

✦ **Adjust the default table.** Because the Insert Table object is, like all Dreamweaver objects, written in HTML, you can alter it to suit your needs. Are most of your tables borderless? Change the object code from `BORDER="1"` to `BORDER="0"`.

Want to make all your tables start at 100 percent instead of 75? Change the code

```
document.theform.width.value="75"
```

to

```
document.theform.width.value="100"
```

For more information about how to modify an existing object, see Chapter 16, "Creating and Using Objects."

✦ **Remember the default cellspacing**. Trying to figure out why you can't close that gap? It could be because, even though the CellSpace text box is blank, Dreamweaver still inserts 2 pixels for cellspacing. Enter a zero as the CellSpace value to clear out the excess air.

Summary

Tables are an extremely powerful Web page design tool. Dreamweaver lets you modify both the appearance and the structure of your HTML tables through a combination of Property Inspectors, dialog boxes, and click-and-drag mouse movements. Mastering tables is an essential task for any modern Web designer, and worth the somewhat challenging learning curve. The key elements to keep in mind are as follows:

✦ An HTML table consists of a series of rows and columns, presented in a gridlike arrangement. Tables can be sized absolutely, in pixels, or relative to the width of the browser's window, in a percentage.

✦ Dreamweaver inserts a table whose dimensions can be altered through the Objects Palette or the Insert ➪ Table menu. Once in the page, the table needs to be selected before any of its properties can be modified through the Table Property Inspector.

✦ Table editing is greatly simplified in Dreamweaver 2. Now you can select multiple cells, columns, or rows — and modify all their contents in one fell swoop.

✦ You can assign certain properties — such as background color, border color, and alignment — for a table's columns, rows, or cells through their respective dialog boxes. A cell's properties override those set for its column or row.

✦ Dreamweaver 2 brings new power to table building with the Format Table and Sort Table commands.

✦ Putting a table within another table — also known as *nesting tables* — is a powerful (and legal) design option in HTML. Nested tables offer a positioning alternative to Dynamic HTML's layers, while retaining backward browser compatibility.

In the next chapter, you learn how to create and use client-side image maps.

✦　　✦　　✦

Making Client-Side Image Maps

By their very nature, HTML images are rectangular. Though you can make portions of a rectangular graphic transparent, giving the impression of an irregularly shaped picture, the image itself — and thus its clickable region — is still a rectangle. For more complex images in which shapes overlap and you want several separate areas of a picture to be hyperlinked, not just the overall graphic, you need an image map.

Dreamweaver includes an easy-to-use tool, the Image Map Editor, for delineating client-side image maps and inserting the proper code in your Web page. This chapter introduces you to that tool and also covers more advanced techniques for creating server-side and rollover image maps.

Client-Side Image Maps

As an almost literal example of an image map, imagine a map of the United States being used on a Web page. Suppose you want to be able to click each state and link to a different page in your site. How would you proceed? With the exception of Colorado and Wyoming, all the states have highly irregular shapes, so you can't use the typical side-by-side arrangement of rectangular images. You need to be able to specify a region on the graphic, to which you could then assign a link. This is exactly what an image map represents.

There are two different kinds of image maps: *client-side* and *server-side*. With a *server-side* image map, all the map data is kept in a file on the server. When the user clicks a particular spot on the image, often referred to as a *hotspot*, the server compares the coordinates of the clicked spot with its imagemap data. If the coordinates match, the server loads the corresponding link. The key advantage to a server-side image map is that it will work with any image-capable browser. The disadvantages are that it consumes more of the server's processing resources and tends to be slower than the client-side version.

With *client-side* image maps, on the other hand, all the data that is downloaded to the browser is kept in the Web page. The comparison process is the same, but it requires a browser that is image-map savvy. Originally, only server-side image maps were possible. It wasn't until Netscape Navigator 2.0 was released that the client-side version was even an option. Microsoft began supporting client-side image maps in Internet Explorer 3.0.

In HTML, there are two parts to a client-side image map. In the ⟨img⟩ tag, Dreamweaver includes a usemap=mapname attribute. The mapname value refers to the second part of the image map's HTML, the ⟨map⟩ tag. One of the first steps in creating an image map is to give it a unique name. Dreamweaver stores all of your mapping data under this map name. Here's an example of the code for an image map with three hot spots:

```
<img src="images/imagemap.jpg" width="640" height="480"
usemap="#navbar"></p>
<map name="navbar">
  <area shape="poly"
coords="166,131,165,131,160,143,164,179,127,180,143,200,156,203
,118,229,119,236,158,229,177,217,199,238,212,247,220,242,196,20
3,232,190,241,189,241,182,223,177,185,182,175,134,166,132"
href="/starpro.html" alt="High Risk Funds">
  <area shape="circle" coords="312,202,56" href="/nestegg.html"
alt="Mutual Funds">
  <area shape="rect" coords="389,138,497,244"
href="/prodfunds.html" alt="Money Markets">
</map>
```

Dreamweaver directly supports client-side image maps. Once you've inserted an image into your Web page, it can be an image map. Select any image and open the expanded version of the Property Inspector. In the lower-right corner you'll see the Map button, as shown in Figure 12-1. This button opens the Image Map Editor.

Map button

Figure 12-1: From the Image Property Inspector, select the Map button to open Dreamweaver's Image Map Editor.

Creating Image Hotspots

Image maps are created with tools similar to those you find in any drawing program. (They're described in detail in the section "Using the drawing tools" later in this chapter.) After you've selected your graphic, you can click a tool to describe a rectangle, oval, or polygon shape.

You can make an image map from any graphic format supported by Dreamweaver: GIF, JPEG, or PNG.

New Feature The initial window for the Image Map Editor displays an area approximately 475 × 200. If your image is larger, you can now resize the Image Map Editor as large as your desktop. To resize the Image Map Editor, position your pointer over any border or corner of its window; when the pointer turns into a two-headed arrow, click and drag the window to its new size.

Follow these steps to create hotspots on an image in Dreamweaver:

1. Select your image and open the Image Property Inspector.

2. Click the Map button to display the Image Map Editor with your selected graphic, as shown in Figure 12-2.

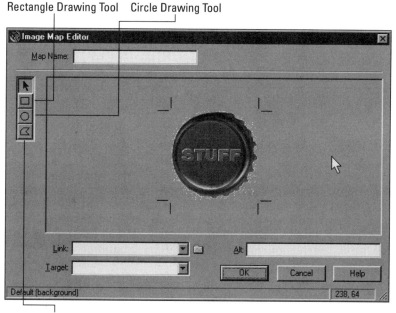

Figure 12-2: The Image Map Editor lets you draw the hotspots directly on your graphic.

3. Enter a unique name for your image map in the Map Name text box.

4. From the toolbar on the left of the Image Map Editor, choose the appropriate drawing tool to outline your hotspot: Rectangle, Circle, or Polygon (see Figure 12-2). Outline one hotspot.

5. Enter the URL for this image map in the Link text box, or click the Folder icon and browse for the file. Then press Tab to go to the next text box (Target).

6. If desired, enter a frame name or other target in the Target text box. Press Tab to go to the next text box (Alt).

A target can refer to a specific section of a frameset or to a new browser window. For more information on using targets in frames, see Chapter 14, "Using Frames and Framesets." To learn more about targeting a new browser window, see "Targeting Your Links" in Chapter 9.

7. In the Alt text box, you can enter text you want to appear as a tool tip that appears when the user's mouse moves over the area.

The information taken from the Alt text box appears as a tooltip only in Netscape browsers. You need to include another attribute, title, equal to the same text to have the tooltip appear in Microsoft browsers. You can enter this code by hand or use Massimo Foti's Title for Maps command (available on the CD-ROM) to automate the process.

8. Repeat Steps 4 through 7 to add additional hotspots to the graphic.

9. Click OK when you're finished.

If the map area you're trying to define is larger than the Image Map Editor window—even when it's stretched to its full size—the solution is to create two or more overlapping areas. Set them all to the same Link and the user will never see the "seam."

Setting the default URL

In addition to joining specific hotspots to a hyperlink, you can also map any undefined areas of the image to a URL. Prior to defining any hotspots with the drawing tools, you notice the phrase "Default (background)" in the status bar of the Image Map Editor (you can see it in Figure 12-2). If you want to set up a default link for the undefined areas, enter the link's Internet address in the Link text box, along with the corresponding Target and Alt information, if any, in their respective text boxes.

When you establish a default, Dreamweaver sets the shape attribute of the <area> tag to "default" in your map data and lists whatever information you've specified.

Caution   Unfortunately, the `<area shape="default" href="url">` code doesn't work in the latest version of Internet Explorer 4.0, so setting the default in the Image Map Editor has no effect in that browser. One workaround to this drawback is to completely cover the graphic with an area, using the Rectangle drawing tool, and then assign the desired default URL.

Using the drawing tools

You'll find the drawing tools in the Image Map Editor to be straightforward and easy to use. Each one produces a series of coordinates that are incorporated into the HTML code. All three tools, when selected, display the crosshair cursor's coordinates in the lower-right corner of the Image Map Editor. These coordinates are also displayed for the arrow pointer.

In the following steps, you'll use the Image Map Editor's Rectangle drawing tool to outline a hotspot:

1. Select the Rectangle tool from the toolbar.
2. Click one corner of the area you want to map, and drag toward the opposite corner to draw a rectangle.
3. Release the mouse button. Dreamweaver inverts the defined area.
4. Fill in the Link, Target, and Alt text boxes.

Follow these steps to use the Circle drawing tool in the Image Map Editor:

1. Select the Circle tool from the toolbar.
2. Click in the center of the area you want to define and drag out the circle until it reaches the correct size.
3. Release the mouse button. Dreamweaver inverts the defined area.
4. As before, complete the Link, Target, and Alt text boxes.

To define an irregularly shaped hotspot, use the Polygon drawing tool. Follow these steps:

1. Select the Polygon tool from the toolbar.
2. Click the first point for your hotspot object.
3. Release the mouse button, and move the mouse to the next point.
4. Continue outlining the object by clicking and moving the mouse.
5. When the hotspot is completely outlined, double-click the mouse to close the area.
6. Fill in the Link, Target, and Alt text boxes.

You can use the drawing tools in any combination. In Figure 12-3, all three drawing tools have been used to create three different hotspots. The star-shaped image is currently selected, as indicated by the inverted colors of that portion. The other two defined areas (the circular and rectangular objects) are shown with thin outlines around them.

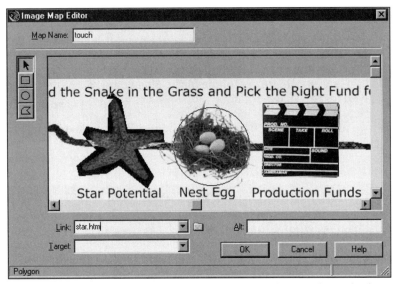

Figure 12-3: The Image Map Editor's drawing tools let you define both regular and irregularly shaped areas.

Modifying an image map

Dreamweaver gives you limited options for modifying the image maps you create. First, you can move any previously defined area by selecting it and then clicking and dragging to a new location. For precise pixel-by-pixel movement, select the area and use the arrow keys to move it in any direction.

Dreamweaver also allows you to delete any existing area. Simply select the area and press the Delete or Backspace key.

Converting Client-Side Maps to Server-Side Maps

Although most Web browsers support client-side image maps, some sites still rely on server-side image maps. You can take a client-side image map generated by Dreamweaver and convert it to a server-side image map — you can even include pointers for both maps in the same Web page, to accommodate older browsers as well as the newer ones. Such a conversion does require, however, that you use a text editor to modify and save the file. You'll also need to add one more attribute, `ismap`, to the `<img>` tag; this attribute tells the server that the image referenced in the `src` attribute is a map.

Adapting the server script

First, let's examine the differences between a client-side image map and a server-side image map from the same graphic. The HTML for a client-side image map looks like this:

```
<map name="navbar">
  <area shape="rect" coords="1,1,30,33" href="home.html"
alt="Home Page">
  <area shape="circle" coords="65,64,62" href="contacts.html"
alt="Information">
  <area shape="default" href="index.html">
</map>
```

The same definitions for a server-side image map are laid out like this:

```
rect home.html 1,1 30,33
circle contacts.html 65,64 62
default index.html
```

As you can see, the server-side image map file is much more sparse. Notice first that all of the `alt="string"` code is thrown out because tooltips can only be shown through client-side image maps.

A server expects the information in this form:

```
shape URL coordinates
```

So, you'll need to remove the `<area>` tag and its delimiters, as well as the phrases `shape=`, `coords=`, and `href=`. Then you reverse the order of the URL and the coordinates.

The last step in this phase of adapting the server-side script is to format the coordinates correctly. The format depends on the shape being defined.

✦ For rectangles, group the *x, y* points into comma-separated pairs with a single space in between each pair.

✦ For circles, separate the center point coordinates from the diameter with a space.

✦ For polygons, group the *x, y* points into comma-separated pairs with a single space in between each pair — just like rectangles.

Your new map file should be stored on your server, probably in a subfolder of the cgi-bin directory.

Caution Not all servers expect server-side image maps in the same format. The format offered here conforms to the NCSA HPPD standard. If you're unsure of the required format, or of where to put your maps on your server, check with your server administrator before creating a server-side image map.

Including the map link

The second phase of converting a client-side map to a server-side one involves making the connection between the Web page and the map file. A client-side image map link directly calls the URL associated with it. In contrast, all references from a server-side link call the map file—which in turn calls the specified URL.

The connection to a server-side map is handled in the normal manner of adding a link to a graphic. You can, of course, do this directly in Dreamweaver. Simply select your graphic, and in the Image Property Inspector insert the map file URL in the Link text box. Be sure the image's Border property is set to zero to avoid the link outline.

The final addition to your script is the `ismap` attribute. Place the `ismap` attribute in the `<img>` tag of the graphic being used for the image map, like this:

```
<img href="images/biglogo.gif" width="200" height="350" ismap>
```

As noted earlier, it is entirely possible to use client-side and server-side image maps together. The easiest way to do it is to keep the image map data as written by Dreamweaver and add the `ismap` attribute. The HTML example seen in the first section, "Client-Side Image Maps," would then read as follows:

```
<a href="http://www.idest.com/cgi-bin/maps/imap.txt">
<img src="images/imagemap.jpg" width="640" height="480"
usemap="#navbar" ismap><a/>
```

Dreamweaver Technique: Building an Image Map Rollover

One of the most popular Web page techniques today is known as a *rollover*. A rollover occurs when a user's mouse moves over a button or graphic in the page, and the button or graphic lights up or changes in some way. You'll see how to create these graphics rollovers in Chapter 8, "Inserting Images." Here in this section, let's try out one method for applying the same technique to an image map. Portions of this technique were adopted from work by Peter Belesis's DHTML Tutorials at Mecklermedia's WebReference (www.webreference.com).

Caution   The following method uses advanced techniques involving JavaScript behaviors and layers. If you're unfamiliar with these concepts, you might want to examine Chapters 17 ("Creating and Using Behaviors") and 25 ("Working with Layers") before proceeding.

Before we get underway, keep in mind that this technique — because it uses layers — works only with 4.0 browsers and higher. Furthermore, though most of these steps can be accomplished in Dreamweaver's visual editor, you will need to tweak the code in your text editor to complete the project.

Step one: Create two images

As with behavior-based button rollovers, you'll use two images to represent the "off" and "on" states of the graphic. However, because we are using image maps here, rather than separate graphics, you'll only need a total of two images (versus two for every button). In our example, there are three buttons "carved" from one graphic; but there very easily could have been eight or a dozen separate buttons, which would have required 16 or 24 separate images. All we need is our two image maps.

After building your first image, bring it into your favorite image-processing program and make the alterations necessary to create the second image. Figure 12-4 shows examples of the two images you need (above and below), inserted into Dreamweaver. As you can see, all that was necessary to make the "on" image was to add a glow effect to each of the three hotspots.

Tip   One of the methods used in this technique involves clipping a region of an image. Presently, layers only support rectangular clipping. Keep this in mind as you build your primary image, and avoid placing hotspots too close together.

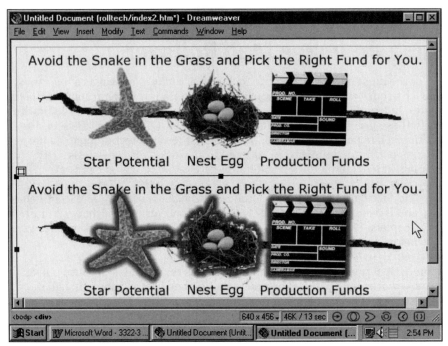

Figure 12-4: You'll need two separate images, representing "on" and "off," for a rollover image map.

Step two: Set up the layers

This technique takes advantage of three different layer properties: absolute positioning, visibility, and clipping. The idea is to display just a portion of a hidden layer during a mouseOver event. So first, we need two layers — one for each of our images.

Follow these steps to establish the initial layers:

1. Choose Insert ➪ Layer or select the Draw Layer button on the Objects Palette to create the onLayer. If you use the menu option instead of drawing out the layer, it will be created as a standard size and you won't have to spend as much time adjusting the layer sizes later.

2. Make sure the cursor is in the layer, and choose Insert ➪ Image or select the Insert Image button on the Objects Palette. Load your "on" graphic. If the layer is smaller than the image, the layer will automatically expand.

3. Repeat Step 1 to create the offLayer. Be sure to give it a unique name.

4. Repeat Step 2 and insert the "off" graphic.

5. If necessary, open the Layers Inspector by choosing Window ⇨ Layers or pressing F11, and make sure of the following:

- Both layers must have unique names. In this example, we use offLayer and onLayer.

- The offLayer must be visible.

- The onLayer must be hidden.

- The onLayer must be on top of the offLayer, so that when you make a portion of the onLayer visible, it will obscure the offLayer.

Figure 12-5 shows how the screen looks with both layers in place and the visibility properties set correctly.

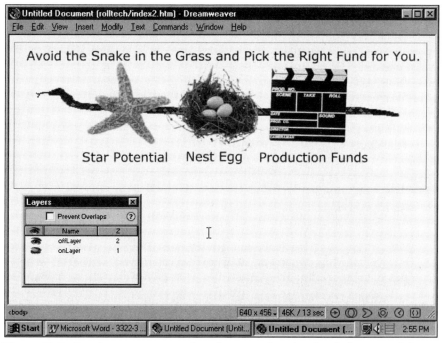

Figure 12-5: Two image maps are placed on top of each other in layers, and the top layer is hidden.

Aligning Layers

Now in Dreamweaver 2, you can use the new layer alignment commands to easily line up the two layers. The commands are covered in detail in Chapter 25, "Working with Layers," but here are the steps briefly. Group the two windows by selecting both layers in the Layer Inspector while pressing the Shift key. Choose two of the Modify ⇨ Layers options — Align Left and Align Top, for example — so that they are in the same position. If the layers are different shapes, you can make them the same size by choosing Modify ⇨ Layers ⇨ Make Same Width and/or Modify ⇨ Layers ⇨ Make Same Height.

Step three: Attach the behavior

Currently, Dreamweaver doesn't support attaching a behavior to an image map. The workaround detailed here involves first attaching the behavior to the full images in each layer, and then cutting and pasting the code built by Dreamweaver. Dreamweaver includes a JavaScript behavior called Show/Hide Layers that does exactly what you need.

Follow these steps to assign the Show/Hide Layers behavior to the layers:

1. Be sure the offLayer (the layer holding the basic, unchanged image) is visible, and the onLayer is hidden. You can select the visibility options in the Layer Inspector, to open and close the "eyes" of the respective layers.

2. Open the Behavior Inspector by clicking the Behavior button in the Launcher or selecting Window ⇨ Behaviors.

3. Select the image in the offLayer.

4. If necessary, choose 4.0 Browsers from the Browser option list.

5. Still in the Behavior Inspector, select the + (Add Behavior) button and choose Show-Hide Layers from the pop-up list.

6. When the Show-Hide Layers dialog box opens, Dreamweaver searches for all the layers in your document. After they are displayed, select the onLayer and click the Show button (see Figure 12-6). Click OK when you've finished.

7. Now we need to change the event that triggers the behavior from `onMouseDown` to `onMouseOver`. To do this, click the Add Event button in the Behavior Inspector. The Add Event button is the down arrow between the Event and Action lists. Choose `onMouseOver` from the Add Event drop-down list.

8. So far, we've assigned one behavior to make the onLayer visible when the pointer is over the image. Now we have to assign another behavior to hide the onLayer when the pointer moves away from the image.

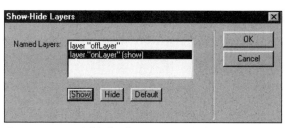

Figure 12-6: Highlight the onLayer and then choose the Show option to ensure that the Show-Hide Layer action makes the appropriate layer visible.

9. Click the Add Behavior button and again select Show-Hide Layers from the option list.

10. Now select the onLayer again and click the Hide button. Click OK when you're finished.

11. Finally, change the Event to `onMouseOut` for this new behavior, following the same procedure as in Step 7.

So what we now have is two behaviors assigned to one image. At this point the Dreamweaver code for the `<body>` of our Web page reads like this:

```
<body bgcolor="#FFFFFF">

<div id="offLayer" style="position:absolute; width:200px;
height:115px; z-index:1; visibility:visible">
  <a href="#" onMouseOver =
"MM_showHideLayers('document.layers[\'onLayer\']',
'document.all[\'onLayer\']','show')"
onMouseOut = "MM_showHideLayers('document.layers[\'onLayer\']',
'document.all[\'onLayer\']','hide')">
<img src="images/imagemap.jpg" width="607" height="191"
border="0"></a>
</div>

<div id="onLayer" style="position:absolute; width:200px;
height:115px; z-index:2; overflow:visible; visibility: hidden">
  <img src="images/imagemap2.jpg" width="607" height="191">
</div>

</body>
```

The `MM_showHideLayers()` JavaScript function called by both `onMouseOver` and `onMouseOut` is automatically written to the `<head>` section. Part of this technique involves adding and modifying that code a bit, which we'll cover in Step 5.

Step four: Make the image maps

You may have noticed that I keep referring to "creating image maps" in the plural. In addition to the map that is used to provide the image-map coordinates, we'll use Dreamweaver's Image Map Editor to draw the coordinates necessary to perform the *clipping* function. When a layer is clipped to a specific rectangle, only that rectangular portion of the layer is visible; the remainder is hidden.

The first part of this step is to make the actual image map that will eventually be used to activate the onMouseOver and onMouseOut events. Follow these steps to complete this task:

1. Select the image in one of the layers. You can use either image (the "on" or the "off") to draw the image map. I preferred the onLayer, with the slightly fuzzier edges.

2. In the extended Image Property Inspector, click the Map button.

3. In the Image Map Editor, give your map a unique name.

4. Draw out the image maps using the drawing tools and give each area a URL in the Link box. Complete the Target and Alt text boxes, if desired. Click the OK button when you're done.

Normally, when building an image map, this is where you would stop. But we're going to stay with the Image Map Editor and use it a second time to find our clipping coordinates for us. Remember, only rectangular clipping is currently supported in Dynamic HTML and CSS; therefore, only the Rectangle tool is used when creating the clipping coordinates.

You can only have one image map per image, but in this technique you have planned ahead and created two identical images to work with. Now you can perform the following steps to build your clipping map:

1. Temporarily reverse the visibility settings of the two layers, so that the layer containing the graphic used to build the image map is hidden.

2. Select the image in the now visible layer. In our example, this is the offLayer.

3. Click the Map button in the extended Image Property Inspector.

4. Give your new image map a temporary name.

5. Select the Rectangle drawing tool, and draw a rectangular area around each of the previously built image map areas. Note: It's important that these areas not overlap, but be drawn side-by-side, as shown in Figure 12-7. Give each area a unique temporary link.

6. Click OK when you've finished.

When Dreamweaver builds code for an image map, it places the first item you define as the last item in the code list, and the last item defined as the first item in the code list. The rectangular coordinates are placed in this order: left, top, right, and bottom, as can be seen in this code fragment:

```
<map name="temp">
  <area shape="rect" coords="365,0,506,176" href="#slate">
  <area shape="rect" coords="236,0,365,176" href="#nest">
  <area shape="rect" coords="93,0,234,176" href="#star">
</map>
```

Notice that, in defining the coordinates, I kept the top (0) and the bottom (176) constant for all three areas. Although this is not essential, it will result in code that is a tad simpler and, if possible, is recommended.

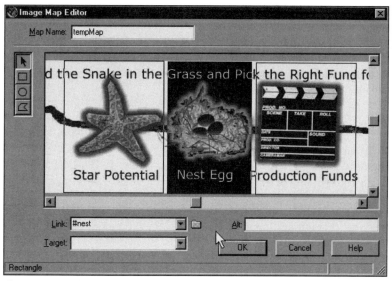

Figure 12-7: Place your rectangular clip regions side by side, without overlapping.

Step five: Complete the code

Let's review what we have done so far:

✦ Before we began working in Dreamweaver, we built two different images — one to depict the regular ("off") state, and another for the "on" state.

✦ We used Dreamweaver to create two identically sized and positioned layers. We then inserted our two images into the hidden layers, with the "on" graphic placed on top.

✦ Next, we used Dreamweaver to assign JavaScript behaviors that reveal the hidden layer when the user's pointer passes over the image.

✦ The last thing we did was to use Dreamweaver's Image Map Editor to build two image maps: one to provide clickable regions on the graphic, and one to provide rectangular coordinates to be used for clipping.

All that is left to do now is tweak the code. Granted, it's going to be a pretty big tweak, but Dreamweaver has really done all the hard work of inserting the layers and writing the cross-browser code for the behaviors. Now it's time to move to your favorite text editor and customize the HTML.

Cutting and pasting the function calls

First, you need to move the JavaScript function calls, `onMouseOver` and `onMouseOut`, away from the image and into each of the image map areas.

1. Cut (Edit ⇨ Cut) the entire function call line from inside the `<a>` tag.

2. Delete the opening `<a>`, and the closing `</a>` tag that follows the `<img>` tag.

3. Move the cursor inside the first `<area>` tag at the end and paste the function calls into the tag. In our example, the code for the circle has been changed from this:

```
<area shape="circle" coords="300,98,56" href="nest.htm">
```

to this:

```
<area shape="circle" coords="300,98,56" href="nest.htm"
onmouseout="MM_showHideLayers('document.layers[\'onLayer\']',
'document.all[\'onLayer\']','hide')"
onmouseover="MM_showHideLayers('document.layers[\'onLayer\']'
,'document.all[\'onLayer\']','show')">
```

4. Repeat this cut-and-paste action for every `<area>` defined in your image map.

Pointing to the right map

You won't be able to test the above changes until you make one more minor change. Remember how, in Step 4 of this technique, you created a temporary image map to grab the clipping coordinates? Part of that process puts a `usemap=mapname` attribute in the `<img>` tag of one of the graphics. Now you need to find that reference and change the `usemap` value so that both images are pointing to the real image map. In the example I built, my two map names are "touch" and "t2"—the latter name is the one assigned to the temporary image map used to get the clipping coordinates. So I needed to change the `<img>` tag from this:

```
<img src="imagemap.jpg" width="607" height="191" border="0"
usemap="#t2">
```

to this:

```
<img src="imagemap.jpg" width="607" height="191" border="0"
usemap="#touch">
```

The section altered in both code lines is in boldface, to make it easy for you to see the change.

Once you've made this change, the image when tested in a 4.0 browser should only change when the pointer passes over the mapped areas. But it's still not quite right: You'll notice that all of the image changes, instead of just one area. It's time to put that clipping function to work.

Building the clipping array

The next step involves taking the coordinates gathered from our pseudo-image map and plugging them into a JavaScript array. Because the top and bottom coordinates were kept constant, we only need to bring in the left and the right values. We also need an identifying number to mark each image map area.

In our example, only three image map buttons were included, so you see only three `setBeginEnd` statements. However, you can have as many buttons as you like.

The following code is included in the `<script>` section, above the Macromedia functions:

```
arClips = new Array();
function setBeginEnd(which,from,to) {
    arClips[which] = new Array();
    arClips[which][0] = from;
    arClips[which][1] = to;
}
setBeginEnd(1,93,234);
setBeginEnd(2,236,365);
setBeginEnd(3,365,506);
clTop = 0;
clBot = 176;
```

The two variables, `clTop` and `clBot`, hold the values for the clip top range and the clip bottom range, respectively. Again, because these are constant, we can go ahead and set them.

Integrating the code

Our last task is to tie all the disparate parts together. First we need to pass the identifying number from each image map area to the function. We do this by adding the number to the end of each function call in each `<shape>` tag. Previously, the code read as follows:

```
<area shape="rect" coords="376,36,486,141" href="slate.htm"
onmouseout="MM_showHideLayers('document.layers[\'onLayer\']','d
ocument.all[\'onLayer\']','hide')"
onmouseover="MM_showHideLayers('document.layers[\'onLayer\']','
document.all[\'onLayer\']','show')">
```

Now, it reads like this (the additions are in bold for easy reference):

```
<area shape="rect" coords="376,36,486,141" href="slate.htm"
onmouseout="MM_showHideLayersIM('document.layers[\'onLayer\']',
'document.all[\'onLayer\']','hide',3)"
onmouseover="MM_showHideLayersIM('document.layers[\'onLayer\']'
,'document.all[\'onLayer\']','show',3)">
```

Be sure to use a unique number to identify each defined shape. In this example, the function name has also been slightly modified with the added IM for image map at the end. This is done to prevent Dreamweaver from overwriting the function if the same behavior is applied elsewhere on the page. Naturally, the name of the actual function needs to be modified as well.

The next step is to modify the Dreamweaver-generated function to read our new value and to act on our array. Listing 12-1 shows the basic Dreamweaver code for showing and hiding layers.

Listing 12-1: **Macromedia's Standard Show/Hide Layers Function**

```
function MM_showHideLayers() { //v2.0
  var i, visStr, args, theObj;
  args = MM_showHideLayers.arguments;
  for (i=0; i<(args.length-2); i+=3) { //with arg triples
(objNS,objIE,visStr)
    visStr   = args[i+2];
    if (navigator.appName == 'Netscape' && document.layers !=
null) {
      theObj = eval(args[i]);
      if (theObj) theObj.visibility = visStr;
    } else if (document.all != null) { //IE
      if (visStr == 'show') visStr = 'visible'; //convert vals
      if (visStr == 'hide') visStr = 'hidden';
      theObj = eval(args[i+1]);
      if (theObj) theObj.style.visibility = visStr;
  } }
```

Cross-Reference Dreamweaver 2's extended Find and Replace capabilities make changes like this a snap. If you're unclear about how to find and replace HTML code, review Chapter 7, "Adding Text to Your Web Page."

Modifying the code involves the following:

✦ Modify the function name to prevent Macromedia from overwriting the customized code, as mentioned at the beginning of this section.

✦ Add needed variables: `clRight` (Right Clip value), `clLeft` (Left Clip value), and `which` (the identifying number of the defined area).

✦ Increase the number of arguments to examine, which is passed by the function call to account for the added value.

✦ Pull the identifying number of the clip from the arguments.

✦ Assign the value to the Left Clip variable, `clLeft`.

✦ Assign the value to the Right Clip variable, `clRight`.

✦ In the Netscape section, set the clipping range for the Left and the Right.

✦ In the Internet Explorer section, set the entire clipping range.

You can see the changes, marked in bold, in Listing 12-2.

Listing 12-2: Modified Image Map Rollover Function

```
function MM_showHideLayersIM() { //v2.0 Modified by jlowery
  var i, visStr, args;
  var clRight, clLeft, which;
  args = MM_showHideLayersIM.arguments;
  for (i=0; i<(args.length-2); i+=4) { //with 4 args
(objNS,objIE,visStr,which)
    visStr   = args[i+2];
    which = args[i+3];
    clLeft = arClips[which][0];
    clRight = arClips[which][1];
    if (navigator.appName == 'Netscape') {
      document.onLayer.clip.left=clLeft
      document.onLayer.clip.right=clRight;
      theObj = eval(args[i]);
      if (theObj) theObj.visibility = visStr;
      } else if (document.all != null) { //IE
      if (visStr == 'show') visStr = 'visible'; //convert vals
      if (visStr == 'hide') visStr = 'hidden';
      document.all.onLayer.style.clip ="rect(" + clTop + " " +
clRight + " " + clBot + " " + clLeft + ")";
      theObj = eval(args[i+1]);
      if (theObj) theObj.style.visibility = visStr;
      }
  }
}
```

Once you've implemented these changes, test your object. You should see the type of reaction demonstrated in Figure 12-8.

Caution   When you go to preview your work in a browser, make sure that visibility is set correctly for each layer.

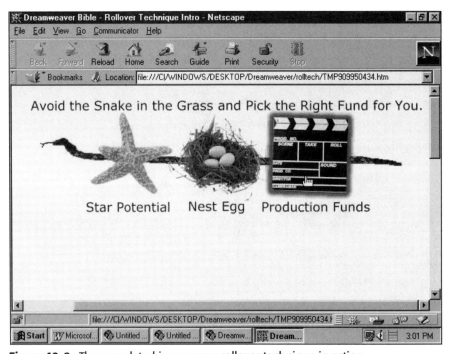

Figure 12-8: The completed image map rollover technique in action.

Summary

Image maps provide a very necessary capability in Web page design. Without them, you wouldn't be able to link irregularly shaped graphics, or to group links all in one image. Dreamweaver's built-in Image Map Editor gives you all the tools you need to create simple, effective client-side image maps.

✦ Image maps let you define separate areas of one graphic and link them to different URLs. There are two kinds of image maps: client-side and server-side. Dreamweaver creates client-side image maps through its Image Map Editor.

✦ The Image Map Editor offers three basic drawing tools for creating rectangular, circular, and irregularly shaped image maps.

✦ If your Web site uses server-side image maps, you can make them by modifying and converting Dreamweaver-generated client-side image maps.

✦ It's possible to create the effect of a graphic rollover, common on Web pages, using client-side image maps. This chapter's Dreamweaver technique shows you how.

In the next chapter you learn about forms in Dreamweaver.

✦   ✦   ✦

Interactive Forms

A form, in the everyday world as well as on the Web, is a type of structured communication. When you apply for a driver's license, you're not told to just write down all your personal info; you're asked to fill out a form that asks for specific parts of that information, one at a time, in a specific manner. Web-based forms are just as precise, if not more so.

Dreamweaver has a robust and superior implementation of HTML forms — from the dedicated Forms panel in the Objects Palette to various form-specific Property Inspectors. In addition to their importance as a tool for communication between the browsing public and Web site administrators, forms are integral to building some of Dreamweaver's own objects.

In this chapter you learn how forms are structured and then created within Dreamweaver. Each form object is explored in detail — text fields, radio buttons, check-boxes, menus and list boxes, command buttons, hidden fields, and password fields.

How HTML Forms Work

Forms have a very special function in HTML: they support interaction. Virtually all HTML elements apart from forms are concerned with design and presentation — delivering the content to the user, if you will. Forms, on the other hand, give the user the ability to pass information back to Web site creators and administrators. Without forms, the Web would be a one-way street.

There are many, many uses for forms on the Web, including surveys, electronic commerce, guest books, polls, and even real-time custom graphic creation. For such feedback to be possible, forms require an additional component to what's seen onscreen so that each form can complete its function. Every form needs some type of connection to a Web server, and usually this connection takes the form of a *common gateway interface (CGI)* script, although JavaScript and Java can also be used. This means that, in addition to designing your forms onscreen, you or someone who works with you must implement a program that collects and manages the information from the form.

Forms, like HTML tables, can be thought of as self-contained units within a Web page. All the elements of a form are contained within the form tag pair, `<form>` and `</form>`. Unlike tables, you cannot nest forms, although there's nothing to stop you from having multiple forms on a page.

The `<form>` tag has three attributes, only two of which are commonly used:

✦ The `method` attribute tells the server how the contents of the form should be presented to the CGI program. The two possible `method` values are `get` and `post`. Get passes the information attached to an URL and is rarely used these days, because it places limitations on the amount of data that can be passed to the gateway program. Post causes the server to present the information as standard input and imposes no limits on the amount of passed data.

✦ The second `<form>` attribute is `action`. The `action` attribute determines what should be done with the form content. Most commonly, `action` is set to a URL for running a specific CGI program or for sending e-mail.

✦ The third, infrequently used attribute for `<form>` is `enctype`, which specifies the MIME media type.

Typical HTML for a `<form>` tag looks something like this:

```
<form method="post" action="http://www.idest.com/
cgi-bin/mailcall.pl">
```

Tip   The `.pl` extension in the preceding example form tag stands for *Perl* — a scripting language often used to create CGI programs. Perl can be edited in any regular text editor.

Within each form is a series of input devices — text boxes, radio buttons, check-boxes, and so on. Each type handles a particular sort of input; in fact, the main tag for these elements is the `<input>` tag. With one exception, the `<textarea>` tag, all form input types are called by specifying the `type` attribute. The text box tag, for example, is written as follows:

```
<input type=text value="lastname">
```

All form-input tags have `value` attributes. Information input by the user is assigned to the given value. Thus, if I were to fill out a form with a text box asking for my last name, like the one produced by the foregoing tag, part of the message sent would include the following string:

```
lastname=Lowery
```

Web servers send all the information from a form in one long text string to whatever program or address is specified in the `action` attribute. It's up to the program or the recipient of the form message to parse the string. For instance, if I were to fill out a small form with my name, e-mail address, and a quick comment like "Good work!" the server would send a text string similar to the following:

```
name=Joseph+Lowery&address=jlowery@idest.com&comment=Good+work%21
```

As you can see, the various fields are separated by ampersands, and the individual words within the responses are separated by plus signs. Characters outside of the lower end of the ASCII set are represented by their hexadecimal value. Decoding this text string is called *parsing* the response.

Tip   If you're not using the `mailto` method for getting your Web feedback, don't despair. Most CGI programs parse the text string as part of their basic functionality before sending it on its way.

Inserting a Form in Dreamweaver

A form is inserted just like any other object in Dreamweaver. Place the cursor where you want your form to start, and then either select the Insert Form button from the Forms panel of the Objects Palette or choose Insert ➪ Form from the menus. Dreamweaver inserts a red dashed outline stretching across the Document Window to indicate the form.

If you have the Property Inspector open, the Form Property Inspector appears when you insert a form. As you can see from Figure 13-1, you can specify only three values regarding forms: the Form Name, the Action, and the Method.

Specifying a form name enables the form to be directly referenced by JavaScript or by other languages. Because of the interactive nature of forms, this feature is often used by Web programmers to gather information from the user.

In the Action text box, you can directly enter an URL or mailto address, or you can select the Folder icon and browse for a file.

Note   Sending your form data via a mailto address is not without its problems. Some browsers, most notably Internet Explorer, are set to warn the user whenever a form button using mailto is selected. While many users will let the mail go through, they do have the option to stop it from being sent.

The method defaults to `Post`, the most commonly used option. You can also choose `Get`; or `Default`, which leaves the method up to the browser. In most cases, you should leave the method set to `Post`.

Form Outline   Insert Form button

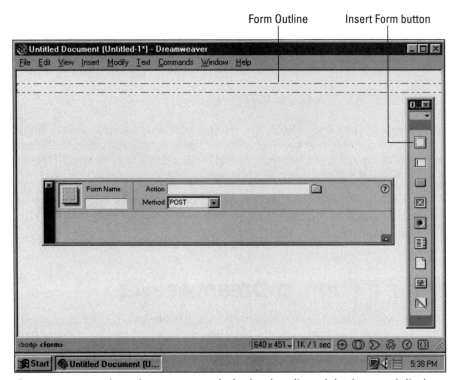

Figure 13-1: Inserting a form creates a dashed red outline of the form and displays the Form Property Inspector, if available.

Note   Forms cannot be placed inline with any other element such as text or graphics.

Keep in mind a few considerations when it comes to mixing forms and other Web page elements:

✦ Forms expand as objects are inserted into them; you can't resize a form by dragging its boundaries.

✦ The outline of a form is invisible; there is no border to turn on or off.

✦ Forms and tables can be used together only if the form either completely encloses or is completely enclosed inside the table. In other words, you can't have a form spanning part of a table.

✦ Forms can be inserted within layers, and multiple forms can be in multiple layers. However, the layer must completely enclose the form. As with forms spanning tables, you can't have a form spanning two or more layers. (A workaround for this limitation is discussed in the "Forms and Layers" section of Chapter 25.)

Tip You can turn off the red dashed form outline in Dreamweaver's preview, if you'd like. Choose Edit ➪ Preferences and, in the Invisible Elements panel, deselect the Form Delimiter option.

Using Text Boxes

Anytime you use a form to gather text information typed in by a user, you use a form object called a *text field*. Text fields can hold any number of alphanumeric characters. The Web designer can decide whether the text field is displayed in one line or several. When the HTML is written, a multiple-line text field uses a

```
<textarea>
```

tag, and a single-line text field is coded with

```
<input type=text>
```

Text fields

To insert a single-line text field in Dreamweaver, you can use any of the following methods:

✦ From the Forms panel of the Objects Palette, select the Insert Text Field button to place a text field at your current cursor position.

✦ Choose Insert ➪ Form Object ➪ Text Field from the menu, which inserts a text field at the current cursor position.

✦ Drag the Insert Text Field button from the Objects Palette to any existing location in the Document Window, and release the mouse button to position the text field.

When you insert a text field, the Property Inspector, when displayed, shows you the attributes that can be changed (see Figure 13-2). The size of a text field is measured by the number of characters it can display at one time. You can change the length of a text field by inserting a value in the Char Width text box. By default, Dreamweaver inserts a text field approximately 20 characters wide. The *approximately* is important here because the *final* size of the text field is ultimately controlled by the browser used to view the page. Unless you limit the number of possible characters by entering a value in the Max Chars text box, the user can enter as many characters as desired and the text box will scroll to display them.

Note that the value in Char Width determines the visible width of the field, while the value in Max Chars actually determines the number of characters that can be entered.

The Init Value text box on the Text Field Property Inspector is used to insert a default text string. The user can overwrite this value, if desired.

Insert Text Field button

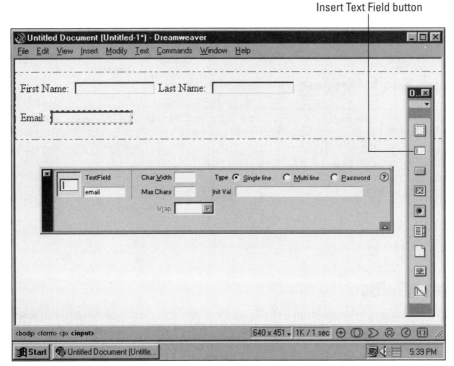

Figure 13-2: The text field of a form is used to allow the user to type in any required information.

Neat Forms

Text field width is measured in a monospaced character width. Because regular fonts are not monospaced, however, lining up text fields and other form objects can be problematic at best. There are two general workarounds: preformatted text and tables.

Switching the labels on the form to preformatted text enables you to insert any amount of whitespace to properly space out ("kern") your text and other input fields. Previously, Web designers were stuck with the default preformatted text format—the rather plain-looking Courier monospaced font. Now, however, newer browsers (3.0 and later) can read the `face=fontname` attribute. So you can combine a regular font with the preformatted text option and get the best of both worlds.

Going the preformatted text route requires you to insert a lot of spaces. So when you are working on a larger, complex form, using tables is probably a better way to go. Besides the speed of layout, the other advantage that tables offer is the ability to right-align text labels next to your text fields. The top form in the following figure gives an example of using preformatted text to get different-sized form fields to line up properly, while the bottom form in the figure uses a table.

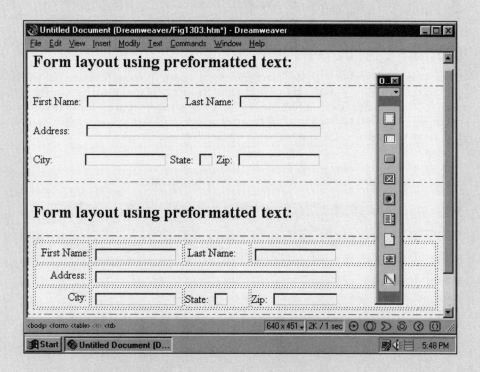

Combining differently sized text fields on a single row—for example, when you're asking for a city, state, and zip code combination—can make the task of lining up your form even more difficult. Most often you'll spend a fair amount of time in a trial-and-error effort to make the text fields match. Be sure to check your results in the various browsers as you build your form.

Password fields

Normally, all text entered into a text field displays as you expect—programmers refer to this process as *echoing*. You can turn off the echoing by selecting the Password option in the Text Field Property Inspector. When a text field is designated as a password field, all text entered by the user will show up as asterisks in Window systems or as dots on Macintoshes.

Use the password field when you want to protect the user's input from prying eyes (as your PIN number is hidden when you enter it at an ATM, for instance). The information entered in a password field is not encrypted or scrambled in any way, and when sent to the Web administrator it displays as regular text.

Only single-line text fields can be set as password fields. You cannot make a multiline `<textarea>` tag act as a password field without employing JavaScript or some other programming.

Multiline text areas

When you want to give your users a generous amount of room to write, set the text field to the Multiline option on the Text Field Property Inspector. This converts the default 20-character width for single-line text fields to a text area approximately 18 characters wide and 3 lines high, with a horizontal and vertical scroll bar. Figure 13-3 shows a typical multiline text field embedded in a form.

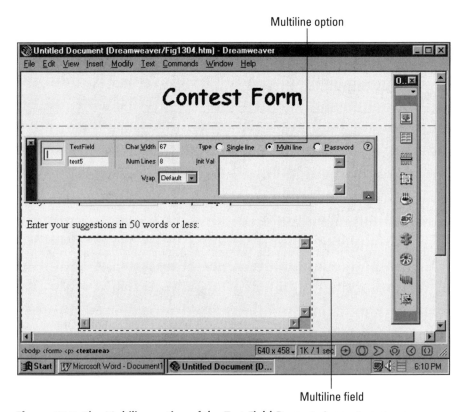

Figure 13-3: The Multiline option of the Text Field Property Inspector opens up a text box for more user information.

You control the width of a multiline text area by entering a value in the Char Width text box of the Text Field Property Inspector, just as you do for single-line text fields. The height of the text area is set equal to the value in the Num Lines text box. As with the default single-line text field, the user can enter any amount of text desired. Unlike the single-line text field, which can restrict the number of characters that can be input through the Max Chars text box, you cannot restrict the number of characters the user enters into a multiline text area.

New Feature By default, text entered into a multiline text field does not wrap when it reaches the right edge of the text area; rather, it keeps scrolling until the user presses Enter (Return). Dreamweaver 2 enables you to force the text to wrap by selecting Virtual or Physical from the Wrap drop-down list. The Virtual option wraps text on the screen but not when the response is submitted. To wrap text in either situation, use the Physical wrap option.

One other option is to preload the text area with any default text you like. Enter this text in the Init Val text box of the Text Field Property Inspector. When Dreamweaver writes the HTML code, this text is not entered as a value, as for the single-line text field, but rather goes in between the `<textarea>...</textarea>` tag pair.

Providing Check-Boxes and Radio Buttons

When you want your Web page reader to choose between a specific set of options in your form, one choice is to use either check-boxes or radio buttons. Check-boxes let you offer a series of options from which the user can pick as many as desired. Radio buttons, on the other hand, give your user a number of selections from which only one is chosen.

Tip You can achieve the same functionality as check-boxes and radio buttons with a different look by using the drop-down list and menu boxes. These options for presenting choices to the user are described shortly.

Check-boxes

Check-boxes are often used in a "Select All That Apply" type of section, when you want to enable the user to choose as many of the listed options as desired. You insert a check-box in much the same way as you do a text box: Select or drag the Insert Check Box from the Objects Palette, or choose Insert ➪ Form Object ➪ Check Box.

Like other form objects, check-boxes can be given a unique name in the text box provided in the Check Box Property Inspector (Figure 13-4). If you don't provide one, Dreamweaver inserts a generic one, such as checkbox4.

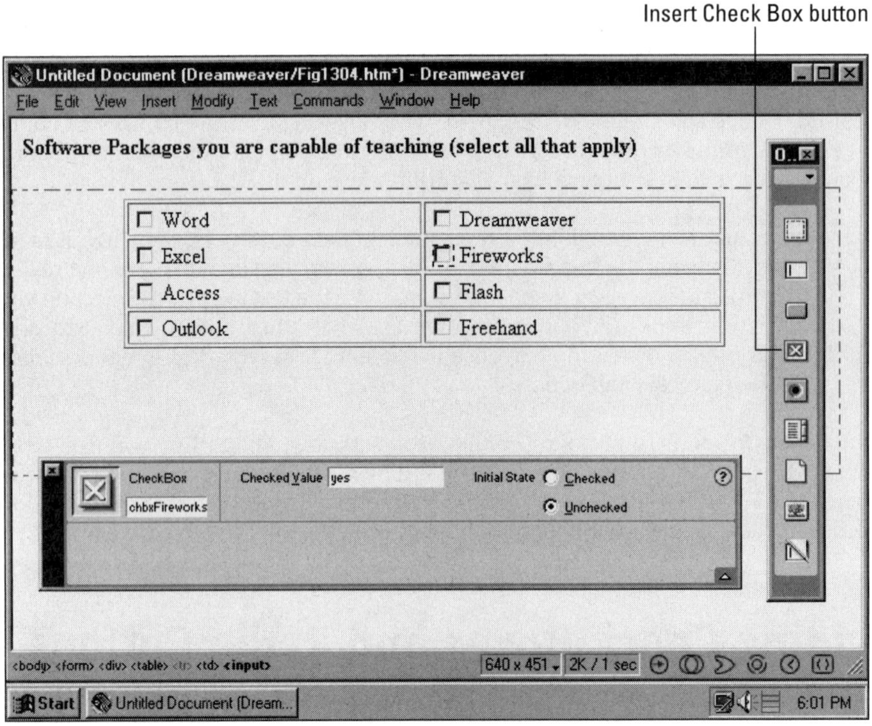

Insert Check Box button

Figure 13-4: Check-boxes are one way of offering the Web page visitor any number of options to choose.

In the CheckedValue text box, fill in the information you want passed to a program when the user selects the check-box. By default, a check-box starts out unchecked, but you can change that by changing the Initial State option to Checked.

Radio buttons

Radio buttons on a form provide a set of options from which the user can only choose one. If users change their mind after choosing one radio button, selecting another one automatically deselects the first choice. You insert radio buttons in the same manner as check-boxes. Choose or drag Insert Radio Button from the Forms panel of the Objects Palette, or choose Insert ➪ Form Object ➪ Radio Button.

Unlike check-boxes and text fields, each radio button in the set does not have a unique name—instead, each *group* of radio buttons does. Giving the entire set of radio buttons the same name enables browsers to assign one value to the radio button set. That value is determined by the contents of the Checked Value text box. Figure 13-5 shows two different sets of radio buttons. One is named `rbComputers` and the other, `rbOpSys`.

Insert Radio button

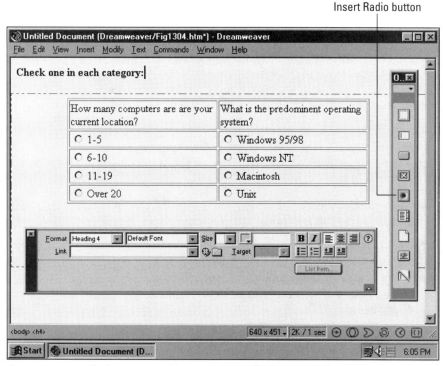

Figure 13-5: Radio buttons enable a user to make just one selection from a group of options.

To designate the default selection for each radio button group, you select the particular radio button and make the Initial State option Checked instead of Unchecked. In the form shown in Figure 13-5, the default selection for the rbOpSys group is Macintosh.

Tip

Because you must give radio buttons in the same set the same name, you can speed up your work a bit by creating one button, copying it, and then pasting the others. Don't forget to change the Checked Value for each button, though.

Creating Form Lists and Menus

Another way to offer your user options, in a more compact form than radio buttons and check-boxes, is with form lists and menus. Both objects can create single-line entries in your form that expand or scroll to reveal all the available options. You can also determine how deep you want the scrolling list to be; that is, how many options you want displayed at a time.

Drop-down menus

A drop-down menu is very familiar to everyday users of computers: the menu is initially displayed as a single-line text box with an option arrow button at the right end; when the button is clicked, the other options are revealed in a list or menu. (Whether the list "pops up" or "drops down" depends on its position in the browser window at the time it is selected. Normally the list drops down, unless it is close to the bottom of the screen.) The user selects one of the listed options and, when the mouse is released, the list closes up and the selected value remains displayed in the text box.

Insert a drop-down menu in Dreamweaver as you would any other form object, with one of these actions:

   ✦ From the Forms panel of the Objects Palette, select the Insert List/Menu button to place a drop-down menu at the current cursor position.

   ✦ Choose Insert ➪ Form Object ➪ List/Menu from the menu to insert a drop-down menu at the current cursor position.

   ✦ Drag the Insert List/Menu button from the Property Inspector to any location in the Document Window, and release the mouse button to position the drop-down menu.

With the List/Menu object inserted, make sure the Menu option (versus the List option) is selected in the Property Inspector, as shown in Figure 13-6. You can also name the drop-down menu by typing a name in the Name text box; if you don't, Dreamweaver supplies a generic "select" name.

Menu values

The HTML code for a drop-down menu uses the `<select>...</select>` tag pair surrounding a number of `<option>...</option>` tag pairs. Dreamweaver gives you a very straightforward user interface for entering labels and values for the options on your menu. The menu item's *label* is what is displayed on the drop-down list; its *value* is what is sent to the server-side processor when this particular option is selected.

To enter the labels and values for a drop-down menu — or for a scrolling list — follow these steps:

   1. Select the menu for which you want to enter values.

   2. From the List/Menu Property Inspector, select the List Values button. The List Values dialog box appears (see Figure 13-7).

Insert List / Menu button

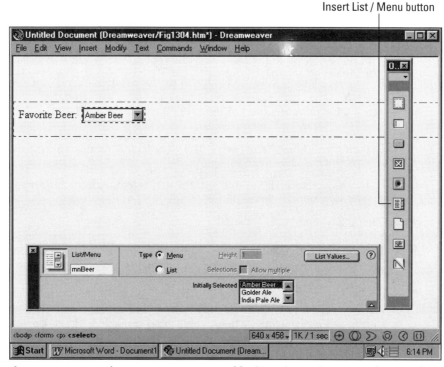

Figure 13-6: Drop-down menus are created by inserting a List/Menu object and then selecting the Menu option in the List/Menu Property Inspector.

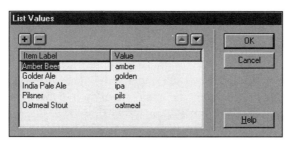

Figure 13-7: Use the List Values dialog box to enter and modify the items in a drop-down menu or scrolling list.

3. In the Item Label column, enter the label for the first item. Press the Tab key to move to the Value column.

4. Enter the value to be associated with this item. Press the Tab key.

5. Continue entering items and values by repeating Steps 3 and 4.

6. To delete an item's label *and* value in the List Values dialog box, highlight it and select the – (minus) button at the top of the list. To delete either the item's label or value, but not both, highlight either the label or the value and press the Delete or Backspace key.

7. To continue adding items, select the + (Add) button or continue using the Tab key (as previously shown in Figure 13-7).

8. To rearrange the order of items in the list, select an item and then press the up or down keys to reposition it.

9. Click OK when you've finished.

If you haven't entered a value for every item, the server-side application receives the label instead. Generally, however, it is a good idea to specify a value for all items.

New Feature

You can preselect any item in a drop-down menu so that it appears in the list box initially and is highlighted when the full list is displayed. Before Dreamweaver 2, you had to accomplish this by entering in the HTML code by hand. Dreamweaver 2 enables you to pick your selection from the Initially Selected menu in the Property Inspector. The Initially Selected menu is empty until you enter items through the List Values dialog box. You can only preselect one item for a drop-down menu.

Scrolling lists

A scrolling list differs from a drop-down menu in three respects. First, and most obviously, the scrolling list field has up and down arrow buttons, rather than an option arrow button, and the user can scroll the list, showing as little as one item at a time, instead of the entire list. Second, you can control the height of the scrolling list, enabling it to display more than one item — or all available items — simultaneously. Third, you can enable the user to select more than one item at a time, as with check-boxes.

A scrolling list is inserted in the same manner as a drop-down menu — through the Objects Palette or the Insert ⇨ Form Object menu. Once the object is inserted, select the List option in the List/Menu Property Inspector.

You enter items for your scrolling list just as you do with a drop-down menu, by starting with the List Values button and filling in the List Values dialog box.

As it does for drop-down menus, Dreamweaver automatically shows the first list item in the scrolling list's single-line text box. However, all the list items are displayed in the Document Window, as shown in Figure 13-8.

Figure 13-8: Scrolling lists enable multiple selections.

By default, the Selections check-box for Allow multiple is enabled in the List/Menu Property Inspector, and the Height box (which controls the number of items visible at one time) is empty.

When multiple selections are enabled (by selecting the Allow multiple check-box), the user can then make multiple selections by using two keyboard modifiers, the Shift and Control keys:

✦ To select several adjacent items in the list, the user must click the first item in the list, press the Shift key, and select the last item in the list.

✦ To select several nonadjacent items, the user must hold down the Control key while selecting the items.

Other than the highlighted text, no other acknowledgment (such as a check mark) appears in the list. As with drop-down menus, the Web designer can determine which options are preselected by highlighting them in the Initially Selected drop-down menu. Use the same techniques with the Shift and Control keys as a user would.

Keep in mind several factors as you are working with scrolling lists:

✦ If you disable the Allow Multiple Selections box and do not set a Height value greater than 1, the list appears as a drop-down menu.

✦ If you do not set a Height value at all, the number of items that appear onscreen is left up to the browser. Internet Explorer, by default, shows four items at a time, and Navigator displays all the items in your list. To exercise control over your scrolling list, it is best to insert a Height value.

✦ The widths of both the scrolling list and the drop-down menu are determined by the number of characters in the longest label. To widen the List/menu object, you must directly enter additional hard spaces ( ) in the HTML code; Dreamweaver does not recognize additional spaces entered through the List Values dialog box. For example, to expand the Favorite Beer List/menu object in our example, you'd need use the HTML Inspector or another editor to change the following code:

```
<option value="oatmeal">Oatmeal Stout</option>
```

to this:

```
<option value="oatmeal">Oatmeal Stout
   </option>
```

Activating Your Form with Buttons

Buttons are essential to HTML forms. You can place all the form objects you want on a page, but until your user presses that Submit button, there's no interaction between the client and the server. HTML provides three basic types of buttons: Submit, Reset, and Command buttons.

Submit, Reset, and Command buttons

A Submit button sends the form to the specified Action (generally an URL of a server-side program, or a mailto address) using the noted Method (generally post). A Reset button clears all the fields in the form. Submit and Reset are both reserved HTML terms used to invoke specific actions.

A Command button permits the execution of functions defined by the Web designer, as programmed in JavaScript or other languages.

To insert a button in Dreamweaver, follow these steps:

1. Position the cursor where you want the button to appear. Then either select the Insert Button icon from the Form pane of the Objects Palette, or choose Insert ➪ Form Object ➪ Button from the menus. Or you can simply drag the Insert Button button from the Objects Palette and drop it into place on an existing form.

2. Choose the button type. As shown in Figure 13-9, the Button Property Inspector indicates that the Submit Form button type is selected. (This is the default.) To make a Reset button, select the Reset Form option. To make a Command button, select the None option.

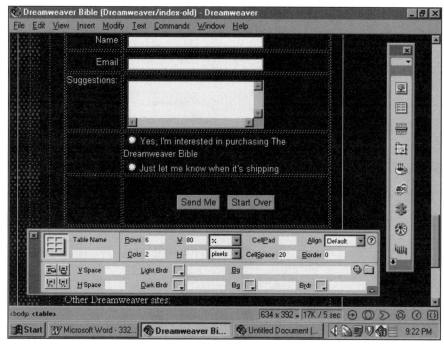

Figure 13-9: You can choose a function and a label for a button through the Button Property Inspector.

3. To change the name of any button as you want it to appear on the Web page, enter the new name in the Label text box.

Tip

When working with Command buttons, it's not enough to just insert the button and give it a name. You have to link the button to a specific function. A common technique is to use JavaScript's `onClick` event to call a function detailed in the `<script>` section of the document:

```
<input type="BUTTON" name="submit2" value="yes"
onClick="doFunction()">
```

Graphical buttons

HTML doesn't limit you to the browser-style default buttons. You can also use an image as a Submit, Reset, or Command button. Dreamweaver now has the capability to add an image field as you do other form elements: Place the cursor in the desired position and choose Insert ➪ Form Object ➪ Image Field, or select the Image Field button from the Forms panel of the Objects Palette. You can use multiple image fields in a form to give the user a graphical choice, as shown in Figure 13-10.

Figure 13-10: Each flag in this page is not just an image; it's an image field that also acts as a Submit button.

When the user clicks the picture that you've designated as an image field for a Submit button, the form is submitted. Any other functionality, such as resetting the fields, must be coded in JavaScript or another language and triggered by attaching an onClick event to the button. This can be handled through the Dreamweaver behaviors, covered in Chapter 17, "Using Behaviors," or by hand-coding the script and inserting the onClick code.

In fact, when the user clicks a graphical button, not only will it submit your form, but it will also pass along the *x, y* coordinates of the image. The *x* coordinate is submitted using the name of the field and an .x attached; likewise, the *y* coordinate is submitted with the name of the field and a .y attached. Although this latter feature isn't often used, it's always good to know all the capabilities of your HTML tools.

Cross-Reference

For detailed information about how to use a graphic as a form button, see the section, "Posting form data with a Submit button" in Chapter 15.

Using the Hidden Field and the File Field

You should also be aware of a couple of other special-purpose form fields. The *hidden field* and *file field* are supported through all major browsers. The hidden field is extremely useful for passing variables to your gateway programs, and the file field enables the user to attach a file to the form being submitted.

The hidden input type

Very often when passing information from a form to a CGI program, the programmer needs to send data that should not be made visible to the user. The data could be a variable needed by the CGI program to set information on the recipient of the form, or it could be an URL to which the CGI program will redirect the user after the form is submitted. To send this sort of information unseen by the form user, you must use a *hidden* form object.

The hidden field is inserted in a form much like the other form elements. To insert a hidden field, place your cursor in the desired position and choose Insert ⇨ Form Object ⇨ Hidden Field or choose the Insert Hidden Field button from the Forms panel of the Objects Palette.

The hidden object is another input type, just like the text, radio button, and check-box types. A hidden variable looks like this in HTML:

```
<input type="hidden" name="recipient"
value="jlowery@idest.com">
```

As you would expect, there is no representation of this tag when it's viewed though a browser. However, Dreamweaver does display a Hidden Form Element Invisible symbol in the Document Window. You can turn off the display of this symbol by deselecting the Hidden Form Element option from the Invisible Elements panel of Preferences.

The file input type

Much more rarely used than the hidden input type is the file input type, which enables any stored computer file to be attached to the form and sent with the other data. Used primarily to allow for the easy sharing of data, the file input type has been largely supplanted by modern e-mail methods, which also allow for files to be attached to any message.

The file field is inserted in a form much like the other form elements. To insert a file field, place your cursor in the desired position, and choose Insert ⇨ Form Object ⇨ File Field or choose the Insert File Field button from the Forms panel of the Objects Palette. Dreamweaver automatically inserts a text box for the filename to be input, with a Browse (Choose) button on the right. In a browser, the user's selection of the Browse (Choose) button displays a standard Open File dialog box, from which a file can be selected to go with the form.

Summary

HTML forms provide a basic line of communication from Web page visitor to Web page creator. With Dreamweaver, you can enter and modify most varieties of form inputs, including text fields and check-boxes.

✦ For the most part, a complete form requires two working parts: the form object inserted in your Web page and a CGI program stored on your Web server.

✦ To avoid using a server-side script, you can use a mailto address rather than an URL pointing to a program in a form's action attribute. However, you will still have to parse the form reply to convert it to a usable format.

✦ The basic types of form input are text fields, text areas, radio buttons, check-boxes, drop-down menus, and scrolling lists.

✦ Once a form is completed it must be sent to the server-side application. This is usually done through a Submit button on the form. Dreamweaver also supports Reset and user-definable Command buttons.

In the next chapter, you learn how to use Dreamweaver to develop frames and framesets.

✦   ✦   ✦

Using Frames and Framesets

✦ ✦ ✦ ✦

In This Chapter

Fundamentals of HTML frames and framesets

Creating frames visually

Altering frames and framesets

Opening links in specific frames

Working with borders, scroll bars, and margins

Inserting frameless content

✦ ✦ ✦ ✦

The first time I fully appreciated the power of frames I was visiting a site that displayed examples of what the Webmaster considered "bad" Web pages. The site was essentially a jump-station with a series of links — the author used a frameset with three frames: one that ran all the way across the top of the page, displaying a logo and other basic information; one narrow panel on the left with a scrolling set of links to the sites themselves, and the main viewing area, which took up two-thirds of the center screen. Selecting any of the links caused the site to appear in the main viewing frame.

I was astounded when I finally realized that each frame was truly an independent Web page, and that you didn't have to use only Web pages on your own site — you could link to any page on the Internet. That was when I also realized the amount of work involved in establishing a frame Web site: Every page displayed on that site used multiple HTML pages.

Dreamweaver takes the head-pounding complexity out of coding and managing frames with a point-and-click interface. You get easy access to the commands for modifying the properties of the overall frame structure as well as each individual frame. This chapter gives you an overview of frames, as well as all the specifics you'll need for inserting and modifying frames and framesets. Special attention is given to defining the unique look of frames through borders, scroll bars, and margins.

Frames constitute one of the Webmaster's major design tools. A frame is a Web page that is subdivided into both static and changing HTML pages. Not too long ago, the evolution of frames was right where Dynamic HTML is today, in terms of general acceptance. The use of frames and framesets has become even more widespread over the last year or so, and the technology is now supported through every major browser version. It's safe to say that every Web designer today needs a working knowledge of frames to stay competitive.

Frames and Framesets: The Basics

It's best to think of frames in two major parts: the frameset and the frames. The *frameset* is the HTML document that defines the framing structure — the number of individual frames that make up a page, their initial size, and the shared attributes among all the frames. A frameset by itself is never displayed. *Frames*, on the other hand, are complete HTML documents that can be viewed and edited separately or together in the organization described by the frameset.

A frameset takes the place of the `<body>` tags in an HTML document, where the content of a Web page is found. Here's what the HTML for a basic frameset looks like:

```
<frameset rows="50%,50%">
  <frame src="top.html">
  <frame src="bottom.html">
</frameset>
```

Notice that the content of a `<frameset>` tag consists entirely of `<frame>` tags, each one referring to a different Web page. The only other element that can be used inside of a `<frameset>` tag is another `<frameset>` tag.

Columns and rows

Framesets, much like tables, are made up of columns and rows. The columns and rows attributes (`cols` and `rows`) are lists of comma-separated values. The number of values indicates the number of either columns or rows, and the values themselves establish the size of the columns or rows. Thus, a `<frameset>` tag that looks like this:

```
<frameset cols="67,355,68">
```

denotes three columns of widths 67, 355, and 68, respectively. And this frameset tag:

```
<frameset cols="270,232" rows="384,400">
```

declares that there are two columns with the specified widths (270 and 232) and two rows with the specified heights (384 and 400).

Sizing frames

Column widths and row heights can be set as absolute measurements in pixels, or expressed as a percentage of the entire screen. HTML frames also support an attribute that assigns the size relative to the other columns or rows. In other words, the relative attribute (designated with an asterisk) assigns the balance of the remaining available screen space to a column or row. For example, the following frameset:

```
<frameset cols="80,*">
```

sets up two frames, one 80 pixels wide and the other as large as the browser window allows. This ensures that the first column will always be a constant size — making it perfect for a set of navigation buttons — while the second is as wide as possible.

The relative attribute can also be used proportionally. When preceded by an integer, as in n*, this attribute specifies that the frame is allocated n times the space it would have received otherwise. So frameset code like this:

```
<frameset rows="4*,*">
```

ensures that one row is proportionately four times the size of the other.

Creating a Frameset and Frames

Dreamweaver offers two ways to divide your Web page into frames and make your frameset. The first method uses the menus. Choose Modify ➪ Frameset, and from the submenu, select the direction in which you would like to split the frame: left, right, up, or down. Left or right splits the frame in half vertically; up or down splits it horizontally in half.

To create a frameset visually using the mouse, follow these steps:

1. Turn on the frame borders in your Dreamweaver Document Window by selecting View ➪ Frame Borders.

   A three-pixel-wide inner border appears along the edges of your Document Window.

2. Position the cursor over any of the frame borders.

3. Press Alt (Option).

If your pointer is over a frame border, the pointer changes into a two-headed arrow when over an edge, and a four-headed arrow (or a drag-hand on the Mac) when over a corner.

4. Drag the frame border into the Document Window. Figure 14-1 shows a four-frame frameset being created.

Dreamweaver initially assigns a temporary filename and an absolute pixel value to your HTML frameset code. Both can be modified later, if you wish.

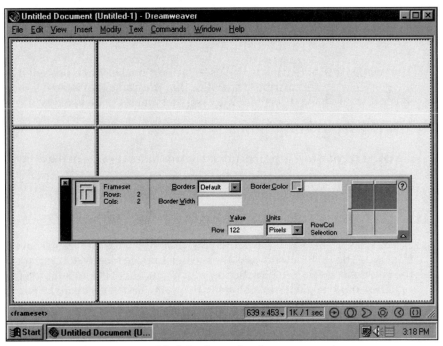

Figure 14-1: After you've enabled the frame borders, you can drag out your frameset structure with the mouse.

Tip

With the menu method of frameset creation, you can only create a two-way frame split, initially. To further split the frame using the menu commands, you must first select each frame. However, by Alt-dragging (Option-dragging) the corner of the frame border, you can quickly create a four-frame frameset.

When the frameset is selected, Dreamweaver displays a black, dotted line along all the frame borders and within every frame. You can easily reposition any frameset border by clicking and dragging it. If you just want to move the border, make sure you don't press the Alt or Option key while dragging the border; this action creates additional frames.

Caution If you create a four-frame frameset in two stages, by first splitting the Web page in one direction and then dragging a frame border to split it in another, you'll find a small aberration in the HTML code. Dreamweaver adds the relative indicator (*) to the second set of frames, as shown in this code:

```
<frameset rows="265,237" cols="323*,455">
```

Although, in most cases, this coding will not create any problems for the user, it could lead to undesired results when the window is resized. To avoid this possible problem, when you know you are building a four-frame frameset, drag the frame border from the corner to create the frameset all at once. If you must create the frameset in two steps, change the relative value to a pixel or percentage value.

Adding more frames

You're not at all limited to your initial frame choices. In addition to being able to move them visually, you can also set the size through the Frameset Property Inspector, as described in the next section. Furthermore, you can continue to split either the entire frame or each column or row as needed. When you divide a column or row into one or more frames, you are actually nesting one frameset inside another.

Tip Once you've created the basic frame structure, you can select View ➪ Frame Borders again (it's a toggle) to turn the borders off and create a more accurate preview of your page.

Using the menus

To split an existing frame using the menus, position the cursor in the frame you want to alter and choose Modify ➪ Frameset ➪ Split Frame Left, Right, Up or Down. Figure 14-2 shows a two-row frameset in which the bottom row was split into two columns and then repositioned. The Frameset Property Inspector indicates that the inner frameset (2 columns, 1 row) is selected.

You can clearly see the "nested" nature of the code in this HTML fragment describing the frameset in Figure 14-2:

```
<frameset rows="163,333" cols="784">
  <frame src="file://Dev/UntitledFrame-34">
  <frameset cols="115,663" rows="*">
    <frame src="file://Dev/UntitledFrame-57">
    <frame src="file://Dev/UntitledFrame-35">
  </frameset>
</frameset>
```

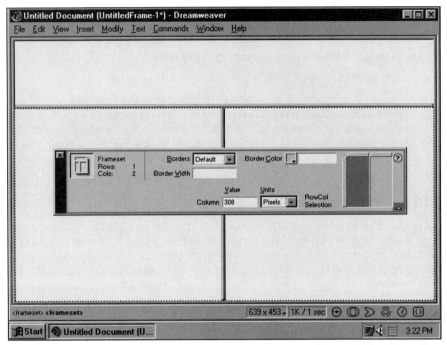

Figure 14-2: Use the Modify ⇨ Frameset menu option to split an existing frame into additional columns or rows and create a nested frameset.

Tip   You can also split an existing frame by Alt-dragging (Option-dragging) the current frame's border, but you have to choose an inner border that does not extend across the page.

Using the mouse

When you need to create additional columns or rows that span the entire Web page, use the mouse method instead of the menus. Option-drag or Alt-drag any of the current frame's borders that go across the entire page, such as one of the outer borders. Figure 14-3 shows a new row added along the bottom of our previous frame structure.

Tip   You can also split a smaller frame by first selecting it and then Alt-dragging or Option-dragging one of its borders. As you'll see in this chapter, you select a frame by Alt-clicking (Windows) or Option-Shift-clicking (Macintosh) inside the frame.

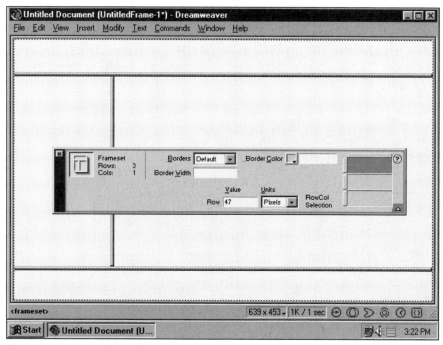

Figure 14-3: An additional frame row was added using the Alt-drag (Option-drag) method.

Working with the Frameset Property Inspector

The Frameset Property Inspector manages those elements, such as the borders, that are common to all the frames within a frameset; it also offers more precise sizing control over individual rows and columns than you can do visually. To access the Frameset Property Inspector, choose Window ➪ Properties if the Property Inspector is not already open, and then select any of the frame borders.

Tip

When a browser visits a Web page that uses frames, it displays the title found in the frameset HTML document for the entire frame. You can set that title in Dreamweaver by selecting the frameset and then choosing Modify ➪ Page Properties. In the Page Properties dialog box, enter your choice of title in the Title text box, as you would for any other Web page. All the other options in the Page Properties dialog box — including background color and text color — apply to the <noframes> content, covered later in "Handling Frameless Browsers."

Resizing frames in a frameset

With HTML, when you want to specify the size of a frame, you work with the row or column in which the frame resides. Dreamweaver gives you two ways to alter a frame's size: by dragging the border or, to be more precise, by specifying a value in the Property Inspector.

As shown in Figure 14-4, Dreamweaver's Frameset Property Inspector contains a Row/Column selector to display the structure of the selected frameset. For each frameset, you select the tab along the top or left side of the Row/Column selector to choose the column or row you want to modify.

Row/Column
Selector tabs

Figure 14-4: In the Frameset Property Inspector, you use the Row/Column Selector tabs to choose which frame you are going to resize.

Tip   The Row/Column Selector shows only one frameset at a time. So if your design uses nested framesets, you won't see an exact duplicate of your entire Web page in the Row/Column Selector.

Whether you need to modify just a row, a column, or both a row and a column depends on the location of the frame.

✦ If your frame spans the width of an entire page, like the top or bottom row in Figure 14-4, select the corresponding tab on the left side of the Row/Column Selector.

✦ If your frame spans the height of an entire page, select the equivalent tab along the top of the Row/Column Selector.

✦ If your frame does not span either height or width, like the middle two rows in Figure 14-4, you need to select both its column and its row, and modify the size of each in turn.

Once you have selected the row or column, follow these steps to specify its size:

1. To specify the size in pixels, enter a number in the Property Inspector's Value text box, and select Pixels as the Units option.

2. To specify the size as a percentage of the screen, enter a number from 1 to 100 in the Value text box, and select Percent as the Units option.

3. To specify a size relative to the other columns or rows, first select Relative as the Units option. Now you have two options:

- To set the size to occupy the remainder of the screen, delete any number that may be entered in the Value text box; optionally, you can enter a 1.

- To scale the frame relative to the other rows or columns, type the scale factor in the Value text box. For example, if you want the frame to be twice the size of another relative frame, put a 2 in the Value text box.

Tip

The Relative size operator is generally used to indicate you want the current frame to take up the balance of the frameset column or row. This makes it easy to specify a size without having to calculate pixel widths, and ensures that the frame will have the largest possible size.

Manipulating frameset borders

By default, Dreamweaver sets up your framesets so all the frames have gray borders that are six pixels wide. You can alter the border color, change the width, or eliminate the borders altogether. All of the border controls are handled through the Frameset Property Inspector.

Tip

There are also border controls for individual frames. Just as table cell settings can override options set for the entire table, the individual frame options override those determined for the entire frameset, as described in the section "Working with the Frame Property Inspector" later in this chapter. Use the frameset border controls when you want to make a global change to the borders, such as turning them all off.

If you are working with nested framesets, it's important that you select the outermost frameset before you begin making any modifications to the borders. You can tell that you've selected the outermost frameset by looking at the Dreamweaver Tag Selector; it will show only one <frameset> in bold. If you select an inner nested frameset, you'll see more than one <frameset> in the Tag Selector.

Eliminating borders

When a frameset is first created, Dreamweaver leaves the borders display up to the browser's discretion. You can expressly turn the frameset borders on or off through the Property Inspector.

To eliminate borders completely, enter a zero in the Border Width text box. Even if there is no width value displayed, the default is a border six pixels wide. If you turn off the borders for your frameset, you can still work in Dreamweaver with the View ⇨ Frame Borders enabled, which gives you quick access to modifying the frameset. The borders will not display, however, when your Web page is previewed in a browser.

Border appearance options

You can control the appearance of your borders to a limited degree. In the Borders drop-down list of options, choosing Yes causes browsers to draw the borders with a 3D appearance. Select No, and the frameset borders will be drawn as a single color. The Default option is generally interpreted by browsers as the three-dimensional look.

Border color options

To change the frameset border color, select the Border Color text box and then enter either a color name or hexadecimal color value. You can also select the color swatch and choose a new border color from the browser-safe color picker. Clicking the Palette icon on the color picker opens the extended color selector, just as for other color swatches in Dreamweaver.

Caution If you have nested framesets on your Web page, make sure you've selected the correct frameset before you make any modifications through the Property Inspector. You can move from a nested frameset to its "parent" by using the keyboard shortcut Alt-Up Arrow (Command-Up Arrow). Likewise, you can move from a parent frameset to its "child" by pressing Alt-Down Arrow (Command-Down Arrow).

Saving a frameset and frames

As mentioned earlier, when you're working with frames, you're working with multiple HTML files. You must be careful to save not only all the individual frames that make up your Web page, but also the frameset itself.

Dreamweaver makes it easy to save framesets and included frames by providing several special commands. To save a frameset, choose File ➪ Save Frameset to open the standard Save File dialog box. You can also save a copy of the current frameset by choosing File ➪ Save Frameset As. You don't have to select the frameset border or position your cursor in any special place to activate these functions.

Saving each frame in the frameset can be a chore unless you choose File ➪ Save All. The first time this command is invoked, Dreamweaver cycles through each of the open frames and displays the Save File dialog box. Each subsequent time you choose File ➪ Save All, Dreamweaver automatically saves every updated file in the frameset.

To copy an individual frame, you must use the regular File ➪ Save As command.

Closing a frameset

There's no real trick to closing a Dreamweaver frameset: just choose File ➪ Close. If the frameset is your last open file, Dreamweaver asks if you'd like to quit the program (unless you've previously selected the "Don't Ask Me Again" option).

Modifying a Frame

What makes the whole concept of a Web page frame work so well is the flexibility of each frame.

✦ You can design your page so that some frames are fixed in size while others are expandable.

✦ You can attach scroll bars to some frames and not others.

✦ Any frame can have its own background image, and yet all frames can appear as one seamless picture.

✦ Borders can be enabled — and colored — for one set of frames, but left off for another set.

Dreamweaver uses a Frame Property Inspector to specify most of a frame's attributes. Others are handled through devices already familiar to you, such as the Page Properties dialog box.

Page properties

Each frame is its own HTML document and, as such, each frame can have independent page properties. To alter the page properties of a frame, position the cursor in the frame and then choose Modify ⇨ Page Properties. You can also use the keyboard shortcuts, Ctrl-J or Command-J. Or you can select Page Properties from the shortcut menu by right-clicking (Control-clicking) any open space on the frame's page.

From the Page Properties dialog box, you can assign a title, although it will not become visible to the user unless the frame is viewed as a separate page. If you plan on using the individual frames as separate pages in your <noframes> content (see "Handling Frameless Browsers" at the end of this chapter), it's good practice to title every page. You can also assign a background and the various link colors by selecting the appropriate color swatch or entering a color name into the correct text box.

Working with the Frame Property Inspector

To access the Frame Property Inspector, you must first select a frame. Selecting a frame is different from just positioning the cursor in the frame. There are two ways to properly select a frame: using the Frames Inspector or using the mouse.

Joining Background Images in Frames

One popular technique is to insert background images into separate frames so they blend into a seamless single image. This takes careful planning and coordination between the author of the graphic and the designer of the Web page.

To accomplish this image consolidation operation, you must first "slice" the image in an image processing program, such as Fireworks or Adobe PhotoShop. Then save each part as a separate graphic, making sure that there is no border around these image sections — each cut-up piece will become the background image for a particular frame. Next, set the background image of each frame to the matching graphic. Be sure to turn off the borders for the frameset, and set the Border Width to zero.

You'll find a Command on the CD-ROM to help you eliminate your borders. Look for the Zero Page Borders Command in Andrew Wooldridge's folder.

Correct sizing of each piece is important, to ensure that no gaps appear in your joined background. A good technique is to use absolute pixel measurements for images that fill the frame and, where the background images tile, set the frame to Relative spacing. In the following figure, the corner frame has the same measurement as the background image (107 × 126 pixels), and all the other frames are set to Relative.

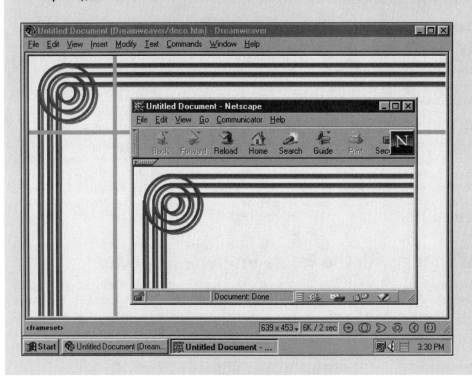

The Frames Inspector shows an accurate representation of all the frames in your Web page. Open the Frames Inspector by choosing Window ➪ Frames. As you can see in Figure 14-5, the Frames Inspector displays names, if assigned, in the individual frames, and (no name) if not. Nested framesets are shown with a heavier border.

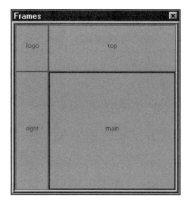

Figure 14-5: Use the Frames Inspector to visually select a frame to modify.

To select a frame, click directly on its represented image in the Frames Inspector. If the Frame Property Inspector is open, it will reflect the selected frame's options. For more complex Web pages, you can resize the Frames Inspector to get a better sense of the page layout. To close the Frames Inspector, select the Close button or choose Window ➪ Frames again.

Tip　　When you are working with multiple framesets, use the Tag Selector together with the Frame Inspector to identify the correct nested frameset. Selecting a frameset in the Tag Selector causes it to be identified in the Frame Inspector with a heavy black border.

To select a frame with the mouse, press Alt (Option-Shift) and click in the desired frame. Once the frame is selected, you can move from one frame to another by pressing Alt (Command) and then using the arrow keys.

Naming your frames

Naming each frame is essential to getting the most power from a frame-structured Web page. The frame's name is used to make the content inserted from a hyperlink appear in that particular frame.

Cross-Reference　　For more information about targeting a link, see "Targeting Frame Content" later in this chapter.

Frame names must follow specific guidelines, as explained in the following steps:

1. Select the frame you want to name. You can either use the Frames Inspector or Alt-click (Option-Shift-click) inside the frame.

2. If necessary, open the Property Inspector by choosing Window ➪ Properties.

3. In the Frame Property Inspector, shown in Figure 14-6, add the frame's name in the text box next to the frame logo. Frame names have the following restrictions:

   • Use one word, with no spaces.

   • Do not use special characters such as quotation marks, question marks, and hyphens. `

   • The underscore character *is* allowed.

   • Certain frame names are reserved: _blank, _parent, _self, and _top.

Frame Name

Figure 14-6: The Frame Property Inspector allows you to name your frame and control all of a frame's attributes.

Opening a Web page into a frame

You don't have to build all Web pages in frames from scratch. You can load an existing Web page into any frame. If you've selected a frame and the Frame Property Inspector is open, just type the link directly into the Src text box or choose the Folder icon to browse for your file. Or, you can position your cursor in a frame (without selecting the frame), and choose File ➪ Open in Frame.

Setting borders

You can generally set most border options adequately in the Frameset Property Inspector; you can also override some of those options, such as color, for each frame. There are, however, practical limitations to these possibilities.

To set borders from the Frame Property Inspector for a selected frame, you can make the borders three-dimensional by choosing Yes in the Borders drop-down option list, or use the monochrome setting by choosing No. Leaving the Borders option at Default gives control to the frameset settings. You can also change a frame's border color by choosing the Border Color swatch in a selected frame's Property Inspector.

Now, about those limitations: They come into play when you try to implement one of your border modifications. Because frames share common borders, it is difficult to isolate an individual frame and have the change affect just the selected frame. As an example, Figure 14-7 shows a frameset in which the borders are set to No for all frames except the one on the lower-right. Notice how the top border of the lower-right frame extends to the left, all the way over the adjacent frame. There are two possible workarounds for this problem. First, you can design your frames so that borders do not touch, as in a multirow frameset. Second, you can create a background image for a frame that includes a border design.

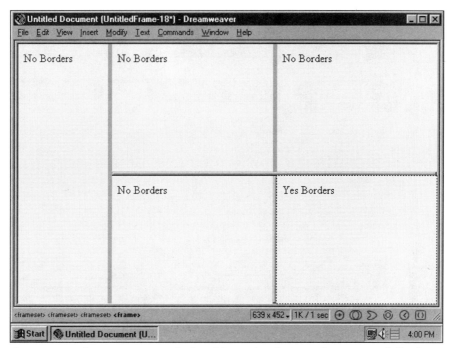

Figure 14-7: If you want to use isolated frame borders, you have to carefully plan your Web page frameset to avoid overlapping borders.

Adding scroll bars

I think one of the features that has given frames the wide use they enjoy of late is the ability to enable or disable scroll bars for each frame. Scroll bars are used when the browser window is too small to display all the information in the Web page frame. The browser window size is completely user-controlled, so the Web designer must apply the various scroll bar options on a frame-by-frame basis, depending on the look desired and the frame's content.

There are four options selectable from the Scroll drop-down list on the Frame
Property Inspector:

✦ **Default.** Leaves the use of scroll bars up to the browser.

✦ **Yes.** Forces scroll bars to appear regardless of the amount of content.

✦ **No.** Disables scroll bars.

✦ **Auto.** Turns scroll bars on if the content of the frame extends horizontally or
vertically beyond what the browser window can display. Figure 14-8 uses an
automatic vertical scroll bar in the lower frame; you can see it on the far right.

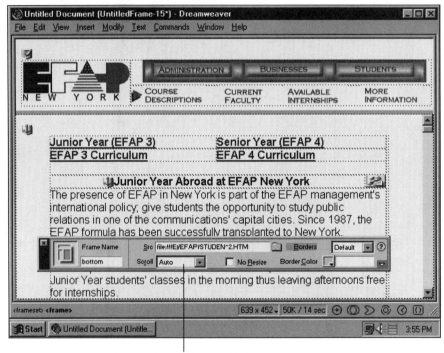

Automatic scroll bar enabled

Figure 14-8: Here, the top frame of the Web page has the scroll bars turned off, and
the bottom frame has scroll bars enabled.

Resizing

By default, all frames are resizable by the user; that is, a visitor to your Web site can
widen, narrow, lengthen, or shorten a frame by dragging the border to a new
position. You can disable this resizing capability, however, on a frame-by-frame
basis. In the Frame Property Inspector, select the No Resize option to turn off the
resizing feature.

Tip
Although it might be tempting to select No Resize for every frame, it's best to allow resizing, except in frames that require a set size to maintain their functionality (for instance, a frame containing navigational controls).

Setting margins

Just as you can pad table cells with additional space to separate text and graphics, you can offset content in frames. Dreamweaver lets you control the left/right margins and the top/bottom margins independently. By default, there is normally about six pixels of space between the content and the left or right frame borders, and about 15 pixels of space between the content and the top or bottom frame borders. You can increase or decrease these margins, but even if you set the values to zero, there is still some room between the borders and the content.

To alter the left and right margins, change the value in the Frame Property Inspector's Margin Width text box; to change the top and bottom margins, enter a new value in the Margin Height text box. If you don't see the Margin Width and Height text boxes, select the Property Inspector expander arrow.

Caution
Dreamweaver currently inserts only the `marginwidth` and `marginheight` attributes when you enter values in the Margin Width and Margin Height text boxes, respectively. The values are not fully recognized by Netscape browsers. To ensure full compatibility, enter the following attributes as well: `topmargin=value` and `leftmargin=value`.

Modifying content

You can update a frame's content in any way you see fit. Sometimes, it's necessary to keep an eye on how altering a single frame's content affects the entire frame. Other times, it is easier — and faster — to work on each frame individually and later load them into the frameset to see the final result.

With Dreamweaver's multiwindow structure, you can have it both ways. Work on the individual frames in one or more windows, and the frameset in yet another.

Although switching back to the frameset window won't automatically update it to show your changed frames, there is one shortcut you can use. After saving changes in the full frame windows, go to the frameset window. Then, in any window you've altered elsewhere, make another small change, such as inserting a space. Finally, choose File ⇨ Revert. This command is normally used to revert to the previously saved version, but in this case you're using it to update your frames.

Caution
To preview changes made to a Web page using frames, you must first save the changed files. Currently, Dreamweaver creates a temporary file of the frameset, but not any of the included frames.

Deleting frames

As you're building your Web page frame, inevitably you'll try a frame design that does not work. How do you delete a frame once you've created it? Click the frame border and drag it into the border of the enclosing, or parent, frame. When there is no parent frame, drag the frame border to the edge of the page. If the frame being deleted contains any unsaved content, Dreamweaver asks if you'd like to save the file before closing it.

Tip Because the enclosing frameset and each individual frame are all discrete HTML pages, each keeps track of its own edits and other changes — and therefore each has its own Undo memory. If you are in a particular frame and try to Undo a frameset alteration, such as adding a new frame to the set, it won't work. To reverse an edit to the frameset, you have to select the frameset and then choose File ⇨ Undo, or use one of the keyboard shortcuts (Ctrl-Z or Command-Z).

Targeting Frame Content

One of the major uses of frames is for navigational control. One frame acts as the navigation center, offering links to various Web pages in a site. When the user selects one of the links, the Web page appears in another frame on the page; and that frame, if necessary, can scroll independently of the navigation frame. This technique keeps the navigation links always visible and accessible.

When you assign a link to appear in a particular frame of your Web page, you are said to be assigning a *target* for the link. You can target specific frames in your Web page, and you can target structural parts of a frameset. In Dreamweaver, targets are assigned through the Text and Image Property Inspectors.

Targeting sections of your frameset

In the earlier section on naming frames, you learned that certain names are reserved. These are the four special names HTML reserves for the parts of a frameset that are used in targeting: _blank, _parent, _self, and _top. With them, you can cause content from a link to overwrite the current frame or to appear in an entirely new browser window.

To target a link to a section of your frameset, follow these steps:

1. Select the text or image you want to use as your link.

2. In the Text (or Image) Property Inspector, enter the URL and/or named anchor in the Link text box. Alternately, you can select the Folder icon to browse for the file.

3. Select the Target text box. You may need to expand the Image Property Inspector to see the Target text box.

4. Select one of the following reserved target names from the drop-down list of Target options (see Figure 14-9), or type an entry into the text box:

- **_blank** opens the link into a new browser window and keeps the current window available.

- **_parent** opens the link into the parent frameset of the current frame, if any.

- **_self** opens the link into the current frame, replacing its contents (this is the default).

- **_top** opens the link into the outermost frameset of the current Web page, replacing all frames.

Figure 14-9: Choose your frame target from the Property Inspector's Target drop-down list.

The generic nature of these reserved target names allows them to be used repeatedly on different Web pages, without your having to code a particular reference each time.

For an example of structural targeting, look at the code for the Dreamweaver Help system. The Index frame, for example, uses the implied _self target whenever a major Help topic is selected, to open an HTML document that shows all the subtopics.

Caution   There is a phenomenon known as *recursive frames* that can be dangerous to your site setup. Let's say you have a frameset named index_frame.html. If you include in any frame on your current page a link to index_frame.html, and set the target as _self, when the user selects that link the entire frameset loads into the current frame — including another link to index_frame.html. Browsers can handle about three or four iterations of this recursion before they crash. To avoid the problem, set your frameset target to _top.

Targeting specific frames in your frameset

Earlier I stressed the importance of naming each frame in your frameset. Once you have entered a name in the Name text box of the Frame Property Inspector, Dreamweaver dynamically updates the Target list to include that name. This feature allows you to target specific frames in your frameset in the same manner that you target the reserved names noted above.

Although you can always type the frame name directly in the Name text box, the drop-down option list comes in handy for this task. Not only do you avoid having to keep track of the various frame names in your Web page, but you avoid typing errors as well. Targets are case-sensitive, and names must match exactly or the browser won't be able to find the target.

Updating two frames or more at once

Sooner or later, most Web designers using frames have the need to update more than one frame with a single click. The problem is, you can't group two or more URLs together in an anchor tag. Here is an easy-to-implement solution, thanks to Dreamweaver's behaviors.

If you're not familiar with Dreamweaver's JavaScript behaviors, you might want to look over Chapter 17, "Using Behaviors," before continuing.

To update more than one frame target from a single link, follow these steps:

1. Select your link in the frame.

2. Open the Behavior Inspector from the Launcher or by choosing Window ⇨ Behaviors.

3. Make sure that 4.0 Browsers is selected in the Show Events For pop-up menu of the Behavior Inspector.

4. Select the + (Add Behavior) button to display the list of available behaviors.

5. Choose Go To URL from the drop-down option list.

6. Dreamweaver displays the Go To URL dialog box (see Figure 14-10) and scans your document for all named frames. Select a target frame from the list of windows or frames.

You won't be able to use this behavior until you name your frames as detailed in the "Naming Your Frames" section of this chapter.

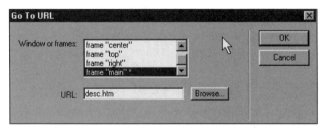

Figure 14-10: You can cause two or more frames to update from a single link by using Dreamweaver's Go To URL behavior.

7. Enter a URL, or choose the Browse (Choose) button to select one.

   Dreamweaver places an asterisk after the targeted frame, to indicate that a URL has been selected for it. You can see this in Figure 14-10.

8. Repeat Steps 6 and 7 for any additional frames you want to target.

9. Click OK when you're finished.

   Dreamweaver automatically selects the `onClick` event for the Go To URL behavior.

Now, whenever you click your one link, the browser opens the URLs in the targeted frames in the order specified.

Handling Frameless Browsers

Not all of today's browsers support frames. Netscape began supporting frames in Navigator version 2.0; Microsoft didn't start until IE version 3.0 — and a few of the earlier versions for both browsers are still in use. There are also less prevalent browsers that don't support frames. HTML has a built-in mechanism for working with browsers that are not frame-enabled: the `<noframes>...</noframes>` tag pair.

When you begin to construct any frameset, Dreamweaver automatically inserts a `<noframes>` area just below the closing `</frameset>` tag. If a browser is not frames-capable, it ignores the frameset and frame information and renders what is found in the `<noframes>` section.

What should you put into the `<noframes>` section? To ensure the widest possible audience, Webmasters typically insert links to a nonframe version of the site. The links can be as obvious or as discreet as you care to make them. Many Webmasters also include links to current versions of Communicator or Internet Explorer, to encourage their nonframe-capable visitors to upgrade.

Dreamweaver includes a facility for easily adding and modifying the `<noframes>` content. Choose Modify ➪ Frameset ➪ Edit NoFrames Content to open the NoFrames Content window. As you can see in Figure 14-11, this window is identical to the regular Dreamweaver Document Window, with the exception of the "NoFrames Content" in the title bar. In this window you have access to all the same objects and palettes as you do normally. When you have finished editing your `<noframe>` content, Choose Modify ➪ Frameset ➪ Edit NoFrames Content again to deselect the option and return to the frameset.

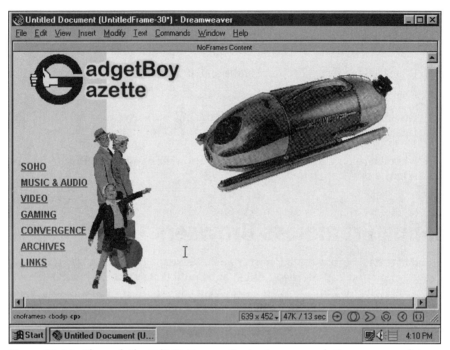

Figure 14-11: Through the Edit NoFrames Content command, Dreamweaver lets you specify what's seen by visitors whose browsers are not frames-capable.

Here are some pointers to keep in mind when working in the NoFrames Content window:

✦ The page properties of the `<noframes>` content are the same as the page properties of the frameset. You can select the frameset and then choose Modify ➪ Page Properties to open the Page Properties dialog box. While in the NoFrames Content window, you can also right-click (Control-click) in any open space to access the Page Properties command.

✦ Dreamweaver disables the File ➪ Open commands when the NoFrames Content window is onscreen. To move existing content into the `<noframes>` section, use Dreamweaver's Copy and Paste features.

✦ The `<noframes>` section is located in the frameset page, which is the primary page examined by search engine "spiders." It's a good idea to enter `<meta>` tag information detailing the site, as described in Chapter 6, "Understanding How HTML Works," in the frameset page. While you're in the NoFrames Content window, you can open the HTML Inspector and add the `<meta>` tags.

Summary

Frames are a significant Webmaster design tool. With frames and framesets, you can divide a single Web page into multiple, independent areas. Dreamweaver gives the Web designer quick and easy access to frame design through the program's drag-and-drop interface.

✦ A framed Web page consists of a separate HTML document for each frame and one additional file that describes the frame structure, called the *frameset*.

✦ A frameset comprises columns and rows, which can be sized absolutely in pixels, as a percentage of the browser window, or relative to the other columns or rows.

✦ Dreamweaver allows you to reposition the frame borders by dragging them to a new location. You can also add new frames by Alt-clicking (Option-clicking) any existing frame border.

✦ Framesets can be nested to create more complex column and row arrangements. Selecting the frame border displays the Frameset Property Inspector.

✦ Select any individual frame through the Frame Inspector or by Alt-clicking (Option-Shift-clicking) within any frame. Once the frame is selected, the Frame Property Inspector can be displayed.

✦ You make your links appear in a specific frame by assigning targets to the links. Dreamweaver supports both structured and named targets. You can update two or more frames with one link by using a Dreamweaver JavaScript behavior.

✦ You should include information and/or links for browsers that are not frames-capable, through Dreamweaver's Edit NoFrames Content feature.

In the next chapter, you learn how to access external programs through your Web pages in Dreamweaver.

✦   ✦   ✦

Extending HTML Through Dreamweaver

Accessing External Programs

♦ ♦ ♦ ♦

In This Chapter

Working with CGI programs

Embedding plug-ins

Using ActiveX controls

Applying Java applets

Including JavaScript or VBScript in Dreamweaver

♦ ♦ ♦ ♦

Until recently, you could create relatively static Web pages made of text and images with "basic" HTML, but you needed additional code for more action. Without using some of the advanced capabilities of Dynamic HTML — viewable only with a fourth-generation browser — animated GIFs have been your sole option for any sort of motion on a self-contained Web page. HTML need not stand alone, however; the language allows for several methods to extend its capabilities.

You can do all of the following using external programs along with HTML:

+ Collect data from the user

+ Add multimedia elements such as audio, video, animation, and virtual reality

+ Enable a Web browser to present almost any kind of information in its native format

+ Dynamically create Web pages based on a user's request

Dreamweaver gives you various methods — some specific to the file type and others more generic — for accessing a full range of external programs invaluable to the Web author. In this chapter, you learn how to send information to and from the server through CGI programs, install feature-extending plug-ins and ActiveX controls, incorporate custom-built Java applets, and work with scripting languages such as JavaScript and VBScript.

Generally, the techniques for melding any of the external capabilities with your Web page are quite straightforward. Often, however, learning to use the outside program takes a fair amount of time — whether that program is writing your

CGI script or encoding your digital video. You may want to approach each specific technique on a project-by-project basis, rather than try to master all of the disciplines at once. No matter how you choose to work, you can always count on Dreamweaver's own extensibility to incorporate every new technology.

Using CGI Programs

When someone clicks a link to a Web page, a message is sent to a particular Web server, which then sends the components of that Web page—the HTML file and any associated graphic files—back to the user. Usually most information is sent over the Web from the server to the client. But how do you send information in the opposite direction, from the client to the server?

The standard method is to use a Common Gateway Interface (CGI) program. CGI programs, or scripts (the terms are used interchangeably), perform many different kinds of Internet functions, but they all entail collecting data from the user and passing it to the server. Whether the server stores the information in a database, manipulates it and passes it on to another system, or generates a new Web page to be sent to the user depends on the design of the CGI program.

Creating and calling scripts

CGI programs can be written in any number of computer languages, including C/C++, Fortran, Perl, TCL, UNIX shell, Visual Basic, AppleScript, and others. The only requirement is that the program must be executable by the type of server processing the information. Perl (Program Extraction and Report Language) is one of the most popular languages used to write CGI programs. Perl is an *interpreted* language—that is, the source code is an ordinary text file compiled at run time, unlike Java or C++ code, which is previously compiled. Because it is text-based, Perl is easy to modify and particularly strong in parsing and manipulating text—an important capability for interpreting data from forms and other Web-based tasks.

Perl is also difficult to debug, however—you don't get much in the way of error reporting from the Perl interpreter.

Note   Keep in mind that with CGI programs, you're essentially running a program on a different, remote computer and what's true for your computer setup may not be true for the server. Your best ally is the system administrator of your Web server. Chances are good that questions about running CGI programs have been asked many times before and there is likely to be a FAQ or equivalent file available.

Every CGI script must be customized to some extent in order to communicate with a particular server. You can develop your custom CGI program in two ways: build it from scratch yourself or modify an existing script. Modifying an existing script is much easier and a customary practice on the Web. Someone else has probably already developed a CGI script for your situation, and it is probably available for download on the Internet.

Tip   Three great sources for CGI scripts are Matt's Script Archives (www.worldwide-mart.com/scripts/), Extropia (formerly Selena Sol's Public Domain Archives) (www.extropia.com), and—for all your scripting needs—The CGI-Resource Index (www.cgi-resources.com).

Once your CGI program is completed, three steps remain before it can be used:

✦ The CGI script must be uploaded to your Web server and stored in a special directory—often named cgi-bin.

✦ The file permissions need to be set depending on the program's function. File permissions determine whether a file can be read, written to, and/or executed and by whom. File permissions are explained in the following section.

✦ The CGI program must be referenced or called from the Web page.

Web designers most often use the HTML <form> structure to call a CGI script and simultaneously pass the data from the user to the server. Dreamweaver enables you to specify the necessary information through various form objects.

Setting file permissions in Dreamweaver

An important aspect of installing CGI programs is properly setting the file permissions for the CGI file. Because of security concerns, most Web servers restrict access on certain files to particular users. A file can be read, overwritten, or executed. With UNIX servers, you can set these three operations for each of three different groups of people: the creator or owner of the file, the group administering the Web server, and outside visitors. These settings are called *file permissions*.

Typically, a CGI file is set to the following parameters:

✦ It can be read, overwritten, or executed by its owner

✦ It can be read and executed by the administrative group, but not overwritten

✦ It can be read and executed by outside visitors, but not overwritten

File permissions are set on a UNIX machine through the site chmod command issued directly to the server. The permissions previously listed are accomplished when the site chmod command is set to 755 and the file name is referenced; an example follows:

```
site chmod 755 mailer.pl
```

To set the file permissions in Dreamweaver, follow these steps:

1. Open the Site Window. Choose File ➪ Open Site (Site ➪ Open Site) and then select the site you want to work with from the submenu.

2. Go online and select the Connect button from the Site Window.

3. From the Site Window menus, choose Window ➪ Site Log (Site ➪ FTP Log).

4. In the Site Log window's FTP command line, use the `site chmod` command with the appropriate code number and filename reference (see the example in Figure 15-1) and press Enter (Return).

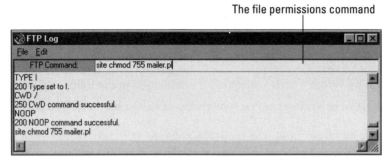

The file permissions command

Figure 15-1: Before a CGI program can be used, the file permissions must be set through Dreamweaver's Site Log window.

Sending data to CGI programs

Two primary methods send data to the Web server for processing by a CGI script. The first technique attaches the information directly to a selected URL; another method uses a form to post the data when the user selects the Submit button. The URL method is useful when you need to send known data.

The form method is useful for sending variable or user-supplied information. Both techniques can be used within the Dreamweaver interface.

Passing data through a URL

Although the URL route is not as commonly employed as the forms method, certain information lends itself well to being passed to the server directly through a URL. Anytime you need to send a specific value to your CGI program, you can use the URL method.

Following is the general syntax of the statement that sends data to the URL. You use a question mark to separate the CGI program address from the data itself. The data takes the following form:

```
1st_field=value+2nd_field=value
```

In practice, information passed to a program via a link looks like the following:

```
<a href= "http://www.testcenter.com/cgi-
bin/response.pl?choice=left+entry=nada_ad">
```

In Dreamweaver, enter the data as part of the Link information, as shown in Figure 15-2. Most often, you should enter the URL to a CGI program as an absolute address, with the full `"http://domain/path"` attached, to properly reference the cgi-bin directory.

Figure 15-2: In the Link text box, enter the specific information to be passed directly to a CGI program.

Using forms to send information

Forms are the most common method to transmit data from the user to a CGI program on a server. With the push of a single Submit button, all of the information the user has filled in or selected on the form — text, menu options, radio button options, and so forth — is sent. The data arrives in the program's standard input. The CGI script manipulates the data before sending it on to a database or in an e-mail message.

Cross-Reference

To find out more about building forms in Dreamweaver and the various form fields, see Chapter 13, "Interactive Forms."

Most CGI scripts require that the form use the `post` method (as opposed to `get`) to send data to the server. When you first insert a form in Dreamweaver, you notice that the default method listed in the form's Property Inspector is POST, as shown in Figure 15-3.

Figure 15-3: Use the POST method to send information via a form to most CGI programs.

Aside from choosing a method, the only other task to ready a form for submission is to assign an Action — which, oddly enough, is really the URL of the CGI program (see the Action box in Figure 15-3).

Again, this URL is most often supplied in absolute address form, like the following:

```
http://www.idest.com/cgi-bin/mailer.pl
```

Posting form data with a Submit button

Once you have set up the form properly and installed the Web page and corresponding CGI program, data is sent to the server when the user selects the Submit button. You don't need to assign an `onClick` or another event to the button.

As noted in Chapter 13, "Submit" and "Reset" are the default labels for these two buttons. You can easily modify the label of a button by entering new text in the Label text box, as shown in Figure 15-4.

Label button

Figure 15-4: Change the text of the Submit and Reset buttons by entering a name in the Label field of the Property Inspector.

With Dreamweaver 1.2, you can also use an image to create a graphical button for handling the submitting chores. However, it's necessary to use a little JavaScript — very little — to accomplish the task. Moreover, you currently have to hand-code the addition. Basically, you have to add a link tag (`<a>...</a>`) around the Image Field button that calls the JavaScript equivalent to Submit or Reset. The code refers to the form in which the button is located (here, "theForm") and uses the following format:

```
<a href="javascript:document.theForm.submit()"><img
src=mySubmit></a>
```

I've bolded the additional code to make it easy to see. To make a Reset button, just substitute `reset()` for `submit()` in the preceding code.

To use an image for a Submit button, follow these steps:

1. Choose Insert ➪ Image or select the Insert Image button from the Common panel of the Objects Palette.

2. In the Insert Image dialog box, enter the path to your image or select the Folder icon to locate the file. The image can be any GIF, JPEG, or PNG format.

3. Give the image a name and, if desired, alternative text using the appropriate text boxes in the Property Inspector (see Figure 15-5).

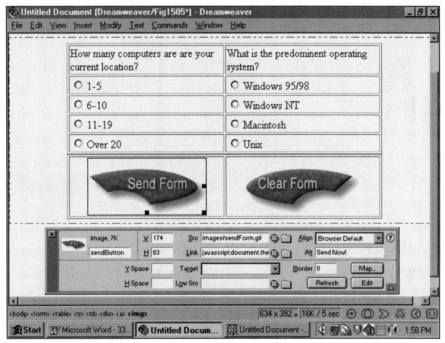

Figure 15-5: You can substitute any valid graphic for the Submit button by using an image and JavaScript.

4. In the Link field of the Property Inspector, enter the following code for a graphical Submit button:

```
javascript:document.theForm.submit()
```

or this code for a Reset button:

```
javascript:document.theForm.reset()
```

Note

Be sure to change the code to reflect your specifics: the name of your form as well as the name of your images.

Using the Hidden Field

Many CGI scripts require that certain information not input by the user be submitted in order to process the form properly. A good example is a text string that tells the CGI program which fields of the form are required. This type of data is hidden from the user and passed to the program through the unseen form object, the appropriately named *Hidden Field*.

Although generally placed at the top of the form, Hidden Fields can be included anywhere between the `<form>` tag pair. You can include a Hidden Field by choosing the Insert Hidden Field button in the Forms panel of the Objects Palette or by selecting Insert ⟿ Form Object ⟿ Hidden Field. Enter the information you want to pass to the CGI program in the Value text box of the Property Inspector, as shown in Figure 15-6.

Figure 15-6: Pass variables that you want to remain unseen by your Web page visitor by using the Hidden Field in your form.

When a Hidden Field is included in your form, Dreamweaver designates it with a Hidden Field icon. Like all invisible elements, the Hidden Field icon can also be hidden by deselecting its option in the Invisible Elements panel of Preferences.

Incorporating Plug-ins

Plug-ins are small software programs introduced by Netscape to enable its browser to display many types of files, not only HTML. Although some of the most well-known plug-ins are employed in the multimedia world — Macromedia's Shockwave, for example — hundreds of different kinds of plug-ins are available for all kinds of files. Plug-ins are generally designed so that the document blends seamlessly with the other portions of the HTML page.

Note   Although the Dreamweaver menus and dialog boxes refer to "inserting a plug-in," a reference to a specific file is actually inserted. That file is of a particular MIME (Multipurpose Internet Mail Extension), which tells the browser what kind of file is being called. Once the browser knows the file's MIME type, it can invoke the correct plug-in. Keep in mind that you're not really inserting a plug-in; you're inserting a file that requires a plug-in.

Just like plug-ins, the code used to insert the plug-in was also originally developed by Netscape. Plug-ins are incorporated into HTML through the `<embed>` tag. Although plug-in features and their associated attributes vary widely, the minimum requirements for a plug-in are the source file and the dimensions (height and width) of the object. Typical HTML for a plug-in looks like the following:

```
<embed src="movies/oscars.avi" height="200" width="300">
```

Note   While the plug-in concept was developed by Netscape, Microsoft has embraced it to some degree. Internet Explorer recognizes the <embed> tag and works with many plug-ins — even if there is not an equivalent ActiveX control available.

Beyond the excitement and novelty that plug-ins can add to your page, one inescapable fact remains: If a user doesn't have the plug-in installed, the plug-in file can't be experienced. Users generally have to download and install the plug-in — and then restart their browsers — before they can perceive any new material. While this sequence is not a particularly difficult task, it nevertheless stops many people from easily viewing your creation in its entirety.

Tip   Plug-in Plaza (www.browserwatch.com/plugins) is an excellent resource for links to the entire spectrum of plug-ins. You can access plug-ins by category or by searching the entire list.

Dreamweaver has an open-ended approach to plug-ins. After you've inserted the Plug-in object, Dreamweaver displays a placeholder for it and enables you to enter the basic attributes through the Property Inspector (see Figure 15-7). Custom attributes are inserted through the Parameters dialog box. You can enter as many attributes as necessary.

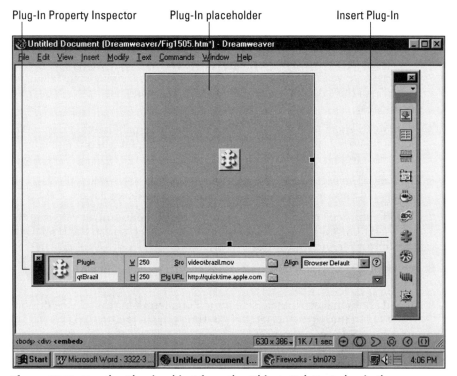

Figure 15-7: Use the Plug-in object from the Objects Palette to begin the process of embedding your plug-in.

Embedding a plug-in

Dreamweaver provides a generic Plug-in object available through the menus or through the Objects Palette. Like any other HTML object, a plug-in can be aligned with text or an image, or even included in a table. Some plug-ins work automatically with no user interaction; others come with their own control panel.

To embed a plug-in into your Web page, follow these steps:

1. Insert the Plug-in object by choosing Insert ➪ Plug-in or by selecting the Plug-in object from the Objects Palette. You can also drag the Insert Plug-in object from the Objects Palette to any place in the Document Window with any existing text or object.

2. In the Select File dialog box, enter the path and filename for your plug-in file in the File Name text box, or select the Browse (Choose) button to locate your file.

   A placeholder icon for the plug-in appears in the Document Window.

3. Size the plug-in placeholder with either of these methods:

   • Enter the appropriate values in the W (Width) and the H (Height) text boxes of the Property Inspector.

   • Click the resizing handles on the plug-in placeholder and drag out the placeholder to a new size.

4. In the Plg URL text box, enter the Internet address where visitors to your Web page can be directed if they do not have the necessary plug-in installed. For example, in the case of QuickTime movies, you would use `http://quicktime.apple.com`.

5. To name the plug-in, enter a unique name in the unlabeled text box on the left side of the Property Inspector. Such names are useful when the plug-in is addressed from a JavaScript function.

6. To change the alignment relative to other inline objects, click the Align arrow button and choose one of the options in the drop-down list.

7. To add additional whitespace around the plug-in, enter pixel values in the V Space text box for the top and bottom of the object, and in the H Space text box for the left and right sides.

8. To surround the plug-in with a border, enter a pixel value in the Border text box.

9. To add additional attributes, select the Parameters button. These options are discussed in the following section, "Setting plug-in parameters."

Once you've entered the basic values for your plug-in, Dreamweaver 2 now enables you to preview it right in the Document Window as well as through an appropriate browser. See the "Playing Plug-ins" section later in this chapter for more details.

Setting plug-in parameters

Because individual attributes for plug-ins can take any form, Dreamweaver offers a completely generic method of entering parameters and associated values. Parameters generally fall into one of two categories: those that take a value and those that stand alone. You can enter both types through the Parameters dialog box.

To set additional parameters to a plug-in, follow these steps:

1. Insert the Plug-in object by choosing Insert ⇨ Plug-in or dragging the Insert Plug-in object from the Objects Palette to a place on your Web page.

2. From the extended Property Inspector, select the Parameters button.

   The Parameters dialog box is displayed with its two columns: Parameters and Values.

3. Click the + (Add) button and type in the first attribute in the Parameter column. Press Tab to move to the Value column, and enter the desired value. If the attribute is a stand-alone and doesn't take a value, simply press Tab again to return to the Parameter column.

4. Repeat Step 3 until all parameters are entered. Press Shift-Tab to move backwards through the list.

5. To delete a parameter, highlight it and select the Minus button.

6. To move a parameter from one position in the list to another, highlight it and select the Up or Down arrow buttons in the Parameters dialog box, as shown in Figure 15-8.

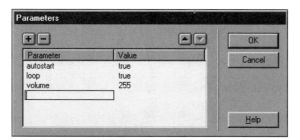

Figure 15-8: Enter specific attributes for each plug-in through the Parameters dialog box.

7. When you are finished inserting your parameters, select the OK button.

Caution Many plug-ins require that the Web server recognize the affiliated MIME types. MIME types are a standard method of specifying various file formats. If your plug-in works locally but not remotely, the server probably needs to be configured for the particular MIME type. Contact your server administrator for further details.

Playing plug-ins

Plug-ins were invented for browsers, by browsers. So the only place you can play a plug-in is in a browser, right? Wrong!—as of Dreamweaver 2, that is. Now you can play any file for which you have a plug-in, right in Dreamweaver's Document Window—and you can keep right on designing. Of course, you could use this capability to play an MP3 music file in the background as you work, but it really has far more practical uses.

New Feature One use for the new Dreamweaver 2 plug-in feature is to align Web page elements with portions of your digitized video or Flash movie. Previously, this process involved a seemingly endless series of flipping back and forth between the Dreamweaver Document Window and the browser preview as you moved elements ever so slightly. Now, Dreamweaver's playback capabilities enable you to line up your static elements with the dynamic ones.

Dreamweaver can play any file that uses plug-ins with the <embed> tag. Naturally, you have to have the plug-in installed on your local system. You can play any one selected plug-in file or all the plug-ins on the page.

Tip Dreamweaver looks in its own Configuration/Plugins folder as well as the Plugins folder of the installed Netscape browser to determine which plug-ins are available. If you have it installed for Netscape, you don't have to reinstall it for Dreamweaver.

To play a selected plug-in, simply click the Play button (the green triangle) in the expanded Property Inspector. You can also choose View ➪ Plugins ➪ Play or use the keyboard shortcut, Ctrl-P (Command-P). To stop the plug-in from playing, click the red Stop button in the Property Inspector (shown in Figure 15-9) or choose View ➪ Plugins ➪ Stop. The keyboard shortcut for stopping a plug-in from playing is Ctrl-. (period) (Command-.).

For the full effect on a media-rich page, play all the embedded plug-ins at once. To do this, choose View ➪ Plugins ➪ Play All or use the keyboard shortcut, Ctrl-Shift-P (Command-Shift-P). You can stop any or all of plug-ins from playing by choosing View ➪ Plugins ➪ Stop All or by using the keyboard shortcut, Ctrl-Shift-. (Command-Shift-.).

 Caution Unfortunately, not all plug-ins are created equally and Dreamweaver can't play every one available. Dreamweaver maintains a list of those it can't play in the file badplugins.cfg found in the Configuration folder. As of this writing, there's only one plug-in noted as being "bad"—Video for Windows. Should you encounter any other plug-in that Dreamweaver can not play, you can add its name to the bad-plugins.cfg file and Dreamweaver will alert you whenever you try to embed a file of this type.

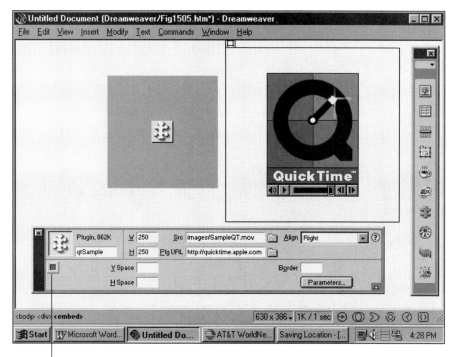

Play/Stop button

Figure 15-9: Files embedded in your Web page, like this QuickTime movie, can now be played back in the Document Window as you design.

Detecting particular plug-ins

When a user visits your Web site via Netscape Navigator 3.0 or higher, you can find out what plug-ins are installed and act accordingly. You may, for example, want to redirect a user who can't accommodate Shockwave files to a separate, less media-intensive page. You can achieve this redirection by creating a mechanism within your page to recognize the Shockwave plug-in.

To detect the presence of a specific plug-in, you need to use a little JavaScript in the <head> section of your document. You also need to know either the official name of the plug-in or its MIME type. As an example, the following code checks for a Shockwave Director plug-in by name; if that name isn't found, the user is redirected to another page:

```
<script language="javascript">
if (!navigator.plugins['Shockwave for Director']){
location="http://www.nadaville.com/simple.html"
}
</script>
```

You can also have your document discover whether a particular MIME type is supported, regardless of which plug-in is used. This next example checks for anything that can play a .wav audio file and, if the means is found, plays some background music:

```
<script language="javascript">
if (navigator.mimetypes['audio/wav']){
document.write('<embed name="audioBG" src="moody.wav" loop=true
autostart=true hidden=true volume=100 height=2 width=2>');
}
</script>
```

Both of these if statements can be used to detect any plug-in and MIME type by simply substituting the appropriate plug-in name and the MIME type you are attempting to detect.

Tip To see which plug-ins are installed in your own system — and their proper names and MIME types — choose Help ⇨ About Plug-ins from within Navigator or Communicator.

Working with ActiveX Components

Microsoft developed ActiveX components largely in response to Netscape's plug-ins, and although the two technologies are similar, some significant differences exist. Standing on the shoulders of Microsoft's Object Linking and Embedding (OLE) technology, ActiveX controls work only with Internet Explorer 3 and later. A plug-in that enables Navigator to run ActiveX components is available, but not widely used.

ActiveX controls, though difficult to develop, are fairly easy to implement in any Web page. Aside from the usual attributes such as a source file and the object dimensions, ActiveX uses two special parameters: a Class ID and the codebase property.

The Class ID is a unique code used to identify the specific ActiveX control. Every ActiveX control has a Class ID that must be used when calling the control. The Class ID is a lengthy combination of numbers and letters; here's the RealPlayer ActiveX Class ID code:

```
CLSID:CFCDAA03-8BE4-11CF-B84B-0020AFBBCCFA
```

To escape the considerable risk of typing errors when entering a Class ID code, you should cut and paste the code.

The codebase property is an Internet location where the ActiveX control can be automatically downloaded and installed if the browser does not find the control on the user's system. The primary difference between the ActiveX's codebase parameter and a plug-in's pluginspage attribute is that the ActiveX control can be transferred and installed without requiring the browser to close and restart. A typical codebase value follows — the Director 7 ActiveX control value:

```
http://download.macromedia.com/pub/shockwave/cabs/director/sw.c
ab#version=7,0,0,0
```

Microsoft uses the `<object>...</object>` tag pair to include ActiveX controls in the HTML code. Unlike Netscape's `<embed>` tag, the `<object>` tag is recognized by the W3C as a valid specification for HTML 3.2 and later.

Note
Optimally, everyone would adhere to the same standard; however, because neither browser recognizes the other's tag 100% of the time, you can actually combine an `<object>` and an `<embed>` tag to cover both browsers. This procedure is explained in the following section.

Dreamweaver provides a separate object for adding ActiveX controls to your Web pages. In addition, Dreamweaver makes it easy to add those complex Class ID codes by maintaining a user-definable list — accessible right from the ActiveX Property Inspector.

Incorporating an ActiveX control

As with plug-ins, Dreamweaver includes an ActiveX object to simplify inserting ActiveX controls. The primary difference between an ActiveX object and a Plug-in object — aside from the two special ActiveX parameters previously noted — is the location for the ActiveX source file. For example, if you want to embed an ActiveX control to show a digital video in AVI format, you first insert the control object by selecting the Insert ActiveX button from the Objects Palette. Then you see the ActiveX Property Inspector (rather than an Insert ActiveX file dialog box). The source file is actually one of the parameters of the `<object>` tag, `FileName`, and must be entered through the Parameters dialog box (Embed Src text box).

Note
Although you'll see a Play button on the ActiveX Property Inspector, like the one on the Embed Property Inspector, you can't actually play ActiveX files in the Document Window. If you have checked the Embed option, the Play button will use the comparable plug-in to play the file, if it's installed on your system.

Follow these steps to insert an ActiveX control into your Web page:

1. Position the cursor where you want the ActiveX file to appear. Choose Insert ⇨ ActiveX or select the Insert ActiveX button from the Objects Palette.

   An ActiveX placeholder appears in the Document Window, and the Property Inspector displays the ActiveX options (see Figure 15-10).

2. In the Class ID text box, enter the Microsoft ID for the ActiveX control.

Tip
If you've previously entered this particular Class ID, select the arrow button and choose the ID from the drop-down list, as shown in Figure 15-10.

Active Property Inspector   AcitveX placeholder   Insert ActiveX

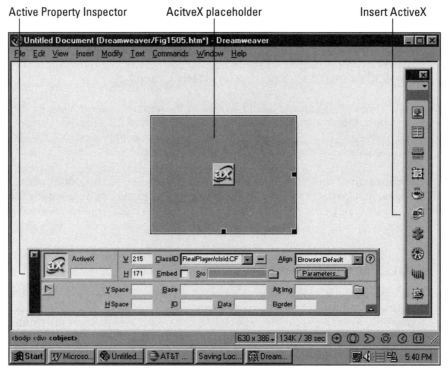

Figure 15-10: ActiveX controls are inserted with the help of Dreamweaver's ActiveX object and its Property Inspector.

3. Change the Width and Height values in the W and H text boxes to match the desired control display.

4. If you know the codebase URL, enter it in the Base text box.

5. Enter other relative parameters for the object as needed (see Table 15-1).

6. Click the Parameters button to display the Parameters dialog box.

7. Click the + (Add) button and enter the first parameter: FileName. Press Tab to move to the Value column, and enter the path and filename for your file.

8. Press Tab, and continue entering the desired parameters in the left column, with their values in the right column. Click OK when you're finished.

9. Preview your ActiveX control in action through Internet Explorer 3 or 4.

Table 15-1
ActiveX Object Properties

ActiveX Object Property	Description
Align	To alter the alignment of the ActiveX control, choose option from the Align drop-down list. In addition to the browser default, your options include Baseline, Top, Middle, Bottom, Texttop, Absolute Middle, Absolute Bottom, Left, and Right.
Alt Image	Enter a path to an alternative image for display to browsers that don't understand the `<object>` tag, like Netscape. The Alt Image is only available if you are not using the Embed option. This image does not display in Dreamweaver.
Border	To place a border around your control, enter a number in the Border text box. The number determines the width of the border in pixels. The default is zero or no border.
Data	Specify a data file for the ActiveX control in this text box. Not all ActiveX controls use this attribute.
Embed	This property designates whether the matching code for the plug-in is to be included (as described in the section "Combining ActiveX controls and plug-in objects" in this chapter).
H Space	You can increase the space to the left and right of the object by entering a value in the H (Horizontal) Space text box. The default is zero.
ID	The ID field is used to define the optional ActiveX ID parameter, most often used to pass data between ActiveX controls.
Name	If desired, you can enter a unique name in the unlabeled field at the left of the Property Inspector. The name is used by JavaScript and VBScript to identify the ActiveX control.
Src	This sets the source for the plug-in, if the Embed check-box is selected (as described in the following section "Combining ActiveX controls and plug-in objects").
V Space	To increase the amount of space between the top and bottom of the ActiveX object and the other elements on the page, enter a pixel value in the V (Vertical) Space text box. The default is zero.

Combining ActiveX controls and plug-in objects

Dreamweaver takes advantage of the fact that Netscape browsers do not recognize the `<object>` tag, and that Microsoft browsers do not recognize the `<embed>` tag placed inside the `<object>` tag. How could this be an advantage, you ask? Because of their mutual exclusivity, you can include both types of tags in the same Web page and still avoid conflicts.

The following example code shows you how the approach works in HTML. The `<embed>` section is bolded to show how one tag fits within another.

```
<object width="137" height="136"
classid="clsid:CFCDAA03-8BE4-11cf-B84B-0020AFBBCCFA">
      <param name="FileName" value="images/braz.wav">
      <embed width="137" height="136"
filename="images/braz.wav"
      src="images/braz.wav"></embed>
   </object>
```

Notice the values common to both tags, including the dimensions and the source file. (The source file is the `src` attribute in `<embed>`, and the `FileName` parameter in the `<object>` tag.) Dreamweaver automatically inserts these values when you enable the Embed option on the ActiveX Property Inspector.

Tip   If you're going to use the Embed option with your ActiveX object, you should wait until you've entered the necessary `FileName` parameter (through the Edit Parameters button) before you select the Embed check-box. When the `FileName` parameter is already specified, Dreamweaver automatically writes the same value in the Embed Scr text box. If you forget and turn on the Embed option before entering the `FileName` parameter, just turn off Embed, reselect it, and the proper value appears as the Embed source file.

Adding Java Applets

Java is a platform-independent programming language developed by Sun Microsystems. Although Java can also be used to write entire applications, its most frequent role is on the Web in the form of an applet. An *applet* is a self-contained program that can be run within a Web page.

Java is a compiled programming language similar to C++. Once a Java applet is compiled, it is saved as a class file. Web browsers call Java applets through, aptly enough, the `<applet>` tag. When you insert an applet, you refer to the primary class file much as you call a graphic file for an image tag.

Each Java applet has its own unique set of parameters — and Dreamweaver enables you to enter as many as necessary, in the same manner as for plug-ins and ActiveX controls. In fact, the Applet object works almost identically to the Plug-in and ActiveX objects.

Note Keep two caveats in mind if you're planning to include Java applets in your Web site. First, most (but not all) browsers support some version of Java—the newest release has the most features but the least support. Second, all the browsers that support Java enable the user to disable it, because of security issues. Make sure to use the Alt property to designate an alternative image or some text for display by browsers that do not support Java.

A Java applet can be inserted in a Web page with a bare minimum of parameters: the code source and the dimensions of the object. Java applets derive much of their power from their configurability, and most of these little programs have numerous custom parameters. As with plug-ins and ActiveX controls, Dreamweaver lets you specify the basic attributes through the Property Inspector, and the custom ones via the Parameters dialog box.

To include a Java applet in your Web page, follow these steps:

1. Position the cursor where you want the applet to originate and choose Insert ➪ Applet. You can also select the Insert Applet button from the Objects Palette.

   The Insert Applet dialog box opens.

2. From the Select File dialog box, enter the path to your class file in the File Name text box or select the Browse (Choose) button to locate the file.

   An Applet object placeholder appears in the Document Window. In the Applet Property Inspector (Figure 15-11), the selected source file appears in the Code text box and the folder appears in the Base text box.

Caution The path to your Java class files cannot be expressed absolutely, but must be given as an address relative to the Web page that is calling it.

3. Enter the height and width of the Applet object in the H and W text boxes, respectively. You can also resize the Applet object by clicking and dragging any of its three sizing handles.

4. You can enter any of the usual basic attributes, such as a name for the object, as well as values for Align, V Space, and/or H Space, Border, and Alt in the appropriate text boxes in the Property Inspector.

5. If desired, enter the online directory where the applet code can be found in the Base text box. If none is specified, the document's URL is assumed to be this attribute, known as the *codebase*.

6. To enter any custom attributes, select the Parameters button to open the Parameters dialog box.

Applet placeholder   Applet Property Inspector   Insert Applet

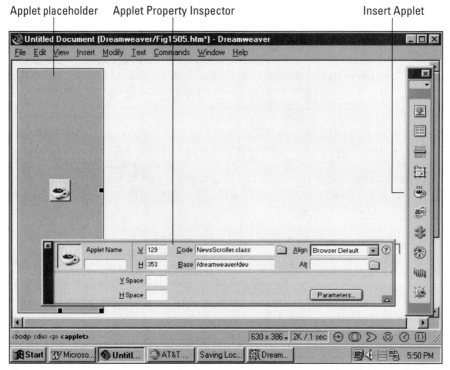

Figure 15-11: Use the Insert Applet button to insert a Java Applet object and display the Applet Property Inspector.

7. Select the + (Add) button and enter the first parameter. Press Tab to move to the Value column.

8. Enter the value for parameter, if any. Press Tab.

9. Continue entering desired parameters in the left column, with their values in the right. Click OK when you're finished.

Tip

Because of the importance of displaying alternative content for users not running Java, Dreamweaver provides a method for displaying something for everyone. To display an image, enter the URL to a graphics file in the Alt text box. To display text as well as an image, you have to do a little hand-coding. First, select a graphics file to insert in the Alt text box, and then open the HTML Inspector. In the ⟨img⟩ tag found between the ⟨applet⟩ tags, add an alt="*your_message*" attribute by hand (where the text you want to display is the value for the alt attribute). Now your Java applet displays an image for browsers that are graphics-enabled but not Java-enabled, and text for text-only browsers such as Lynx.

Some Java class files have additional graphics files. In most cases, you need to store both the class files and the graphics files in the same folder.

Adding JavaScript and VBScript

When initially developed by Netscape, JavaScript was called LiveScript. This browser-oriented language did not gain importance until Sun Microsystems joined the development team and the product was renamed JavaScript. Although the rechristening was a stroke of marketing genius, it has caused endless confusion among beginning programmers — JavaScript and Java have almost nothing in common outside of their capability to be incorporated in a Web page. JavaScript is used primarily to add functionality on the client side of the browser (for tasks such as verifying form data and adding interactivity to interface elements), or to script Netscape's servers on the server side. Java, on the other hand, is an application development language that can be used for a wide variety of tasks.

Conversely, VBScript is a full-featured Microsoft production. Both VBScript and JavaScript are scripting languages — which means you can write the code in any text editor and compile it at run time. JavaScript enjoys more support than VBScript — JavaScript can be rendered by both Netscape and Microsoft browsers, whereas VBScript is read only by Internet Explorer — but both languages have their fans. In Dreamweaver, both types of code are inserted in the Web page in the same manner.

Inserting JavaScript or VBScript

If only mastering JavaScript or VBScript itself were as easy as inserting the code in Dreamweaver! Simply go to the Objects Palette's Invisibles pane and select the Insert Script button, or choose Insert ⇨ Script from the menus, and enter your code in the small Insert Script window. After you click OK, a Script icon appears in place of your script.

Of course, any JavaScript or VBScript instruction is beyond the scope of this book, but any working Web designer must have an understanding of what these languages can do. Both languages refer to and, to varying degrees, manipulate the information on a Web page. Over time, you can expect significant growth in the capabilities of the JavaScript and VBScript disciplines.

 Dreamweaver, through the application of its behaviors, goes a long way toward making JavaScript useful for nonprogrammers. To learn more about Behaviors, see Chapter 17, "Using Behaviors."

Use the Script Property Inspector (Figure 15-12) to select an external file for your JavaScript or VBScript code. You can also set the language type by opening the Language drop-down list and choosing either JavaScript or VBScript. Because different features are available in the various releases of JavaScript, you can also specify JavaScript 1.1 or JavaScript 1.2. If you need to choose a specific version of JavaScript, you must do it when you initially insert the script — you cannot change the setting from the Script Property Inspector. Naturally, you could also make the adjustment in the HTML Inspector.

Figure 15-12: Insert either JavaScript or VBScript through the Objects Palette's Script object available on the Invisibles panel.

When you choose JavaScript or VBScript as your Language type, Dreamweaver writes the code accordingly. Both languages use the `<script>` tag pair, and each is specified in the `language` attribute, as follows:

```
<script language="JavaScript">alert("Look Out!")</script>
```

New Feature With Dreamweaver 2, you are no longer restricted to inserting code in just the `<body>` section of your Web page. Many JavaScript and VBScript functions must be located in the `<head>` section. To insert this type of script, first select View ⇨ Head Content. Next, select the now-visible `<head>` window and choose Insert ⇨ Script or click the Insert Script object. Enter your script as described earlier in this section and then select the main Document Window or choose View ⇨ Head Content again to deselect it.

You can also indicate whether your script is client-side or server-side-based by choosing the Type option from the Property Inspector. If you choose server-side, your script is enclosed in `<server>`...`</server>` tags and is interpreted by the Web server hosting the page.

Editing JavaScript or VBScript

Dreamweaver provides a large editing window for modifying your script code. To open this Script Properties window, select the placeholder icon for the script you want to modify and then choose the Edit button on the Script Property Inspector. You have the same functionality in the Script Properties window as in the Script Property Inspector; namely, you can choose your language or link to an external script file. In Figure 15-13, the Script Properties window has only a vertical scroll bar — not a horizontal scroll bar.

Tip Some older browsers "break" when loading a JavaScript Web page and display the code written between the `<script>`...`</script>` tag pair. Although Dreamweaver doesn't do it by default, you can use a trick to prevent this anomaly. In the HTML Inspector or your external editor, insert the opening comment tag (`<--`) right after the opening `<script>` tag. Then insert the closing comment tag (`-->`), preceded by two forward slashes, right before the closing `</script>`. An example follows:

```
<script language="Javascript">
<!--
[JavaScript code goes here]
//-->
</script>
```

The comment tags effectively tell the older browser to ignore the enclosed content. The two forward slashes in front of the closing comment tag are JavaScript's comment indicator, and tell it to ignore the rest of the line.

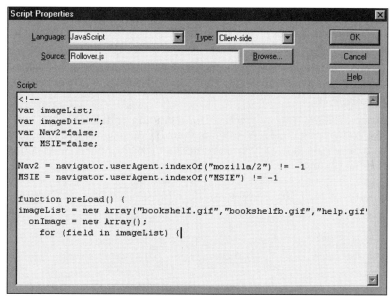

Figure 15-13: The generous Script Properties window provides plenty of room for modifying your JavaScript or VBScript.

Summary

To paraphrase a popular commercial, "Web pages aren't just for HTML anymore." The horizons of possibility expand tremendously when you start to explore any of the technologies discussed in this chapter: CGI, plug-ins, ActiveX, Java, and JavaScript or VBScript. Dreamweaver maintains an open-ended design for external programs.

✦ CGI scripts are primarily used to send information back and forth between the user and the Web server. The Web server can then, under direction of the CGI program, store the information in a database or forward it to another URL or e-mail address.

✦ Plug-ins enable browsers to display formats other than HTML. A plug-in can display multimedia content inline with other HTML objects such as images and tables. Dreamweaver supports a Plug-in object that enables the `<embed>` code to be customized through the Parameters dialog box.

✦ Dreamweaver 2 now enables you to play any or all of the plug-ins — right in the Document Window as you're creating your Web page.

✦ ActiveX controls are employed by Microsoft browsers in a manner similar to Netscape's plug-ins. Each ActiveX control has its own unique Class ID, as well as a codebase attribute that enables users to get the control without interrupting their workflow. The Dreamweaver ActiveX object enables you to easily combine both ActiveX controls and their corresponding plug-in with the Embed option.

✦ Java applets can be inserted as Applet objects in a Dreamweaver Web page. Java source files, called *classes,* can be linked to the Applet object through the Property Inspector.

✦ Dreamweaver offers a simple method for including both JavaScript and VBScript code in the <body> section of your HTML page. Script functions that need to be inserted in the <head> section can now be added by selecting View ➪ Head Content.

In the next chapter, you learn how you can use and create your own Dreamweaver objects.

✦   ✦   ✦

Creating and Using Objects

Sometimes the simplest ideas are the most powerful. The Dreamweaver development team had a simple idea: Why not code the insertable objects in HTML? After all, when you choose to insert anything into a Web page — from a horizontal rule to a Shockwave Director movie — you are just putting HTML in the page. If the objects are just HTML files, what are the possible benefits? For one, the objects can be easily modified. Also, HTML requires no special program to code, and coding the language itself is not extraordinarily difficult. In addition, the core users of Dreamweaver are experts in HTML. Now, a simple idea is turned into a powerful tool.

All the objects included with Dreamweaver can be modified and customized to fit any Web designer's working preferences. Furthermore, custom objects can easily be created. This capability not only enables you to include regular HTML tags that repeatedly occur in your designs, but it also opens the door to an impressive new level of expandability. Dreamweaver's capability to accommodate any number of custom objects means you can take advantage of new technologies immediately.

Building a site that needs the latest tags just released by the W3C? Go right ahead — make an object that inserts any or all of the tags. You may not be able to see the result in Dreamweaver, but if your browser can handle the tags, you can preview them there.

Find yourself including the same ActiveX control over and over again, with only one change in the parameters? Create a custom object that inserts that control, with all the constant attributes — and add a parameter form to enter the variable attributes.

This chapter shows you the tremendous potential of Dreamweaver objects. After studying the use of the standard objects, you learn how you can customize your object working environment. Then, you find out how to create your own objects and take advantage of the new features in Dreamweaver 2.

Inserting Dreamweaver Objects

If you've been using Dreamweaver, you've been using objects. Even if your first exposure to Dreamweaver has been working through the first 15 chapters of this book, you've already used several types of objects. Aside from text, everything inserted in a Web page can be considered an object: images, comments, plug-ins, named anchors — they're all objects and are all extremely easy to use.

Dreamweaver offers several ways to include any object. For a few objects, you even have as many as four different techniques from which to choose:

✦ From the main menu, choose Insert and then any of the listed objects.

✦ From the Objects Palette (see Figure 16-1), click any button on the four standard panes — Common, Forms, Head, and Invisibles — to insert an object in the current cursor position.

✦ Drag any button off the Objects Palette and drop it next to any existing content on your Web page.

✦ Many objects have a keyboard shortcut, such as Ctrl-Alt-I (Command-Alt-I) for Image or Ctrl-Alt-F (Command-Alt-F) for a Flash movie. Keyboard shortcuts insert the chosen object at the current cursor location.

Figure 16-1: You'll find yourself returning to the Objects Palette as an easy way to include HTML elements.

Tip

When you insert one of the objects from the Invisibles panel — such as the Line-Break, Comment, or Named Anchor — Dreamweaver by default inserts an icon to show the object's placement. If you find these icons distracting, you can turn them all off by choosing the toggle command, View ➪ Invisible Elements. If you have an Invisible Element "turned off" in Preferences, you will never see the icon, regardless of the status of the View menu command.

Modifying the Objects Palette

The Objects Palette is one of the most customizable of all of Dreamweaver's features. In addition to the flexibility of having it "float" anywhere on the screen, you can also resize and reshape the Palette to your liking — you can even dock it with other floating windows in Dreamweaver 2. Most important, you can rearrange its contents, add new panes, and, as noted earlier, include custom objects.

Moving and reshaping the Objects Palette

If you work with your Document Window fully expanded, you'll often find yourself repositioning the Objects Palette. Just click-and-drag the title bar on top of the Palette to quickly move it out of the way. You can also press F4 to send the Objects Palette (and any other open palette or inspector) behind the Document Window or Site Window. Pressing F4 again brings them back to the front.

If you don't like the long, vertical shape that Dreamweaver uses by default for the Objects Palette, you can change its appearance. Place your pointer over any border of the Palette until the usual pointing arrow changes into a two-headed arrow — now you can click and drag the Objects Palette into a new shape. You can drag any corner to form a rectangular shape, as shown in Figure 16-2, or you can make the Palette extend horizontally instead of vertically.

Figure 16-2: Reshape the Objects Palette to your liking.

When screen real estate is at a premium, you can reduce the overall size of the Objects Palette — even down to just a one-button size. If you shrink it down small enough so that all the buttons don't show at once, one or two scroll arrows appear. Click an arrow to see the next button in the Palette.

New Feature The Objects Palette is the only one of the "big three" floating windows — Objects, Properties, and Launcher — that can be included in Dreamweaver 2's new docking system. If you're working with a variety of Dreamweaver's other features, such as layers, templates, behaviors, and so on, you might want to group the Objects Palette with these other windows to reduce your workspace clutter.

Reorganizing the objects and adding panes

The four panes of the Objects Palette — Common, Forms, Head, and Invisibles — correspond to the three folders found in the Dreamweaver Configuration\Objects directory. Each folder has two items for each object: an HTML file and a GIF file. The HTML file is the source code for the object, and the GIF file is the button image. If you want to move an item from one Objects Palette pane to another, just transfer the two files related to that object from one folder to the other.

For example, let's say you're doing a lot of JavaScript work and you want to move the Insert Script object from the Invisibles pane to the Common pane. To accomplish this task, you need to move script.htm and script.gif from the Invisibles folder to the Common folder. You can click-and-drag the files, or cut-and-paste them. You must restart Dreamweaver to see the changes.

You're not limited to the four panes on the Objects Palette. The standard panes — Common, Forms, Head, and Invisibles — correspond to identically named subfolders in the Objects directory. If you want to add another pane, simply add a new subfolder. For example, I've developed a number of custom objects for inserting sound and digital video files, which I wanted to group on a new pane of the Objects Palette. In my file management program, I created a folder called Media within the Dreamweaver\Configuration\Objects\ folder and moved all my special object files into the new folder. After restarting Dreamweaver, Media appears as my fifth pane in the Objects Palette.

 Caution   Dreamweaver only recognizes one level of subfolders within the Objects folder as new Objects Palette panes. You cannot, for instance, create a subfolder called Videos within the Media subfolder that will be recognized by Dreamweaver as a submenu.

Dreamweaver alphabetizes the Object panes by folder name. If you want your new custom pane to appear first on the Objects Palette, you must name its folder so that it appears further down alphabetically (that is, closer to *A*) than the Common folder. Use one of two tricks: You can start the custom folder name with a tilde (~), such as ~Media, for instance; or you can rename the Common folder so that its name appears later in the alphabet.

Customizing the Insert Menu

Just as you can reorganize the Objects Palette to your working style, you can also restructure the Insert menu. To a degree, the Insert menu can control the appearance of the Objects Palette. You can create keyboard shortcuts for objects, and make subfolders for existing and new objects. The capability to create custom objects is an invaluable design feature; as a significant bonus, Dreamweaver enables you to reference custom objects.

The key to the Insert menu is a file called InsertMenu.htm, stored in Dreamweaver's Configuration\Object folder. Because InsertMenu.htm is an HTML file, you can make your modifications directly in Dreamweaver. After you're done, just save the file and restart Dreamweaver to see your changes take effect.

Altering the InsertMenu file

The InsertMenu file uses basic HTML—bulleted lists and underlining—to build the familiar drop-down menu. Three items make up each item in the list:

1. The object name as it appears in the Insert menu. In Windows systems, one letter, unique to the list, is underlined; this letter is used together with the Alt key to call the object.

2. A single letter used in combination with the Ctrl-Alt (Command-Alt) keys to make up the keyboard shortcut.

3. The object HTML file.

The standard InsertMenu file, shown in Figure 16-3, begins as follows:

```
•Image, I, Image.htm
•Table, T, Table.htm
•Horizontal Rule, , HR.htm
•----------
•Layer, , Layer.htm
•----------
•Applet, , Applet.htm
•ActiveX, , ActiveX.htm
•Plugin, , Plugin.htm
•----------
•Flash, F, Flash.htm
•Shockwave, D, Shockwave.htm
•Rollover Image, , Rollover.htm
•----------
•Form, , Form.htm
•Form Object
   •Text Field, , Text Field.htm
   •Button, , Button.htm
   •Check Box, , Checkbox.htm
   •Radio Button, , Radio.htm
   •List/Menu, , List Menu.htm
   •File Field, , File Field.htm
   •Image Field, , Image Field.htm
   •Hidden Field, , Hidden Field.htm
•----------
•Named Anchor, A, Anchor.htm
•Comment, , Comment.htm
•Script, , Script.htm
•Line Break, , Line Break.htm
•Non-Breaking Space, , NBSP.htm
•Server-Side Include, , SSI.htm
•----------
•Head
   •Meta, , Meta.htm
   •Keywords, ,Keywords.htm
   •Description, ,Description.htm
```

```
•Refresh, , Refresh.htm
•Base, , Base.htm
•Link, , Link.htm
```

Caution   Before you alter the InsertMenu.htm file, save a spare copy of the file. Open the file in Dreamweaver, choose File ⇨ Save As, and enter a different name in the File Name text box — something like **InsertMenu-Original** (the .htm extension is automatically attached). Then, just to make sure that copy is left unchanged, close your renamed file and reopen InsertMenu.htm.

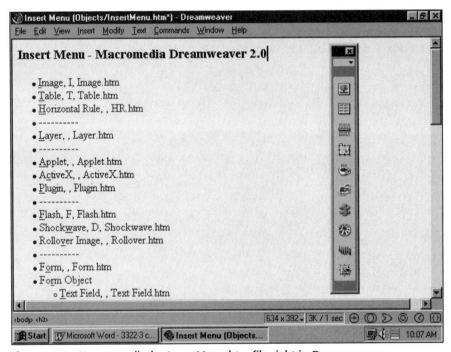

Figure 16-3: You can edit the InsertMenu.htm file right in Dreamweaver.

Once you have the InsertMenu.htm file open, take a look at the HTML. Notice that each object is one list item, $\langle li \rangle$, in an unordered list, $\langle ul \rangle$ — even the separator lines made up of dashes are list items. To rearrange one or more items to a different location in the list, select the entire line for the object you want to move. Then choose Edit ⇨ Cut or use the keyboard shortcut, Ctrl-X (Command-X). Move your cursor to the front of the line below where you want your cut line to appear, and choose Edit ⇨ Paste or Ctrl-V (Command-V).

Tip   Dreamweaver even lets you specify the order of the buttons that appear in the Objects Palette. The order is the same as in the Insert menu, which is determined by the InsertMenu.htm file. When you alter the order of the items in this file, the Objects Palette buttons reflect the same sequence the next time you start Dreamweaver.

You can also group items in submenus, such as the submenu for Form Objects. To achieve this effect, highlight the item you want to appear in a submenu and, from the Property Inspector, choose the Indent button—you can also select Text ⇨ Indent in the menus. Because all items are in an unordered list, the submenu items appear with a different bullet in the HTML file, but render normally in the list.

Adding items and keyboard shortcuts

Once you start making your own objects—and installing other prebuilt ones like those included on this book's CD-ROM—you'll eventually want to modify the InsertMenu.htm file to incorporate your creations. Again, this procedure is straightforward; just follow the format of the objects already in the file.

Tip

In addition to adding new objects with keyboard shortcuts, you can also add a keyboard shortcut to any existing object that doesn't have a shortcut. The single letter that denotes the shortcut can be uppercase or lowercase; Dreamweaver doesn't care. You can also use the single-digit numbers, 0–9.

To add a new object to the InsertMenu.htm file, follow these steps:

1. From within Dreamweaver, open the file Dreamweaver\Configuration\Objects\InsertMenu.htm.

2. Position the text cursor at the end of the line above where you want to insert the object.

3. Press Enter (Return) to make a new bulleted entry.

4. Enter the object name, the shortcut letter (if any), and the object source file—separated by commas. Even if you don't use a shortcut letter, you still must include both commas.

   The format for this entry follows:

   ```
   Objectname, X, objectfile.htm
   ```

   where *Objectname* is the name of the object, with the Alt- letter underlined; *X* is the Ctrl-Alt- (Command-Alt) shortcut letter; and *objectfile* is the .htm or .html file name of the object. Be sure you enter the filename exactly, with the correct extension.

5. When you've completed your editing of the InsertMenu.htm file, choose File ⇨ Save or press Ctrl-S (Command-S) to save the file.

6. Quit and restart Dreamweaver.

Adding Other Objects

Before you begin building your own custom objects, you may want to look around and see if someone else has already created something similar. In addition to having the standard objects that ship with Dreamweaver, numerous Web sites have objects (and behaviors) that are available for download. You can even search an ongoing database of Dreamweaver objects (as well as behaviors, commands, and so on) at the Dreamweaver Extension Database, located on my site, "Dreamweaver etc." (www.idest.com/dreamweaver). Of course, a wide variety of objects are available on the CD-ROM accompanying this book. You can find these objects in the folder Dreamweaver\Configuration\Objects.

No matter where you get your objects, the procedure for installing them is the same. To incorporate new objects into your Dreamweaver system, follow these steps:

1. Uncompress the files if necessary. Object files come with an HTML file and a GIF file, and the two files are usually compressed for easy download or transfer.

2. If necessary, make a new folder for your objects. All objects must be stored in a subfolder of the Dreamweaver\Configuration\Objects folder. You can either store the object files in a standard subfolder (Common, Forms, Head, or Invisibles, for instance) or in a new folder that you create.

3. Transfer the object files to the desired folder. Be careful: Make sure you transfer both the HTML and the GIF file together.

4. Open InsertMenu.htm in Dreamweaver, and modify the file to include your new objects. Follow the steps described in the preceding section "Altering the InsertMenu file."

5. Restart Dreamweaver.

Online Sources for Dreamweaver Extensions

There are numerous online sources for new objects and behaviors. However, like traditional Web development, creating Dreamweaver extensions is an ever-growing affair—if you can't find what you're looking for at any one site, visit the Dreamweaver Extension Database hosted by Dreamweaver etc.

Macromedia

    http://www.macromedia.com/support/dreamweaver/upndown/objects

The official Object and Behavior Exchange site accepts objects submitted from all over. After evaluations by the Dreamweaver engineers, objects are posted for downloading. Before you can access this area of the Macromedia site, you must accept the terms of a licensing agreement.

Dreamweaver Depot

`http://people.netscape.com/andreww/dreamweaver/`

Run by Andrew Wooldridge, the Dreamweaver Depot initially specialized in Netscape-only objects and behaviors, but the site now offers cross-browser and Internet Explorer-specific extensions as well. The Depot also has a forum and a chat room for Dreamweaver aficionados.

Dreamweaver's Fan Page

`http://www.cybernet.ch/users/massimo/`

Massimo Foti produces high-quality extensions that fulfill many specific functions faced by a Web developer. For example, his site features extensions devoted to redirecting browsers as well as controlling remote windows and scrolling layers.

Excellent Dreamweaver Supply Bin

`http://home.att.net/~JCB.BEI/Dreamweaver/`

This site, chaired by Kevin Bartz, focuses primarily on objects and behaviors that take advantage of Internet Explorer's special features. The Supply Bin also has a good supply of cross-browser objects and behaviors.

Webmonkey Editor Extensions Collection

`http://www.hotwired.com/webmonkey/javascript/code_library/ed_ext`

Although this area on the Hot Wired site could potentially hold other Web authoring tools' extensions, Dreamweaver is currently the only one on the market with the capability. You'll find several professional-quality objects and behaviors, both cross-browser and browser-specific.

Yaromat

`http://www.yaromat.com/`

Featuring objects, commands, and behaviors by Jaro von Flocken, Yaromat houses some of the most creative Dreamweaver extensions on the Web. His Layer f(x) behavior brings mathematical precision to layer movements, and his other creations are equally dramatic.

Dreamweaver etc.

`http://www.idest.com/dreamweaver/`

Maintained by Joseph Lowery, author of this book, the Dreamweaver etc. site includes all the objects found on this book's CD-ROM, plus new ones posted after this book's publication.

Creating Custom Objects

Each custom object, like standard objects, is made from two files: an HTML file describing the object, and a GIF file depicting the button. The complexity of the HTML depends on the complexity of the object. You can build just about anything — from a simple object that replicates a repeatedly used item, to a high-end object that uses advanced JavaScript techniques for creating special function layers and windows. You can even make objects that create other objects.

To support the "higher end" of the custom object scale, Dreamweaver 2 includes proprietary extensions to JavaScript and a Document Object Model (DOM), which combines a subset of Netscape Navigator 3.0's DOM with a subset of the DOM established by the W3C. You study these techniques further into the chapter. As the following section shows, however, many objects don't require any JavaScript and are easy to construct.

Making simple objects

To make a simple object that inserts any HTML-created item, put only the code necessary to create the object into a file, and then save the file in one of the object folders. The key phrase in the preceding sentence is *only the code necessary*. Unlike a regular Web page, for a simple custom object you don't include the framing `<html>...<body>...</body>...</html>` sections — all you need is the essential code necessary to make the object.

For example, let's say you are asked to enhance 100 Web pages and make each page capable of showing a different VDOLive movie. Each of the .avi files is different, so you can't use Dreamweaver's Library feature. The easiest way to handle this situation is to create a dummy version of what you need and then turn that dummy into an object.

Step 1: Creating the item

First, create your item as you normally would in Dreamweaver. For this example, let's insert a plug-in and add all the standard attributes: `name`, `height` and `width`, `pluginspage`, `border`, `v space`, and `h space` — and even a few special parameters like `autostart` and `stretch`. The only attribute that the example omits is the attribute that changes: the file source. You also want the movie to be centered, wherever it's located, and you center the plug-in. When finished, the complete code for the page and plug-in, as generated by Dreamweaver, looks like the following:

```
<html>
<head>
<title>Untitled Document</title>
<meta http-equiv="Content-Type" content="text/html;
charset=iso-8859-1">
</head>
<body bgcolor="#FFFFFF">
<div align="center">
```

```
    <embed src="" width="135" height="135" name="vdoMovie"
pluginspage="http://www.vdo.net/download/" vspace="5"
hspace="5" border="5" stretch="true" autostart="false"></embed>
</div>
</body>
</html>
```

Step 2: Creating the object

To create a simple object from the preceding, just cut everything in the code but the item (or items) you want repeated. In the HTML Inspector, select all the code from the opening `<html>` tag up to and including the `<body>` tag, and then delete. Then delete the closing tags, `</body>` and `</html>`. The only remaining code is the following:

```
<div align="center">
    <embed src="" width="135" height="135" name="vdoMovie"
pluginspage="http://www.vdo.net/download/" vspace="5"
hspace="5" border="5" stretch="true" autostart="false"></embed>
</div>
```

After you eliminate all the code except for your object's code and return to the visual editor, the Document Window changes from a white background to a dark-gray background. This change occurs because Dreamweaver makes the `bgcolor` attribute of the `<body>` tag white by default — to create a simple object, you need to delete the entire `<body>` tag, including the color information.

Step 3: Saving the object

Now your object is ready to be saved. For Dreamweaver to recognize this or any other snippet of code as an object, the file must be saved in the Configuration\ Objects folder. You can choose to save your object in any of the existing subfolders — Common, Forms, Head, or Invisibles — or you can create a new subfolder within the Objects folder. For this example, create a new folder called Media for this and other similar objects.

Caution   You must save your new object in a subfolder within the Objects folder. Dream-weaver doesn't recognize objects saved individually in the Objects folder.

After the file is saved, you can restart Dreamweaver to test your object — or you can use the new Reload Objects feature.

New Feature   To force Dreamweaver to reload objects, behavior, inspectors, and commands, click the expander arrow on the Objects Palette while holding down the Ctrl (Command) key. In addition to the different Objects Palette panes, Dreamweaver 2 displays the Reload Objects menu item, as shown in Figure 16-4. Select this option and soon your new objects will be available — although there's one final step to consider.

Figure 16-4: Press the Ctrl (Command) key and click the Objects Palette expander arrow to access the Reload Objects command.

Step 4: Creating a button for the object

As shown in Figure 16-5, Dreamweaver displays an "image not found" placeholder in the Objects Palette, because you haven't yet made a button image for the vdoMovie object. In addition, unless you specifically include the new object in the InsertMenu.htm file, the object is listed in the bottom portion of the Insert menu. This arrangement is fine for debugging, but if you want to continue using your object, it's more efficient to create a button image for it and revise the InsertMenu.htm file to include it. The following section shows you how to complete this task.

Building an object button

Object buttons are GIF files, ideally sized at 18 pixels square. To make the object button, you can use any graphics-creation program that can save GIF files. If your button image file is not 18 pixels by 18 pixels, Dreamweaver resizes it to those dimensions. Although Dreamweaver uses a specific color scheme, you are not limited to the same palette. Your button can be as colorful as you want — as long as it can still fit in an 18-pixel square.

Tip

To create an object button, you can open and modify any of the existing GIF files for the standard buttons. Just be sure to use the Save As command of your paint program — and not the Save command — to save your modified version.

After you've created your button image, save the GIF file in the same folder as the HTML file for the new object. At this time, you may also want to modify the InsertMenu.htm file as already described.

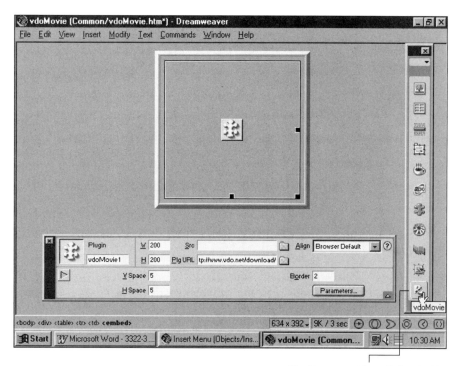

The "image not found" placeholder

Figure 16-5: You can create custom objects like the vdoMovie object shown here.

Putting JavaScript to Work in Custom Objects

The remaining sections of this chapter deal with using JavaScript to create more complex objects.

Caution   If you're totally unfamiliar with JavaScript, you might want to review this section with a good supporting resource at hand. An excellent choice is Danny Goodman's *JavaScript Bible*, published by IDG Books Worldwide.

Using the objectTag() function

When Macromedia built a JavaScript interpreter into Dreamweaver, a number of extensions were included to facilitate object and behavior creation. One of these functions, `objectTag()`, is the key to building advanced objects. All of the standard Dreamweaver-built objects use the `objectTag()` function. This function has a single purpose: it writes any specified value into the HTML document.

New Feature

Prior to Dreamweaver 2, the `objectTag()` function could only write code into the `<body>` of a file. With the current release, however, `objectTag()` can insert code in the `<head>` as well as the `<body>`. Moreover, the function handles the placement intelligently; `objectTag()` knows which tags should be placed where. Consequently, you don't have to make any special declarations to place code in the `<head>` section.

You can see a simple use of the `objectTag()` function by looking at the source code for Dreamweaver's Insert Line-Break object. In the Objects\Invisibles folder, open line_break.htm and look at the code for this object in the HTML Inspector. Just like most JavaScript functions that can affect any portion of the page, the `objectTag()` function is written in the `<head>` section. Here's the function in its entirety:

```
function objectTag() {
   // Return the html tag that should be inserted
   return "<BR>";
}
```

Tip

You can designate a tooltip to appear when your mouse passes over your new object's button. Enter the desired name in the `<title>` section of the HTML object file. The designated `<title>` also appears on any dialog boxes used by the object.

Aside from the comment line, `objectTag()` only returns a value. In the preceding example, the value happens to be "`<BR>`". You can insert any HTML code as the return value. However, because JavaScript formats any value as a string, you need to apply JavaScript string-formatting syntax, as follows:

✦ To use the `objectTag()` function to return an HTML tag and a variable, use quotes around each string literal but not around the variable, and join the two with a plus sign. For example, the following `objectTag()` function code inserts `<img src=images/whatzit.gif>` in the current cursor position:

```
nada = "images/whatzit.gif"
return "<img src=" + nada + ">";
```

✦ To make an object that returns separate lines of code, put each tag on its own line, with the symbol for a newline, \n, at the end of the string, surrounded by quotes; then add a plus sign at the end of the line. For example, the following `objectTag()` function inserts a Flash movie of a particular size and shape:

```
function objectTag() {
  // Return the html tag that should be inserted
  return '\n' +
'<object classid="clsid:D27CDB6E-AE6D-11cf-96B8-444553540000'
\n' +
'codebase="http://download.macromedia.com/pub/shockwave/cabs/
flash/swflash.cab#3,0,0,0". "width="145" height="135"> \n' +
' <param name="movie" value="newMovie.swf"> \n' +
' <param name="PLAY" value="false"> \n' +
```

```
' <embed src="newMovie.swf" \n' +
'pluginspage="http://www.macromedia.com/shockwave/download/"
width="145" height="135" play="false"></embed> \n' +
'</object>'
}
```

Some developers prefer to set the entire collection of strings to a variable and return that variable. In this case, you'd be better served by using JavaScript's add-by-value operator (+=), as in this example:

```
var retval = ''
retval += '<table width="' + newWidth + '" height="' +
newHeight + '" border="0" cellspacing="0" cellpadding="0">\n'
retval += '   <tr>\n'
retval += '      <td>' + newCode + '</td>\n'
retval += '   </tr>\n'
retval += '</table>\n'
return retval
```

✦ Use single quotes to surround the return values that include double quotes. Make sure that for every opening quote of one kind, there is a matching closing quote of the same kind. For example:

```
return '<img src="images/eiffel.jpg">'
```

✦ Use the backslash character, \, to display special inline characters such as double and single quotes or newline.

```
return "<strong>You\'re Right!</strong>"
```

Tip

Unless you're mixing variables with the HTML you're using for your object, you should use the "object-only" method described in the previous section, "Making simple objects." Reserve the objectTag() function for your intermediate-to-advanced object-creation projects.

Offering Help

As objects grow in their features, they often grow in their complexity. An object with multiple parameters — especially if it is intended for public release — could potentially benefit from a Help button. Dreamweaver 2 offers just such a button to aid custom object builders and their users.

New Feature

Including the displayHelp() function causes Dreamweaver 2 to display a Help button, directly beneath the OK and Cancel buttons found to the right of a user-created parameter form. When selected, this button calls whatever is defined in the function.

For example, if you wanted to define a Help button that would put up an informative message within Dreamweaver, you might code the displayHelp() function this way:

```
displayHelp() {
  alert("Be sure to name all your layers first")
}
```

You're not restricted to in-program alerts. If you have a much larger Help file, you can have it displayed in your primary browser by using Dreamweaver 2's built-in `browseDocument()` function. With the following definition, when the Help button is selected, Dreamweaver first opens the primary browser (if it's not already running) and shows the object-specific Help file:

```
displayHelp() {

dreamweaver.browseDocument("http://www.idest.com/dreamweaver/he
lp/entitiesHelp.htm")
}
```

Note that the above code includes an absolute URL that pulls a page off the Web. You can also reference a file locally. The best way to do this is to use another Dreamweaver JavaScript function, `getConfigurationPath()`. Just as it sounds, this function returns the current path to the Configuration folder. Using this as a base, you can reference other files installed on the system. In this example, the Help file is stored in a folder called HelpDocs, which in turn is stored within the Configuration folder:

```
function displayHelp() {
  var helpPath = dreamweaver.getConfigurationPath() +
"/HelpDocs/replicatorHelp.htm"
  dreamweaver.browseDocument(helpPath)
}
```

Attaching a parameter form

To be truly useful, many objects require additional attributes. Several of the standard objects in Dreamweaver use parameter forms to simplify entry of these attributes. A *parameter form* is the portion of the object code that creates a dialog box. Dreamweaver uses the HTML form commands for handling the parameter form duties.

To see how a parameter form is structured, look at the parameter forms used in the standard objects. Select the Insert Script button in the Invisibles panel of the Objects Palette. The Insert Script dialog box that appears on the screen is a basic parameter form.

Next, open the Script object source file (Objects\Invisibles\script.htm) in Dreamweaver to see how the parameter form is built. As shown in Figure 16-6, the `<body>` of the file consists of a single `<form>` element with two items inside, a text field and a menu list.

Parameter form

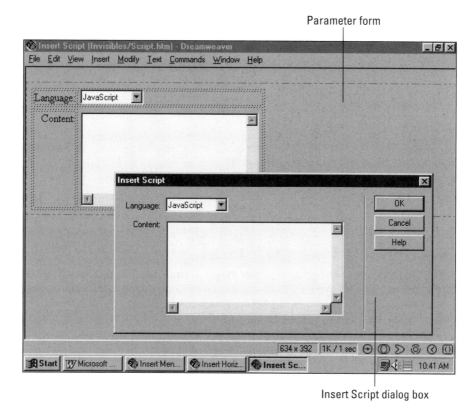

Insert Script dialog box

Figure 16-6: To see how the parameter form is used, compare the Script source file to its completed object.

The ⟨body⟩ section of the HTML source code for the Script object contains only the ⟨form⟩ with two fields: a ⟨select⟩ field (the menu list used to select the language) and a ⟨textarea⟩ field for the actual script:

```
<FORM NAME="theform">
  <table>
    <tr>
      <td align="right">Language:</td>
      <td>
        <select name="Language">
          <option value="JS" selected>JavaScript</option>
          <option value="JS11">JavaScript 1.1</option>
          <option value="JS12">JavaScript 1.2</option>
          <option value="VB">VBScript</option>
        </select>
      </td>
    </tr>
    <tr>
      <td align="right" height="5"></td>
```

```
      <td rowspan="2">
        <textarea name="script" cols="50" rows="8"></textarea>
      </td>
    </tr>
    <tr>
      <td align="right" valign="top">Content:</td>
    </tr>
  </table>
</FORM>
```

When the parameter form is displayed as an object, Dreamweaver automatically adds the OK, Cancel, and Help buttons. When you select the OK button, the `objectTag()` function combines the values in the `<select>` and `<textarea>` tags with the necessary HTML tags to write the Script code.

Sizing the Parameter Form Dialog Box

Although you cannot control all aspects of your parameter form — Dreamweaver automatically inserts the OK and Cancel buttons on the upper-right — you can designate the dimensions of the parameter's dialog box. Normally, Dreamweaver automatically sizes the dialog box, but for a complex object, you can speed up the display by using the `windowDimensions()` function. Moreover, if your object is intended for general distribution, you can set different window dimensions for the Macintosh and Windows platforms.

The `windowDimensions()` function takes one argument, `platform`, and returns a string in the following form:

```
"width_in_Pixels,height_in_Pixels"
```

The size specified should not include the area for the OK and Cancel buttons. If the dimensions offered are too small to display all the options in the parameter form, scroll bars automatically appear.

The following example of the `windowDimensions()` function creates a parameter form dialog box 650 pixels by 530 pixels if viewed on a Macintosh, and 670 pixels by 550 pixels if viewed on a Windows system:

```
function windowDimensions(platform){
    if (platform.charAt(0) == 'm'){ // Macintosh
      return "650,530";
    }
    else { // Windows 95 or NT
      return "670,550";
    }
  }
```

Macromedia recommends that you not use the `windowDimensions()` function unless you want your dialog box to be larger than 640 × 480 pixels. Like all Dreamweaver extensions to the Application Programming Interface (API), the `windowDimensions()` function can be used to build both objects and actions.

Using the form controls

Dreamweaver uses the HTML `<form>` tag and all of its various input types to gather attribute information for objects. To use the form elements in a parameter form, their input data must be passed to the JavaScript functions. Because Dreamweaver uses a subset of the Navigator 3.0 Document Object Model (DOM), as shown in Table 16-1, you are restricted to using specific methods for the various input types to gather this information. Properties marked with an asterisk are read-only.

Table 16-1			
Form Elements in the Dreamweaver Document Object Model			
Object	*Properties*	*Methods*	*Events*
form	elements* (an array of button, checkbox, password, radio, reset, select, submit, text, and text area objects) child objects by name	None	None
button reset submit	form*	blur() focus()	onClick
checkbox radio	checked form*	blur() focus()	onClick
password text textarea	value form*	blur() focus() select()	onBlur onFocus
select	form* options[n].defaultSelected* options[n].index* options[n].selected* options[n].text* options[n].value* selectedIndex	blur() (Windows only) focus() (Windows only)	onBlur (Windows only) onChange onFocus() (Windows only)

Note   JavaScript uses a hierarchical method of addressing the various elements on any given Web page. Moving from most general to most specific, each element is separated by a period. For example, the background color property of a page would be `document.bgColor`. The status of a check-box named "sendPromo" on a form called "orderForm" would be `document.orderForm.sendPromo.checked`. The more complex your objects, the more important it is for you to master this syntax.

Text, textarea, and password fields

When information is entered in one of the text input type fields, the data is stored in the value property of the specific object. For example, look again at the code for the Plug-in object, and notice the text field where the selected file's name is displayed:

```
<INPUT TYPE="text" name="pluginfilename" size="30">
```

When the `objectTag()` function is run, the contents of that text box is assigned to a variable, and that variable is included in the output written to the Web page:

```
function objectTag() {
  // Return the html tag that should be inserted
  var retval = '<EMBED SRC="' +
escape(document.forms[0].pluginfilename.value) + '"></EMBED>';

  // clear the field for next insertion
  clearForm();
  return retval;
}
```

In the preceding case, the input filename is located in:

```
document.forms[0].pluginfilename.value
```

Because the form was also named ("theForm"), this same value could also be written as follows:

```
document.theForm.pluginfilename.value
```

Note

> The "escape" function is a JavaScript internal function that converts a text string so that it can be read by a Web server. Any special characters are encoded into their hexadecimal ASCII equivalents. A single space between words, for instance, is converted to %20.

The text input types recognize two events in the Dreamweaver Document Object Model: `onBlur` and `onFocus`. When a user selects a text field, either by tabbing or clicking into it, that text field is said to have *focus* — and the `onFocus` event is fired. When the user leaves that field, the field loses focus or *blurs* — and the `onBlur` event is triggered. Because the DOM does not recognize the `onChange` event handler with text fields, you can use a combination of `onFocus` and `onBlur` to check for changes and act accordingly.

Submit, Reset, and Command buttons

The button input types are used in parameter forms to trigger custom JavaScript functions. Instead of sending data to an external server, the data is sent to a specified internal function. The buttons respond only to `onClick` events and cannot pass any particular properties of their own, such as value or name.

Command buttons are used extensively in the Character Entities object shown in Figure 16-7. (The object is available on this book's CD-ROM.) Each character entity is a separate Command button, written in the following form:

```
<input type="BUTTON" value="&#161;"
onClick="getChar('&amp;#161;','&#161;')">
```

Figure 16-7: This custom Character Entities object (available on the CD-ROM) uses 97 separate Command buttons.

Each character entity symbol in each line has a specific purpose. The value is the character displayed on the button; the first argument in the getChar() function is written to a hidden field and eventually sent to the Web page; and the second argument is used to display the selected character in a text box.

```
function getChar(val,val2) {
  document.theForm.charValue.value=val
  document.theForm.txChar.value=val2
}
```

When this object is at work, the user makes a selection and clicks OK, and the objectTag() function reads the value from the hidden field and writes it into the Web page:

```
function objectTag() {
  return document.theForm.charValue.value;
}
```

Command buttons can be used to fire any custom JavaScripts and pass any necessary information to be eventually processed by the objectTag() function.

Check-boxes

Check-boxes allow an option to be selected or deselected, so the only information that a function needs from a check-box is whether it has been selected. Dreamweaver's DOM lets you read the checked property of the Check-box object and act accordingly. The Character Entities object discussed in the preceding section, for instance, uses a check-box to turn on and off the Multiple Characters option. If the check-box (named cbMultiple) is selected, then document.theForm.cbMultiple.checked is true and one set of statements is executed; otherwise, the second set of statements is run. The code for check-boxes follows:

```
function getChar(val,val2) {
if(document.theForm.cbMultiple.checked) {
  document.theForm.charValue.value=
  document.theForm.charValue.value+val
  document.theForm.txChar.value=
  document.theForm.txChar.value+val2
  } else {
  document.theForm.charValue.value=val
  document.theForm.txChar.value=val2
  }
}
```

Check-boxes are excellent for setting up either/or situations. You can also use check-boxes to set (turn on) particular attributes. You may, for instance, use a check-box to let the user enable an automatic startup for an .avi movie, or to turn the control panel on or off.

Radio buttons

Radio buttons offer a group of options, from which the user can only select one. The group is composed of <input type=radio> tags with the same name attribute; there can be as few as two in the group or as many as necessary.

The input type radio, like checkbox, makes use of the checked property to see which option was selected. The method used to figure out which of the radio buttons was chosen depends on the number of buttons used on the form:

✦ With just two or three buttons, you may want to use a simple if-else construct to determine which radio button was selected.

✦ If you are offering many options, you can use a loop structure to look at the checked property of each radio button.

With only a couple of radio buttons in a group, you can examine the one radio-type item in the array (starting with 0) and see if it was checked. In the following code, if one radio button is selected, the variable (theChoice) is set to one value—otherwise, it is set to the other value:

```
if (document.forms[0].comm[0].checked == "1")
    theChoice = "left";
else
    theChoice = "right";
```

When you have many radio buttons, or you don't know how many radio buttons you will have, use a counter loop such as this next example from the Enhanced LineBreak object (available on the CD-ROM):

```
for (var i = 0; i < document.theForm.lbreak.length; i++) {
    if (document.theForm.lbreak[i].checked) {
        break
    }
}
```

In this example, `lbreak` is the name of the group of radio buttons on the parameter form, and the `length` property tells you how many radio buttons are in the group. When the loop finds the selected radio button in the array, the loop is broken and the program proceeds to the next group of statements.

Unfortunately, once you know which radio button is checked, there's no easy way to get its value. The Dreamweaver DOM doesn't support the value property for the radio input type. As a result, you have to assign the value to a variable based on which radio button was selected. You can complete this task in a simple series of if-else statements:

```
if (i == 0){
val = ""
    } else {
    if (i == 1) {
    val = "left"
        } else {
        if (i == 2) {
        val = "right"
            } else {
            val = "all"
            }
        }
    }
```

Alternatively, you can put all the values in an array and assign them in a statement like the following:

```
return "<br clear=" + newValue[i].name + ">"
```

List boxes and drop-down menus

List boxes and drop-down menus are perfect for offering a variety of options in a compact format. Drop-down menus enable the user to choose an option from a scrolling list; list boxes offer multiple choices from a similar list. Both use the

`<select>` tag to set up their available options. When you include a list box or drop-down menu from Dreamweaver, you enter the options by selecting the List Value button and entering the item labels and their associated values in the dialog box. The code for the Direction list box — taken from Matthew David's Marquee object, which is shown in Figure 16-8 and is available on the CD-ROM — is written as follows:

```
<select name="direction">
    <option value="LEFT" selected>LEFT</option>
    <option value="RIGHT">RIGHT</option>
    <option value="UP">UP</option>
    <option value="DOWN">DOWN</option>
</select>
```

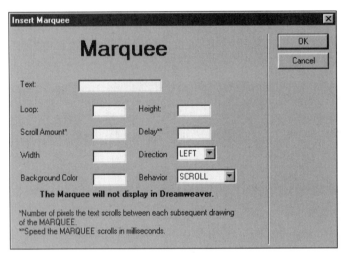

Figure 16-8: The Marquee custom object is designed to take advantage of an Internet Explorer special function: the capability to make a scrolling text display.

Each list box or drop-down menu must have a unique name — in the preceding code, that name is "direction," given in the `<select>` tag. To discover which option the user selected when working with a drop-down menu, you need to examine the selected Index property of the named `<select>` object. Each `<option>` in a `<select>` tag is placed in an array in the order listed in the displayed menu. Remember, arrays always start with a 0 in JavaScript.

The following code looks at each member of the array; if that option is the one in which the `selectedIndex` property is true, then the proper value is assigned to a variable:

```
if(document.forms[0].direction.selectedIndex == 0) {
  direct_choice = 'LEFT'
    } else {
    if(document.forms[0].direction.selectedIndex == 1) {
  direct_choice = 'RIGHT'
  } else {
      if(document.forms[0].direction.selectedIndex == 2) {
      direct_choice = 'UP'
  } else {
      if(document.forms[0].direction.selectedIndex == 3) {
      direct_choice = 'DOWN'
  }
 }
}
}
```

The process is slightly different when you allow multiple options in a list box. In this situation, you should set up a loop to examine the `options[n].selected` property. All the options in a `<select>` tag set have additional properties that can be read by Dreamweaver's DOM, as follows:

Select Options	Description
`options[n].defaultSelected`	Returns True for the option (or options, when multiple selections are enabled) for every `<option>` tag with a `selected` attribute
`options[n].index`	Returns the option's position in the array
`options[n].selected`	Returns True if the option is chosen by the user
`options[n].text`	Returns the text of the item as it appears in the list
`options[n].value`	Returns the value of the item assigned in the `<option>` statement

The following method cycles through all of the <options> to find which one(s) were selected:

```
for (var i = 0; i < document.theForm.optList.length; i++) {
  if (document.theForm.optList.options[i].selected) {
      result += "n\ " + document.theForm.optList.options[i].
      value
      }
  }
return result
}
```

Adding images to your objects

Custom objects don't have to be just text, of course. You can include images in your object, just as you would in a regular Web page — with one catch: Dreamweaver has to be able to find your image files. If you are not distributing your custom object, you can use images from any folder on your system. On the other hand, if your objects are going out to other users, you have to either include the image files with the object or use existing graphics stored in known locations.

What existing graphics are on every Dreamweaver system in specific locations? The GIF files for each object, of course. The button for the custom Character Entities object (previously shown in Figure 16-7) is used in the dialog box for the object itself. Because the two files always have to be in the same folder, you can include the image file on the same level. The size of the GIF files is fairly small (18 pixels by 18 pixels), so you can simply double the size of the image and let Dreamweaver rescale it.

Of course, you can create your own custom graphics for your objects and include those files with the associated HTML and GIF button files. You can even spice up your Dreamweaver standard objects, as shown in Figure 16-9.

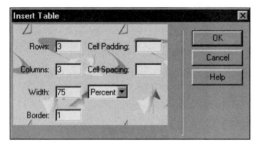

Figure 16-9: You can include graphics in custom objects; in this Insert Table dialog box, the standard Dreamweaver object is altered.

Tip

You can count on two other useful graphical objects: the "plus" and "minus" buttons used in the Dreamweaver dialog boxes for behaviors and parameters. The GIF files for these buttons (`btnAdd.gif` and `btnDel.gif`) are found in the Configuration\Behaviors\Actions folder.

Using layers and Flash movies in objects

The capability to use layers in Dreamweaver objects and behaviors was introduced in Dreamweaver 1.2. With the expansive possibilities of layers, you can build a Wizard-type object that leads users through a series of complex steps, with instructions on every screen. You can also use layers to describe the effect of the user's choices.

Dreamweaver 2 has cleaned up much of the known problems found in the earlier implementation. For an excellent example of the use of layers to create a Dreamweaver extension, take a look at the Drag Layer behavior, discussed in Chapter 17. This behavior uses five different layers to reveal new options as the user makes certain choices; there's even an error level to inform the user of a precondition to using the object.

Note

Layers allow you to pack in a lot of information — and amass a great deal of input — in a single parameter form. One of the best examples of a multilayered object is Dreamweaver Attain's Knowledge object. Dreamweaver Attain is a version of the program customized for Web learning and the Knowledge object is the primary interface. Amazingly enough, all the key functionality of the program is contained in the one object.

Another innovation in Dreamweaver objects now available is the ability to use Flash movies — or any plug-in on the system — within the parameter form. All that's required is that the user have the same plug-in available on his or her system.

New Feature

With Flash's scalable vector graphics, animation capabilities, and interactivity, user interfaces have the potential to take a tremendous leap forward. Instead of a Help message, you could build in a training video that demonstrates particularly difficult concepts.

Incorporating a Flash file in your object's parameter form is no different from using it in your Web page. Just choose Insert ⇨ Flash, or select the Insert Flash button from the Objects Palette. Dreamweaver 2 automatically reads the correct size from the Flash file. Make sure any other parameters you desire are set and you've just created an advanced user interface! To get an idea of what's possible, take a look at Figure 16-10, which shows a new Insert Flash 3 object that uses Flash as the interface, playing in Dreamweaver.

On the CD-ROM

If the Insert Flash 3 object shown in Figure 16-10 intrigues you, feel free to check it out personally. You'll find it on the CD-ROM under the Spooky and the Bandit folder.

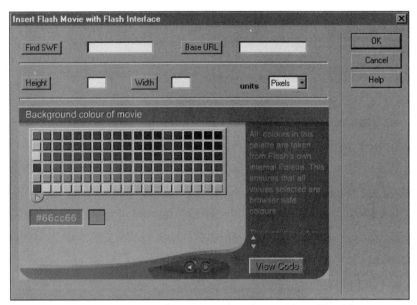

Figure 16-10: Spice up your object's user interface with a , like this
Insert Flash 3 object from the Web designer team of Spooky and the Bandit.

Summary

In one sense, objects are analogous to the macros in a word-processing program
that allow repetitive work to be greatly simplified. Objects can be so much more
than just duplication tools, however — they can extend the reach of Dreamweaver's
power and instantly incorporate new standards and technology. The standard
Dreamweaver objects can be used effortlessly. Just like all objects, they are simply
HTML files, and thus provide excellent examples for creating custom objects.

✦ Objects can be inserted from either the Objects Palette or the Insert menu.✦
Both the Objects Palette and the Insert menu can be easily modified by
adjusting the InsertMenu.htm file.

✦ Simple objects can be created by inserting the HTML code necessary to make
the object into a file, and then saving the file in one of the object's subfolders.

✦ More complex objects can take advantage of Dreamweaver's built-in
JavaScript interpreter, its Document Object Model, special JavaScript
functions, and enhanced Application Programming Interface (API).
Dreamweaver even allows layers to be used in the construction of
custom objects.

In the next chapter, you learn how to use Dreamweaver behaviors.

✦   ✦   ✦

Using Behaviors

Behaviors are truly the power tools of Dreamweaver. With Dreamweaver behaviors, any Web designer can make layers appear and disappear, execute any number of rollovers, or control a Shockwave movie—all without even knowing even a snippet of JavaScript. In the hands of an accomplished JavaScript programmer, Dreamweaver behaviors can be customized or created from scratch to automate the most difficult Web effect.

Creating behaviors is one of the more challenging Dreamweaver features to master. Implementing these gems, however, is a piece of cake. This chapter examines the concepts behind and the reality of using behaviors—detailing the use of all the behaviors included with Dreamweaver and from other notable third-party sources. Also, you'll find tips on managing your ever-increasing library of behaviors.

Here's a guarantee for you: Once you get the hang of using Dreamweaver behaviors, your Web pages will never be the same.

Understanding Behaviors, Events, and Actions

A *behavior*, in Macromedia parlance, is the combination of an event and an action. In the electronic age, one pushes a button (the event) and something (the action) occurs—like changing the channel on the TV. In Dreamweaver, events can be anything as interactive as a user's click on a link, or something as automatic as the loading of a Web page. Behaviors are said to be *attached* to a specific element on your page, whether it's a text link, an image, or even the <body> tag.

New Feature   Dreamweaver 2 has simplified the process of working with behaviors by including default events in every possible object on the Web page. Now, instead of having to think about both *how* you want to do something and *what* you want to do, you only have to focus on the *what*—the action. Users of previous versions of Dreamweaver might find the change a bit disconcerting, but it's really a much more natural way to work with behaviors.

To help you understand conceptually how behaviors are structured, let's examine the four essential steps for adding a behavior to your Web page:

Step 1: Pick a tag. All behaviors are connected to a specific HTML element. You can attach a behavior to everything from the `<body>` to the `<textarea>` of a form. If a certain behavior is unavailable, it's because the necessary element isn't present on the page.

Step 2: Choose your target browser. Different browsers — and the various browser versions — support different events. Dreamweaver lets you choose either a specific browser, such as Internet Explorer 4, or a browser range, such as 3.0 and 4.0 browsers.

Step 3: Select an action. Dreamweaver makes active only those actions available to your specific page. You can't, for instance, choose the Show-Hide Layer action until you insert one or more layers. Behaviors guide you to the workable options.

Step 4: Enter the parameters. Behaviors get their power from their flexibility. Each action comes with a specific parameter form (which represents the dialog box that the user sees) designed to customize the JavaScript code output. Depending on the action, you can choose source files, set attributes, and enable features. The parameter form can even dynamically update to reflect your current Web page.

Dreamweaver 2 comes with 19 cross-browser-compatible actions, and third-party developers have made many additional actions available, with even more in the works. Behaviors greatly extend the range of possibilities for the modern Web designer — without learning to program JavaScript. All you need to know about attaching behaviors is presented in the following section.

Attaching a Behavior

When you see the code generated by Dreamweaver, you understand why setting up a behavior is also referred to as attaching a behavior. As previously noted, Dreamweaver needs a specific HTML tag in order to assign the behavior (Step 1). The link tag `<a>` is often used because, in JavaScript, links can respond to several different events, including `onClick`. Here's an example:

```
<a href="#" onClick="MM_popupMsg('Thanks for coming!')">Exit
Here</a>
```

You're not restricted to one event per tag or even one action per event. Multiple events can be attached to a tag to handle various user actions. For example, you may have an image that does all of the following things:

✦ Highlights when the user's pointer moves over the image

✦ Reveals a hidden layer in another area of the page when the user clicks the mouse button over on the image

✦ Makes a sound when the user releases the mouse button over the image

✦ Starts a Flash movie when the user's pointer moves away from the image

Likewise, a single event can trigger several actions. Updating multiple frames though a single link used to be difficult — but no more. Dreamweaver makes it easy by enabling you to attach several Go to URL actions to the same event, onMouseClick. In addition, you are not restricted to attaching multiple instances of the same action to a single event. For example, in a site that uses a lot of multimedia, you could tie all of the following actions to a single onClick event:

✦ Begin playing an audio file (with the Control Sound action).

✦ Move a layer across the screen (with the Play Timeline action).

✦ Display a second graphic in place of the first (with the Swap Image action).

✦ Show the copyright information for the audio piece in the status bar (with the Display Status Message action).

You can even determine the order in which the actions connected to a single event are executed.

With Dreamweaver behaviors, hours of complex JavaScript coding is reduced to a handful of mouse clicks and a minimum of data entry. All behavior assigning and modification are handled through the Behavior Inspector.

Using the Behavior Inspector

The Behavior Inspector is a two-paned window (see Figure 17-1) that neatly sums up the behaviors concept in general. A list of assigned events is located on the left side of the window. The selected tag is displayed at the top of the events pane, with a drop-down list of browsers, which includes the following:

✦ 3.0 and 4.0 Browsers

✦ 4.0 Browsers

✦ IE 3.0

✦ IE 4.0

✦ Netscape 3.0

✦ Netscape 4.0

When you select one of these options, the default event for the selected tag is noted by Dreamweaver. After you've selected an action and completed the dialog box, the default event appears in the Event pane alongside the action in the Actions pane. You can choose a different event by selecting the down arrow next to the default event. Select any event in the drop-down list. Double-click the action to open the associated Parameter window, where you can modify the action's attributes.

Selected tag   Browser drop-down list

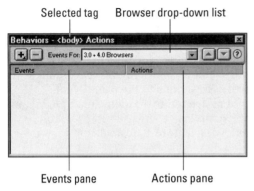

Events pane   Actions pane

Figure 17-1: You can handle everything about a behavior through the Behavior Inspector.

As usual in Dreamweaver, you have your choice of methods for opening the Behavior Inspector:

✦ Choose Window ➪ Behaviors.

✦ Select the Show Behaviors button from either Launcher.

✦ Use the keyboard shortcut, F8 (an on/off toggle).

Tip   The Behavior Inspector can be closed by toggling it off with F8, or hidden with the other floating windows by pressing F4.

After you have attached a behavior to a tag and closed the associated action's parameter form, Dreamweaver writes the necessary HTML and JavaScript code into your document. Because it involves functions that can be called from anywhere in the document, the JavaScript code is placed in the <head> section of the page, and the code that links the selected tag to the functions is written in the <body> section. A few actions, including Control Sound, place additional HTML code at the bottom of the <body>, but most of the code — there can be a lot of code to handle all the cross-browser contingencies — is placed in the <head> HTML section.

Adding a behavior

Now let's look more closely at the procedure for adding (or attaching) a behavior. As noted earlier, you can only assign certain events to particular tags, and those options are further defined by the type of selected browser.

Note   Even in the latest browsers, key events such as onMouseDown, onMouseOver, and onMouseOut only work with anchor tags. To circumvent this limitation, Dreamweaver can enclose an element, such as <img>, with an anchor tag that links to nowhere — src="#". Events that use the anchor tag in this fashion are seen in parentheses in the pop-up menu of events.

To add a behavior to your Web page, follow these steps:

1. Select an object in the Document Window.

Tip

If you want to assign a behavior to the entire page, select the `<body>` tag from the Tag Selector.

2. Open the Behavior Inspector by choosing Window ➪ Behaviors or selecting the Show Behaviors button from either Launcher. You can see the selected tag at the top of the Events pane.

3. If necessary, select a different browser target from the drop-down list in the Events pane.

4. Select the + (Add Action) button to reveal the available options, as shown in Figure 17-2. Choose one from the pop-up menu.

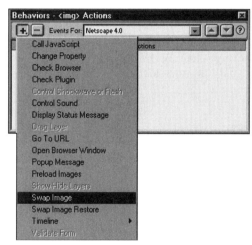

Figure 17-2: The Add Action pop-up menu dynamically changes according to what's on the current page and which tag is selected.

5. Enter the necessary parameters in the Actions dialog box.

6. Click OK when you're finished.

The standard events

Every time Dreamweaver 2 attaches a behavior to a tag, it also inserts an event for you. The default event that is chosen is based on two selections: the browser type and the tag selected. The different browsers in use have widely different capabilities, notably when it comes to understanding the various event handlers and associated tags.

For every browser and browser combination shown in the Browser drop-down list, Dreamweaver has a corresponding file in the Configuration\Behaviors\Events folder. Each of the tags listed in each file, such as I.E. 4.0.htm, has at least one event associated with it. The entries look like this:

```
<INPUT TYPE="Text" onBlur="*" onChange="" onFocus=""
onSelect="">
```

The default event for each tag is marked with an asterisk; in the example, onBlur is the default event. After you've selected an action and completed the dialog box, the default event appears in the Events pane alongside the action in the Actions pane.

Tip   If you find yourself changing a particular default event over and over again to some other event, you might want to modify the Event file to pick your alternative as the default. To do this, open the relevant browser file found in the Configuration\Behaviors\Events folder in a regular text editor (not Dreamweaver) and move the asterisk to a different event for that particular tag. Resave the file and restart Dreamweaver to try out your new default behavior.

Should the default event not be the one you prefer to use, you can easily choose another. Choose a different event by selecting the down arrow next to the displayed default event in the Behavior Inspector and select any event in the drop-down list (see Figure 17-3).

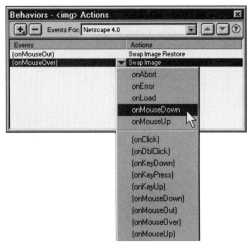

Figure 17-3: In Dreamweaver 2, you can change the default event by selecting the Events arrow button.

Dreamweaver ships with a set list of events recognized by particular browsers. The Dreamweaver\Configuration\Behaviors\Events folder contains HTML files corresponding to the six browsers offered in the Events pane's drop-down list. You can open these files in Dreamweaver, but Macromedia asks that you not edit them—with one exception. Each file contains the list of tags that have supported *event handlers* (the JavaScript term for events) in that browser.

The older the browser, the fewer event handlers are included—unfortunately, this also means that if you want to reach the broadest Internet audience, your event options are limited. In the broadest category, 3.0 and 4.0 browsers, only 13 different tags can receive any sort of event handler. This is one of the reasons why, for example, Internet Explorer 3 can't handle rollovers: the browser doesn't understand what an onMouseOut event is and so the image can't revert to its original state.

If you do open and examine an event file in Dreamweaver, notice a group of yellow tags and a few form objects (see Figure 17-4). The yellow tags identify what Dreamweaver sees as invalid HTML. Those form objects—the buttons, check-box, radio button, and text—render normally but aren't active.

Caution　It's far better to use a standard text editor such as HomeSite or BBEdit to open and modify an event file than to use Dreamweaver. By default, Dreamweaver attempts to correct the invalid HTML it finds in the file and if you save the file with these unwanted corrections in place, your file will be corrupted and you'll lose access to certain events.

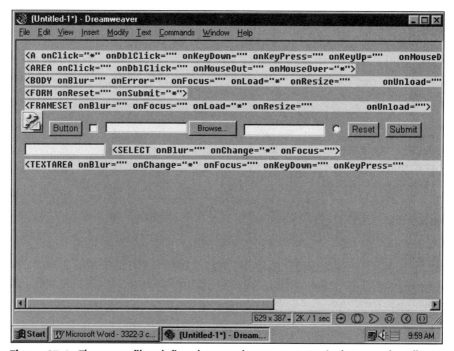

Figure 17-4: The event files define the tags that support particular event handlers in a selected browser.

In this case, viewing the HTML is far more instructive than the Document Window, as you can see by looking at Listing 17-1. This example gives the event handler definitions for the 3.0 and 4.0 Browsers category.

Listing 17-1: **The Events File for 3.0 and 4.0 Browsers**

```
<A onMouseOver="*">
<AREA onClick="" onMouseOut="" onMouseOver="*">
<BODY onLoad="*" onUnload="">
<FORM onReset="" onSubmit="*">
<FRAMESET onLoad="*" onUnload="">
<INPUT TYPE="Button" onClick="*">
<INPUT TYPE="Checkbox" onClick="*">
<INPUT TYPE="Radio" onClick="*">
<INPUT TYPE="Reset" onClick="*">
<INPUT TYPE="Submit" onClick="*">
<INPUT TYPE="Text" onBlur="*" onChange="" onFocus=""
onSelect="">
<SELECT onBlur="" onChange="*" onFocus="">
<TEXTAREA onBlur="" onChange="*" onFocus="" onSelect="">
```

By contrast, the events file for Internet Explorer 4.0 shows support for every tag under the HTML sun — 79 in all — with almost every tag able to handle any type of event.

Tip   Although any HTML tag could potentially be used to attach a behavior, the most commonly used by far are the `<body>` tag (for entire-page events such as `onLoad`), the `<img>` tag when used as a button, and the link tag, `<a>`.

To locate the default events for any tag as used by a particular browser, consult Table 17-1. The table also shows, at a glance, which browsers support which tags to receive events.

Table 17-1
Default Events by Browser

Tag	3.0 + 4.0 Browsers	4.0 Browsers	IE 3.0	IE 4.0	Netscape 3.0	Netscape 4.0
`<a>`	onMouseOver	onClick	onMouseOver	onClick	onClick	onClick
`<address>`				onClick		
`<applet>`				onLoad		
`<area>`	onMouseOver	onMouseOver		onClick	onMouseOver	onMouseOver
`<b>`				onMouseOver		
`<big>`				onMouseOver		
`<blink>`				onMouseOver		
`<body>`	onLoad	onLoad	onLoad	onLoad	onLoad	onLoad
`<button>`				onClick		
`<caption>`				onMouseOver		
`<center>`				onMouseOver		
`<cite>`				onMouseOver		
`<code>`				onMouseOver		
`<col>`				onMouseOver		
`<dd>`				onMouseOver		
`<dfn>`				onMouseOver		
`<dir>`				onMouseOver		
`<div>`				onClick		
`<dl>`				onMouseOver		
`<dt>`				onMouseOver		
`<em>`				onMouseOver		
`<embed>`				onLoad		

Continued

Table 17-1 (continued)

Tag	3.0 + 4.0 Browsers	4.0 Browsers	IE 3.0	IE 4.0	Netscape 3.0	Netscape 4.0
`<fieldset>`				onClick		
`<font>`				onMouseOver		
`<form>`	onSubmit	onSubmit	onSubmit	onSubmit	onSubmit	onSubmit
`<frame>`				onLoad		
`<frameset>`	onLoad	onLoad	onLoad	onLoad	onLoad	onLoad
`<iframe>`				onFocus		
`<ilayer>`					onLoad	onLoad
`<h1>-<h6>`				onMouseOver		
`<hr>`				onMouseOver		
`<I>`				onMouseOver		
`<img>`		onMouseDown		onClick	(None selected)	onMouseDown
`<input type=button | checkbox | image | radio | reset | submit>`	onClick	onClick	onClick	onClick	onClick	onClick
`<input type=file | password>`		onChange		onChange	onChange	onChange
`<input type=text>`	onBlur	onBlur	onBlur	onBlur	onBlur	onBlur
`<ins>`				onMouseOver		
`<kbd>`				onClick		
`<label>`				onClick		
`<layer>`						onMouseOver
`<li>`				onMouseOver		
`<listing>`				onMouseOver		

Tag	3.0 + 4.0 Browsers	4.0 Browsers	IE 3.0	IE 4.0	Netscape 3.0	Netscape 4.0
`<map>`				onClick		
`<marquee>`				onMouseOver		
`<menu>`				onMouseOver		
`<nobr>`				onMouseOver		
`<object>`				onLoad		
`<ol>`				onMouseOver		
`<p>`				onMouseOver		
`<plaintext>`				onMouseOver		
`<pre>`				onMouseOver		
`<q>`				onMouseOver		
`<s>`				onMouseOver		
`<samp>`				onMouseOver		
`<select>`	onChange	onChange	onChange	onChange	onChange	onChange
`<small>`				onMouseOver		
`<span>`				onMouseOver		
`<strike>`				onMouseOver		
`<strong>`				onMouseOver		
`<sub>`				onMouseOver		
`<sup>`				onMouseOver		
`<table>`				onMouseOver		
`<tbody>`				onMouseOver		
`<td>`				onMouseOver		
`<textarea>`	onChange	onChange	onChange	onChange	onChange	onChange
`<tfoot>`				onMouseOver		

Continued

Table 17-1 *(continued)*

Tag	3.0 + 4.0 Browsers	4.0 Browsers	IE 3.0	IE 4.0	Netscape 3.0	Netscape 4.0
`<th>`				onMouseOver		
`<thead>`				onMouseOver		
`<tr>`				onMouseOver		
`<tt>`				onMouseOver		
`<u>`				onMouseOver		
`<ul>`				onMouseOver		
`<var>`				onMouseOver		
`<xmp>`				onMouseOver		

Standard actions

As of this writing, 19 standard actions ship with Dreamweaver 2. Each action operates independently and differently from the others, although many share common functions. Each action is associated with a different dialog box or parameter form to enable easy attribute entry.

The following sections describe each of the standard actions: what the action does, what requirements must be met for it to be activated, what options are available, and most important of all, how to use it. Each action is written to work with all 4.0 browsers; however, some actions do not work as designed in the older browsers. The charts included with every action show the action's compatibility with older browsers. (The information in these charts was adapted from the Dreamweaver Help pages and is used with permission.)

Note   The following descriptions assume that you understand the basics of assigning behaviors and that you know how to open the Behavior Inspector.

Call JavaScript

Dreamweaver 2 only includes one completely new behavior that was not in previous versions of the program — but it's an extremely powerful one. With Call JavaScript, you can execute any JavaScript function — standard or custom — with a single mouse click or other event. As your JavaScript savvy grows, you'll find yourself using this behavior again and again.

New Feature   Call JavaScript is very straightforward to use; simply type in the JavaScript code or the name of the function you want to trigger into the dialog box. If, for example, you wanted to get some input from a visitor, you could use JavaScript's built-in `prompt()` method, like this:

```
result=prompt("Whom shall I say is calling?","")
```

When this code is triggered, a small dialog box appears with your query (here, "Whom shall I say is calling?") and a space for an input string. The second argument in the `prompt()` method enables you to include a default answer — to leave it blank, just use two quotes.

Note   You can use either single or double quotes in your Call JavaScript behavior; Dreamweaver automatically adjusts for whichever you choose. However, I find it easier to use single quotes because Dreamweaver translates double quotes into character entities; that is, " becomes `&quot;`.

Naturally, you could use Call JavaScript to handle much more complex chores as well. To call a specific custom function that is already in the `<head>` section of your page, just enter its name — along with any necessary arguments — in the Call JavaScript dialog box, shown in Figure 17-5.

Figure 17-5: Trigger any JavaScript function by attaching a Call JavaScript behavior to an image or text.

To use the Call JavaScript behavior, follow these steps:

1. Select the object to trigger the action.
2. From the Behavior Inspector, select the Add Action button and choose Call JavaScript.
3. In the Call JavaScript dialog box, enter your code in the text box.
4. Click OK when you're done.

Note   In the following charts that detail action behaviors for both newer and older browsers, the phrase "Fails without error" means that the action won't work in the older browser, but neither does it generate an error message for the user to see. Where the table indicates "error," it means the user receives a JavaScript alert message.

Here's the browser compatibility chart for the Call JavaScript behavior:

JavaScript	Netscape 2.x	Netscape 3.x	Internet Explorer 3.0	Internet Call Explorer 3.01
Macintosh	OK	OK	Fails without error	OK
Windows	OK	OK	OK	OK

Change Property

The Change Property action enables you to dynamically alter a property of one of the following tags:

```
<layer>      <div>      <form>      <textarea>
<span>       <img>      <select>
```

You can also alter the following `<input>` types:

```
radio        checkbox      text        password
```

Exactly which properties can be altered depends on the tag as well as on the browser being targeted. For example, the `<div>` tag and Internet Explorer 4.0 combination enables you to change virtually every style sheet option on the fly.

The Change Property dialog box (see Figure 17-6) offers a list of the selected tags in the current page.

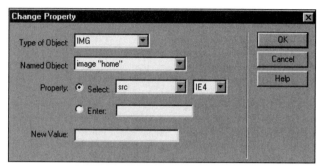

Figure 17-6: The Change Property action enables you to alter attributes of certain tags dynamically.

 Caution   It's important that you name the objects you want to alter so that Dreamweaver can properly identify them. Remember to use unique names that begin with a letter and contain no spaces or special characters.

This behavior is especially useful for changing text onscreen in a form's textarea or text field. Be sure to name the form if you wish to use Change Property in this manner.

To use the Change Property action, follow these steps:

1. Select the object to trigger the action.

2. From the Behavior Inspector, select the Add Action button and choose Change Property.

3. In the Change Property dialog box, choose an object type, such as DIV or TEXTAREA, from the Type of Object drop-down list.

4. In the dynamic Named Object drop-down list, choose the object on your page you wish to affect.

5. Click the Select radio button. Select the target browser in the small list box on the far right, and then choose the property to change. If you don't find the property in the drop-down list box, you can type it yourself into the Enter text box.

 Note   Many properties in the various browsers are read-only and cannot be dynamically altered.

6. In the New Value text box, type the property's new value to be inserted when the event is fired.

7. Click OK when you're done.

Here's the browser compatibility chart for the Change Property behavior:

Change Property	Netscape 2.x	Netscape 3.x	Internet Explorer 3.0	Internet Explorer 3.01
Macintosh	OK; fails without error for objects in layers	OK; fails without error for objects in layers	Fails without error	OK
Windows	OK; fails without error for objects in layers	OK; fails without error for objects in layers	OK	OK

Check Browser

Increasingly, Web sites are splitting into multilevel versions of themselves to gracefully handle the variety of browsers in operation. The Check Browser action acts as a type of browser "router" capable of sending browsers to appropriate URLs, or just letting them stay on the current page. Generally, the Check Browser action is assigned to the <body> tag and uses the onLoad event. If used in this fashion, it's a good idea to keep the basic page accessible to all browsers, even those with JavaScript disabled.

The Check Browser parameter form (see Figure 17-7) is quite flexible and enables you to specify decimal version numbers for the two main browsers. For instance, you may want to let all users of Navigator 4.04 or later stay on the current page, and send everyone else to an alternative URL. The URLs can be either relative, like alt/index.html, or absolute, like http://www.idest.com/alt/index.html.

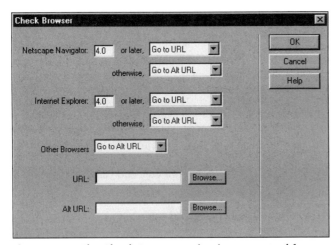

Figure 17-7: The Check Browser action is a great tool for segregating old and new browsers.

To use the Check Browser action, follow these steps:

1. Select the object to trigger the action.

2. From the Behavior Inspector, select the Add Action button and choose Check Browser.

3. Specify the Netscape Navigator and Internet Explorer versions, and whether you want the browser to stay on the current page, go to another URL, or proceed to a third alternative URL.

Note With both major browsers, you can specify the URL that the lower version numbers should visit.

4. Set the same options for all other browsers, such as Opera and Linux.

5. Enter the URL and alternate URL options in their respective text boxes, or select the Browse (Choose) button to locate the files.

Cross-Reference The Check Browser action works well with another Dreamweaver feature: Convert to 3.0 Compatible. Learn all about this new capability in Chapter 33, "Publishing Via Site FTP."

Here's the browser compatibility chart for the Check Browser behavior:

Check Browser	Netscape 2.x	Netscape 3.x	Internet Explorer 3.0	Internet Explorer 3.01
Macintosh	OK; fails without error for objects in layers	OK; fails without error for objects in layers	Fails without error	OK
Windows	OK; fails without error for objects in layers	OK; fails without error for objects in layers	OK	OK

Check Plugin

If certain pages on your Web site require the use of one or more plug-ins, you can use the Check Plugin action to see if a visitor has the necessary plug-in installed. Once this has been examined, Check Plugin can route users with the appropriate plug-in to one URL, and users without it to another URL. You can only look for one plug-in at a time, but you can use multiple instances of the Check Plugin action, if needed.

By default, the parameter form for Check Plugin (see Figure 17-8) offers five plug-ins: Shockwave Flash, Shockwave for Director, LiveAudio, Netscape Media Player, and QuickTime Plug-in. You can check for any other plug-in by entering its name in the Enter text box; use the name that appears when choosing Help ➪ About Plugins in the Navigator menus.

Tip   If you use a particular plug-in regularly, you may want to also modify the Check Plugin.js file found in your Actions folder. Add your new plug-in name to the PLUGIN_NAMES variable in the initGlobal function.

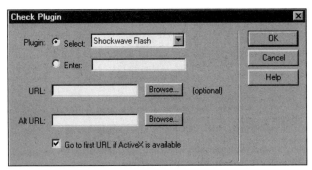

Figure 17-8: Running a media-intensive site? Use the Check Plugin action to divert visitors without plug-ins to alternative pages.

Although Check Plugin cannot check for specific ActiveX controls, this action can route the Internet Explorer user to the same page as users who have plug-ins. The best way to handle both browsers is to use both ActiveX controls and plug-ins, through the `<object>` and `<embed>` methods explained in Chapter 15, "Accessing External Programs."

On the CD-ROM   Another method for determining whether a plug-in or other player is available is to use the Check MIME action included on the CD-ROM. This action works in the same way as the Check Plugin action, except you enter the MIME type.

To use the Check Plugin action, follow these steps:

1. Select the object to trigger the action.

2. From the Behavior Inspector, select the Add Action button and choose Check Browser.

3. Select a plug-in from the drop-down list. You can also type another plug-in name in the Enter text box.

4. If you want to send users who are confirmed to have the plug-in to a different page, enter that URL (absolute or relative) in the URL text box, or use the Browse (Choose) button to locate the file. If you want them to stay on the current page, leave the text box empty.

5. In the Alt URL text box, enter the URL for users who do not have the required plug-in.

6. If you do not want Internet Explorer users to go to the same location chosen for users with the plug-in, deselect the "Go to first URL if ActiveX is available" check-box. In this case, users are sent to the Alt URL address.

Here's the browser compatibility chart for the Check Plugin behavior:

Check Plugin	Netscape 2.x	Netscape 3.x	Internet Explorer 3.0	Internet Explorer 3.01
Macintosh	OK	OK	Fails without error	OK
Windows	OK	OK	OK	OK

Control Shockwave or Flash

The Control Shockwave or Flash action enables you to command your Shockwave and Flash movies through external controls. With Control Shockwave or Flash, you can build your own interface for your Shockwave or Flash material. This action can be used in conjunction with the `autostart=true` attribute (entered through the Property Inspector's Parameter dialog box for the Shockwave or Flash file), to enable a replaying of the movie.

You must have a Shockwave or Flash movie inserted in your Web page in order for the Control Shockwave or Flash action to be available. The parameter form for this action (see Figure 17-9) lists all the Shockwave or Flash movies by name that are found in either an `<embed>` or `<object>` tag. You can set the action to control the movie in one of four ways: Start, Stop, Rewind, or Go to Frame. You can only choose one option each time you attach an action to an event. If you choose the last option, you need to specify the frame number in the text box. Note that specifying a Go to Frame number does not start the movie there; you will need to attach a second Control Shockwave or Flash action to the same event to play the file.

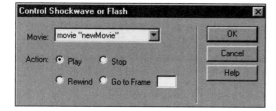

Figure 17-9: Build your own interface, and then control a Shockwave and Flash movie externally with the Control Shockwave or Flash action.

> **Tip**
> Be sure to name your Shockwave or Flash movie. Otherwise, the Control Shockwave or Flash action lists both `unnamed <embed>` and `unnamed <object>` for each file, and you cannot write to both tags as you can with a named movie.

To use the Control Shockwave or Flash action, follow these steps:

1. Select the object to trigger the action.

2. From the Behavior Inspector, select the Add Action button and choose Control Shockwave or Flash.

3. In the Control Shockwave or Flash dialog box, select a movie from the Named Shockwave Object drop-down list.

4. Select a control by choosing its radio button:

    • **Play** begins playing the movie at the current frame location.

    • **Stop** stops playing the movie.

    • **Rewind** returns the movie to its first frame.

    • **Go to Frame** displays a specific frame in the movie. Note: for this option, you must enter a frame number in the text box.

5. Select OK when you're done.

Here's the browser compatibility chart for the Control Shockwave or Flash behavior:

Control Shockwave or Flash	Netscape 2.x	Netscape 3.x	Internet Explorer 3.0	Internet Explorer 3.01
Macintosh	Fails without error	OK	Fails without error	Fails without error
Windows	Fails without error	OK	OK	Fails without error

Control Sound

The Control Sound action is used to add external controls to an audio file that normally uses the Netscape LiveAudio plug-in or the Windows Media Player. Supported audio file types include .wav, .mid, .au, and .aiff files — generally to add background music with a hidden sound file. The Control Sound action inserts an `<embed>` tag with the following attributes set:

✦ `loop=false`

✦ `autostart=false`

✦ `mastersound`

✦ `hidden=true`

✦ `width=0`

✦ `height=0`

Instead of automatically detecting which sound files have been inserted in the current Web page, Control Sound needs the sound file to be inserted though the action's parameter form (see Figure 17-10). Once the file has been inserted through the Control Sound action, the file appears in the Stop Sound drop-down list when you next invoke this action.

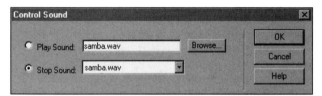

Figure 17-10: Give your Web page background music and control it with the Control Sound action.

New Feature Dreamweaver 2 can detect if a visitor's browser has the Windows Media Player installed and, if so, issues the appropriate commands.

To use the Control Sound action, follow these steps:

1. Select the object to trigger the action.

2. From the Behavior Inspector, select the Add Action button and choose Control Sound.

3. To play a sound, select the Play Sound radio button, and enter the path to the audio file in the Play Sound text box, or select the Browse (Choose) button to locate the file.

4. To stop a sound, select the Stop Sound radio button and select the audio file to control from the Stop Sound drop-down list.

Note Only audio files that have been previously inserted through the Play Sound option are listed.

5. Select OK when you're done.

Here's the browser compatibility chart for the Control Sound behavior:

Control Sound	Netscape 2.x	Netscape 3.x	Internet Explorer 3.0	Internet Explorer 3.01
Macintosh	Error	OK	Fails without error	OK
Windows	Fails without error	OK	OK	OK

Display Status Message

Use the Display Status Message action to show your choice of text in a browser's status bar, based on a user's action such as moving the pointer over an image. The message stays displayed in the status bar until another message replaces it. System messages, such as URLs, tend to be temporary and only visible when the user's mouse is over a link.

The only limit to the length of the message is the size of the browser's status bar; you should test your message in various browsers to make sure that it is completely visible.

Tip　To display a message only when a user's pointer is over an image, use one Display Status Message action, attached to an `onMouseOver` event, with your associated text. Use another Display Status Message action, attached to an `onMouseOut` event, that has a null string (a couple of spaces) as the text.

All text is entered in the Display Status Message parameter form (see Figure 17-11) in the Message text box.

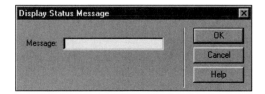

Figure 17-11: Use the Display Status Message action to guide your users with instructions in the browser window's status bar.

To use the Display Status Message action, follow these steps:

1. Select the object to trigger the action.
2. From the Behavior Inspector, select the Add Action button and choose Display Status Message.
3. Enter your text in the Message text box.
4. Click OK when you're done.

Here's the browser compatibility chart for the Display Status Message behavior:

Display Status Message	Netscape 2.x	Netscape 3.x	Internet Explorer 3.0	Internet Explorer 3.01
Macintosh	Error	OK	Fails without error	OK
Windows	Fails without error	OK	OK	OK

Drag Layer

Introduced to Dreamweaver in version 1.2, the Drag Layer action provides some spectacular effects with little effort. Now, in Dreamweaver 2, the behavior has been redesigned for easier use and significantly more power. Drag Layer enables your Web page visitors to move layers — and all that they contain — around the screen with the drag-and-drop technique. With the Drag Layer action, you can easily set up the following capabilities for the user:

✦ Enable layers to be dragged anywhere on the screen.

✦ Restrict the dragging to a particular direction or combination of directions — a horizontal sliding layer can be restricted to left and right movement, for instance.

✦ Limit the drag handle to a portion of the layer such as the upper bar, or enable the whole layer to be used.

✦ Provide an alternative clipping method by enabling only a portion of the layer to be dragged.

✦ Enable changing of the layers' stacking order while dragging or on mouse release.

✦ Set a snap-to target area on your Web page for layers that the user releases within a defined radius.

✦ Program a JavaScript command to be executed when the snap-to target is hit, or every time the layer is released.

Cross-Reference

Layers are one of the more powerful features of Dreamweaver. To get the most out of the layer-oriented behaviors, familiarize yourself with layers by examining Chapter 25, "Working with Layers."

Layers must be inserted in your Web page before the Drag Layer action becomes available for selection from the Add Action pop-up menu. You must attach the action to the <body> — you can, however, attach separate versions of Drag Layer to different layers for different effects.

Drag Layer's parameter form (see Figure 17-12) includes a Get Current Position button that puts the left and top coordinates of a selected layer into the appropriate boxes for the Get Target parameters. If you plan on using targeting, place your layer at the target location before attaching the behavior.

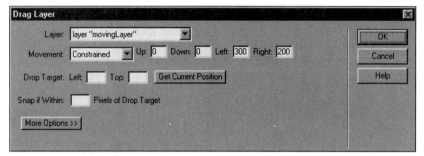

Figure 17-12: With the Drag Layer action, you can set up your layers to be repositioned by the user.

To use the Drag Layer action, follow these steps:

1. Select the <body> tag.

2. From the Behavior Inspector, select the Add Action button and choose Drag Layer.

3. In the Layer drop-down list of the parameter form, select the layer you want to make draggable.

4. To limit the movement of the layer, change the Movement option from Unconstrained to Constrained. Text boxes for Up, Down, Left, and Right appear. Enter pixel values in the text boxes to control the range of motion:

   • To constrain movement vertically, enter positive numbers in the Up and Down text boxes and zeros in the Left and Right text boxes.

   • To constrain movement horizontally, enter positive numbers in the Left and Right text boxes and zeros in the Up and Down text boxes.

   • To enable movement in a rectangular region, enter positive values in all four text boxes.

5. To establish a location for a target for the dragged layer, enter coordinates in the Drop Target: Left and Top text boxes. Select the Get Current Position button to fill these text boxes with the layer's present location.

6. To set a snap-to area around the target coordinates where the layer falls, if released in the target location, enter a pixel value in the Snap if Within text box.

7. For additional options, select the More Options button.

   The additional options appear.

8. If you want to limit the area to be used as a drag handle, select the radio button for Drag Handle: Area Within Layer. Left, Top, Width and Height text boxes appear. In the appropriate text boxes, enter the Left and Top coordinates of the drag handle in pixels, as well as the Width and Height dimensions.

Note   If you want to enable the whole layer to act as a drag handle, make sure the Drag Handle: Entire Layer radio button is selected.

9. To control the positioning of the dragged layer, set the following While Dragging options:

   • To keep the layer in its current depth and not bring it to the front when it is dragged, deselect the check-box for While Dragging: Bring Layer to the Front.

   • To change the stacking order of the layer when it is released, select either Leave on Top or Restore z-order from the drop-down list.

10. To execute a JavaScript command while the layer is being dragged, enter the command or function in the Call JavaScript text box.

11. To execute a JavaScript command when the layer is dropped on the target, enter the code in the When Dropped: Call JavaScript text box. If you want the JavaScript to execute only when the layer is snapped to its target, select the Only if snapped option — this option requires that a value be entered in the Snap if Within text box.

12. Click OK when you're done.

Here's the browser compatibility chart for the Drag Layer behavior:

Drag Layer	*Netscape 2.x*	*Netscape 3.x*	*Internet Explorer 3.0*	*Internet Explorer 3.01*
Macintosh	Fails without error	Fails without error	Fails without error	Fails without error
Windows	Fails without error	Fails without error	Fails without error	Fails without error

Go to URL

Dreamweaver brings the same power of links — with a lot more flexibility — to any event with the Go to URL action. One of the trickier tasks in using frames on a Web page is updating two or more frames simultaneously with a single button click. The Go to URL action handily streamlines this process for the Web designer. Go to URL can also be used as a preload router that sends the user to another Web page once the onLoad event has finished.

The dialog box for Go to URL (see Figure 17-13) displays any existing anchors or frames in the current page or frameset. To load multiple URLs at the same time, open the drop-down list and select the first frame that you want to alter; then enter the desired page or location in the URL text box. Select the second frame from the list and enter the next URL (or Browse/Choose to find it). If you select a frame to which you have previously assigned a URL, that address appears in the URL text box.

Figure 17-13: Update two or more frames at the same time with the Go to URL action.

To use the Go to URL action, follow these steps:

1. Select the object to trigger the action.

2. From the Behavior Inspector, select the Add Action button and choose Go to URL.

3. From the Go to URL dialog box, select the target for your link from the list in the Open In window.

4. Enter the path of the file to open in the URL text box or click the Browse (Choose) button to locate a file.

   An asterisk appears next to the frame name to indicate that a URL has been chosen.

5. To select another target to load a different URL, repeat Steps 3 and 4.

6. Click OK when you're done.

Here's the browser compatibility chart for the Go to URL behavior:

Go to URL	Netscape 2.x	Netscape 3.x	Internet Explorer 3.0	Internet Explorer 3.01
Macintosh	Works in a frame. In main window, fails without error if applied to a link.	OK	Fails without error	OK
Windows	OK	OK	OK	OK

Open Browser Window

Want to display your latest design in a borderless, nonresizable browser window that's exactly the size of your image? With the Open Browser Window action, you can open a new browser window and specify its exact size and attributes. You can even set it up to receive JavaScript events.

You can also open a new browser window with a regular link by specifying `target="_blank"`, but you can't control any of the window's attributes with that method. You do get this control with the parameter form of the Open Browser Window action (see Figure 17-14); here you can set the width and height, and whether or not to display the Navigation Toolbar, Location Toolbar, Status Bar, Menu Bar, Scrollbars, and Resize Handles. You can also name your new window, a necessary step for advanced JavaScript control.

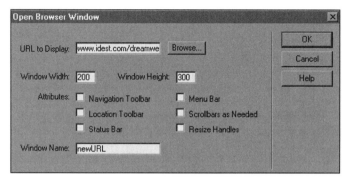

Figure 17-14: Use the Open Browser Window action to program in a pop-up advertisement or remote control.

You have to explicitly select any of the attributes you want to appear in your new window. Your new browser window contains only the attributes you've checked, plus basic window elements such as a title bar and a Close button.

To use the Open Browser Window action, follow these steps:

1. Select the object to trigger the action.

2. From the Behavior Inspector, select the Add Action button and choose Open Browser Window.

3. In the URL to Display text box, enter the address of the Web page you want to display in the new window. You can also select the Browse (Choose) button to locate the file.

4. To specify the window's size and shape, enter the width and height values in the appropriate text boxes.

Note You must enter both a width and height measurement, or the new browser window opens to its default size.

5. Check the appropriate Attributes check-boxes to enable the parameters you want.

6. If you plan on using JavaScript to address or control the window, type a unique name in the Window Name text box. This name cannot contain spaces

or special characters. Dreamweaver alerts you if the name you've entered is unacceptable.

7. Click OK when you're done.

Here's the browser compatibility chart for the Open Browser Window behavior:

Open Browser Window	Netscape 2.x	Netscape 3.x	Internet Explorer 3.0	Internet Explorer 3.01
Macintosh	OK	OK	Fails without error	OK
Windows	OK	OK	OK	OK

Popup Message

You can send a quick message to your users with the Popup Message action. When triggered, this action opens a JavaScript Application Alert with your message. You enter your message in the Message text box on the action's parameter form (see Figure 17-15).

Figure 17-15: Send a message to your users with the Popup Message action.

To use the Popup Message action, follow these steps:

1. Select the object to trigger the action.
2. From the Behavior Inspector, select the Add Action button and choose Popup Message.
3. Enter your text in the Message text box.
4. Click OK when you're done.

Here's the browser compatibility chart for the Popup Message behavior:

Popup Message	Netscape 2.x	Netscape 3.x	Internet Explorer 3.0	Internet Explorer 3.01
Macintosh	Fails without error	OK	Fails without error	OK
Windows	OK	OK	OK	OK

Preload Images

Designs commonly require a particular image or images to be displayed immediately when called by an action or a timeline. Because of the nature of HTML, all graphics are separate files that normally are downloaded when needed. To get the snappy response required for certain designs, graphics need to be *preloaded* or *cached* so that they will be available. The Preload Images action performs this important service. You designate the images you want to cache for later use through the Preload Images parameter form (see Figure 17-16).

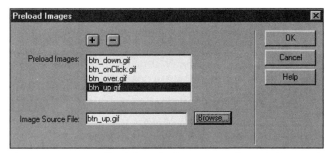

Figure 17-16: Media-rich Web sites respond much faster when images have been cached with the Preload Images action.

Note　　You don't need to use the Preload Images action if you're creating rollovers. Both the Rollover object and the Swap Image action enable you to preload images from their dialog boxes.

To use the Preload Images action, follow these steps:

1. Select the object to trigger the action.

2. From the Behavior Inspector, select the Add Action button and Preload Images.

3. In the action's parameter form, enter the path to the image file in the Image Source File text box, or select the Browse (Choose) button to locate the file.

4. To add another file, click the + (Add) button and repeat Step 2.

Caution　　After you've specified your first file to be preloaded, be sure to press the + (Add) button for each successive file you want to add to the list. Otherwise, the highlighted file is replaced by the next entry.

5. To remove a file from the Preload Images list, select it and click the – (Delete) button.

6. Click OK when you're done.

Here's the browser compatibility chart for the Preload Images behavior:

Preload Message	Netscape 2.x	Netscape 3.x	Internet Explorer 3.0	Internet Explorer 3.01
Macintosh	Fails without error	OK	Fails without error	OK
Windows	Fails without error	OK	Fails without error	OK

Show-Hide Layer

One of the key features of Dynamic HTML layers is their ability to appear and disappear on command. The Show-Hide Layer action gives you easy control over the visibility attribute for all layers in the current Web page. In addition to explicitly showing or hiding layers, this action can also restore layers to the default visibility setting.

Typically, the Show-Hide Layer action reveals one layer while concealing another; however, you are not restricted to hiding or showing just one layer at a time. The action's parameter form (see Figure 17-17) shows you a list of all the layers in the current Web page, from which you can choose as many as you want to show or hide.

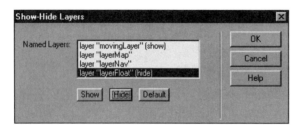

Figure 17-17: The Show-Hide Layers action can make any number of hidden layers visible, hide any number of visible layers, or both.

To use the Show-Hide Layer action, follow these steps:

1. Select the object to trigger the action.

2. From the Behavior Inspector, select the Add Action button and choose Show-Hide Layer.

   When the dialog box opens, the parameter form shows a list of the available layers in the open Web page.

3. To reveal a hidden layer, from the Show-Hide Layer dialog box select the layer from the Named Layers list and click the Show button.

4. To hide a visible layer, select its name from the list and click the Hide button.

5. To restore a layer's default visibility value, select the layer in the list and click the Default button.

Here's the browser compatibility chart for the Show-Hide Layer behavior:

Show-Hide Layer	Netscape 2.x	Netscape 3.x	Internet Explorer 3.0	Internet Explorer 3.01
Macintosh	Fails without error	Fails without error	Fails without error	Fails without error
Windows	Fails without error	Fails without error	Fails without error	Fails without error

Swap Image and Swap Image Restore

Button rollovers are one of the most commonly used techniques in Web design today. In a typical button rollover, a user's pointer moves over one image and the graphic appears to change in some way, seeming to glow or change color. Actually, the onMouseOver event triggers the almost instantaneous swapping of one image for another. Dreamweaver automates this difficult coding task with the Swap Image action and its companion, the Swap Image Restore action.

New Feature
In recognition of how rollovers most commonly work in the real world, Dreamweaver 2 now makes it possible to combine the Swap Image and Swap Image Restore in one easy operation — as well as preload all the images. Moreover, you can use a link in one frame to trigger a rollover in another frame without having to tweak the code as you did in previous versions.

When the parameters form for the Swap Image action opens, it automatically loads all the images it finds in the current Web page (see Figure 17-18). You select the image you want to change — which could be the same image to which you are attaching the behavior — and enter the address for the file you want to replace the rolled-over image. You can swap more than one image with each Swap Image action. For example, if you want an entire submenu to change when a user rolls over a particular option, you can use a single Swap Image action to switch all of the submenu button images.

If you choose not to enable the Restore Images onMouseOut option, which changes the image back to the original, you need to attach the Swap Image Restore action to another event. The Swap Image Restore action can be used only after a Swap Image action. No parameter form exists for the Swap Image Restore action — just a dialog box confirming your selection.

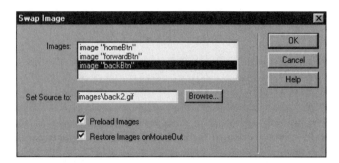

Figure 17-18: The Swap Image action is used primarily for handling button rollovers.

Tip   If the swapped-in image has different dimensions than the image it replaces, the swapped-in image is resized to the height and width of the first image.

To use the Swap Image action, follow these steps:

1. Select the object to trigger the action.

2. From the Behavior Inspector, select the Add Action button and choose Swap Image.

3. In the parameter form, choose an available image from the Named Images list of graphics on the current page.

4. In the Set Source To text box, enter the path to the image that you want to swap in. You can also select the Browse (Choose) button to locate the file.

   An asterisk appears at the end of the selected image name to indicate an alternative image has been selected.

5. To swap additional images using the same event, repeat Steps 3 and 4.

6. To preload all images involved in the Swap Image action when the page loads, make sure the Preload Images option is checked. Click OK.

7. To cause the selected images to revert to their original source, make sure that the Restore Images onMouseOut option is selected.

8. Click OK when you're done.

Here's the browser compatibility chart for the Swap Image and Swap Image Restore behaviors:

Swap Image and Swap Image Restore	Netscape 2.x	Netscape 3.x	Internet Explorer 3.0	Internet Explorer 3.01
Macintosh	Fails without error	OK	Fails without error	OK
Windows	Fails without error	OK	Fails without error	OK

Timelines: Play Timeline, Stop Timeline, and Go to Timeline Frame

Any Dynamic HTML animation in Dreamweaver happens with timelines, but a timeline can't do anything without the actions written to control it. The three actions in the timeline set — Play Timeline, Stop Timeline, and Go to Timeline Frame — are all you need to set your Web page in motion.

Before the Timeline actions become available, there must be at least one timeline on the current page. All three of these related actions are located in the Timeline pop-up menu. Generally, when you are establishing controls for playing a timeline, you first attach the Go to Timeline Frame action to an event and then attach the Play Timeline action to the same event. By setting a specific frame before you let the timeline start, you ensure that the timeline always begins at the same point.

Cross-
Reference

For more detailed information on using timelines, see Chapter 26, "Working with Timelines."

The Play Timeline and Stop Timeline actions have only one element on their parameter form: a drop-down list box offering all timelines in the current page.

The Go to Timeline Frame action's parameter form (see Figure 17-19), aside from enabling you to pick a timeline and enter a specific go-to frame, also gives you the option to loop the timeline a set number of times.

Tip

If you want the timeline to loop an infinite number of times, leave the Loop text box empty, and turn on the Loop option in the Timeline Inspector.

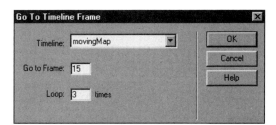

Figure 17-19: Control your timelines through the three Timeline actions. The Go to Timeline Frame parameter form lets you choose a go-to frame and designate the number of loops for the timeline.

To use the Go to Timeline Frame action, follow these steps:

1. Select the object to trigger the action.

2. From the Behavior Inspector, select the Add Action button and choose Go to Frame.

3. In the dialog box Timeline list, choose the timeline for which you want to set the start frame.

4. Enter the frame number in the Go to Frame text box.

5. If you want the timeline to loop a set number of times, enter a value in the Loop text box.

6. Click OK when you're done.

To use the Play Timeline action, follow these steps:

1. Select an object to trigger the action, and then choose Timeline ⇨ Play Timeline from the Add Action pop-up menu in the Behavior Inspector.

2. In the parameter form's Timeline list, choose the timeline that you want to play .

To use the Stop Timeline action, follow these steps:

1. Select an object to trigger the action, and then choose Timeline ⇨ Stop Timeline from the Add Action pop-up menu in the Behavior Inspector.

2. In the parameter form's Timeline list, choose the timeline that you want to stop.

Note

You can also choose All Timelines to stop every timeline on the current Web page from playing.

Here's the browser compatibility chart for the Timeline behaviors:

Timelines: Play Timeline, Stop Timeline, and Go to Timeline Frame	Netscape 2.x	Netscape 3.x	Internet Explorer 3.0	Internet Explorer 3.01
Macintosh	Error	Image source animation and invoking behaviors work, but layer animation fails without error.	Fails without error	Fails without error
Windows	Error	Image source animation and invoking behaviors work, but layer animation fails without error.	Fails without error	Fails without error

Validate Form

When you set up a form for user input, each field is established with a purpose. The name field, the e-mail address field, the zip code field — each has its own requirements for input. Usually, unless the CGI program is specifically written to check the user's input, forms take input of any type. Even if the CGI program can handle it, this server-side method ties up server time, and is relatively slow. The Validate Form action checks any text field's input and returns the form to the user if any of the entries are unacceptable. You can also use this action to designate any text field as a required field.

Validate Form can be used either to check individual fields or to check multiple fields for the entire form. Attaching a Validate Form action to an individual text box alerts the user to any errors as the form is being filled out. To check the entire form, the Validate Form action must be linked to the form's Submit button.

The Validate Form dialog box (see Figure 17-20) lets you designate any text field as required, and you can evaluate its contents. You can require the input of a text field to be a number, an e-mail address (for instance, jdoe@anywhere.com), or a number within a range. The number range you specify can include positive whole numbers, negative numbers, or decimals.

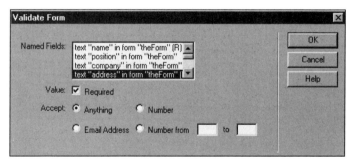

Figure 17-20: The Validate Form action can check your form's entries without CGI programming.

To use the Validate Form action, follow these steps:

1. Select the form object, such as a Submit button or text field, to trigger the action.

Tip

You can also attach the Validate Form to a check-box or radio button, but it's really only useful if you want to require the field.

2. From the Behavior Inspector, select the Add Action button and choose Validate Form.

3. If validating an entire form, select a text field from the Named Fields list.

If you are validating a single field, the selected form object is chosen for you and appears in the Named Fields list.

4. To make the field required, select the Value: Required check-box.

5. To set the kind of input expected, choose from one of the following Accept options:

- **Anything** accepts any input.

- **Number** allows any sort of numeric input. You cannot mix text and numbers, however, as in a telephone number like (212) 555-1212.

- **Email Address** looks for an e-mail address with the @ sign.

- **Number Range** lets you enter two numbers, one in each text box, to define the number range.

6. Click OK when you're done.

On the CD-ROM   Date validation is currently problematic when attempted with Dreamweaver's Validate Form action — you can't enter a date such as "011298" and have it recognize the entry as a number. For easy date validation, use the Plus Validate Form action included on the CD-ROM in the Configuration\Actions folder.

Here's the browser compatibility chart for the Validate Form behavior:

Validate Form	Netscape 2.x	Netscape 3.x	Internet Explorer 3.0	Internet Explorer 3.01
Macintosh	Fails without error	OK	Fails without error	OK
Windows	Fails without error	OK	Fails without error	OK

Managing and Modifying Your Behaviors

The standard behaviors that come with Dreamweaver are indeed impressive — but they're really just the beginning. Because existing behaviors can be modified and new ones created from scratch, you can continue to add behaviors as you need them.

The process of adding a behavior is simplicity itself. Just copy the HTML file to the Configuration\Behaviors\Actions folder and restart Dreamweaver.

If you find that your Add Action pop-up list is starting to get a little unwieldy, you can create subfolders to organize the actions better. When you create a folder within the Actions folder, that subfolder appears on the Add Action pop-up menu as a submenu, as you saw when you worked with the Timelines actions in a preceding section. Figure 17-21 shows a sample arrangement. This example has a subfolder called New to centralize the nonstandard but useful actions. You can even create sub-subfolders to maintain several levels of nested menus.

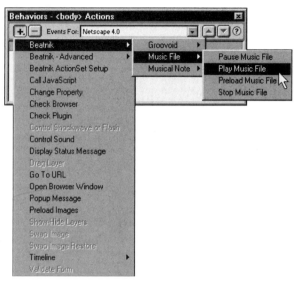

Figure 17-21: To create a new submenu in the Actions pop-up menu, just create a folder in the Actions directory.

Altering the parameters of a behavior

You can alter any of the attributes for your inserted behaviors at any time. To modify a behavior you have already attached, follow these steps:

1. Open the Behavior Inspector (go to Window ➪ Behaviors or click the Show Behaviors button in either Launcher, or press F8).
2. Select the object in the Document Window or the tag in the Tag Selector to which your behavior is attached.
3. Double-click the action that you want to alter. The appropriate dialog box opens, with the previously selected parameters.
4. Make any modifications to the existing settings for the action.
5. Click OK when you are finished.

Sequencing your behaviors

When you have more than one action attached to a particular event, the order of the actions is often important. For example, you should generally implement the Go to Timeline Frame action ahead of the Play Timeline action. To specify the sequence in which Dreamweaver triggers the actions, reposition as necessary in the Actions page by highlighting one and using the up and down arrow buttons to reposition it in the list.

Deleting behaviors

To remove a behavior from your list of actions attached to a particular event, simply highlight the behavior and select the – (Delete) button. If the removed behavior is the last action added, the event is also removed from the list; this process occurs after you select any other tag or click anywhere in the Document Window.

Summary

Dreamweaver behaviors can greatly extend the Web designer's palette of possibilities — even a Web designer who is an accomplished JavaScript programmer. Behaviors simplify and automate the process of incorporating common, and not so common, JavaScript functions. The versatility of the behavior format enables anyone proficient in JavaScript to create custom actions that can be attached to any event. When considering behaviors, keep the following points in mind:

✦ Behaviors are a combination of events and actions.

✦ Behaviors are written as in HTML and are completely customizable from within Dreamweaver.

✦ Different browsers support different events. Dreamweaver enables you to select a specific browser or a browser range, such as all 4.0 browsers, on which to base your event choice.

✦ Dreamweaver includes 19 standard actions. Some actions are not available unless a particular object is included on the current page.

In the next chapter, you learn how to create your own behaviors using Dreamweaver's custom JavaScript extensions.

✦   ✦   ✦

Creating a Behavior

In This Chapter

The basics of
building a behavior

Working with the
Document Object
Model

Exploring the
Dreamweaver API

Streamlining your
code with common
functions

Accessing useful
behavior techniques

The technology of a Dreamweaver behavior is open, and
anybody with the requisite JavaScript and HTML skills
can write one. To talk about "writing" a behavior, though, is a
bit of a misnomer. You never actually touch the event portion
of the behavior—you only work on the action file. To help the
creation process, Macromedia has a complete Extending
Dreamweaver document covering all the custom functions,
JavaScript extensions, and the Document Object Model (DOM)
that Dreamweaver recognizes.

Behaviors in Dreamweaver 2 have expanded considerably in
their functionality and implementation. By incorporating a
much broader DOM, Dreamweaver 2 can read and affect
virtually any element on the current HTML page. You can even
use behaviors to open other existing documents or create new
Web pages from scratch. Furthermore, the JavaScript API
(built-in JavaScript extensions) has expanded from four
functions to 26 to make behavior-building as smooth as
possible. You'll also find many helpful—and reusable—
functions built by the master coders on the Dreamweaver
team incorporated in the standard behaviors. This chapter
covers all these new features, but first let's get an overview of
the process of creating a behavior.

Creating a Behavior from Scratch

Writing a behavior is not so complex when you take it one
step at a time. In all, there are six basic steps to creating a
behavior from scratch:

> **Step 1: Define your behavior.** A behavior is an
> automatic method of incorporating a particular
> JavaScript function. The best way to begin building your
> behavior is to write that function. The function that you
> write is actually incorporated into the Dreamweaver
> action.

Step 2: Create the action file. One of the key functions in Dreamweaver behaviors is, aptly enough, `behaviorFunction()`, which inserts your function into the `<head>` section of the Web page. Dreamweaver 2 lets you include multiple functions as well as single ones.

Step 3: Build the user interface. As you look through the standard Dreamweaver behaviors, you see a dialog box that acts as the user interface in all but a few instances. The user interface that you create is based on HTML forms and is alternately referred to as a *parameter form*.

Step 4: Apply the behavior. Both an event and an action are required to make up a behavior. The `applyBehavior()` function ties your new function to a specific tag and event. The `applyBehavior()` function also passes the necessary arguments to the function in the `<head>` section.

Step 5: Inspect the behavior. From a user's point of view, building a Web page is often a trial-and-error process. You try one setting and if it doesn't work, you try another. To modify settings for a particular behavior, the user double-clicks the behavior name to reopen the dialog box and change the settings. The `inspectBehavior()` function handles the restoration of the previous values to the parameters form for easy editing.

Step 6: Test your behavior. The final step, as in any software development, is testing. You need to try out your new behavior in a variety of Web browsers and debug it, if necessary. (And it's always necessary.)

To demonstrate the process of creating a behavior, the next few sections take you through a real-world example: the construction of an Add a Groovoid action. A Groovoid is one of 72 sound effects incorporated into the Beatnik plug-in. Groovoids can be used for one-shot user interface feedback or for seamlessly repeating background music.

Cross-Reference For more on Headspace's Beatnik and Groovoids, see the "Making music with Beatnik" section of Chapter 21, "Using Audio on Your Web Page." You'll also find an official Groovoid behavior from Headspace described — one that's found in the Beatnik Action Set and included on the CD-ROM.

Step 1: Define your behavior

Behaviors are born of need, desire, or a combination of both. After repeating a single operation a thousand times, you probably find yourself thinking, There's got to be a better way. The better way usually automates the process in any possible way. In the case of inserting JavaScript functions into Web pages, the better way is to create a behavior.

Starting from this vantage point already accomplishes the first phase of behavior creation: defining the behavior. For example, suppose you've been using the Groovoid feature of the Beatnik plug-in to attach particular user-interface sounds to particular events, mostly `onMouseOver` and `onClick`. Rather than continue to enter the function by hand repeatedly, and having to look up the exact titles of the Groovoid samples, it would be easier to incorporate them into an action.

Here's a complete listing of my Groovoid-adding function as I routinely use it:

```
<html>
<head>
  <title>Groovoid Sample</title>
  <meta http-equiv="Content-Type" content="text/html;
charset=iso-8859-1">
<script SRC="images/music-object.js"></script>
<script language=JavaScript>
function doGroovoid(looping,groovoidName) {
  myMusicObject.playGroovoid(looping,groovoidName);
}
myMusicObject = new musicObject ("myMusicObject")
myMusicObject.stubEmbed('images/stub.rmf')
</script>
</head>
<body bgcolor="#FFFFFF">
<a href="#" onClick="doGroovoid(false,'Fanfare-Arrival')"><img
src="images/button01.gif" width="63" height="37"
name="playButton" border="0"></a>
</body>
</html>
```

Notice the lines in boldface. These are the key parts in the file: the function in the `<script>` section (the action) and the run-time function call attached to the button image (the event). After testing in several browsers, I know my function is sound (no pun intended, but welcome) and can be made into a behavior.

When you define your behavior in this manner, it tells you the arguments you need to generalize. In my Groovoid example, there are two: `looping` and `groovoidName`. Ideally, your action should be flexible enough to enable any argument to be user-defined. So now I know that in my user interface, I'll have at most two attributes to take in through my parameter form and pass to my function.

Once you've created and tested your function in Dreamweaver, save it. I've found it helpful to go back to the original file as I build my action and verify that I have everything in working order.

Step 2: Create the action file

In the next phase of behavior creation, you build the skeleton of the action file and begin filling in the necessary JavaScript functions. Each action file must have, at a minimum, the following four functions:

✦ `canAcceptBehavior()` determines if the behavior should be available. If it is not to be available, the entry in the Add Action pop-up menu is not selectable.

✦ `behaviorFunction()` inserts the general function in the `<head>` section of the Web page.

✦ `applyBehavior()` attaches the run-time function to the selected tag and inserts the chosen event.

✦ `inspectBehavior()` enables the user to reopen the parameter form and make modifications to the original settings.

The easiest way to start an action file is to adapt one that is already built. You can open and modify any of the existing Dreamweaver standard actions, as long as you remember to use the File ➪ Save As feature command and give your file a new name.

New Feature

Beginning with Dreamweaver 1.2, behaviors and other extensions could include external JavaScript files through the `<script language="javascript" src="script.js"></script>` construct. All of the Dreamweaver 2 behaviors have been rewritten to take advantage of this facility. The key benefit of this approach is to enable easy sharing of JavaScript code between functions. Although you can still combine the user interface and JavaScript aspects of a behavior in one file, the standard practice now is to store your parameter form instructions in the HTML file, like Control Sound.htm, and the JavaScript in a .js file with an identical name, such as Control Sound.js. My example incorporates the external JavaScript file technique.

Here are the steps to follow in this phase, with descriptions of what to do in creating the Add a Groovoid action:

1. Open a simple action file to serve as a template. I chose the Display Status Message action, contained in two files: Display Status Message.htm and Display Status Message.js.

2. Choose File ➪ Save As to save your file under a new name.

3. Open the HTML Inspector or your favorite text editor to work on the code for your new action.

Tip

It's best to work on the parameter form — the user interface — in Dreamweaver and, if your function code is extensive, work on your JavaScript file in an external editor, such as HomeSite or BBEdit.

4. Replace every instance of the old primary function name and arguments with the name of your function — normally this occurs in two functions: `behaviorFunction()` and `applyBehavior()`. In my case, the original function was `MM_displayStatusMsg (msgStr)`, and the new one was `doGroovoid (looping, groovoidName)`. Be sure to make this replacement in both the .htm and the .js files.

Whenever you first open the Behavior Inspector, Dreamweaver checks to see if there are multiple function names. If you don't replace the run-time functions, Dreamweaver recognizes the earlier file, but not the later one.

Tip

Use Dreamweaver 2's new extended Find and Replace capabilities to make sure you've retrieved all instances of a function's name — in one easy operation.

5. Replace the original function with your new function copied from your function test file. It's easiest to just copy-and-paste from one document to the other.

Note

You'll notice that nothing was done with the `canAcceptBehavior()` function. This function determines whether or not the action is available based on the elements in the current page. For instance, the Swap Image and Swap Image Restore actions are not available unless the Web page contains one or more images. In most cases where you want the function to be generally available, including our Groovoid example, you won't have to modify this function at all. Should you have to, look at the standard .js files that use this criteria, including Drag Layer, Control Shockwave or Flash, and Swap Image.

Because Dreamweaver 1.2, `behaviorFunction()` can return function names instead of definitions. First, insert your function in the JavaScript file, like this:

```
function doGroovoid(looping,groovoidName,uniqueName) {
  myMusicObject.playGroovoid(looping,groovoidName);
}
```

Once your function is included, you can call it with `behaviorFunction()`:

```
function behaviorFunction(){
  return "doGroovoid";
}
```

Moreover, `behaviorFunction()` is no longer limited to returning just one function. You can also use it to return multiple functions. For more on this capability, see "Dreamweaver Behavior Techniques" later in this chapter.

Step 3: Build the user interface

The user interface of a behavior is a parameter form, constructed with HTML form elements. The key indicator of what you'll need to include in your action's parameter form is the number and type of arguments required by your completed function.

In the Groovoid example, the function requires two primary arguments: `looping` and `groovoidName`. The interface needs to enable the user to choose the looping parameter (whether or not to loop the sample and, if so, for how many times) and the Groovoid name. One of the time-consuming aspects of attaching a Groovoid to an event is entering the exact name — there are 70 Groovoids and using the exact name is essential. To be useful, the action should make it easy to find and select a Groovoid name, automatically placing it in the function.

To make the behavior as universal as possible, I've also enabled the user to specify the paths to two necessary helper files: music-object.js and stub.rmf. The standard mechanism enables the path to be entered by hand or by browsing a Select File dialog box; Dreamweaver supplies prebuilt functions to help implement a browse button.

All user interface constructions are contained in the `<body>` section of your HTML action file. You can use Dreamweaver's visual editor to create and modify your form quickly. Many Web designers use tables to line up the various form elements; if you use this approach, be sure to place the table inside the form and not the other way around. Although you could insert a form in the cell of a table, you are limited to just entering form elements in that cell—and you return to no structure at all.

Follow these steps to create your user interface:

1. Open your HTML action file in Dreamweaver.

2. Choose Insert ➪ Form or select the Insert Form button from the Forms panel of the Objects Palette. Name the form in the Property Inspector for easy JavaScript identification.

3. For better alignment, place a table in your form by choosing Insert ➪ Table or selecting the Insert Table button from the Common panel of the Objects Palette.

4. Enter your form elements as needed. Be sure to name each one individually (with the exception of a radio button grouping) for JavaScript purposes.

Note   As with Dreamweaver objects, you don't see the OK, Cancel, and Help buttons that appear when the parameter form is actually used. Dreamweaver automatically applies these buttons to the upper-right part of your interface.

The interface for the Add a Groovoid action, as shown in Figure 18-1, uses a pair of text boxes for the necessary paths and a series of list boxes and radio buttons to select the Groovoid name. Another couple of radio buttons and a check-box handle the looping parameters. Because the example has two different sets of radio buttons, each set has its own unique name.

Building a Browse (Choose) button

The user input for getting a file path typically consists of two parts: a text box and a form button. If the user wants to just type in the path for the files, the text box is used. Often, however, it's much simpler for the user to click a Browse (Choose) button and choose the file from the standard Select File dialog box. The Browse button concept is so often used that Dreamweaver includes its mechanism in the _common.js file with other useful, generic functions. To use these functions, insert the following line in the `<head>` section of your HTML file:

```
<script language="javascript" src="_common.js"></script>
```

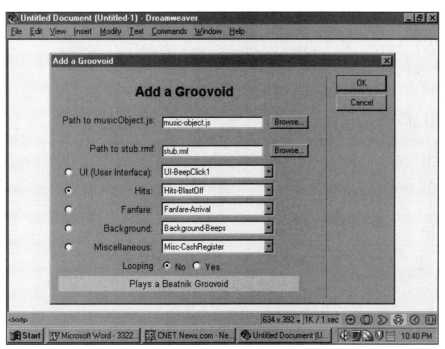

Figure 18-1: The parameter form uses a form to gather the user input and transmit it to the proper functions.

To make a Browse (Choose) button for a Dreamweaver dialog box, follow these steps:

1. Insert a regular form button in your form.

2. Set the button parameters, first changing it to a "None" button type from its default "Submit" type. You should also perform the following two steps:

   - **Name the button.** This is essential for straightforward JavaScript programming.

   - **Label the button.** Typically, you would use the label "Browse..." for a button of this type.

3. Add the function call to the button. You can do this in one of two ways:

   - While the button is selected, open the HTML Inspector and enter the following code in the `<input>` tag:

     ```
     onClick="browseFile(document.theForm.theTextField)"
     ```

     where *theForm* is the name of the form and *theTextField* is the name of the associated text field. This ensures that the name of the selected file appears in the text box next to the Browse (Choose) button.

• Attach the Call JavaScript button to the Browse (Choose) button. In the Call JavaScript dialog box, enter the just the function call:

```
browseFile(document.theForm.theTextField)
```

where, again, *theForm* is the form name and *theTextField* is the name of the text box adjacent to the button.

Initializing the user interface

The last part of setting up the user interface writes a function that activates the interface and sets the cursor in the right text box, or whatever is applicable. To complete this task, use the `initializeUI()` function, generally located in the Local Functions section of the JavaScript code. My example needs to have the cursor put in the first text box; in programmer parlance, you're said to be giving *focus* to a particular text field. If you have a text box in which you want to place the cursor, the `initializeUI()` function would read as follows:

```
function initializeUI() {
  document.theForm.textName.focus();
}
```

Finally, you need to attach the `initializeUI()` to `<body>` with an `onLoad` event in the HTML file. Again, you can proceed in one of two ways. First, you can locate the `<body>` tag and amend it so that it reads as follows:

```
<body onLoad="initializeUI()">
```

The second method uses the Call JavaScript behavior as described in the previous "Building a Browse (Choose) button" section. In this case, enter only the code

```
intializeUI()
```

in the Call JavaScript dialog box.

Step 4: Apply the behavior

Now you can write the code that links your function to a specific tag and event. You can think of this process in three steps:

1. Make sure that the user entered information in the right places.

2. Put the user's input on the parameter form into a more usable format.

3. Return the run-time function call.

All of these steps are contained in the `applyBehavior()` function maintained in the JavaScript file.

You gather information from an action's parameter form in the same way that you gather data from a custom object. Using the same techniques discussed in Chapter 16, "Creating and Using Objects," you receive the input information and usually convert it to local variables that are easier to handle. The number of variables is equal to the number of arguments expected; in the case of the Add a Groovoid action, there are two variables: `looping` and `groovoidName`.

Tip   If any of the input from the parameter form potentially may be sent out to a Web server — say, a URL or a file — you need to encode the text string so that it can be read by UNIX servers. Use the built-in JavaScript function `escape` to convert space and special characters in the URL to UNIX-friendly strings. The companion function, `unescape()`, reverses the process and is used in the `inspectBehavior()` function.

Follow these steps to build your `applyBehavior()` function:

1. Make the necessary variables:

```
var looping
var nameGroovoid
```

2. Get the information from the form. This process depends on the type of input field used. For the radio buttons, you can use a simple if-else test:

```
if (document.theForm.radioLoop[0].checked == "1")
    looping = "false";
else
    looping = "true";
```

3. Return the function run-time call, incorporating the variables. The `applyBehavior()` function must return a complete string. Enclose the argument variables with single quotes. If you use any internal quotes, they should be preceded by or escaped with a backslash.

4. Run an error check to see if values are entered where necessary; if not, inform the user.

```
if (nameGroovoid) {
return "doGroovoid(\'" + looping + "\',\'" + groovoidName +
"\')";
} else {
return "Please pick a Groovoid."
```

Only one more step remains before you're ready to begin testing your action.

Step 5: Inspect the behavior

Now it's time to can add the `inspectBehavior()` function to the JavaScript file. Basically, this function is called when the user double-clicks the action in the Behavior Inspector. It restores the information already entered through the parameter form and enables the user to change the parameters. In many ways, `inspectBehavior()` can be considered the reverse of the `applyBehavior()`

function: rather than reading the form and writing the information to the Web page, `inspectBehavior()` reads the information and writes the information back to the form.

Interpreting the string of information from a form is referred to as *parsing the string*. The Add a Groovoid action passes a message string similar to the following:

```
doGroovoid('false','Fanfare-Arrival')
```

Dreamweaver uses several built-in functions to aid the parsing process, but the key function is `getTokens()`. The `getTokens()` function accepts a string to parse and the separators for which to look. It returns an array of strings. You can call `getTokens()`, passing the function call string as the first argument. The second argument should contain parentheses, a quote, and a comma as separators, as follows:

```
var argArray = getTokens(msgStr,"()',");
```

Once the string arguments are in an array, they can be extracted and placed back in the parameter form. Follow these steps to write the `inspectBehavior()` function:

1. Declare a variable and set it equal to the `getTokens()` function.

2. Assign the array elements to the same variables you used in the `applyBehavior()` function:

```
If (argArray.length == 3) {
    var looping = argArray[1];
    var groovoidName = argArray[2];
```

3. Now put the variables back in the form:

```
document.theForm.radioLoop = looping
document.theForm.radioCat = groovoidName
```

4. The complete `inspectBehavior()` function looks like the following:

```
function inspectBehavior(msgStr) {
    var argArray = getTokens(msgStr,"()',");
    If (argArray.length == 3) {
    var looping = argArray[1];
        var groovoidName = argArray[2];
document.theForm.radioLoop = looping
document.theForm.radioCat = groovoidName
    }
}
```

Tip

This example is a fairly simple `inspectBehavior()` function. Keep in mind that the more input you allow from your user, the more complicated it is to restore the information through this function. As with many aspects of building behaviors, one of the best ways to construct your `inspectBehavior()` function is by examining the code of working examples provided in the Macromedia-built behaviors, as well as examples contributed by other developers.

Step 6: Test your behavior

Testing and debugging is the final, necessary phase of building an action. To test your behavior, follow these steps:

1. Restart Dreamweaver.

2. Insert an image or a link in a blank Web page.

3. Select the element to use as your trigger.

4. Open the Behavior Inspector.

5. Select `onClick` from the Add Event pop-up menu.

6. Select the + (Add) Action button and choose your behavior.

7. Fill out the parameters form as required. Your action's name appears in the Actions pane.

8. Double-click the action to verify that your prior choices have been restored.

9. Test the behavior in various Web browsers.

Caution   When you first select an event to add, Dreamweaver examines all of the actions in the Actions folder. If a problem is found, such as two files having the same function name, you are alerted to the conflict and the list only displays the older file. You have to correct the problem with the other action and restart Dreamweaver before the file appears in the list again.

If your action is intended for distribution and not your own personal use, you should expand your testing considerably, especially on the user-interface side. As the action programmer, you know what values are expected and know — often subconsciously — how to avoid the pitfalls into which a new user may easily stumble. Be especially mindful of accepting input through a text box. Unless you're just passing a message to be displayed onscreen or in the browser status bar, you often have to validate the incoming text string. Telling the user to enter a number in a particular range doesn't guarantee correct results.

Debugging the behavior

Finding a bug is every programmer's least favorite moment — but getting rid of that bug can be the best. Basic JavaScript debugging techniques, including using the `alert()` function to keep track of variables, are without a doubt your first course of action. With its built-in JavaScript interpreter, Dreamweaver can give you error messages in the same manner as a browser. You'll find that Dreamweaver 2's error handling has improved significantly, with more error messages pointing directly to the problem code.

If the errors are severe enough to stop Dreamweaver from recognizing your action file as such, the file is not listed in the Action pop-up menu until the problem is resolved. Generally this situation means that you must restart Dreamweaver after each modification until the problem is resolved. Once you are debugging and modifying the minor errors, the following technique enables you to make changes without restarting Dreamweaver:

1. First, open your Action file and make the necessary changes. Save the file.

2. Assign your action to a tag and open the behavior's dialog box. Without entering any parameters, click Cancel to close the parameter form.

3. Remove the action from the Actions pane by selecting the Delete button.

4. Reassign your action, and Dreamweaver loads the new version.

Tip Remember that JavaScript is case-sensitive. If you get a message that a function cannot be found, make sure the names match exactly.

Extending Dreamweaver Documentation

To help developers create behaviors, Macromedia has released the Extending Dreamweaver documentation. Extending Dreamweaver is the background documentation of the various functions available for building behaviors. As such, it provides a useful framework for discussing the underpinnings of Dreamweaver behaviors and how you can use the extensions and built-in functions.

Although Extending Dreamweaver covers all types of Dreamweaver extensions, behavior developers will be interested in three main sections: the Document Object Model, the Dreamweaver JavaScript API, and the Behaviors chapter. The more you understand about each of the various components and their included functions, the more flexibility you have in building your behaviors.

The most recent version of Extending Dreamweaver, as of this writing, is included on the CD-ROM. Macromedia plans to continue to expand the documentation, however; check Macromedia's Web site to see if an updated version is available.

Caution The material in this section is intended for programmers familiar with JavaScript and, as such, is fairly advanced.

Document Object Model

JavaScript is an interpreted programming language that addresses elements in the browser and on the Web page in a hierarchical fashion. To access the properties of any object on the page, JavaScript employs a Document Object Model (DOM). The DOM breaks down the page into successively smaller parts, until each element and its specific properties are identified.

New Feature As noted in the introduction, Dreamweaver 2 has significantly expanded the DOM by integrating a subset of the Netscape 3.0 DOM from the earlier version of Dreamweaver with a subset of the W3C's new implementation of the DOM. They've also tossed in a couple of features not implemented in either specification, but incredibly useful nonetheless.

Understanding nodes

Dreamweaver's DOM makes available, or *exposes*, virtually every element on a Web page. The DOM is often described using a tree metaphor, with the HTML document as the trunk. Instead of regarding the `<head>` and the `<body>` as the major branches, however, Dreamweaver's DOM, like the W3C DOM, uses four separate branches, or *nodes*, to divide the document:

✦ **DOCUMENT_NODE** enables access to objects directly relating to the overall document.

✦ **ELEMENT_NODE** contains references to all tags in the HTML document.

✦ **TEXT_NODE** describes the contiguous block of text within tags.

✦ **COMMENT_NODE** represents the comments within an HTML document and the text strings they contain.

Just as one tree branch can lead to another, nodes can contain other nodes. For example, a layer can contain a table that holds table rows that, in turn hold table data. One node containing another is said to be in a *parent-child* relationship and a node that cannot contain any other nodes is referred to as a *leaf node*, as it is incapable of supporting any more "branches." Figure 18-2 illustrates the node concept.

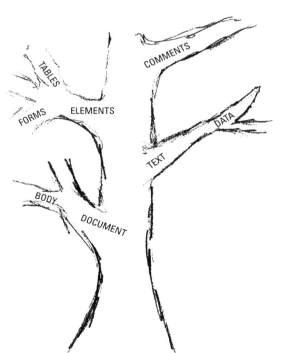

Figure 18-2: Nodes are used to express the structure of the HTML document and its relationship to the browser.

DOM Properties

When referencing a specific tag, the DOM syntax goes from the most general to the most specific. For example, let's say you want to find out what a user entered into a specific text box, a property called *value*. You need to start from the document itself and work your way down, as follows:

```
var theText = document.theForm.textboxName.value
```

The DOM dictates what properties are accessible and in what form. Not all properties and methods are supported. You can't, for instance, directly reference the value of a button on a form. Instead, you have to assign that value to a hidden or other text field, and access that value.

The portion of the DOM relating directly to forms and form elements is discussed in Chapter 16, "Creating and Using Objects." The same rules of use and the same restrictions for implementing forms in objects apply likewise to implementing forms in behaviors. Additionally, the Dreamweaver DOM addresses other major objects as outlined in Table 18-1. Read-only properties are marked with an asterisk; otherwise, properties can be both read and set.

Table 18-1
Dreamweaver Document Object Model Properties

Property	Nodes	Description	Return Values
nodeType*	All	Returns the node of the current selection	DOCUMENT_NODE ELEMENT_NODE TEXT_NODE COMMENT_NODE
parentNode*	All	Returns the parent tag or, if the HTML tag is selected, the document object	Any node
parentWindow*	DOCUMENT_NODE		A string
childNodes*	All	Returns the nodelist of immediate children to the current selection	An array
documentElement*	DOCUMENT_NODE	Corresponds to the `<html>` tag of the current document	"`<html>` `<head>`... `</body>` `</html>`" (when used with outerHTML)

Property	Nodes	Description	Return Values
`body*`	`DOCUMENT_NODE`	**Corresponds to** `<body>` **tag of the current document**	`"<body>...` `</body>"` (when used with `outerHTML`)
`URL*`	`DOCUMENT_NODE`	Returns the current document's path for example	`"FILE://C|/` `DOCS/NEW.HTML"`
`tagName*`	`ELEMENT_NODE`	**The HTML name for a tag**	`"IMG"` or `"TABLE"` for example
`attrName`	`ELEMENT_NODE`	Returns the value of the named attribute	"grey" or "#33CC66" for example
`innerHTML`	`ELEMENT_NODE`	**Returns the HTML source within the specified tag**	"<b>*First Name*</b>"
`outerHTML`	`ELEMENT_NODE`	**Returns the HTML source, including the specified tag**	"<p><b>*First Name*</b></p>"
`data`	`TEXT_NODE` `COMMENT_NODE`	**Returns the text string contained within a specified tag or comment**	`"J. Lowery"` where the tag reads `<p>J.` `Lowery</p>`

DOM Methods

Methods, in programming, are functions attached to a particular object, such as the document object. Dreamweaver 2 includes several methods in the new DOM to help manipulate the HTML page. With the node structure, you can apply these methods to the current document, frameset, frame, or a selected object.

Using these methods, your behaviors can inspect the current page and, if desired, change or even delete any attributes found. Table 18-2 outlines the methods contained in the Dreamweaver 2 DOM.

Table 18-2
Dreamweaver DOM Methods

Method	Returns	Description
getElementsByTagName(tagName)	A nodelist	Builds an array of the specified tag on the current page
hasChildNodes()*	True or False	Determines if current selection has children
getAttribute(attrName)	The value	Gets the value of a named attribute
setAttribute(attrName,attrValue)	Nothing	Sets a particular attribute to the specified value
removeAttribute(attrName)	Nothing	Deletes the specified attribute

Dreamweaver JavaScript API extensions

To make the behavior programmer's life a little easier, Dreamweaver 2 has added numerous built-in API extensions to the regular set of JavaScript functions. In addition to giving the Dreamweaver behavior programmer far more control over the current Web page, the Dreamweaver JavaScript extensions can open, create, browse, and save external Web pages.

New Feature   You'll notice that the API extensions have "dreamweaver." as a prefix. This procedure was actually started with Dreamweaver 1.2, but is fully implemented with version 2. These functions, described in the following sections, can be used in the main behavior JavaScript section or in objects. Table 18-3 gives an overview of the general extensions.

These functions can be used in all of Dreamweaver's customizable extensions, including objects, commands, inspectors, and translators. You'll also find several Dreamweaver behavior APIs explained later in this chapter.

Table 18-3
Overview of Dreamweaver JavaScript Extensions

Function	Role
dreamweaver.getDocumentDOM()	Accesses a tree of objects in a document
dreamweaver.getSelection()	Returns the current selection as memory offsets

Function	Role
`dreamweaver.setSelection()`	Sets the selection in the current document
`dreamweaver.offsetsToNode()`	Returns the node at specified memory offsets
`dreamweaver.nodeToOffsets()`	Returns the location of a node as memory offsets
`dreamweaver.getTokens()`	Parses a string into separate elements or tokens
`dreamweaver.getObjectTags()`	Returns an array of specified tags in a document
`dreamweaver.getObjectRefs()`	Returns an array of specified tags in a browser-specific format
`dreamweaver.getElementRef()`	Returns an object reference for a specified tag in a browser-specific format
`dreamweaver.getBehaviorEvent()`	Returns the event triggering the behavior
`dreamweaver.getBehaviorTag()`	Returns the tag associated with the behavior
`dreamweaver.getBehaviorElement()`	Returns the DOM object of the tag associated with the behavior
`dreamweaver.browseForFileURL()`	Enables a user to locate a file through a dialog box
`dreamweaver.getDocumentPath()`	Returns the path of the specified document
`dreamweaver.getConfigurationPath()`	Returns the path to the Dreamweaver Configuration folder
`dreamweaver.getSiteRoot()`	Returns the path to the local root folder
`dreamweaver.releaseDocument()`	Frees a document from memory
`dreamweaver.browseDocument()`	Opens a specified document in the primary browser
`dreamweaver.openDocument()`	Opens an existing document in Dreamweaver
`dreamweaver.createDocument()`	Opens a new document in Dreamweaver
`dreamweaver.saveDocument()`	Stores a specified document, locally

Continued

Table 18-3 (continued)	
Function	**Role**
`dreamweaver.editLockedRegions()`	Locks or unlocks a template region
`dreamweaver.popupCommand()`	Runs the specified command
`dreamweaver.popupAction()`	Runs the specified action
`dreamweaver.latin1ToNative()`	Changes a specified string from Latin 1 encoding to the encoding of the user's system
`dreamweaver.nativeToLatin1()`	Changes a specified string from the encoding of the user's system to Latin 1

The dreamweaver.getDocumentDOM() function

The `getDocumentDOM()` function is the starting point for many Dreamweaver JavaScript manipulations. Setting this function equal to a variable returns the entire Document Object Model of the specified document, enabling the DOM (and thus the document) to be read and edited. Generally, `getDocumentDOM()` is used in this fashion:

```
var theDom = dreamweaver.getDocumentDOM("document")
```

Here, `theDom` now represents the root of the current document and everything connected to it. Once you have accessed the DOM in this manner, you need to request more specific information. If, for example, you wanted to examine the `<body>` of the current document, you could code it this way:

```
var theDom = dreamweaver.getDocumentDOM("document")
var theBody = theDom.body
```

You could also use JavaScript dot notation to shorten the code:

```
var theBody = dreamweaver.getDocumentDOM("document").body
```

Tip   Many behaviors require repeated access to the DOM; it's good practice to set it to one variable early on in your script.

The `getDocumentDOM()` function requires one argument, *sourceDoc*, which, as expected, refers to the source document. The argument must be one of the following:

✦ `"document"` sets the reference to the current document. While the `"document"` argument can be used from anywhere to read the DOM, any edits applied using it must be ultimately called from within the `applyBehavior()`, `deleteBehavior()`, or `objectTag()` functions — or any function in a Command or Property Inspector file.

✦ **"parent"** sets the source document to the parent of the current document. This argument is generally used to determine if a document is within a frameset, like this:

```
var frameset = dreamweaver.getDocumentDOM("parent");
if (frameset) { ... do code ... }
```

✦ **"parent.frames[number]"** or **"parent.frames['framename']"**. To access another document in the frameset of which the current document is a member, use one of these two argument forms. The first, "parent. frames[number]", is usually used when the names of the current frames are unknown or to cycle through any number of frames. The second, "parent.frames['framename']", is applied in specific cases where the names of the other frames are known and modifications need to be made only to them.

✦ **A URL.** Occasionally, the behavior builder needs to reference existing documents, either locally or on the Web. Using a URL — either absolute or relative — as an argument enables you to retrieve information on almost any document you can specify. When using a relative URL, like this one from Dreamweaver's displayHelp.js file,

```
var idRoot =
dreamweaver.getDocumentDOM('../../../Help/contextID.html')
```

the URL is relative to the location of the behavior or other extensibility file.

The dreamweaver.getSelection() function

Quite often, how a behavior performs is dictated by what tag the user selects prior to attaching the behavior. The getSelection() function is the *first step* toward getting all the information necessary to control your behavior based on a user selection. I emphasize "first step" because this function returns the selection in the form of *byte offsets in memory*. A *byte offset* is a number that points to a memory address. In the case of the getSelection() function, the two byte offsets that are returned mark the beginning and end of the selection in memory. For example, say you open a new page in Dreamweaver, type in a phrase like "The Key Points" and then select the first word. If you used the getSelection function like this:

```
var selArray = dreamweaver.getSelection()
alert(selArray)
```

the message box would return

```
161,164
```

which denotes the beginning byte (161) and the ending byte (164) offset of the selected word, "The". If your beginning and ending byte offsets are the same (as in "164,164"), then nothing is selected. This fact comes in handy when you want to make sure that the user has selected something before proceeding.

To examine what is contained within the byte offsets returned by the `getSelection()` function, you have to use the `offsetsToNode()` function, explained later in this section.

The dreamweaver.setSelection() function

Just as `getSelection()` retrieves the memory offsets of the current selection, the `setSelection()` function sets a new pair of memory offsets and thus a new selection. The `setSelection()` function takes two arguments: *offsetBegin* and *offsetEnd*.

Most often, `setSelection()` is used to restore a user's selection after various document manipulations have taken place. In this example, the selection is first stored in a variable via `getSelection()` and then, after much document modification, restored by `setSelection`:

```
var currSelection = dreamweaver.getSelection()
// document altering code goes here
dreamweaver.setSelection(currSelection[0],currSelection[1])
```

Note   Should the new setting not conform to a valid HTML selection, such as the attributes within a tag, the selection expands to include the entire tag.

You can also use `setSelection` to deselect anything on the page after completing a behavior. All that's required is that the two arguments be equal. Using the preceding example, the following code:

```
dreamweaver.setSelection(currSelection[1],currSelection[1])
```

would place the cursor after the previous selection, while

```
dreamweaver.setSelection(currSelection[0],currSelection[0])
```

would place it before.

The dreamweaver.offsetsToNode() function

The `offsetsToNode()` function serves as a translator, converting the byte memory offsets retrieved by `getSelection()` into readable data. For this reason, you'll often see the following code combination:

```
selArr = dreamweaver.getSelection();
selObj = dreamweaver.offsetsToNode(selArr[0],selArr[1]);
```

where `getSelection()` returns the array of the selection and returns the object referenced by that array. As indicated, `offsetsToNode()` takes two arguments: *offsetBegin* and *offsetEnd*, usually expressed as the initial (0) and next (1) array elements.

Once you've used `offsetsToNode` to get the selected object, you can examine or manipulate it. For example, in the custom Replicator command (included on the CD-ROM), I used `offsetsToNode` to see if the selection made was appropriate (text only) and if not, call a help function:

```
var offsets = dreamweaver.getSelection()
var selObj = dreamweaver.offsetsToNode(offsets[0],offsets[1])
if (selObj.nodeType == Node.TEXT_NODE) {
  helpMe2()
}
```

The dreamweaver.nodeToOffsets() function

As the name indicates `nodeToOffsets()` is the inverse of `offsetsToNode()`. Instead of converting memory offsets to an object, `nodeToOffsets` takes an object reference and returns its memory offsets. This is useful when you need to manipulate a substring of the selection, usually text.

For example, in the custom command Change Case (included on the CD-ROM), after the selected object is retrieved via `getSelection` and `offsetsToNode`, `nodeToOffsets` expresses it in an array that can be uppercased or lowercased at the click of a button. Here's a fragment of the code from the custom `upperCase()` function:

```
var theDom = dreamweaver.getDocumentDOM("document");
var offsets = dreamweaver.getSelection()
var theNode = dreamweaver.offsetsToNode(offsets[0],offsets[1])
if (theNode.nodeType == Node.TEXT_NODE) {var nodeOffsets =
dreamweaver.nodeToOffsets(theNode)
offsets[0] = offsets[0]-nodeOffsets[0]
offsets[1] = offsets[1]-nodeOffsets[0]
var nodeText = theNode.data
theNode.data = nodeText.substring(0,offsets[0]) +
 nodeText.substring(offsets[0], offsets[1]).toUpperCase() +
 nodeText.substring(offsets[1], nodeText.length);
```

Because `nodeToOffsets` returns two memory offsets, you can use these as the arguments in `setSelection` to choose an object on the page. If, for instance, you wanted to select the first link on the page, you could use the code as follows:

```
var theDom = dreamweaver.getDocumentDOM("document")
var theLink = theDom.links[0]
var offsets = dreamweaver.nodeToOffsets(theLink)
dreamweaver.setSelection(offsets[0],offsets[1])
```

The dreamweaver.getTokens() function

The `getTokens()` function is often used in the `inspectBehavior()` function because it does such a good job of parsing a string. A *token* is a group of text characters that do not contain any of the specified separators. Generally, the *separators* in a function are the parentheses that surround the arguments and the commas that separate them.

The getTokens() function takes two arguments — the string to be parsed and the separators — and puts the results in an array. For example, note the following string:

```
doGroovoid('false','Fanfare-Arrival')
```

To extract the two arguments from this statement, use the getTokens() function as follows:

```
getTokens("doGroovoid('false','Fanfare-Arrival')","'(),")
```

If you set this function equal to an array called argArray, you get the following results:

```
argArray[0] = 'doGroovoid'
argArray[1] = 'false'
argArray[2] = 'Fanfare-Arrival'
```

Usually the first element of the array, the function name, is ignored.

The dreamweaver.getObjectTags() function

The canApplyBehavior() function often uses the getObjectTags() function to see if particular HTML objects exist on the current page. If getObjectTags() doesn't find them, the behavior cannot be applied and the item is inactive on the Add Action pop-up menu. Because the getObjectTags() function places the found tags in an array, the function can also be used to extract the unique names of those tags. This procedure is used in both the Control Shockwave and Show-Hide Layers actions.

The getObjectTags() function takes two arguments: either document or parent, and a list of tags for which to search. If the first argument is document, then the current page is assumed to be searched; the parent argument is used when the Web page is a member of a frameset. Each tag in the second argument is surrounded by quotes and separated by commas. For example, note the following statement:

```
getObjectTags("document","embed")
```

The preceding looks for all the <embed> tags in the current document and returns the entire tag in an array. The array can then be examined to see if it has the desired property — for example, a Flash movie file extension.

Note two special cases with the getObjectTags() function. First, if layer is specified, the function returns all <layer> and <ilayer> tags and all absolutely positioned <div>, <span>, and <img> tags. Second, if input is in the tag list, all

`<input>` types are returned. To get a specific input type (such as a radio button), you specify **input/*type***, where *type* is button, text, radio, checkbox, password, textarea, select, hidden, reset, or submit.

The dreamweaver.getObjectRefs() function

Netscape and Internet Explorer format some tags differently, especially those dealing with layers. To look for the appropriate tags coded for a particular browser, you need to use the getObjectRefs() function. The getObjectRefs() function examines the current Web page using the DOM of either Netscape 4.0 or Internet Explorer 4.0 as its guide.

The getObjectRefs() function takes three arguments:

- ✦ **NS 4.0 or IE 4.0.** Sets the browser conditions for which to look.
- ✦ **Document or parent.** The parent argument is used if the page to be examined is in a frameset.
- ✦ **The tag list.** Tags are enclosed in quotes and separated by commas. If no list is given, all the tags are put into the array.

The getObjectRefs() function is used in the Change Property action to look for the various layer tag formats.

Caution The getObjectRefs() function does not return references for unnamed objects. If an object does not contain either a name or an id attribute, Dreamweaver returns unnamed <tag>. As always, you should name any object potentially referenced by JavaScript.

The dreamweaver.getElementRef() function

Similar to getObjectRefs, the getElementRef() function is used to gather browser-specific references to a particular object. The primary difference is that getElementRef() is used when investigating a single object, and getObjectRefs is used for an array of objects.

The getElementRef() function takes two arguments: the first argument is either "NS 4.0" or "IE 4.0," which reference the Netscape and Internet Explorer formats, respectively; and the second argument is the tag being examined. The string returned puts the specified tag in the format of the named browser. If, for example, getElementRef() is used to get the object reference to a specific layer in Netscape terms, like this:

```
var theObjNS = dreamweaver.getElementRef("NS 4.0", tagArr[i])
```

the variable, theObjNS, would be set to something like:

```
document.layers['newLayer']
```

On the other hand, the same layer, in Internet Explorer terms, like this:

```
var theObjNS = dreamweaver.getElementRef("IE 4.0", tagArr[i])
```

would return a string like `document.all.newLayer1`.

Both `getElementRef()` and `getObjectRefs()` return browser-correct references
for both browsers for the following tags: `<a>`, `<area>`, `<applet>`, `<embed>`,
`<select>`, `<option>`, `<textarea>`, `<object>`, and `<img>`. Additionally, references
for the tags `<div>`, `<span>`, and `<input>` are returned correctly for Internet
Explorer, as `<layer>` and `<ilayer>` are for Netscape. Absolutely positioned `<div>`
and `<span>` tags are also returned correctly for Netscape, but others return the
message "`cannot reference <tag>`".

Caution   Naming objects and layers is often critical in JavaScript, as it certainly is with
`getElementRef()` and `getObjectRef()`. Dreamweaver can't return refer-
ences for unnamed objects; for these you'll get back an "`unnamed <tag>`" message. Furthermore, Dreamweaver can't handle references to a named object if it is
in an unnamed layer or form. While Dreamweaver automatically names layers as
they are created, forms require that names be entered by the designer, in the
Property Inspector.

The dreamweaver.getBehaviorEvent() function

Introduced in version 1.2, the `getBehaviorEvent()` function is used to find which
event is selected for the chosen behavior. In Dreamweaver 2, actions are chosen
prior to events, so this function is little used. Macromedia has officially deprecated
`getBehaviorEvent()`.

When used, `getBehaviorEvent()` takes no argument and is generally found in the
user interface initialization routines, where it is used to ascertain the event chosen
and, if not as desired, inform the user or deny access to the behavior.

The dreamweaver.getBehaviorTag() function

Similar to `getBehaviorEvent()`, the `getBehaviorTag()` function returns the tag
selected to implement the current behavior. And, like `getBehaviorEvent()`,
`getBehaviorTag()` can also be incorporated into the behavior setup code to steer
the user in the appropriate direction.

The `getBehaviorTag()` returns the entire tag—attributes, values, and any text
selected. For this reason, you need to seek out only the relevant portion of tag. One
technique for doing this is to use JavaScript's `indexOf` property to determine if the
tag is within the returned string. To make this even easier, it's best to uppercase or
lowercase the tag. As an example, the following code looks to see if the tag selected
for the behavior is an `<img>` tag, and, if it's not, alerts the users to what's required:

```
function initializeUI(){
var theTag = dreamweaver.getBehaviorTag().toUpperCase();
if (theTag.indexOf('IMG') != -1)){
```

```
// Behavior UI initilaization goes here
} else{
alert("This behavior requires you select an IMAGE to proceed.")
}
}
```

Note   This is different from using the `canAcceptBehavior` function to block access to a behavior. With the `getBehaviorTag()` technique, the user is informed of what the problem is, rather than simply being denied access.

The dreamweaver.getBehaviorElement() function

Another method to discover which tag was selected for the invoked behavior is the `getBehaviorElement()` function. The major difference between this function and the `getBehaviorTag()` function is that the former returns the DOM reference to the tag, whereas the latter returns the tag itself. Once you have the DOM reference of the behavior tag, you can uncover a terrific amount of information about the tag and its attributes.

Like `getBehaviorTag()`, `getBehaviorElement()` is most often used to determine if the user has selected an appropriate tag for the chosen behavior. If the tag is inappropriate, a helpful message can be displayed to guide the user to a better option. The `getBehaviorElement()` function returns either a DOM reference or `null`. Circumstances under which `null` is returned by `getBehaviorElement()` are as follows:

✦ The function was not invoked from a script called by the Behavior Inspector.

✦ The behavior called is part of a timeline.

✦ The function was invoked from a script called by `dreamweaver.popupAction()`.

✦ The function was invoked as part of a Behavior Inspector that is attaching an event to a link wrapper (`<a href="#">...</a>`) and the link wrapper has not yet been created.

✦ The function is called outside of a behavior.

The following example assumes that the required tag must be an embedded plug-in that is visible on the page:

```
function initializeUI(){
var theTag = dreamweaver.getBehaviorElement();
var tagGood = (theTag.tagName == "EMBED" &&
theTag.getAttribute("HIDDEN") == null);
if (tagGood) {
// Behavior User Interface code goes here
} else{
alert("This behavior can not be applied to hidden plug-ins")
}
}
```

The dreamweaver.browseForFileURL() function

The `browseForFileURL()` function enables the user to locate a file via a dialog box, rather than enter the entire path by hand. The function has been reworked for Dreamweaver 2 and now is far more flexible. You can now specify whether you want an Open, Save, or Select style dialog box, as well as the label in the title bar. You can even enable the Preview panel for images. No matter which options you choose, the `browseForFileURL()` function returns the path and filename in the form of a relative URL.

The `browseForFileURL()` function follows this syntax:

```
browseForFileURL('Open'|'Save'|'Select', 'Title Bar Label',
true|false)
```

The first argument, either `Open`, `Save` or `Select`, specifies the type of dialog box. The Select File dialog box displays additional local root information in its lower portion. The second argument is displayed in the title bar of the dialog box; if you don't want to insert your own title you must use two quotes, as in this example:

```
browseForFileURL('open','',false)
```

The final argument is a Boolean and indicates whether the Preview panel for selecting images is to be displayed or not. If no title bar label is given and the Preview panel argument is true, the title displayed is "Select Image Source."

The `browseForFileURL()` function is generally contained within another function that is called by an `onClick` event attached to a Browse (Choose) button, which in turn is next to a text field that enables the user to enter the path by hand. Standard now, in the _common.js file, is the `browseFile()` function, which takes one argument, `fieldToStoreURL`. For instance, the code for a Browse (Choose) button may read as follows:

```
<input type="text" name="textFile">
<input value="Browse..." type="button"
onClick="browseFile(document.theForm.textFile.value)"
name="button">
```

The `browseFile()` function then calls the built-in `browseForFileURL()` function, which opens the Select File dialog box and, if the dialog is returned with a filename, assigns that filename to a variable. In the standard `browseFile()` function, shown here, the returned filename is then assigned to a textbox value for the given field, which makes the name appear in the text box:

```
function browseFile(fieldToStoreURL){
  var fileName = "";
  fileName = browseForFileURL();  //returns a local filename
  if (fileName) fieldToStoreURL.value = fileName;
}
```

The `browseForFileURL()` function does not return absolute URLs.

The dreamweaver.getDocumentPath() function

Dreamweaver 2 adds several local document functions that aid in the reading, editing, and storing of current and external documents. The getDocumentPath() function is one of these; as the name states, this function returns the path of the specified document. The path returned is in the file:// URL format, so that a file located at c:\sites\index.html would return file://c|/sites/ as its path.

The getDocumentPath() function takes one argument: the source document. This argument can be "document", "parent", "parent.frames[number]", or "parent.frames[framename]" as described earlier in the getDocumentDOM() function. If the document specified has not been saved, getDocumentPath() returns an empty string.

The dreamweaver.getConfigurationPath() function

The Configuration folder can be considered the hub of Dreamweaver extensibility. Not only does it contain all the standard HTML files, such as the behaviors and objects, that are read into the system when Dreamweaver starts, but it also holds various other files that control the look and feel of the menus in other areas. As such, it's often useful to be able to find the path to the Configuration folder so that other files can be created, read, edited, and stored. And that's exactly what getConfigurationPath() does.

One sample use of this function included with Dreamweaver 2 is part of the secret behind the Rollover object. To a trained eye, the Rollover object is unlike any other — in fact, it's not really an object at all, it's a command masquerading as an object. You'll find that the getConfigurationPath() function plays a key role in the JavaScript file, rollover.js, with this code:

```
var rolloverCmdURL = dreamweaver.getConfigurationPath() +
"/Commands/Rollover.htm";
    var rolloverDoc    = dreamweaver.getDocumentDOM(
rolloverCmdURL );
```

In the first line, getConfigurationPath is used to locate the Rollover.htm file in the Command subfolder and assign it to a variable. This then enables the object to retrieve the DOM for manipulation with the getDocumentDOM() function.

Note   Like getDocumentPath(), getConfigurationPath() formats the path as a file:// URL.

The dreamweaver.getSiteRoot() function

Dreamweaver depends on the establishment of a local site root for much of its Web site management facility: All site root relative links and references are based upon the location of the site root folder. The capability to uncover its file location is important for any behaviors or other extensibility files that work on the site root level. Dreamweaver supplies such a capability with the getSiteRoot() function.

Very straightforward to use, `getSiteRoot()` does not take an argument and returns a file:// URL format reference to the local site root of the currently selected document. If an empty string is returned, it means that the file has not been saved.

The dreamweaver.releaseDocument() function

If you're working with a complex document with a lot of images, layers, tables, and text, you're going to have a lot of HTML to deal with. Accessing the DOM for that page can take up a significant chunk of your memory. If you're working with multiple pages, you could begin to run low on memory before the behavior closes and the memory is automatically freed. With the `releaseDocument()` function, you can get back the memory as soon as possible, whenever you request it.

The `releaseDocument` function's one argument is the DOM of the document in question. This is acquired by using the `getDocumentDOM()` function. You can see this function demonstrated in Dreamweaver's displayHelp.js file, which is used to direct all the help requested, contextually.

The dreamweaver.browseDocument() function

Should a Help file get too big for an alert dialog box, you might need to provide access to a larger file. Dreamweaver 2 lets you open any specified file — including an expanded Help file — within the primary browser. The `browseDocument()` function takes one argument, the path to the required file:

```
dreamweaver.browseDocument("http://www.idest.com/help/etable.
htm")
```

As noted in Chapter 16, "Creating and Using Objects," you can use `browseDocument` to access an absolute URL from the Web or a file from a local drive. To display a local file you need to combine `browseDocument` with another function such as `getConfigurationPath()`. The example offered here shows how to use the two functions together to programatically display Dreamweaver's InsertMenu.htm file:

```
function displayMenu() {
  var menuPath = dreamweaver.getConfigurationPath() +
"/Objects/InsertMenu.htm"
  dreamweaver.browseDocument(menuPath)
}
```

The dreamweaver.openDocument() and dreamweaver.createDocument() functions

The `openDocument()` and `createDocument()` functions provide similar capabilities while possessing similar restrictions. The `openDocument()` function is equivalent to selecting File ⇨ Open and selecting a file from the dialog box. The `createDocument()` function, as the name implies, creates a new, blank document, based on the standard Default.htm file. In either case, the document loads into a Dreamweaver window and is brought forward.

The createDocument() function does not need an argument to work and automatically returns the DOM of the new document. For example, the following code:

```
var theNewDoc = dreamweaver.createDocument()
```

is the same as using getDocumentDOM() for a new page.

The openDocument() function requires an argument in the form of a file:// URL. If the URL is given in relative terms, the file is relative to the extensibility file calling the function. For instance, to open a file located one directory up from the Command folder, you would need to refer to it as follows in a custom command:

```
dreamweaver.openDocument("../Extensions.txt")
```

You can also use the same technique referred to earlier in the browseDocument() function to access files with the Configuration folder as a base.

Note While this function and its companion, createDocument(), cannot be used within a behavior, they can be called from a custom command or Property Inspector. Therefore, it's possible to use the popupCommand() function to access a command that employs openDocument() or createDocument().

The dreamweaver.saveDocument() function

Once all your edits and modifications have been finished, you need a way to store that file. The aptly named saveDocument() function performs just that chore for you. This function takes two arguments, *documentObject* and *fileURL*; the first corresponds to the DOM of the file desired to be saved and the second is the address for it to be saved to. Again the *fileURL* is relative to the extensibility file.

The saveDocument function returns true if successful and false if the file-storing attempt fails. If the file specified is noted as read-only, Dreamweaver attempts to check it out; if it is unsuccessful, an error message will appear.

The dreamweaver.editLockedRegions() function

Dreamweaver 2 templates are based on a combination of locked and editable regions. Normally, these regions are designated in the Document Window, but you can use the editLockedRegions() function to lock and unlock a template's regions programatically. The editLockedRegions() function works by entering true as the function's argument if you want to unlock all of the current document's locked regions, and entering false to lock them again. After the routine calling editLockedRegions() ends, all regions revert to their default status.

Caution Due to the potential undesirable results using this function, Macromedia recommends that only custom data translators use the editLockedRegions() function.

The dreamweaver.popupAction() and dreamweaver.popupCommand() functions

While the popupAction() and popup.Command() functions are not directly useful to behavior creators, because they cannot be called from within a behavior, they do allow considerable cross-pollination of Dreamweaver extensible objects. Invoking these functions calls an existing behavior or command and presents its dialog box to the user — except you use these functions to call the behaviors or commands from within a custom object, command, or Property Inspector.

The popupAction() function takes two arguments: the name of the action file and the general function call of the action. The action chosen must be in the Action subfolder. For example, code to call the Control Sound behavior could look like this:

```
var goCS = dreamweaver.popupAction("Control
Sound.htm","MM_controlSound(,,)")
```

Tip To call an action in a subfolder of the Action subfolder, you need to specify the path. For example, if you want to call one of the standard Timeline actions, it's necessary to state the action name as "Timeline/Go to Frame.htm".

The general function call can be found near the end of the applyBehavior() function, where the return value is specified, or as the behaviorFunction() return value. The popupAction() function returns the completed function call, including whatever parameters are selected by the user. In the previous example, if the user had chosen "Play" and selected "brazil.mid" as the file, the result (goCS) would be similar to the following:

```
"MM_controlSound('play',document.CS911946210190.'brazil.mid')"
```

Note The second argument is a unique name generated by Dreamweaver as part of the function.

Everything is written into the user's page, except the event handler and its corresponding function call. This is left to the calling object, command, or Property Inspector to handle.

The popup.Command() function is a bit simpler; this function only requires one argument: the name of the command file. Any file named must be located in the Commands folder. The popup.Command() function does not return a value, but simply executes the specified command.

The dreamweaver.latin1ToNative() and dreamweaver.nativeToLatin1() functions

Dreamweaver 2 provides two new functions to help with the localization of your behaviors around the globe. Many countries use font encodings other than Latin 1, which is standard in the U.S. and several Western European countries. To convert a string of text for a user interface from Latin 1 encoding to that of the user's machine, use the latin1ToNative() function. The argument, a text string, should be already translated into the other language. To convert a text string from the user's encoding system to Latin 1, use the inverse function, `nativeToLatin1()`.

Note

Neither of these functions has an effect in Windows systems, which are already based on Latin 1.

The dreamweaver.relativeToAbsoluteURL() function

As more programs like Fireworks and Director 7 are capable of outputting HTML, behaviors and other extensions are being employed to access their documents. It's often necessary to find the absolute URL of a selected file in order to get the document's DOM or open it. The `relativeToAbsoluteURL()` function returns this needed information, given three arguments:

✦ **docBaseURL.** The portion of the current document's relative path name excluding the filename. For example, if the file in question were to be found at `images/austria.gif`, the docBaseURL would be `images/`.

✦ **siteRootURL.** The file URL of the current site root, as returned from the `getSiteRoot()` function.

✦ **relativeURL.** The full relative path name of the selected file (for example, `images/austria.gif`).

The syntax for the function is as follows:

```
var absoluteURL = dreamweaver.relativeToAbsoluteURL(
docBaseURL, siteRootURL, relativeURL )
```

Of the three arguments, only docBaseURL is a little tricky to get. Once you have the relativeURL, which can be returned from the `browseForFileURL()` function, you need to examine the path name and extract the first part of the path leading up to the actual filename. To do this, use the JavaScript function `lastIndexOf` to find the final "/" character and extract the previous substring. For example:

```
function docBase() {
var docURL = dreamweaver.getDocumentPath("document");
var index = docURL.lastIndexOf('/');
if ( -1 == index ){ // If there is no additional path
  return "";      // return nothing.
  }
  else {
  return docURL.substring(0, index);
  }
}
```

Behavior API

You've seen most of the behavior API functions applied in a previous section, "Creating the Action file." The API is used to create a behavior. The primary functions are as follows:

Function	Role
`canAcceptBehavior()`	Determines whether an action is available
`windowDimensions()`	Sets the width and height of the parameter form
`applyBehavior()`	Attaches the behavior function to the selected tag
`inspectBehavior()`	Restores user-selected values to the parameter form for reediting
`behaviorFunction()`	Writes a function into the `<head>` of the HTML file
`behaviorObjects()`	Writes a function into the `<body>` of the HTML file
`deleteBehavior()`	Removes a behavior from the HTML file
`identifyBehaviorArguments()`	Notes the behavior arguments that need to be altered if the file is moved
`displayHelp()`	Attaches a Help button to the behavior's dialog box

For discussions of the uses of the `canAcceptBehavior()`, `applyBehavior()`, `inspectBehavior()`, and `behaviorFunction()` functions, see the preceding sections. Following are discussions of the other behavior API functions.

The windowDimensions() function

To speed display, the `windowDimensions()` function sets specific dimensions for the parameters form that the user sees as the dialog box. If this function is not defined, the window dimensions are computed automatically. This function takes one argument, `platform`, which is used to specify whether the user's system is Macintosh or Windows. The function returns a string with the width and height in pixels. For example:

```
function windowDimensions(platform){
if (platform.charAt(0) == 'm'){ // Macintosh
      return "650,500";
      }
      else { // Windows 95 or NT
      return "675,525";
}
}
```

You can see this function in some of the standard behaviors. However, Macromedia recommends that it only be used when you need the behavior's dialog box to be larger than 640 × 480.

The behaviorObjects() function

Just as `behaviorFunction()` returns information that is included in the `<head>` section, the `behaviorObjects()` function returns information that is included in the `<body>` section of the current Web page. The `behaviorObjects()` function can only be placed at the very top of the section, just after the `<body>` tag. You can see this function in the Control Sound action, where an `<embed>` tag is written into the `<body>` section, as follows:

```
<!-- #BeginBehavior MM_controlSound1 -->
<embed name='MM_controlSound1' src='/images/Braz.mid'
loop=false autostart=false mastersound hidden=true width=0
height=0></embed>
<!-- #EndBehavior MM_controlSound1 -->
```

The comments that surround the implanted `<embed>` tag are used as identifiers so that Dreamweaver can remove the tag later if necessary. The function takes one argument, *uniquename*, which in the preceding example is expressed as `MM_controlSound1`. The *uniquename* is generated by Dreamweaver and is in the form of function-number. If you place another Control Sound action in the same document, the unique name increments to `MM_controlSound2`.

The deleteBehavior() function

Normally, Dreamweaver automatically handles removal of a behavior's event handler and associated JavaScript when the user chooses the Remove Behavior button in the Behavior Inspector. However, as behaviors grow in complexity and become capable of adding additional support code to the HTML document, it becomes necessary to use the `deleteBehavior()` function on a case-by-case basis. To better understand how `deleteBehavior()` is used, it's best to look at a couple of examples.

Two standard behaviors, Control Sound and Swap Image, use the `deleteBehavior()` function. Control Sound inserts an `<embed>` tag that contains a unique ID. To remove the code, `deleteBehavior()` first reads a function call string, just like the one returned by `applyBehavior()`. If the function finds an `<embed>` tag with the matching ID that is not referenced elsewhere on the page, the code is deleted. Here's the implementation of `deleteBehavior()` for Control Sound:

```
function deleteBehavior(fnCallStr) {
  var argArray,sndName,doc,tagArray,i,embedName;

  argArray = extractArgs(fnCallStr);
  if (argArray.length > 2) {
    sndName = dreamweaver.getTokens(argArray[2],".")[1];
//remove "document.", use unique name
    //Find all EMBED calls that we created (name starts with
"CS"), add to menu
    doc = dreamweaver.getDocumentDOM("document"); //get all
    tagArray = doc.getElementsByTagName("EMBED");
    for (i=0; i<tagArray.length; i++) {  //with each EMBED tag
      embedName = tagArray[i].name;
      if (embedName == sndName) { //if same embed
        if ( -1 == doc.body.outerHTML.indexOf( argArray[2] ) )
// and embed ref'd no where else
          tagArray[i].outerHTML = "";
```

```
        break;
    } } }
  }
```

Swap Image doesn't insert additional `<embed>` or other tags; it inserts additional event handlers to make implementing rollovers a one-step process. When a Swap Image behavior is deleted from the page, all the additional event handlers must be stripped out as well. To do this, the `deleteBehavior()` function first reads in the behavior function call string and then searches for the *Preload ID*. This is a unique name inserted by Dreamweaver if the user checked the Preload option when running the behavior. If the Preload ID is found, the preload handler, such as `onLoad = MM_preloadImages()`, is removed. Next, the Swap Image `deleteBehavior()` searches to see if the Swap Image Restore code was added — and if so, deletes that event handler as well.

The identifyBehaviorArguments() function

If you've ever had to relocate a Web site from one directory to another, you know the laborious job of making sure all your references are intact. Dreamweaver 2 takes some of the tedium out of this chore. When you use Save As from Dreamweaver, all of the file paths within HTML attributes, such as the image source files and links, are automatically updated. Dreamweaver now extends the same functionality to URLs contained within behaviors.

For example, suppose you have constructed a Web page that uses the Check Browser action to route users to various URLs, depending on the browser they are using. Should you elect to save your Web page in a different folder, for whatever reason, Dreamweaver automatically updates the referenced URLs.

For this property to work correctly, a new function must be included in the behavior. The function, `identifyBehaviorArguments()`, passes the argument structure to Dreamweaver so it can update the URLs, if necessary. The function also identifies the layer objects in the behavior that Dreamweaver must correct if the Convert Layers to Tables command is used.

The `identifyBehaviorArguments()` function accepts a string that contains the behavior function call, with arguments. The function then extracts the arguments into an array and identifies which arguments in the array are URLs, which ones are layer objects, and which ones are neither. Four identifying values are returned:

✦ **URL** when the argument is a file or file path.

✦ **NS4.0ref** when the argument identifies a layer in Netscape syntax, such as `document.layers[\'Layer1\']`.

✦ **IE4.0ref** when the argument identifies a layer in Internet Explorer syntax, such as `document.all[\'Layer1\']`.

✦ **Other** when the argument is none of the above.

You can see an example of the `identifyBehaviorArguments()` function in the Check Plugin action:

```
function identifyBehaviorArguments(fnCallStr) {
  var argArray;

  argArray = extractArgs(fnCallStr);
  if (argArray.length == 5) {
    return "other,URL,URL,other";
  }
}
```

As with the `inspectBehavior()` function, the array for the function-call string is one element longer than the number of arguments — the initial array element is the function name itself.

The displayHelp() function

The `displayHelp()` function inserts a Help button on your custom behavior dialog boxes, below the standard OK and Cancel buttons.

New Feature

Introduced in Dreamweaver 2, this function takes no arguments and is usually defined to display a Help message or file. The two typical techniques are to use either the `alert()` method or the Dreamweaver JavaScript extension, `browseDocument()`.

To display a brief message, use the `alert()` method, like the following code:

```
function displayHelp() {
  alert("This behavior works only with .rmf files.")
}
```

When you need to bring up a much longer file, use the `browseDocument()` function:

```
function displayHelp() {

dreamweaver.browseDocument("http://www.idest.com/help/rep.htm")
}
```

You can also reference local files using `browseDocument()`. See the `browseDocument()` description in the section "Dreamweaver JavaScript API extensions."

Caution

Do not include the JavaScript file displayHelp.js in your behaviors. This is the Dreamweaver file used for calling its own Help pages.

Useful Common Functions

As with most other object-oriented programming languages, it's good programming practice to build a function once and recall it when needed. Dreamweaver 2 includes a library of such useful functions, which are maintained in the _common.js file. While they are used extensively throughout the standard behaviors, there is no reason you can't use them in your own routines. To access them, you only need insert a line in your behavior JavaScript file like this:

```
<script language="javascript" src="_common.js"></script>
```

Table 18-4 shows a breakdown of the 16 functions available in the _common.js file.

Table 18-4 Dreamweaver Standard Common Functions	
Function	**Description**
extractArgs()	Takes a function call and extracts the arguments into an array without quotes
escapeQuotes()	Reviews a strings and adds the escape character, \, in front of any single quote, double quote, or backslash found
unescapeQuotes()	Removes any escape characters found in a string
browseFile()	Opens the Select File dialog box and inserts the results into a specified text box
stripStar()	Removes asterisks from the end of a string
stripValue()	Removes any specified value from the end of a string
addStarToMenuItem()	Adds an asterisk to a selected menu item on the end, as in Swap Image
addValueToMenuItem()	Adds any specified value to a selected menu item, as (show), (hide), and (default) are added in Show/Hide Layers
niceNames()	Changes JavaScript object references like document.layers['onLayer'].document.theForm to a more readable format such form "theForm" in layer "onLayer"
nameReduce()	Extracts object names and array numbers and quotes them, if necessary

Function	Description
errMsg()	Concatenates strings given in an argument. For example, errMsg("Now is the %s for %s to fight", *var1*, *var2*) returns "Now is the time for all men to fight" if *var1* is set to "time" and *var2* is set to "all men". However, if *var1* is set to "not the time" and *var2* is set to "anyone", then errMsg returns "Now is not the time for anyone to fight."
findObject()	Returns the JavaScript object reference for any named object. For example, if you have an image named imgOne in a form in a layer, onLayer, findObject("imgOne") returns document.layers['onLayer'].imgOne.
getParam()	Returns an array of named objects within a given tag found on the current page
badChars()	Removes inappropriate characters such as ~!@#$%^&*()_+|`-=\\{}[]:\";'<>,./, and space
getAllObjectRefs()	Returns an array of object references for any specified tag in the current document or, if the document is in a frameset, in all frames
getAllObjectTags()	Returns an array of tags for any specified tag in the current document or, if the document is in a frameset, in all frames

Dreamweaver Behavior Techniques

Quite often, creating a behavior is far more than just stringing a number of predefined functions together. Specific techniques exist for many special needs and, if you don't know them, you can spend many hours redeveloping the wheel. In this section, you learn several methods that can help you streamline your work.

Specifying an event

In Dreamweaver 2, every tag capable of being used to launch a behavior has a default event. While you can alter the default events for various tags by editing the HTML files in the Events folder, as described in Chapter 17, these changes only affect your own system, not those of other users. You can, however, specify the desired event on a behavior-by-behavior basis — in fact, you can specify a series of desired events.

The event specification takes place in the canApplyBehavior() function. Usually, this function returns either true or false depending on whether the proper conditions for implementing the behavior have been met. If, however, the conditions have been met *and* you want to specify an event to use, canApplyBehavior() can be set to return a string of acceptable events.

In the following example, the page is inspected and if a layer is found, the default event is overridden in favor of onKeyDown:

```
function canAcceptBehavior(){
  var nameArray = dreamweaver.getObjectRefs("NS
4.0","document","LAYER");
  if (nameArray.length > 0){
    return "onKeyDown";
  }else{
  return FALSE;
}
```

It's also possible to specify a series of preferred events, in reverse order of preference, like this:

```
return "onKeyDown, onKeyPress, onKeyUp"
```

If one event handler is not available — perhaps because the user specified an older browser — the next is selected.

Returning a value

Most event handlers don't require a return value to be implemented, but some, such as onMouseOver and onMouseOut, do. Generally, Dreamweaver behaviors don't take this into account, but you can by declaring a special variable, document.MM_returnValue. You can see the return value variable in operation in the standard Display Status Message behavior.

The document.MM_returnValue variable is declared as the last line in the function definition. Thus, Display Status Message reads as follows:

```
function MM_displayStatusMsg(msgStr) { //v2.0
  status=msgStr;
  document.MM_returnValue = true;
}
```

Naturally, the return value can also be false.

Including multiple functions

Although little known, the ability to return multiple functions began in Dreamweaver 1.2. Previously, all behavior functions had to be self-contained and one could not call on any helper functions. Now, however, multiple functions can easily be defined and returned via behaviorFunction(). Once written into the user's page, all the returned functions are stored in a single <script></script> tag pair.

The technique for inserting multiple functions is fairly straightforward. First, list your defined functions in a comma-delimited string in `behaviorFunction()`. The one trick is to make sure that your primary function — the one called by the event handler — is listed last. This technique is illustrated in the following code for my custom Resize Layer Patch behavior:

```
function behaviorFunction(){
  return 'reDo,resizePatch';
}
```

Here, my primary function is `resizePatch()` and is used as such in `applyBehavior()`:

```
function applyBehavior() {
  return 'resizePatch()';  //return fn call with args
}
```

Hava Edelstein, an engineer on the Dreamweaver team specializing in JavaScript, has provided a number of commands and utility functions that are very useful in building behaviors and other Dreamweaver extensions. You'll find them in the folder with her name on the CD-ROM.

Summary

While creating a custom behavior is not a simple task, it is a vastly rewarding one — both from the programmer's and the user's perspective. Dreamweaver gives you tremendous power to automate advanced Web page techniques and Dreamweaver 2 has greatly enhanced that power with an expanded Document Object Model. As you ponder building your own behaviors, remember the following:

✦ If you can achieve a result in JavaScript, chances are good you can make a behavior to automate that task.

✦ Dreamweaver 2 includes an expanded Document Object Model (DOM) that enables the programmer to examine and modify virtually every aspect of an HTML page.

✦ You can use Dreamweaver's built-in JavaScript extensions and API functions to build your own actions.

✦ Dreamweaver's JavaScript extensions enable you to open existing documents, as well as create and save new ones.

✦ Many useful functions can be found in the standard _common.js file.

In the next chapter, you learn how to customize Dreamweaver further through commands, Property Inspectors, and more.

✦   ✦   ✦

Customizing Dreamweaver

✦ ✦ ✦ ✦

In This Chapter

Automating Web
development with
commands

Including custom
XML tags

Examining new
Property Inspectors

Expanding
Dreamweaver's core
functionality

Translating server-
side content

✦ ✦ ✦ ✦

The Web is a very dynamic environment, with new
technologies continually emerging. Until recently, HTML
standards were changing every year or so and even now,
products are routinely introduced that use the Web as a
jumping-off place for new methods and tools. Keeping pace
with the constantly shifting work environment of the Web was
beyond the abilities of any suite of Web authoring tools, much
less a single one—until Dreamweaver debuted, of course.
The initial version of Dreamweaver had a high degree of
extensibility built right in, with its customizable HTML objects
and JavaScript behaviors.

Macromedia takes this core of flexibility to new heights with
Dreamweaver 2. With the introduction of the W3C Document
Object Model, objects and behaviors have been beefed up so
that they are much more powerful than ever. In addition,
Dreamweaver 2 presents a host of new ways to extend its
power:

✦ **Commands.** Commands are JavaScript and HTML code
that manipulate the Web page during the design phase,
much as behaviors are triggered at run time.

✦ **Custom tags.** With the rapid rise of XML, custom tag
support becomes essential in a professional Web
authoring tool. Dreamweaver 2 gives you the power to
create any custom tag and control how it displays in the
Document Window.

✦ **Property Inspectors.** Custom Property Inspectors go
hand-in-hand with custom tags, permitting the
straightforward entry of attributes and values in a
manner consistent with the Dreamweaver user interface.

✦ **C-level extensions.** Some special uses require a root-
level addition to Dreamweaver's capabilities.
Macromedia's engineers have "popped the hood" on
Dreamweaver and made it possible for a C or C++
language library to interface with it through C-level
extensions.

✦ **Translators.** Translators allow server-side content to be viewed in the Document Window at design time, as well as in the browser at run time.

While a few of these extension features require programming skills outside of those common to the typical Web designer, most are well within the reach of an HTML and JavaScript-savvy coder. As with behaviors and objects, the source code for all but the C-level extensions is readily available and serves as an excellent training ground. This chapter, combined with these standard scripts, provides all the tools you need to begin carving out your own, personalized version of Dreamweaver.

Adding New Commands

By their very nature, objects and behaviors are single-purpose engines. A custom object inserts a single block of HTML into the <body> of a Web page, while custom behaviors add JavaScript functions to the <head> and attributes of one tag. Commands, on the other hand, are multifaceted, multipurpose, go-anywhere and do-anything mechanisms. Commands can do everything objects and behaviors can do, combined — and more. In fact, commands can even masquerade as objects.

New Feature
For all their power, however, commands are one of the most accessible of the Dreamweaver 2 extensions. This section describes the basic structure of commands as well as the use of the standard commands that ship with Dreamweaver 2. You'll also find information about how to create your own commands and control their integration into Dreamweaver.

Understanding Dreamweaver commands

When I first encountered commands, I thought, Great! Dreamweaver now has a macro language, and I envisioned instantly automating simple Web design tasks. Before long, I realized that commands were even more powerful — and a bit trickier than a macro recorder. Dreamweaver 2's adoption of the W3C Document Object Model (DOM) is one of the factors that makes commands feasible. The DOM in Dreamweaver makes available, or *exposes*, every part of the HTML page — every tag, every attribute, every bit of content — which can then be read, modified, deleted, or added to. Moreover, Dreamweaver commands can open, read, and modify other files on local systems.

The command can have a parameter form or not, depending on how the command was written. Generally, commands are listed in the Commands menu, but by altering the CommandMenu.htm file (as described later in the chapter), you can cause your command to appear as part of any other menu — or to not appear at all. Because one command can call another, such hidden commands are more easily modified.

But how specifically are commands being used? Here's a short list of the commands that have been built by Web designers outside of Macromedia in the brief time that the technology has been publicly available:

✦ **iCat Commands** open up a browser window and connect you to the iCat Web site for online e-commerce registration. Additional commands build the database of online store items and synchronize the information on both local and remote servers. By Eric Greene for iCat.

✦ **Site Log** keeps track of the changes made to a Web site for team development use. By Andrew Wooldridge.

✦ **Tag Killer** removes all instances of any tag from a Web page. By Massimo Foti.

✦ **Scratch Pad** keeps snippets of code available for easy cutting and pasting on a single page or across Web sites. By Andrew Wooldridge.

✦ **Borderless Frames** sets all frames in a frameset to no borders. By Massimo Foti.

✦ **Quick Site** prototypes a simple Web site by creating files and generating a navigation bar to all pages. By Andrew Wooldridge.

✦ **Replicator** duplicates any selected element any number of times. By this book's author, Joseph Lowery.

As should be obvious from this list, commands come close to being limited only by the author's imagination. The next section takes a brief look at the commands that ship with Dreamweaver 2 and their uses.

Dreamweaver 2 ships with five standard commands that, in addition to adding some extra functionality, give you a taste of just how powerful commands can be:

✦ **Clean Up HTML** removes unnecessary or redundant HTML for a smaller file size and more readable code.

✦ **Apply Source Formatting** styles the HTML in Web pages created outside of Dreamweaver to resemble Dreamweaver-created code.

✦ **Set Color Scheme** selects the colors for the current page's background, text, and link states.

✦ **Sort Table** performs a one- or two-level sort on any table, using any column in an ascending or descending manner.

✦ **Format Table** applies one of 17 different predesigned formats or any designated custom format to the selected table.

Cross-Reference

Three of the standard commands are described in detail elsewhere in the book. A description of Set Color Scheme can be found in Chapter 6, "Understanding How HTML Works" and the two Table commands are covered in Chapter 11, "Setting Up Tables."

The Clean Up HTML command

Even if you never open the HTML Inspector or touch the code in an external editor, your HTML can still become unwieldy. One of the most common problems is redundant `<font>` tags that result from doing something like selecting some text and then first changing the font itself, and next the font size, and finally the font color. This is likely to give you code that resembles the following:

```
<font face="Arial"><font size="4"><font
color="green">Bonanza!</font></font></font>
```

The Clean Up HTML command is, quite literally, custom made to consolidate code like this and remove some of the code clutter that can accumulate during a page's design. In all, you have six different cleansing operations from which to choose. The Clean Up HTML command is only applicable to the current page and cannot be applied sitewide.

To use the Clean Up HTML command, follow these steps:

1. Choose Commands ➪ Clean Up HTML.

   The Clean Up HTML dialog box appears, as shown in Figure 19-1.

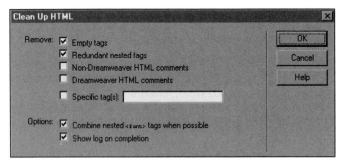

Figure 19-1: Reduce your page's file size and make your HTML more readable with the Clean Up HTML command.

2. To delete tag pairs with no code between them (such as `<i></i>`), make sure the Remove: Empty Tags option is selected.

3. To eliminate superfluous tags that repeat the same code as the tags surrounding them, as in this example:

   ```
   <font color="white">And the <font color="white">truth</font>
   is plain to see.</font>
   ```

   choose the Remove: Redundant Tags option.

4. To delete any HTML comments not created by Dreamweaver to mark a Library or Template item, choose Remove: Non-Dreamweaver HTML Comments.

5. To clear all Dreamweaver specific comments, such as:

```
<! #BeginEditable "openingPara" -->
```

select the Remove: Dreamweaver HTML Comments option.

6. To erase any specific tag and its attributes, select the Remove: Specific Tag(s) option and enter the tag name(s) in the text box.

Note   Tag names are entered without angle brackets; separate multiple tags with a comma.

7. To consolidate `<font>` tags, select the Combine Nested `<font>` Tags When Possible option.

8. To view a report of the changes applied to your document, select the Show Log on Completion option.

9. Click OK when you're done.

Dreamweaver performs the actions requested on the current document. If the Show Log option has been selected, an alert displays the changes made, if any.

The Apply Source Formatting command

All the code created by Dreamweaver is structured according to a document called the Source Format Profile. The Source Format Profile controls which codes are indented and which are on their own line, as well as numerous other specifications of HTML writing. Occasionally, a Web designer must work with Web pages created earlier or by other designers using other programs, or even by hand. The Apply Source Formatting command can rewrite the original code so that it is structured according to the current Source Format Profile. The more accustomed your eye is to following Dreamweaver-style HTML, the more you'll value this command.

Cross-Reference   To learn more about the Source Format Profile, see Chapter 3, "Setting Your Preferences."

The Apply Source Formatting command is an example of a Dreamweaver command that doesn't display a dialog box to gather the user's selected parameters — because there are no parameters to set. To invoke the command, choose Commands ➪ Apply Source Formatting. The command is applied immediately, with no confirmation or feedback offered indicating that it is complete.

Tip   The Clean Up HTML and Apply Source Formatting commands make a powerful toolset. Together, these two commands are especially useful at simplifying HTML pages created in word-processing programs like Microsoft Word.

Creating commands

Commands, like most behaviors, are a combination of JavaScript functions and HTML forms; the HTML provides the user interface for any parameters that need to be set and the JavaScript carries out the particular command. Although you can combine both languages in a single HTML file, many programmers, including those from Macromedia, keep the JavaScript in a separate .js file that is incorporated in the HTML file with a ⟨script⟩ tag, like this one:

```
<SCRIPT LANGUAGE="javascript" SRC="Clean Up HTML.js">
```

This separation enables easy modification of the user interface and the underlying code, and the sharing of the JavaScript functions.

Commands are very open-ended. In fact, only two Dreamweaver functions are specific to Commands — canAcceptCommand() and commandButtons() — and neither function is required.

Cross-
Reference

The DOM in Dreamweaver is covered in great detail in Chapter 18, "Creating a Behavior."

The canAcceptCommand() function controls when the command is active in the menus and when it is ghosted. If canAcceptCommand() is not defined, the command is always available. This function returns True or False; if False is returned, the command is ghosted in the menus.

You can see canAcceptCommand() in action in both the Sort Table and Format Table commands. For either of these commands to be effective, a table must be indicated. Rather than require that a table be selected, the canAcceptCommand() function calls a subroutine, findTable(), which returns true if the user's cursor is positioned inside a table:

```
function canAcceptCommand(){
  if (findTable())
    return true;
  else
    return false;
}

function findTable(){
  var tableObj="";
  var selArr = dreamweaver.getSelection();
  var selObj = dreamweaver.offsetsToNode(selArr[0],selArr[1]);

  while (tableObj=="" && selObj.parentNode){
    if (selObj.nodeType == Node.ELEMENT_NODE &&
selObj.tagName=="TABLE")
    tableObj=selObj;
  else
    selObj = selObj.parentNode;
  }
```

```
    return tableObj;
}
```

Macromedia recommends that the `canAcceptCommand()` function not be defined unless there is at least one case in which the command should not be available. Otherwise, the function is asked to run for no purpose, which degrades performance.

The `commandButtons()` function defines the buttons that appear on the parameter form to the right. This expanded functionality is extremely useful when developing commands. Some commands require that an operation be allowed to run repeatedly and not just the one time an OK button is selected. As noted earlier, you don't have to declare the function at all, in which case the form expands to fill the dialog box entirely.

Each button that is declared has a function associated with it, which is executed when the user selects that particular button. All the buttons for a command are listed in an array, returned by `commandButtons()`. The following example declares three buttons: OK, Cancel, and Help:

```
function commandButtons() {
   return new
Array("OK","goCommand()","Cancel","window.close()","Help","disp
layHelp()")
}
```

Notice that two of the buttons, OK and Help, call custom functions; but the Cancel button simply calls a built-in JavaScript function to close the window. There are no real limitations to the number of buttons a command can hold other than user interface design sense.

The remainder of the user interface for a command — the parameter form — is constructed in the same manner, using the same tools as objects and behaviors. A command parameter form or dialog box uses an HTML `<form>` in the `<body>` of the file. If no `<form>` is declared, the command executes without displaying a dialog box. All of the form elements used in objects — text boxes, radio buttons, check-boxes, and lists — are available in commands.

Cross-Reference For detailed information about how to retrieve information in a parameter form, see Chapter 16, "Creating and Using Objects."

Dreamweaver Techniques: Useful command routines

Quite often when programming a command, I'll get stuck on one small point. "If only I knew how to _____ , I'd be home free," is my usual refrain. The following routines and explanations are presented in the interest of helping you to "fill in the blank" as you begin to construct your own custom commands.

Getting a user's selection

Although many commands work with the entire HTML document, some require just a portion of text or an object that has been selected by the user. While it seems like a simple task, some quirks in the API make getting a selection a little tricky.

Selecting text

The usual method for finding out—and acting on—what the user has selected requires the getSelection() function. As discussed in Chapter 18, "Creating a Behavior," getSelection() returns two byte offsets that mark the beginning and end of the user's selection. The difficulty appears when you try to extract the character data that corresponds to those byte offsets. The offsetsToNode() function, which is used to make this translation, expands the offsets to the nearest tag—the innerHTML, in other words. For example, the following function attempts to get the user's selection and report it, in an alert:

```
function testCase() {
 var theDom = dreamweaver.getDocumentDOM("document");
 var offsets = dreamweaver.getSelection()
 var theNode = dreamweaver.offsetsToNode(offsets[0],offsets[1])
 var nodeText = theNode.data
 alert(nodeText)
}
```

If a user selects the word "grey" in the paragraph "The old grey mare just ain't what she used to be," the function returns the entire line. In order get just what is selected, you need to use the nodeToOffsets() function in combination with offsetsToNode() and the JavaScript substring() function.

The example code in Listing 19-1 demonstrates the proper substring technique; it is taken from the Change Case command, included on the CD-ROM:

Listing 19-1: **Getting Selected Text**

```
function lowerCase(){
 var theDom=dreamweaver.getDocumentDOM("document");
 var offsets = dreamweaver.getSelection()
 var theNode = dreamweaver.offsetsToNode(offsets[0],offsets[1])
 if (theNode.nodeType == Node.TEXT_NODE) {
 var nodeOffsets = dreamweaver.nodeToOffsets(theNode)
 offsets[0] = offsets[0]-nodeOffsets[0]
 offsets[1] = offsets[1]-nodeOffsets[0]
 var nodeText = theNode.data
 theNode.data = nodeText.substring(0,offsets[0]) +
  nodeText.substring(offsets[0], offsets[1]).toLowerCase() +
  nodeText.substring(offsets[1], nodeText.length);
 window.close()
 } else { //it's not a TEXT_NODE
 var nodeOffsets = dreamweaver.nodeToOffsets(theNode)
```

```
offsets[0] = offsets[0]-nodeOffsets[0]
offsets[1] = offsets[1]-nodeOffsets[0]
var nodeText = theNode.innerHTML
theNode.innerHTML = nodeText.toLowerCase()
window.close()
  }
}
```

In the example function, you'll notice two conditions — either the selected string is text (a TEXT_NODE) or it's not. If the node is something other than a TEXT_NODE, the `data` property is not available and `innerHTML` must be used instead. This situation occurs when a user selects an entire paragraph. In fact, all the user has to select is the last character before the closing tag — such as a period at the end of a paragraph — and the node type switches to ELEMENT_NODE.

Selecting objects

By comparison, you have far fewer hoops to jump through to reference a selected object. To find a selected object, you only need to get its `outerHTML` property, as shown in Listing 19-2.

Listing 19-2: **Getting a Selected Object**

```
function replicate(){
  var theDom = dreamweaver.getDocumentDOM("document");
  var offsets = dreamweaver.getSelection()
  var selObj = dreamweaver.offsetsToNode(offsets[0],offsets[1])
  if (selObj.nodeType == Node.TEXT_NODE) {
    helpMe2()
    window.close()
    return;
  }
  var theCode = selObj.outerHTML
```

Listing 19-2 also includes a small error routine that looks to see if the user's selection is text (`selObj.nodeType == Node.TEXT_NODE`) and if so, puts up an advisory and then closes the window to allow the user to reselect.

Using a command as an object

Commands offer a tremendous range of power and can perform actions not available to behaviors or objects. To take advantage of this power with a point-and-click interface, it's best to "disguise" your command as an object. As an object, your command appears in both the Objects Palette and the Insert menu.

Usually, a Dreamweaver object consists of two files: an HTML file for the code and a GIF image for the button, all in the Object folder. When using a command as an object, however, you can have as many as five files split between the Object and Command folder. The standard Rollover object is a good example: there are three associated Rollover files in the Object folder and two in the Command folder. Here is how they are used:

✦ **Object\Rollover.gif.** The image for the Rollover button that appears in the Objects Palette

✦ **Object\Rollover.htm.** A shell file (called by the Rollover button) that reads Object\Rollover.js

✦ **Object\Rollover.js.** Contains the `objectTag()` function, which references the Command\Rollover.htm file

✦ **Command\Rollover.htm.** Builds the user interface for the "object" and reads all external JavaScript files, including Command\Rollover.js

✦ **Command\Rollover.js.** Contains the actual code for the function that performs the required operations, which returns its value to the Object\Rollover.htm file by way of the Object\Rollover.js file

The key to understanding how to use a command as an object is the code linking the two. In the Object\Rollover.js file, you'll find the `objectTag()`, which is used to write an object into an existing Web page with its return value. In this case, the function first gets the Document Object Model of the relevant Command file (Command\Rollover.htm); this procedure allows the current function to reference any variable set in the other file. Then the `popupCommand` is executed, which runs Command\Rollover.htm — which in turn launches the dialog box and gets the user parameters. Finally, a result from that command is set to the return value of `objectTag()` and written into the HTML page. Here's the `objectTag()` function in its entirety from Object\Rollover.js:

```
function objectTag() {
    var rolloverCmdURL = dreamweaver.getConfigurationPath() +
"/Commands/Rollover.htm";
    var rolloverDoc    = dreamweaver.getDocumentDOM(
rolloverCmdURL );
    dreamweaver.popupCommand( "Rollover.htm" );
    return( rolloverDoc.parentWindow.getRolloverTag() );
}
```

Some custom commands disguised as objects make the DOM connection in the command file, rather than the object file. The iCat objects, for example, all establish the link in the primary functions of their command JavaScript files, in this manner:

```
    var dom = dreamweaver.getDocumentDOM("../Objects/iCat/Add To
Cart.htm");
    dom.parentWindow.icatTagStr = icatTagStr;
```

Then, the corresponding `objectTag()` function simply returns the `icatTagStr` variable.

Placing code in the `<head>` section

It's fairly straightforward to insert text wherever the cursor has been set in the document—you just set a text string equal to the [`innerHTML` | `data`] property of the DOM at that point. But how do you insert code in the `<head>` section of a Web page where the cursor is generally not found? Certain code, such as `<script>` tags that hold extensive JavaScript functions, needs to be inserted in the `<head>`. By design, behaviors return code specifically intended for the `<script>` tag—except you can't easily use a behavior to include a line like

```
<script language="Javascript" src="extend.js"></script>
```

You can insert such a line with commands, however; and this technique, developed by Dreamweaver extensions author Massimo Foti, shows the way.

Unfortunately, no equivalent to the .body property exists in the Dreamweaver DOM for the `<head>` section. The way around this minor limitation is to first locate the sole `<head>` tag in a document. This task can be accomplished in two lines of JavaScript code:

```
theDom = dreamweaver.getDocumentDOM("document")
theHeadNode = theDom.getElementsByTagName("HEAD")
```

Now the script variable needs to be set. Whenever Dreamweaver encounters a closing `<script>` tag (such as `</script>`) in a JavaScript function, the tag is flagged because it seems to be missing a mate. To avoid this problem, split the tag up into two concatenated strings, like this:

```
theScript = '<script language="Javascript"
src="extend.js"><scr' + 'ipt>'
```

Finally, find the first item in the `<head>` section and append the script to its `innerHTML` property:

```
theHeadNode.item(0).innerHTML = theHeadNode.item(0).innerHTML +
theScript
```

The full function looks like this:

```
function insertScript() {
  var theDom, theHeadNode, theScript
  theDom = dreamweaver.getDocumentDOM("document")
  theHeadNode = theDom.getElementsByTagName("HEAD")
  theScript = '<script language="Javascript"
src="extend.js"><scr' + 'ipt>'
}
```

You'll find numerous examples of Massimo Foti's commands and other extensions on the CD-ROM. Just look in the Configuration folder under Commands, Actions, and Objects.

Using commands to call other commands

In the earlier section "Using a command as an object," the `popupCommand()` function plays a key role. It's worth emphasizing that this same function is used when you want one command to invoke another command. The proper syntax is

```
var doNew = popupCommand("commandFileName")
```

where *commandFileName* is the name of an HTML file in the Command folder. No value is returned with `popupCommand()`; the function just executes whatever command is called. The called command's dialog box is presented and must be completed or canceled before the originating command is able to continue.

Creating a blank document

Commands aren't limited to working on the current document — you can use a command to read, modify, and even create new files. Any new file created using the `createDocument()` function is an HTML page based on the Default.htm file found in the Configuration\Templates folder — this is the same file used as the base for any files created when File ⇨ New is chosen.

Occasionally, however, a command needs to make a new non-HTML document, such as an XML or SMIL file or other file type that doesn't use the `<html>`...`</html>` structure. To accomplish this task, you first create an HTML file and then replace its entire contents with your own data — or nothing at all. The following custom function, developed by Andrew Wooldridge, makes and saves a new, blank text file:

```
function doNew() {
var newDOM = dreamweaver.createDocument();
var theDoc = newDOM.documentElement;
theDoc.outerHTML = ".";
theDoc.innerHTML = " ";
dreamweaver.saveDocument(newDOM, '../../empty.txt');
}
```

Remember, all the Dreamweaver document functions — such as `saveDocument()` — use addresses relative to the file calling them. For example, if the `doNew()` function just described is included in a command, and therefore stored in the Commands folder, the empty.txt document will be saved two folders above the Commands folder or in the Dreamweaver root directory, as the full path to the Commands folder is Dreamweaver\Configuration\Commands.

You'll find a command incorporating this technique on the CD-ROM along with many others by Andrew Wooldridge. Andrew has a deep understanding of commands and continually stretches the boundaries of what they can accomplish.

Commands from a Developer's Developer

Hava Edelstein, a JavaScript engineer with Macromedia, has contributed five commands especially valuable for developers. You'll find them on the CD-ROM under her name, as well as on her Web site (www.hava.com). Here is an overview of these very useful commands:

✦ **Eval.** This command allows you to quickly spot check JavaScript statements and perform one-time alterations to your document. A must-have for the serious command developer.

✦ **Show Browser References.** Navigator and Internet Explorer handle objects references — especially those objects in layers — quite differently. This command allows you to select any object on the page and then find its proper JavaScript reference, which can be easily cut-and-pasted into your code.

✦ **Show Document Tree.** Want to see how the current document is structured from a DOM point of view? Run this command to create a new document with all the details, most notably the Node_Type of each node. Included in this command is a very useful subroutine, traverseNodes(), which travels recursively through a document's nodes.

✦ **Set All Checkboxes.** If you've ever had to work with a large form with many check-boxes, you'll appreciate this command. Each check-box on the page is presented and can be set as checked or unchecked. Of special note to programmers is the included function, setSingleWordAttribute(), which allows an attribute such as hidden or checked to be set; this functionality is not present in the standard Dreamweaver function setAttribute().

✦ **Show Table Properties.** While the ability to display the properties of a selected table may not seem all that compelling, it's what's under the hood here that counts. This command encompasses three useful utility functions: getTagAttributes(), stripQuotesIfTheyExist(), and deleteExtraWhiteSpace().

You'll find all of Hava's commands to be heavily commented and very worthwhile for programmers of any level.

Changing the command order

In order to run a command, you must access it through the menu or a keyboard shortcut. Unlike Dreamweaver objects, commands have no floating palette to choose from. The Command menu is structured by an HTML file named, appropriately enough, CommandMenu.htm. The CommandMenu.htm file is similar to the InsertMenu.htm and also consists of a series of list items to represent the menu items. Here's the code for the standard CommandMenu file:

```
• Clean Up HTML, ,Clean Up HTML.htm
• Apply Source Formatting, ,Apply Source Formatting.htm
• -----
• Set Color Scheme, ,Set Color Scheme.htm
```

- `- - - - -`
- `Sort Table, ,Sort Table.htm`
- `Format Table, ,Format Table.htm`
- `, ,Rollover.htm`

Each unordered list item has three parts, separated by commas: the command name, the keyboard shortcut (if any), and the HTML file with the code for the command. Separators, in the form of a dashed line are used to group items; the number of dashes is irrelevant, as long as the first character is a hyphen.

Tip   In Windows systems, you can also select the mnemonic that appears underlined in the menu. To do this, select the letter you want to act as the mnemonic in the unordered list and choose Text ⇨ Style ⇨ Underline.

To group commands under a submenu, use an indented unordered list. You can easily indent a grouping by selecting the list items and then choosing Text ⇨ Indent or selecting the Indent button on the Property Inspector. Here's the code for a grouping installed with the iCat e-commerce objects (not all objects installed are shown here):

```
<li>----------</li>
<li><u>i</u>Cat
  <ul>
    <li>Sign<u>u</u>p, , iCat Signup.htm</li>
    <li><u>S</u>ynchronize, , iCatSynchronize.htm</li>
    <li><u>E</u>dit Store, , iCat Edit Store.htm</li>
    <li></li>
  </ul>
```

Any changes made to the CommandMenu.htm file do not take effect until Dreamweaver is restarted.

Hiding commands

If the command name is omitted as the first of the three parts of a list item, as is the case with Rollover.htm in the standard CommandMenu.htm file, the command is not shown on the menu. Why would you want to hide a command? If a command is intended to be called from another Dreamweaver custom extension, such as an object or a behavior, you hide the command from the menu so that it is not accessed inappropriately. Any command not explicitly hidden by listing only `filename` in the CommandMenu.htm file is added dynamically to the bottom portion of the Command menu.

The hiding technique is used extensively in third-party objects that rely heavily on commands, but require the Objects Palette for ease of use.

Adding commands to other menus

Commands have the potential to affect virtually every design operation; you're not limited to listing them just in the Command menu — you can add a command to any other existing menu as well. Moreover, commands can appear in an existing submenu or you can create their own. The key to making a command appear on a different menu is to create a separate unordered list in the CommandMenu.htm file, after the command listing.

The existing menu items are specified in the followings format:

```
topLevelMenuItem | menuItem | subMenuItem
```

The *topLevelMenuItem* variable is one of the existing primary menu categories: File, Edit, View, and so on. The *menuItem* variable refers to an existing menu item under a given category, such as Convert (under the File menu). The *subMenuItem* variable is an existing submenu under the specified *menuItem*, such as Tables to Layers under Convert; the *subMenuItem* variable is optional. For example, to cause the custom command Replicator to appear under the File ⇨ Convert ⇨ Tables to Layers menu item, as shown in Figure 19-2, I would include a separate unordered list in the CommandMenu.htm file, like this:

```
<p>File | Convert | Tables to Layers</p>
<ul>
  <li>----</li>
  <li>Replicator, , Replicator.htm</li>
  <li>----</li>
</ul>
```

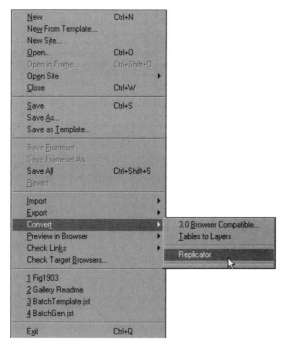

Figure 19-2: You can display custom commands from standard menus by altering the CommandMenu.htm file.

The menu item variables designating where the command should appear can either be a name or a number. The `topLevelMenuItem` is numbered 1 through 9, where 1 is File, 2 is Edit, and so on. When using numbers to represent `menuItems` and `subMenuItems` (such as Undo, Redo, etc.), positive numbers are counted from the top of the menu strip; negative numbers are counted from the bottom. For example, to cause a new command to appear under the View ⇨ Invisible Elements menu, specify 3 | 2 or `View` | 2 as the heading for the separate unordered list. If a zero is used, commands are inserted at the top of a menu; and if a -1 is used, at the bottom.

Tip   It's also possible to cause Dreamweaver objects to appear in menus other than Insert by applying this same technique to the InsertMenu.htm file.

Working with Custom Tags

With the advent of XML — where there are no standard tags — an ability to handle custom tags is essential in a Web authoring tool. Dreamweaver 2 adds this ability through its third-party tag feature. After you've defined a third-party tag, Dreamweaver displays it in the Document Window by highlighting its content, inserting a user-defined icon, or neither. Third-party tags are easily selected through the Tag Selector on the status bar and, thus, easy to cut, copy, and paste or otherwise manipulate. Perhaps most important, once a third-party tag is defined, you can apply a custom Property Inspector that permits tag attributes to be entered in a standardized user interface.

New Feature   Third-party tags can now be defined directly within Dreamweaver 2. Just as Object files use HTML to structure HTML code for easy insertion, Dreamweaver uses XML to make an XML definition for the custom tag. A custom tag declaration consists solely of one tag, `<tagspec>`, with up to seven attributes. The attributes for `<tagspec>` are as follows:

✦ **tag_name.** Defines the name of the tag as used in the markup. Any valid name — no spaces or special characters allowed — is possible. A tag with the attribute `tag_name="invoice"` is entered in the document as `<invoice>`.

✦ **tag_type.** Determines whether the tag has a closing tag (`nonempty`) and is thus capable of enclosing content or if the tag describes the content itself (`empty`). For example, the `<invoice>` tag could have a `tag_type="nonempty"` because all the content is between `<invoice>` and `</invoice>`.

✦ **render_contents.** Sets whether the contents of a non-empty type tag are displayed or not. The `render_contents` attribute value is either `true` or `false`; if `false`, the tag's icon is displayed instead of the contents.

✦ **content_model.** Establishes valid placement and content for the tag in the document. The three possible options are as follows:

- **block_model.** Tags defined with `content_model="block_model"` only appear in the `<body>` section of a document and contain block-level HTML tags, such as `<p>`, `<div>`, `<blockquote>`, and `<pre>`.

- **head_model.** To define a tag that appears in the `<head>` section and can contain text, set `content_model="head_model"`.

- **marker_model.** Tags with the attribute `content_model=marker_model` are capable of being placed anywhere in the document with no restrictions on content. The `marker_model` value is most often used for inline tags that are placed within a paragraph or division.

✦ **icon.** Empty tags or non-empty custom tags with the `render_content` disabled require a GIF file to act as an icon in the Document Window. The icon attribute should be set to any valid URL, relative or absolute (as in `icon="images/invoice.gif"`).

✦ **icon_width.** Sets the width in pixels of the icon used to represent the tag. The value can be any positive integer.

✦ **icon_height.** Sets the height in pixels of the icon used to represent the tag. The value can be any positive integer.

Tip   The icons used by Dreamweaver to represent the Invisible Elements such as the `<br>` tag are 16 pixels wide by 14 pixels high.

Here's the complete code for a sample custom tag, the Cold Fusion Directory tag:

```
<tagspec tag_name="CFDIRECTORY" tag_type="empty"
render_contents="false" content_model="marker_model"
icon="ColdFusion.gif" icon_width="16"
icon_height="16"></tagspec>
```

You can see an example of the Cold Fusion custom tags in Figure 19-3.

Note   If the content is to be rendered for a custom tag, you can easily view it in the Document Window by enabling the Third-Party Tags Highlighting option in Preferences. Make sure that View ➪ Invisible Elements is enabled.

Once a custom tag is defined, the definition is saved in an XML file in the ThirdPartyTags folder, found in the Configuration directory. If you are establishing a number of custom tags, you can place all the definitions in the same file. Macromedia refers to this as the Tag DB or Database.

On the CD-ROM   Andrew Wooldridge has created an extremely useful command called Build_Custom_Tag for defining XML third-party tags. You'll find it in the Configuration\Commands folder of the CD-ROM.

Custom icon   Highlighted content for Third-Party Tags

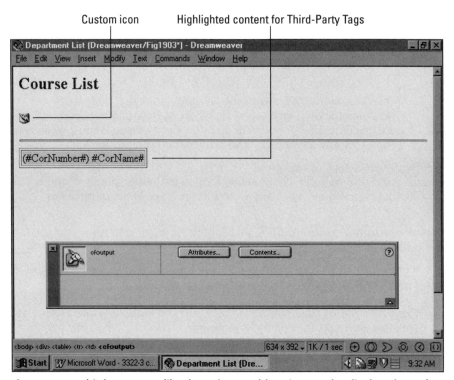

Figure 19-3: Third-party tags like these from Cold Fusion can be displayed — and manipulated — in the Document Window.

Customizing Property Inspectors

The Property Inspector is used throughout Dreamweaver to display the current attributes of many different types of tags: text, images, layers, plug-ins, and so on. Not only do Property Inspectors make it easy to see the particulars for an object, they make it a snap to modify the same parameters. With the addition of custom tags in Dreamweaver 2, the ability to add custom Property Inspectors is a natural parallel. Moreover, you can create custom Property Inspectors for existing tags, which display in place of the built-in Property Inspectors.

New Feature

Like objects, commands, and behaviors, custom Property Inspectors are composed of HTML and JavaScript; the Property Inspector HTML file itself is stored in the Configuration\Inspectors folder. However, the layout of the Property Inspector is far more restrictive than it is with the other Dreamweaver extensions. The dialog box for an object, command, or behavior can be any size or shape desired — any custom Property Inspector must fit the standard Property Inspector dimensions and design. Because of the precise positioning necessary to insert parameter form items such as text boxes and drop-down menu lists, layers are used extensively to create the layout.

Quite elaborate Property Inspectors are possible. The XSSI IF Property Inspector built by Webmonkey, shown in Figure 19-4, has three separate tabs (based on layers) for accessing different possible parameters of the object. Property Inspectors, like other extension types, can also incorporate CSS styles, Flash movies, and Shockwave files.

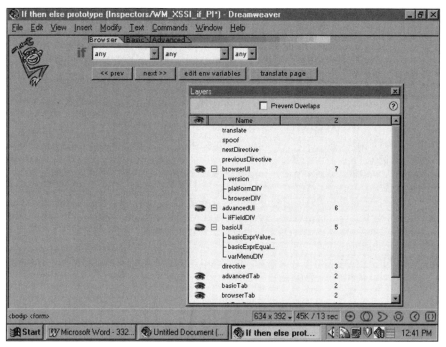

Figure 19-4: Some custom Property Inspectors, like this one from Webmonkey, take advantage of Dreamweaver's layer and CSS styles support.

Coding a Property Inspector

Like many of the other standard extension files, most of the Property Inspector files that ship with Dreamweaver 2 are composed of an HTML file that calls a separate JavaScript file. It is entirely possible, however, to combine HTML and JavaScript into a single file. No matter how it's structured, a custom Property Inspector HTML file needs three key elements to be properly defined:

✦ An initial HTML comment line that identifies which tag the Property Inspector is for.

✦ The function `canInspectSelection()`, which determines if the Property Inspector should be displayed according to the current selection.

✦ A second function, `inspectSelection()`, that updates the tag's HTML when new values are entered in the Property Inspector.

If any of these elements are missing or incorrectly declared, Dreamweaver ignores the file and does not display the Property Inspector.

Cross-Reference

In addition to the mandatory functions and definition, custom Property Inspectors are capable of using any of the other Dreamweaver JavaScript functions described in Chapter 18, "Creating a Behavior," with the exception of the `getBehaviorTag()` and `getBehaviorElement` functions. If you include the `displayHelp()` function, a small question mark in a circle appears in the upper-right corner of your custom Property Inspector, which, when selected by the user, executes whatever routines your Help function has declared.

The Property Inspector definition

The initial HTML comment — placed above the `<html>` tag — defines the Property Inspector. More than one Property Inspector can be defined for a particular tag, making it possible for separate Inspectors to be used if different attributes are specified. Therefore, each Property Inspector is assigned a priority that determines the one to be displayed. Property Inspectors are further defined by whether the current selection is within the tag indicated or contains the entire tag; this feature enables two different Property Inspectors to be defined, as with the `<table>` tag. Finally, optional graphic elements are definable: a horizontal line to delineate the upper and lower portions of a Property Inspector, and a vertical line to separate the object's name from the other parts of the Property Inspector.

The Property Inspector definition follows this syntax:

```
<!-- tag:ID,priority:Number,selection:Type,hline,vline -->
```

For example, the Property Inspector for the `<link>` tag (a `<head>` element) is defined like this:

```
<!-- tag:LINK,priority:5,selection:within,vline,hline -->
```

The individual sections of the definition are as follows:

✦ **tag.** The name of the tag for which the Property Inspector is intended. Although it's not mandatory, the tag name is customarily uppercased. The tag ID can also be one of three keywords: *COMMENT*, when a comment class tag is indicated; *LOCKED*, when a locked region is to be inspected; or *ASP*, for all ASP elements.

Note

The asterisks on either side of the tag keywords are mandatory.

✦ **priority.** The priority of a Property Inspector is given as a number from 1 to 10. The highest priority, 10, means that this Property Inspector takes precedence over any other possible Property Inspectors. The lowest priority, 1, marks the Property Inspector as the one to use when no other Property Inspector is available.

Note An example of how `priority` is used can be found in the `<meta>` tag and the Description and Keyword objects. The Property Inspectors for Description and Keyword have a higher priority than the one for the basic `<meta>` tag, which permits those Inspectors to be shown initially if the proper criteria is met; if the criteria is *not* met, the Property Inspector for the `<meta>` tag is displayed.

✦ **selection.** Depending on the current selection, the cursor is either within a particular tag or exactly enclosing it. The `selection` attribute is set to `within` or `exact`, according to the condition under which the Property Inspector should be displayed.

✦ **hline.** Inserts a one-pixel horizontal gray line (see Figure 19-5) dividing the upper and lower halves of the expanded Property Inspector.

✦ **vline.** Places a one-pixel vertical gray line (see Figure 19-5) between the tag's `name` field and the other properties on the upper half of the Property Inspector.

Figure 19-5: The Property Inspector for the `<img>` tag uses both the `hline` and `vline` attributes.

The canInspectSelection() function

To control the circumstances under which your custom Property Inspector is displayed, use the `canInspectSelection()` function. Like `canAcceptBehavior()` and `canAcceptCommand()` for behaviors and commands, respectively, if `canInspectSelection()` returns `true`, the Property Inspector is shown; if it returns `false`, the custom Property Inspector is not shown.

As noted earlier, the `canInspectSelection()` function is mandatory. If there are no conditions under which the Property Inspector should not be displayed, use the following code:

```
function canInspectSelection(){
  return true;
}
```

Several of the standard Dreamweaver <head> elements have Property Inspector files that use the canInspectSelection() function to limit access to specific tags. In this example, drawn from the <meta> Description object, the current selection is examined to see if a <meta> tag is selected, and the name attribute is set to description:

```
function canInspectSelection(){
  var selArr=dreamweaver.getSelection();
  var metaObj = dreamweaver.offsetsToNode(selArr[0],selArr[1]);
  return (metaObj.tagName && metaObj.tagName == "META" &&
       metaObj.getAttribute("name") &&
     metaObj.getAttribute("name").toLowerCase()=="description");
}
```

The inspectSelection() function

The inspectSelection() function is the workhorse of the custom Property Inspector code and is responsible for pulling the information from the selected tag for display in the various Property Inspector fields. Depending on the code design, the inspectSelection() function can also be used to update the HTML code when the attribute values are modified in the Property Inspector.

Here's a simple example of how the inspectSelection() function is used, drawn from the Link Property Inspector file:

```
function inspectSelection(){
  var Href = findObject("Href");

  if (linkObj.getAttribute("href"))
    Href.value=linkObj.getAttribute("href");
  else
    Href.value = "";
}
```

In this example, if an attribute (href) exists, its value is assigned to the Property Inspector's appropriate text box value (Href.value). The remainder of the inspectSelection() function for the <link> tag consists of a series of statements like those in the example code.

Tip   You can design a Property Inspector that displays a different interface depending on whether it is expanded or not, as the Keywords Property Inspector does. If an Inspector is not expanded, the argument(0) property is set to the value min; when it is expanded, argument(0) is equal to the value max.

Many Property Inspectors update their HTML tags when there is a change in one of the input boxes. There is no real standard method of accomplishing this, due to the many possible variations with Property Inspectors. However, one of the most commonly used events is onBlur(), as in this example, again taken from the Link Property Inspector file:

```
<input type="text" name="Rel" onBlur="setLinkTag()"
style="width:120">
```

The `setLinkTag()` function that is called is a local one that reads the new value in the current text box and sets it equal to the corresponding attribute.

Designing a Property Inspector

All the attributes for a Property Inspector must fit into a tightly designed space. While it's helpful to look at examples found in the Inspectors folder, many of the standard Property Inspectors are built-in to the core functionality of the program and are not immediately accessible on the design level. The following specifications and tips are offered to make it easier for you to design your own custom Property Inspectors:

✦ The full dimensions of available layout space in a Property Inspector are 482 pixels wide by 87 pixels high.

✦ The top (unexpanded) portion of the Property Inspector is 42 pixels high, while the bottom portion is 44 pixels high.

✦ If the `hline` attribute is specified in the Property Inspector definition, a single-pixel line is drawn the entire width of the Inspector, 43 pixels from the top.

✦ If the `vline` attribute is specified, a single-pixel line is drawn across the top half of the Property Inspector, 118 pixels from the left.

✦ The background color for the Property Inspector is a light gray, which translates into #D0D0D0FF in hexadecimal, or an RGB value of 208, 208, 208.

✦ The default text displayed within a Property Inspector is from the Arial, Helvetica, sans-serif font families, sized at 9 points. If you enter text with the standard Default text selected, it will be rendered in this style.

✦ The image placed on the upper left of the Property Inspector is generally sized at 36 pixels square and placed 3 pixels from the top and 2 pixels from the left. Although you are under no requirement to keep this size image — or its placement — following these guidelines will help your custom Property Inspectors to resemble the standard Dreamweaver ones.

✦ It's a good idea to lay out your Property Inspector with the View ⇨ Invisible Elements command disabled. The small icons that indicate layers can alter the perceived spacing.

✦ Keep the Layer palette visible. Many custom Property Inspectors use multiple layers to position the elements exactly — several of the Webmonkey-designed XSSI Property Inspectors employ upwards of 20 layers, as shown in Figure 19-6 — and the Layer palette makes selecting individual layers for adjustment a snap.

✦ Use nested layers to position and group associated items in the Property Inspector. Almost all form objects used in Property Inspectors for user input, such as text boxes and drop-down lists, are identified by labels. Placing both label and text boxes in their own layers, while grouping them under one parent layer, provides maximum flexibility and ease of placement.

✦ Apply CSS styles within the Property Inspector to easily manage font sizes and design your Property Inspector in a WYSIWYG environment.

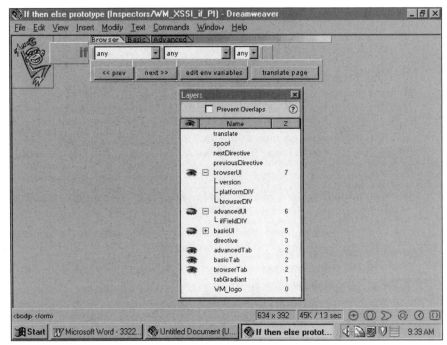

Figure 19-6: Property Inspectors, like Webmonkey's custom XSSI IF inspector, use absolute and relative layers to position layout components and toggle different options.

Translators

In order for any markup tag to be depicted in the Document Window — whether it's <b> for bold or a custom third-party tag like Tango's <@cols> — it must be *translated*. Dreamweaver's built-in rendering system translates all the standard HTML code, along with a few special custom tags like those for ASP and Cold Fusion. However, in order to display any other custom tags, or those that perform special functions such as server-side includes, a special translator must be built.

New Feature

As part of its expansion efforts, Dreamweaver 2 permits the inclusion of custom translators. This enhancement allows programs that output non-standard HTML to be displayed on screen integrated with the regular code. One of Dreamweaver's main claims to fame is its ability to accept code without rewriting it. Now, with Dreamweaver 2 translators, custom code can not only be inserted, it can be shown — and edited — visually.

Here's a brief overview of how translators work:

1. When Dreamweaver starts, all the properly coded translators in the Configuration\Translators folder are initialized.

2. If a document is loaded with non-standard HTML, the code is checked against the installed translators.

3. The Translator Preferences are examined. Should the translator in question be set for automatic translation, the next step is carried through. Otherwise, the translation does not take place until the user chooses Modify ⇨ Translate ⇨ *TranslatorName*.

4. The code is processed with the translator and temporarily converted to a format acceptable to Dreamweaver.

5. Dreamweaver renders the code on screen.

6. If a change is made to the page, Dreamweaver retranslates the document and refreshes the screen. (There are numerous other conditions under which Dreamweaver translates a page, all of which are detailed in the following section, "Enabling Translators.")

7. When the page is saved, the temporary translation is discarded and the original code, with any modifications, is stored.

In the short time that Dreamweaver 2 has been available, developers have broken new ground with the use of translators. Some of the translators that have been developed so far include those for the following:

✦ **Server-Side Includes.** Standard with Dreamweaver 2, the SSI translator effortlessly inserts at design time files that you normally don't see until delivered by the Web server. (To learn more about SSI, see Chapter 32, "Using the Repeating Elements Library.")

✦ **XSSI.** The Extended Server-Side Include (XSSI) extension, developed by Webmonkey authors Alx, Nadav, and Taylor for Macromedia, includes a translator that brings the Apache-served code right in the Document Window. (See the XSSI sidebar in Chapter 32, "Using the Repeating Elements Library.")

✦ **Live Picture.** The code for a Live Picture graphic, which allows for panning and zooming, is structured inside a `<meta>` tag. The translator for this code incorporates a temporary JPEG representation of the more detailed image in the page for a smoother design session. (You'll find details on the Live Picture enhancement in Chapter 28, "Adding Multimedia Code Through SMIL.")

✦ **Tango.** Developed by Pervasive Software, the Tango translator compensates for differences between their database-oriented code and standard HTML. Additionally, Tango includes a manually controlled Sample Data translator that enables the Web designer to view the page complete with example database output. (Tango is covered in Chapter 29, "Dynamic Database Content.")

Enabling translators

As noted earlier, you can determine when you want a particular translator to do its job. Translation can be fully automatic or completely manual — or one of several states in between. You can even determine the order in which the translators look at a page. All of these features are controlled by the Translation panel in the Dreamweaver Preferences dialog box.

Some extensions handle the translator setup automatically; others require that you specify certain translation options before the custom translator is fully enabled. To access the Translator controls, choose Edit ➪ Preferences and select the Translation category. The Translation panel, as shown in Figure 19-7, appears.

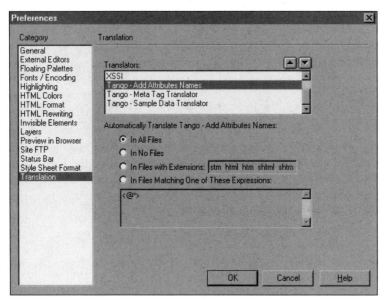

Figure 19-7: Setting your Translation preferences gives you control over results appearing in the Document Window.

There are four basic possibilities for automatic translation to occur:

✦ **In All Files.** Translation takes place whenever a modification or other qualifying condition (as noted in the following section) takes place.

✦ **In No Files.** The user must select the proper Translate command from the menu.

✦ **In Files with Extensions.** Translation is limited to specific file types, as identified by their file extension.

✦ **In Files Matching One of These Expressions.** Translation takes place only if the code includes one of the Regular Expressions listed. (Regular Expressions are a Find and Replace technology discussed in Chapter 7, "Adding Text to Your Web Page.")

Sometimes it's necessary for one translator to set the stage for another. In these cases, you can select a particular translator from the list and use the up and down arrows to move it higher or lower on the list. The higher translators are invoked before the lower ones.

For all but the manual option (In No Files), the translation is triggered by any of the following events in Dreamweaver:

✦ A file is opened

✦ A change is made in the HTML Inspector and then refreshed in the Document Window

✦ An object is inserted through the Objects Palette or the Insert menu

✦ The Document Window is updated after a change to the current file has occurred in another application such as HomeSite or BBEdit

✦ A dependent file, such as an image, is edited and the modifications are stored

✦ The `innerHTML` or `outerHTML` property of any tag object, or the data property of any comment object, is set in a DOM-related JavaScript function

✦ The properties of an object are altered

✦ Any of the conversion or layout commands are chosen: Convert ⇨ 3.0 Browser Compatible; Convert ⇨ Tables to Layers; Layout ⇨ Reposition Content Using Layers; or Layout ⇨ Convert Tables to Layers

To manually trigger a translation, choose Modify ⇨ Translate ⇨ *TranslatorName,* where *TranslatorName* is any of the installed custom translators.

Translator functions

Like other Dreamweaver extensions such as behaviors and commands, translators are HTML files with JavaScript. Because there is no user interface for a translator — other than deciding when to invoke it, there are no parameters to set or options to choose from; all the pertinent code is in the `<head>` section of a translator. In the translator's `<head>`, along with any necessary support routines, you'll find two essential JavaScript functions: `getTranslatorInfo()` and `translateMarkup()`. Any other Dreamweaver JavaScript API functions not specific to behaviors can be used in a translator as well.

Note   Due to the limitations of JavaScript, much of the heart of custom translation is handled by specially written C-level Extensions. These compiled code libraries enhance Dreamweaver's capabilities so that new data types can be integrated. C-level Extensions are covered later in this chapter.

The getTranslatorInfo() function

The settings that appear for each selected translator in the Translation panel of Preferences are determined by the getTranslatorInfo() function. The function itself simply sets up and returns an array of text strings that are read by Dreamweaver during initialization.

The structure of the array is fairly rigid. The number of array elements is specified when the Array variable is declared, and a particular text string must correspond to the proper array element. The array order is as follows:

✦ **translatorClass.** The Translator's unique name used in JavaScript functions. The name has to begin with a letter and can contain alphanumeric characters as well as hyphens or underscores.

✦ **title.** The title listed in the menu and the Translation panel. This text string can be no longer than 40 characters.

✦ **nExtensions.** The number of file extensions, such as .cfml, to follow. This declaration tells Dreamweaver how to read the next portion of the array. If this value is set to 0, then all files are acceptable.

✦ **extension.** The actual file extension without the leading period.

✦ **nRegularExpressions.** The number of Regular Expressions to be declared. Should this value be equal to 0, the array is closed.

✦ **RegularExpression.** The Regular Expression to be searched for by Dreamweaver.

The number of array elements — and thus, the detail of the function — depends entirely on the translator. Here, for example, is the code for getTranslatorInfo() from Live Picture's translator, where a file must have a particular <meta> tag to be translated:

```
function getTranslatorInfo(){
  returnArray = new Array( 5 )
  returnArray[0] = "FPX";       // translatorClass
  returnArray[1] = "Flashpix Image Translator";    // title
  returnArray[2] = "0"         // number of extensions
  returnArray[3] = "1";        // number of expressions
  returnArray[4] = "<meta http-equiv=\"refresh\"
content=\"0;url=http://";
  return returnArray
}
```

By comparison, the standard SSI translator's getTranslatorInfo() function has 10 array elements and Webmonkey's XSSI has 17.

The translateMarkup() function

While the getTranslatorInfo() function initializes the translator, the translateMarkup() function actually does the work. As noted earlier, most of the translators rely on a custom C-level Extension to handle the inner-workings of the function, but `translateMarkup()` provides the JavaScript shell.

The `translateMarkup()` function takes three arguments, which must be declared but whose actual values are provided by Dreamweaver:

- ✦ ***docName.*** The file URL for the file to be translated.
- ✦ ***siteRoot.*** The site root of the file to be translated. Should the file be outside the current site, the value would be empty.
- ✦ ***docContent.*** A text string with the code for the page to be translated.

Typically, the *docContent* text string is parsed using either JavaScript or a C-level Extension within the `translateMarkup()` function that returns the translated document. This translated document is then displayed by Dreamweaver.

Here's the `translateMarkup()` function from the standard SSI translator:

```
function translateMarkup( docNameStr, siteRootStr, inStr ) {
   var outStr = ""
   if ( inStr.length > 0 )
   {
   outStr = SSITranslator.translateMarkup( docNameStr,
siteRootStr, inStr )
   }
   return outStr
}
```

Notice that in this example, the translated document in the form of `outStr` is created by the custom function `SSITranslator.translateMarkup()`. The `SSITranslator` portion of this function calls the C-level Extension, built by Macromedia for this purpose.

Locking code

Translations are generally intended for on-screen presentation only. Although there's no rule saying that translated content can't be written out to disk, most applications need the original content to run. To protect the original content, Dreamweaver 2 includes a special locking tag. This XML tag pair, `<MM:BeginLock>...<MM:EndLock>`, stops the enclosed content (the translation) from being edited, while simultaneously storing a copy of the original content in a special format.

The `<MM:BeginLock>` tag has several attributes:

- ✦ **translatorClass.** The identifying name of the translator as specified in `getTranslatorInfo()`. Required.
- ✦ **type.** The type or tag name for the markup to be translated.

✦ **depFiles.** A comma-separated list of any files on which the locked content depends. If any of the listed dependent files are altered, the page is retranslated.

✦ **orig.** A text string with the original markup before translation. The text string is encoded to include three standard HTML characters. The "<" becomes %3C; the ">" becomes %3E; and the quote character is converted to %22.

To see how the special locking tag works, look at an example taken from the Tango Sample Data translator. Tango uses what are called "meta tags" that begin with an @ sign, like the <@TOTALROWS> tag. The Tango Sample Data translator replaces what will be a result drawn from a database with a specified sample value. The original code is

```
<@TOTALROWS samptotalrows=23>
```

Once the code is translated, Dreamweaver refreshes the screen with this code:

```
<MM:BeginLock translatorClass="TANGO_SAMPLEDATA"  type
="@TOTALROWS" orig="%3C@TOTALROWS
samptotalrows=23%3E">23<MM:EndLock>
```

The "23" in bold is the actual translated content that appears in Dreamweaver's Document Window.

Note   You don't actually see the locking code — even if you open the HTML Inspector when a page is translated. To view the code, select the translated item, copy it, and then paste it in another text application, or use the Paste As Text feature to see the results in Dreamweaver.

Extending C-level Libraries

All programs have their limits. Most limitations are intentional and serve to focus the tool for a particular use. Some limitations are accepted because of programming budgets — for both money and time — with the hope that the boundaries can be exceeded in the next version. With Dreamweaver 2, one small section of those high, sharply defined walls has been replaced with a doorway: C-level Extensions. Now, with the proper programming acumen, you can customize Dreamweaver to add the capabilities you need.

New Feature   Like most modern computer programs, the core of Dreamweaver is developed using C and C++, both low-level languages that execute much faster than any noncompiled language, such as JavaScript. Because C is a compiled language, you can't just drop in a function with a few lines of code and expect it to work — it has to be integrated into the program. The only possible way to add significant functionality is through another compiled component called a *library*. With the C-level Extensions capability, Dreamweaver 2 permits the incorporation of these libraries, known as DLLs (Dynamic Load Libraries) on Windows systems and CFMs (Code Fragment Managers) on Macintosh systems.

One excellent example of the extended library is `DWFile`. This C-level Extension is used by several Dreamweaver partners, including RealNetworks and iCat, to perform tasks outside the capabilities of JavaScript; namely, reading and writing external text files. By adding this one library, Dreamweaver can now work with the support files necessary to power a wide range of associated programs. `DWFile` is described in detail later in this section.

C-level Extensions are also used in combination with Dreamweaver's new Translator feature. As discussed earlier in this chapter, translators handle the chore of temporarily converting nonstandard code to HTML that Dreamweaver can present on screen — while maintaining the original code in the file. Although much of this functionality isn't impossible for JavaScript, the conversion would be too slow to be effective. C-level Extensions are definitely the way to go when looking for a powerful solution.

Note   Programming in C or C++, as required by C-level Extensions, is beyond the scope of this book. Developers are encouraged to examine Macromedia's Extending Dreamweaver PDF file found on the Dreamweaver Web site.

Calling a C-level Extension

C-level Extensions, properly stored in the Configuration\JSExtensions folder, are read into Dreamweaver during initialization when the program first starts. The routines contained within the custom libraries are accessed through JavaScript functions in commands, behaviors, objects, translators, and other Dreamweaver extensions.

As an example, let's take a look at how Macromedia's C-level Extensions `DWFile` is used. `DWFile` has seven main functions:

✦ **exists()** checks to see if a specified filename exists. This function takes one argument, the filename.

✦ **read()** reads a text file into a string for examination. This function also takes one argument, the filename.

✦ **write()** outputs a string to a text file. This function has three arguments; the first two — the name of the file to be created and the string to be written — are required. The third, the mode, must be the word "append." This argument, if used, causes the string to be added to the end of the existing text file; otherwise the file is overwritten.

✦ **getAttributes()** returns the attributes of a specified file or folder. Possible attributes are R (Read-Only), D (Directory), H (Hidden), and S (System file or folder).

✦ **getModificationDate()** returns the date a specified file or folder was last modified.

✦ **createFolder()** creates a folder, given a file URL.

✦ **listFolder()** lists the contents of a specified folder in an array. This function takes two arguments: the file URL of the desired folder (required) and a Keyword, either "files" (which returns just file names) or "directories" (which returns just directory names). If the Keyword argument is not used, You'll get both files and directories.

The following JavaScript function, which could be included in any Dreamweaver extension, uses DWFile to see if a file, named in a passed argument, exists. If it does, the contents are read and presented in an alert; if the file doesn't exist, the function creates it and writes out a brief message.

```
function fileWork(theFile) {
  var isFile = DWFile.exists(theFile)
  if (isFile) {
      alert(DWFile.read(theFile))
  } else {
    DWFile.write(theFile,"File Created by DWFile")
  }
}
```

Note how the C-level Extension name, DWFile, is used to call the library and its internal functions. Once the library has been initialized, it can be addressed like any other internal function and its routines are simply called as methods of the function using JavaScript dot notation, such as DWFile.exists(theFile).

Building C-level Extensions

A C-level Extension must follow strict guidelines in order to be properly recognized by Dreamweaver. Specifically, two files must be included in the library when created in C and each function must be declared for correct interpretation by Dreamweaver's JavaScript interpreter.

Macromedia engineers have developed a C-level Extension API in the form of a C header, mm_jsapi.h. This header contains definitions for over 20 data types and functions. To insert mm_jsapi.h in your custom library, add the following statement:

```
#include "mm_isapi.h"
```

You can find the latest version of mm_jsapi.h on the Dreamweaver Web site.

After you've included the JavaScript API header, you need to declare a specific macro, MM_STATE. This macro, contained within the mm_jsapi.h header, holds definitions necessary for the integration of the C-level Extension into Dreamweaver's JavaScript API. The MM_STATE must be defined only once.

Each library can be composed of numerous functions available to be called from within Dreamweaver. For Dreamweaver's JavaScript interpreter to recognize the functions, each one must be declared in a special function, JS_DefineFunction(), defined in the library. All of the JS_DefineFunction() functions are contained in the MM_Init() function. The syntax for JS_DefineFunction() is as follows:

```
JS_DefineFunction(jsName, call, nArgs)
```

where *jsName* is the JavaScript name for the function, *call* is a pointer to a C-level function, and *nArgs* is the number of arguments that the function can expect. For example, the MM_Init() function for DWFile might look like this:

```
void

  MM_Init()
  {
    JS_DefineFunction("exist", exist, 1);
    JS_DefineFunction("read", exist, 1);
    JS_DefineFunction("write", exist, 2);
  }
```

Because MM_Init() depends on definitions included in the C header, mm_jsapi.h, it must be called after the header is included.

Tip　　If you're building cross-platform C-level Extensions, consider using Metrowerks CodeWarrior integrated development environment. CodeWarrior can edit, compile, and debug C, C++, and even Java or Pascal for both Windows and Macintosh operating systems. Perhaps most important, Macromedia engineers used CodeWarrior to test C-level Extensions.

Summary

Dreamweaver's commitment to professional Web site authoring is at its most profound when examining the program's customization capabilities. Virtually every Web site production house can benefit from some degree of personalization—and some clients absolutely require it. As you consider making your productive life easier by extending Dreamweaver, keep the following points in mind:

✦ Dreamweaver 2 includes a full range of customizable features: objects, behaviors, commands, third-party tags, Property Inspectors, and translators. You can even extend the program's core feature set with the C-level Extensibility option.

✦ You can use commands to affect any part of your HTML page and automate repetitive tasks.

✦ In addition to accessing custom commands through the Command menu, you can configure them as objects for inclusion in the Objects Palette. You can also make a command appear in any other standard Dreamweaver menu by altering the CommandMenu.htm file.

✦ To make it easy to work with XML and other non-HTML tags, Dreamweaver enables you to create custom tags complete with individual icons or highlighted content.

✦ Attributes for third-party tags are viewable — and modifiable — by creating a custom Property Inspector.

✦ Dreamweaver's C-level Extensibility feature allows C and C++ programmers to add new core functionality to a program.

✦ Tags from server-side applications can be viewed in the Document Window, just as they would be when browsed online, when a custom translator is used. A custom translator often requires a C-level Extension.

In the next chapter, you learn how to add all types of digital video — including streaming video — to your Web page.

✦   ✦   ✦

Adding Multimedia Elements

Adding Video to Your Web Page

In a world accustomed to being entertained by moving images 50 feet high, it's hard to understand why people are thrilled to see a grainy, jerky, quarter-screen-sized video on a Web page. And in truth, it's the promise of video on the Web, not the current state of it, that has folks excited. Many of the industry's major players, including Microsoft and Apple, are spending big bucks to bring that promise a little closer to reality.

No one standard for video on the Web has yet to emerge, although QuickTime and RealVideo are the most popular formats on the Web and both are cross-platform. Dreamweaver therefore handles the various flavors through open-ended HTML commands. Video can be downloaded to the user and then automatically played with a helper application, such as Microsoft's Window's Media Player or QuickTime's MoviePlayer.

Streaming video, which enables the movie to begin playing as it is being downloaded, is a relatively recent innovation that has taken the Internet by storm. This chapter looks at all the different methods for incorporating video—whether you're downloading an MPEG file or streaming a RealVideo movie—into your Web pages through Dreamweaver.

Video on the Web

It may be hard for folks not involved in the technology of computers and the Internet to understand why the high-tech Web doesn't always include something as "low-tech" as video. After all, television has been around for over 50 years, right? The difficulties arise from the fundamental difference between the two media: television and radio signals are analog, and computers work with digital signals. Sure, you can convert an analog signal to a digital one—but that's just the beginning of the solution.

Any digital equivalent of an analog file is enormous by comparison: A two-hour movie fits on a single video cassette, but uncompressed digital video uses roughly 27 megabytes per second; a two-hour show equals almost 2,000,000MB (2,000 gigabytes) of storage. And large file sizes translate into enormous bandwidth problems when you are transmitting video over the Web.

To resolve this issue of megasized files, industry professionals and manufacturers have developed various strategies, or *architectures*, for the creation, storage, and playback of digital media. Each architecture has a different file format, and thus each requires the user to have a playback system — whether a plug-in, ActiveX control, or Java applet — capable of handling that particular format.

In an effort to keep file sizes as small as possible, Web videos are often presented relatively small. It's not uncommon to display a video in one-quarter of the screen or less. Furthermore, in terms of smoothness of the action, you'll notice a major difference between conventional and Web-based video. Film is shown at 24 frames per second, while video uses roughly 30 frames per second. The best Web video rarely gets above 15 frames per second — almost guaranteeing a choppiness of motion, depending on the footage. The faster the action, the more noticeable the frame rate.

Given all the restrictions that video on the Web suffers, why use it at all? Simply because there is nothing else like it, and when you need video you have to use video. Take heart, though. Advances are occurring at a very rapid rate, both in the development of new video architectures and codecs, as well as in new, higher-speed Internet delivery systems such as cable modems. What you learn in this chapter enables you to include video in your Dreamweaver-built Web pages today, and gives you a good foundation for accommodating future enhancements.

The leading digital video architectures are described briefly in the following sections.

MPEG

Developed by the Motion Picture Experts Group, MPEG is to moving pictures what JPEG is to still images. Several different versions of MPEG have been developed by the standards group. Of these, MPEG-1 is the most widely supported, although MPEG-2 probably has enough market penetration to be useful. Filename extensions are either .mpg or .mpeg.

QuickTime

Originally developed by Apple as a multiplatform multimedia solution, QuickTime has proved so successful that version 3.0 is the basis for the latest MPEG standard. Aside from the regular QuickTime, Apple has also released QuickTime VR, which provides panoramic views. Filename extensions are either .qt or .mov.

RealVideo

RealNetworks released the first streaming media system—RealAudio—in 1995. The current version, RealVideo, supports streaming playback for both audio and video. Filename extensions include .ra, .rpm, and .ram.

ActiveMovie and Video for Windows

Years ago, in the light of QuickTime's success on the Macintosh, Microsoft released its own video format, Video for Windows. All Windows systems are equipped with players for any .avi file. These .avi files are not cross-platform, however. So although the format is standard for all Windows systems, its inability to "play well with others" has made Video for Windows less popular on the Web.

Microsoft has released a flurry of video formats and components as the company tries to gain a foothold on the digital video market. The ActiveMovie component was released as part of the ActiveMedia suite of programs and was largely comparable to the Video for Windows format. Most recently, the Windows Media Player (WMP) was released and incorporated into the latest versions of Internet Explorer. While this player can handle both downloaded and streaming video, as well as many other media types, its introduction has caused numerous problems due to its incompatible playback command syntax. Luckily, Dreamweaver 2 includes a "detect WMP" routine that makes seamless playback a possibility again.

Inserting Simple Video Capabilities

Once you've digitized your video, the easiest way to make it available on your Web page is to treat it as an ordinary link. Then, when the link is selected, the video downloads to the user's machine. What happens next depends on what Helper applications are on the user's system. Most modern systems come equipped with multimedia players that can handle the common video file formats: MPEG, QuickTime, and Video for Windows.

To include a digitized video file on your Web page in Dreamweaver, follow these steps:

1. Select the text or image that you want to serve as the link to the video file.

2. In the Property Inspector, enter the name of the video file in the Link text box, or select the folder icon to browse for the file.

3. Because video files can be quite large, it's also good practice to note the file size next to the link name or enter it in the Alt text box, as shown in Figure 20-1.

Figure 20-1: You can insert any video file for user download by including it as a link to a selected graphic or text.

Tip

Don't expect to automatically see an image from the linked video file in Dreamweaver's Document Window or in your browser preview. Many Web designers grab a still image from the video, convert it to GIF or JPEG format, and use that as the linked graphic.

Using Inline Video

Microsoft's Internet Explorer has a very useful proprietary attribute capable of producing *inline video*. Inline video is digital video that can be played back within the Web page itself, "in line with" other elements such as text and graphics. You can't depend on it for full Internet access; nevertheless, the dynamic source attribute, dynsrc, enables a Web designer working with an Internet Explorer intranet to easily include and control any Video for Windows (.avi) file. The attribute is inserted in the ⟨img⟩ tag, like this:

```
<img src="images/logo.gif" dynsrc="images/logo.avi">
```

A browser not supporting the dynsrc attribute displays the normally referenced image source, and an Internet Explorer browser automatically displays the image after it is transferred. Like the linked video files noted in the preceding section, a dynamic source video has to be completely downloaded before it can begin playing. Unless you're using a custom object in Dreamweaver, you have to code all the dynamic source attributes by hand. The dynamic source attribute enables some degree of control in displaying your .avi file.

Additional attributes of the `<img>` tag are described in Table 20-1. You can also use any of the regular `<img>` tag attributes, including `height`, `width`, `border`, `hspace`, and `vspace`.

Table 20-1	
Attributes for Internet Explorer Inline Video	
<img> Attribute	**_Purpose_**
`start`	By default, the video begins playing once the file download from the Web server is completed. Using the `start` attribute, you can specify when you want the video to play, either on `fileopen` or `mouseover`. You can also include both values to make your video play when it is first downloaded and then repeat whenever the user's mouse is passed over the image.
`controls`	To add the standard control panel to your video, insert the attribute `controls` by itself in any dynamic source object.
`dynsrc`	This attribute sets the .avi file to be displayed.
`loop`	Set the number of times you want your video clip to repeat by giving a value to the `loop` attribute. To make your video repeat continuously, use either `loop=-1` or `loop=infinite`.
`loopdelay`	Use this attribute to insert a delay between each repeat of a video clip. Insert `loopdelay=n`, where n is the time in milliseconds; for example, `loopdelay=5000` would create a five-second delay between loops.

On the CD-ROM Dreamweaver's interface doesn't by default support the `<dynsrc>` dynamic source attribute, so normally you'd have to enter these attributes and values by hand. You can, however, use the Dynamic Source object found on the CD-ROM to easily insert your .avi video clip. Just transfer dynsrc.htm and dynsrc.gif from the Dreamweaver/ Configuration/Objects/Media folder.

Playing Videos Within Dreamweaver

Until Dreamweaver 2, inline videos could only be viewed through a browser. This restriction made designing a Web page with a video component very tricky and largely a trial-and-error operation. Now, however, Dreamweaver can play back — in the Document Window—most digital video formats that use a plug-in, such as QuickTime movies and RealVideo files.

New Feature   Whenever a file is embedded for playback via a plug-in, a green Play button appears in the Property Inspector. To play a particular digital video in Dreamweaver's Document Window, all you have to do is select the plug-in place-holder and click the Play button. The video begins playing and the green Play button becomes a red Stop button—to end playback, just click the Stop button.

You can also use the menus and the corresponding keyboard shortcuts to control the digital video in the Document Window: View ➪ Plugins ➪ Play or Ctrl-P (Command-P), and View ➪ Plugins ➪ Stop or Ctrl-. (period) (Command-.). Finally, if you have multiple videos inserted on the page, you can play them all by choosing View ➪ Plugins ➪ Play All or by using the keyboard shortcut Ctrl-Shift-P (Command-Shift-P), and stop them with View ➪ Plugins ➪ Stop All or Ctrl-Shift-.(Command-Shift-.).

Caution   Unfortunately, the one plug-in identified as "bad" by Macromedia in the BadPlugins.cfg file is the Video for Windows plug-in. For the time being, you'll still have to preview your .avi files through the browser.

Installing QuickTime and QuickTime VR Movies

QuickTime has become a leading format for cross-platform multimedia content. Developed by Apple, the QuickTime architecture encompasses still pictures, digitized video, audio, drawing, and even panoramic virtual reality environments. Because QuickTime output can be played on multiple platforms, it has substantial support in the industry. If I had to guess which architecture would become the standard, I'd bet on QuickTime.

QuickTime attributes

To view a QuickTime movie in your Web page, your users need to have a QuickTime plug-in installed. The HTML command for incorporating a QuickTime movie (or any other media that requires a plug-in) is the `<embed>` tag. Because so many different types of plug-ins exist, Dreamweaver uses a generic Plug-in Inspector that enables an unlimited number of parameters to be specified.

Only three parameters are required for a QuickTime movie: the source of the file, the movie's width, and the movie's height. If you don't know the dimensions of your QuickTime movie, open the file with the MoviePlayer program that comes with QuickTime and choose Movie ➪ Get Info.

Note   When specifying the height of the movie, add 24 pixels to leave room for the controller panel, unless you've specifically turned off the controller.

To insert a QuickTime movie in your Web page, follow these steps:

1. First, insert the Plug-in object. Choose Insert ⇨ Plug-in or select the Plug-in object from the Common pane of the Objects Palette, or drag the Plug-in object to a location on your Web page.

2. In the Insert Plug-in dialog box, enter the QuickTime file's path and name in the Plug-in Source text box, or select the folder to browse for the file. Click OK when you're done.

3. In the Plug-in Inspector (see Figure 20-2), enter the width and height values in the W and H text boxes, respectively. Alternately, you can drag any of the sizing handles on the Plug-in placeholder in the Document Window to a new size. Remember to add 24 pixels to the height if you are using the controller panel.

Figure 20-2: When inserting a QuickTime movie, specify the properties and values in the Plug-in Inspector.

4. In the Plg URL text box, enter the Internet address to which you want visitors to your Web page directed if they do not have the necessary plug-in installed. (Note: In the case of QuickTime movies, use `http://quicktime.apple.com`.)

5. Select the Parameters button to open the Parameters dialog box. Enter the QuickTime parameters in the left column and the desired values in the right column. Press Tab to move from one column to another. Table 20-2 describes the available parameters for a QuickTime movie.

6. Dreamweaver's Plug-in Inspector also enables you to enter several other attributes generally used with other objects, such as images. These other attributes include `Align` (alignment), `V Space` (vertical space), `H Space` (horizontal space), and `Border` (border). You can also enter a name in the Plug-in text box if you plan on referring to your QuickTime file in a JavaScript or other program.

On the CD-ROM   While you can certainly use the Plug-in Inspector to fill out your QuickTime parameters, you can also make your life a little easier by using the QuickTime object found on the CD-ROM. Just copy the two files from Dreamweaver/Configuration/Objects/Media (qtime.htm and qtime.gif) to your folder and restart Dreamweaver. You'll find all the parameters necessary for including a QuickTime or QuickTime VR movie.

Table 20-2
QuickTime Movie Parameters

QuickTime Parameter	Description
autoplay	Enables the QuickTime movie to start playing as soon as the movie data has sufficiently downloaded. You can set autoplay to either true or false (the default).
bgcolor	Sets the background color for the QuickTime movie (QuickTime 3 only).
cache	Informs the user's browser to cache the movie, as with other documents. The values for cache are true (the default) or false. Note: This parameter is currently supported only by Netscape 3.0 browsers.
controller	Displays the controller panel attached to the QuickTime movie. You can set controller to either true (the default) or false. If the controller is enabled, add 24 pixels to the height of the movie.
hidden	If hidden is included as a parameter, the QuickTime movie is not displayed, but the audio soundtrack is played. This parameter does not take any values.
href	Establishes a link to a URL when the movie is selected by the viewer. You can supply either an absolute or a relative Internet address.
loop	Causes the movie to loop continuously. In addition to true and false (the default) values, the loop parameter also can take a palindrome value, which causes the QuickTime movie to play alternately forward and backward.
playeveryframe	When enabled, this parameter forces the movie to play every frame, even if it must do so at a slower rate than is optimum. Possible values are true and false (the default). Do not enable playeveryframe if the QuickTime movie includes an audio or MIDI track, because it will disable the sound.
scale	Resizes the QuickTime movie. By setting scale to tofit, you can scale the movie to the dimensions of the embedded box as specified by the height and width values. Setting scale to aspect resizes the movie to the height and width dimensions, but maintains the aspect ratio of the original movie. You can also set scale to a number; if, for example, you want to resize the movie to two-and-a-half times the original size, you would set the scale value to 2.5. The default is scale=1.

QuickTime Parameter	Description
target	Enables the link specified in the href parameter to be targeted to a specific frame or named anchor. You can use any of the standard target values, including _self, _parent, _top, or _blank.
volume	Controls the volume of the QuickTime audio track. Possible values are 0 (no sound) to 256 (loudest). The default is volume=256.

QuickTime VR

QuickTime has one feature that no other video architecture can match: QuickTime VR (QTVR). QuickTime VR enables the user to "look around" in the view being offered—this range is often a 180° panoramic view and sometimes has complete 360° capability. QTVR is also used for "object movies," in which the camera rotates around an object at its center point in three dimensions. In addition, QuickTime VR enables the designer to designate certain areas as *hotspots* that, when selected by the user, activate a link to another page or another movie. Though purists will argue that QTVR is not *really* virtual reality, the technology has made tremendous progress toward acceptance on the Web.

QuickTime VR's attributes are entered in the same manner as the regular QuickTime movie attributes—through the Parameters button in the Plug-in Parameters dialog box (see Figure 20-3).

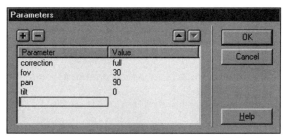

Figure 20-3: Use the Plug-in Parameters dialog box to enter attributes for any plug-in. This example is for a QuickTime VR movie.

QTVR's special capabilities require special attributes, as listed in Table 20-3.

Table 20-3
Parameters for QuickTime VR Movies

QuickTime VR Parameter	Description
correction	Applies the correction filter. Settings are none, partial, or full (the default).
fov	Specifies the initial field-of-view angle. The range of values goes from 0 (maximum zoom) to 90 (narrowest zoom). The default is fov=0.
hotspot	Defines the URL for any designated hotspot. The syntax is hotspot n=URL, where n is the identification number given the hotspot during QTVR authoring, and URL is any valid Internet address. Note: Because of this attribute's syntax, you can't use the Parameters dialog box to enter a hotspot; you must either enter its value by hand or through a custom object.
node	Determines the initial node for a QTVR multinode movie. Nodes are specified during QTVR authoring and given numeric IDs. Set node to a new integer to override the default initial node.
pan	Sets the initial pan angle, in degrees, of a QuickTime VR movie. The range of values for a typical movie is from 0.0_ to 360.0_. The default is pan=0.
tilt	Sets the initial tilt angle, in degrees, of a QuickTime VR movie. The range of values for a typical movie is from –42.5 to 42.5 degrees. The default is tilt=0.

As with a regular QuickTime movie, the only *required* parameters for a QTVR movie are the source file, movie width, and movie height. Remember to add an additional 24 pixels to the height measurement for the controller.

 Caution   Some parameters meaningful to regular QuickTime movies are not appropriate for QuickTime VR movies. These include autoplay, controller, hidden, href, loop, playeveryframe, target, and volume.

Working with Streaming Video

If you've ever downloaded a few minutes of digital video over a slow modem connection, you know the reason why streaming video was invented. In an age where immediacy rules, waiting until the complete video file is transferred and then loaded into the video player can seem to last an eternity. *Streaming*, on the other hand, enables the multimedia content to begin playing as soon as the first complete packet of information is received, and then to continue playing as more digital information arrives. Video is just one form of media to get the streaming treatment: You can also stream audio, animation, text, and other formats.

As with other digital video, no clear standard exists for streaming video. Most solutions require special software on the server side, as well as client-side plug-ins. Many companies are competing in the market. Dreamweaver uses the Plug-in object and Plug-in Inspector to insert and configure the parameters for the various streaming video formats: RealVideo, NetShow, VXtreme, and VDOLive, to name a few.

Tip   All of the video solutions require that the digital content be compressed or encoded with a system-specific encoder. Visit specific companies' Web sites to get more information — and, in some cases, the necessary software — for this process.

Regardless of which streaming video protocol you use, the procedure for incorporating the file on your Web page is basically the same, although the details (such as filename extensions) differ. In order to demonstrate the general technique and still offer some specific information you can use, the next section details how to include streaming RealVideo clips with Dreamweaver. Check with the streaming video developer you plan to use to get the precise installation details.

A RealVideo example

The earliest streaming system (and one of today's most prevalent) was developed by RealNetworks (`www.real.com`). RealNetworks offers a free multimedia player, RealPlayer, for anyone wishing to see or hear the content of these systems. An enhanced player product is also available at low cost. The latest version of the RealPlayer is known as the RealPlayer G2, for Generation 2, and allows other Real media types, such as RealFlash, RealText and RealPix to be played, as well as RealVideo and RealAudio.

When incorporating RealVideo into your Web pages, you have a variety of playback options. You can set the video so that a free-floating RealPlayer is invoked, or you can specify that the video appear inline on your Web page. You can also customize the controls that appear on your Web page so that only the ones you want — at the size you want — are included.

New Feature   Dreamweaver 2 includes a full set of Real media objects — collectively called *RealSystem G2 objects* — which were developed in partnership with RealNetworks. You can find instructions for using these new objects later in this chapter.

Creating RealVideo metafiles

RealVideo uses its own specialized server software to transmit encoded video files called RealServer. Rather than call this server and the digital video file directly, RealVideo uses a system of *metafiles* to link to the RealVideo server and file. A metafile is an ordinary text file containing the appropriate URL pointing to the RealServer and video file.

The metafiles are distinguished from the media files by their filename extensions:

.rm   RealVideo files

.ra   RealAudio files

.ram   Metafile that launches the independent RealPlayer

.rpm   Metafile that launches the RealPlayer plug-in

Caution   For your RealVideo file to play properly, the Web server administrator must config-
ure your Web server to understand that the extensions .ra and .ram refer to the
MIME type audio/x-pn-realaudio, and that the extension .rpm refers to the
MIME type audio/x-pn-realaudio-plugin.

To create the metafile, open your favorite text editor and insert one or more lines
pointing to your server and the video files. Instead of using the http:// locator
seen with most URLs, the latest RealVideo files address the RealSystem G2 server
with a rtsp:// (Real Time Streaming Protocol) indicator. The contents of the file
should take the following form:

```
rtsp://hostname/path/file
```

where *hostname* is the domain name of the server where the RealVideo files are
stored, *path* is the path to the file, and *file* is the name of the RealVideo file. For
example, to display a training video, the metafile contents might look like the
following:

```
rtsp://www.trainers.com/videos/training01.rm
```

You can include multiple video clips by putting each one on its own line, separated
by a single return. RealVideo plays each clip in succession and the user can skip
from one clip to another.

Inserting RealVideo in your Web page

Once you've created both the encoded RealVideo file and the metafiles, you're
ready to insert them into your Web page. You have two basic techniques for
including RealVideo: as a link, and using the <embed> tag.

Using a link

Generally, if you want to invoke the free-floating RealPlayer, you use a link; the href
attribute is set to an address for a metafile, like this:

```
<a href="videos/howto01.ram">Demonstration</a>
```

When the link is selected, it calls the metafile that, in turn, calls the video file on the
RealServer. As the file begins to download to the user's system, the RealPlayer
program is invoked and starts to display the video as soon as possible through the

independent video window, as shown in Figure 20-4. The link can be inserted in Dreamweaver through either the Text or Image Property Inspector.

Figure 20-4: You can set up your RealVideo clip so that it plays inline, or in a separate player as illustrated here.

Using <embed>

If, on the other hand, you'd like to make the video appear inline with the Web page's text or graphics, you use Dreamweaver's Plug-in object to insert an <embed> tag. Position the pointer where you want the RealVideo to be displayed, and either choose Insert ➪ Plug-in or select Insert Plug-in from the Objects Palette. After the Insert Plug-in dialog box appears, enter the path and filename for the video's metafile in the Plug-in Source text box.

When the Plug-in object representing the RealVideo clip is selected, the Property Inspector lets you enter values for the <embed> tag. As with the QuickTime object, the only attributes required for a RealVideo clip are the file source and the width and height of the movie. And, also like QuickTime, you can choose from a healthy number of attributes to control your RealVideo movie. Attributes are entered by selecting the Parameters button on the Plug-in Inspector, and entering attributes and their values in the Parameters dialog box (shown earlier in Figure 20-3).

RealVideo attributes are listed in Table 20-4.

Table 20-4
Parameters for RealVideo Movies

RealVideo Parameter	Description
autostart	Enables the RealVideo clip to start playing as soon as content is available. You can set autostart to either true (the default) or false.
console	Determines the console name for each control in a Web page having multiple controls. To force controls on a page to refer to the same file, use the same console=name attribute. The console name _master links to all controls on a page, whereas _unique connects to no other instances.
controls	Enables the placement of individual control panel elements in the Web page. You can use multiple controls in one attribute or multiple <embed> tags to build a custom RealVideo interface. The separate controls are as follows: all controlpanel imagewindow infovolumepanel infopanel playbutton positionslider positionfield statuspanel statusbar stopbutton statusfield volumeslider
nolabels	Suppresses the Title, Author, and Copyright labels in the Status panel. If you set nolabels to true, the actual data is still visible. The default is nolabels=false.

Using the RealSystem G2 object set

Macromedia has partnered with Real Networks to provide a full set of objects to ease the implementation of Real media in Dreamweaver. The RealSystem G2 object set includes drop-in objects to play RealAudio, RealVideo, RealPix, RealText, RealFlash, and SMIL presentations. You'll also find an array of control panel options for building your own interface.

Cross-Reference

The RealVideo object is covered later in this chapter. The RealAudio object is covered in Chapter 21, "Using Audio on Your Web Page"; and the other Real media in Chapter 28, "Adding Multimedia Extensions."

HTTP Streaming

To gain the maximum throughput of your RealVideo files, it's best to use the RealServer software. Occasionally, however, you'll encounter Web site clients who must economize and can't afford the specialized server. Not widely known is the fact that you can use a regular World Wide Web server to stream RealVideo and other RealMedia files.

Two prerequisites exist for HTTP streaming: Your system administrator must first correctly configure the MIME types and you must provide multiple files to match the right user-selectable modem speeds. The proper MIME types are as follows:

✦ audio/x-pn-RealAudio (for .ra, .rm or .ram files)

✦ audio/x-pn-RealAudio-plugin (for .rpm files)

✦ video/x-pn-RealVideo (for .ra, .rm or .ram files)

✦ video/x-pn-RealVideo-plugin (for .rpm files)

RealServer automatically selects the right file for the user's modem connection. If you are using HTTP streaming capabilities, you should offer multiple files to accommodate the various modem connection rates, such as 28.8K and 56K.

Other than a reduction in download speed, the other disadvantage to using HTTP streaming over RealServer streaming is the reduced number of simultaneous users who can be served. RealServer can handle hundreds of connections at the same time; HTTP streaming is far more limited.

Installing RealSystem G2 objects

The RealSystem G2 objects need to be installed before they can be used and, naturally, you'll need the RealPlayer G2 on your system as well. To install the objects, follow these steps:

1. Uncompress the RealSystem G2 objects using one of the following methods:

   • For Windows systems, open the g2_obj.zip file using a system utility such as WinZip or PKZip.

   • For Macintosh systems, use a compression utility such as Stuffit Expander to open the file, realg2.sit.hqx.

2. After you've uncompressed the files, run the setup program and follow the on-screen instructions.

   A new folder, RealSystem G2, is created to contain all the various files.

3. Restart Dreamweaver.

One Dreamweaver has reopened, you'll find another pane added to the Objects Palette: RealSystem G2. There are objects for six media types, including RealVideo and seven control panel options. You may need to expand or scroll the Objects Palette to see buttons for all the objects.

Control options for RealSystem G2 objects

You can also use the RealSystem G2 objects to build your own interface that incorporates parts of the standard control panel. A separate control panel element works with any file or other element with the same `console` name. For example, if you have two RealVideo files on your Web page, you could have separate Play buttons (each pointing to a different `console` value, say `video1` and `video2`) while having one volume slider controlling all sound with the console name `_master`. Table 20-5 displays the various control options available to all RealSystem G2 objects.

Table 20-5
RealSystem G2 Control Options

Icon	G2 Object	Description
	Insert Full Controls	Shows the Control Panel, Information and Volume Panel, and the Status Bar.
	Insert Control Panel	Shows the Play/Pause button, the Stop button, Fast Forward and Rewind controls, and the position slider.
	Insert Play Button	Shows the Play and Pause buttons.
	Insert Stop Button	Shows only the Stop button.
	Insert Volume Slider	Shows the vertical volume control slider.
	Insert Status Panel	Shows the Status panel, which displays messages, current place in the presentation timeline, and total clip length.
	Insert InfoVolumePanel Control	Shows the title, author, and copyright information panel, as well as the volume slider.
	AboutReal	Displays the Help file for installing and running RealSystem G2 objects.

Inserting a RealVideo object

With the RealVideo object, all you need to know is the name of your source file and its dimensions—all the other factors are handled for you. The RealVideo object inserts a combination of tags to call both an ActiveX control and a plug-in so that the file can be played with both Internet Explorer and Netscape Navigator. You can also add new parameters after the object has been inserted through the Property Inspector's Edit Parameters button.

To insert a RealVideo object, follow these steps:

1. Choose Insert ➪ RealSystem G2 Object ➪ RealVideo or select the Insert RealVideo button from the RealSystem G2 panel of the Objects Palette.

The Insert RealVideo dialog box (shown in Figure 20-5) opens.

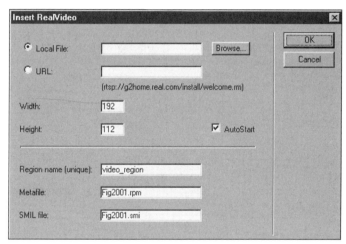

Figure 20-5: The RealVideo object makes inserting streaming video a simple process.

2. Enter the source file by choosing one of the following radio buttons:

- **Local File.** Enter the path name of a file found on the local system in the Local File text box or choose the Browse (Choose) button to locate the file.

- **URL.** Enter the absolute address of a file located on the Internet in the URL text box. The example address, `rtsp://g2home.real.com/ install/welcome.rm`, is displayed beneath the URL text box.

3. Enter the dimensions of the RealVideo movie in the Width and Height text boxes.

The default measurements of 192 pixels wide by 112 pixels high are suggestions only and do not necessarily reflect the accurate size of your file.

4. If you don't want your file to begin playing automatically, deselect the Autostart option.

5. The remaining text boxes, Region name, Metafile, and SMIL file, are automatically filled out. Alter any name by entering the modification in the text box.

6. Click OK when you're done.

Note
The RealVideo object creates both a metafile and a SMIL presentation file. When selected by the user to play (or playing automatically), the original file first calls the metafile, which in turn, calls the SMIL file. For this reason, if you ever need to change the source of the original file, you'll have to open and edit the referenced SMIL file — or delete the RealVideo object and reinsert it with the new filename.

By default, the RealVideo object is inserted with the controls set to the ImageWindow option, which shows only the RealVideo movie with no control panel. To incorporate a control panel into the video file, you need to first choose the Edit Parameters button from the Property Inspector. Next, change the `controls` attribute from `imagewindow` to one of the other options, such as `All`, `ControlPanel`, or `PlayButton`.

Summary

Digital video on the Web is in its infancy. Bandwidth is still too tight to enable full-screen, full-motion movies, no matter what the format. However, you can include downloadable as well as streaming video content through Dreamweaver's Plug-in object and Plug-in Inspector.

✦ Converting analog video to digital video requires special compressing or encoding systems. Even with the highest degree of compression, digital video has enormous storage and download requirements.

✦ You can include a digital video movie to be downloaded in your Web page by using the anchor tag, `<a>`, and setting the `href` attribute to the file's location on your Web server.

✦ Use Dreamweaver's Plug-in object when you want your video to be presented inline on your Web page. The Plug-in Inspector then lets you alter the video's parameters for any video architecture.

✦ QuickTime is an excellent example of cross-platform digital video that offers a full range of options — including QuickTime VR for displaying panoramic movies.

✦ To enable your visitors to view your digital video clips as soon as possible, use a streaming video technology such as RealVideo. RealVideo files can be displayed either in a separate player or embedded in the Web page. Dreamweaver 2 includes a set of RealSystem G2 objects for easy inclusion.

In the next chapter you learn how Dreamweaver helps you incorporate background music, sound effects, and streaming audio into your Web pages.

Using Audio on Your Web Page

✦   ✦   ✦   ✦

In This Chapter

Inserting and
embedding sound

Using plug-ins for
greater control

Working with the
Beatnik objects

Adding a
background
audio layer

Accessing streaming
audio

✦   ✦   ✦   ✦

Web sites tend to be divided into two categories: those totally without sound and those that use a lot of it — there's not much middle ground. Music and entertainment sites rely heavily on both downloadable and streaming audio.

You'll likely find that the major stumbling block for putting audio on the Web is not the HTML implementation, but achieving the conversion from analog to digital sound. Once you have the necessary equipment and the expertise for this task, however, the ability (via Dreamweaver) to add an audio layer to a site will greatly enhance your Web designer palette of skills.

In this chapter you'll learn how to use audio in the Web pages you design with Dreamweaver. You'll be able to include simple audio that must be fully downloaded before it can play, as well as streaming audio that starts playing as soon as the opening bars have been transferred. In addition to the better-known music formats such as .wav, MIDI, and RealAudio, this chapter also examines a relative newcomer to the audio scene: Rich Music Format, including its plug-in component, Beatnik, and its advanced JavaScript capabilities.

With Dreamweaver 2, adding audio to your Web pages just got a whole lot easier — and more interesting. This version of Dreamweaver comes with two significant additions in sound objects: the RealSystem G2 objects, including a RealAudio object for streaming audio; and Headspace's Beatnik ActionSet, which includes an astounding 48 behaviors to aid in the complete sonification of your Web page. But before we leap into those deep waters, let's get an overview of audio on the Web.

Digital Audio Fundamentals

Audio on the Internet has been around longer than video, but there's still no one standard. Outside of a single proprietary

Internet Explorer tag, no direct HTML command exists to include sound in your Web page. Dreamweaver, therefore, uses a generic plug-in approach to handle the various audio options.

Like digital video, digital audio requires all analog signals — voice, music, and sounds — to be converted. And, again like digital video, the resulting files can be quite hefty. Many different formats for digital audio files are in use today across the various computer platforms. These formats can be identified by their unique file name extensions, described in Table 21-1.

Table 21-1 Digital Audio File Formats	
Audio File Name Extension	*Format Description*
.au	Used by NeXT and Sun UNIX systems, the .au format is important because many of the earliest Internet audio files were available for UNIX only.
.aiff	The Audio Interchange File Format was developed by Apple and is also used by Silicon Graphics machines.
.midi or .mid	The MIDI format consists of instructions on re-creating a musical performance, rather than specific notes.
.mp3	The MPEG2 Audio Layer 3 format features high-quality digital audio files with excellent compression. Used very heavily for downloading long audio samples.
.ra or .ram	RealAudio, developed by Progressive Networks, was the first streaming audio format.
.rmf	The Rich Music Format, developed by musician Thomas Dolby and his company, Headspace, is used by the Beatnik plug-in.
.swa	Shockwave Audio, developed by Macromedia and based on MP3; this format can be streamed or downloaded.
.wav	Codeveloped by Microsoft and IBM, the waveform audio file format is heavily used in Windows systems.

Which audio format should you choose? That depends on a combination of factors, including your target audience, available bandwidth, and the purpose of the audio's content. Live broadcasts over the Internet, for example, must be created in RealAudio (or one of the other streaming technologies). Short sound effects can be handled by most of the formats, so you'll need to weigh the more prevalent accessibility of .wav files against the higher fidelity of a plug-in such as Beatnik. It's not uncommon for a sound file to be offered in multiple formats.

Linking Audio Files

If you're working with .wav, .mid, .mp3, or other common audio files, you can easily incorporate them into your Web design. The simplest way to add these sound files to a Web page is to include them as a link. From Dreamweaver's Text or Image Property Inspector, you enter the path to your audio file in the Link text box or select the Folder icon to browse for the file. When the user selects that link, the sound file downloads, and whatever program has been designated to handle that type of file opens in a separate window and begins playing the music (see Figure 21-1).

Figure 21-1: The audio file included in this page can be downloaded and played by the user. The file has been entered as a link through the Dreamweaver Property Inspector.

Tip

Dreamweaver lets you search for files of a specific type with a simple trick. Limit the selection that appears in the Select File dialog box by typing the asterisk (*) wildcard character, followed by the file name extension of the desired type of files. For example, if you were looking for MIDI files, you would enter ***.mid**. Only MIDI files will be displayed for your selection.

The Netscape and Microsoft browsers both come with their own players — or connections to multimedia players — for handling the various audio formats, including .wav, MIDI, .au, and .aiff. Each player is a little different, but they all offer simple, familiar controls such as Pause, Stop, and Volume buttons (you can see the Netscape browser and Windows Media Player in Figure 21-1). Each audio link in your Web page opens a separate player.

When you use the link technique for incorporating sound, you have no control over the position or appearance of the floating player window. However, you can control these factors and more by embedding your audio.

Embedding Sounds and Music

To truly integrate audio files into your Web page — and to avoid a free-floating sound control panel — the files must be embedded. Embedding the sound files also gives you a much higher degree of control over every element of audio presentation, including the following:

✦ The clip's play volume

✦ Which part, if any, of the controls are visible

✦ The starting and ending points of the music clip

As with any other embedded object, you can present the visual display inline with other text elements — aligned to the top, middle, or bottom of the text, or blocked left or right to allow text to flow around it. Dreamweaver controls all of these various parameters through two different objects: the Plug-in object and the ActiveX object. Each type of object calls a specific type of player. For example, the default Plug-in object calls the LiveAudio Plug-in in a Netscape browser, and the Windows Media Player control in Internet Explorer. Calling the Windows Media Player as an ActiveX object explicitly enables you to modify a great number of parameters for Internet Explorer — which are completely ignored by Navigator. You'll learn all of your embedding options, including techniques for cross-browser audio, in the next few sections.

As with the basic video file, Dreamweaver uses the generic Plug-in object to embed audio in your Web page. The object requires only three parameters: the source of the audio file, and the width and height of the object. To embed an audio file in your Web page, follow these steps in Dreamweaver:

1. Position the cursor where you want the control panel for the audio file to appear.

2. Insert the Plug-in object by choosing Insert ➪ Plug-in or by selecting the Plug-in object from the Objects Palette.

3. In the Property Inspector, enter the path and filename for your audio file in the Plug-in Source text box. Select Browse (Choose) to choose your file from the Select File dialog box.

4. Use either of the following techniques to size the plug-in placeholder:

- Enter the appropriate values in the W (Width) and the H (Height) text boxes of the Property Inspector.

- Click the resizing handles on the plug-in placeholder and drag it out to a new size.

Tip For a default audio plug-in, use a width of 144 pixels and a height of 60 pixels. These dimensions are slightly larger than necessary for Internet Explorer's audio controls, but they fit Navigator's controls perfectly, and the control panel will not appear to be "clipped" when viewed through any browser.

When the Plug-in object is inserted, Dreamweaver displays the generic plug-in icon instead of any control panel (as with other placeholders). The type of control panel displayed depends on the browser used, as shown in Figure 21-2. Here you can see the differences between Dreamweaver in the top window, Netscape Navigator in the lower-left, and Internet Explorer in the lower-right.

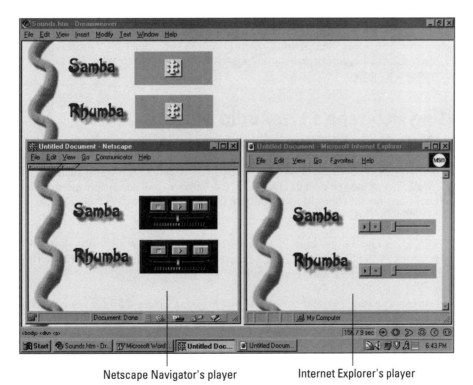

Netscape Navigator's player   Internet Explorer's player

Figure 21-2: With a basic embedding technique, the type of player is set by the browser.

Incorporating Enhanced Plug-ins

Because there's really no one standard yet for Internet audio, you can exercise a much finer degree of control of the audio in your pages by calling specific plug-ins. The trade-off, unfortunately, is that by designating a plug-in, you reduce the size of your potential audience. Some plug-ins are specific to a browser or browser version. Moreover, plug-ins that aren't distributed with the major browsers face an uphill battle in terms of market penetration. If you use a plug-in, you can always expect some folks to be resistant to downloading the necessary software. Before you incorporate any plug-in, you must weigh these issues against your overall design plan.

Tip   A great number of audio plug-ins are available and offer a broad variety of functionality and features. A good place to see a list of those available is the Plug-in Plaza (`www.browserwatch.com/plug-in.html`). In addition to offering complete descriptions, this site also has links directly to the download areas.

To represent the wide range of audio plug-ins, this chapter examines two of the major players in the field: Netscape's LiveAudio and Headspace's Beatnik. LiveAudio has the advantage of being included with Netscape Navigator/Communicator (since Navigator 3.0), and Beatnik provides excellent fidelity and next-generation features — and is also included in versions of Netscape Navigator 4.5 and above.

Using Netscape's LiveAudio plug-in

LiveAudio is Netscape's default audio player and is used when you do basic embedding of an audio file, as well as when you attach a sound file to a URL. Both of these methods of incorporating audio, however, barely scratch the surface of what LiveAudio is capable of doing. LiveAudio uses up to 13 different parameters to shape its appearance and functionality in the Web page, and also accepts a full range of JavaScript commands.

To take advantage of LiveAudio's full capabilities, you must enter the audio file's parameters and values through Dreamweaver's Property Inspector. Follow these steps to specify the parameters for your Plug-in object:

1. Insert the Plug-in object — either by choosing Insert ⇨ Plug-in or by dragging the Plug-in object from the Objects Palette to a place on your Web page.

2. From the extended Property Inspector, select Parameters.

    The Parameter dialog box is displayed with its two columns: Parameter and Value (see Figure 21-3).

Figure 21-3: Enter all the LiveAudio attributes and their values through the Parameters dialog box.

3. Click in the Parameter column and type in the first parameter. Press Tab to move to the Value column and enter the desired value. Press Tab again to move to the next parameter.

   • Press Shift-Tab if you need to move backwards through the list.

   • To delete a parameter, highlight it and select the – (minus) button at the top of the parameters list.

   • To add a new parameter, select the + (plus) button to move to the first blank line and press Tab to move to the next parameter.

   • To move a parameter from one position in the list to another, highlight it and select the up or down arrow buttons at the top of the parameters list.

   For most plug-ins, including LiveAudio, the order of the parameters is irrelevant.

4. Repeat Step 3 until all parameters are entered.

5. Click OK when you're done.

The parameters for LiveAudio affect either the look of the player or the qualities of the sound. The main parameter for altering the player's appearance is `controls`. Depending on the value used, you can display the default control panel, a smaller version, or individual controls.

You can embed individual controls anywhere on your Web page. To link the various controls, you use the `mastersound` keyword in each `<embed>` statement and set the name parameter to one unique value for all files. Finally, set the source in one `<embed>` tag to the actual sound file, and the other sources in the other files to a dummy file called a *stub* file.

Table 21-2 contains all the parameters available for LiveAudio, except those set by Dreamweaver's Property Inspector (source, height, width, and alignment).

Table 21-2
LiveAudio Parameters

Parameter	Acceptable Values	Description
autostart	true or false	If autostart is set to true, the audio file begins playing as soon as the download is completed. The default is false.
controls	console, smallconsole, playbutton, pausebutton, stopbutton, or volumelever	Sets the sound control to appear. The default is console.
endtime	minutes:seconds; for example, 00:00	Determines the point in the sound clip at which the audio stops playing.
hidden	true	Expressly hides all the audio controls; sound plays in the background.
loop	true, false, or an integer	Setting loop to true forces the sound file to repeat continuously until the Stop button is selected or the user goes to another page. To set the number of times the sound repeats, set loop equal to an integer. The default is false.
mastersound	None	Enables several <embed> tags to be grouped and controlled as one. Used in conjunction with the <name> attribute.
name	A unique name	Links various <embed> tags in a file to control them as one. Used in conjunction with the <mastersound> attribute.
starttime	minutes:seconds; for example, 00:00	Determines the point in the sound clip at which the audio begins playing.
volume	1 to 100	Sets the loudness of the audio clip on a scale from 1 to 100 percent.

Caution   Although LiveAudio enjoys the distribution of being bundled with Netscape Navigator, keep in mind that most plugs-ins by themselves don't work in Internet Explorer.

Making music with Beatnik

Beatnik is a recent but very powerful entry into the audio plug-in field. Developed by Headspace, Inc., an audio technology company headed by musician Thomas Dolby, Beatnik plays Rich Music Format (RMF) files. RMF playback compares favorably with high-end PC wavetable sound cards, even though the processing is entirely software-based. Beatnik can also play other traditional audio-file formats, including .wav, .aiff, MIDI, and MOD.

In addition to offering excellent sound, the other advantage that Beatnik offers is interactivity. Beatnik supports a comprehensive JavaScript command set. With Beatnik, you can play sounds or music in response to mouse clicks, mouse movements, and other user events. In addition, the audio can be altered in its tempo, volume, pitch, or mix.

Beatnik includes one additional special feature worth noting. Included with each Beatnik plug-in are 72 user-interface sounds, known as *Groovoids*. Groovoids are short sounds — a cash register ring, teletypes, fanfares, chimes, and musical snippets — built into the Beatnik memory. Because they are incorporated in the plug-in, there's no additional download time. Thus, a Web designer can use the Groovoids to provide aural feedback for user selections, or as a type of hold music while a Web page is loading.

New Feature Dreamweaver 2 now comes with the Beatnik ActionSet. The Beatnik ActionSet is a comprehensive collection of Dreamweaver behaviors — 48 in all — developed by Headspace. Actually, the standard free ActionSet only comes with 31 behaviors; the other 17 are part of a Pro series that can be purchased as an upgrade from the Headspace Web site. This section covers all the behaviors, however, so you'll know what the possibilities are.

The only downside to Beatnik is that it is subject to the quirks inherent to advanced plug-ins. First, the Beatnik plug-in only works with the newer browsers, 3.0 and higher, because Beatnik relies on JavaScript. Second, your users must have the plug-in (or ActiveX control) installed before they can experience the RMF and Groovoid sounds.

Installing the Beatnik ActionSet

Before you can use the Beatnik ActionSet in Dreamweaver, you have to install it. Follow these steps:

1. Close Dreamweaver if it is running.

2. Double-click the `beatnik-actionset-111-dw` file to begin the installation process.

On the CD-ROM If you don't have a fairly recent version of the Beatnik Player, use the Beatnik plug-in located on this book's CD-ROM in the External Programs folder. Unfortunately, only the Netscape plug-in is on the CD; the ActiveX control was still in beta when this book went to press. However, you can download the ActiveX control from Headspace's Web site at `www.headspace.com`.

3. When prompted, enter the location of Dreamweaver 2 or accept the entry found.

   When the installation is complete, the documentation for the Beatnik ActionSet automatically opens in your system browser.

4. When you're ready to begin investigating the Beatnik ActionSet, start Dreamweaver.

Cross-Reference

If you've never worked with behaviors before, you might want to review Chapter 17, "Using Behaviors," before proceeding.

Using the Beatnik ActionSet

As befits a revolutionary technology, the Beatnik ActionSet must be used with special care. While it's still possible to use the `<embed>` tag to insert Beatnik RMF files as detailed later in this chapter, the Beatnik ActionSet works in a significantly different fashion. Following are the key points:

✦ **Players.** Beatnik, unlike many other Web audio technologies, is capable of playing eight different audio files simultaneously. When the Beatnik ActionSet is initialized, the eight different voices are established, although one is reserved to play musical notes. Many of the Beatnik behaviors allow you to assign a specific player or to use the next available player. Unless you wish to exercise ongoing control over a specific voice, it's generally best to choose the available player option.

✦ **Interface.** Under the new Beatnik ActionSet philosophy, you won't find a series of control panels from which to choose — in fact, you won't find one. Rather than hard-code a VCR-like panel into the system, all Beatnik audio events occur via user interaction using either a custom interface or no interface whatsoever. While this may seem daunting at first, it actually gives the Web designer tremendous freedom, and works effectively to better integrate the sound design into the page.

✦ **Settings.** Adding music to the Web page often requires much fine-tuning and trial-and-error. The Beatnik ActionSet includes a series of settings that recognize this real-world requirement. At the least, you'll find Default Settings for using preset configurations, Previously Used Settings for your last configuration, and New Settings, which reflect the latest modifications. You can switch back-and-forth between these settings to find exactly the right sound.

Initializing a page

Each of the behaviors in the Beatnik ActionSet use a JavaScript library found in the file `beatnik-actionset.js` as well as a dummy music file called `stub.rmf`. In order to use any of the behaviors, a page must first be initialized and these files located. To simplify this task, Beatnik includes a special behavior, the Beatnik ActionSet Setup.

To initialize a page for Beatnik behaviors, follow these steps:

1. Select the `<body>` tag from the Tag Selector in the status bar.

2. Open the Behavior Inspector by choosing Window ➪ Behaviors or selecting the Show Behaviors button from either Launcher.

3. Click the Add Behavior button (the + sign) and choose Beatnik ActionSet Setup from the drop-down list.

   The Beatnik ActionSet Setup dialog box opens, as shown in Figure 21-4.

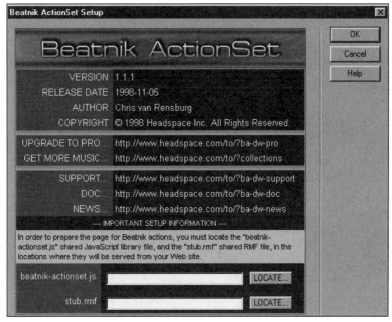

Figure 21-4: You must initialize your Web page with the Beatnik ActionSet Setup before you can use any of the Beatnik behaviors.

4. Enter the path to the `beatnik-actionset.js` file in the appropriate text box or select the Locate button to browse for the file.

Tip   Initially, the beatnik-actionset.js file is located in the Configuration\Behaviors\ Help\Beatnik-ActionSet\javascript folder. It's good practice to copy the file to the local root folder of your working site and assign that file in the Setup behavior. Keeping it in the local root folder makes it easier to upload when publishing the page.

5. Next, enter the path to the `stub.rmf` file in the text box or select the Locate button to browse for the file.

Tip

You'll find a copy of the stub.rmf file in the Configuration\Behaviors\Help\ BeatnikActionSet\music folder. Again, it's a good idea to copy this file to your working site directory and choose that file in the Beatnik Setup.

6. Click OK when you're done.

Caution

Should you ever relocate a page that has been Beatnik-initialized, Headspace recommends that you use Dreamweaver 2's advanced Find and Replace features to update the pages with the new location for these two files. Currently, it's not possible to delete and reapply the Setup behavior.

Adding Groovoids

As mentioned earlier, Groovoids are short musical riffs and sound effects intended to add an interactive sound dimension to your Web page. The Beatnik player includes 72 such samples in five categories: User Interface, Hits, Fanfare, Background, and Miscellaneous. Groovoids are used in two different ways:

✦ As a repeating background theme, generally begun when the page is loading

✦ As an interactive audio cue based on a user's actions and attached to a specific button or link

The Beatnik ActionSet has a section devoted to Groovoids with three behaviors:

✦ **Play Groovoid** starts a specified Groovoid when triggered.

✦ **Pause Groovoid** pauses or restarts a Groovoid. The pause can incorporate a fade of user-definable length.

✦ **Stop Groovoid** stops the specified Groovoid from playing; the Stop action can also fade out.

To insert a Play Groovoid behavior, follow these steps:

1. Set up the Web page as outlined in the earlier "Initializing a Page" section, if you've not done so already.

2. Select the tag you'd like to attach the Play Groovoid behavior to.

3. From the Behavior Inspector, choose Beatnik ➪ Groovoid ➪ Play Groovoid.

   The Play Groovoid dialog box opens, as shown in Figure 21-5.

4. If desired, enter a unique player name in the Target Player text box. Generally, Groovoids use the [available player] setting.

5. Select the looping option. Choose Yes to cause the Groovoid to repeat, No for it to play once, and Auto for automatic looping. Under the Auto setting, background music loops and user interface selections do not.

Figure 21-5: Use the Play Groovoid behavior to insert ongoing background music or short user-interface sounds.

6. Choose the Groovoid Name from the drop-down list. The Groovoids are grouped by category.

7. Select the Volume from the drop-down list, where 100 is the loudest and 0 is mute.

8. To return to the original settings, choose Default Settings from the Presets option box. If you are editing a behavior, you can choose Previous Settings to return to your prior options, or New Settings to display the latest changes.

9. Click OK when you're done.

Because of the ongoing nature of the Groovoid background music, it is sometimes helpful to pause the audio. The Pause Groovoid behavior allows you to stop and restart the music from where it stopped. Applying a second Pause Groovoid behavior causes the music to restart, as can triggering the behavior again. Moreover, you can fade the music out and back in again. Naturally, a Groovoid must be playing before it can be paused.

To insert a Pause Groovoid behavior, follow these steps:

1. Select the tag to which you'd like to attach the Pause Groovoid behavior.

2. From the Behavior Inspector, choose Beatnik ⇨ Groovoid ⇨ Pause Groovoid.

   The Pause Groovoid dialog box opens.

3. Enter the Target Player in the text box, if specified earlier. Otherwise, leave Target Player with its default setting, [matching Groovoid].

4. Select the name of the Groovoid you wish to pause.

5. If desired, enter the fade out/fade in time in the Fade Time text box, in milliseconds.

   You can use the VCR-like controls to choose a Fade Time. The Go To Beginning, Fast Reverse, and Reverse buttons decrement your value (0, –1,000, and –100, respectively), while the Play button increases it 100 milliseconds; the Fast Forward button, 1,000 milliseconds; and the Go to End button, 100,000 milliseconds (100 seconds or 1.6 minutes).

6. Click OK when you're done.

The Stop Groovoid behavior is structured exactly like Pause Groovoid and is implemented in the same fashion.

Playing Beatnik music

While Groovoids are great for providing aural feedback or "canned" background music, you can't use them to play user-designated music files. Beatnik supports a wide range of music formats: Rich Music Format (.rmf), WAV (.wav), MIDI (.mid or .midi), MOD, Audio Interchange File Format (.aiff or .aif), and AU (.au). Unlike Groovoids, these file types have to be completely downloaded before they can begin playing on the user's system. To prevent unwanted delays in playback, Beatnik includes a Preload behavior.

In all, the Beatnik ActionSet provides four commands for working with music files:

✦ **Play Music File** starts the selected file to play. The file can also be designated as looping or nonlooping.

✦ **Pause Music File** pauses and restarts the selected file with or without fades.

✦ **Stop Music File** stops the music from playing with or without a fade.

✦ **Preload Music File** loads the selected file into memory before it begins to play.

All of the behaviors function in a very similar fashion. Like the Groovoids, a Target Player is chosen initially; however, in the case of music files, it is often better to designate a Target Player, rather than leave the default selection of [available player]. By designating a Target Player, you reserve one of the eight voices for the particular file and are assured of uninterrupted play. You can also adjust the parameters of the music file while it is playing by referring to the Target Player in another behavior.

To use the Play Music File behavior, follow these steps:

1. Set up the Web page as outlined in the earlier "Initializing a Page" section, if you've not done so already.

2. Select the tag to which you'd like to attach the Play Music File behavior.

3. From the Behavior Inspector, choose Beatnik ➪ Music File ➪ Play Music File.

   The Play Music File dialog box opens, as shown in Figure 21-6.

Figure 21-6: Start any .rmf, .wav, .au, .aiff, MIDI, or MOD file through the Play Music File behavior.

4. If desired, enter a unique player name in the Target Player text box. Otherwise, leave the default [available player] setting.

5. To cause a file to play repeatedly, change the Looping option to Yes.

6. Enter the path to the music file in the File URL text box or use the ... (Browse/Choose) button to the right of the text box to locate the file.

7. Select the loudness setting for the file from the Volume option box, where 100 is the loudest and 0 is mute.

Tip   The mute or zero setting should only be chosen if you intend to fade up the music at a later time.

8. You can inspect previous configurations by choosing one of the Preset options: Default Settings, Previous Settings, or New Settings.

9. Click OK when you're finished.

The Pause Music File and Stop Music File are used in exactly the same manner as Pause Groovoid and Stop Groovoid. If you've given the music file a unique Target Player name, use that in the Pause and Stop Music File behaviors. If, on the other hand, you left the Target Player at the [available player] setting, choose [matching file] for Target Player and enter the file's path in the File URL text box.

Hitting all the notes

If you're a musician first and a Web designer second, you'll appreciate the total control Beatnik gives you over the music. Beatnik has a fully functional built-in software synthesizer that is capable of playing notes over the 16 MIDI channels using any one of over 500 instruments. Moreover, you can alter the velocity, duration or sustain, volume, and pan settings of any note.

Tip   You can easily play chords by assigning multiple Play Musical Note behaviors to a single tag and event. Just change the note settings while maintaining the same instrument in all behaviors. Of course, you could also have multiple instruments playing the same note — or any variation of the above.

There are only two behaviors in this category: Play Musical Note and Stop Musical Note. All settings are established in the Play Musical Note dialog box, shown in Figure 21-7. Generally, it's best to leave the Target Player setting at its default [reserved player] setting, although you can also specify a player already declared for a Groovoid or music file. Entering a new, previously unused value is not permitted. Likewise, leaving the Channel parameter set to [auto] allows the Beatnik Music Management System to handle note assignment. Change this setting to a specific MIDI channel only if you want to halt its playing with the Stop Musical Note behavior at some point.

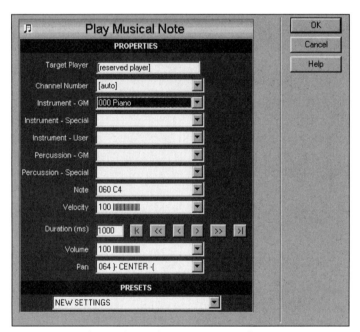

Figure 21-7: Choose from almost 350 musical MIDI instruments to play any of 128 notes over a 10-octave range with the Play Musical Note behavior.

To assign a Play Musical Note behavior, follow these steps:

1. Set up the Web page as outlined in the earlier "Initializing a Page" section, if you've not done so already.

2. Select the tag to which you'd like to attach the Play Musical Note behavior.

3. From the Behavior Inspector, choose Beatnik ⇨ Musical Note ⇨ Play Musical Note.

   The Play Musical Note dialog box opens.

4. Enter a unique name in Target Player text box, if desired. Otherwise, leave the default [reserved player] setting.

5. If a specific MIDI channel is desired, choose a new number from the Channel Number drop-down list. Otherwise, leave the default [auto] setting.

6. Choose a musical instrument from one of the following five categories:

   - **Instrument – GM.** The general MIDI soundbank, modeled after industry-standard instruments.

   - **Instrument – Special.** Variations on the general MIDI soundbank.

   - **Instrument – User.** User-defined instrumentation for RMF music files, set up by Beatnik authoring software. (These files are dependent on the selected music file and not present when the stub.rmf file is used.)

   - **Percussion – GM.** General MIDI percussive instruments.

   - **Percussion – Special.** Variations on the general MIDI percussive instruments.

Caution

Although the behavior's user interface allows you to choose multiple instruments from different categories, only the first one is valid. Therefore, make sure that only the final choice is displayed in the chosen category list box; all other list boxes should display the blank value, found at the top of the list options.

7. Choose a note pitch from C-1 (C in octave –1) to G9 (G in the ninth octave) by selecting an option from the Note drop-down list.

   The notes are shown with the corresponding MIDI number (0–127) first, followed by the musical note name. Middle C, for example, is displayed as 060 C4 — which represents the C note in the 4th octave. Sharps are designated with a hash mark (#).

8. Select the velocity (how hard the note is struck) of the musical note from the Velocity drop-down list.

   The Beatnik velocity scale goes from the hardest note struck (100) to the softest (0) and corresponds to the MIDI rates of 127-0. The default is 100.

9. Select the duration for the musical note from the Duration (ms) VCR-style controls.

   The duration is given in milliseconds. The default is 1,000 or 1 second.

10. Choose the loudness setting for the musical note from the Volume option box.

11. Choose the pan setting from the Pan option box.

    The default pan setting is the audio center, between the left and right speakers. Beatnik allows you to choose from 21 pan positions in all, from all the way to the left to all the way to the right.

12. You can inspect previous configurations by choosing one of the Preset options: Default Settings, Previous Settings, or New Settings.

13. Click OK when you're finished.

Incorporating advanced Beatnik features

Beatnik really gets its power from making your Web page audio interactive — and much of that interactivity comes from using the behaviors found under the Beatnik - Advanced category. In all, there are 22 different behaviors divided into the four main advanced sections: Channels, Global, Player, and Tracks. Virtually any of the attributes previously explored in the music file or musical note behaviors can be modified on the fly with the advanced behaviors, including the volume, pan setting, and instrument. Moreover, you can adjust the tempo, transpose the music, and instantly mute all but one of the instruments for a solo.

All the behaviors function in a similar fashion to those already described. Rather than detailing the use of each of the 22 behaviors, the remainder of this section describes their effects. The advanced Beatnik behaviors are categorized according to what they control:

✦ Channel behaviors control individual MIDI channels.

✦ Global behaviors affect all Beatnik sounds.

✦ Player behaviors pinpoint specific, named voices or players.

✦ Track behaviors target any one of the possible 64 tracks in a Beatnik MIDI or RMF composition.

Tip   Any behavior that starts with the word Adjust, such as Adjust Channel Pan, is used relatively; while any one that starts with Set, such as Set Channel Pan, is used absolutely.

Table 21-3 describes the Beatnik Channel behaviors. These behaviors are applied by selecting a tag and, from the Behavior Inspector, choosing Beatnik - Advanced ⇨ Channels and then the desired behavior. In all cases, choose either the matching Target Player or the number of the MIDI channel already playing that you wish to alter.

Caution   A known problem emerges when Adjust Channel Volume is used with the current Beatnik player (version 1.3.2). Headspace advises that this behavior not be used until a new version of the player that addresses this problem is released.

Table 21-3
Beatnik Advanced Channel Behaviors

Behavior	Description
Adjust Channel Pan	Moves the left-to-right speaker pan relative to the current setting.
Adjust Channel Volume	Changes the loudness of the selected player or channel relative to the current setting.
Set Channel Instrument	Selects a different instrument for the selected player or channel.
Set Channel Monophonic	Changes the MIDI setting from polyphonic (multivoiced) to monophonic (single-voiced) or vice versa. A Toggle option allows the setting to alternate each time it is selected.
Set Channel Mute	Turns the mute setting on or off for the selected channel or player. A Toggle option allows the setting to alternate each time it is selected.
Set Channel Pan	Selects a new left-to-right speaker pan setting for the selected player or channel.
Set Channel Solo	Changes the solo status from the unsolo setting to solo or vice versa. A Toggle option allows the setting to alternate each time it is selected.
Set Channel Volume	Selects a new loudness setting for the specified channel or player.

The Global Beatnik behaviors apply to all eight player voices, affecting every sound emanating from the Beatnik sound engine. There are only two behaviors in this category:

✦ **Set Global Mute.** This behavior effectively mutes or unmutes all Beatnik sound. The behavior can be set to one option or the other, or used as a toggle to alternate between the two states.

✦ **Set Reverb Type.** *Reverb* can be thought of as the amount of echo in a sound. Beatnik has one reverb setting for all of its sounds, which can be altered globally through this behavior. There are six different reverb options, each expressed as the size of a room, ranging from zero to the most reverb:

- No Reverb (Default)
- Closet
- Garage
- Acoustic Lab
- Cavern
- Dungeon

Caution   The Global Reverb setting should be judiciously applied. If an instrument relies heavily on reverb for its effect, changing the Global setting will significantly alter what is heard.

When you want to alter one of Beatnik's eight players on a page, use one of Beatnik's Advanced Player behaviors. These behaviors can be used in concert with the Channel behaviors to affect the sound experience. Before any of the Player behaviors can be used, a Groovoid, music file, or musical note must be inserted with a named player. Table 21-4 describes the Advanced Player behaviors.

Table 21-4
Beatnik Advanced Player Behaviors

Behavior	Description
Adjust Position	Resets the playback position relative to its current position. This behavior can be used to build a VCR-like control with fast-forward and reverse features. A positive value (measured in milliseconds) moves the position forward and a negative value moves it backward.
Adjust Tempo	Alters the playback speed of a selected player relative to the current speed. Values are measured in beats per minute; a positive number speeds up the music, while a negative number slows it down.
Adjust Transposition	Alters the pitch of a selected player relative to the current setting. Possible values range from up three octaves to down three octaves.
Adjust Volume	Modifies the current loudness setting relative to the current setting for a selected player.
Release Player	Frees one of the eight Beatnik player slots previously reserved.
Set Position	Resets the playback position to an absolute position. This behavior can be used to build a VCR-like control with a Rewind feature. A positive value (measured in milliseconds) moves the position forward and a negative value moves it backward.
Set Tempo	Resets the playback speed of a selected player to a new speed. Values are measured in beats per minute; a positive number speeds up the music, while a negative number slows it down.
Set Transposition	Resets the pitch of a selected player to a new setting. Possible values range from up three octaves to down three octaves.
Set Volume	Resets the current loudness setting relative to a new setting for a selected player.
Show Copyright Info	Displays the detailed copyright information available in every RMF file in a separate system window.

Caution Headspace has acknowledged a problem with the Show Copyright Info behavior when viewed using the current version of Beatnik, v.1.3.2. The company advises that this behavior not be used until the problem has been corrected in a future version of the Beatnik player.

The final advanced Beatnik category affects music tracks. Both RMF and Beatnik MIDI files allow composers to create their music with up to 64 different tracks. The tracks are identified by their number, 1 to 64. The two Track behaviors are as follows:

✦ **Set Track Mute** mutes or unmutes the sound on a specified track. The behavior can be set to one option or the other, or used as a toggle to alternate between the two states.

✦ **Set Track Solo** sets a specified track to solo or unsolo status. A toggle option allows the choice to alternate.

Pro Beatnik features

As noted in the introduction to the Beatnik behaviors, the ActionSet comes in both a free and upgrade version. The free version includes all the standard and advanced Beatnik behaviors; the upgrade version, purchasable from Headspace's Web site, adds the Pro Beatnik behaviors. While it's beyond the scope of this book to cover all the Pro Beatnik features in detail, knowing what additional features it offers can help you make a decision to upgrade or not.

The Pro behaviors both simply sonifying a Web page and extend its capabilities. Following are the four categories included in the Pro Beatnik behaviors:

✦ **Compatibility.** This allows the Web page designer to specify a specific minimum version requirement for the Beatnik player. Without this behavior, any system with the Beatnik player installed — regardless of version — will attempt to run the page.

✦ **Dynamic.** Often the difference between a great sound effect and an annoying one is the number of times the same sound is heard. The Dynamic category allows for Groovoids, music files, and musical notes to be chosen for a specified group and played randomly, thus varying the musical experience of a Web page.

✦ **Sonification Wizards.** The form is perhaps the most interactive of all Web page elements. Rather than undergo the tedious procedure of adding feedback sounds to each and every form check-box, radio button, or text box, Beatnik provides a Sonify Forms with Groovoids wizard, shown in Figure 21-8, for an all-in-one solution. Additionally, form elements can be used to trigger any JavaScript function by using Beatnik's Sonify Forms with Handlers. This behavior extends beyond an audio capability and allows, for example, a layer to be made visible when a text box receives focus, and disappear when it loses focus.

✦ **Synchronization.** With the Synchronization category of behaviors, Beatnik can use events in the music — such as a chorus change or the beginning of lyrics — to trigger specific JavaScript functions. These music events are incorporated into the RMF file by the composer and can be referenced generically (such as all the choruses in a song) or specifically (such as one particular lyric).

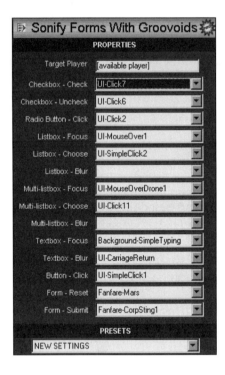

Figure 21-8: The Sonify Forms with Groovoids behavior allows you to attach aural feedback cues to any or all form elements on a page.

The Pro Beatnik behaviors are extremely powerful and allow an integration of music and visuals limited only by the imagination — and, because they're Dreamweaver behaviors, you can do it all without coding the JavaScript.

Embedding a Beatnik object in your page

Once the Beatnik object is installed in Dreamweaver, you'll find that incorporating RMF and other files to use the plug-in is a very straightforward process. As with other plug-ins, simply position the cursor where you want the Beatnik object to appear, and select it from the Objects Palette. (You can also choose Insert ➪ Beatnik from the menus.) When the Insert Beatnik dialog box opens, enter a file source in the RMF File Source text box. This can be the name of any RMF file or other audio format file. As usual, you can also select Browse to choose your file from a Select File dialog box. Click OK when you're finished.

Tip

Once you've learned how to include a Beatnik object, you can really indulge yourself. You can embed—and play!—up to eight Beatnik objects on a page (although some systems may have problems playing more than four at a time).

After you've picked your file, the Property Inspector displays your filename in the src text box, along with other information about the Beatnik object, including the following attributes:

✦ **Width and Height.** The preset dimensions conform to the size of the default Beatnik controls. As with LiveAudio objects, you can vary the size and number of Beatnik controls through the parameters.

✦ **Plg URL.** When a user doesn't have the appropriate plug-in, this attribute provides a link to get one. The Beatnik plug-in URL address is http://www. headspace.com/beatnik/?plug-in.

Caution

At a minimum, always keep the width and height attributes set to a value of at least 2, even when using the hidden parameter. Enter the width and height pixel sizes in the W and H text boxes on the Property Inspector, respectively. Otherwise, your plug-ins are not backwardly compatible with earlier versions of Netscape Navigator.

Beatnik parameters

When you click Parameters in the Beatnik object's Property Inspector, you get access to the parameters described in Table 21-5.

Table 21-5
Beatnik Object Parameters

Beatnik Parameter	Description
autostart	This attribute is set to true, which allows the audio to begin playing as soon as the file has completely downloaded. Use false if you want to control the playing of the audio independently.
Display	Determines which graphic is used to represent the Beatnik object. Options are song, which shows copyright information, or system (the default), which enables the user to toggle between the song information, output meters, or oscilloscope.
Hidden	Hides the controls; no value is specified.
Type	Sets the MIME type. If the audio file is in RMF format, this attribute is set to audio/rmf.
mode	Sets which of three graphics is to be displayed initially as the Beatnik plug-in— scope, meters, or copyright. When display=song, then only the copyright value is available.

Continued

Table 21-5 *(continued)*	
Beatnik Parameter	**Description**
loop	If set to true, this attribute causes the file to repeat continuously. If set to false (the default), the file plays once only. The value for loop can also be an integer to determine the number of times the file repeats.
volume	Preset to the loudest value (100); this attribute can be any number from 1 to 100.

Using the Windows Media Player to Play Audio

The Windows Media Player is Internet Explorer's multimedia player. As such, you can use it to play the standard audio files, including .wav, .midi, .aiff, or .au. In fact, when you add an audio file as a link, or embed it without any other specifications, Internet Explorer automatically calls Windows Media Player to play the file. Calling Windows Media Player directly as an ActiveX control, however, gives you far more flexibility over your player's appearance and functionality.

Cross-Reference

If you're unfamiliar with ActiveX controls, you might want to look over the "Incorporating an ActiveX control" section of Chapter 15 before proceeding.

Calling the Windows Media Player ActiveX control

To incorporate the Windows Media Player ActiveX control, follow these steps:

1. Position the cursor where you would like the Windows Media Player control panel to appear. Choose Insert ➪ ActiveX or select Insert ActiveX from the Objects Palette.

   The Property Inspector displays the ActiveX options.

2. In the ClassID text box, enter the ID for the Windows Media Player control: CLSID:22d6f312-b0f6-11d0-94ab-0080c74c7e95.

Tip

If you've entered this *long* Windows Media Player Class ID previously, you can click the arrow button and choose the ID from the drop-down list.

3. Change the width and height values in the W and H text boxes to match the desired control display.

   The Windows Media Player display resizes to match your dimensions as closely as possible.

Tip

If you want to show both the controls and the timer display, you can use a value of 100 for both the width and height dimensions. If you want to just show the control panel, without the timer display, make the height a minimum of 20 pixels.

4. Click Parameters in the Property Inspector.

5. Select the Add (+) button and enter the first parameter: FileName. Press Tab to move to the Value column.

6. Enter the path and filename for your audio file. Press Tab.

7. Continue entering the desired parameters and values for your audio file.

8. Click OK when you're finished.

Like LiveAudio, the ActiveX Windows Media Player control has many parameters to choose from — 34, to be exact. Explaining all of these parameters is beyond the scope of this book, but Table 21-6 lists the key parameters that parallel the LiveAudio attributes. For more detailed information on using the Windows Media Player ActiveX control, visit Microsoft's Web site DirectX section, at http://www. microsoft.com/directx/.

Table 21-6
Windows Media Player Parameters

Windows Media Player Parameter	Possible Values	Description
AutoStart	true or false	Determines if the sound begins playing when the download is complete. The default is true.
FileName	Any valid URL	Specifies the sound file to be played.
PlayCount	Any integer	Sets the number of times the file should repeat. If the value is 0, the sound loops continuously. The default is 1.
SelectionStart	Number of seconds	Determines the beginning point for the audio clip, relative to the start of the file.
SelectionEnd	Number of seconds	Determines the ending point for the audio clip, relative to the start of the file.
ShowControls	true or false	Hides the control panel if set to true. The default is false.
ShowDisplay	true or false	Hides the display panel if set to true. The default is false.
Volume	Any integer, from 10000 to 0 The default is the highest volume, 0.	Sets the loudness of the audio playback.

Using Embed with ActiveX

All ActiveX controls are included in HTML's `<object>`...`</object>` tag pair. Dreamweaver codes this for you when you insert any ActiveX control. Of course, Netscape doesn't recognize the `<object>` tag, just as Internet Explorer doesn't recognize Netscape's plug-ins. However, you can use a simple technique in Dreamweaver to ensure cross-browser compatibility for ActiveX objects.

After you've entered the `FileName` parameter and value for the ActiveX Windows Media Player control, select the Embed check-box in the Property Inspector. The same name that you specified as the `FileName` now appears in the Embed text box. Dreamweaver takes advantage of the fact that Netscape doesn't recognize the `<object>` tag by inserting the `<embed>` tag inside the `<object>`...`</object>` tag pair. The resulting HTML looks like the following:

```
<object width="200" height="18" classid="CLSID:05589FA1-
C356-11CE-BF01-00AA0055595A" border="2">
     <param name="FileName" value="images/Braz.mid">
     <param name="ShowDisplay" value="False">
     <embed width="200" height="18" border="2"
filename="images/Braz.mid" showdisplay="False"
src="images/Braz.mid"></embed>
    </object>
```

Note that Dreamweaver picks up the attributes and parameters from the ActiveX control to use in the `<embed>` tag. Often you'll have to adjust these, especially when specifying a narrow ActiveX control and a taller Netscape object.

Playing Background Music

Background music, played while the user is viewing online material, is one of the Web's hidden treasures. When used tastefully, background music can enhance the overall impact of the page. Two methods are necessary to cover the major browsers in use: the `<bgsound>` tag for Internet Explorer, and a hidden `<embed>` tag for Netscape. You can use both without fear of conflict.

For Internet Explorer: <bgsound>

Microsoft uses a proprietary HTML command to implement background sound, `<bgsound>`; although the tag has been officially deprecated, it still works in even the most current version of Internet Explorer. The `<bgsound>` tag must be coded by hand or through a custom object in Dreamweaver. The background sound command takes the following attributes:

<bgsound> Attribute	*Description*
src	Sets the URL of the background sound to be played.
loop	Determines the number of times that a file repeats. You can set the value to any integer. To cause the audio clip to repeat continually, make loop=infinite or loop=-1.

The complete HTML for a continuously looping background sound looks like this:

```
<bgsound src="sounds/bgtrack1" loop=infinite>
```

As noted earlier, the <bgsound> tag is ignored by all browsers except Internet Explorer.

For other browsers: Hidden <embed>

To make sure your background sound is heard by Netscape and other browsers besides Internet Explorer, use a hidden <embed> tag. You embed a background sound as described in the earlier section "Basic audio embedding." All you need do, once the sound is embedded, is to add the necessary parameters, and you have instant background music.

Caution   This technique "breaks" when the current version of the Windows Media Player is installed and only works for those Netscape Navigator users who have LiveAudio set up as their default player.

Follow these steps to embed background music in a Web page to be viewed in browsers other than Internet Explorer:

1. Position the cursor near the top of your Web page. Choose Insert ➪ Plug-in or select the Plug-in object from the Objects Palette.

2. Enter the path to your audio file in the Plug-in Source text box, or select Browse to locate the file.

3. In the Property Inspector, enter a 2 in both the H (Height) and W (Width) text boxes.

4. Click Parameters.

5. In the Parameters dialog box, select the Add (+) button and enter **hidden** in the Parameter column. Press Tab and enter **true** in the Value column.

6. Enter **autostart** as the next parameter and give it the value **true**.

7. To make the audio clip repeat, enter **loop** as the next parameter, and in the Value column enter the number of times you want the sound to repeat. To make the audio repeat endlessly (or until the user goes to another Web page), enter **true** as the value.

8. Click OK to finish.

Dreamweaver automatically adds the necessary parameters, such as `hidden` and `autostart`, to hide and automatically play the file.

Caution

To preserve backward compatibility with earlier Netscape versions, it's important to enter a small value in the Height and Width text boxes for the background music object, even though the control is hidden.

Installing Streaming Audio

Although audio files are not as time-consuming as video, downloading them can take a long time. Audio-on-demand — or *streaming audio* — has emerged as an alternative to such lengthy downloads. The recognized leader in the streaming audio field is RealAudio, a format developed by RealNetworks (`www.real.com`).

Cross-Reference

Streaming audio files work much the same as streaming video files, as covered in Chapter 20, "Adding Video to Your Web Page." Both these streaming formats use metafiles to call the actual media files. For details on creating metafiles, see the "Creating RealVideo metafiles" section in Chapter 20.

As with RealVideo, you can have the RealAudio player either appear to be free-floating or embedded in the Web page. Embedding a RealAudio file is explained in the next section. To insert a RealAudio streaming audio file with a free-floating player, follow these steps:

1. Select the link or image that you want to use to begin the RealAudio file.

2. In the Property Inspector, enter the path to the RealAudio metafile in the Link text box or select Browse to locate the file.

You'll want to make sure that the metafile has the .ram extension.

Using the RealAudio object

Embedding a streaming audio file has been greatly simplified with the introduction of the RealAudio object.

New Feature   In Dreamweaver 2, all you need to know is the location of the source file — whether it's on a local system or on the Web — and the RealAudio object handles the rest. The RealAudio object is virtually identical to the RealVideo object included with the RealSystem G2 objects. (To learn how to install the RealSystem G2 objects (and attach individual controls), see Chapter 20, "Adding Video to Your Web Page".)

After you've installed the RealSystem G2 objects, you can insert the RealAudio object in one of two ways. You can choose Insert ⇨ RealSystem G2 Object ⇨ RealAudio or you can select the Insert RealAudio object from the RealSystem G2 panel of the Objects Palette. Once you've inserted the object, the Insert RealAudio dialog box appears, as shown in Figure 21-9. All you need to do is to enter the path to the streaming audio file either in the Local File text box or in the URL text box; be sure to select the appropriate radio buttons for your choice. After you click OK, the object verifies the creation of two additional support files, the metafile and the SMIL file, and your file is ready to stream.

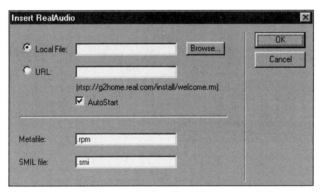

Figure 21-9: The Insert RealAudio object, part of the RealSystem G2 object set, makes embedding a streaming file into your Web page a snap.

Accessing RealAudio parameters

Only the source of the player and the dimensions are required, but it will come as no surprise to you that a great number of attributes are available for a RealAudio file. You can add any of the attributes found in Table 21-7 through the Parameters button of the selected RealAudio file's Property Inspector.

Table 21-7
RealAudio Parameters

Attributes	Possible Values	Description
autostart	true or false	Enables the RealAudio clip to start playing as soon as content is available. The default is autostart=true.
console	_master or _unique	Determines the console name for each control in a Web page that uses multiple controls. To force controls on a page to refer to the same file, use the same console=name attribute. The console name _master links to ll controls on a page; _unique connects to no other instances.
controls	all, controlpanel, infovolumepanel, infopanel, statuspanel, statusbar, playbutton, stopbutton, volumeslider, positionslider, positionfield, or statusfield	Enables the placement of individual control panel elements in the Web page. You can use multiple controls in one attribute, or multiple `<embed>` tags to build a custom RealAudio interface.
nolabels	true or false	Suppresses the Title, Author, and Copyright labels in the Status panel. If you set nolabels to true, the actual data is still visible. The default is nolabels=false.

Summary

Adding sound to a Web page indeed brings it into the realm of multimedia. Dreamweaver gives you numerous methods to handle the various different audio formats, both static and streaming. With custom Dreamweaver objects and actions, enhancing your Web site with audio is, quite literally, a snap.

✦ Audio must be digitized before it can be sent over the Web. The leading audio file formats are .wav, .au, .aiff, .rmf, and .midi (for sound that must be downloaded before it can be played).

✦ You can either link to a sound or embed it in your Web page. With standard audio, the linking technique calls an independent, free-floating player; the embedding technique incorporates the player into the design of the page.

✦ Plug-ins offer far greater control over the appearance and functionality of the sound than relying on common players; to use a plug-in, however, your user must download it.

✦ The Beatnik plug-in provides excellent fidelity and JavaScript interaction.

✦ You can include a background sound for both major browsers by using two separate but compatible techniques.

✦ Streaming audio gives almost instant access to large audio files; RealAudio is the recognized standard in the field and the inclusion of the RealSystem G2 objects simplifies embedding streaming players.

In the next chapter you learn how to incorporate Shockwave Director and Flash multimedia elements in your Dreamweaver Web pages.

✦   ✦   ✦

Inserting Shockwave Movies

CHAPTER

22

To many Web designers, Shockwave has represented the state-of-the-art in Internet multimedia since Macromedia first released the compression scheme in 1995. With Shockwave, multimedia files created in Macromedia's flagship authoring package, Director, could be compiled to run in a browser window. This gave Web designers the ability to build just about anything — from interactive Web interfaces with buttons that look indented and clicked when pushed, to arcade-style games, multimedia Web front-ends, and complete Web sites built entirely in Director — bringing a CD-ROM "look and feel" to the Web.

Macromedia's strategy was to enable the output of *all* of its products to the Web. Soon Web sites sported "Shocked" real-time scalable maps and diagrams from Freehand (a vector graphics package), and tutorials from Authorware (an instructional design package). In short order, a vector-based animation package called FutureSplash was acquired as a source of Shocked animations for Web pages, and repackaged as Macromedia Flash. Today the company offers options for streamed animation, audio, and multimedia as well.

As you might expect, Macromedia carefully paved the way for Shockwave and Flash files to be incorporated into Dreamweaver. Both of these formats have special objects that provide control over virtually all of their parameters through the Property Inspector — and each format is cross-browser-compatible by default. To take full advantage of Shockwave's multimedia capabilities, you need to understand the differences between Director and Flash, as well as the various parameters available to each format. In addition to covering this material, this chapter also shows you how to use independent controls — both inline and with frames — for your Shockwave and Flash movies.

Shockwave and Flash: What's the Difference?

Because both Director and Flash movies can be "shocked" and saved as Shockwave files, how do you choose which program to use? Each has its own special functions, and each excels at producing particular types of effects. Director is more full-featured, with a complete programming language (Lingo). And Director movies can include Flash animations. Director also has a much steeper learning curve than does Flash. Flash is terrific for short, low-bandwidth animations with or without a synchronized audio track; however, the interactive capabilities in Flash are limited.

Director is really a multimedia production program used for combining various elements: backgrounds, foreground elements called *sprites*, and various media such as digital audio and video. With Director's Lingo programming language, you can build extraordinarily elaborate demos and games — you can even use an extension called NetLingo with Internet-specific commands. When you need to include a high degree of interactivity, build your movie with Shockwave.

One of the primary differences between Director and Flash is the supported graphic formats. Director is better for *bitmap graphics*, in which each pixel is mapped to a specific color; both GIF and JPEG formats use bitmap graphics. Flash, on the other hand, uses primarily *vector graphics*, which are drawing elements described mathematically. Because vector graphics use a description of a drawing — a blue circle with a radius of 2.5 centimeters, for instance — rather than a bitmap, the resulting files are much smaller. An animation included with Flash might be only 40K — however, a comparable QuickTime movie (for which the vector graphics are converted to bitmap graphics) would be over ten times larger at 430K.

Aside from file size, the other feature that distinguishes vector graphics from bitmap graphics is the smoothness of the line. When viewed with sufficient magnification, bitmap graphics always display telltale "stair-steps" or "jaggies," especially around curves. Vector graphics, on the other hand, are almost smooth. In fact, Flash takes special advantage of this characteristic and enables users to zoom into any movie — an important effect that saves a lot of bandwidth when used correctly.

However, these differences have been significantly blurred with the release of Director 7, which now incorporates much of Flash's vector functionality. Director can now, without the assistance of any Xtra (a Director plug-in), create and show vector graphics, but Flash still needs to convert bitmaps to vectors before it can display them.

Flash animations can be used as special effects, cartoons, and navigation bars within (or without) frames. Although Flash isn't the best choice for games and other complex interactive elements, you can use Flash to animate your navigation system — complete with sound effects for button-pushing feedback.

If Flash 3 is a power-tool, Director is a bulldozer. Director 7 has been significantly expanded to handle a wide variety of file types, such as QuickTime and MP3, with advanced streaming capabilities. Supporting multimedia interactivity is Director's own programming language, Lingo, which has also been enhanced for version 7. Furthermore, Director 7 includes multiplayer support for network games play and chat rooms, XML parsing, embedded compressed fonts, up to 1,000 sprite channels, and a potential frame rate of 999 frames per second. Luckily, Dreamweaver lets you pack all that power into a Web page with its Shockwave object.

Including Shockwave Movies in Dreamweaver Projects

Dreamweaver makes it easy to bring Shockwave and Flash files into your Web pages. The Objects Palette provides an object for both types of movie, located in the Common panel.

New Feature

Because Shockwave and Flash objects insert both an ActiveX control and a plug-in, Dreamweaver 2 enables you to play the movie in the Document Window. First it displays a plug-in placeholder icon (see Figure 22-1).

Flash placeholder

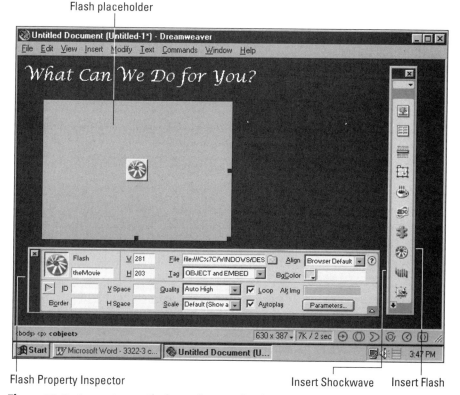

Flash Property Inspector   Insert Shockwave   Insert Flash

Figure 22-1: Lay out your Flash or Director Shockwave movie and preview it in any compatible browser.

Before you can successfully include a Flash or Shockwave file, you need to know one small bit of information — the dimensions of your movie. Now, Dreamweaver 2 automatically reads the dimensions of your Flash file when you use the Insert Flash Movie object.

Unfortunately, if you're incorporating a Shockwave movie, you still need to enter the dimensions by hand in the

To check the width and height of your movie in Director, load your file and then choose Modify ➪ Movie ➪ Properties to open the Movie Properties dialog box.

Tip   It is essential to have the movie's height and width before you can include it successfully in Dreamweaver-built Web pages. During the development phase of a Dreamweaver project, I often include the movie dimensions in a filename, as an instant reminder to take care of this detail. For example, if I'm working with two different Shockwave movies, I can give them names like navbar125 x 241.dcr and navbar400 x 50.dcr. (The .dcr extension is automatically appended by Director when you save a movie as a Shockwave file.) By consistently putting width before height in the file name, this trick saves me the time it would take to reopen Director, load the movie, and choose Modify ➪ Movie to check the measurements in the Movie Properties dialog box.

To include either a Shockwave or Flash file in your Web page, follow these steps:

1. Position the cursor in the Document Window at the point where you'd like the movie to appear.

2. Insert the movie using any of these methods:

   • Choose Insert ➪ Shockwave or Insert ➪ Flash from the menus.

   • In the Common panel of the Objects Palette, select either the Insert Shockwave or Insert Flash button.

   • Drag the movie object from the Objects Palette to any location in the Document Window.

3. In the Select File dialog box, enter the path and the filename in the File Name text box or select the Browse (Choose) button to locate the file. Click OK.

   Dreamweaver inserts a small plug-in placeholder in the current cursor position, and the Property Inspector displays the appropriate information for Shockwave or Flash.

4. Preview the Flash or Shockwave movie in the Document Window by selecting the Play button found in the extended Property Inspector. You can also choose View ➪ Plugins ➪ Play.

5. End the preview of your file by selecting the Stop button in the extended Property Inspector or selecting View ➪ Plugins ➪ Stop.

Tip   If you have more than one Flash or Shockwave movie on your page, you can control them all by choosing View ⇨ Plugins ⇨ Play All and View ⇨ Plugins ⇨ Stop All. If your files appear in different pages in a frameset, you'll have to repeat the Play All command for each page.

As noted earlier, you must specify the dimensions of your file in the Property Inspector before you can preview the movie in a browser; again, Dreamweaver 2 now supplies this information automatically for Flash files, but you'll have to enter it yourself for Shockwave movies. Although they produce basically the same kind of file, Shockwave and Flash have some different features in the Dreamweaver Property Inspector. These differences are covered separately in the following sections.

On the CD-ROM   You'll find a custom Command that automates this process for you called Insert Shockwave HTML in the Configuration\Commands folder.

Specifying Shockwave properties

Once you've inserted your Shockwave file, you're ready to begin entering the specific parameters in the Property Inspector. The Property Inspector takes care of all but one Shockwave attribute, the `palette` parameter. Some of the information, including the ActiveX Class ID, is automatically set in the Property Inspector when you insert the movie.

Generating HTML Within Director

Starting with Director 7, you can now generate a file with all the appropriate HTML code at the same time that you save your Shockwave movie, with just the selection of a check-box. When you choose File ⇨ Save as Shockwave Movie in Director, the dialog box now contains a Generate HTML option. Selecting this option causes Director 7 to save an HTML file with the same name as your Shockwave movie, but with an appropriate file extension (.html for Macintosh and .htm for Windows). You can easily copy-and-paste this HTML code directly into Dreamweaver.

When you open the Director-generated HTML file, you'll see the name of your file and the Shockwave placeholder, correctly sized and ready to preview. To move this object into another Web page in progress, just select the Shockwave object and choose Edit ⇨ Copy. Then switch to your other page and choose Edit ⇨ Paste. Naturally, you can also use the keyboard shortcuts or, if both pages are accessible, just drag-and-drop the object from one page to another.

To set or modify the parameters for a Shockwave file, follow these steps:

1. Select the Shockwave placeholder icon.

2. In the Shockwave Property Inspector, enter the width and the height values in the W and H text boxes, respectively, as shown in Figure 22-2. Alternately, you can click and drag any of the three resizing handles on the placeholder icon.

Note Pressing the Shift key while dragging the corner resizing handle maintains the current aspect ratio.

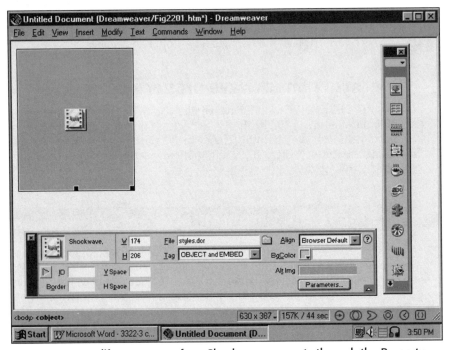

Figure 22-2: Modify parameters for a Shockwave property through the Property Inspector.

3. To designate how the Shockwave HTML code is written, select one of these three options from the Tag drop-down list:

   • **Object and Embed.** This is the default option and ensures that code is written for both Internet Explorer and Netscape Navigator/Communicator. Use this option unless your page is on an intranet where only one browser is used.

- **Object only.** Select this option to enable your movie to be viewed by Internet Explorer-compatible browsers.

- **Embed only.** Select this option to enable your movie to be viewed by Navigator/Communicator-compatible browsers.

4. Set and modify other object attributes as needed; see Table 22-1 for a list.

Table 22-1
Property Inspector Options for Shockwave Objects

Shockwave Property	Description
Align	Choose an option to alter the alignment of the movie. In addition to the browser default, your options include Baseline, Top, Middle, Bottom, Texttop, Absolute Middle, Absolute Bottom, Left, and Right.
Alt Image	The Alt Image file is displayed in browsers that do not support the `<object>` tag, and is available if you select Object Only. This image does not display in Dreamweaver. Enter the path to the alternate image, or select the Folder icon to open a Select Image Source dialog box.
BgColor	The background color is only visible if the width and height of the plug-in are larger than the movie. To alter the background color of your plug-in, choose the color swatch and select a new color from the pop-up menu; or enter a valid color name in the BgColor text box.
Border	To place a border around your movie, enter a number in the Border text box. The number determines the width of the border in pixels. The default is zero or no border.
H Space	You can increase the space to the left and right of the movie by entering a value in the H (Horizontal) Space text box. The default is zero.
ID	The ID field is used to define the optional ActiveX ID parameter, most often used to pass data between ActiveX controls.
(Name)	If desired, you can enter a unique name in this unlabeled field on the far left of the Property Inspector. The name is used by JavaScript and other languages to identify the movie.
V Space	To increase the amount of space between other elements on the page, and the top and bottom of the movie plug-in, enter a pixel value in the V (Vertical) Space text box. Again, the default is zero.

Additional parameters for Shockwave

As with other plug-ins, you can pass other attributes to the Shockwave movie via the Parameters dialog box—available by clicking the Parameters button on the Property Inspector. Press the Add (+) button to begin inserting additional parameters. Enter the attributes in the left column and their respective values in the right. To remove an attribute, highlight it and select the Delete (–) button.

Automatic settings for Shockwave files

When you insert a Shockwave or Flash file, Dreamweaver writes a number of parameters that are constant and necessary. In the `<object>` portion of the code, Dreamweaver includes the ActiveX Class ID number as well as the `codebase` number; the former calls the specific ActiveX control, and the latter enables users who don't have the control installed to receive it automatically. Likewise, in the `<embed>` section, Dreamweaver fills in the `pluginspage` attribute, designating the location where Navigator users can find the necessary plug-in. Be sure you don't accidentally remove any of this information—however, if you should, all you have to do is delete and reinsert the object.

The palette parameter

Only one other general attribute is usually assigned to a Shockwave file, the `palette` parameter. This parameter takes a value of either `foreground` or `background`.

✦ If `palette` is set to `background`, the movie's color scheme does not override that of the system; this is the default.

✦ When `palette` is set to `foreground`, then the colors of the selected movie are applied to the user's system—which includes the desktop, scroll bars, and so forth.

Note that `palette` is not supported by Internet Explorer.

Caution

Web designers should take care when specifying the `palette=foreground` parameter. This effect is likely to prove startling to the user; moreover, if your color scheme is sufficiently different, the change may render the user's system unusable. If you do use the `palette` parameter, be sure to include a Director command to restore the original system color scheme in the final frame of the movie.

Designating Flash attributes

Flash movies require the same basic parameters as their Director counterparts—and Flash movies have a few additional optional ones as well. As it does for Shockwave files, Dreamweaver sets almost all the attributes for Flash movies through the Property Inspector. The major difference you'll notice is that several more parameters are available.

To set or modify the attributes for a Flash file, follow these steps:

1. After your Flash movie has been inserted in the Document Window, make sure it's selected. Then insert the width and height dimensions in the W and H text boxes of the Property Inspector.

2. Set the other attributes in the Property Inspector, as needed for your Flash movie. (Refer to the previous descriptions of these attributes in the "Specifying Shockwave parameters" section.) In addition, you can also set the parameters described in Table 22-2.

Table 22-2		
Property Inspector Options for Flash Objects		
Flash Parameter	**Possible Values**	**Description**
Autoplay	Checked (default) or unchecked	Enables the Flash movie to begin playing as soon as it has completely downloaded or, if streaming, as soon as enough has loaded.
Loop	Checked (default) or unchecked	If Loop is checked, the movie plays continuously; if unchecked, the movie plays once.
Quality:		Controls anti-aliasing during playback.
	High	Anti-aliasing is turned on.
	Low	The animation begins in high quality (with anti-aliasing) and switches to normal if the host computer is too slow.
	AutoHigh (default)	No anti-aliasing is used; this setting is best for animations that must be played quickly.
	AutoLow	Starts the animation in normal quality (no anti-aliasing) and then switches to high quality if the host machine is fast enough.
Scale:		Scale determines how the movie fits into the dimensions as specified in the width and height text boxes.
	ShowAll (default)	Displays the entire movie in the given dimensions while maintaining the file's original aspect ratio. Some of the background may be visible with this setting.
	ExactFit	Scales the movie precisely into the dimensions without regard for the aspect ratio. It is possible that the image could be distorted with this setting.
	NoBorder	Fits the movie into the given dimensions so that no borders are showing, and maintains the original aspect ratio. Some of the movie may be cut off with this setting.

Setting the scale in Flash movies

Be careful with your setting for the Scale parameter. It is important that you supply the exact dimensions of your Flash movie. Note in Figure 22-3 the comments below each of the four examples. The example in the lower-right corner of this figure is the only one with the exact measurements and the only one that is displayed properly.

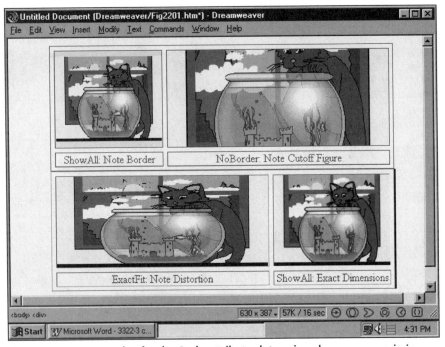

Figure 22-3: Your setting for the Scale attribute determines how your movie is resized within the plug-in width and height measurements.

Tip   Dreamweaver makes it easy to rescale a Flash movie. First, from the Property Inspector, enter the precise width and height of your file in the W and H text boxes. Then, while holding the Shift key, click and drag the corner resizing handle of the Flash placeholder icon to the new size for the movie. By Shift-dragging, you retain the aspect ratio set in the Property Inspector. This lets you quickly enlarge or reduce your movie without distortion.

Additional parameters for Flash

Flash has two additional attributes that can be entered through the Parameters dialog box (click the Parameters button on the Property Inspector): salign and swliveconnect. The salign attribute determines how the movie aligns itself to the surrounding frame when the Scale attribute is set to ShowAll. In addition, salign determines which portion of the image gets cut off when the Scale attribute is set to NoBorder. The alignment can be set to L (left), R (right), T (top), or B (bottom). You can also use these values in combination. For example, if you set `salign=RB`, the movie aligns with the right-bottom edge or the lower-right corner of the frame.

The `swliveconnect` attribute comes into play when you're using FSCommands or JavaScripting in your Flash 3 movies. FSCommands are interactive commands, such as Go to URL, issued from inside the Flash movie. The latest versions of the Netscape browser initialize Java when first called — and if your Flash movie uses FSCommands or JavaScript, it uses Java to communicate with the Netscape plug-in interface, LiveConnect. Because not all Flash movies need the LiveConnect connection, you can prevent Java from being initialized by entering the `swliveconnect` attribute in the Parameters dialog box and set its value to `false`. When the `swliveconnect=false` parameter is found by the browser, the Java is not initialized as part of the loading process — and your movie loads quicker.

Working with the Aftershock Utility

To play Director's and Flash's Shockwave files, a plug-in or an ActiveX control is required. If a user doesn't have the necessary plug-in or control, one will have to be downloaded and installed before the user can view your Shockwave page. Macromedia does, however, offer a nonplug-in alternative: the Aftershock utility.

Aftershock enables Flash movies to be converted to Java applets, which can be played through any browser that supports Java without a plug-in. It's even possible to build your Flash Web pages so that they gracefully "degrade," depending on the user's system. If the user has the Flash plug-in, play the regular Flash movie; if the user doesn't have the plug-in but is Java-enabled, show the Java version; if neither the plug-in nor Java is available, show a still from the Flash movie in JPEG format.

Tip You can force Aftershock to degrade to an animated GIF by exporting your movie in that format from Flash and then substituting the JPEG <img> source for that of the newly generated GIF animation.

Aftershock 2.5 comes complete with a Dreamweaver object for straightforward use and editing. Install the Aftershock object by copying Aftershock.htm and Aftershock.gif to one of the standard Configuration\Objects subfolders such as Common, or to a new subfolder that you've created, and restart Dreamweaver.

Caution A couple of known problems exist with installing Aftershock. First, some early copies of Dreamweaver did not include the button for the Aftershock object, Aftershock.gif. You'll find a copy of it on this book's CD-ROM in the Configuration\ Objects\Common folder. Second, the version of Aftershock included with Director 7 is 2.5, but the About command lists the version as 2.0. If you're unsure which version you have, be sure to download the latest version from Macromedia's Web site.

Once you've installed the Aftershock object, it's a two-step process to insert — and convert — a Flash movie to take advantage of Aftershock capabilities. To use Aftershock in Dreamweaver, follow these steps:

1. Choose Insert ➪ Aftershock or select the Aftershock button from the Objects Palette.

   The Aftershock dialog box appears.

2. Enter the path to the Flash or Shockwave file to insert with Aftershock in the text box or use the Browse (Choose) button to locate the file.

   Once you've chosen a file, Dreamweaver puts a placeholder icon on screen and the Aftershock Property Inspector is made available. Select the Play button on the extended Property Inspector to run the Flash movie.

3. Before you modify your Aftershock settings, you must save the HTML file.

   If you haven't saved your file, Dreamweaver alerts you to the problem.

4. Select the Launch Aftershock button on the Property Inspector.

   Aftershock opens, as shown in Figure 22-4.

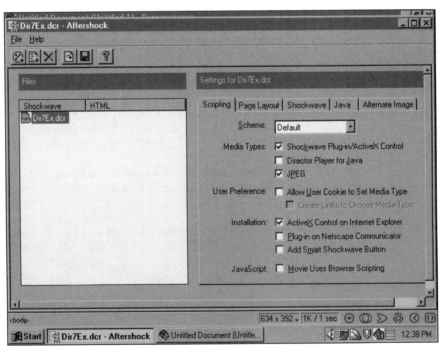

Figure 22-4: Aftershock enables browsers without the Flash plug-in to view Java or animated GIF versions of your Flash movie.

5. A file requester appears on top of Aftershock asking that you locate the referenced Flash movie. Use the Browse (Choose) button to locate the file and click Select.

6. Choose your settings in the Aftershock utility.

Note Aftershock offers many different parameters and settings, and covering them all is beyond the scope of this book. For more information about using this utility, see the Aftershock Help pages or your Flash manual, or visit the Aftershock support center on Macromedia's Web site at `http://www.macromedia.com/support/flash/how/subjects/aftershock/`.

7. When you're ready, save your Aftershock file by selecting the Save button or choosing File ➪ Save Changes.

As the file is saved, the code is written into the Dreamweaver page that follows your settings with built-in browser detection.

Configuring MIME Types

As with any plug-in, your Web server has to have the correct MIME types set before Shockwave files can be properly served to your users. If your Web page plays Shockwave and Flash movies locally, but not remotely, chances are good the correct MIME types need to be added. Configuring MIME types is generally handled by the system administrator.

The system administrator needs to know the following information in order to correctly configure the MIME types:

Application	MIME Type	File Extension
Shockwave	application/x-director	*.dcr, *.dir, *.dxr
Flash	application/x-shockwave-flash	*.swf

Both Shockwave and Flash are popular plug-ins, and it's likely that the Web server is already configured to recognize the appropriate file types.

Tip Movies made by an earlier version of Flash, called FutureSplash, can also be played by the Flash plug-in—but only if the correct MIME type is added: `application/futuresplash` with the file extension, *.spl.

Providing User Interaction with Shockwave Movies

What happens once you've installed your Director or Flash Shockwave files? Many movies are set to play automatically or upon some action from the user, such as a mouse click on a particular hotspot within the page. The Show Me movies used in the Dreamweaver Help Pages are good examples of the kind of interactivity you can program within a Director Shockwave movie. But what if you want the user to be able to start or stop a movie in one part of the page, using controls in another part? How can controls in one frame affect a movie in a different frame?

Dreamweaver includes a Control Shockwave or Flash behavior that makes inline controls — controls on the same Web page as the movie — very easy to set up. However, establishing frame-to-frame control is slightly more complex in Dreamweaver and requires a minor modification to the program-generated code. You'll find all you need to know in this section, for using both techniques.

Both of the following step-by-step techniques rely on Dreamweaver behaviors. If you're unfamiliar with using behaviors, you will want to review Chapter 17, "Using Behaviors," before proceeding.

Dreamweaver Technique: Creating inline Shockwave controls

Certainly it's perfectly acceptable to make your Director or Flash movies with built-in controls for interactivity, but sometimes you'll want to separate the controls from the movie. Dreamweaver includes a JavaScript behavior called Control Shockwave or Flash. With this behavior, you can set up external controls to start, stop, and rewind Shockwave and Flash movies.

To create inline Shockwave or Flash controls:

1. Insert your Shockwave or Flash file by choosing either the Insert Shockwave or Insert Flash button from the Objects Palette.

2. From the Select File dialog box, enter the path to your file in the File Name text box, or select the Browse (Choose) button to locate your file.

3. For Shockwave, enter the width and height of your movie in the W and H text boxes, respectively, in the Property Inspector. The dimensions for Flash movies are entered automatically.

4. Enter a unique name for your movie in the text box provided.

5. If you are inserting a Flash movie, deselect the Autoplay and Loop options.

6. To insert the first control, position the cursor where you'd like the control to appear on the page.

7. Select Insert Image from the Objects Palette or select some text.

8. In the Link box of the Property Inspector, enter a dummy link or just a hash symbol, #, to create an empty target.

9. Open the Behavior Inspector by selecting the Behavior button from the Launcher or by pressing F8.

10. If necessary, change the selected browser to 4.0 Browsers; you can do this by opening the drop-down list at the top of the Browser Inspector.

11. Select the + (Add) Action button and choose Control Shockwave or Flash from the drop-down list.

12. In the Control Shockwave or Flash dialog box (see Figure 22-5), select the movie you want to affect from the Movie drop-down list.

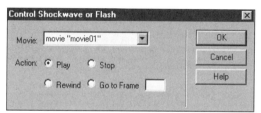

Figure 22-5: In the Control Shockwave or Flash dialog box, you assign a control action to an image button or link.

13. Now select the desired action for your control. Choose from the four options: Play, Stop, Rewind, and Go to Frame. If you choose the Go to Frame option, enter a frame number in the text box.

14. Click OK to close the Control Shockwave or Flash dialog box.

15. Repeat Steps 6–14 for each movie control you'd like to add. Figure 22-6 shows a sample Web page with three different controls in various places on the page.

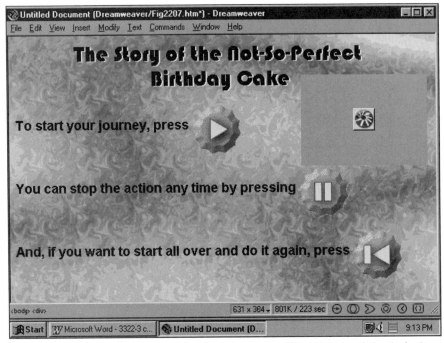

Figure 22-6: This Web page contains three controls—Play, Stop, and Rewind—inserted via the inline Control Shockwave or Flash technique.

Dreamweaver Technique: Playing Shockwave movies in frames

Framesets and frames are great for Web sites in which you want your navigation and other controls kept in one place, in one frame, and the freedom to vary the content in another frame. It's entirely possible to set up your movie's playback buttons in one frame and the Shockwave movie in another. The method and the tools used are very similar to those used in the preceding technique for adding same-page controls to a Shockwave movie. For this technique using frames, some HTML hand-coding is necessary, but it is relatively minor—only one additional line per control!

As you saw in the previous section, Dreamweaver's Control Shockwave or Flash behavior lists all the Shockwave movies, both Flash and Director, on the Web page and lets you choose the one you want to affect (as previously shown in Figure 22-4). Unfortunately, the behavior as currently constructed only looks on one page and not through an entire frameset. However, with a little sleight-of-hand and a bit of JavaScript, you can get the effect you want.

Tip

Before you begin applying this technique, you should have constructed (and saved) your frameset and individual frames. Be sure to name each frame uniquely, because you'll have to provide the names in order to address the correct frames.

To place Shockwave controls in frames:

1. In one frame, insert the images or links that are going to act as the Shockwave controls. (For this demonstration, the control frame is named `frControl`.)

2. In another frame, insert the Shockwave file (either Shockwave or Flash) by choosing the appropriate object from the Objects Palette. (For this demonstration, the movie frame is named `frMovie`.) In Figure 22-7, `frControl` is on the left of the page, and `frMovie` is on the right.

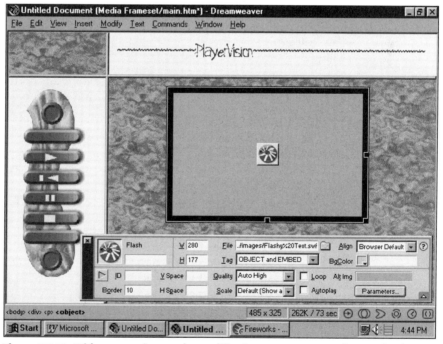

Figure 22-7: With some minor code modification, you can control your Shockwave movies from a different frame.

3. Be sure to modify the Shockwave Property Inspector with the necessary parameters: name, width, height, and source; and, if you're inserting a Flash file, deselect the Autoplay and Loop check-boxes.

4. Copy the Shockwave placeholder by selecting it and choosing Edit ➪ Copy.

5. Position the cursor in the `frControl` frame, and paste the placeholder in a temporary position by choosing Edit ⇨ Paste. At this point, the placement for the placeholder is not critical, as long as it is in the same frame as the images or links you are going to use as controls. The placeholder will be deleted shortly.

   Instead of using the Copy and Paste commands, you can hold down Ctrl (Command), and click and drag the placeholder to its new temporary position.

6. Now select the first image or link you want to use as a control. As described in the preceding technique, attach the Control Shockwave or Flash behavior to the selected object. As you learned in the preceding exercise, this entails the following actions:

   • With the image or link selected, open the Behavior Inspector.

   • Add the Control Shockwave or Flash action.

   • In the Control Shockwave or Flash dialog box, specify the movie and select the required action (Play, Rewind, Stop, or Go to Frame).

7. The major work is finished now. All you still need to do is add a little HTML. Open the HTML Inspector or use your favorite external editor to edit the file.

8. Locate the image or link controls in the code. Each JavaScript routine is called from within an `<a>` tag and will read something like the following, where `fMovie` is the name of the Flash movie:

   ```
   <a href="#" onClick="MM_controlShockwave('document.fMovie',
   'document.fMovie','Play')">
   ```

9. Wherever you see the JavaScript reference to `document`, change it to

   ```
   parent.frameName.document
   ```

   where `frameName` is the unique name you gave to the frame in which your movie appears. In our example, `frameName` is `frMovie`, so after the replacement is made the tag reads as follows:

   ```
   <a href="#" onClick="MM_controlShockwave('parent.frMovie.
   document.fMovie','document.fMovie','Play')">
   ```

   By making this substitution, you've pointed the JavaScript function first to the "parent" of the current document — and the parent of a frame is the entire frameset. Now that we're looking at the entire frameset, the next word (which is the unique frame name) points the JavaScript function directly to the desired frame within the frameset.

   Tip   If you have a number of controls, you might want to use Dreamweaver 2's advanced Find and Replace features to ensure that you've updated all the code.

10. After you've made the alterations to all of your controls, close the HTML Inspector or external editor.

11. Finally, delete the temporary Shockwave movie that was inserted into the frame containing the controls.

Test the frameset by pressing F12 (primary browser) or Shift-F12 (secondary browser). If you haven't changed the Property Inspector's default Tag attribute (the default is Object and Embed), the Shockwave movie should work in both Netscape Navigator and Internet Explorer.

Summary

Shockwave makes a strong case for being the king of all multimedia. Together, the interactive power of Shockwave and the speedy glitz of Flash can enliven a Web page's content like nothing else. Dreamweaver is extremely well-suited for integrating and displaying Shockwave movies.

✦ Shockwave is a compression/playback system developed by Macromedia. Both Director and Flash enable creations called movies to be exported into the Shockwave format. Shockwave movies are played on the Web with the help of a plug-in, Java Applet, or ActiveX control.

✦ Dreamweaver has built-in objects for both Director and Flash versions of Shockwave files. All the important parameters are accessible directly through the Property Inspector.

✦ You only need three parameters to incorporate a Shockwave movie: the file's location, height, and width. Dreamweaver 2 now automatically imports a Flash movie's dimensions. You can get the exact measurements of a Shockwave movie from within Director.

✦ Dreamweaver comes with a JavaScript behavior for controlling Shockwave movies. This Control Shockwave or Flash behavior can be used as-is for adding external controls to the same Web page or — with a minor modification — for adding the controls to another frame in the same frameset.

In the next chapter you'll begin to learn about Dynamic HTML.

✦   ✦   ✦

Dynamic HTML and Dreamweaver

◆ ◆ ◆ ◆

What's Dynamic HTML?

✦ ✦ ✦ ✦

In This Chapter

Dynamic HTML fundamentals

Using the DHTML features of Navigator

Applying DHTML techniques in Internet Explorer

✦ ✦ ✦ ✦

Dynamic HTML sounds like an ad slogan for the latest technology, doesn't it? In this case, the word *dynamic* refers to the capability to change, evolve, grow, shift, and otherwise metamorphose into a different state. With Dynamic HTML (or DHTML), almost everything on the heretofore static Web page can change. Moreover, these dynamic transitions are not generated from the server side of the Internet, but inherent in the programming language itself.

Depending on the implementation, Dynamic HTML enables an amazing range of effects to take place:

✦ Objects fly in from all corners of the screen and assemble into a coherent, integrated portion of the page.

✦ Text and logos suddenly materialize and instantly disappear from the screen.

✦ Web pages aren't two-dimensional — now objects can be in front of or behind other objects.

✦ Outlines expand to reveal details and collapse to provide an overview; content changes with the interactive click of a button.

✦ The design on the Web appears as it was designed off the Web; designers can make their Web layouts appear just the way they want, without complicated tables or single-pixel spacers.

✦ Tables are automatically generated according to the data returned from a query, and then updated globally with input from the user.

These capabilities barely scratch the surface of the Dynamic HTML possibilities. With Dreamweaver's advanced interface, challenging and code-intensive projects become intuitively achievable. Dreamweaver is among the first Web authoring tools to take full advantage of Dynamic HTML capabilities.

With its history of open standards and competing commercial visions, however, the Web doesn't yet have a smooth road with Dynamic HTML. In theory, both Netscape and Microsoft have fully embraced DHTML, but the reality is that both companies have adopted divergent models of the standard. Dreamweaver rises above the fray and makes cross-browser Dynamic HTML really work — with little or no assistance from the Web designer.

This chapter has a dual purpose. First and foremost, it introduces you to the concepts of DHTML and provides an overview of the current state of implementation in the two primary browsers. Second, it examines the browser-specific Dynamic HTML features and shows you how to employ them in Dreamweaver.

Tip For a taste of the possibilities with Dynamic HTML, visit Macromedia's Dynamic HTML Zone at www.dhtmlzone.com and select the Tutorials option. Once you're in the tutorial screen, click the Launch Superfly button. This demo not only shows the excitement Dynamic HTML can generate, but also acts as an excellent tutorial. (While you're in the Dynamic HTML Zone, be sure to also check out the Spotlight sites for further demonstrations.)

Fundamentals of Dynamic HTML

What makes Dynamic HTML so, well . . . dynamic? No single factor can take all the credit. Rather, DHTML is really a combination of new technologies that are coming to be regarded as the next generation of Web development. In this section, you examine the roles of the components that make up DHTML:

✦ **Cascading Style Sheets.** CSS give the Web designer control over the many characteristics of the Web page, whether designated by a standard or custom HTML tag.

✦ **Absolute positioning.** This feature enables pixel-precise placement of any Web object.

✦ **Dynamic content.** The Web page can have content added or deleted on the fly.

✦ **Downloadable fonts.** Web designers can embed specific fonts to control a Web page's typography.

✦ **Data binding.** Server-side data is linked to a table or form on a Web page, which can dynamically update without redrawing the entire page.

Not all of this functionality is cross-browser, but all these features are possible in one configuration or another. As a whole, Dynamic HTML brings a more responsive, media-rich Web environment to the Web designer's palette — one that more closely resembles multimedia CD-ROM productions, while still maintaining the unique hyperconnectivity of the Internet. Best of all, Dynamic HTML is far more internalized than earlier HTML implementations, relying less on Helper applications and plug-ins to achieve its state-of-the-art effects.

Cascading Style Sheets

As sanctioned by the HTML-governing body, the World Wide Web Consortium (W3C), the Cascading Style Sheet (CSS) specification is at the core of DHTML. CSS was the first step toward making traditional HTML more flexible and malleable. In a nutshell, CSS enables a Web designer to specify the attributes of an HTML tag — whether in a single page or through an entire site — with one command.

Take the ⟨h1⟩ tag, for instance. Does management want all headlines across the company's Web site during July to be Helvetica 24-point and blue-green? CSS can handle this request in one line:

```
h1 {  font: 24pt Helvetica; color: green}
```

If you're a print-oriented layout artist who has been trying to adjust to HTML, you'll appreciate not only the flexibility and control of Cascading Style Sheets, but also their implementation. CSS uses the well-established language of print designers. Fonts, for example, can be sized in points or picas, instead of with relative sizes 1–6.

The Cascading Style Sheets technology not only affects the standard attributes of HTML tags, but also extends the number and variety of properties that can be modified. For instance, CSS now enables Web designers to specify the line height of any given tag, whether to make a paragraph of text double-spaced, or to tighten the leading (line-spacing) for subheads. CSS offers entire categories of new elements, such as boxes, that can be added to the designer's palette and the Web page. Moreover, CSS power is not limited to existing standard tags — you can create custom styles and assign them special characteristics. For instance, a large organization may define a "legal" style to be used in disclaimers and other fine print.

The important aspect of CSS from the standpoint of DHTML is that CSS begins to control the elements on the page in a systematic fashion. In the fullest implementation of CSS, scripting languages such as JavaScript can address any declared style and modify its properties interactively.

Cross-Reference Dreamweaver uses an intuitive interface for working with CSS. To learn more about this topic, see Chapter 24, "Building Style Sheet Web Pages."

Absolute positioning

From a print designer's viewpoint, perhaps the single most aggravating aspect of working on the Web has been the inability to easily place type or graphics anywhere on the page. Designers have had to go to elaborate lengths, using complex nested tables and one-pixel images as spacers, in attempts to achieve a faithful online representation of their designs.

An extension of Cascading Style Sheets now provides a more elegant solution: *absolute positioning*. Known as CSS-P, the standard for positioning has been adopted fully by Microsoft and to a lesser extent by Netscape. CSS-P forms the basis for layers.

Layers are invisible containers that can hold any type and amount of Web elements — and most important, they can be positioned anywhere on a Web page to exact pixel coordinates.

The power of layers goes farther than absolute positioning, however. Layers and their contents can be made invisible or visible with a change of one property. Because CSS employs a concept known as *inheritance*, in which related styles take on the characteristics of the parent style, many layers can be manipulated at once. As the term implies, layers bring an illusion of depth to the Web page. By design, each layer exists in its own three-dimensional plane. You can stack one layer on top of another or you can change their stacking order interactively.

Just as regular CSS elements can be updated dynamically, so can the position of layers — which makes the look of animation possible. Just as one second in a movie is actually 24 static images shown rapidly, layers can be quickly repositioned, appearing to move from point A to point B. This animation quality is one of the most striking features of Dynamic HTML. For the first time, movement on the Web is not generated from a source external to the Web page itself, whether it is server-push, an animated GIF, or a plug-in. This capability accelerates the display of pages online and enables Web pages to be viewed offline in a more easy and complete manner.

 To learn more absolute positioning and layers, refer to Chapter 25, "Working with Layers."

Dynamic content

So far, Dynamic HTML can change the look of a Web page's elements with CSS and control the placement of a Web page's objects with layers — but what about the content? Only Microsoft has currently taken the challenge of creating dynamic content. Because Internet Explorer 4.0 has complete control over the Document Object Model (DOM), any element or tag can be updated on the fly. This capability includes the content or value of tags.

Dynamic content is extremely useful when working with outline-based documents. With dynamic content links, you can show only the heading of a document, which when selected by the user, expands to present the substance — no matter how many paragraphs exist. Select the same heading again, and the expanded outline collapses. Expanding and collapsing outlines can be implemented in both primary 4.0 browsers. Only Microsoft, however, uses true dynamic content; Netscape uses a technique involving layers.

When you build an expanding outline in a Web page, you initially include all the content. Then, you designate the heading and the content and apply the appropriate styles, as illustrated in Figure 23-1.

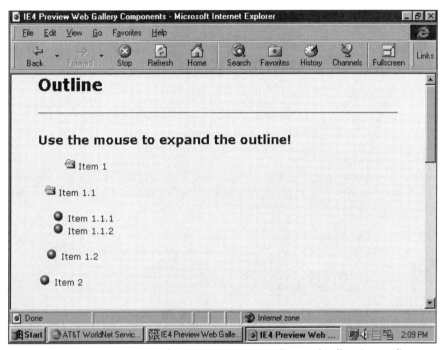

Figure 23-1: Dynamic content lets you create expanding and collapsing outlines.

Downloadable fonts

Increased font control tops the wish list for most Web designers — and this capability does not mean font size or color. For too long, Web pages have been limited to the most generic of typefaces (primarily Times and Helvetica), because HTML could only access the fonts on the user's system. Dynamic HTML promises to change this deficiency with downloadable fonts. As the term implies, *downloadable fonts* enable the Web designer to embed a specific font within a DHTML page, and the font is temporarily transferred to the Web site visitor's system.

Unfortunately, at the present time, the key word in the preceding paragraph is "promises." Both Microsoft and Netscape have implemented their own mutually incompatible versions of downloadable fonts. The demand for this capability is so strong, however, that it is only a matter of time before downloadable fonts become a cross-browser reality and a working standard. In the meantime, you can apply Open Font in Internet Explorer 4.0 and Dynamic Font technology in Communicator 4.0 simultaneously.

Tip

You can embed fonts capable of being read by both browsers with the help of Bitstream's TrueDoc technology. While it's native to Navigator, Internet Explorer users only need an ActiveX control, which can be automatically downloaded.

Data binding

Tying an online database to a Web page has never been a trivial matter. Any Web page had to be server-side generated in order to post the most current information — until the emergence of Dynamic HTML's *data binding* feature. With data binding, the tables, forms, and other elements of the page used to present the information can also receive information and can be dynamically restructured. Once data has been received on the client side, data binding enables the information to be filtered, sorted, and represented — only the elements affected need be redrawn, rather than the entire page.

Presently, only Internet Explorer 4.0 supports data binding, which is a proposed specification of the W3C at this writing. Microsoft's support is extensive, however; key innovations include the following:

✦ **Full object model access to data binding attributes** enables Web designers to use JavaScript to add, delete, and modify bindings at run time.

✦ **Table paging** provides the capability to limit the number of records displayed in a repeated table and move the starting record forward and backward in the data set.

✦ **Table and form generation** offers automatic building of table rows from data records and data-bound form fields.

For more on data binding, see the section "Delivering Data Binding" later in this chapter.

Accessing DHTML in Netscape Communicator

The Navigator 4 component of Communicator contains three features that comprise Netscape's Dynamic HTML effort: style sheets, positionable content, and downloadable fonts. The Netscape version of DHTML only partially conforms to the standard outlined by the W3C. For instance, Netscape supports two different types of style sheets: the W3C-standard Cascading Style Sheets, and the company's own JavaScript Style Sheets (JSS).

The following sections discuss Netscape's methods of implementing Dynamic HTML and show you how to implement those methods in Dreamweaver.

Creating style sheets

Let's take a closer look at Netscape's support of the standard Cascading Style Sheet as well as its own proprietary JSS method. In brief, CSS uses the `<style>` tag to apply new attributes to an existing HTML tag or a custom tag known as a *class*. The CSS style tag format looks like the following:

```
<STYLE TYPE="text/css">
<!--
P {font-size:18pt; margin-left:20pt;}
H1 {color:blue;}
-->
</STYLE>
```

JavaScript Style Sheets also use the `<style>` tag but take advantage of the DOM to format the JSS specifications. The DOM is a hierarchical system that identifies each page element by its type of object (or by its assigned name). Once you have properly identified an element, you can then change its properties. The preceding CSS style sheet example looks like the following in JSS:

```
<STYLE TYPE = "text/javascript">
tags.P.fontSize = "18pt";
tags.P.marginLeft = "20pt";
tags.H1.color = "blue";
</STYLE>
```

Caution   Do not use the HTML comment tags with JavaScript Style Sheets.

Dreamweaver outputs CSS-formatted code and previews the changes as well. Although you cannot preview JSS-formatted code within Dreamweaver, JSS renders properly when previewed in a compatible browser.

To be frank, JSS has not received serious support in the Web developer community, and because the standard CSS format works in both browsers, JSS has little chance of becoming popular. If, however, you develop pages that use JSS, you can continue to code them in Dreamweaver—just not as conveniently.

Making positionable content

With positionable content, Netscape again supports two possibilities. Although Navigator 4.0 essentially supports the CSS-P style layers created using the `<div>` and `<span>` tags with the style attributes, it also puts forth its own proprietary `<layer>` and `<ilayer>` tags. Aside from these syntax differences, some differences also exist between what Navigator 4.0 supports in the properties for CSS-P style positioning and the proprietary `<layer>` tags. That said, all of the tags form the basis for layers, which can be placed anywhere on the page.

Relative positioning represents perhaps the biggest difference between the two implementations. Usually when you place a layer in your Web page, the `left` and `top` attributes define the layer's absolute position on the screen. When the `position` attribute is set to `relative`, however, the `left` and `top` values relate to whatever contains the layer, whether it is a table or another layer. Relative positioning using the CSS convention of `position:relative` simply doesn't work in the current release of Navigator 4.05. Instead, you should use the `<layer>` and `<ilayer>` tags. The `<layer>` is used for absolute positioning and the `<ilayer>` is used for relative positioning—or what Netscape calls *inflow-positioning*. Dreamweaver supports all four of the layer tag variations.

Several other properties for positionable content are supported differently in Netscape than in the CSS standard. In most cases, when Netscape doesn't support the CSS standard, it offers its own variation for the `<layer>` and `<ilayer>` tags and for the CSS style use. Table 23-1 describes these equivalents.

Tip
You can include both the CSS standard and the Netscape variation of an attribute in a `<style>` tag for cross-browser compatibility without dire consequences. In Dreamweaver, however, you need to add the Netscape syntax by hand, preferably after the CSS standard syntax.

Table 23-1
Differences Between CSS and Netscape Layer Properties

CSS Term	*Layer Property*	*Netscape Equivalent*
`include-source:url ("filename.htm")`	`SRC="filename.htm"`	`source-include:url ("filename.htm")`
`background-color: colorname`	`BGCOLOR="colorname"`	`layer-background-color:colorname`
`background-image:url ("filename")`	`BACKGROUND="filename"`	`layer-background-image:filename`

Using downloadable fonts

Fonts in HTML have only recently started to get a little respect. A `<font>` tag wasn't supported until HTML 3.2—and the support is strictly limited. Attributes for the `<font>` tag enable you to specify a number of font face options from which the user's system can choose, such as the following:

```
<font face="Arial, Helvetica, sans-serif">
```

Until Dynamic HTML, however, a designer could not use a typeface that the user did not have on his or her system and still expect to have the layout viewed correctly. Netscape's method for implementing downloadable fonts requires that the fonts be contained in a font definition file on the same Web server as the Web page. When the page is served to the user, the font definition file is downloaded with the HTML file, in the same way as a GIF or JPEG file. The font definition file is loaded asynchronously so that the HTML page doesn't have to wait while the fonts are loading.

Note To protect the copyrights of font designers, the downloaded font remains on the user's system only while the page is in the browser's cache; the fonts cannot be copied for personal use.

Font definition files are generated with a special authoring tool, such as Typograph from HexMac (www.hexmac.com), Bitstream's WebFont Maker (www.truedoc.com), or the Font Composer Plug-in for Communicator. The process involves opening your Web page in the authoring tool, selecting text, and applying the font to it. You then burn (process) the file, which saves the document, creates a font definition file containing the fonts used by the file, and also links the font definition file to the document. Font definition files can only be used by one domain at a time, and the domain is specified at the time you burn the file.

Once the font definition file is created, you link the font through a style tag, such as the following:

```
<STYLE TYPE="text/css"><!--
@fontdef url(http://home.netscape.com/fonts/sample.pfr);
--></STYLE>
```

You can also use a <link> tag, as follows:

```
<LINK REL="fontdef" SRC="fontdef1.pfr">
```

The final step in getting the user's system to recognize Netscape downloadable fonts adds a new MIME type to the Web server, application/font-tdpfr, with a filename extension of .pfr (Portable Font Resource).

Once you've linked the font to your page, you can include it in a font tag, just like a regular system font. For example, if you've included a font called "BurnOut," you could include a font family definition by choosing Text ➪ Font ➪ Edit Font List. Then, when applying the font to a particular bit of text, the HTML could read as follows:

```
"<font face="BurnOut, Arial, Helvetica, sans-serif">
```

To support the new capabilities of downloadable fonts, Netscape includes two new attributes: point-size and weight. The point-size attribute enables you to set exact sizes for your font (unlike the regular size attribute for the <font> tag, which works relatively). The weight attribute enables you to alter the boldness of the font. The weight value is from 100 to 900, inclusive (in steps of 100), where 100 indicates the least bold value, and 900 indicates the boldest value. Specifying the <b> tag causes Netscape to render the boldest font possible.

The amount of work involved to achieve downloadable fonts is a factor in Web designers' reluctance to use the technique. As you can see in Figure 23-2, however, the results can be spectacular.

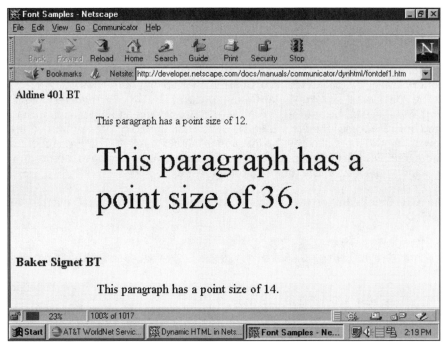

Figure 23-2: You can access a wide range of fonts and font sizes with Netscape's downloadable font technology.

Tip
You can certainly use Netscape's downloadable fonts in Dreamweaver, but keep in mind that you have to add all the special code by hand. Also, Dreamweaver does not preview the font changes.

Viewing Netscape Embedded Fonts in Internet Explorer

As noted earlier, Internet Explorer browsers can use Netscape embedded fonts with the aid of a small ActiveX control. The ActiveX control is added simply by inserting the following lines after the <link> code:

```
<script language="JavaScript"
src="http://www.truedoc.com/activex/tdserver.js"></script>
```

When the Internet Explorer browser loads the page, the user's system is inspected to determine if the proper ActiveX control is already installed. If not, the user is asked if the ActiveX control should be downloaded.

The easiest way to include TrueDoc fonts in a page is to use Simon White's PFR command, included on this book's CD-ROM. The command searches for a PFR file and then inserts the necessary code for the link and the ActiveX control.

Working with DHTML and Internet Explorer

With Internet Explorer 4.0, Microsoft adopted Dynamic HTML with a vengeance. At least partially supporting all the W3C official recommendations as well as numerous proposals, Internet Explorer 4.0 advances DHTML to the extreme. Included in Microsoft's rendition are the following features:

✦ **Dynamic Styles** includes a robust implementation of the CSS Level 1 specification for controlling style sheets.

✦ **Dynamic Content** enables the Web page to be redrawn after it has been downloaded.

✦ **Positioning and animation** provide a full implementation of the CSS-P specification for layers and movement.

✦ **Filters and transitions** permits designers to use special effects applied to images, text, or entire Web pages.

✦ **Open fonts** lets the Web page specify a font that is automatically downloaded, used for that page, and then discarded.

✦ **Data Binding** links Web elements such as tables to an external source, either a server database or a comma-delimited file, for automatic updating.

✦ **Dynamic HTML Object Model** gives complete access to all of the page elements and their properties through an extensive list of events.

Dreamweaver directly supports all the Internet Explorer 4.0 Dynamic HTML features that are cross-browser-compatible, including style sheets, layers, and a large portion of the Object Model. Other elements, such as filters and transitions, can be applied through Dreamweaver's Style Sheet Inspector, but cannot be previewed in the Document Window.

This book does not cover all the details of Internet Explorer 4.0's DHTML implementation, but the remainder of this section covers those features not duplicated in any other browser.

Creating Dynamic Content

Dynamic Content has been made possible by Internet Explorer 4.0's complete support of the Dynamic HTML Object Model, a superset of Netscape's own Document Object Model. Essentially, the DHTML Object Model gives you full access to all the elements in a document — and here's the innovation — even after the document has been downloaded to the user.

The most obvious use for Dynamic Content is with outline-oriented Web pages. Dynamic Content enables outlines to expand and collapse at the click of a mouse. The key property to activate Dynamic Content is the `display` property, because you can name or identify any block of text or element and then alter its `display` property on the fly.

The following code hides the `<ul>` list elements until the user clicks the heading above it, and then hides the list again when the same heading is double-clicked:

```
<a href=# onClick="javascript:document.all.MyList.style.display
= ''"
onDblClick="javascript:document.all.MyList.style.display='none'
" border=0>
<h1>Notes on Installation</h1>
</a>
<ul ID=MyList STYLE="display:none" >
  <li>Item #1...</li>
  <li>Item #2...</li>
  <li>Item #3...</li>
</ul>
<p>More information to follow...</p>
```

When viewed in Dreamweaver's Document Window, you see all the elements, and you must preview it in Internet Explorer 4.0 to see the Dynamic Content in action. Currently, you have to code this sort of structure in Dreamweaver by hand or through a custom object.

Using filters and transitions

Looking for a little sparkle in your Web page? Internet Explorer 4.0's filters and transitions are quite spectacular. A filter is a special effect, such as a drop shadow, that you can apply to an element (usually text or an image) through CSS. Transitions are used when one image is exchanged with another, or one Web page with another.

The number of available filters and the range of their parameters is mind-boggling. The list shown in Table 23-2 gives an overview of the filters, but doesn't hint at the amount of variety available from changing their attributes.

Table 23-2
CSS/Internet Explorer 4.0 Filters

Filter	Description
Alpha	Sets a uniform transparency level
Blend	Sets a transition blending between two objects
Blur	Creates the impression of moving at high speed
Chroma	Makes a specific color transparent
DropShadow	Creates a solid silhouette of the object
FlipH	Creates a horizontal mirror image
FlipV	Creates a vertical mirror image
Glow	Adds radiance around the outside edges of the object

Filter	Description
Gray	Drops color information from the image
Invert	Reverses the hue, saturation, and brightness values
Light	Projects a light source onto an object
Mask	Creates a transparent mask from an object
Shadow	Creates an offset solid silhouette
Reveal	Sets a transition's revealing of a hidden object
Wave	Creates a sine wave distortion along the horizontal axis
Xray	Shows just the edges of the object

Filters can be coded in the `<style>` tag or as a `style` attribute and are generally applied to a class object. The syntax follows:

```
filter:filtername(parameter_1, parameter_2, ...)
```

As you can see from Figure 23-3, the effects are quite amazing — especially when you consider that they all can be performed interactively.

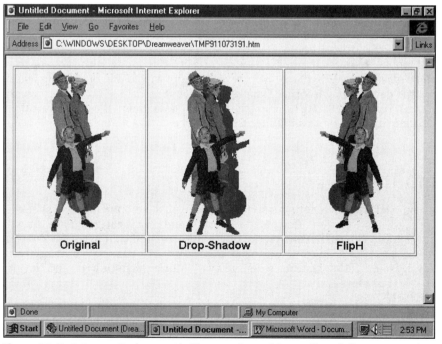

Figure 23-3: Internet Explorer 4.0's filters and transitions offer a full spectrum of graphic effects.

Delivering Data Binding

Much of the business of the Web depends on database-driven Web sites — virtual storefronts, online catalogs, and special information servers all require a strong connection between client-side requests and server-side answers. Microsoft's Dynamic HTML data binding links individual elements in your document, such as tables and forms, to data from another source, such as a database on a server or a comma-delimited text file. When the Web page with the data-bound tag is loaded, the data is automatically retrieved from the source, formatted, and displayed within the tag.

You can use Internet Explorer 4.0's Data Binding feature to generate tables in your Web page automatically and dynamically by binding a `<table>` tag to a data source. When the Web page is viewed, a new row is created in the table for each record retrieved from the source, and the cells of each row are filled with text and data from the fields of the record. Because this eneration is dynamic, the user can view the document even while new rows in the table are being created. Moreover, once all the table data is present, you can sort or filter it without requiring the server to send additional data. The table is simply regenerated, using the previously retrieved data to fill the new rows and cells of the table.

You can also bind one or more tags in the Web page to specific fields of a record. When the page is browsed, the tags are filled with text and data from the fields in the current record. This technique can be used to generate form letters on the Web from a remote database. You can also bind the form tags to record fields, which gives the user the opportunity to view the information and, if necessary, change it. Then the record can be submitted to the server and reentered into the database.

Data binding requires that a data source object be included in the Web page. A *data source object* is an ActiveX control (or a Java applet) capable of communicating with the data source. Internet Explorer 4.0 offers two data source objects with Internet Explorer 4.0: one for comma-delimited data in text files, and the other for SQL data in SQL Servers and other ODBC sources.

Summary

Dynamic HTML is a quantum leap forward in Web development. Style sheets, layers, dynamic content, downloadable fonts, and other features make the 4.0 generation of browsers faster, more client-side-oriented, and more designer-friendly.

✦ Dynamic HTML features work only with Internet Explorer 4.0 and Navigator 4.0 browsers and above.

✦ Much of the DHTML feature set is based on the Cascading Style Sheet specification recommended by the World Wide Web Consortium.

✦ The Dynamic HTML components of Netscape Navigator 4.0 are a blend of W3C standards and proprietary tags.

✦ Microsoft's Internet Explorer 4.0 offers the widest support of Dynamic HTML innovations through its Dynamic HTML Object Model, combined with comprehensive support of the CSS Level 1 standard.

In the next chapter, you study more specifics about how to use Cascading Style Sheets.

✦　　✦　　✦

Building Style Sheet Web Pages

In This Chapter

Cascading Style
Sheets basics

Defining and
inserting styles

Dreamweaver
Technique: Clearing
underlines in links

Style sheet options:
Eight categories of
attributes

Using external style
sheets

All publications, whether on paper or the Web, need a balance of style and content to be effective. Style without content is all flash with no real information. Content with no style is flat and uninteresting, thus losing the substance. Traditionally, HTML has tied style to content wherever possible, preferring logical tags like <strong> to indicate emphasis to physical tags like <b> for bold. But while this emphasis on the logical worked for many single documents, its imprecision made it unrealistic, if not impossible, to achieve style consistency across a broad range of Web pages.

The Cascading Style Sheets specification has changed this situation — and much more. As support for Cascading Style Sheets (CSS) grows, more Web designers can alter font faces, type size and spacing, and many other page elements with a single command — and have the effect ripple not only throughout the page, but also throughout a Web site. Moreover, an enhancement of CSS called CSS-P (for positioning) is the foundation for what has commonly become known as *layers*.

Dreamweaver is one of the first Web authoring tools to make the application of Cascading Style Sheets user-friendly. Through Dreamweaver's intuitive interface, the Web designer can access over 70 different CSS settings affecting everything from type specs to multimedia-like transitions. Dreamweaver lets you work the way you want: Create your style sheet all at once and then link it when you're ready, or make up your styles one-by-one as you build your Web page.

In this chapter, you find out how CSS works and why you need it. A Dreamweaver Technique for removing underlines from links walks you through a typical style sheet session. With that experience under your belt, you're ready for the sections with detailed information on the current CSS commands and how to apply them to your Web page and site. Also, the section on defining styles helps you understand what's what in the Style Definition dialog box. Finally, you learn how you can create external style sheets to create — and maintain — the look and feel of an entire Web site with a single document.

Understanding Cascading Style Sheets

The Cascading Style Sheets system significantly increases the design capabilities for a Web site. If you are a designer used to working with desktop publishing tools, you will recognize many familiar features included in CSS, including the following:

✦ Commands for specifying and applying font characteristics

✦ Traditional layout measurement systems and terminology

✦ Pinpoint precision for page layout

Cascading Style Sheets are able to apply many features with a simple syntax that is easy to understand. If you're familiar with the concept of using styles in a word processing program, you'll have no trouble grasping style sheets.

Here's how the process works: CSS instructions are given in rules; a style sheet is a collection of these rules. A rule is a statement made up of an HTML or custom tag called a *selector*; and its defined properties, referred to as a *declaration*. For example, a CSS rule that makes the contents of all <h1> tags (the selector) red in color (the declaration) looks like the following:

```
h1 {color:red}
```

In the following sections, you see the various characteristics of CSS — grouping, inheritance, and cascading — working together to give style sheets their flexibility and power.

Grouping properties

A Web designer often needs to change several style properties at once. CSS allows declarations to be grouped by separating them with semicolons. For example:

```
h1 {color:red; font-family:Arial,Helvetica,sans-serif; font-size:18pt}
```

The Dreamweaver interface provides a wide range of options for styles. Should you ever need to look at the code, you'll find that Dreamweaver groups your selections exactly as shown in the preceding example. Although Dreamweaver keeps each selector in its own rule, when you are hand-coding your style sheets you can group selectors as well as declarations. Grouped selectors are separated by commas, rather than semicolons. For example:

```
h1, h2, p, em {color:green; text-align:left}
```

Inheritance of properties

CSS rules can also be applied to more than one tag through inheritance. Most, but not all, CSS declarations can be inherited by the HTML tags enclosed within the CSS selector. Suppose you set all <p> tags to the color red. Any tags included within a <p>...</p> tag pair then inherit that property and are also colored red.

Inheritance is also at work within HTML tags that involve a parent-child relationship, as with a list. Whether numbered (or ordered, <ol>) or bulleted (or unordered <ul>), a list comprises any number of list items, designated by a <li> tag. Each list item is considered a child of the parent tag, <ol> or <ul>. Take a look at the following example:

```
ol {color:red}
ul {color:blue}
```

With the preceding example, all ordered list items appear in red, while all unordered list items appear in blue. One major benefit to this parent-child relationship is that you can change the font for an entire page with one CSS rule. The following statement accomplishes this change:

```
body {font-family: Arial}
```

The change is possible in the previous example because the <body> tag is considered the parent of every HTML element on a page.

Tip

There's one exception to the preceding rule: tables. Netscape (through version 4.5) treats tables differently than the rest of the HTML <body> when it comes to style sheets. To change the font of a table, you'd have to specify something like the following:

```
td {font-family: Arial}
```

Because every cell in a table uses the <td> tag, this style sheet declaration affects the entire table. Dreamweaver 2 is uneven in its application of this treatment. Setting the entire <body> to a particular font family is displayed correctly in the Document Window, with even tables being affected. However, changing the color of a font in the <body> style sheet declaration does not alter the font color of text in a table in the Document Window.

Cascading characteristics

The term *cascading* describes the capability of a local style to override a general style. Think of a stream flowing down a mountain; each ledge encountered by the stream has the potential to change its direction. The last ledge determines the final direction of the stream. In the same manner, one CSS rule applying generally to a block of text can be overridden by another rule applied to a more specific part of the same text.

For example, let's say you've defined, using style sheets, all normal paragraphs — <p> tags — to be in a particular font in a standard color, but you mark one section of the text using a little-used tag such as <samp>. If you make a CSS rule altering both the font and color of the <samp> tag, the section takes on the characteristics of that rule.

The cascading aspect of style sheets also works on a larger scale. One of the key features of CSS is the capability to define external style sheets that can be linked to individual Web pages, acting on their overall look and feel. Indeed, you can use the cascading behavior to fine-tune the overall Web site style based on a particular page or range of pages. Your company may, for instance, define an external style sheet for the entire company intranet, and each division could then build upon that overall model for its individual Web pages. For example, let's say that the company style sheet dictates that all <h2> headings are in Arial and black. One department could output their Web pages with <h2> tags in Arial, but colored red rather than black, while another department could make them blue.

Defining new classes for extended design control

Redefining existing HTML tags is a step in the right direction toward consistent design, but the real power of CSS comes into play when you define custom tags. In CSS-speak, a custom tag is called a *class,* and the selector name always begins with a period. Here's a simple example: To style all copyright notices at the bottom of all pages of a Web site to be displayed in Helvetica, 8-point type, and all caps, you could define a tag like this:

```
.cnote {font-family:Helvetica; font-size:8pt; font-
transform:uppercase}
```

If you define this style in an external style sheet and apply it to all 999 pages of your Web site, you only have to alter one line of code (instead of all 999 pages) when the edict comes down from management to make all the copyright notices a touch larger. Once a new class has been defined, you can apply it to any range of text, from one word to an entire page.

How styles are applied

CSS applies style formatting to your page in one of three ways:

✦ Via an internal style sheet

✦ Via an external, linked style sheet

✦ Via embedded style rules

Internal style sheets

An internal style sheet is a list of all of the CSS styles for a page.

Dreamweaver inserts all of the style sheets at the top of a Web page within a `<style>...</style>` tag pair. Placing style sheets within the header tags has become a convention that many designers use, although you can also apply a style sheet anywhere on a page.

The `<style>` tag for a Cascading Style Sheet identifies the type attribute as `text/css`. A sample internal style sheet looks like the following:

```
<style type="text/css">
<!--
p {  font-family: "Arial, Helvetica, sans-serif"; color:
#000000}
.cnote {  font: 8pt "Arial, Helvetica, sans-serif"; text-
transform: uppercase}
h1 {  font: bold 18pt Arial, Helvetica, sans-serif; color:
#FF0000}
-->
</style>
```

The HTML comments `<!--` and `-->` prevent older browsers that can't read style sheets from displaying the CSS rules.

External style sheets

An external style sheet is a file containing the CSS rules; it links one or more Web pages. One benefit of linking to an external style sheet is that you can customize and change the appearance of a Web site quickly and easily from one file.

Two different methods exist for working with an external style sheet: the `link` method and the `import` method. Dreamweaver lets you choose your preferred method.

For the `link` method, a line of code is added outside of the `<style>` tags, as follows:

```
<link rel="stylesheet" href="mainstyle.css">
```

The `import` method writes code within the style tags, as follows:

```
<style type="text/css">
@import "newstyles.css";
</style>
```

Between the `link` and the `import` methods, the `link` method is generally better supported among browsers.

Embedded rules

The final method of applying a style inserts it within HTML tags using the `style` attribute. This method is the most "local" of all the techniques; that is, it is closest to the tag it is affecting and therefore has the ultimate control — because of the cascading nature of style sheets as previously discussed.

When you create a layer within Dreamweaver, you notice that the positioning attribute is a Cascading Style Sheet embedded within a `<div>` tag like the following:

```
<div id="Layer1" style="position:absolute; visibility:inherit;
left:314px; top:62px; width:194px; height:128px; z-index:1">
</div>
```

For all its apparent complexity, the Cascading Style Sheets system becomes straightforward in Dreamweaver. Often, you won't have to write a single line of code. But even if you don't have to write code, you should understand the CSS fundamentals of grouping, inheritance, and cascading.

Creating and Applying a Style Sheet in Dreamweaver

Dreamweaver uses three primary tools to implement Cascading Style Sheets: the Styles Palette, the Edit Style Sheet dialog box, and the Style Definition dialog box. Specifically, the Styles Palette is used to apply styles created in the Edit Style Sheet dialog box and specified with the Style Definition dialog box. With these three interfaces, you can accomplish the following:

✦ Apply styles to selected text or to a particular tag surrounding that text

✦ View and edit many of the attributes included in the official release of CSS Level 1

✦ Modify any styles you have created

✦ Link or import all of your styles from an external style sheet

Caution   The fourth-generation browsers support many of the attributes from the first draft of the Cascading Style Sheets standard. Neither Netscape Navigator 4.0 nor Microsoft Internet Explorer 4.0 fully supports CSS Level 1, however. Of the earlier browsers, only Internet Explorer 3.0 supports a limited set of the CSS Level 1 features: font attributes, indents, and color. However, this support is rendered differently in Internet Explorer 3.0 and 4.0. Netscape Navigator 3.0 does not support any of the features of CSS Level 1.

Dreamweaver Technique: Eliminating underlines from links

Because Dreamweaver's interface for CSS has so many controls, initially creating and applying a style can be a little confusing. Before delving into the details of the various palettes, dialog boxes, and floating windows, let's quickly step through a typical style sheet session. Then you'll have an overall understanding of how all the pieces fit together.

Note Don't panic if you encounter unfamiliar elements of Dreamweaver's interface in this introductory technique. You see them at work again and again as you work through the chapter.

One of the modifications most commonly included in style sheets is disabling the underline for the anchor tag, `<a>`, which is normally associated with any hyperlinked text. To accomplish this task, follow these steps:

1. Open the Styles Palette by choosing Windows ⇨ Styles or selecting the Show Styles button from either Launcher.

2. In the Styles Palette, select the Style Sheet button. This sequence opens the Edit Styles dialog box.

3. In the Edit Styles dialog box, select the New button. This sequence opens the New Style dialog box.

4. In the New Style dialog box, select Redefine HTML Tag and choose the anchor tag, a, from the drop-down list. Click OK, and the Style Definition window opens.

Tip You can also select the Use CSS Selector option and choose a link from the drop-down list. You cannot preview this altered style in Dreamweaver, however.

5. In the Style Definition window, make sure that the correct pane is displayed by selecting Type from the list of categories.

6. In the Decoration section of the Type pane, select the none option. You can also make any other modifications to the anchor tag style, such as color or font size. Click OK when you're done.

   The Style Definition window closes, and any style changes instantly take effect on your page. If you have any previously defined links, the underline disappears from them.

7. In the Edit Style dialog box, select the Done button.

Now, any links that you insert on your page still function as links — the user's pointer still changes into a pointing hand, and the links are active — but no underline appears.

Tip   This technique works for any text used as a link. To eliminate the border around an image designated as a link, the image's border must be set to zero in the Property Inspector. Dreamweaver 2 handles this automatically when a graphic is made into a link.

Using the Styles Palette to apply styles

The Styles Palette, shown in Figure 24-1, is a flexible and easy-to-use interface with straightforward command buttons listing all available style items. Like all of Dreamweaver's primary palettes, you can open the Styles Palette in several ways:

✦ Choose Windows ⇨ Styles

✦ Select the Show Styles button from either Launcher

✦ Press F7

Figure 24-1: The Dreamweaver Styles Palette helps you apply consistent styles to a Web page.

The Styles Palette has three simple but important elements. The Apply To drop-down list shows the current tags available to the present cursor location. The tags in this list correspond to those found in the Tag Selector at any given time. One other item in the Apply To list is Selection, which attaches any defined style to any selected portion of your HTML page. The Apply To list enables you to focus quickly on whatever portion of the Web page to which you're applying a new style.

The main part of the Styles Palette is the list of defined custom styles or classes. Every custom tag you create is listed alphabetically in this window. Once you've chosen the portion of your HTML document that you're stylizing, you can choose one of the custom styles listed here by simply selecting it.

At the bottom of the Styles Palette is the Style Sheet button. Clicking this button opens the multifaceted Edit Style Sheet dialog box, in which you can create a new style, link a style sheet, edit or remove an existing style, or duplicate a style that you can then alter. Before you can begin applying styles to a Web page or site, the styles must be defined, and using the Edit Style Sheet dialog box is the pain-free method of accomplishing this task. You can, of course, open the HTML Inspector and add the style by hand, but you can avoid this process with the Edit Style Sheet dialog box. You'll get a good close look at this tool in the upcoming section "Editing and managing style sheets with the Edit Style Sheet dialog box."

To apply an existing style, follow these steps:

1. Choose Windows ⇨ Styles or select the Show Styles button from either Launcher to open the Styles Palette.

2. To apply the style to a section of the page enclosed by an HTML tag, select the tag from the Apply To drop-down list or from the Tag Selector.

    To apply the style to a section that's not enclosed by a single HTML tag, use your mouse to select that section in the Document Window. The section is highlighted, and a Selection option then appears in the Apply To list.

3. To apply the style you want to the chosen section of the page, simply select it in the Styles Palette.

As you might expect, Dreamweaver offers a second way of applying a style to your pages. The following quick method, using the menus, does not employ the Styles Palette:

1. Highlight the text to which you're applying the style, either through the Tag Selector or by using the mouse.

2. Select Text ⇨ Custom Style ⇨ Your Style.

Editing and managing style sheets with the Edit Style Sheet dialog box

The Edit Style Sheet dialog box, shown in Figure 24-2, displays all of your current styles — including HTML and custom styles — and provides various controls to link a style sheet and edit, create, duplicate, or remove a style.

Figure 24-2: The Edit Style Sheet dialog box lists and defines any given style, in addition to presenting several command buttons for creating and managing styles.

> **Tip**   To start editing one of your styles immediately, double-click the style in the list
> window of the Edit Style Sheet dialog box. This sequence takes you to the Style
> Definition dialog box, in which you redefine your selected style.

Use the five command buttons along the right side of the Edit Style Sheet dialog box
to create new external sheets or manage your existing style sheets:

✦ **Link** lets you create an external style sheet or link to an existing external
style sheet.

✦ **New** begins the creation of a new style by first opening the New Style dialog
box, described in the following section.

✦ **Edit** modifies any existing style.

✦ **Duplicate** makes a copy of the selected style as a basis for creating a new style.

✦ **Remove** deletes an existing style.

Defining new styles with the New Style dialog box

Selecting the New button in the Edit Style Sheet dialog box brings up a new dialog
box called New Style (see Figure 24-3). In this dialog box, you specify the type of
style you're defining, along with its name. The following sections explain the three
style types:

✦ Make Custom Style (class)

✦ Redefine HTML Tag

✦ Use CSS Selector

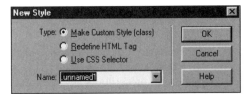

Figure 24-3: The first step in
defining a new style is to select
a style type and enter a name
for the style.

Make Custom Style (class)

Making a custom style is the most flexible way to define a style on a page. The first
step in creating a custom style is to give it a name; this name is used in the `class`
attribute. The name for your class must start with a period and must be
alphanumeric without punctuation or special characters. If you do not begin the
name of your custom style with a period, Dreamweaver inserts one for you.

Following are typical names you can use:

```
.master
.pagetitle
.bodytext
```

Caution Although you can use names such as `body`, `title`, or any other HTML tag, this approach is not a good idea. Dreamweaver warns you of the conflict if you try this method.

Redefine HTML Tags

The second radio button in the New Style dialog box is Redefine HTML Tags. This type of style is an excellent tool for making quick, global changes to existing Web pages. Essentially, the Redefine HTML Tags style enables you to modify the features of your existing HTML tags. When you select this option, the drop-down list displays over 40 HTML tags in alphabetical order. Select a tag from the drop-down list and click OK.

Use CSS Selector

When you use the third style type, Use CSS Selector, you define what are known as *pseudo-classes*. A pseudo-class is a cross between a custom style and a redefined HTML tag. The pseudo-classes in CSS are associated with the `<a>` tag used to create hypertext links.

When you choose Use CSS Selector, the drop-down list box contains four customization options:

✦ `a:active` customizes the style of a link when selected by the user

✦ `a:hover` customizes the style of a link while the user's mouse is over it

Note This pseudo-class is a CSS Level 2 specification and is currently only supported by Internet Explorer 4.0 and above.

✦ `a:link` customizes the style of a link that has not been visited recently

✦ `a:visited` customizes the style of a link to a page that has been recently visited

Tip Dreamweaver does not preview pseudo-class styles, although they can be previewed through a supported browser.

Styles and Their Attributes

After you've selected a type and name for a new style or chosen to edit an existing style, the Style Definition dialog box opens. A Category list from which you select a style category (just as you select a category of preferences in Dreamweaver's Preferences dialog box) is located on the left side of this dialog box.

Dreamweaver offers you eight categories of CSS Level 1 styles to help you define your style sheet:

Type	Box	Positioning
Background	Border	Extensions
Block	List	

You can apply styles from one or all categories. The following sections describe each style category and its available settings.

Note Dreamweaver doesn't preview all the possible CSS attributes. Those attributes that can't be seen in the Document Window are marked with an asterisk in the Style Definition dialog boxes.

Type options

The Type category (see Figure 24-4) specifies the appearance and layout of the typeface for the page in the browser window. The Type category is one of the most widely used and supported categories — it can be rendered in Internet Explorer 3.0 and above and Navigator 4.0 and above. Table 24-1 explains the settings available in this category.

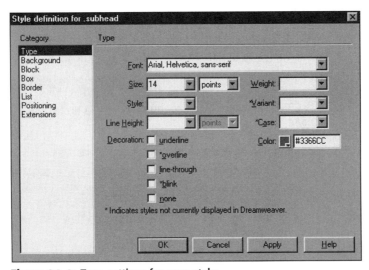

Figure 24-4: Type settings for your style.

Table 24-1
CSS Type Attributes

Type Setting	Description
Font	Specifies the font or a collection of fonts, known as a font family. You can edit the font list by selecting Edit Font List from the drop-down list. (This sequence opens the Edit Font List dialog box, as described in Chapter 7.)
Size	Selects a size for the selected font. If you enter a value, you can then select the measurement system in the adjacent text box (the default is points). The relative sizes, such as small, medium, and large, are set relative to the parent element.
Style	Specifies a normal, oblique, or italic attribute for the font. An oblique font may have been generated in the browser by electronically slanting a normal font.
Line Height	Sets the line height of the line (known as *leading* in traditional layout). Typically, line height is a point or two more than the font size, although you can set the line height to be the same as or smaller than the font size, for an overlapping effect.
Decoration	Changes the decoration for text. Options include underline, overline, line-through, blink, and none. The blink decoration is only displayed in Netscape browsers.
Weight	Sets the boldness of the text. You can use the relative settings (light, bold, bolder, and boldest) or apply a numeric value. Normal is around 400; bold is 700.
Variant	Switches between normal and small caps. Small-caps is a font style that displays text as uppercase, but the capital letters are a slightly larger size. The Variant option is not currently fully supported by either primary browser.
Case	Forces a browser to render the text as uppercase, lowercase, or capitalized.
Color	Sets a color for the selected font. Enter a color name or select the color swatch to choose a browser-safe color from the pop-up menu.

Background options

Since Netscape Navigator 2, Web designers have been able to use background images and color. Thanks to CSS Background attributes, designers can now use background images and color with increased control. Whereas traditional HTML background images are restricted to a single image for the entire browser window, CSS backgrounds can be specified for a single paragraph or any other CSS selector. (To set a background for the entire page, apply the style to the <body> tag.)

Moreover, instead of an image automatically tiling to fill the browser window, CSS backgrounds can be made to tile horizontally, vertically, or not at all (see Figure 22-5). You can even position the image relative to the selected element.

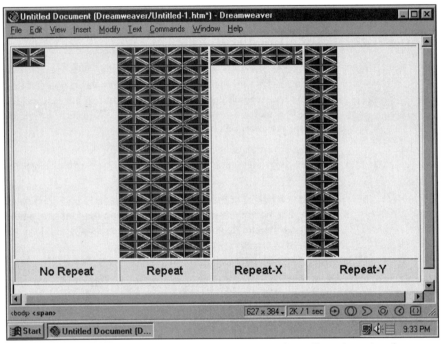

Figure 24-5: You can achieve a number of different tiling effects by using the Repeat attribute of the CSS Background category.

Neither of the primary browsers fully supports the CSS Background attributes shown in Figure 24-6 and listed in Table 24-2. The Repeat attribute enjoys full support, but Positioning and Attachment are only rendered in Internet Explorer 4.0 and above.

Table 24-2
CSS Background Attributes

Background Setting	Description
Background Color	Sets the background color for a particular style. Note that this setting enables you to set background colors for individual paragraphs or other elements.
Background Image	Specifies a background image.

Background Setting	Description
Repeat	Determines the tiling options for a graphic: **no repeat** displays the image in the upper-left corner of the applied style. **repeat** tiles the background image horizontally and vertically across the applied style. **repeat-x** tiles the background image horizontally across the applied style. **repeat-y** tiles the background image vertically down the applied style.
Attachment	Determines whether the background image remains fixed in its original position or scrolls with the page. This setting is useful for positioned elements. Often, if you use the overflow attribute, you want the background image to scroll in order to maintain layout control.
Horizontal Positioning	Controls the positioning of the background image in relation to the style sheet elements (text or graphics) along the horizontal axis.
Vertical Positioning	Controls the positioning of the background image in relation to the style sheet elements (text or graphics) along the vertical axis.

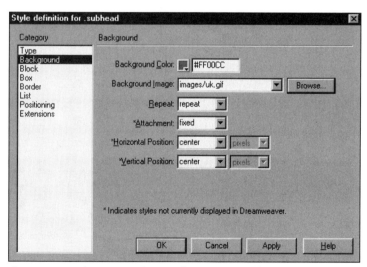

Figure 24-6: The CSS Background options enable a much wider range of control over background images and color.

Block options

One of the most common formatting effects in traditional publishing long absent from Web publishing is justified text — text that appears as a solid block. Justified text is now possible with the Text Align attribute, one of the six options available in the CSS Block category, as shown in Figure 24-7. Indented paragraphs are also a new possibility. Table 24-3 lists the CSS Block options.

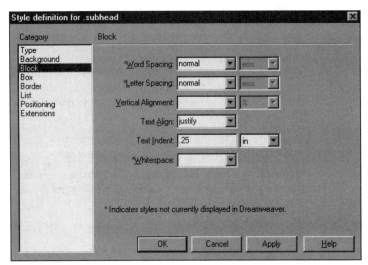

Figure 24-7: The Block options give the Web designer enhanced text control.

Table 24-3
CSS Block Attributes

Block Setting	Description
Word Spacing	Defines the spacing between words. You can increase or decrease the spacing with positive and negative values.
Letter Spacing	Defines the spacing between the letters of a word. You can increase or decrease the spacing with positive and negative values.
Vertical Alignment	Sets the vertical alignment of the style. Choose from baseline, sub, super, top, text-top, middle, bottom, text-bottom, or add your own value.

Block Setting	Description
Text Align	Sets text alignment (left, right, center, and justified)
Text Indent	Indents the first line of text on a style by the amount specified
Whitespace	Controls display of spaces and tabs. The normal option causes all whitespace to collapse. The pre option behaves similarly to the \<pre\> tag; all whitespace is preserved. The nowrap option enables text to wrap if a \<br\> tag is detected.

Box options

The Box attribute defines the placement and settings for elements (primarily images) on a page. Many of the controls (shown in Figure 24-8) emulate spacing behavior similar to that found in \<table\> attributes. If you are already comfortable using HTML tables with cell padding, border colors, and width/height controls, you will quickly learn how to use these Box features, which are described in Table 24-4.

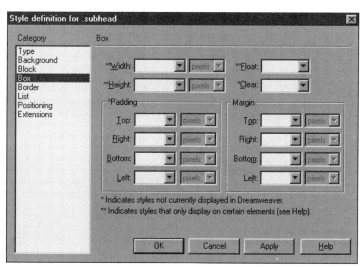

Figure 24-8: The CSS Box attributes define the placement of HTML elements on the Web page.

Dreamweaver imposes some specific restrictions on which Box attributes can and cannot be previewed in the Document Window. For example, the Float and Clear attributes can only be previewed when applied to an image. The Margin attributes can be previewed when applied to block-level elements, such as any of the \<h1\> through \<h6\> tags or the \<p\> tag. Padding is not displayed within Dreamweaver.

Table 24-4
CSS Box Attributes

Box Setting	Description
Width	Sets the width of the element.
Height	Defines the height of the element.
Float	Places the element at the left or right page margin. Any text that encounters the element wraps around it.
Clear	Sets the side on which layers are not allowed to be displayed next to the element. If a layer is encountered, the element with the Clear attribute places itself beneath the layer.
Margin	Defines the amount of space between the border of the element and other elements in the page.
Padding	Sets the amount of space between the element and the border or margin, if no border is specified. You can control the padding for the left, right, top, and bottom independently.

Border options

With Cascading Style Sheets, you can specify many parameters for borders surrounding text, images, and other elements such as Java Applets. In addition to specifying separate colors for any of the four box sides, you can also choose the width of each side's border, as shown in the CSS Border panel (see Figure 24-9). You can use eight different types of border lines, including solid, dashed, inset, and ridge. Table 24-5 lists the Border options.

Table 24-5
CSS Border Attributes

Border Setting	Description
Top	Sets the color and settings for a border along the top of an element
Right	Sets the color and settings for a border along the right-hand side of an element.
Bottom	Sets the color and settings for a border along the bottom of an element.
Left	Sets the color and settings for a border along the left-hand side of an element.
Style	Sets the style of the border. You can use any of the following as a border: Dotted, Dashed, Solid, Double, Groove, Ridge, Inset, and Outset.

Tip   The CSS Border attributes are especially useful for highlighting paragraphs of text with a surrounding box. Use the Box panel's Padding attribute to inset the text from the border.

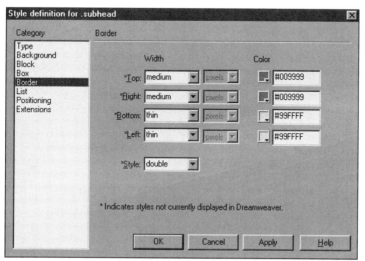

Figure 24-9: Borders are useful when you need to highlight a section of text or a graphic.

List options

CSS gives you greater control over bulleted points. With Cascading Style Sheets, you can now display a specific bulleted point based on a graphic image, or you can choose from the standard built-in bullets, including disc, circle, and square. The CSS List pane also lets you specify the type of ordered list to use, including decimal, roman numerals, or A-B-C order.

Figure 24-10 shows, and Table 24-6 describes, the settings for lists.

Table 24-6	
List Category for Styles	

List Setting	Description
Type	Selects the built-in bullet type. The options include: disc, circle, square, decimal, lowercase roman, uppercase roman, lowercase alpha, and uppercase alpha.
Bullet	Sets an image to be used as a custom bullet. Enter the path to the Image image in the text box.
Position	Determines if the list item wraps to an indent (the default) or to the margin.

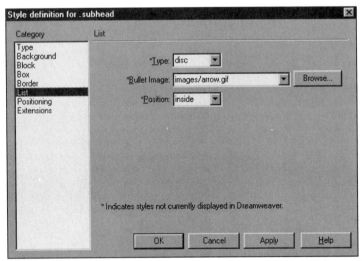

Figure 24-10: Specify a graphic to use as a bullet through the CSS List pane.

Positioning options

For many designers, positioning has increased creativity in page layout design. With positioning, you have exact control over where an element will be placed on a page. Figure 24-11 shows the various attributes that provide you with this pinpoint control of your elements on a page. The options are described in Table 24-7.

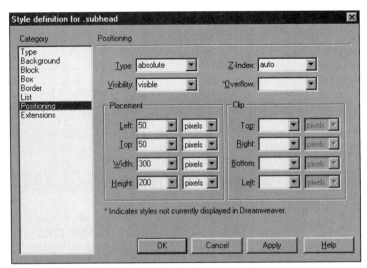

Figure 24-11: Control over the placement of elements on a page frees the Web designer from the restrictions imposed with HTML tables and other old style formats.

Dreamweaver layers are built upon the foundation of CSS positioning. For a complete explanation of layers and their attributes, see Chapter 25, "Working with Layers."

<table>
<tr><td colspan="2" align="center">**Table 24-7**
CSS Positioning Attributes</td></tr>
<tr><td>*Positioning Setting*</td><td>*Description*</td></tr>
<tr><td>Type</td><td>Determines whether an element can be positioned absolutely or relatively on a page. The third option, static, does not allow positioning.</td></tr>
<tr><td>Visibility</td><td>Determines whether the element is visible, hidden, or inherits the property from its parent.</td></tr>
<tr><td>Z-Index</td><td>Sets the apparent depth of a positioned element. Higher values are closer to the top.</td></tr>
<tr><td>Overflow</td><td>Specifies how the element is displayed when it's larger than the dimensions of the element. Options include the following: Clip, where the element is partially hidden; none, where the element is displayed and the dimensions are disregarded; and Scroll, which inserts scroll bars to display the overflowing portion of the element.</td></tr>
<tr><td>Placement</td><td>Sets the styled element's placement with the left and top attributes; and the dimensions with the width and height attributes.</td></tr>
<tr><td>Clip</td><td>Sets the visible portion of the element through the left, top, width, and height attributes.</td></tr>
</table>

Extensions options

The specifications for Cascading Style Sheets are rapidly evolving, and Dreamweaver has grouped some cutting-edge features in the Extensions category. As of this writing, Extensions attributes (see Table 24-8) are only supported by Internet Explorer 4.0 and above, although support is planned for Netscape Navigator 5.0. The Extensions settings shown in Figure 24-12 affect three different areas: page breaks for printing, the user's cursor, and special effects called *filters*.

One of the problems with the Web's never-ending evolution of page design is evident when you begin to print the page. The pagebreak attribute alleviates this problem by enabling the designer to designate a style that forces a page break when printing; the break can occur either before or after the element is attached to the style. While no browser currently supports this feature, it's a good candidate for support by future browsers.

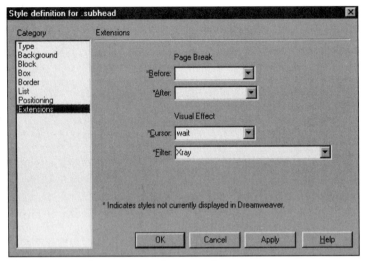

Figure 24-12: The CSS Extensions panel.

Table 24-8
CSS Extensions Attributes

Extensions Setting	Description
Pagebreak	Inserts a point on a page where a printer sees a page break. Not supported by any current browser.
Cursor	Defines the type of cursor that appears when the user moves the cursor over an element. Currently supported only by Internet Explorer 4.0.
Filter	Filters enable you to customize the look and transition of an element without having to use graphic or animation files. Currently supported only by Internet Explorer 4.0 and above.

The Filter attribute offers 16 different special effects that can be applied to an element. Many of these effects, such as wave and xray, are quite stunning. Several effects involve transitions, as well. Table 24-9 details all of these effects.

Table 24-9
CSS Filters

Filter	Syntax	Description
Alpha	alpha(Opacity=*opacity*, FinishOpacity=*finishopacity*, Style=*style*, StartX=*startX*, StartY=*startY*, FinishX=*finishX*, FinishY=*finishY*) *Opacity* is a value from 0 to 100, where 0 is transparent and 100 is fully opaque. *style* can be 0 (uniform), 1 (linear), 2 (radial), or 3 (rectangular).	Sets the opacity of a specified gradient region. This can have the effect of creating a burst of light in an image
BlendTrans*	blendtrans(duration=*duration*) *Duration* is a time value for the length of the transition, in the format of *seconds.milliseconds*.	Causes an image to fade in or out over a specified time
Blur	blur(Add=*add*, Direction=*direction*, Strength=*strength*) *Add* is any integer other than 0. *Direction* is any value from 0 to 315 in increments of 45. *Strength* is any positive integer representing the number of pixels affected.	Emulates motion blur for images
Chroma	chroma(Color= *color*) *Color* must be given in hexadecimal form, for example, #rrggbb.	Makes a specific color in an image transparent
DropShadow	dropshadow(Color=*color*, OffX=*offX*, OffY=*offY*, Positive=*positive*) *Color* is a hexadecimal triplet. *OffX* and *OffY* are pixel offsets for the shadow. *Positive* is a Boolean switch; use 1 to create shadow for nontransparent pixels, and 0 to create shadow for transparent pixels.	Creates a drop shadow of the applied element, either image or text, in the specified color
FlipH	FlipH	Flips an image or text horizontally
FlipV	FlipV	Flips an image or text vertically
Glow	Glow(Color=*color*, Strength=*strength*) *Color* is a hexadecimal triplet. *Strength* is a value from 0 to 100.	Adds radiance to an image in the specified color

Continued

	Table 24-9 *(continued)*	
Filter	**Syntax**	**Description**
Gray	Gray	Converts an image in grayscale
Invert	Invert	Reverses the hue, saturation, and luminance of an image
Light*	Light	Creates the illusion that an object is illuminated by one or more light sources
Mask	Mask(Color=*color*) *Color* is a hexadecimal triplet.	Sets all the transparent pixels to the specified color and converts the nontransparent pixels to the background color
RevealTrans*	RevealTrans(duration=*duration*, transition=*style*) *Duration* is a time value that the transition takes, in the format of *seconds.milliseconds*. *Style* is one of 23 different transitions.	Reveals an image using a specified type of transition over a set period of time
Shadow	Shadow(Color=*color*, Direction=*direction*) *Color* is a hexadecimal triplet. *Direction* is any value from 0 to 315 in increments of 45.	Creates a gradient shadow in the specified color and direction for images or text
Wave	Wave(Add=*add*, Freq=*freq*, LightStrength=*strength*, Phase=*phase*, Strength=*strength*) *Add* is a Boolean value, where 1 adds the original object to the filtered object and 0 does not. *Freq* is an integer specifying the number of waves. *LightStrength* is a percentage value. *Phase* specifies the angular offset of the wave, in percentage (for example, 0% or 100% = 360 degrees, 25% = 90 degrees) *Strength* is an integer value specifying the intensity of the wave effect.	Adds sine wave distortion to the selected image or text
Xray	Xray	Converts an image to inverse grayscale for an X-rayed appearance

* These three transitions require extensive documentation beyond the scope of this book.

Linking to an External Style Sheet

The external style sheet is an essential tool in the Web designer's CSS toolbox. Certainly, with Cascading Style Sheets, you can change all of a particular tag's attributes in a single page fairly quickly. But changing all the pages on a large Web site can still take an enormous amount of time. With an external style sheet linked to most, if not all, of a Web site's pages, the workload is cut down substantially.

To link to a separate style sheet, follow these steps:

1. Open the Styles Palette.
2. Select the Style Sheet button.
3. In the Edit Style dialog box, select the Link command button.
4. The Link External Style Sheet dialog box pops up, where you can access all your style sheets, by browsing and linking (see Figure 24-13).

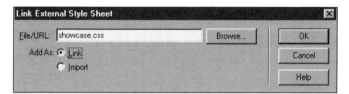

Figure 24-13: You can link an external style sheet to one Web page or your entire site through the Link External Style Sheet dialog box.

5. Either type in the file/URL path or select the Browse (Choose) button to locate a style sheet; the Cascading Style Sheet file has the .css filename extension on your hard drive. If you have not already created a style sheet, you can do so by locating the place you want to have the style sheet and then creating a name for it. Useful names for style sheets can be master.css, contents.css, or body.css.
6. Choose either the Link or Import radio button.

   To add a CSS style to a page, you have to either link or import the file. Both of these features work for linking a style sheet; however, the link method is supported in more browsers.

Tip Once you've defined your external style sheet, there are a couple of shortcuts to the Edit Style Sheet dialog box. First, you can press the Ctrl (Command) key and click the Style Sheet button in the Styles Palette. Rather than displaying the Edit Style Sheet dialog box with a link to your external style sheet (which you'd have to double-click or highlight and select Edit to modify), you'll see the dialog box for the external style sheet immediately.

The second method is useful if you have the Site Window open. Just double-click any .css file and the Edit Style Sheet dialog box for that file opens instantly.

When you go back to the Edit Style Sheet dialog box, you see a link file referenced in the listing above all of the styles. You can double-click the linked file to open a new Edit Style Sheet dialog box for your linked style sheet file. The defined styles within the linked style sheet then appear in the Styles Palette.

New Feature

If you've already defined styles in the current document and you want to convert them to an external style sheet, Dreamweaver 2 has you covered. Just choose File ➪ Export CSS Styles and enter a filename in the Export Styles as CSS File dialog box. Follow the directions in this section for linking this newly created file to your other Web pages as a style sheet.

Summary

In this chapter, you discovered how you can easily and effectively add and modify Cascading Style Sheets. You can now accomplish all of the following:

✦ Update and change styles easily with the Styles Palette

✦ Easily apply generated styles to an element on a page

✦ Apply a consistent look and feel with linked style sheets

✦ Position fonts and elements, such as images, with pinpoint accuracy

✦ Exercise control over the layout, size, and display of fonts on a page

✦ Define external style sheets to control the look and feel of an entire site

In the next chapter, you learn how to position elements on a page in Dreamweaver using layers.

✦   ✦   ✦

Working with Layers

For many years, page designers have taken the capability of placing text and graphics anywhere on a printed page for granted — even enabling graphics, type, and other elements to "bleed" off a page. This flexibility in design has eluded Web designers until recently. Lack of absolute control over layout has been a high price to pay for the universality of HTML, which makes any Web page viewable by any system, regardless of the computer or the screen resolution.

Lately, however, the integration of positioned layers within the Cascading Style Sheets specification has brought true absolute positioning to the Web. Page designers with a yen for more control can move to the precision offered with Cascading Style Sheets-Positioning (CSS-P).

Dreamweaver's implementation of layers turns the promise of CSS-P into an intuitive, designer-friendly, layout-compatible reality. As its name implies, layers offer more than pixel-perfect positioning. You can stack one layer on another, hide some layers while showing others, move a layer across the screen — and even move several layers around the screen simultaneously. Layers add an entirely new dimension to the Web designer's palette. Dreamweaver 2.0 even enables you to create page layouts using layers, and then convert those layers to tables that are viewable by earlier browsers.

This chapter explores every aspect of how layers work in HTML — except for animation, which is saved for Chapter 26, "Working with Timelines." With the fundamentals under your belt, you learn how to create, modify, populate, and activate layers on your Web page.

Layers 101

When the World Wide Web first made its debut in 1989, few people were concerned about the aesthetic layout of a page. In fact, because the Web was a descendant of SGML — a multiplatform, text document, and information markup specification — layout was trivialized. Content and the newfound capability to use hypertext to jump from one page to another were emphasized. After the first graphical Web browser software (Mosaic) was released, it quickly became clear that a page's graphics and layout could enhance a Web site's accessibility and marketability. Content was still king, but design was moving up quickly.

The first attempt at Web page layout was the server-side image map. This item was a typically large graphic (usually too hefty to be downloaded comfortably) with hotspots. A click on a hotspot sent a message to the server, which returned a link to the browser. The download time for these files was horrendous, and the performance varied from acceptable to awful, based on the server's load.

The widespread adoption of tables, released with HTML 2.0 and enhanced with HTML 3.2, radically changed layout control. Designers gained the ability to align objects and text — but a lot of graphical eye candy was still left to graphic files strategically located within the tables. The harder designers worked at precisely laying out their Web pages, the more they had to resort to workarounds such as nested tables and one-pixel-wide GIFs used as spacers. To relieve the woes of Web designers everywhere, the W3C included a feature within the new Cascading Styles Sheet specifications that allows for absolute positioning of an element upon a page. Absolute positioning enables an element, such as an image or block of text, to be placed anywhere on the Web page. Both Microsoft Internet Explorer 4.0 and Netscape Navigator 4.0 (and later) support layers under the Cascading Style Sheet-Positioning specification.

The addition of the third dimension, depth, truly turned the positioning specs into layers. Now objects can be positioned side-by-side, and they have a *z-index* property as well. The z-index gets its name from the geometric practice of describing three-dimensional space with x, y, and z coordinates; z-index is also called the *stacking order* because objects can be stacked upon one another.

A single layer in HTML looks like the following:

```
<div id="Layer1" style="position:absolute; visibility:inherit;
width:200px; height:115px; z-index:1"></div>
```

Positioned layers are most commonly placed within the `<div>` tag. Another popular location is the `<span>` tag. These tags were chosen because they are seldom used in the HTML 3.2 specification (Dreamweaver supports both tags). Both Microsoft and Netscape encourage users to employ either of these tags, because the two primary browsers are designed to credit full CSS-P features to either the `<div>` or `<span>` tag. You should generally use the `<div>` tag when cross-browser compatibility is important.

Positioning Measurement

The positioning of layers is determined by aligning elements on an x-axis and a y-axis. In CSS, the x-axis (defined as "Left" in CSS syntax) begins at the left-hand side of the page, and the y-axis (defined as "Top" in CSS syntax) is measured from the top of the page down. As with many of the other CSS features, you have your choice of measurement systems for Left and Top positioning. All measurements are given in Dreamweaver as a number followed by the abbreviation of the measurement system (without any intervening spaces). The measurement system options follow:

Unit	Abbreviation	Measurement
Pixels	px	Relative to the screen
Points	pt	1 pt = 1/72 in
Inches	in	1 in = 2.54 cm
Centimeters	cm	1 cm = 0.3937 in
Millimeters	mm	1 mm = 0.03937 in
Picas	pc	1 pc = 12 pt
EMS	em	The height of the element's font
Percentage	%	Relative to the browser window

If you don't define a unit of measurement for layer positioning, Dreamweaver defaults to pixels. If you decide to edit out the unit of measurement, the Web browser defaults to pixels.

Note Netscape has developed two additional proprietary tags for using layers: ⟨layer⟩ and ⟨ilayer⟩. The primary difference between the two tags has to do with positioning: the ⟨layer⟩ tag is used for absolute positioning, and the ⟨ilayer⟩ tag for relative positioning. Unfortunately, layers created by the ⟨div⟩ tag and the ⟨layer⟩ tag have different feature sets. Because Netscape recognizes both tags to some degree, you cannot combine them in the same way that you can use both the ⟨object⟩ and ⟨embed⟩ tags.

Creating Layers with Dreamweaver

Dreamweaver enables you to create layers creatively and precisely. You can drag out a layer, placing and sizing it by eye, or choose to do it by the numbers — it's up to you. Moreover, you can combine the methods, quickly eyeballing and roughing out a layer layout and then aligning the edges precisely. For Web design that approaches conventional page layout, Dreamweaver even includes rulers and a grid to which you can snap your layers.

Creating layers in Dreamweaver can be handled in one of three ways:

✦ You can drag out a layer, after selecting the Draw Layer button from the Objects Palette.

✦ You can put a layer in a predetermined size by choosing Insert ⇨ Layer.

✦ You can create a layer with mathematical precision through the Style Sheet Palette.

The first two methods are quite intuitive and explained in the following section. The Style Sheet Palette method is examined later in this chapter.

Inserting a layer object

When you want to draw out your layer quickly, use the object approach. If you come from a traditional page-designer background and are accustomed to using a program like Quark Express or PageMaker, you're already familiar with drawing out frames or text boxes with the click-and-drag technique. Dreamweaver uses the same method for placing and sizing new layer objects.

To draw out a layer as an object, follow these steps:

1. From the Common pane of the Objects Palette, select the Draw Layer button. Your pointer becomes a crosshair cursor. (If you decide not to draw out a layer, you can press Shift-Esc at this point or just click once without dragging to abort the process.)

2. Click anywhere in your document to position the layer, and drag out a rectangle. Release the mouse button when you have an approximate size and shape with which you're satisfied (see Figure 25-1).

After you've dragged out your layer, notice several changes to the screen. First, the layer now has a small box on the outside of the upper-left corner. This box, shown in Figure 25-2, is the selection handle, which you can use to move an existing layer around the Web page. When you click on the selection handle, eight sizing handles appear around the perimeter of the layer.

Another subtle but important addition to the screen is the Layer icon. Like the other Invisibles icons, the Layer icon can be cut, copied, pasted, and repositioned. When you move the Layer icon, however, its corresponding layer does not move — you are actually only moving the code for the layer to a different place in the HTML source. Generally, the layer code's position in the HTML is immaterial — however, you may want to locate your layer source in a specific area to be backwardly compatible with 3.0 browsers. Dragging and positioning the Layer icon one after another is a quick way to achieve this task.

Layer icon   Selected Layer

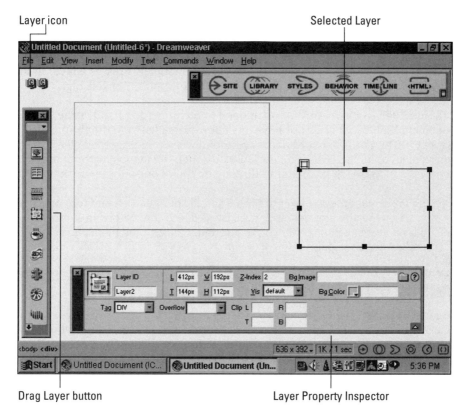

Drag Layer button   Layer Property Inspector

Figure 25-1: After selecting the Drag Layer object in the Objects Palette (Common), the pointer becomes crosshairs when you are working on the page. Click and drag to create the layer.

Selection handle

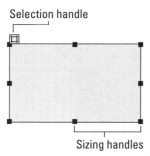

Sizing handles

Figure 25-2: Once a layer is created, you can move it by dragging the selection handle and size it with the sizing handles.

Using the Insert ⇨ Layer command

The second method to create a layer is through the menus. Instead of selecting an object from the Objects Palette, choose Insert ⇨ Layer. Unlike the click-and-drag method, inserting a layer through the menu automatically creates a layer in the upper-left corner; the default size is 200 pixels wide and 115 pixels high.

Although the layer is by default positioned in the upper left-hand corner of the Document Window, it does not have any coordinates listed in the Property Inspector. The position coordinates are added when you drag the layer into a new position. If you repeatedly add new layers through the menus, without moving them to new positions, each layer stacks directly on top of one another, with no offset.

Caution
It's important for every layer to have a specific position (left and top) assigned to it. Otherwise, the browser displays all layers directly on top of one another. To give a layer measurements, after you've inserted it through the menu, be sure to drag the layer, even slightly.

Setting default characteristics of a layer

You can designate the default size — as well as other features — of the layer that is inserted with Insert ⇨ Layer. Choose Edit ⇨ Preferences or use the keyboard shortcut Ctrl-U (Command-U) to open the Preferences dialog box. Select the Layers category. The Layers Preferences panel (see Figure 25-3) helps you to set the following layer attributes listed in Table 25-1.

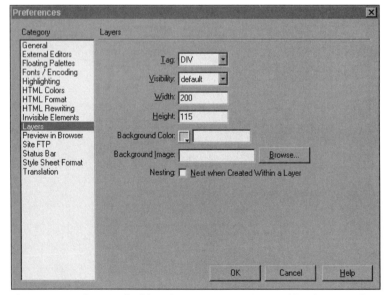

Figure 25-3: If you're building layers to a certain specification, use the Layers Preferences panel to designate your options.

Table 25-1 **Layer Preferences**	
Layer Preferences	*Description*
Tag	Sets the HTML code to use when creating layers. The options are `<div>` (the default), `<span>`, `<layer>`, and `<ilayer>`.
Visibility	Determines the initial state of visibility for a layer. The options are `default`, `inherit`, `visible`, and `hidden`.
Width	Sets the width of the layer in the measurement system of your choice. The default is 200 pixels.
Height	Sets the height of the layer in the measurement system of your choice. The default is 115 pixels.
Background Color	Sets a color for the layer background. Select the color from the pop-up menu of Web-safe colors.
Background Image	Sets an image for the layer background. In the text box, enter the path to the graphics file, or click the Browse (Choose) button to locate the file.
Nesting Option	If you want to nest layers when one layer is placed in the other automatically, check the Nest When Created Within an Existing Layer check-box.

Embedding a layer with style sheets

In addition to laying out your layer by eye, or inserting a default layer with Insert ⇨ Layer, you can also specify your layers precisely through style sheets. Although this method is not as intuitive as either of the preceding methods, creating layers through style sheets has notable advantages:

✦ You can enter precise dimensions and other positioning attributes.

✦ The placement and shape of a layer can be combined with other style factors such as font family, font size, color, and line spacing.

✦ Layer styles can be saved in an external style sheet, which enables similar elements on every Web page in a site to be controlled from one source.

Cross-Reference

If you haven't yet read Chapter 24, "Building Style Sheet Web Pages," you may want to look it over before continuing here.

To create a layer with style sheets, follow these steps:

1. Choose Window ⇨ Styles or select the Show Styles button from the Launcher. This selection opens the Styles Palette.

2. From the Styles Palette, select the Style Sheet button. This selection opens the Edit Style Sheet dialog box.

3. From the Edit Style Sheet dialog box, select the New button.

4. From the New Style dialog box, keep the Type option set to Make Custom Style (class). Enter a name for your new style and click OK.

5. Next up is the Style Definition dialog box. Select the Positioning category.

6. From the Positioning panel (see Figure 25-4), enter the desired attributes: Type, Visibility, Z-Index, Overflow, Placement (Left, Top, Width, and Height), and Clip settings (Top, Right, Bottom, Left).

   The Type attribute offers three options: Absolute, Relative, and Static. While you are familiar with the first two options, the third option, Static, is probably new to you. Use Static when you don't want to add a layer or specify a position, but you still want to specify a rectangular background.

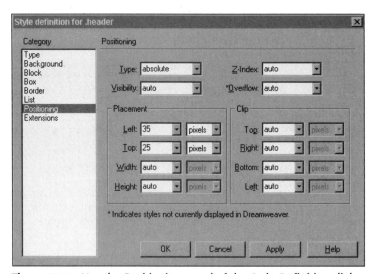

Figure 25-4: Use the Positioning panel of the Style Definition dialog box to set layer attributes in an internal or external style sheet.

7. If appropriate, select other categories and enter any additional style sheet attributes desired. Click OK when you're done.

Keep in mind that layers are part of the overall Cascading Style Sheet specification and can benefit from all of the features of style sheets. You may decide that a specific area of text — a header, for instance — must always be rendered in a bold, red, 18-point Arial font with a green background, and that it should always be placed 35 pixels from the left margin and 25 pixels from the top of the page. You can place the style sheet within a .CSS file, have your Web pages link to this file, and receive a result similar to what's shown (in black and white) in Figure 25-5. Within one component—the Cascading Style Sheet file—you can contain all of your positioning features for a page's headers, titles and other text, graphics, or objects. This capability gives you the benefit of controlling the position and look of every title linked to one style sheet.

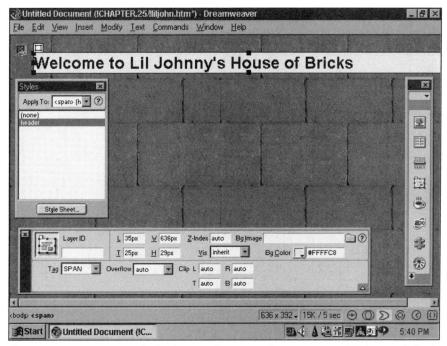

Figure 25-5: You can apply the layer style to any element on any Web page linked to the style sheet.

Choosing relative instead of absolute positioning

In most cases, absolute positioning uses the top-left corner of the Web page or the position where the <body> tag begins as the point of origin from which the Web browser determines the position of the text, image, or object. You can also specify measurements relative to objects. Dreamweaver offers two methods to accomplish relative positioning.

Using the relative attribute

In the first method, you select Relative as the Type attribute in the Style Sheet Positioning category. Relative positioning does not force a fixed position; instead, the positioning is guided by the HTML tags around it. For example, you may place a list of some items within a table and set the positioning relative to the table. You can see the effect of this sequence in Figure 25-6. In this illustration's Positioning

Panel, the Type attribute is set to Relative and the Placement/Left value is set to .5 inch for a style applied to the listed items.

Note Dreamweaver 2.0 doesn't preview relative positioning, so you should check your placement by previewing the page in a browser, as shown in Figure 25-6.

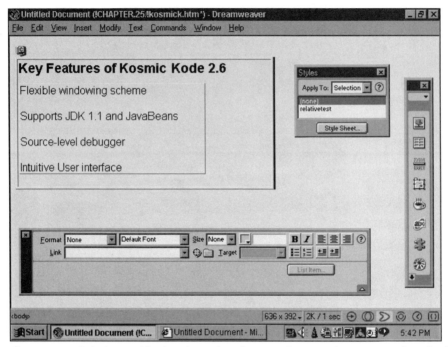

Figure 25-6: Relative positioning through styles can give your document a clean look, although the effect is not previewed in Dreamweaver.

Relative attributes can be useful, particularly if you want to place the positioned objects within free-flowing HTML. Free-flowing HTML repositions itself if the browser window is larger or smaller than the designer is aware. When you're using this technique, remember to place your relative layers within absolutely positioned layers. Otherwise, when the end user resizes the browser, the relative layers position themselves relatively to the browser and not to the absolutely positioned layers. This situation can produce messy results — use relative positioning with caution when mixed with absolute layers.

Using nested layers

The second technique for positioning layers relatively uses nested layers. Once you nest one layer inside another, the inner layer uses the upper-left corner of the outer layer as its orientation point. For more details about nesting layers, refer to "Nesting with the Layers Palette" later in this chapter.

Modifying a Layer

Dreamweaver helps you deftly alter layers once you have created them. Because of the complexity of managing layers, Dreamweaver offers an additional tool to the usual Property Inspector: the Layers Palette. This tool enables you to select any of the layers on the current page quickly, change layer relationships, modify their visibility, and adjust their stacking order. You can also alter the visibility and stacking order of a selected layer in the Property Inspector, along with many other attributes. Before any modifications can be accomplished, however, you have to select the layer.

Selecting a layer

You can choose from several methods to select a layer for alteration (see Figure 25-7). Your choice will most likely depend on the complexity of your page layout:

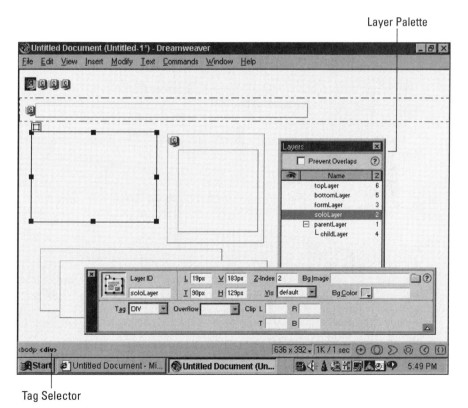

Figure 25-7: You have four different methods for selecting a layer to modify.

✦ When you have only a few layers that are not overlapping, just click the selection handle of the layer with which you want to work.

✦ When you have layers placed in specific places in the HTML code (for example, a layer embedded in a table), choose the Layer icon.

✦ When you have many overlapping layers that are being addressed by one or more JavaScript functions, use the Layers Palette to choose the desired layer by name.

✦ When you're working with invisible layers, click the ⟨div⟩ tag in the Tag Selector to reveal the outline of the layer.

Resizing a layer

To resize a layer, position the pointer over one of the eight sizing handles surrounding the selected layer. When over the handles, the pointer changes shape to a two- or four-headed arrow. Now click and drag the layer to a new size and shape.

You can also use the arrow keys to resize your layer with more precision. The following keyboard shortcuts change the width and height dimensions while the layer remains anchored by the upper-left corner:

✦ When the layer is selected, press Ctrl-arrow (Option-arrow) to expand or contract the layer by one pixel.

✦ Press Shift-Ctrl-arrow (Shift-Option-arrow) to increase or decrease the selected layer by the current grid increment. The default grid increment is 5 pixels.

Tip   You can quickly preview the position of a layer on a Web page without leaving Dreamweaver. Deselecting the View ⇨ Layer Borders option leaves the layer outline displayed only when the layer is selected, but otherwise it is not shown.

Moving a layer

The easiest way to reposition a layer is to drag the selection handle. If you don't see the handle on a layer, click anywhere in the layer. You can drag the layer anywhere on the screen — or off the bottom or right side of the screen. To move the layer off the left side or top of the screen, enter a negative value in the left and top (L and T) text boxes of the Layer Property Inspector.

Tip   To hide the layer completely, match the negative value with the width or height of the layer. For example, if your layer is 220 pixels wide and you want to position it off screen to the left (so that the layer can slide on at the click of a mouse), set the Left position at −220 pixels.

As with resizing layers, you can also use the arrow keys to move the layer more precisely:

✦ Press any arrow key to move the selected layer one pixel in any direction.

✦ Use Shift-arrow to move the selected layer by the current grid increment.

Using the Layer Property Inspector

You can modify almost all the CSS-P attributes for your layer right from the Layer Property Inspector (Figure 25-8). Certain attributes, such as width, height, and background image and color are self-explanatory or recognizable from other objects. Other layers-only attributes such as visibility and inheritance require further explanation. Table 25-2 describes all the Layer properties, and the following sections discuss the features unique to layers.

Figure 25-8: The Layer Property Inspector makes it easy to move, resize, hide, and manipulate all of the visual elements of a layer.

Table 25-2 Layer Property Inspector Options		
Layer Attribute	*Possible Values*	*Description*
BgColor	Any hexadecimal or valid color name	Background color for the layer
BgImage	Any valid graphic file	Background image for the layer
Clip (Top, Bottom, Left, Right)	Any positive integer	Measurements for the displayable region of the layer. If the values are not specified, the entire layer is visible
H (Height)	Any integer measurement in pixels, centimeters, millimeters, inches, points, percentage, ems, or picas	Vertical measurement of the layer

Continued

	Table 25-2 *(continued)*	
Layer Attribute	*Possible Values*	*Description*
L (Left)	Any integer measurement in pixels, centimeters, millimeters, inches, points, percentage, ems, or picas	Distance measured from the origin point on the left
Name	Any unique name without spaces or special characters	Labels the layer so that it can be addressed by style sheets or JavaScript functions
Overflow	visible, scroll, hidden, or auto	Determines how text or images larger than the layer should be handled
T (Top)	Any integer measurement in pixels, centimeters, millimeters, inches, points, percentage, ems, or picas	The distance measured from the origin point on the top
Tag	span, div, layer, or ilayer	Type of HTML tag to use for the layer
Vis (Visibility)	default, inherit, visible, or hidden	Determines whether a layer is displayed. If visibility is set to inherit, then the layer takes on the characteristic of the parent layer
W (Width)	Any integer measurement in pixels, centimeters, millimeters, inches, points, percentage, ems, or picas	The horizontal measurement of the layer
Z-Index	Any integer	Stacking order of the layer in relation to other layers on the Web page. Higher numbers are closer to the top

Name

Names are important when working with layers. To refer to them properly for both CSS and JavaScript purposes, each layer must have a unique name: unique among the layers and unique among every other object on the Web page. Dreamweaver automatically names each layer as it is created in sequence: Layer1, Layer2, and so forth. You can enter a name that is easier for you to remember by replacing the provided name in the text box on the far left of the Property Inspector.

Caution

Netscape Note: Netscape Navigator 4.0 is strict with its use of the ID attribute. You must ensure that you call the layer with an alphanumeric name that does not use spacing or special characters such as the underscore or percentage sign. Moreover, make sure your layer name begins with a letter and not a number — in other words, `layer9` works but `9layer` can cause problems.

Tag attribute

The Tag drop-down list contains the HTML tags that can be associated with the layer. By default, the positioned layer has `<div>` as the tag, but you can also choose `<span>`, `<layer>`, or `<ilayer>`. As previously noted, the `<div>` and `<span>` tags are endorsed by the World Wide Web Consortium group as part of their CSS standards. The `<layer>` and `<ilayer>` tags are Netscape Navigator proprietary tags, although Netscape also supports the CSS tags.

Indeed, if you are working on a Navigator-based intranet, you may want to change the default layer tag. Choose Edit ➪ Preferences and then, from the Layers category, select either `<layer>` or `<ilayer>` from the Tag drop-down list.

Visibility

Visibility (`Vis` in the Property Inspector) defines whether or not you can see a layer on a Web page. Four values are available:

✦ **Default** allows the browser to set the visibility attribute. Most browsers use the `inherit` value as their default.

✦ **Inherit** sets the visibility to the same value as that of the parent layer, which enables a series of layers to be hidden or made visible by changing only one layer.

✦ **Visible** causes the layer and all of its contents to be displayed.

✦ **Hidden** makes the current layer and all of its contents invisible.

Remember the following when you're specifying visibility:

✦ Whether or not you can see a layer, you must remember that the layer still occupies space on the page and demands some of the page loading time. Hiding a layer does not affect the layout of the page, and invisible graphics take just as long to download as visible graphics.

✦ When you are defining the visibility of a positioned object or layer, you should not use `default` as the visibility value. A designer does not necessarily know whether the site's end user has set the default visibility to `visible` or `hidden`. Designing an effective Web page can be difficult without this knowledge.

Overflow

Normally, a layer expands to fit the text or graphics inserted into it. You can restrict the size of a layer by changing the height and width values in the Property Inspector, however. What happens when you define a layer to be too small for an image, or when an amount of text depends on the setting of the layer's `overflow` attribute? CSS layers (the `<div>` and `<span>` tags) support four different `overflow` settings:

✦ **Visible (Default).** All of the overflowing text or image is displayed, and the height and width settings established for the layer are ignored.

✦ **Hidden.** The portion of the text or graphic that overflows the dimensions is not visible.

✦ **Scroll.** Horizontal and vertical scroll bars are added to the layer regardless of the content size or amount, and regardless of the layer measurements.

✦ **Auto.** When the contents of the layer exceeds the width and/or height values, horizontal and vertical scroll bars appear.

Currently, support for the `overflow` attribute is spotty at best. Dreamweaver doesn't display the result in the Document Window; it must be previewed in a browser to be seen. Navigator offers limited support: Only the attribute's hidden value works correctly and, even then, just for text. Only Internet Explorer 4.0 renders the `overflow` attribute correctly, as shown in Figure 25-9.

Caution

Netscape Note: The Overflow property is not recognized by the Netscape proprietary layer tags, `<layer>` and `<ilayer>`.

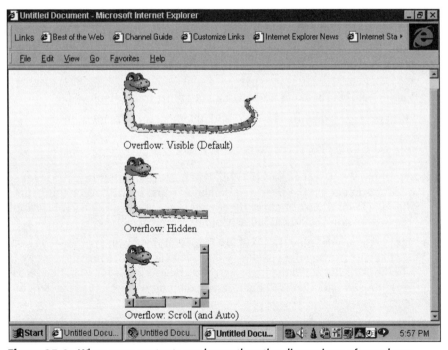

Figure 25-9: When your contents are larger than the dimensions of your layer, you can regulate the results with the `overflow` attribute.

Clipping

If you're familiar with the process of cropping an image, you'll quickly grasp the concept of clipping layers. Just as desktop publishing software hides but doesn't delete the portion of the picture outside of the crop marks, layers can mask the area outside the clipping region defined by the Left, Top, Right, and Bottom values in the Clip section of the Layer Property Inspector.

All clipping values are measured from the upper-left corner of the layer. You can use any CSS standard measurement system: pixels (the default), inches, centimeters, millimeters, ems, or picas.

The current implementation of CSS only supports rectangular clipping. When you look at the code for a clipped layer, you see the values you inserted in the Layer Property Inspector in parentheses following the `clip` attribute, with the `rect` (for rectangular) keyword, as follows:

```
<div id="Layer1" style="position:absolute; left:54px; top:24px;
width:400px; height:115px; z-index:1; visibility:inherit; clip:
rect(10 100 100 10)">
```

Generally, you specify values for all four criteria: Left, Top, Right, and Bottom. You can also leave the Left and Top values empty or use the keyword `auto` — which causes the Left and Top values to be set at the origin point: 0,0.

Tip   You can clip layers dynamically. In fact, this property is the basis for the image map rollover technique discussed in Chapter 12, "Making Client-Side Image Maps."

A Visual Clipping Technique

Dreamweaver doesn't allow you to draw the clipping region visually — the values have to be explicitly input in the Clip section of the Layer Property Inspector. That said, a trick using a second temporary layer can make it easier to position your clipping. Follow these steps to get accurate clipping values:

1. Insert your original layer and image.

2. Nest a second, temporary layer inside the first, original layer (select the Draw Layer button in the Objects Palette and draw out the second layer inside the first).

If you have your Layer Preferences set so that a layer does not automatically nest when created inside another layer, press the Ctrl (Command) key while you draw your layer, to override the preference.

3. Position the second layer over the area you want to clip. Use the layer's sizing handles to alter the size and shape, if necessary.

Continued

4. Note the position and dimensions of the second layer (the Left, Top, Width, and Height values).

5. Delete the second layer.

6. In the Property Inspector for the original layer, enter the Clip values as follows:

- **L** — Enter the Left value for the second layer.

- **T** — Enter the Top value for the second layer.

- **R** — Add the second layer's Left value to its Width value.

- **B** — Add the second layer's Top value to its Height value.

Dreamweaver displays the clipped layer after you enter the final value. The following figure shows the original layer and the temporary layer on the left, and the final clipped version of the original layer on the right.

Z-Index

One of a layer's most powerful features is its capability to appear above or below other layers. You can change this order, known as the *z-index*, dynamically.

Whenever a new layer is added, Dreamweaver automatically increments the z-index — layers with higher z-index values are positioned above layers with lower z-index values. The z-index can be adjusted manually in either the Layer Property Inspector or the Layers Palette. The z-index must be an integer, either negative or positive.

Tip Although some Web designers use high values for the z-index, such as 3,000, the z-index is completely relative. The only reason to increase a z-index to an extremely high number is to ensure that that particular layer remains on top.

The z-index is valid for the CSS layer tags as well as the Netscape proprietary layer tags. Netscape also has two additional attributes that can affect the apparent depth of either the <layer>- or <ilayer>-based content: above and below. With above and below, you can specify which existing layer is to appear directly on top of or beneath the current layer. You can only set one of the depth attributes, the z-index, or above or below.

Caution Certain types of objects — including Java Applets, plug-ins, and ActiveX controls — ignore the z-index setting when included in a layer, and always appear as the uppermost layer.

When you designate the layer's tag attribute to be either <layer> or <ilayer>, the Property Inspector displays an additional field: the A/B attribute for setting the above or below value, as shown in Figure 25-10. Choose either attribute from the A/B drop-down list and then select the layer from the adjacent list. The layer you choose must be set up in the code before the current layer. You can achieve this condition in the Document Window by moving the icon for the current layer to a position after the other layers. Although you must use either <layer> or <ilayer> to specify the above or below attribute, the layer specified can be either a CSS or Netscape type.

Figure 25-10: Choosing the Netscape-specific tags LAYER or ILAYER from the Property Inspector causes several new options to appear, including the A/B switch for the Above/Below depth position.

Caution Working with the above and below attributes can be confusing. Notice that they determine which layer is to appear on top of or underneath the current layer, and not which layer the present layer will be above or below.

Background image or color

Inserting a background image or color with the Layer's Property Inspector works in a similar manner to changing the background image or color for a table (as explained in Chapter 11, "Setting Up Tables"). To insert an image, enter the path to the file in the Bg Image text box, or select the Folder icon to locate the image file on your system or network. If the layer is larger than the image, the image will be tiled, just as it would in the background of a Web page or table.

To give a layer a background color, enter the color name (either in its hexadecimal or nominal form) in the Bg Color text box. You can also select the color swatch to pick your color from the color picker.

Additional Netscape properties

In addition to the `above` and `below` values for the `z-index` attribute, two other Netscape variations are worth noting — both of which appear as options in the Property Inspector when either `<layer>` or `<ilayer>` is selected as the layer tag.

When either `<layer>` or `<ilayer>` is selected, the Page X and Page Y options become available as radio buttons in the Property Inspector in addition to Left and Top. With Netscape layers, Left and Top place the layer relative to the top-left corner of its parent (whether that's the page or another layer if the layer is nested). Page X and Page Y, on the other hand, position the layer based on the top-left corner of the page, regardless of whether the layer is nested.

The other additional Netscape layer attribute is the `source` property. You can specify another HTML document to appear within a `<layer>` or `<ilayer>` — much like placing other Web pages in frames. To specify a source for a Netscape layer, enter the path to the file in the Src text box, or select the Folder icon to locate the file.

The Layers Palette

Dreamweaver offers another tool to help manage the layers in your Web page: the Layers Palette. Although this tool doesn't display as many properties about each element as the Property Inspector, the Layers Palette gives you a good overview of all the layers on your page. It also provides a quick method of selecting a layer — even when it's off screen — as well as enabling you to change the z-index and the nesting order.

The Layers Palette, shown in Figure 25-11, can be opened either through the Window menu (Window ➪ Layer) or by pressing the keyboard shortcut, F11.

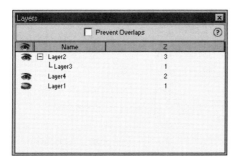

Figure 25-11: Use the Layers Palette to select quickly or alter the visibility or relationships of all the layers on your page.

Modifying properties with the Layers Palette

The Layers Palette lists the visibility, name, and z-index settings for each layer. All of these properties can be modified directly through the Layers Palette.

The visibility of a particular layer is noted by the eye symbol in column one of the Inspector. Selecting the eye symbol cycles you through three different visibility states:

✦ **Eye closed** indicates that the layer is hidden.

✦ **Eye open** indicates that the layer is visible.

✦ **No eye** indicates that the visibility attribute is set to the default (which, for both Navigator 4.0 and Internet Explorer 4.0, means `inherit`).

You can also change a layer's name (in the second column of the Layers Palette). Just double-click the current layer name in the Inspector; the name will be highlighted. Type in the new name and press Enter (Return) to complete the change.

The z-index (stacking order) in the third column can be altered in the same manner. Double-click on the z-index value; then type in the new value and press Enter (Return). You can enter any positive or negative integer. If you're working with the Netscape proprietary layer tags, you can also alter the `above` or `below` values previously set for the z-index through the Property Inspector. Use A for Above and B for Below.

Tip   To change a layer's z-index interactively, you can drag one layer above or below another in the Layers Palette.

Nesting with the Layers Palette

Another task managed by the Layers Palette is nesting or unnesting layers. This process is also referred to as creating parent-child layers. To nest one layer inside another through the Layers Palette, follow these steps:

1. Choose Window ➪ Layers or press F11 to open the Layers Palette.

2. Press the Ctrl (Command) key, and then click on the name of the layer to be nested (the child) and drag it on top of the other layer (the parent).

3. When you see a rectangle form around the parent layer's name, release the mouse.

   The child layer is indented underneath the parent layer, and the parent layer has a minus sign (a down-pointing triangle on the Mac) attached to the front of its name.

4. To hide the child layer from view, select the minus sign (down-pointing triangle) in front of the parent layer's name. Once the child layer is hidden, the minus sign turns into a plus sign (a right-pointing triangle on the Mac).

5. To reveal the child layer, select the plus sign (right-pointing triangle on the Mac).

6. To undo a nested layer, select the child layer and drag it to a new position in the Layers Palette.

Caution   When it comes to nested layers, Netscape Navigator 4.0 does not "play well with others." In fact, the expected results are so rarely achieved that it's best to avoid nested layers in cross-browser sites for the time being.

You can use the nesting features of the Layers Palette to hide many layers quickly. If the visibility of all child layers is set to default — with no eye displayed — then by hiding the parent layer you cause all the child layers to inherit that visibility setting and also disappear from view.

Tip   You can also delete a layer from the Layers Palette. Just highlight the layer to be removed and press Delete. Dreamweaver does not enable you to delete nested layers as a group, however — you have to remove each one individually.

Aligning layers with the ruler and grid

With the capability to position layers anywhere on a page comes additional responsibility and potential problems. In anything that involves animation, correct alignment of moving parts is crucial. As you begin to set up your layers, their exact placement and alignment becomes critical. Dreamweaver includes two tools to simplify layered Web page design: the ruler and the grid.

Rulers and grids are familiar concepts in traditional desktop publishing. Dreamweaver's ruler shows the x- and y-axis in pixels, inches, or centimeters along the outer edge of the Document Window. The grid crisscrosses the page with lines to support a visual guideline when you're placing objects. You can even enable a snap-to-grid feature to ensure easy, absolute alignment.

Using the ruler

Until now, "eyeballing it" was the only option available for Web page layout. The absolute positioning capability of layers has changed this deficiency, however. Now online designers have a more precise and familiar system of alignment: the ruler. Dreamweaver's ruler can be displayed in several different measurement units and with your choice of origin point.

To enable the ruler in Dreamweaver, choose View ➪ Rulers ➪ Show or use the keyboard shortcut, Ctrl-Alt-Shift-R (Command-Option-Shift-R). Horizontal and vertical rulers appear on along the top and the left sides of the Document Window, as shown in Figure 25-12. As you move the pointer, a light-gray line indicates the position on both rulers.

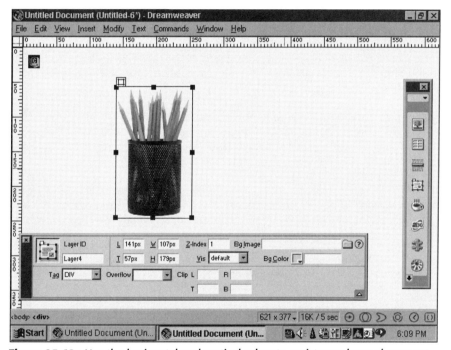

Figure 25-12: Use the horizontal and vertical rulers to assist your layer placement and overall Web page layout.

By default, the ruler uses pixels as its measurement system. You can change the default by selecting View ➪ Rulers and choosing either inches or centimeters.

Dreamweaver also lets you move the ruler origin to a new position. Normally, the upper-left corner of the page acts as the origin point for the ruler. On some occasions, it's helpful to start the measurement at a different location — at the bottom-right edge of an advertisement, for example. To move the origin point, select the intersection of the horizontal and the vertical rulers and drag the crosshairs to a new location. When you release the mouse button, both rulers are adjusted to show negative values above and to the right of the new origin point. To return the origin point to its default setting, choose View ➪ Rulers ➪ Reset Origin or you can simply double-click the intersection of the rulers.

Tip   You can access a ruler shortcut menu by right-clicking (Ctrl-clicking) the ruler itself. The shortcut menu lets you change the system of measurement, reset the origin point, or hide the rulers.

Lining up with the grid

Rulers are generally good for positioning single objects, but a grid is extremely helpful when aligning one object to another. With Dreamweaver's grid facility, you can align elements visually or snap them to the grid. You can set many of the grid's other features, including grid spacing, color, and type.

To turn on the grid, choose View ➪ Grid ➪ Show or press Ctrl-Alt-Shift-G (Command-Option-Shift-G). By default, the grid is displayed with light-blue lines set at 50-pixel increments.

The snap-to-grid feature is enabled by choosing View ➪ Grid ➪ Snap To or with the keyboard shortcut, Ctrl-Alt-G (Command-Option-G). When activated, Snap to Grid causes the upper-left corner of a layer to be placed at the nearest grid intersection when the layer is moved.

Like most of Dreamweaver's tools, the grid can be customized. To alter the grid settings, choose View ➪ Grid ➪ Settings. In the Grid Settings dialog box, shown in Figure 25-13, you can change any of the following settings (just click OK when you're done):

Grid Setting	Description
Visible Grid	A check-box toggle to show or hide the grid.
Spacing	Adjust the distance between grid points by entering a numeric value in the text box.
Spacing Unit of Measure	Select Pixels, Inches, or Centimeters from the Spacing drop-down list.
Color	Change the default color (light-blue), selecting the color swatch to bring up a pop-up menu of color options.
Display	Choose either solid lines or dots for the gridlines.
Snapping	Check-box toggle to enable or disable the Snap to Grid feature.
Snap Every	Adjust the distance between snap-to points (the points to which Dreamweaver snaps selected objects). Enter a number in the text box, and select the distance measurement unit from the drop-down list.

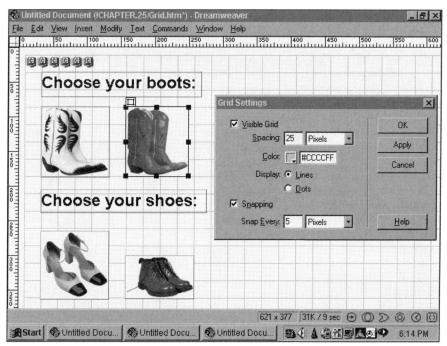

Figure 25-13: Dreamweaver's grid feature is extremely handy for aligning a series of objects.

Adding Elements to a Layer

Once you have created and initially positioned your layers, you can begin to fill them with content. Inserting objects in a layer is just like inserting objects in a Web page. The same insertion methods are available to you:

✦ Position the cursor inside a layer, choose Insert in the menu bar, and select an object to insert.

✦ With the cursor inside a layer, select any object from the Objects Palette. Note: you cannot select the Draw Layer object.

✦ Drag an object from the Objects Palette and drop it inside the layer.

Netscape Note: A known problem exists with Netscape Navigator 4.0 and nested layers — and layers in general — using the <div> tag. Whenever the browser window is resized, the layers lose their left and top position and are displayed along the left edge of the browser window or parent layer. As a workaround, use the AutoFix Layer object from the CD-ROM in the Dreamweaver Behaviors folder, which is attached to the <body> tag and uses the onLoad event.

Forms and layers

When you're mixing forms and layers, follow only one rule: Always put the form completely inside the layer. If you place the layer within the form, all form elements after the layer tags are ignored. With the form completely enclosed in the layer, the form can safely be positioned anywhere on the page and all form elements still remain completely active.

Although this rule means you can't split one form onto separate layers, you can set up multiple forms on multiple layers — and still have them all communicate to one final CGI or other program. This technique uses JavaScript to send the user-input values in the separate forms to hidden fields in the form with the Submit button. Let's say, for example, that you have three separate forms gathering information in three separate layers on a Web page. Call them formA, formB, and formC on layer1, layer2, and layer3, respectively. When the Submit button in formC on layer3 is selected, a JavaScript function is first called by means of an `onClick` event in the button's `<input>` tag. The function, in part, looks like the following:

```
function gatherData() {
  document.formC.hidden1.value = document.formA.text1.value
  document.formC.hidden2.value = document.formB.text2.value
}
```

Notice how every value from the various forms gets sent to a hidden field in formC, the form with the Submit button. Now, when the form is submitted, all the hidden information gathered from the various forms is submitted along with formC's own information.

Note

Netscape Note: The code for this separate-forms approach, as written in the preceding listing, works in Internet Explorer. Navigator, however, uses a different syntax to address forms in layers. To work properly in Navigator, the code must look like the following:

```
document.layers["layer3"].document.formC.hidden1.value
=document.layers["layer1"].document.formA.text1.value
```

To make the code cross-browser-compatible, you can use an initialization function that allows for the differences, or you can build it into the `onClick` function. (For more information on building cross-browser-compatible code, see Chapter 31, "Maximizing Browser Targeting.")

Creating Your Page Design with Layers

While the advantage to designing with layers is the greater flexibility it affords, one of the greatest disadvantages of using layers is that they are viewable in only the most recent generation of browsers. Dreamweaver 2.0 enables you to get the best of both worlds by letting you use layers to design complex page layouts, and then transforming those layers into tables that can be viewed in earlier browsers. Designing this way has some limitations — you can't, for example, actually layer items on top of each other. Nevertheless, Dreamweaver's ability to convert layers to tables (and tables to layers) enables you to create complex layouts with ease.

Using the Tracing Image

Page-layout artists are often confronted with Web-page designs that have been mocked up in a graphics program. Dreamweaver's Tracing Image function enables you to use such images to guide the precise placement of graphics, text, tables, and forms in your Web page, enabling you to match the original design as closely as possible.

In order to use a Tracing Image, the graphic must be saved in either a JPG, GIF, or PNG format. Once the Tracing Image has been placed in your page, it is viewable only in Dreamweaver — it will never appear in a browser. A placed Tracing Image will hide any background color or background graphic in your Web page. Preview your page in a browser, or hide the tracing layer, to view your page without the Tracing Image.

Adding the Tracing Image to your page

To add a Tracing Image to your Dreamweaver page, select View ⇨ Tracing Image ⇨ Load. This brings up a Select Image Source dialog box that enables you to select the graphic you would like to use as a Tracing Image. Clicking Select brings up the Page Properties dialog box, as shown in Figure 25-14, where you may specify the opacity of the Tracing Image, from Transparent (0%) to Opaque (100%). You can change the Tracing Image or its transparency at any point by selecting Modify ⇨ Page Properties to bring up the Page Properties dialog box. You can toggle between hiding and showing the Tracing Image by selecting View ⇨ Tracing Image ⇨ Show. The Tracing Image can also be inserted directly in the Page Properties dialog box by entering its path in the Tracing Image text box or selecting the Browse (Choose) button to locate the image.

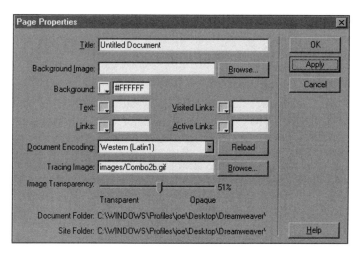

Figure 25-14: Setting the transparency of the Tracing Image to a setting like 51% can help you differentiate between it and the content layers you are positioning.

Moving the Tracing Image

The Tracing Image cannot be selected and moved the same way as other objects on your page. Instead, you must move the Tracing Image using menu commands. You have several options for adjusting the Tracing Image's position to better fit your design. First, you can align the Tracing Image with any object on your page by first selecting the object and then choosing View ⇨ Tracing Image ⇨ Align with Selection. This will line up the upper-left corner of the Tracing Image with the upper-left corner of the bounding box of the object you've selected.

To precisely or visually move the Tracing Image to a specific location, select View ⇨ Tracing Image ⇨ Adjust Position. Then enter the X and Y coordinates into the boxes in the Adjust Tracing Image Position dialog box, as shown in Figure 25-15. For more hands-on positioning, use the arrow keys to nudge the tracing layer up, down, left, or right 1 pixel at a time. Holding down the Shift key while pressing the arrow keys will move the Tracing Image in 5-pixel increments. Finally, you can return the Tracing Image to its default location of 9 pixels down from the top and 11 pixels in from the left by selecting View ⇨ Tracing Image ⇨ Reset Position.

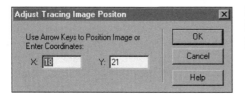

Figure 25-15: Use the Adjust Tracing Image Position dialog box to precisely place your graphic template.

Preventing overlaps

In order to place layers on your page that can later be converted to a table, the layers must not overlap one another. Before you begin drawing out your layers, either open the Layers Palette by selecting Windows ⇨ Layers or pressing F11, and put a check mark in the Prevent Overlap box at the top of the Inspector window. You can also select View ⇨ Prevent Layer Overlaps to toggle overlap protection on.

Designing precision layouts

As noted earlier, layers brought pixel-perfect positioning to the Internet. Now, Web designers can enjoy some of the layout capabilities assumed by print designers. Unfortunately, you need a 4.0 browser to view any page created with layers, and a fair portion of the Web audience is still using 3.0 or older browsers. The previous version of Dreamweaver introduced the capability to make a 3.0-compatible version of a completed 4.0 layer-based page, and now Dreamweaver 2 makes that capability a round-trip feature.

New Feature

With two new Layout commands, Web designers can now freely design their page and then lock it into position for posting. Moreover, if the design needs adjustment — and all designs need adjustment — the posted page can be temporarily converted back to layers for easy repositioning. The Reposition Content Using Layers and Convert Layers to Tables menu commands work terrifically together and greatly enhance the designer's workflow.

The two commands are described in detail in the following sections, but let's examine a typical Dreamweaver layout session to see how they function together:

1. The Web designer is handed a comp or layout design created by another member of the company or a third-party designer.

2. After creating the graphic and type elements, the Web designer is ready to compose the page in Dreamweaver.

3. Ideally, the comp is converted to an electronic graphic format and brought into Dreamweaver as a Tracing Image.

4. If at all possible, it's best for conversion purposes to not overlap any layers, so the Web designer enables the Prevent Overlap option.

5. Each element is placed in a separate layer and placed in position, following the Tracing Image, if any.

6. With one command (Convert Layers to Tables), the layout is restructured from appearing in layers to being in tables for backward browser compatibility.

7. After the client has viewed the page — and made the inevitable changes — the page is converted from tables to layers. Again, in Dreamweaver 2, this process is triggered by one command (Reposition Content Using Layers) and takes seconds to complete.

8. The trip from tables to layers and back again is made as many times as necessary to get the layout pixel-perfect.

Reposition Content to Layers and Convert Layers to Tables is a one-two combination that cuts layout time tremendously and frees the designer to create visually instead of programmatically.

Converting content to layers

Dreamweaver 2.0 enables you to take any page and enclose all the contents in layers for easy design layout with drag-and-drop ease. Reposition Content Using Layers is very flexible and enables the designer to convert pages previously constructed either partially or totally with tables or ones that already have layers in place. You can even quickly convert an all-text page into a layer.

Tip   One valuable use for this command is to better prepare a page to use another Dreamweaver feature: Convert to 3.0 Browser Compatible. While you no longer have to have every page element in a layer to use this feature, if you use the Reposition Content Using Layers command first, you'll get better results.

With the page open in Dreamweaver, select Modify ➪ Layout ➪ Reposition Content Using Layers to view the command's dialog box, shown in Figure 25-16. By default, each of the following Layout Tool options are enabled:

✦ **Prevent Layer Overlaps.** You will want this option turned on if you plan to convert the layers back to a table.

✦ **Show Layer Palette.** This automatically opens the Layer palette for you with each layer given a default name by Dreamweaver.

✦ **Show Grid.** This options reveals the grid overlay that can help with precision layout.

✦ **Snap to Grid.** With this turned on, layers will snap to the nearest gridlines as they are moved onscreen.

You can uncheck any of these options before you convert the page.

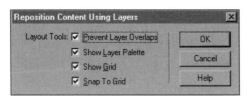

Figure 25-16: Choose the appropriate Layout Tools to help you reposition your content using layers.

Tip   Turn off Show Grid and Snap to Grid if you are laying out objects on top of a Tracing Image, as they may interfere with the absolute positions that you are trying to achieve.

Converting layers to tables

To convert a Web page that has been designed with layers into a table for viewing in older browsers, simply select Modify ➪ Layout ➪ Convert Layers to Tables. This will open the Convert Layers to Table dialog box, shown in Figure 25-17, with the following options:

✦ **Most Accurate.** This will create as complex a table as is necessary to guarantee that the elements on your Web page appear in the exact locations that you've specified. This is the default setting.

✦ **Smallest.** Collapse empty cells less than *n* pixels wide: Selecting this option will simplify your table layouts by joining cells that are less than the number of pixels wide that you specify. This may result in a table that takes less time to load; however, it will also mean that the elements on your page may not appear in the precise locations that you've placed them.

✦ **Use Transparent GIFs.** When you select this option, Dreamweaver will fill all empty cells with a transparent spacer graphic to ensure that the table will look the same across a variety of browsers. When Dreamweaver creates the table layout, it places a file called transparent.gif in the same folder as your Web page. You must make sure to include this file when you upload your page to your server in order for it to display correctly.

✦ **Center on Page.** Selecting this option will put `<div align=center>` tags around your table so that it displays in the middle of a browser window. Deselecting this option will leave out those tags so that the table will start from its default position in the upper-left corner of a browser.

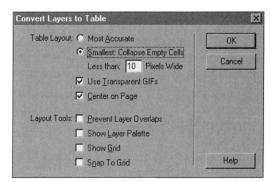

Figure 25-17: Choose Layout Tools to help reposition your content using layers.

Once you have converted your layout into a table, as shown in Figure 25-18, you should preview it in your browser. If you aren't happy with the way your layout looks, or if you wish to do further modifications, you can convert the table back into layers by selecting Modify ⇨ Layout ⇨ Reposition Content Using Layers as described previously, selecting the layers to drag and drop the contents into new positions. Finally, transform your layout back into a table, and preview it again.

Tip It's worth pointing out that the two Modify ⇨ Layout commands can be easily reversed by choosing Edit ⇨ Undo, whereas the corresponding File ⇨ Convert commands cannot.

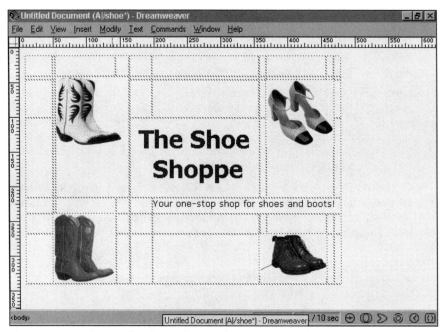

Figure 25-18: The results of transforming layers into a table, using the default settings.

Activating Layers with Behaviors

While absolute positioning is a major reason to use layers, you may have other motives for using this capability. All the properties of a layer — the coordinates, the size and shape, the depth, the visibility, and the clipping — can be altered dynamically and interactively as well. Normally, resetting a layer's properties dynamically entails some fairly daunting JavaScript programming. Now, with one of Dreamweaver's hallmarks — those illustrious behaviors — activating layers is possible for nonprogrammers as well.

Cross-Reference   In case you missed it, Chapter 17, "Using Behaviors," describes Dreamweaver's rich Behaviors feature.

Behaviors consist of two parts, the event and the action. In Dreamweaver 2.0, two standard actions are designed specifically for working with layers:

✦ **Drag Layer** enables the user to move the layer and get a response to that movement.

✦ **Show-Hide Layers** controls the visibility of layers, either interactively or through some pre-programmed action on the page.

You can find detailed information about these actions in their respective sections in Chapter 17. The following sections outline how to use these behaviors to activate your layers.

Drag Layer

For the Web designer, positioning a layer is easy: click the selection handle and drag the layer to a new location. For the readers of your pages, moving a layer is next to impossible—unless you incorporate the Drag Layer action into the page's design.

With the Drag Layer action, you can set up interactive pages in which the user can rearrange elements of the design to achieve an effect or make a selection. Drag Layer includes an option that enables you to execute a JavaScript command if the user drops the layer on a specific target. In the example shown in Figure 25-19, each pair of shoes is in its own layer. When the user drops a pair in the bag, a one-line JavaScript command opens the desired catalog page and order form.

Figure 25-19: On this interactive page, visitors can drop merchandise into the shopping bag; this feature is made possible with the Drag Layer action.

After you've created all your layers, you're ready to attach the behavior. Because Drag Layer initializes the script to make the interaction possible, you should always associate this behavior with the `<body>` tag and the `onLoad` Event.

Follow these steps to use the Drag Layer action, and to designate the settings for the drag operation:

1. Choose the `<body>` tag from the Tag Selector in the status bar.

2. Choose Window ⇨ Behaviors or select the Show Behaviors button from either Launcher. The Behavior Inspector opens.

3. In the Behavior Inspector, make sure that 4.0 Browsers is displayed in the browser list.

4. Click the + (Add) Action button and choose Drag Layer from the Add Action pop-up menu.

5. In the Drag Layer dialog box, select the layer you want to make available for dragging.

6. To limit the movement of the dragged layer, select Constrained from the Movement drop-down list. Then enter the coordinates to specify the direction to which you want to limit the movement in the Up, Down, Left, and/or Right text boxes.

7. To establish a location for a target, enter coordinates in the Drop Target: Left and Top text boxes. You can fill these text boxes with the selected layer's present location by clicking the Get Current Position button.

8. You can also set a snap-to area around the target's coordinates. When released in the target's location, the dragged layer snaps to this area. Enter a pixel value in the Snap if Within text box.

9. Click the More Options button.

10. Designate the drag handle:

    • To allow the whole layer to act as a drag handle, select Entire Layer from the drop-down menu.

    • If you want to limit the area to be used as a drag handle, select Area within Layer from the drop-down menu. Enter the Left and Top coordinates as well as the Width and Height dimensions in the appropriate text boxes.

11. If you want to keep the layer in its current depth and not bring it to the front, deselect the check-box for While Dragging: Bring Layer to the Front. To change the stacking order of the layer when it is released after dragging, select either Leave on Top or Restore z-index from the drop-down list.

12. To execute a JavaScript command when the layer is dropped on the target, enter the code in the Call JavaScript text box. If you want the script to execute every time the layer is dropped, enter the code in the When Dropped: Call JavaScript text box. If the code should execute only when the layer is dropped on the target, make sure there's a check in the Only if Snapped check-box.

13. To change the event that triggers the action (the default is `onLoad`) select an event from the drop-down menu in the Events column.

Targeted JavaScript Commands

The following simple yet useful JavaScript commands can be entered in the Snap JavaScript text box of the Drag Layer dialog box:

✦ To display a brief message to the user after the layer is dropped, use the `alert()` function:

```
alert("You hit the target")
```

✦ To send the user to another Web page when the layer is dropped in the right location, use the JavaScript location object:

```
location = "http://www.yourdomain.com/yourpage.html"
```

The location object can also be used with relative URLs.

Show-Hide Layers

The ability to implement interactive control of a layer's visibility offers tremendous potential to the Web designer. The Show-Hide Layers action makes this implementation straightforward and simple to set up. With the Show-Hide Layers action, you can simultaneously show one or more layers while hiding as many other layers as necessary. Create your layers and give them a unique name before invoking the Show-Hide Layers action.

To use Show-Hide Layers, follow these steps:

1. Select an image, link, or other HTML tag to which you'll attach the behavior.

2. Choose Window ➪ Behaviors or select the Show Behaviors button from either Launcher to open the Behavior Inspector.

3. Choose Show-Hide Layers from the + (Add) Action pop-up menu. The parameters form (Figure 25-20) shows a list of the available layers in the open Web page.

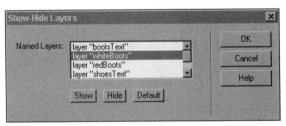

Figure 25-20: With the Show-Hide Layers behavior attached, you can easily program the visibility of all the layers in your Web page.

4. To cause a hidden layer to be revealed when this event is fired, select the layer from the list and choose the Show button.

5. To hide a visible layer when this event is fired, select its name from the list and select the Hide button.

6. To restore a layer's default visibility value when this event is fired, select the layer and choose the Default button.

7. Click OK when you are done.

8. If the default event is not suitable, use the drop-down menu in the Events column to select a different one.

Dreamweaver Technique: Creating a Loading Layer

As Web creations become more complex, most designers want their layers to zip on and off screen or appear and disappear as quickly as possible for the viewer of the page. A layer can act only when it has finished loading its content — the text and images. Rather than have the user see each layer loading in, some designers use a *loading layer* to mask the process until everything is downloaded and ready to go.

A loading layer is fairly easy to create. Dreamweaver 2 supplies all the JavaScript necessary in one behavior, Show-Hide Layers. Keep in mind that because this technique uses layers, it's only good for 4.0 browsers and above. Use the following steps to create a loading layer:

1. Create all of your layers with the contents in place, and the visibility property set as normal.

2. Create the loading layer. (Choose Insert ➪ Layer or select the Draw Layer button from the Objects Palette.)

3. Create one additional layer — the loading layer.

4. Enter and position whatever contents you want displayed in the loading layer while all the other layers are loading.

5. Open the Layers Palette (F11).

6. Turn off the visibility for all layers except the loading layer. In essence, you're hiding every other layer.

7. Select the `<body>` tag from the Tag Selector.

8. Choose Window ⇨ Behaviors or select Show Behaviors from either Launcher to open the Behavior Inspector.

9. Select the + (Add) Action button and choose Show-Hide Layers from the pop-up menu.

10. In the Show-Hide Layers dialog box, select the loading layer and then click the Hide button.

11. Select all the other layers and set them to Show. Click OK when you are done.

12. Leave `onLoad` (the default) as the event to trigger this action.

Now, when you test your Web page, you should see only your loading layer until everything else is loaded, and then the loading layer disappears and all the other layers are made visible.

 Note A loading layer may be the last bastion of the `<blink>` tag. Created by Netscape fairly early in the history of the Web, the `<blink>...</blink>` tag pair was grossly overused and is today generally shunned. However, if you apply it (by hand in the HTML Inspector) just to the ellipse following the term "Loading..." like this:

```
<h2>Loading<blink>...</blink></h2>
```

you'll get a small bit of movement on the page, similar to a blinking cursor. The `<blink>` tag is only supported by Netscape Navigator.

Summary

Layers are effective placement tools for developing the layout of a page. Anyone used to designing with desktop publishing tools can quickly learn to work layers effectively.

✦ Layers are only visible on fourth-generation and later browsers.

✦ Layers can be used to place HTML content anywhere on a Web page.

✦ You can stack layers on top of one another. This depth control is referred to as the *stacking order* or the *z-index*.

✦ Dreamweaver can convert layers to tables for viewing in earlier browsers, and back again for straightforward repositioning.

✦ Layers can be constructed so that the end user can display or hide them interactively, or alter their position, size, and depth dynamically.

✦ Dreamweaver gives you rulers and grids to help with layer placement and alignment.

✦ Layers can easily be activated by using Dreamweaver's built-in JavaScript behaviors.

In the next chapter, you learn how to develop timelines, which enable layers and their contents to move around the Web page.

✦   ✦   ✦

Working with Timelines

Motion implies time. A static object, like an ordinary HTML Web page, can exist either in a single moment or over a period of time. Conversely, moving objects (such as Dynamic HTML layers flying across the screen) need a few seconds to complete their path. All of Dreamweaver's DHTML animation effects use the Timeline feature to manage this conjunction of movement and time.

Timelines can do much more than move a layer across a Web page, however. A timeline can coordinate an entire presentation: starting the background music, scrolling the opening rolling credits, and cueing the voice-over narration on top of a slideshow. These actions are all possible with Dreamweaver because, in addition to controlling a layer's position, timelines can also trigger any of Dreamweaver's JavaScript behaviors on a specific frame.

This chapter explores the full and varied world of timelines. After an introductory section brings you up to speed on the underlying concepts of timelines, you learn how to insert and modify timelines to achieve cutting-edge effects. A Dreamweaver Technique shows you, step-by-step, how to create a multiscreen slideshow complete with fly-in and fly-out graphics. From complex multilayer animations to slideshow presentations, you can do it all with Dreamweaver timelines.

Note Because timelines are so intricately intertwined with layers and behaviors, you need to have a good grasp of these concepts. Before examining the topic of timelines, make sure to read Chapter 17, "Using Behaviors," Chapter 18, "Creating a Behavior," and Chapter 25, "Working with Layers."

Into the Fourth Dimension with Timelines

Until recently, Web designers have had little control over the fourth dimension and their Web pages. Only animated GIFs, Java, or animation programs such as Macromedia's Flash could create the illusion of motion events. Unfortunately, all of these technologies have some limitations.

The general problem with animated GIF images is related to file size. An animated GIF starts out as an image for every frame. Therefore, if you incorporate a three-second, 15-frames-per-second animation, you are asking the user to download the compressed equivalent of 45 separate images. Even though an animated GIF is an index color file with a limited 256 colors and uses the format's built-in compression, the GIF file is still a relatively large graphic file. Moreover, for all their apparent animated qualities, GIFs allow no true interaction other than as a link to another URL. Animations created with Dynamic HTML and Dreamweaver's timelines, on the other hand, do not significantly increase the overall size of the Web page and are completely interactive.

DHTML is not the only low-bandwidth approach to animations with interactive content for the Web. You can create animations, complete with user-driven interactions, with Java — as long as you're a Java programmer. Certainly Java development tools are making the language easier to use, but you still must deal with the rather long load time of any Java applet and the increasing variety of Java versions. As another option, Macromedia Director movies can be compressed or "shocked" to provide animation and interactivity in your pages. Like Java, the Director approach requires a bit of a learning curve. Shockwave movies can also have long load times and require the user to have a plug-in to be viewed.

Macromedia's Flash is another alternative to GIF images, though Flash has its own set of caveats to keep in mind. On the plus side, Flash files are small and can be streamed through their own player. This arrangement is tempting, and if you just want animation on a page, Flash is probably a superior choice to any of the approaches previously described. On the minus side, Flash is limited to its own proprietary features and functions, and every user must have the Flash plug-in or ActiveX control installed. Moreover, a Flash image cannot execute behavior commands, and you cannot layer Flash animation on top of other layers on a page. Once you or another designer has created a Flash animation, the animation must be edited with the same animation package.

Timeline capabilities

Dreamweaver timelines are part of the HTML code. For the movement of one layer straight across a Web page, Dreamweaver generates about 70 lines of code devoted to initializing and playing the timeline. But just what is a timeline? A timeline is composed of a series of frames. A frame is a snapshot of what the Web page, more specifically, the objects on the timeline, look like at a particular moment. You probably know that a movie is made up of a series of still pictures; when viewed quickly, the pictures create the illusion of movement. Each individual picture is a frame; movies show 24 frames per second, and video uses about 30 frames per second. Web animation, on the other hand, generally displays about 15 frames per second (fps). Not surprisingly, Dreamweaver's timeline is similar to the one used in Macromedia's timeline-based, multimedia authoring tool and animation package, Director 7.0.

If you have to draw each frame of a 30-second animation, even at 15 fps, you won't have time for other work. Dreamweaver uses the concept of *keyframes* to make a simple layer movement workable. Each keyframe contains a change in the timeline object's properties, such as position. For example, let's say you want your layer to start at the upper-left (represented by the coordinates 0,0) and travel to the lower-right (at 750,550). To accomplish this task, you need only specify the layer's position for the two keyframes — the start and the finish — and Dreamweaver generates all the frames in between.

Timelines have three primary roles:

✦ A timeline can alter a layer's position, dimensions, visibility, and depth.

✦ Timelines can change the source for any image on a Web page and cause another graphic of the same height and width to appear in the same location.

✦ Any of Dreamweaver's JavaScript behaviors can be triggered on any frame of a timeline.

A few ground rules

Keep the following basic guidelines in mind when you're using timelines in the Web pages you create with Dreamweaver:

✦ Timelines require a 4.0 or later browser.

✦ For a timeline to be able to animate an object, such as text, the object must be within a layer. If you try to create a timeline with an element that is not in a layer, Dreamweaver warns you and prevents you from adding the object to the timeline.

✦ Events don't have to start on the beginning of a timeline. If you want to have an action begin five seconds after a page has loaded, you can set the behavior on frame 60 of the timeline, with a frame rate of 15 frames per second.

✦ The selected frame rate is a "best-case scenario," as the actual frame rate depends on the user's system. A slower system or one that is simultaneously running numerous other programs can easily degrade the frame rate.

✦ You can include multiple animations on one timeline. The only restriction? You can't have two animations affecting the same layer at the same time. Dreamweaver prevents you from making this error.

✦ You can have multiple timelines that animate different layers simultaneously or the same layer at different times. Although you can set two or more timelines to animate the same layer at the same time, the results are difficult to predict and generally unintended.

Creating Animations with Timelines

Dreamweaver provides an excellent tool for managing timelines — the Timelines Inspector. Open this tool by choosing Window ➪ Timelines, selecting the Show Timelines button from either Launcher, or using the keyboard shortcut, F9.

The Timelines Inspector uses VCR-style controls combined with a playback head, which is a visual representation showing which frame is the current one. As shown in Figure 26-1, the Timelines Inspector gives you full control over any of the timeline functions. The Timelines Inspector has four major areas:

✦ **Timeline Controls.** Includes the Timeline pop-up menu for selecting the current timeline; the Rewind, Back, and Play buttons, the Fps (frame rate) text box; and the Autoplay and Loop check-boxes.

✦ **Behavior Channel.** Shows the placement of any behaviors attached to specific frames of the timeline.

✦ **Frames.** Displays the frame numbers for all timelines, and the playback head showing the current frame number.

✦ **Animation Channels.** Represents the animations for any included layers and images.

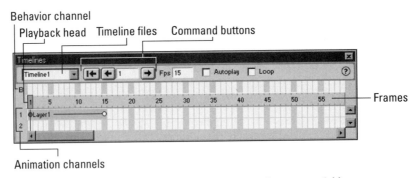

Figure 26-1: Dreamweaver's Timelines Inspector lets you quickly and easily master animation control.

Adding Layers to the Timelines Inspector

As with many of Dreamweaver's functions, you can add a layer or an image to the Timelines Inspector in more than one way. You can either insert a layer into a timeline through the menus (Modify ➪ Add Object to Timeline), or you can drag and drop an object into a timeline. The default timeline is set at a frame rate of 15 fps. When you add an object to a timeline, Dreamweaver inserts an animation bar of 15 frames in length, labeled with the object's name. The animation bar shows the duration (the number of frames) for the timeline's effect on the object. An animation bar is initially created with two initial keyframes: the start and the end.

To add a layer or image to the Timelines Inspector through the menus, follow these steps:

1. Choose Window ⇨ Timelines, or select the Show Timelines button from either Launcher to open the Timelines Inspector.

2. In the Document Window, select the layer or image you want to add to the timeline.

3. Choose Modify ⇨ Add Object to Timeline. An animation bar appears in the first frame of the timeline, as shown in Figure 26-2.

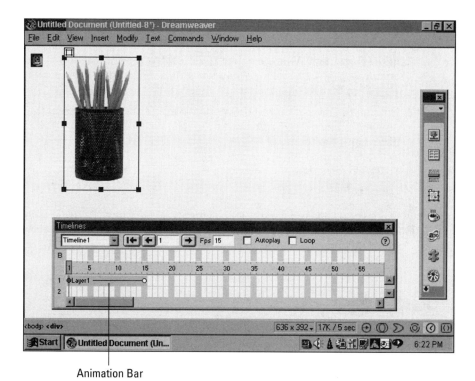

Animation Bar

Figure 26-2: The default animation bar is set at 15 frames, but can easily be modified.

4. To add another object, repeat Steps 2 and 3. Each additional animation bar is inserted beneath the preceding bar.

Tip

The first time you add an image or layer to the Timelines Inspector, Dreamweaver displays an alert message that details the limitations of timelines. If you don't want to see this alert, turn it off by checking the Don't Show Me This Message Again check-box.

As previously noted, you can add as many objects to a timeline as you desire. If necessary, increase the size of the Timelines Inspector by dragging any border of its window.

You have a little more flexibility when you add an object by dragging it into the timeline. Instead of the animation bar always beginning at frame 1, you can drop the object in to begin on any frame. This approach is useful, especially if you are putting more than one object into the same animation channel.

To place an object in a timeline with the drag-and-drop method, follow these steps:

1. Open the Timelines Inspector by choosing Window ⇨ Timelines or selecting the Show Timelines button from either Launcher.

2. In the Document Window, select the object you want to add to the timeline and drag it to the Timelines Inspector. As soon as the object is over the Timelines Inspector, a 15-frame animation bar appears.

3. Holding the mouse button down, position the animation bar so that the animation begins in the desired frame. Release the mouse button to drop the object into the timeline.

Note

Your placement does not have to be exact; you can modify it later.

Placing a layer or image on a timeline is just the beginning. To begin using your timeline in depth, you have to make changes to the object for the keyframes and customize the timeline.

Modifying a Timeline

When you add an object — either an image or a layer — to a timeline, you'll notice that the animation bar has an open circle at its beginning and end. An open circle marks a keyframe. As previously explained, the designer specifies a change in the state of the timeline object in a keyframe. For example, when you first insert a layer, the two generated keyframes have identical properties — the layer's position, size, visibility, and depth are unchanged. For any animation to occur, you have to change one of the layer's properties for one of the keyframes.

For example, let's move a layer quickly across the screen. Follow these steps:

1. Create a layer. If you like, add an image or a background color so that the layer will be more noticeable.

2. Open the Timelines Inspector (go to Window ⇨ Timelines, select the Show Timelines button from the Launcher, or press F9).

3. Drag the layer into the Timelines Inspector and release the mouse button.

4. Select the ending keyframe of the layer's animation bar. The playback head moves to the new frame.

5. In the Document Window, grab the layer's selection handle and drag the layer to a new location. A thin line connects the starting position of the layer to the ending position, as shown in Figure 26-3. This line is the *animation path*.

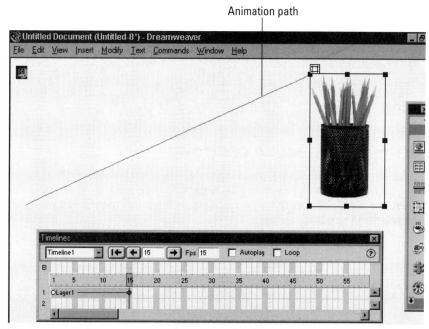

Figure 26-3: When you move a layer on a timeline, Dreamweaver displays an animation path.

6. To play your animation, first click the Rewind button in the Timelines Inspector; then click and hold down the Play button.

If you want to change the beginning position for your layer's movement, select the starting keyframe and then move the layer in the Document Window. To alter the final position for your layer's movement, select the ending keyframe and then move the layer.

Tip For more precise control of your layer's position in a timeline, select a keyframe and then, in the layer's Property Inspector, change the Left and/or Top values. You can also select the layer and use the arrow keys to move it.

Altering the animation bars

A Web designer can easily stretch or alter the range of frames occupied by a layer or image in an animation bar. You can make an animation longer, smoother, or have it start at an entirely different time. You can also move the layer to a different animation channel so it runs before or after another animation.

Use the mouse to drag an animation bar around the timeline. Click on any part of the bar except on the keyframe indicators, and move it as needed. To change the length of an animation, select the first or final keyframe and drag it forward or backward to a new frame.

You can remove an animation bar in two ways: select it and press Delete, or choose Modify ➪ Timeline ➪ Remove Object.

Using the Timeline controls

As you probably noticed if you worked through the example in the preceding section, you don't have to use a browser to preview a timeline. The Timeline controls shown in Figure 26-4 enable you to fine-tune your animations before you view them through a browser.

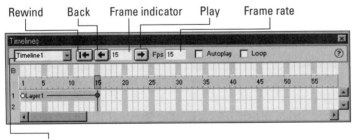

Figure 26-4: The Timeline controls let you move back and forth in your timeline, easily and precisely.

At the top-left corner is the Timeline pop-up menu, which is used to indicate the current timeline. By default, every new timeline is given the name Timeline*n*, where *n* indicates how many timelines have been created. You can rename the timeline by selecting it and typing in the new name. As you accumulate and use more timelines, you should give them recognizable names.

Tip   If you change the timeline name, you must enter a one-word name using alphanumeric characters that always begin with a letter. Netscape Navigator 4.0 cannot read spaces or special characters in JavaScript.

The next three buttons in the control bar enable you to move through the frames of a timeline. From left to right:

✦ **Rewind** moves the playback head to the first frame of the current timeline.

✦ **Back** moves the playback head to the previous frame. You can hold down the Back button to play the timeline in reverse.

✦ **Play** moves the timeline forward one frame at a time; hold down the Play button to play the timeline normally. When the last frame is reached, the playback head moves to the first frame of the current timeline and continues playing it.

The field between the Back and Play buttons is the frame indicator text box. To jump to any specific frame, enter the frame number in this box.

The next item in the control bar is the Fps (frames per second) text box. To change the frame rate, enter a new value in the Fps text box and press Tab or Enter (Return). The frame rate you set is an ideal number that a user's browser attempts to reach. The default rate of 15 frames per second is a good balance for both Macintosh and Windows systems.

Tip   Because browsers play every frame regardless of the frame rate setting, increasing the frame rate does not necessarily make your animations smoother. A better method for creating smooth animation is to drag the end keyframe farther out and therefore increase the number of frames used by your animation.

The next two check-boxes, Autoplay and Loop, affect how the animation is played.

Autoplay

If you mark the Autoplay check-box, the current timeline begins playing as soon as the Web page is fully downloaded. Dreamweaver alerts you to this arrangement by telling you that the Play Timeline action is attached to an onLoad event. Autoplay is achieved by inserting code into the <body> tag that looks similar to the following:

```
<body bgcolor="#FFFFFF" onload="MM_timelinePlay('timeline1')">
```

Note   If you don't use the Autoplay feature, you must attach the Play Timeline action to another event and tag, such as an `onMouseClick` event and a button graphic. Otherwise, the timeline does not play.

Looping

Mark the Loop check-box if you want an animation to repeat once it has reached the final frame. When Loop is enabled, the default causes the layer to replay itself an infinite numbers of times; you can change this setting, however.

When you first enable the Loop check-box, Dreamweaver alerts you that it is placing a Go to Frame action after the last frame of your current timeline. To set the number of repetitions for a timeline, follow these steps:

1. In the Timelines Inspector, check the Loop check-box.

2. Dreamweaver displays an alert informing you that the Go to Timeline Frame action is being added one frame past your current final frame. To disable these alerts, select the Don't Show Me This Message Again option.

3. In the Behavior channel (above the Frame numbers and playback head), double-click the behavior you just added.

Note   When you first add a behavior to a timeline, Dreamweaver presents a dialog box reminding you how to perform this action. Select the Don't Show Me This Message Again option when you've mastered the technique.

The Behavior Inspector opens, with an `onFrame` event in the Events pane and a Go To Timeline Frame action showing in the Actions pane.

4. Double-click the `onFrame` event. The Go to Timeline Frame dialog box opens (see Figure 26-5).

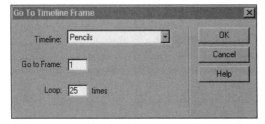

Figure 26-5: Selecting the Loop option on the Timelines Inspector adds a Go to Timeline Frame action, which you can customize.

5. Enter a positive number in the Loop text box to set the number of times you want your timeline to repeat. To keep the animation repeating continuously, leave the Loop text box blank.

6. Click OK when you are finished.

Tip

Your animations don't have to loop back to the beginning each time. By entering a different frame number in the Go to Frame text box of the Go to Timeline Frame dialog box, you can repeat just a segment of the animation.

Adding keyframes

Animating a timeline can go far beyond moving your layer from point A to point B. Layers (and the content within them) can dip, swirl, zigzag, and generally move in any fashion — all made possible by keyframes in which you have entered some change for the object. Dreamweaver calculates all the differences between each keyframe, whether the change is in a layer's position or size. Each timeline starts with two keyframes, the beginning and the end; you have to add other keyframes before you can insert the desired changes.

You can add a keyframe to your established timeline in a couple of different ways. The first method uses the Add Keyframe command, and the second method uses the mouse to click a keyframe into place.

Adding keyframes with the Add Keyframe command

To add a keyframe with the Add Keyframe command, follow these steps:

1. In the Timelines Inspector, select the animation bar for the object with which you are working.

2. Select the frame in which you want to add a keyframe.

3. Add your keyframe by either of the following methods:

- Choose Modify ➪ Timeline ➪ Add Keyframe.
- Right-click (Control-click) the frame in the animation bar and, from the shortcut menu, choose Add Keyframe.

A new keyframe is added on the selected frame, signified by the open circle in the animation bar.

While your new keyframe is selected, you can alter the layer's position, size, visibility, or depth. For example, if your animation involves moving a layer across the screen, you can drag the layer to a new position while the new keyframe is selected. The animation path is redrawn to incorporate this new positioning, as illustrated in Figure 26-6.

Altered animation path   Repositioned layer

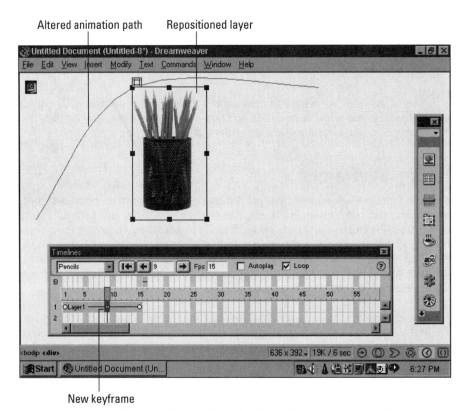

New keyframe

Figure 26-6: Repositioning a layer while a keyframe is selected can redirect your animation path.

Adding a keyframe with the mouse

The second method for adding a keyframe is quicker. To add a keyframe using the mouse, simply hold down the Ctrl (Command) key. Then click anywhere in the animation bar where you want to add a keyframe. Your cursor will turn into a small open circle when it is over the Timeline Window to show that it is ready to add a new keyframe.

What if you want to move the keyframe? Simply click and drag the keyframe to a new frame, sliding it along the animation bar in the Timelines Inspector.

Tip

If, after plotting out an elaborate animation with a layer, you discover that you need to shift the entire animation—say, 6 pixels to the right—you don't have to redo all your work. Just select the animation bar in the Timelines Inspector and then, in the Document Window, move the layer in question. Dreamweaver shifts the entire animation to your new location.

Removing timeline elements

The easiest way to remove an object, keyframe, or behavior from the Timelines Inspector is to select the element and press Delete. You cannot use this technique to delete individual frames or entire timelines, however. For these situations, you must use the menus:

✦ To remove the whole timeline, choose Modify ⇨ Timeline ⇨ Remove Timeline.

✦ To remove an individual frame, choose Modify ⇨ Timeline ⇨ Remove Frame.

The Timelines Inspector's shortcut menu also contains all the removal commands. Right-click (Control-click) the Timelines Inspector anywhere below the control bar, and in the shortcut menu (see Figure 26-7) choose the removal command you need: Remove Keyframe, Remove Behavior, Remove Object, Remove Frame, or Remove Timeline.

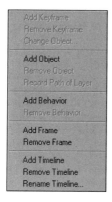

Figure 26-7: The Timelines Inspector's shortcut menu is extremely handy for doing quick edits.

Changing animation speed

You can alter your Dynamic HTML animation speed with two different methods that can be used separately or together.

✦ Drag the final keyframe in the animation bar out, to cover additional frames; or back, to cover fewer frames. Any keyframes within the animation bar are kept proportional to their original settings. This method works well when altering the speed of an individual animation bar.

✦ Change the frames per second value in the Fps text box of the Timelines Inspector. Increasing the number of frames per second accelerates the animation, and vice versa. Adjusting the Fps value affects every layer contained within the timeline; you cannot use this method for individual layers.

Caution   Browsers play every frame of a Dynamic HTML animation, regardless of the systems resources. Some systems, therefore, play the same animation faster or slower than others. Don't depend on every system to have the same timing.

Recording a layer's path

Plotting keyframes and repositioning your layers works well when you need to follow a pixel-precise path but it can be extremely tedious when you're trying to move a layer more freely on the screen. Luckily, there is another, easier method for defining a movement path for a layer. In Dreamweaver 2.0, you can simply drag your layer around the screen to create a path, and refine the path or its timing afterward.

New Feature   The new Record Path of Layer command automatically creates the necessary series of keyframes, calculated from your dragging of the layer. To fine-tune your work, you can select any keyframes and reposition the layer or even delete it entirely. This new feature is a definite timesaver for quickly inserting your DHTML animation.

Keep in mind that a timeline not only represents positions but positions over time, and thus, movement. The Record Path of Layer command is very smart when it comes to time; the slower you drag the layer, the more keypoints are plotted. You can vary the positioning of the keyframes by changing the tempo of your dragging. Moreover, the duration of the recorded timeline reflects the length of time spent dragging the layer.

To record a layer's path, do the following:

1. In the Document Window, select the layer you are going to move.

Caution   Make sure that you've selected the layer itself and not its contents. If you've correctly selected the layer, it will have eight selection boxes around it.

2. Drag the layer to the location in the document where you want it to be at the start of the movement.

3. From the menu bar, select Modify ➪ Record Path of Layer. You can also right-click (Control-click) the selected layer and choose Record Path from the shortcut menu.

   If it's not already open, the Timelines Inspector appears.

4. Click on the layer, and drag it around onscreen to define the movement. As you drag the layer, Dreamweaver draws a gray dotted line that shows you the path it is creating (see Figure 26-8).

   Each gray dot represents a keyframe. The slower you draw, the closer the keyframes are placed; moving quickly across the Document Window causes Dreamweaver to space out the keyframes.

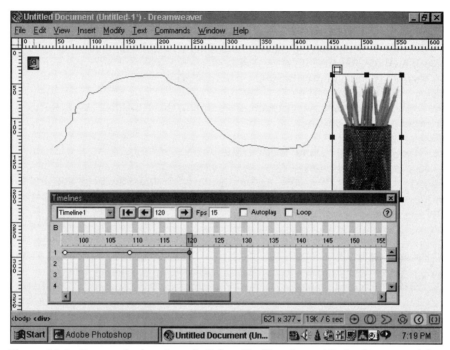

Figure 26-8: To record a layer's path, Select Modify ⇨ Record Path of Layer, and then drag your layer in the Document Window.

5. Release the mouse. This ends the recording.

    Dreamweaver displays an alert reminding you of the capabilities of the Timelines Inspector. Select the Don't Show Me This Message Again option to prevent this dialog box from re-appearing.

After you've finished recording a layer's movement, you will see a new animation bar in the Timelines Inspector, representing the motion you just recorded. The duration of the new timeline matches the duration of your dragging of the layer. A number of keyframes that define your layer's movement will already be inserted in this animation bar. You can use any of the procedures described earlier in this chapter to modify the timeline or its keyframes. If you select the same layer at the end of the generated timeline and perform the Record Path operation again, another animation bar is added at the end of the current timeline.

Caution   Any new paths recorded with the same layer are added after the last animation bar. You can't select a keyframe in the middle of a path and then record a path from that point; the starting keyframe of the newly recorded path corresponds to the position of the layer in the last keyframe.

Triggering Behaviors in Timelines

Adding a behavior to a timeline is similar to adding behaviors to any object on a Web page. Because timelines are written in JavaScript, they behave exactly the same as any object enhanced with JavaScript.

You'll use the behaviors channel section of the Timelines Inspector to work with behaviors in timelines.

You can attach a behavior to a timeline in four ways:

✦ Highlight the frame in which you wish to have the behavior, and then right-click (Control-click). Select Add Behavior from the shortcut menu.

✦ Highlight the frame in which you want to activate the behavior, and choose Modify ➪ Add Behavior to Timeline.

✦ Open the Behavior Inspector and click the frame you wish to modify in the Behavior channel.

✦ Double-click the frame for which you want to add a behavior in the Behavior channel.

After a behavior is attached to a frame and you open the Behavior Inspector, you see that the event inserted in the Events pane is related to a frame number; for example, `onFrame20`. Each frame can trigger multiple actions.

Cross-Reference For more specifics about Dreamweaver behaviors, see Chapter 17, "Using Behaviors," and Chapter 18, "Creating a Behavior."

Behaviors are essential to timelines. Without these elements, you cannot play or stop your timeline-based animations from running. Even when you select the Autoplay or Loop options in the Timelines Inspector, you are enabling a behavior. The three behaviors always deployed for timelines are Play Timeline, Stop Timeline, and Go to Timeline Frame.

If you are not using the Autoplay feature for your timeline, you must explicitly attach a Play Timeline behavior to an interactive or another event on your Web page. For example, a timeline is typically set to start playing once a specific picture has loaded, if the user enters a value in a form's text box, or — more frequently — when the user selects a Play button. You could use the Stop Timeline behavior to pause an animation temporarily.

To use the Play Timeline or Stop Timeline behavior, follow these steps:

1. In the Document Window, select a tag, link, or image that you want to trigger the event.

2. Choose Window ➪ Behaviors or select the Show Behavior button from the Launcher to open the Behavior Inspector.

3. In the Behavior Inspector, click the + (Add) Action button, and from the pop-up menu choose either of the following methods:

- Timeline ⇨ Play Timeline to start a timeline.
- Timeline ⇨ Stop Timeline to end a timeline.

4. In the Play Timeline or Stop Timeline dialog box (see Figure 26-9), choose the timeline that you want to play (or stop) from the appropriate Timeline drop-down list.

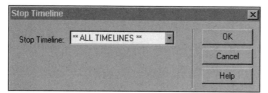

Figure 26-9: The Stop Timeline behavior can be used to stop all timelines or a specific timeline from playing.

5. Click OK when you are finished.

6. Select an event to trigger the behavior from the drop-down menu in the Events column.

When you select the option to loop your timeline, Dreamweaver automatically inserts a Go to Frame behavior — with the first frame set as the target. You can display any frame on your timeline by inserting the Go to Frame behavior manually. To use the Go to Frame behavior, follow these steps:

1. In the Document Window, select a tag, link, or image that you want to have trigger the event.

2. Choose Window ⇨ Behaviors or select the Show Behavior button from the Launcher to open the Behavior Inspector.

3. In the Behavior Inspector, select the + (Add) Action button and choose Timeline ⇨ Go to Timeline Frame from the drop-down list.

4. Choose the timeline you want to affect from the Timeline drop-down menu.

5. Enter the frame number in the Go to Frame text box.

6. If you'd like the timeline to loop a set number of times, enter a value in the Loop text box.

Remember, if you don't enter a value, the timeline loops endlessly.

7. Click OK when you are finished.

8. Choose an event to trigger the behavior from the drop-down menu in the Events pane.

Tip Depending on the type of effect desired, you may want to use two of the Timeline behaviors together. To ensure that your timeline always starts from the same point, first attach a Go to Timeline Frame behavior to the event, and then attach the Play Timeline behavior to the same event.

Dreamweaver Technique: Creating a Multiscreen Slideshow

Moving layers around the screen is pretty cool, but you've probably already figured out that you can do a lot more with timelines. One of the possibilities is a graphics slideshow displaying a rotating series of pictures. To demonstrate the range of potential available to timelines, the following sample project shows you how to construct a slideshow with more than one screen, complete with moving layers and triggered behaviors.

This technique has four steps:

> **Step 1: Preparing the graphic elements.** The process is easier if you have most (if not all) of your images for the slideshow—as well as the control interface—ready to go.

> **Step 2: Creating the slideshow timeline.** In this project, one timeline is devoted to rotating images on four different "screens."

> **Step 3: Creating the moving layers timeline.** The slideshow begins and ends with a bit of flair, as the screens fly in and fly out.

> **Step 4: Adding the behaviors.** The slideshow includes controls for playing, pausing, restarting, and ending the slideshow, which then takes the user to another Web page.

This technique is intended to act as a basis for your own creations, not as an end in itself. You can add many variations and refinements; for example, you can preload images, make rollover buttons, and add music to the background. Following is a fundamental structure focused on the use of timelines, which you can expand with additional objects as needed.

Note The end result of this Dreamweaver Technique can only be viewed by 4.0 browsers or later.

Step 1: Preparing the graphic elements

You'll find only one restriction to using a timeline for a slideshow presentation, but the qualification is significant—all the graphics in one "screen" must have the same dimensions. The timeline doesn't actually change the image tag; it only changes the file source for the tag. Thus, the height and width of the last image inserted overrides all the values for the foregoing graphics.

Luckily, all major image-processing software can resize and extend the canvas of a picture with little effort. When creating a slideshow, you may find it useful to do all of the resizing work at one time. Load in your images with the greatest width and height — they may or may not be the same picture — and use these measurements as your common denominators for all graphics.

Go ahead and create your interface buttons earlier rather than later. Experience shows that the more design elements you prepare ahead of time, the less adjusting you have to do later. Also, activating a timeline with a behavior is a straightforward process, and a finished interface enables you to incorporate the buttons quickly.

Finally, you should create and place the layers you'll be using. The sample Web page in this technique is built of four screens, all of the same dimensions. The four different layers are uniquely named, but they all have the same size.

Tip   If you are making multiple versions of the same layer, consider changing the default layer size to fit your design. Choose Edit ➪ Preferences and open up the default Layers preferences. Once you've customized the height and width values, all the layers incorporated in the Web page with the Insert ➪ Layer command automatically size correctly. You only have to position these layers.

To recap, use the following steps to prepare your graphics:

1. Create all the images to be used as slides. All the slides must be the same height and width.

2. Prepare and place your interface buttons.

3. Create the number of layers that you'll need for the different screens in the slideshow.

4. Position your layers so that each can hold a different slide. The preceding example has four layers, centered on the screen in two rows.

5. Insert your opening slides into each of the layers.

Note   Your opening slide doesn't have to be a graphic image. You could also use a solid-colored GIF or a slide with text.

Try to work backward from a final design whenever layer positioning is involved. At this stage, all of the elements are in their ending placement, ready for the slideshow to begin (see Figure 26-10). Next, you can activate the slideshow.

Figure 26-10: Before activating any layers or setting up the slideshow, design the layout.

Step 2: Creating the slideshow timeline

For all the attention that timelines and layers receive, you may be surprised that one of the best features of Dreamweaver timelines has nothing to do with layers. You can use timelines to change images anywhere on your Web page—whether or not they are in layers. As explained in Step 1, the timeline doesn't actually replace one <img> tag with another, but rather alters an image by swapping the src attribute value. The src changes just as changes in a layer's position, shape, or depth must happen at a keyframe.

In planning your slideshow, you need to decide how often a new slide appears, because you need to set keyframes at each of these points. If you are changing your slides every few seconds, you can change the frame rate to 1 fps. This setting helps you easily keep track of how many seconds occur between each slide change (and because no animation is involved with this timeline, a rapid frame rate is irrelevant). Note, however, that on the other timeline—involving moving layers—the frame rate should be maintained at around 15 fps. Each timeline can have its own frame rate.

The only other choices involve the Autoplay and Loop options. As with frame rate, you can set each timeline to its own options without interfering with another timeline. This example has the slideshow loop but not start automatically. Use the Play button to enable the user to start the show. But first, let's add the images to the slides.

To put images into a slideshow on a timeline, follow these steps:

1. Choose Window ➪ Timelines or select the Show Timelines button from the Launcher to open the Timelines Inspector.

2. If desired, rename Timeline1 by selecting the name and typing your own unique name.

3. Select one image from those onscreen in the positioned layers, and drag the graphic to the Timelines Inspector.

Be sure to grab the image, not the layer.

4. Release the animation bar at the beginning of the timeline.

5. Repeat Steps 3 and 4 for each image until all images are represented on the timeline.

6. Change the frame rate by entering a new value in the Fps text box. This example changes the frame rate to 1.

7. Select the Loop or Autoplay option, if desired.

8. On one of the animation bars representing images, select the frame for a keyframe.

9. Choose Modify ➪ Timeline ➪ Add Keyframe, right-click (Control-click) the frame on the timeline, and choose Add Keyframe from the shortcut menu, or hold down the Ctrl (Command) key and click on the animation bar.

10. In the Image Property Inspector, select the Src folder to locate the graphic file for the next slide image.

11. Repeat Steps 9 and 10 until every animation bar has keyframes for every slide change, and each keyframe has a new or different image assigned.

This example changes slides every five seconds, as you can see in Figure 26-11 by looking at the keyframe placement. Although the slideshow has all four images changing simultaneously, you can also stagger the timing of the image changes. Simply drag one or more of the animation bars a few frames forward or backward after the keyframes have been set.

To preview your slide changes, you don't have to go outside of Dreamweaver. Just click and hold down the Play button on the Timelines Inspector.

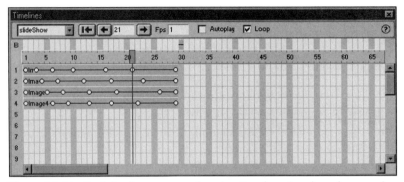

Figure 26-11: Each keyframe on each animation bar signals a change of the slide image.

Step 3: Creating the moving layers timeline

At this stage, the slideshow is functional, but a little dull. To add a bit of showmanship, you can "fly in" the layers from different areas of the Web page to their final destination. This task is easy—to complete the effect, the layers "fly out" when the user is ready to leave.

You can achieve these fly-in/fly-out effects in several ways. You can put the opening fly-in on one timeline and the ending fly-out on another. A more concise method combines the fly-in and fly-out for each layer on one timeline—separating them with a Stop Timeline behavior. After the fly-in portion happens when the page has loaded (because the example selects the Autoplay option for this timeline), the fly-out section does not begin to play until signaled to continue with the Play Timeline behavior.

To create the moving layers' opening and closing for the slideshow, follow these steps:

1. Choose Modify ➪ Timeline ➪ Add Timeline, or right-click (Ctrl-click) the Timelines Inspector and choose Add Timeline from the shortcut menu.

2. Rename your new timeline if desired.

3. Select the Autoplay check-box so that this timeline begins playing automatically when the Web page is loaded.

4. Select any one of the layers surrounding your images and drag it onto the Timelines Inspector.

Caution

This time, make sure you move the layers — not the images.

5. To set the amount of time for the fly-in section to span, drag the final keyframe of the animation bar to a new frame. The example sets the end at 30 frames, which at 15 fps lasts two seconds.

6. From the Document Window, select the same layer again and drag it to the Timelines Inspector. Place it directly after the first animation bar. This animation bar becomes the fly-out portion.

7. Drag the final keyframe to extend the time, if desired.

8. At this point, all four keyframes — two for each animation bar — have exactly the same information. Now change the positions for two keyframes to allow the layer to move. Select the first keyframe in the opening animation bar.

9. Reposition the layer so that it is offscreen. Although you can complete this task manually to the right or bottom of the screen by dragging the layer to a new location, you can also use the Layer Property Inspector to input new values directly for the Left and Top attributes.

Tip

Use negative numbers to move a layer offscreen to the left or top of the browser window.

10. From the Timelines Inspector, select the last keyframe of the closing animation bar.

11. Reposition the layer offscreen. If you want the layer to return in the same manner as it arrived, enter the same values for the Left and Top attributes as in the first keyframe of the opening animation bar.

12. Repeat Steps 4 through 11 for every layer.

Now, when you preview this timeline, the layers fly in and immediately fly out again. Figure 26-12 shows the layers in the example in mid-animation. In the final phase of the technique, you add behaviors to put the action under user control.

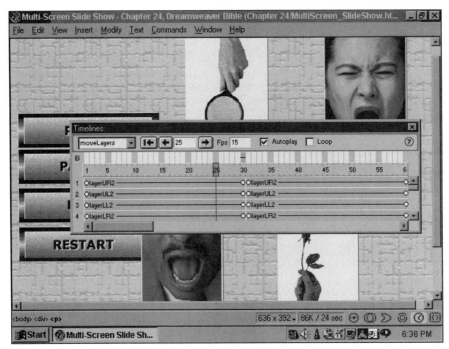

Figure 26-12: You can use two animation bars side-by-side to achieve a back-and-forth effect.

Step 4: Adding the behaviors

Although it may be fun to watch an unexpected effect take place, giving the user control over aspects of a presentation is much more involving — for the designer as well as the user. The example is ready to incorporate the user-interaction aspect by attaching Dreamweaver behaviors to the user interface and to the behavior channel of the Timelines Inspector.

Two timeline behaviors have already been attached to the example — when the Loop option is selected in Step 2 for the slideshow timeline, Dreamweaver automatically includes a Go to Timeline Frame behavior after the final frame that sends the timeline back to the first frame. In the moving layers timeline, enabling the Autostart option causes Dreamweaver to attach a Play Timeline behavior to the onLoad event of the Web page's <body> tag. To complete the project, five behaviors need to be added.

First, you need a behavior to stop the moving layers from proceeding after the fly-in portion of the animation:

1. From the Timelines Inspector, double-click the final frame of the first animation bar in the Behavior channel.

2. In the Behavior Inspector, select Timeline ⇨ Stop Timeline from the + (Add) Actions pull-down menu.

3. From the Stop Timeline dialog box, select the timeline that contains the moving layers.

4. Click OK. An `onFrame` event is set for the Stop Timeline action by default.

Second, you need a behavior to let the user begin playing the slideshow:

1. In the Document Window, select the Play button.

2. In the Behavior Inspector, select the Timeline ⇨ Play Timeline action from the + (Add) Action drop-down list.

3. In the Play Timeline dialog box, choose the timeline representing the slideshow.

4. Click OK. An `onMouseDown` event is set to trigger the action by default.

The next behavior enables the user to stop the slideshow temporarily:

1. In the Document Window, select the Pause button.

2. In the Behavior Inspector, select Timeline ⇨ Stop Timeline from the + (Add) Actions drop-down list.

3. Choose the layer representing the slideshow in the Stop Timeline dialog box.

4. Click OK. An `onMouseDown` event is set to trigger the action by default.

To enable the user to begin the slideshow from the beginning, follow these steps:

1. In the Document Window, select the Restart button.

2. In the Behavior Inspector, add the Timeline ⇨ Go to Timeline Frame action.

3. In the Go to Timeline Frame dialog box, choose the layer representing the slideshow.

4. Enter a 1 in the Frame text box.

5. Click OK. An `onMouseDown` event is set to trigger the action by default.

6. Add the next action. In the Behavior Inspector, select Timeline ⇨ Play Timeline from the + (Add) Action drop-down list.

7. In the Play Timeline dialog box, choose the layer representing the slideshow.

8. Click OK. An `onMouseDown` event is attached to the action by default.

To end the presentation and move the user on to the next Web page, follow these steps:

1. In the Document Window, select the End button.

2. In the Behavior Inspector, select the Timeline ⇨ Play Timeline action from the + (Add) Action drop-down list.

3. Choose the timeline representing the moving layers in the Play Timeline dialog box and click OK. The timeline begins playing where it last stopped — just before the layers are about to fly out. An `onMouseDown` event is set to trigger the action by default.

4. Add the next behavior. Select the Go to URL action from the + (Add) drop-down list.

5. In the Go to URL dialog box, enter the path to the new page in the URL text box; or select the Browse (Choose) button to locate the file. Click OK when you are finished.

The project is complete and ready to test. Feel free to experiment, trying out different timings to achieve different effects.

You can test the final working version by just using your browser to view the Multiscreen Slideshow Demo in the Dreamweaver Bible Code section of the CD-ROM.

Summary

Timelines are effective tools for developing pages in which events need to be triggered at specific points in time.

✦ Timelines can affect particular attributes of layers and images, or they can start any Dreamweaver behavior.

✦ Use the Timelines Inspector to set an animation to play automatically, to have it loop indefinitely, and to change the frames-per-second display rate of the timeline.

✦ You must use one of the timeline behaviors to activate your timeline if you don't use the Autoplay feature.

In the next chapter, you learn how you can use Dreamweaver to explore the brave new world of XML, the Extensible Markup Language.

Creating Next-Generation Code with Dreamweaver

◆ ◆ ◆ ◆

◆ ◆ ◆ ◆

Extending with XML

XML, short for *Extensible Markup Language*, is quickly becoming a powerful force on the Web and an important technology for Web designers to master. XML allows the parts of any document — from Web page to invoice — to be defined in terms of how those parts are used. When a document is defined by its structure, rather than its appearance, as it is with HTML, the same document can be read by a wide variety of systems and put to use far more efficiently.

With Dreamweaver 2, Macromedia introduces *Roundtrip XML*, a complement to Dreamweaver's Roundtrip HTML core philosophy. Roundtrip HTML ensures that the defined tags of HTML remain just as you've written them. With XML, there is no one defined set of tags — XML tags can be written for an industry, a company, or just a Web site. Roundtrip XML permits Web designers to export and import XML pages based on their own structure. This chapter explores the basics of XML as well as the implementation of Roundtrip XML in Dreamweaver.

Understanding XML

XML is to structure as Cascading Style Sheets (CSS) are to format. While CSS controls the look of a particular document on the Web, XML makes the document's intent paramount. Because there are almost as many ways that the parts of documents can be described as there are types of documents, a set language, such as HTML, could never provide enough specification to be truly useful. This is why, with XML, you create your own custom tags to describe the page — XML is truly an extensible language.

XML became a W3C Recommendation in February, 1998, after a relatively brief two-year study. The speed with which the recommendation was approved speaks to the need for the technology. XML has been described as a more accessible version of SGML (*Standard Generalized Markup Language*), the widely used text processing standard. In fact, the XML Working Group that drafted the W3C recommendation started out as the SGML Working Group.

What can XML do that HTML can't? Let's say you have a shipping order that you want to distribute. With HTML, each of the parts of the document — such as the billing address, the shipping address, and the order details, to name a few — are enclosed in tags that describe their appearance, like this:

```
<h2 align="center">Invoice<bold>
<p align="left">Ship to:</p>
<p>J. Lowery<br>
101 101st Avenue, Ste. 101<br>
New York, NY 10000</p>
```

With XML, each section of the page is given its own set of tags, according to their meaning, like this:

```
<documentType>Invoice</documentType>
<ship-toHeader>Ship to:</ship-toHeader>
<customer>J. Lowery<br></customer>
<ship-toAddress>101 101st Avenue, Ste. 101<br>
New York, NY 10000</ship-toAddress>
```

Like HTML, XML is a combination of content and markup tags. Markup tags can be in pairs, like `<customer></customer>`, or they can be singular. A single tag is called an *empty tag*, because no content is included. Single tags in XML must include an ending slash — as in `<noTax/>`, for example — and are used to mark where something occurs. In the example, `<noTax/>` indicates that no sales tax is to be applied to this invoice.

XML tags can, again like HTML, also include attributes and values. As with HTML, XML attributes further describe the tag, much like an adjective describes a noun. For example, another way to write the `<ship-toHeader>` tag would be

```
<header type="Ship To">
```

With a more generalized tag such as this one, you could easily change values, as in `<header type="Bill To">`, rather than include another new tag.

In all, XML recognizes six kinds of markups:

✦ **Elements.** Elements are more commonly known as tags and, as in HTML, are delimited by a set of angle brackets, <>. As noted previously, elements can also have attributes set to particular values.

Caution While surrounding values with quotes — such as in `color="white"` — is optional in HTML, it's mandatory in XML.

✦ **Entity References.** Certain characters in XML, such as the delimiting angle brackets, are reserved in order to permit markup to be recognized. These characters are represented by entities in XML. As in HTML, character entities begin with an ampersand and end with a semicolon. For example `&lt;Content&gt;` is XML code to represent `<Content>`.

✦ **Comments.** XML comments are identical to HTML comments; they both begin with `<!--` and end with `-->`.

✦ **Processing instructions.** XML processing instructions are similar to server-side includes in that the XML processor (like the server) passes them on to the application (like the browser).

✦ **Marked sections.** XML can pass blocks of code or other data without parsing the markup and content. These blocks of character data are marked with `<![CDATA[` at the beginning and `]]>` at the end. For example:

```
<![CDATA[If age < 19 and age > 6, then the kids are in
school]]>
```

Communication between XML and HTML is greatly eased because large blocks of data can be passed in this fashion.

✦ **Document type declarations.** Because every XML document is capable of containing its own set of custom tags, a method for defining these tags must exist. While a discussion of the formats of such document type declarations are beyond the scope of this book, it's helpful to know that such declarations can be made for elements, attributes, character entities, and notations. *Notations* refer to external binary data, such as GIFs, that are passed through the XML parser to the application.

XML documents may begin with an XML declaration that specifies the version of XML being used. The XML declaration for a document compliant with the 1.0 specification looks like the following:

```
<?xml version="1.0"?>
```

A much more detailed *document type declaration* (DTD), in which each tag and attribute is described in SGML, is also possible. XML documents including these types of DTDs are labeled *valid XML documents*. Other documents that respect the rules of XML regarding nesting of tags and other matters, but don't include DTDs for the elements, are known as *well-formed XML*. Dreamweaver exports well-formed XML documents, but can import either well-formed or valid XML.

Exporting XML

How do you make an XML page? In Dreamweaver 2, you can convert an existing document into XML format with one command. Currently, Dreamweaver creates its XML pages based on a template's editable regions. This approach allows the true content of a page—what distinguishes it from all other pages of the same type—to be separated and applied independently of the original Web page. In other words, once the XML information is culled from a Web page, it can be imported into any other application to be displayed, read, spoken, translated, or acted upon.

Dreamweaver templates are composed of locked and editable regions; the locked regions are repeated for each page created from the template, while the content in the editable regions is added per page. The connection between XML and templates is similar to the relationship between a database form and its data. In a database, each field has a unique name, such as LastName, FirstName, and so on. When you create a database form to present the data, the placeholders for the data use the same field names. Then, when data from one record flows into the form, the information from the field goes into the areas with the corresponding field names. Likewise, each editable region has a unique name—in essence, a field name. The content within the editable region is the field's data. When exported as an XML file, the name of the editable region is converted to an XML tag that surrounds its data.

For example, Figure 27-1 shows a Dreamweaver template for a purchase order. On the left are the headings (To, Company, Address, etc.) for the information in a locked area, while the specific shipping data on the right resides in a series of editable regions, each with its own name. When exported as XML by Dreamweaver, the resulting XML file looks like the following:

```
<?xml version="1.0"?>
<doctitle><![CDATA[<title>Purchase Order</title>]]></doctitle>
<Customer><![CDATA[Jose Bleau]]></Customer>
<Company><![CDATA[Kreamhorn, Inc. ]]></Company>
<Address><![CDATA[155 Somerton Ave.<br>
                  West Therea, TX]]></Address>
<PO_Date><![CDATA[January 2, 1999]]></PO_Date>
<Ship_Via><![CDATA[FedEx]]></Ship_Via>
```

Cross-Reference

To get a better idea of how to use XML, you need to first understand Dreamweaver templates. Learn more about Dreamweaver templates in Chapter 34, "Using Dreamweaver Templates."

Note several important items about the XML file. First, notice the use of self-evident labels for each of the tags, such as `<Customer>` and `<Ship_Via>`; such names make it very easy to understand an XML file. Even the one tag not based on a user-defined name, `<doctitle>` is very straightforward. Second, all the data included in the XML tags is marked as a CDATA area; this ensures that the information is conveyed intact, just as it was entered. Finally, if you look at the `<Address>` tag data, you'll see that even HTML tags (here, a `<br>` tag) are included in the CDATA blocks. This practice allows basic formatting to be carried over from one page to the next. You can avoid this by selecting just the inner content—without any of the formatting tags—to be marked as an editable region.

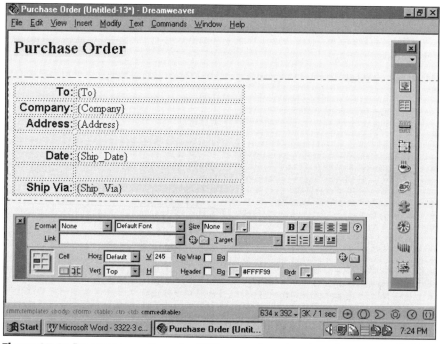

Figure 27-1: Dreamweaver 2 creates XML pages based on templates and editable regions.

Dreamweaver can create one of two different types of XML tags during its export operation. The first is a referred to as *Dreamweaver Standard XML* and uses an ⟨item⟩ tag with a name attribute set to the editable region's name. For example, if the editable region was named Ship_Via, the Dreamweaver Standard tag would be

```
<item name="Ship_Via">Content</item>
```

The Dreamweaver Standard XML file has one other distinguishing characteristic. The XML file is saved with a reference to the defining Dreamweaver template, like this:

```
<templateItems template="/Templates/PO.dwt">
```

When importing a Dreamweaver Standard XML file, if the specified template cannot be found, a dialog box appears asking that you select another template.

The other option is to use what Dreamweaver refers to as *Editable Region Name* tags. This method uses the editable region names themselves as tags. In the case of the editable region name Ship_Via, the tag pair under this method would be ⟨Ship_Via⟩⟨/Ship_Via⟩.

To create an XML file from within Dreamweaver, follow these steps:

1. Open a Dreamweaver document based on a template that has at least one editable region.

2. Choose File ⇨ Export ⇨ Export Editable Regions As XML.

   The Export Editable Regions As XML dialog box opens, as shown in Figure 27-2.

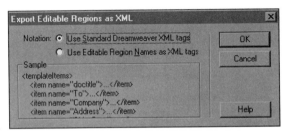

Figure 27-2: Convert any template-based page to an XML document with the Export Editable Regions As XML command.

3. Choose the format for the XML tags by selecting one of the Notation options:

   • **Use Standard Dreamweaver XML Tags.** Select this option to produce `<item>` tags with `name` attributes set to the names of the editable regions.

   • **Use Editable Region Names as XML Tags.** Select this option to produce XML tags that use the editable region names directly.

   Selecting either option displays sample tags in the preview area of the dialog box.

4. Select OK when you're done.

   An Export Editable Regions As XML Save File dialog box appears.

5. Enter the path and name of the XML file you wish to save in the File Name text box or select the Browse (Choose) button to locate another folder. Click Save when you're done.

Importing XML

As part of Roundtrip XML, Dreamweaver 2 includes an Import XML command. Like the Export XML command, Import XML works with Dreamweaver templates. The content information in the XML document fills out the editable regions in the template, much as data fills out a form in a database.

With this import capability, content can be independently created and stored in an XML file and then, to publish the page to the Web, simply imported into the Dreamweaver template.

Note While currently there are not many tools on the market to create separate XML files, many are in development and should be available shortly.

To import an XML file into a Dreamweaver template, follow these steps:

1. If desired, open a file based on a Dreamweaver template.

Tip You don't have to have a page created from a template open in order to access the XML information — Dreamweaver automatically opens one for you.

2. Choose File ⇨ Import XML into Template.

   The Import XML dialog box opens.

Caution Any existing information in the Dreamweaver document in the editable regions will be replaced by the information in the corresponding tags of the XML document.

3. Select an XML file from the Import XML dialog box.

4. Choose Open when you're done.

   The XML file is imported into Dreamweaver and the editable region placeholder names are replaced with the data in the XML document.

Summary

XML is a vital future technology that is knocking on the door of virtually every Web designer in business. As the development tools become more common, the Roundtrip XML ability within Dreamweaver will make interfacing with this new method of communication straightforward and effortless. Keep the following points in mind about XML:

✦ XML (Extensible Markup Language) allows content to be separated from the style of a Web page, creating information that can be more easily used in various situations with different kinds of media.

✦ Tags in XML reflect the nature of the content, rather than its appearance.

✦ Dreamweaver 2 includes a Roundtrip XML facility that allows for the export and import of XML files through Dreamweaver templates.

In the next chapter, you learn how Dreamweaver can extend the multimedia reach of your Web pages through custom objects developed with partners such as Real Networks, IBM, and Live Picture.

✦   ✦   ✦

Adding Multimedia Extensions

Dreamweaver has become the Web authoring tool of choice among many professionals — especially those designers responsible for building cutting-edge sites. Not only does Dreamweaver integrate well with other hot Web technologies from Macromedia — like Shockwave and Flash — but Dreamweaver's extensibility makes it possible to create custom objects for other emerging media. When Dreamweaver 2 was announced, so were partnerships with RealNetworks, IBM, Hewlett-Packard, and Live Picture that extend Dreamweaver's capabilities into several exciting new areas.

Integrating new technologies into a Web site is far from a no-brainer. Before a Web designer can commit to using any nonstandard component — that is, anything not accessible by the basic browser — the market for the Web site must be evaluated. Some Web site audiences follow every trend and always have the latest in browser versions and plug-ins — a crowd like this is ready for anything new. Other markets are more conservative and only the most generic Web sites need apply. The general Web audiences are somewhere in between, with pockets of intranets where a particular plug-in is a given.

In this chapter, you'll explore some of the newest of the new media and learn how Dreamweaver eases the learning curve of adopting a new technology. The first part of the chapter covers streaming multimedia presentations from RealNetworks using the W3C recommendation SMIL to integrate RealVideo, RealAudio, and other Real media types. Next, you'll see how IBM is integrating multimedia into Web advertising with the HotMedia technology. This chapter also covers two methods — one from Hewlett-Packard and one from Live Picture — for allowing Web browsers to zoom into photographs to reveal astounding detail. No doubt about it: if you're looking for the multimedia edge, you'll find it in Dreamweaver.

Understanding SMIL

SMIL, which stands for *Synchronized Multimedia Integration Language*, truly puts the "multi" back in multimedia. This new standardized language, developed by the W3C, is used when several streaming media types — video, audio, animation, text, or straight graphics — are displayed in one presentation. SMIL (pronounced "smile") uses a simple markup similar to HTML to coordinate the final display.

RealNetworks is best known for their pioneering efforts in the field of streaming media, primarily audio and video. The latest version of their player, the Real G2 (for Generation 2) Player, can handle far more than single RealVideo or RealAudio files, however. Through SMIL, the RealPlayer G2 plays multiple media streams — whether two or more videos or a video and an audio track. Moreover, additional media types can be integrated into a SMIL presentation:

✦ **RealFlash.** Animated movies in the form of Flash files, synchronized with a RealAudio file and played from a RealServer.

✦ **RealText.** Streaming text files used to create low-bandwidth credits, ticker tapes, or other text-based displays.

✦ **RealPix.** Slideshows of high-quality JPEG photographs, with programmable transitions.

The RealSystem G2 objects for Dreamweaver 2 include an object for each of these new media types as well as for a inserting a completed SMIL presentation.

Cross-Reference

Streaming audio and video are now mainstays of the Web. To learn more about streaming video, see Chapter 20, "Adding Video to Your Web Page"; for details on streaming audio, see Chapter 21, "Using Audio on Your Web Page."

Creating SMIL presentations

While detailing how you script an entire presentation is beyond the scope of this book, it's interesting to see how the SMIL code works. As with HTML, SMIL is composed of a series of tags with varying attributes — it, too, is a text-based file. The basic tag pair is `<smil></smil>`, which forms the shell for any SMIL file. For example, a complete SMIL presentation that displays three streaming audios, one after the other, looks like this:

```
<smil>
  <body>
    <audio src="rtsp://realserver.company.com/one.ra"/>
    <audio src="rtsp://realserver.company.com/two.ra"/>
    <audio src="rtsp://realserver.company.com/three.ra"/>
  </body>
</smil>
```

Note

The `rtsp://` prefix seen in the previous example replaces the `pnm://` prefix used by RealServer systems before the G2 player was introduced.

SMIL files can have both `<head>` and `<body>` sections, but the `<head>` section isn't required, unlike in an HTML document. If present, the `<head>` section is generally used to display information in the RealPlayer, such as creator or copyright information. All tags and attributes are entered in lowercase, although the attribute values, enclosed in double quotes, can be mixed-case. Not all SMIL tags come in pairs. As with XML, single SMIL tags, like `<audio>` or `<video>` end with a forward slash before the closing angle bracket, like this:

```
<video src="video/highlights.rm"/>
```

The `src` attribute for any media type can be either absolute or relative, as with HTML. Other similarities to HTML include using the same type of comment in SMIL (`<!-- -->`) as well as identical character entities for special characters such as the quote (`&quot;`), apostrophe (`&apos;`), ampersand (`&amp;`), left angle bracket (`&lt;`), and right angle bracket (`&gt;`).

If playing different media in sequence were all that SMIL did, it wouldn't be so exciting. What makes SMIL really shine is its ability to play different media streams at the same time and to synchronize them. To play different media streams simultaneously, use the parallel tag pair, `<par></par>`, as follows:

```
<par>
  <video src="videos/newsong.rm"/>
  <textstream src="lyrics/newsong.rt"/>
</par>
```

In this example, both the RealVideo file and the RealText file play together or in parallel. You can also play media in sequence and in parallel in the same presentation. To specify a sequence, use the `<seq></seq>` tag pair. In this example, after the first clip plays, the second and third play at the same time—and when they end, the fourth clip plays:

```
<seq>
    clip 1
    <par>
      clip 2
      clip 3
    </par>
    clip 4
</seq>
```

Synchronizing a parallel presentation can be handled in several ways. You can force all clips in a `<par>` group to end when one finishes or when they all do. You can also cause them all to stop after a certain time interval. If you wanted to end

playback of a streaming audio file when the streaming text file ends, your code
might look like this:

```
<par endsync="id(vid)">
  <video id="vid" src="videos/newsong.rm"/>
  <textstream src="lyrics/newsong.rt"/>
</par>
```

while the actual presentation could resemble the SMIL screen shown in Figure 28-1.

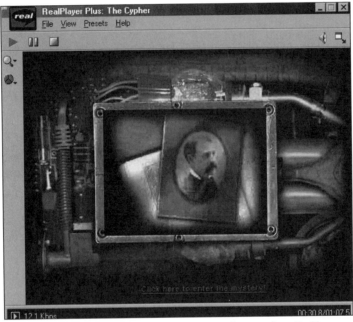

Figure 28-1: SMIL presentations, like any other RealMedia file, can
be shown in a separate player or embedded in the page, as in
this example.

The `endsync` attribute is set to the ID for the streaming audio file, `aud`. Note that
the `id` attribute is used in the `<audio>` tag, much like JavaScript uses the `name`
attribute.

Note   Suffice it to say that SMIL is a very full-featured language. To learn more about the
intricacies of SMIL, visit the Developer Center on RealNetwork's Web site
(`www.real.com`) or the Just SMIL Web site (`www.justsmil.com`).

Using the Real G2 objects

In addition to the RealAudio, RealVideo, and control panel control objects (covered in Chapters 20 and 21), the RealSystem G2 objects for Dreamweaver 2 make it easy to insert RealFlash, RealPix, RealText, and SMIL files. Inserting the objects is very straightforward—you only need to know the name of the file you're inserting and its dimensions. Currently, SMIL documents themselves must be created by hand; but once done, you can easily integrate them into your Dreamweaver pages.

Note   Want to try out the RealSystem G2 objects, but didn't get Dreamweaver yet? No problem—you'll find the newest version of the Real objects on the Dreamweaver Web site in the Extensions section (http://www.macromedia.com/software/dreamweaver/download/extensions/).

The RealText, RealFlash, and RealPix objects function in exactly the same manner. To insert one of these types of RealSystem objects, follow these steps:

1. Choose Insert ⇨ RealSystem G2 Object and select either RealText, RealFlash, or RealPix—or select the desired object from the RealSystem G2 panel of the Objects Palette.

Caution   Make sure you save your file before beginning to insert any of the RealSystem G2 objects. Otherwise, a system alert reminds you and will not let you proceed until you do so.

The appropriate RealSystem dialog box opens. Figure 28-2 shows the Insert RealText dialog box.

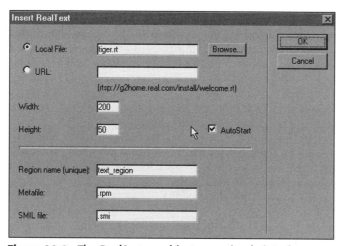

Figure 28-2: The RealSystem objects use simple interfaces like this Insert RealText dialog box to insert a variety of streaming media types into your Web page.

2. Enter the source file by choosing one of the following radio buttons:

- **Local File.** Enter the pathname of a file found on the local system in the Local File text box, or choose the Browse (Choose) button to locate the file.

- **URL.** Enter the absolute address of a file located on the Internet in the URL text box. The example address, `rtsp://g2home.real.com/install/welcome.rm`, is displayed beneath the URL text box.

3. Enter the dimensions of the RealSystem file in the Width and Height text boxes.

Note   Both the RealFlash and RealPix objects suggest dimensions of 320 pixels wide by 240 pixels high; the RealText object uses 200 pixels by 30 pixels as its base. Keep in mind that these measurements are suggestions only and should be altered to reflect the actual size of the player you want to use.

4. If you don't want your file to begin playing automatically, deselect the AutoStart option.

5. The remaining text boxes, Region name, Metafile, and SMIL file, are automatically filled out. Alter any name by entering the modification in the text box.

6. Click OK when you're done.

As with RealAudio and RealVideo objects, these RealSystem objects create both a metafile and a SMIL presentation file. When selected by the user to play (or when playing automatically), the original file first calls the metafile, which in turn calls the SMIL file. By default, the RealVideo object is inserted with the controls set to the ImageWindow option, which shows only the RealVideo movie with no control panel. To incorporate a control panel into the video file, you need to first choose the Edit Parameters button from the Property Inspector. Next, change the `controls` attribute from `imagewindow` to one of the other options, such as `All`, `ControlPanel`, or `PlayButton`.

Cross-Reference   The control panel options — and their corresponding objects — are explained in detail in Chapter 20, "Adding Video to Your Web Page."

The SMIL object is just a tad different. Because you don't need one SMIL file to play another, only the additional metafile is created for the SMIL object. Otherwise, the procedure is the same: Insert the SMIL object and, in the dialog box, enter the name of the SMIL file or its URL and the dimensions of the player.

Caution   If you find that your Real media types are not playing correctly — or at all — check all the paths. The paths to the RealSystem G2 metafiles and SMIL files may need to be adjusted by hand in the code. This is especially true if the HTML page, or any metafile, is moved.

IBM HotMedia

The standard Web ad banner is, at most, an animated GIF linked to the promoter's home page. IBM has developed a Windows-only Java-based technology that significantly sharpens the cutting edge in interactive advertising. With IBM's HotMedia technology, a single ad banner can integrate all of the following:

✦ Animated GIFs

✦ Panning and scrolling images

✦ Multitrack animations

✦ 3D object movies

✦ Zoomable, multi-resolution images

✦ Audio and video clips

✦ 360-degree panoramas

Unlike many other multimedia solutions, HotMedia requires no additional plug-ins or special server, but rather works with a series of compact Java players published from a standard HTTP server. Taking advantage of Java's inherent modularity, HotMedia delivers only the Java applet code and the source files necessary for the requested display. Moreover, the media itself — such as digitized video — is delivered progressively, in a fashion similar to streaming. Each separate media component can be triggered by mouse-click or set to occur automatically.

HotMedia features

The initial image in a HotMedia file is called a *thumbnail*. A thumbnail is a static image in either JPEG or GIF format. To attract interest to the graphic, HotMedia thumbnails are capable of several effects. The image can scroll from left to right, either smoothly or in frames. The scrolling effect can be set to play once, loop, or ping-pong (go to the end and play in reverse).

Perhaps the biggest innovation, however, is HotMedia's linking capability. *Links* can call other HotMedia files or jump to a standard Web page. Two different types of links are possible: *spatial* and *temporal*. A spatial link can be placed on objects in any image, panorama, animation, and video media, while a temporal link is associated with a specific time in a presentation, as when an audio announcement says, "Click now!" The Web designer can decide whether to display the links, as red rectangles, or not.

HotMedia files are composed using IBM's HotMedia Assembly utility. The Assembly program, shown in Figure 28-3, combines output from other programs, such as image editors like Adobe Photoshop or Macromedia's Fireworks, into one file that is saved with a .mvr extension. As of this writing, the current version of the Assembly utility (1.0) only supports the thumbnail and animation media — panorama, audio, and video are still to come.

Note   Currently, the HotMedia Assembly program and the HotMedia Dreamweaver objects are only available for Windows systems; however, the completed files play-back on any Java-enabled browser.

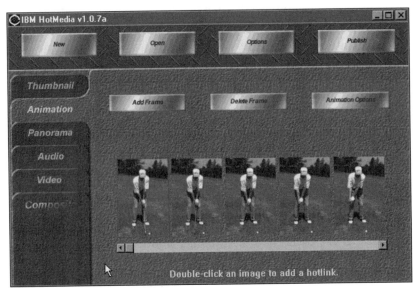

Figure 28-3: The IBM HotMedia Assembly utility combines numerous media types to create compelling interactive advertising.

Using the HotMedia object

IBM developed an object to insert the applet code for HotMedia files into your Dreamweaver pages. The HotMedia object is inserted into the Common panel of the Objects Palette during the HotMedia installation. The HotMedia Assembly program, with sample files and documentation, is also installed.

Caution   Make sure you enable object dialog boxes before attempting to insert a HotMedia object. Otherwise, you'll get an error message indicating that a file was not cho-sen — with no option to choose one.

To insert a HotMedia published file, follow these steps:

1. Position your cursor where you'd like the HotMedia file to appear on your page and select the HotMedia object from the Common panel of the Objects Palette.

   The Insert HotMediaPlayer dialog box, shown in Figure 28-4, appears.

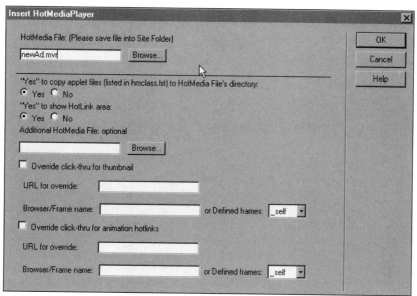

Figure 28-4: With the HotMedia object, you can specify alternative URLs — and even page-specific frames — or additional HotMedia files to link to.

2. Enter the path to the HotMedia file (with file extension .mvr) in the HotMedia File text box or select the Browse (Choose) button to locate the file.

3. To automatically copy the HotMedia .class files to the same directory as the selected file, leave the Copy Applet Files option set to Yes.

4. To display a red rectangle when the user's mouse passes over the defined link area, keep the Show HotLink Area option set to Yes.

5. Enter any additional HotMedia files you wish to link to in the Additional HotMedia File text box.

6. Generally, links are inserted into HotMedia files at authoring time. However, you can specify a different URL in two different locations: in the initial thumbnail image or during an animation:

   • To insert a different link in the opening thumbnail image, select the "Override click-thru for thumbnail image" option and then enter the new link in the "URL for override" text box. If you'd like the URL to appear in a specific browser window or frame, enter its name in the Browser/Frame Name text box or choose one of the frame targets from the Defined Frames drop-down list.

   • To insert a different link in an animated sequence, select the "Override click-thru for animation hotlinks" option and then enter the new link in the "URL for override" text box. If you'd like the URL to appear in a specific browser window or frame, enter its name in the Browser/Frame Name text box or choose one of the frame targets from the Defined Frames drop-down list.

7. Click OK when you're done.

Note

If the browser cannot run the applet, the class files have probably not been found. When the HotMedia applet is selected in Dreamweaver, select the Code Folder icon and choose the HM.class file. This forces the Base value to update properly.

Zooming into Graphics

The standard for photographic images on the Web, the JPEG format, is great for depicting detailed images — but only as a single, flat view. If you try to magnify any JPEG photograph, you'll quickly find yourself faced with an incomprehensible series of blurred, blocky pixels, and panning anywhere on the image is just not possible. These limitations are no longer a factor when using the new technologies from Hewlett-Packard and Live Picture. Both companies have developed software that enables users to zoom into photographs with amazing clarity and detail.

Whereas before JPEG images with resolutions higher than 800×600 were impractical for the Web because of the extremely large file size, now, using Hewlett-Packard's OpenPix or Live Picture's Zoom format, detailed images of $2,000 \times 3,000$ are just the beginning. Most important, these special photographic formats can easily be inserted into your Web pages using their custom objects with Dreamweaver.

Both technologies use server-side components to power their enhanced imagery. Hewlett-Packard's ImageIgniter software works with Unix and NT servers, while the Live Picture Image Server software must be deployed to view their Zoom images.

Using OpenPix images

OpenPix, Hewlett-Packard's entry, inserts additional attributes in the `<img>` tag to integrate into standard HTML; the added parameters are parsed by the ImageIgniter server, but otherwise ignored by browsers. An OpenPix entry looks like the following:

```
<img Src="../images/kidsworld.JPG"
          OPXSrc="../images/kidsworld.fpx"
          OPXVType="Auto"
          OPXVStyle="popup"
          BGColor="#FFFFFF"
          Align="middle"
          Alt="Kids with Globe Image"
          Coords="0.0,0.0,1.0,1.0"
          Width="260"
          Height="268">
```

Such code is used to insert an OpenPix image like the one shown in Figure 28-5. Note the control panel beneath the photograph that is used to zoom into and out of the image, as well as pan in any direction.

Figure 28-5: Hewlett-Packard's OpenPix software lets you select a region to zoom into for sharp details.

The three attributes starting with OPX convey the special information needed for viewing the detailed photographs. The actual OpenPix file is listed in the OPXSrc attribute — the .fpx file extension stands for FlashPix, the same high-end image format used by Live Picture. Viewing OpenPix images requires the use of an ActiveX control, Netscape plug-in, or Java viewer on the client side. The OPXVType attribute enables you to either choose a specific method of delivery or leave it up to the server. The OPXVStyle attribute specifies the kind of control panel, used for zooming or panning the image, to be displayed; the options are as follows:

> ✦ **PopUp.** The control panel overlays the bottom of the image when the user's mouse passes over the image.

> ✦ **Bottom.** The control panel overlays the bottom of the image.

> ✦ **Under.** The control panel is shown beneath the image.

✦ **None.** No control panel is displayed. However, a right-click in Windows systems or hold-click in Macintosh systems brings up a shortcut menu when the viewer uses either an ActiveX control or plug-in.

Using the OpenPix object

Before you can use the OpenPix object, you have to install the Hewlett-Packard custom software. Initiate the installation by double-clicking the OpenPix setup icon found in the Hewlett-Packard subfolder, under Extensions to Dreamweaver on the Dreamweaver 2 CD-ROM. Follow the step-by-step instructions and when finished, restart Dreamweaver. You'll find the Insert OpenPix Image button added to the Objects Palette.

To insert an OpenPix image, follow these steps:

1. Position your cursor where you'd like the OpenPix file to appear on your page and select the Insert OpenPix Image object from the Common panel of the Objects Palette.

   The Insert OpenPix Image dialog box, shown in Figure 28-6, appears.

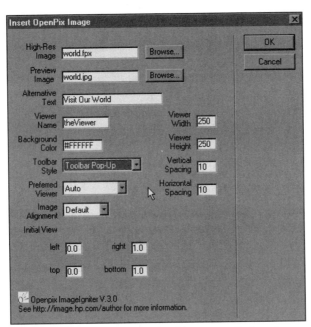

Figure 28-6: Use the OpenPix object to easily insert high-resolution, zoom-capable photographs.

2. Enter the path to the FlashPix format graphics file in the High-Res Image text box or choose the Browse (Choose) button to locate the file.

3. Enter the path to the JPEG-format graphics file in the Preview Image text box or choose the Browse (Choose) button to locate the file.

4. If desired, enter the <alt> tag text in the Alternative Text text box.

5. Enter the viewer attributes in the following areas:

- **Viewer Name.** Enter a unique name if you wish to control the viewer through JavaScript.

- **Viewer Width.** Enter the width of the image in pixels.

- **Viewer Height.** Enter the height of the image in pixels.

- **Vertical Spacing.** Enter the number of pixels, if any, to use as a top and bottom margin around the image.

- **Horizontal Spacing.** Enter the number of pixels, if any, to use as a left and right margin around the image.

- **Background Color.** Enter, in hexadecimal format, the color of the image background displayed in ActiveX controls and plug-ins.

- **Toolbar Style.** Select the type of control panel to use from the drop-down list: Toolbar at Bottom, Toolbar Underneath, Toolbar Popup, or None.

- **Preferred Viewer.** Select the type of image viewer to use from the drop-down list: Auto, Interactive, Print, ActiveX Control, Java Applet, Plug in, or Flat Image.

Note

Interactive is currently the same as Auto and permits the server software to choose the best player.

- **Image Alignment.** Choose the alignment on the page from the drop-down list: Left, Right, Middle, Top, Bottom, Texttop, Absbottom, Absmiddle, or Baseline. The default is Middle.

6. Set the coordinates for the initial view of the image by entering values into the Initial View left, top, right, and bottom text boxes. The values are percentage-based and range from 0.0 to 1.0. For example, to set the initial view to the upper-right quadrant of a picture, enter the following values: left - 0.5; top - 0.0; right - 1.0; bottom - 0.5.

7. Click OK when you're done.

Caution

Hewlett-Packard recommends that no more than eight viewers be employed on any one Web page, particularly if the Java player is specified. The browser can become very sluggish or even lock up when more than the recommended number of images is present.

Integrating Zoom pictures with Live Picture

The Live Picture Zoom object is slightly different from Hewlett-Packard's OpenPix object. To begin with, each image needs to be inserted into its own page and displayed independently or, more likely, in a frame as part of a frameset. When inserting the image, all you have to do is select the FlashPix-formatted file—the object does the rest. There are no additional parameters to specify. The control panel is automatically presented underneath the image, and the dimensions of the image are automatically calculated. The Zoom object also takes advantage of Dreamweaver's extensibility and works with a translator to display the JPEG version of the FlashPix image in Dreamweaver.

Note   The current version of the Live Picture Zoom object supports zoomable photographs but does not yet support zoomable panoramas and 3D image objects.

Before you can insert a Zoom object file, you must install the Live Picture software. Double-click the `zoomobject` executable to begin the installation process. After following the step-by-step instructions, restart Dreamweaver. To preview the Live Picture file in Dreamweaver, you must first enable the translator. To do this, choose Edit ➪ Preferences and select the Translator category. From the Translator panel, highlight the FlashPix image translator in the Translator list and then choose the In All Files option under Automatically Translate Server-Side Includes.

Inserting a Live Picture object is a straightforward process. Simply select the page or frame to insert your image in and position your cursor where you'd like the image to appear. Next, select the FlashPix button from the Common panel of the Objects Palette. The standard Select Image dialog box appears. Select your .fpx file from the FPX Images folder or one of its subfolders and click OK when you're done. The JPEG preview image is displayed, with the Zoom control panel, in the Dreamweaver page.

Note   To interact with the FlashPix file, you must view it through a browser reading the image from a Live Picture Server.

The Live Picture object doesn't insert a modified `<img>` tag like the OpenPix object does. Rather, it inserts a `<meta>` tag that calls the Live Picture Server to deliver the proper image. This is why each Live Picture file must be on its own page.

Once you've inserted the FlashPix file, you can modify its parameters by selecting it and using the custom Live Picture Property Inspector.

The Live Picture Property Inspector gives you access to the following options:

✦ **Filename.** The name of the FlashPix file. You can switch to a different file by selecting the Folder icon and choosing a new image.

✦ **Server.** The domain name or IP address of the Live Picture Server to be used.

✦ **Port.** The server port used by the Live Picture Server. By default the port is set to 8087.

✦ **Width.** The width of the image to be displayed. The height is automatically calculated to maintain the proper aspect ratio. Changing the width rescales the final image and the preview image.

✦ **Relative-path.** The path to the selected image, including any folders or directories, on the Live Picture Server.

Caution There is a known problem with early versions of the Live Picture object. When inserting the `<meta>` tag that calls the image, the URL encoding replaces the initial spaces with the Unix code for a space, %20. A new version of the Live Picture object that corrects this problem should be available on the Live Picture Web site at `http://www.livepicture.com/products/misc/dwzoom.html`.

Summary

As the Web strives for a richer media experience, more and more multimedia forms are developed. Dreamweaver's extensibility makes it perfectly adaptable to incorporate new technologies such as SMIL, HotMedia, OpenPix, and Zoom images. When you're looking to expand your Web page beyond the standard media formats, keep the following factors in mind:

✦ The Synchronized Multimedia Integration Language (SMIL) developed by RealNetworks permits multiple media types to be combined into a single streaming presentation.

✦ IBM's HotMedia object enables you to insert interactive advertising with pan-capable images, animation, audio, and programmable hotlinks.

✦ With Hewlett-Packard's OpenPix and Live Picture's FlashPix technology, very high resolution images — with zooming and panning enabled — can be included in your Web pages, but you must have their server software installed.

In the next chapter, you learn how Dreamweaver can be used to connect with a variety of database technologies to deliver Web pages with dynamic content.

✦   ✦   ✦

Connectivity Through Dreamweaver

Dynamic Database Content

Initially, the Internet was a vehicle for simple documents —
basic communication, reports on laboratory findings, and
scholarly papers — and the Web consisted of basically static,
unchanging pages, each one separate and independent. As the
Web exploded and the need for more up-to-date information
grew, the practice of building or continually modifying a Web
page soon became impractical. Not only were special skills
required, such as an understanding of HTML coding, but data
was often taken from an existing system and reentered onto a
Web page, thus duplicating effort unnecessarily. A link
between the Web and existing database structures was forged
to create dynamic Web pages capable of displaying the most
current content in a structured, easy-to-navigate format.

Database connectivity is a strong and growing aspect of the
Web. Without a strong connection between the Web and
databases, e-commerce could not thrive, news bureaus would
be buried under a glut of information, and intranets would be
continually out-of-date. Numerous companies are involved in
the field: Microsoft pioneered Active Server Pages for their
servers, while companies like Allaire, Oracle, and Tango
produce alternative technologies for others.

Until recently, Internet database connectivity was an art form
practiced only by the most adept programmers. If you didn't
understand the inner workings of ODBC, SQL, and other
database acronyms, you could forget it. However, if you want
to keep your client base happy and growing, that won't be an
option for long — many businesses are demanding database
connectivity for the Web sites. Now, with products like
Dreamweaver 2, bringing a page to life through active
database content is only a click or two away. Dreamweaver,

in its current release, has partnered with several of the top companies to smooth this tortuous path. This chapter first explains the ins and outs of database connectivity and then explores all the options presently available—even as more are on the way, thanks to Dreamweaver 2's inherent extensibility.

Understanding Active Content

For many Web designers, databases are a completely foreign territory—and how you build a bridge from their Web pages to one is a total mystery. Before you implement a database-oriented Web site, it's helpful to understand the fundamentals of databases and gain an overview of the connectivity processes involved. For some Web production companies, the designer is responsible for all aspects of site creation; here, a firm understanding of the new possibilities and technologies of an active content page is essential.

Note   If you're familiar with databases and connectivity, feel free to skip this introductory section.

Database basics

Databases store information, systematically. Here, the key word is "systematically." Many other technologies, both low- and high-end, store information—a shelf of books, a shoebox full of receipts, even a collection of Web pages—but few store the information in such a way that retrieval is structured and uniform. Naturally, the precise nature of the structure varies from one type of database to another, but fundamentally they are all the same.

A database is made up of a series of *records*. Each record can be thought of as a snapshot of a particular set of details. These details are known as *fields* and each field contains the pertinent information or data. A single database record can be made up of any number of fields of varying types—some fields hold only numbers or only dates, while others are open-ended and can hold any type of information. A series of database records, all with the same fields, are commonly referred to as a *table*—a simple table is also known as a *flat-file database*. Like a word-processing or an HTML table, a database table has rows and columns. Each column represents a field, while each row represents a record. For example, the following table describes a series of books that I call `BookTitles`:

Title	Author	Pages	Published
JavaScript Bible	Danny Goodman	1,015	1998
HTML Manual of Style	Larry Aronson and Joseph Lowery	385	1997
Netrepreneur	Joseph Lowery	424	1998

The first row in the table contains the field names: Title, Author, Pages, and Published. Each subsequent row contains a complete record. As presented here, this table is in no particular order; however, one of the reasons databases are so powerful is their *sorting* ability. If I were to sort the `BookTitles` table by page count, listing the books with the fewest pages first, it would look like this:

Title	*Author*	*Pages*	*Published*
HTML Manual of Style	Larry Aronson and Joseph Lowery	385	1997
Netrepreneur	Joseph Lowery	424	1998
JavaScript Bible	Danny Goodman	1,015	1998

Most modern databases can sort a table on any field, using any criteria. Many databases require that a table have an *index field* where each entry is unique, to simplify data manipulation. In the prior table example, the Title field could serve as an index because each title is unique; however, this is often not the case and a separate field is created.

Index fields, also referred to as *key fields*, become an absolute necessity when two or more tables — or flat-file databases — are combined to create a *relational database*. As the name implies, a relational database presents information that is related. For example, let's say we created another table called `BookSales` to accompany our previous book database example, like this:

Region	*Sales*	*Book*
East	10,000	*JavaScript Bible*
South	20,500	*JavaScript Bible*
West	42,000	*JavaScript Bible*
North	25,000	*JavaScript Bible*
East	15,000	*Netrepreneur*
South	12,000	*Netrepreneur*
West	8,000	*Netrepreneur*
North	21,000	*Netrepreneur*
East	8,330	*HTML Manual of Style*
South	6,500	*HTML Manual of Style*
West	8,000	*HTML Manual of Style*
North	7,400	*HTML Manual of Style*

To get a list of authors, sorted according to sales figures, you have to combine or join the two databases. A field common to both tables is used to create the juncture, or *join* — here, the common field is the index field, Title. While flat-file databases can be used in many situations, most industrial-strength applications use relational databases to access information.

In addition to changing the sort order of a table, database information can also be selectively retrieved by using a *filter*. A filter is often represented by a *where* statement, as in "Show me the books where regional sales were over 10,000 but under 20,000." Applying this filter to the BookSales table would result in the following table:

Region	*Sales*	*Book*
East	10,000	*JavaScript Bible*
East	15,000	*Netrepreneur*
South	12,000	*Netrepreneur*

The common language understood by many Web-available databases is SQL, which stands for *Structured Query Language*. An SQL statement tells the database precisely what information you're looking for and what form you want it in. Although they can become quite complex, a relatively simple SQL statement has just four parts:

✦ **Select** picks the fields to display.

✦ **From** chooses the databases from which to gather the information.

✦ **Where** describes the filter criteria and/or the joins.

✦ **Order** gives the sorting criteria.

A sample SQL statement translation of our "Show me the books where regional sales were over 10,000 but under 20,000" example would look like this:

```
SELECT Title
FROM BookSales
WHERE (Sales > 10000) & (Sales < 20000)
ORDER by Sales
```

Joins between two or more tables are depicted in SQL with an equal sign and are considered part of the filter in the WHERE statement. To show the sales by author's name, I'd have to revise my SQL statement so it read as follows:

```
SELECT Title, Author
FROM BookTitles, BookSales
WHERE BookTitles = BookSales & ((Sales > 10000) & (Sales <
20000))
ORDER by Author
```

Tip

The quick way to display all the fields in a table is to use an SQL statement with a wildcard, like this:

```
SELECT * FROM Booktitles
```

The asterisk indicates that you want to choose every field.

How active content pages work

The journey for a static Web page from user to server is very straightforward, even for the most complex, graphic-laden and JavaScript-laden page. The user clicks on a link that sends a signal to the server to send that page. An active content page — with full database connectivity — travels a much different route, however.

An active content page is a blend of traditional HTML and a database server language, such as ASP or Cold Fusion Markup Language (CFML). When a user accesses an active content page, the requested page is passed through the database server where the code is processed and a new HTML page is generated. This page is then returned to the regular Web server and sent on to the user. Figure 29-1 illustrates this process.

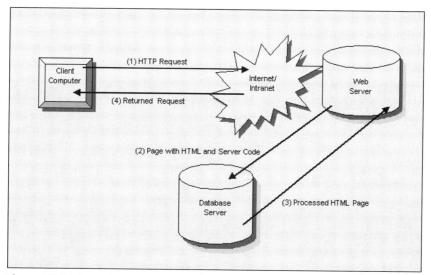

Figure 29-1: An active content page is processed by a database server prior to being sent to the user.

Active content servers can connect to more than databases, however. Other possibilities include the following:

✦ **Directory servers.** Directory servers control the permissions for large corporations and determine who is granted access to what group of files. With a directory server, two people — with different clearances — could see two different pages when clicking on the same link.

✦ **Mail servers.** E-mail communication can be fully automated through a mail server: responses to forms are categorized and forwarded to the proper parties; mass mailings can go out at the click of a button; and messages can be automatically incorporated into Web pages.

✦ **File servers.** By and large, HTML by itself has no file manipulation capabilities. However, with a file server, files can be uploaded, copied, renamed, moved, deleted, and more.

The primary HTML vehicle for interfacing with a database server is the form.

Most Web databases are Open Database Connectivity (ODBC) compliant. ODBC is a standard that allows virtually any type of database to be accessed — if the database has an ODBC driver. Similar to printer drivers that enable your computer to communicate with a wide variety of printers, an ODBC driver translates data to and from the database program. When setting up your database on the Web server, you may need to declare the ODBC driver for the file, as well as establish the Data Source Name (DSN). The DSN is used to simplify query building by giving each database a unique name to be referenced. Most servers require that the ODBC driver and DSN name be handled by the system administrator, or someone with that level of access.

Dreamweaver Database Partners

Developing connectivity for a Web authoring tool requires a close alliance with the database company. Macromedia has established partnerships with several of the leaders in Internet database technology and is in the process of releasing a series of solutions with each of them. As of this writing, the partnership with Allaire has brought the Cold Fusion extensions to fruition, and the Tango extensions from Pervasive are soon to be released. Both are covered extensively in the remainder of this chapter.

Other partnerships are underway. Macromedia has announced similar arrangements with Oracle, Broadvision, and Apple. Oracle is just now releasing their database product geared for the Web, Oracle 8i. Oracle has many adherents, and their new technology, combined with Dreamweaver, promises to be a winning combination. Broadvision is a developer of high-end database solutions used for tracking personal access on the Web; their primary Web development tool is Dreamweaver. Database integration for Broadvision means a much smoother workflow for complex Web sites.

Support for Apple's WebObjects 4 was recently announced in some detail. By the time this book was published, Macromedia and Apple plan to release a suite of 17 Dreamweaver objects in support of WebObjects. Apple touts WebObjects as the leading application server platform for development of Internet and intranet applications, with more than 3,000 customers globally. WebObjects supports the Power Macintosh G3 systems as well as Unix and Windows NT platforms.

Dreamweaver's extensibility makes it the ideal Web authoring tool for customization and use by the various connectivity solutions. Be sure to keep an eye on the official Dreamweaver Web site (`www.dreamweaver.com`) for further announcements and software releases.

Working with Cold Fusion

If you're a Windows Dreamweaver user, you're probably familiar with Allaire, makers of the bundled external editor, HomeSite 4. Allaire is perhaps better known in the general computing world for Cold Fusion, the development system that integrates browser, server, and database technologies. The Cold Fusion Application Server, now in version 4, works with all major Web servers to deploy active content pages on the Internet.

One of Allaire's strongest features is its use of the Cold Fusion Markup Language (CFML). Like HTML, CFML consists of a series of tags that is interpreted at run time to build a viewable page. The primary difference is that HTML is interpreted by the browser, or client-side; and CFML is interpreted server-side. The Cold Fusion Application server reads in a Web page with both HTML and CFML, and processes the CFML tags to convert them to HTML. The real power is in the CFML processing as database content is accessed and blended with the existing page before being returned for viewing.

With Dreamweaver 2, Allaire partners with Macromedia to integrate CFML into an advanced Web authoring tool. Included with Dreamweaver 2 are 12 objects for inserting CFML tags into the page, as well as a trial version of the Cold Fusion Application Server for a single user on Windows systems. The Cold Fusion Application Server program enables you to develop and test Cold Fusion-compatible pages on your system prior to publishing them to the Web.

So what's a typical Cold Fusion page look like? Let's take a look at a sample application that exports all the information from a small database onto a Web page. To do this, the page first must request or *query* the database for the data. Then, the data is *output* onto the page. The code for such a page is a mix of regular HTML and Cold Fusion CFML tags, like the following:

Using the Cold Fusion Application Server

The trial version of the Cold Fusion Application Server included with Dreamweaver 2 offers a unique opportunity for Web developers to get up to speed with database technology on their own systems. If you're new to the server side of Web design, it's important to understand that the Cold Fusion Application Server works along with Web servers, but does not replace them. To use Cold Fusion, you'll need to have a Web server already installed; typical choices are the Personal Web Server from Microsoft or O'Reilly's WebSite Professional Web Server.

Once you've installed the Web server software, double-click the icon for Cold Fusion Application Server to start the installation process. Follow the prompts; when finished, the program is set to automatically start when your system boots. You'll find a great deal of documentation available in the Cold Fusion 4.0 program group in HTML format for easy browsing.

To preview your new Web documents locally, you'll need to establish a new site where the local root folder points to the public folder of the Web server. With WebSite Professional (and many other servers), this is the htdocs folder. Cold Fusion installs a subfolder in the Web server's public folder called cfdocs. You can build your test pages in the cfdocs folder. Before you can preview them locally however, you'll need to change the Preferences to enable this feature. Choose Edit ➪ Preferences and, from the Preview in Browser tab, select the Preview Using Local Server option. Now you can preview your Cold Fusion files using any of the browsers you've set up with the press of a button (F12 or Shift-F12) or the click of a mouse (File ➪ Preview in Browser). The browser will use the URL `http://localhost/` as the base address to find the Dreamweaver pages.

You must use caution with this feature, however. If you've enabled the Preview Using Local Server option, you won't be able to preview any sites previously established that aren't included in the Web server folder. To preview these as before, deselect the Preview Using Local Server option.

```
<cfquery name="empNames" datasource="employees">
  select * from CurrentEmployees
  order by LastName
</cfquery>

<h2>Current Employee Listing</h2>

<cfoutput query="empNames">
<b>#LastName#</b>, #FirstName#<br>
</cfoutput>
```

In this example, a query is first created from a database with the Data Source Name, "employees." The query itself is named "empNames"; you must name any queries so that they may be referenced later. The CurrentEmployees table is targeted and the query asks that all fields be retrieved and placed in an alphabetical last-name-first order. Next, a heading, "Current Employee Listing," is placed on the page with a regular HTML heading style, `<h2>`. Any HTML tags and content — images, layers, whatever — could have been placed here.

The final section, in the `<cfoutput>`...`<cfoutput>` tag pair determines what form the displayed data takes. Each field called from the CurrentEmployees table of the employees database is marked on either side with hash marks, #. Notice that HTML code as well as regular text can be interspersed with the CFML code to achieve the desired effect. Here, information from the Lastname field is put in bold and followed by a comma. Then the employee's first names are displayed. The line-break tag, `<br>`, is added to ensure that every entry appears on its own line. Figure 29-2 shows how this page looks both in Dreamweaver and in its sample output.

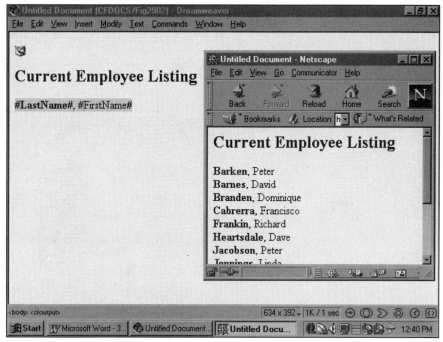

Figure 29-2: The Dreamweaver page displays the CFML code that translates into the browser output once processed.

Applying the Cold Fusion objects

Dreamweaver 2 comes with a set of a dozen Cold Fusion objects to simplify adding CFML code to your HTML page. CFML tags look very similar to the familiar HTML elements. For example, to add a form to your Cold Fusion page, you would add the following:

```
<cfform name="employeeUpdate" action="empUpdate.cfm"></cfform>
```

CFML tags also use attributes and values such as name="employeeUpdate"; all CFML tags begin with the Cold Fusion initials, cf. Like HTML, form elements such as text fields and Submit buttons are placed in-between the opening and closing tags.

Note   To identify any Web page that should be processed by the Cold Fusion Application Server, the file extension .cfm or .cfml is added. Dreamweaver handles this automatically when you save your document and select Cold Fusion Templates from the Files of Type list in the Save File dialog box.

When a CFML tag is inserted into a Web page in Dreamweaver — whether by hand or via one of the Cold Fusion objects — Dreamweaver designates it as a third-party tag. As such, it is highlighted in the document, as shown in Figure 29-3, if the Preferences option is enabled. To turn on CFML (and other third-party tag) highlighting, choose Edit ➪ Preferences and select the Highlighting category. Make sure the Show option of Third-Party Tags is selected. If you don't like the default highlight color, choose another one by clicking the color swatch next to the Third-Party Tags label.

Cold Fusion icon

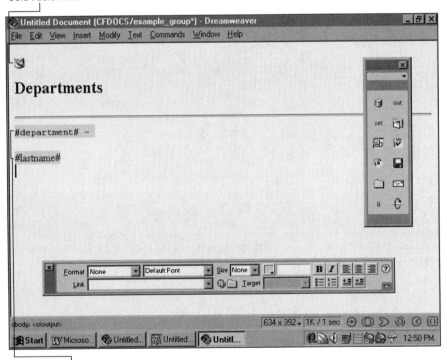

Third-Party Tag highlighting

Figure 29-3: Third-Party tags like those from Cold Fusion can be highlighted in the Document Window.

For most CFML objects, Dreamweaver also inserts a Cold Fusion icon, similar to those for the `<br>` tag or layers, as a placeholder to represent the code. You can enable or disable the appearance of the CFML icon through the Cold Fusion option on the Invisibles panel of Preferences. Like all other placeholders, Cold Fusion icons can be cut, copied-and-pasted, or moved via the drag-and-drop method.

The Cold Fusion Dreamweaver objects fall into four categories:

✦ **Database Setup.** Two objects, Query and Output, are used for reading information from a database and displaying it.

✦ **Forms.** Similar to their HTML counterparts, these four objects — Form, Text, Checkbox, and Radio — offer special capabilities in the database server environment.

✦ **Programming.** One key advantage to server-side processing is the ability to use conditional commands, such as the Set, If, and Loop objects found here.

✦ **Other Servers.** As noted earlier, the Cold Fusion Application Server can interact with more than databases. These objects — Mail, File, and Directory — enable the Web designer to handle e-mail, file manipulation, and directory management.

Database setup

Arguably, two of the most important tags in the Cold Fusion Markup Language are `<cfquery>` and `<cfoutput>`. The first, `<cfquery>`, is responsible for establishing contact with the database and passing it SQL statements. The second, `<cfoutput>`, is the basic output mechanism for the results of the query and, as such, shapes much of what is seen on the screen. Dreamweaver 2 translates these two important commands into two easy-to-use Cold Fusion objects: Query and Output.

The Query object

The Query object is the main conduit for transmitting SQL statements to a data source. Generally the SQL statements take the form of a query; however, `<cfquery>`, the tag inserted by this object, is not limited to passing queries — any SQL statement is valid.

The Query object is set up in two parts: Basic Settings and Advanced Settings. Use the Basic Settings panel to enter the primary required information:

✦ **Query Name.** A unique name given to the query itself so that it may be called by other tags. The query name must start with a letter and use only letters, numbers, and the underscore character; query names with spaces are not acceptable.

✦ **Data Source.** This is the name registered with the ODBC DSN program for the database to be accessed.

✦ **Query.** SQL statements define the operation to be performed on the data. Four main types of SQL statements are supported: `Select`, `Insert`, `Update`, and `Delete`.

In the Advanced Settings panel, password information, if necessary to access the database, can be supplied. The maximum number of rows to show on a page can also be set on this panel. You can also set a timeout value and enable the debugger for the query.

Note   The Query object must be placed before any other object, such as the Output object, that references it on the HTML page. Traditionally, when coding a `<cfquery>` tag by hand, it is placed above the `<html>` tag. However, this is not possible in Dreamweaver and is not necessary if you ensure that other objects are located further down the page.

To use the Query object, follow these steps:

1. Place your cursor near the top of the HTML page.

2. Select the Query object from the Cold Fusion panel of the Objects Palette.

   The Cold Fusion Query dialog box (shown in Figure 21-4) is displayed.

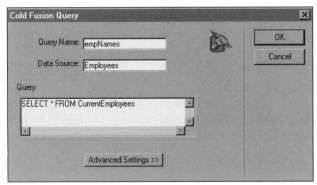

Figure 29-4: The Cold Fusion Query object is used to send SQL statements to the selected database.

3. Enter a unique name for the query in the Query Name text box. Make sure that the name begins with a letter and does not contain spaces. Press Tab to continue.

4. Enter the name of the database in the Data Source text box. Press Tab to continue.

Caution   Data Source names are case-sensitive. Be sure to enter the exact name as found in the ODBC driver manager.

5. Enter your SQL statements in the Query text area.

   By default, the Query text area already has the often used `SELECT * FROM` phrase inserted. To define a table from which records should be pulled, enter the name of the table after the phrase. For example:

```
SELECT * FROM Employees
```

where Employees is the name of one table in the selected database.

6. To enter additional settings, click the Advanced Settings button.

7. If needed, enter the user name to access the database in the User text box; and the password in the Password text box.

8. Enter a maximum time, in milliseconds, for the query to execute before returning an error message in the Server Timeout text box.

Note   Currently, only SQL Server version 6.x and above support the Timeout feature.

9. To limit the number of rows displayable on the resulting page, enter a value in the Max Rows text box.

10. To provide debugging information when the query is run, select the Debug option.

   If the query runs with no errors, Debug reports the number of records returned and the length of time the query took to run, and recaps the SQL statements — all at the bottom of the HTML page, after the database output.

Once the Query object has been inserted on the page, it can be easily modified. To change the settings or SQL statements associated with a Query object, select its icon in the Document Window. The Cold Fusion Property Inspector displays the name of the tag and two buttons: Attributes and Contents. Choose the Attributes button to alter any of the settings, such as the Query Name or Data Source; a Parameter dialog box opens with the attributes on the left and their values on the right. Enter new attributes by choosing the Add button (the plus sign) and inserting the parameter and corresponding value. Attributes can be removed by selecting them and choosing the Remove button (the minus sign).

To revise the SQL statements of a Query object, select the Contents button. A large text edit dialog box appears with the existing SQL statements. Make any necessary modifications and then press OK.

The Output object

Once the data is retrieved through the Query object, the Output object displays it, in whatever format specified. While the Output object and its corresponding CFML tag, `<cfoutput>`, frequently handle database queries, results from built-in functions, such as those dealing with date and time, are also displayable. The `<cfoutput>` tag is very versatile and can be used as often as required on any given page. You could, for example, use it to create a form letter, filling in the variables (like Name and Address) with information from a database.

Caution   The only restriction on the `<cfoutput>` tag is that it cannot be nested. In other words, the following code is not valid:

```
<cfoutput>Hi I'm #name# from
<output>#store#</output></output>
```

To use the Output object, follow these steps:

1. Position your cursor on the page where you'd like the output to appear.

   The result output can be placed inline with other text on the page or in a separate table. Output object results can also be used to populate a drop-down option list.

Tip Keep your Invisible Elements turned on so you can be sure to place the Output object after the Query object.

2. Select the Output object from the Cold Fusion panel of the Objects Palette.

   The Cold Fusion Output dialog box appears, as shown in Figure 29-5.

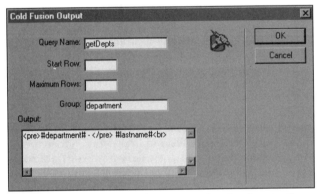

Figure 29-5: The Output object controls what is actually integrated into the Web page for viewing — both the content and the format.

3. If you want to display records from a particular query already on the page, enter the name of the query in the Query Name text box.

4. To begin displaying records other than from the beginning, enter the number of the beginning record in the Start Row text box.

5. If you want to limit the number of rows that can be displayed at one time, enter a value in the Maximum Rows text box.

6. To eliminate duplicates in a recordset, enter the name of the sort field in the Group text box.

   For example, if you wanted to sort some output by state, but only wanted the name of the state to appear once, the State field would be entered in the Group text box as well as used in the SQL statement, Order By.

7. Enter the desired output format in the Output text area.

Fields are designated with hash marks on either side, as in #employees#. HTML code is used to format the code. For example:

```
<a href=#Link#>#Site#</a>: <font
color="red">#Creator#</font><br>
```

outputs a hyperlink list of Web sites, followed by the name of the site's creator, in red.

8. Click OK when you're done.

For simple lists, the `<pre>` tag is often used to format output where the initial field is a constant size, as in this example where the Department ID is always four digits and the phone extension is three:

```
<pre>#dept_ID#    #dept_ext#  #dept_head#</pre><br>
```

How do you structure output for which the field results are varied in length? Just as you would if you were "hard-wiring" the data on a page — with a table. There are several ways to implement a table in Cold Fusion. CFML has its own table tag, `<cftable>`, which uses the `<pre>` tag to line up fields. When used with the `<cfcol>` tag, the heading for each column of data can be specified. For example, this code:

```
<cftable query="tryMe" colheaders>
  <cfcol header="ID" width="5" align="right"
text="<b>#Emp_ID#</b>">
  <cfcol header="First Name" width="30" text="#FirstName#">
  <cfcol header="Last Name" width="30" text="#LastName#">
</cftable>
```

creates a table based on the query tryMe. Next, three columns are created, each designated with the label specified by the header attribute in the `<cfcol>` tag.

Tip   To create an HTML style table with `<cftable>` add the `htmltable` attribute to the CFML tag. With the `htmltable` attribute, column widths are interpreted as percentages, rather than as a number of characters.

Gathering data through forms

Databases aren't necessarily a one-way street. Through forms, you can enable users to insert new information into a database or revise existing information. Both the insert and updating operations are generally handled in two pages: a page that takes in the information on a form and a page that processes the input and displays a confirmation. In Cold Fusion, the form page can use form tags from HTML, CFML, or a combination of both; the processing page, however, must be a CFML page.

To use traditional HTML forms for the input page, you first need to set the `action` attribute of the `<form>` tag equal to the Cold Fusion processing page, using the `post` method. Next, the names of `input` tags should match the names of the fields.

The submit and reset buttons do not require any special attention. For example, the following form enables the updating of a Web site link page, taking in the name of the site, its creator, and the link information:

```
<form method="post" action="site_insert.cfm" name="theForm">
  <pre>
    Site: <input type="text" name="Site" size="40"><br>
 Creator: <input type="text" name="Creator" size="40"><br>
    Link: <input type="text" name="Link" size="40"><br>
          <input type="submit" name="Submit" value="Insert
Info">
          <input type="reset" name="reset" value="Clear
Form"></pre>
</form>
```

To process this insert request, you can use one of two methods: via an SQL statement or by use of the <cfinsert> tag. On the CFML process page that is called by the action attribute of the form, the code is generally entered at or near the top of the page. The Dreamweaver Query object can be used to enter the SQL statements. As before, enter a unique name for the query and the DSN name for the data source. Then the SQL statements are formatted as follows:

```
INSERT INTO TableName (Field1, Field2, Field3)
VALUES ('#Form.FieldName1#','#Form.FieldName2#',
'#Form.FieldName3#')
```

For the balance of the page, you can enter any sort of confirmation message desired, in regular HTML.

The other method for processing is slightly less complicated, but because there are no Dreamweaver objects, the code must be entered by hand. The <cfinsert> tag requires the names of the data source, the table, and the fields. In the previous example, the <cfinsert> tag would look like this:

```
<cfinsert datasource="extensions" tablename="Sites"
formfields="Site,Creator,Link">
```

The Form object

While the regular HTML <form> tag can be used without difficulty in Cold Fusion, the proprietary <cfform> tag—implemented by the Cold Fusion Form object in Dreamweaver—adds a tremendous degree of functionality. In addition to using any of the standard HTML form objects, <cfform> also enables its own parallel brand of objects, with the ability to require or validate any response. Moreover, with <cfform> you have access to a full complement of Java-based input types, including a tree control for depicting collapsible lists, a grid control for organizing data, and even a slider control for mouse input.

To use the Cold Fusion Form object, follow these steps:

1. Position your cursor where you'd like the form to appear on the Web page.

2. Select the Form object from the Cold Fusion panel of the Objects Palette.

   The Cold Fusion Form dialog box appears, as shown in Figure 29-6.

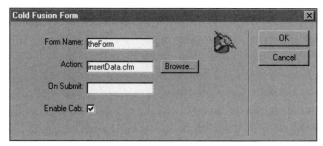

Figure 29-6: With the Cold Fusion Form object, a user's input can be automatically validated and the form can include advanced Java input types such as a slider control.

3. Enter a unique name in the Form Name text box.

4. Enter the path to a Cold Fusion file in the Action text box or select the Folder icon to locate the file.

5. If you'd like to pre-process the input before passing it to Cold Fusion, enter the JavaScript function to call in the On Submit text field.

6. To permit Microsoft browser users without the required Java classes to download the necessary cabinet (*.cab) files for the Java applet based controls, select the Enable Cab option.

7. Click OK when you're done.

Caution   Because the `<cfform>` is not visible onscreen, unlike the standard `<form>` outline, it can be difficult to place input objects inside the tag. I recommend that you keep the HTML Inspector open to ensure that the objects are properly inserted.

The Input objects: Text, Checkbox, and Radio

The key advantage offered by all the Cold Fusion input objects — Text, Checkbox, and Radio — is validation. Cold Fusion offers ten different types of validation: everything from a date to a credit card number. Any field can be required and numbers can be checked to see if they fall in a particular range. Web designer–defined messages are displayed upon a validation error to help the user. Or, if you prefer, validation can be handled by a custom JavaScript function.

To use any of the Cold Fusion input objects — Text, Checkbox, or Radio — follow these steps:

1. Position your cursor where you'd like the form to appear on the Web page.

2. Select the Text, Checkbox, or Radio object from the Cold Fusion panel of the Objects Palette.

Note   The Cold Fusion input objects are used like their HTML equivalents. Text enables any user input; Checkbox enables users to select one or several options; and Radio enables a user to select one of a group.

The specified object's dialog box appears. Figure 29-7 displays the Cold Fusion Text dialog box.

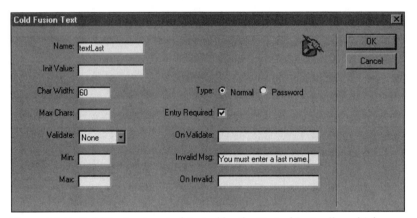

Figure 29-7: Cold Fusion input objects, like the Text object, offer a high degree of validation possibilities.

3. Enter a unique name for the input object in the Name text box.

4. For a Text object, you can also enter the following information:

   • **Char Width.** The width of the text box, in number of characters.

   • **Max Chars.** The maximum number of allowable characters.

   • **Password.** To mask the input, select the Type: Password option.

5. For a Checkbox or Radio object, you can also select the following options:

   • **Checked Value.** The value that is passed if the check-box or radio button is selected.

   • **Initial State.** Displays the check-box or radio button as selected or unselected.

Note
For a radio button group, make sure that the names of all the buttons in the group are identical.

6. For all Cold Fusion input objects, the following validation options are available:

- **Entry Required.** When selected, the user must enter a value for the field.
- **Validate.** (Text object only.) Select one of ten types of validation.
- **Date.** Entry must be in U.S. date format: mm/dd/yy.
- **Eurodate.** Entry must be in a European date format: dd/mm/yy.
- **Time.** Entry must be in the form hh:mm:ss.
- **Float.** Entry must be a floating-point number.
- **Integer.** Entry must be an integer.
- **Telephone.** Entry must be in the format ###-###-###, where the first digit is not zero.
- **Zipcode.** Entry must be a five- or nine- digit number in the form #####-####.
- **Credit Card.** Entry must be in a credit card format.
- **Social Security Number.** Entry must be in the form ###-##-####.
- **Min.** The minimum allowable value for numeric entries.
- **Max.** The maximum allowable value for numeric entries.
- **On Validate.** A custom JavaScript function used to perform validation instead of the selected Cold Fusion validation routine.
- **Invalid Msg.** Message to be displayed if validation fails.
- **On Invalid.** A custom JavaScript function that executes if validation fails.

7. Click OK when you're done.

Programming with Cold Fusion objects

Just as client-side scripting is made possible by JavaScript's programming capabilities, server-side scripting works with Cold Fusion's programming features. Dreamweaver 2 includes three objects to enable easy code insertion: Set, If, and Loop.

The Set object

The Cold Fusion Set object is used to create and define variables through the `<cfset>` tag. Using the Set object is very straightforward. Simply select the Set object from the Cold Fusion panel of the Objects Palette and enter the variable and its equivalent value in the dialog box, like this:

```
bookCode = "H23"
```

If a variable has been previously declared, it is set to the new value. The `<cfset>` tag can be used to establish static variables, with strings of text or numeric values, or dynamic variables that depend on a database relationship. To set a variable to the data in a queried field, format the Set object code like this:

```
<cfset currentBook = "bookbase.title">
```

where `bookbase` is the table name and `title` is a field in that table. You can also define a variable to represent a combination of text and dynamic data, like this:

```
<cfset bestBook = "#bookbase.title# is the most frequently read
book this week">
```

You can also use the Set object to represent mathematical expressions, either by themselves or in combination with other text, as in the following examples:

```
<cfset totalTax = (8.25 * 19.95) + 19.95>
<cfset owedAmt = "You owe " & (8.25 * 19.95) + 19.95>
```

Note that an ampersand is used to concatenate a text string and an expression.

The If object

Much programming depends on conditionals — if X is true do this; otherwise, do that. Cold Fusion uses the `<cfif>`, `<cfelseif>`, and `<cfelse>` tags to create both simple and compound conditional statements. In general, the syntax for a conditional block in CFML is as follows:

```
<cfif expression>
HTML and CFML tags go here
  <cifelse expression >
  HTML and CFML tags go here
<cfelse>
HTML and CFML tags go here
</cfif>
```

Should the *expression* prove true, the initial statements are processed; otherwise, the `<cfelseif>` condition is checked and those statements are processed. If both conditions fail, the statements following `<cfelse>` are executed.

Aside from regular numeric and Boolean operators, Cold Fusion also uses a series of decision operators in conditional statements. The decision operators, and their alternative notations, are as follows:

Operator	Alternative
IS	EQUAL, EQ
IS NOT	NOT EQUAL, NEQ
CONTAINS	n/a

Operator	Alternative
DOES NOT CONTAIN	n/a
GREATER THAN	GT
LESS THAN	LT
GREATER THAN OR EQUAL TO	GTE, GE
LESSER THAN OR EQUAL TO	LTE, LE

In Dreamweaver, all three conditional statements are accessed through the Cold Fusion If object. While you can insert conditionals directly in the Document Window, it's a good idea to have the HTML Inspector open, particularly if you are using the Else If and Else forms.

To use the Cold Fusion If object, follow these steps:

1. Position your cursor where you'd like the conditional block in the code.

2. Select the If object from the Cold Fusion panel of the Objects Palette.

   The Cold Fusion If dialog box appears, as shown in Figure 29-8.

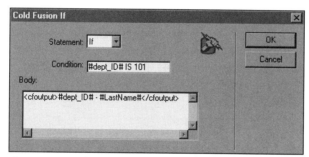

Figure 29-8: The Cold Fusion If object handles all three stages of conditionals: If, Else If, and Else.

3. Select which of the three tags you wish to insert from the Statement option list: If, Else If, or Else.

> **Note** The If statement must be chosen first.

4. Enter the expression to be evaluated in the Condition text box.

5. Enter the statements to be executed in the Body text area.

6. Click OK when you're done.

Tip   To add Else If or Else conditionals to an existing If conditional, you must position your text cursor before the closing `</cfif>` tag. While this can be accomplished through the Document Window, it's much easier to use the HTML Inspector.

The Loop object

Looping, the ability to cycle through a series of operations, is just as important as conditionals in any type of programming. The Cold Fusion implementation is especially noteworthy as it supports five different types of loops:

✦ **Indexed Loop.** Statements are repeated for a set range of values.

✦ **Conditional Loop.** Statements are repeated while a particular condition remains true.

✦ **Looping over a Query.** Statements are repeated for every record in a range of a recordset.

✦ **Looping over a List.** Statements are repeated for every element in a particular list.

✦ **Looping over a COM collection.** Statements are repeated for every member of a Component Object Model collection or structure.

The Dreamweaver 2 Cold Fusion Loop object incorporates all five loop types.

To begin to set up any of the loop types, first choose the Loop object from the Cold Fusion panel of the Objects Palette. In the Loop dialog box, select the Loop Type from the drop-down box. For each type, a different set of options is displayed; in every case, the statements to be executed during the loop are entered into the Body text area. Table 29-1 explains the options for each `<cfloop>` type; optional arguments are marked with an asterisk.

Table 29-1
Cold Fusion Loop Types

Loop Type	Attribute	Description
Indexed Loop	Index Name	Defines the variable that is used as the loop counter
	From	The initial value of the index
	To	The ending value of the index
	Step*	The value that the index is incremented with each loop. The Step value can be a positive or negative whole number where the default is 1

Loop Type	Attribute	Description
Conditional Loop	Condition	The expression that is evaluated with each loop. When the expression is no longer true, the loop ends.
Query Loop	Query Name	The name of the previously defined query that controls the loop
	Start Row*	The first row of the query to be included in the loop
	End Row*	The last row of the query to be included in the loop
List Loop	Index Name	Defines the variable that is used as the loop counter
	List	The list items to be processed. The items can be directly entered, as in "Baker, Barber, Sailor, Cook," or pulled from a variable.
	List Delimiters	The separators used to divide the list. In the previous example, commas would be listed as the delimiters. Multiple delimiters, such as ",.\" can be entered.
COM Collection Name	Collection Name	The name of the COM collection to be accessed during the loop
	Item Name	The variable assigned from the member of the collection referenced during the loop

*Optional

Accessing other servers

As already noted, the Cold Fusion Application Server isn't just for communicating with databases. One of Cold Fusion's key advantages is its ability to integrate with a wide variety of server types. For example, because Cold Fusion can work with a mail server, it's possible to coordinate mass e-mailings from within the program. Moreover, you can use Cold Fusion — and its corresponding Dreamweaver objects — to handle both file and directory functions.

The Mail object

E-mail is a fact of modern communication; to some, e-mail is the "killer app" for which the Internet was designed. While unsolicited bulk e-mailings (also known as *spam*) have earned their undesirable reputation, automated e-mails are an effective way for a business to handle today's increased communication load. With Cold Fusion, you can output to a mail server to send e-mail just as easily as you can to a Web server to deliver an HTML page.

The Cold Fusion Mail object inserts the `<cfmail>` tag, which outputs Simple Mail Transfer Protocol (SMTP) type e-mail. SMTP e-mail is the standard form of text-only e-mail and can be read by all mail programs. The best way to think of `<cfmail>` is as a close relative to `<cfoutput>` — they're identical in functionality except that instead of sending processed output formatted as HTML to a browser as `<cfoutput>` does, `<cfmail>` sends its processed output as e-mail to an SMTP server.

As an example of how `<cfmail>` can automate communication, consider the customer inquiry form. Generally, the interested customer fills it out and clicks the Submit button, where the information may be collected for later retrieval or sent directly to Sales and Marketing. When the Submit button is chosen, if the form has a CFML page set as its `action` attribute, that page is processed by Cold Fusion. To automatically send the customer inquiry form to a department (or an individual), the `<cfmail>` tag is added to the CFML page that also serves as a thank-you to the customer. Here's some sample `<cfmail>` code for such an operation:

```
<cfmail from="#form.emailAddress#"
        to="sales@idest.com"
        subject="Sales Inquiry" >
This customer is interested in our product - call today!

Customer: #form.FirstName# #form.LastName#
Product: #form.ProductSelected#

Comments: #form.Comments#
</cfmail>
```

The Cold Fusion Mail object in Dreamweaver 2 has a wide range of attributes that can be employed; however, only a few are required. Parameters such as To, From, and Subject can all be generated on-the-fly by Cold Fusion's database connection, which allows for a very flexible mail-management technology.

To insert a Cold Fusion Mail object into your Web page, follow these steps:

1. Place your cursor on the page where you want the Mail object code to appear.
2. Choose the Mail object from the Cold Fusion panel of the Objects Palette.

   The Cold Fusion Mail dialog box appears, as shown in Figure 29-9.
3. Enter the e-mail address of the recipient in the To text box.
4. Enter the e-mail address of the sender in the From text box.
5. Enter the e-mail address of any additional recipients in the CC text box.
6. Enter the topic of the e-mail in the Subject text box.
7. Enter the server address of the SMTP system sending the mail. If no server is listed, the server name specified in the Cold Fusion Administrator is used.
8. Enter the content of your message in the Body text area.

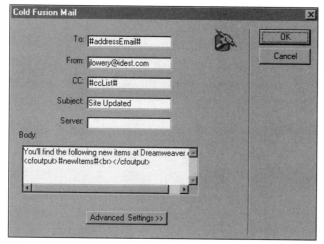

Figure 29-9: Output to e-mail as easily as you output to screen by using the Cold Fusion Mail object.

9. To enter any advanced parameters, choose the Advanced Settings button.

10. Enter a query name, if any, to be referenced in the Query Name text box.

11. Enter the first row in the query to be included in processing in the Start Row text box.

12. Enter the total number of rows in the query to be included in processing in the Max Row text box.

13. Enter the field name of the query to group the results in the Group text box.

14. Enter the mail type, if other than straight text, in the Mail Type text box.

Note As of this writing, the only valid entry here is "HTML."

15. Enter the mail server port in the Server Port text box, if different from the standard port number, 25.

16. Enter the number of seconds to wait before the connection to the SMTP server expires in the Timeout text box.

17. Enter the path of a file to be attached to the e-mail in the Attachment text box or select the Browse button to locate a file.

18. Click OK when you're done.

The File object

One of JavaScript's primary limitations — but also one of the reasons it is so widely accepted — is its inability to manage directories or files. While that makes sense for a client-side application, such capabilities are sorely needed in a server-side program. New data is constantly being added, whether temporarily or permanently. Cold Fusion provides numerous methods for creating and modifying files as needed, and Dreamweaver's File object puts all the parameters at your fingertips.

Note   If you're having trouble getting results from the File or Directory objects, be sure to check with the Cold Fusion administrator for the server. Anyone with administrator clearance can disable file and directory functions.

The File object and its corresponding tag, `<cffile>`, control eight different file operations:

✦ **Upload** transfers a file from the user to the server. File types can be limited to specific MIME types and/or file formats.

✦ **Move** moves a file from one directory to another.

✦ **Rename** renames a file on the server.

✦ **Copy** copies a file from one directory to another.

✦ **Delete** removes a file from the server.

✦ **Read** reads an existing text file, such as an access log.

✦ **Write** writes a new text file, including HTML pages.

✦ **Append** adds text to an existing text file.

To set up any of the `<cffile>` types, first choose the File object from the Cold Fusion panel of the Objects Palette. In the File dialog box, shown in Figure 29-10, select the Action drop-down box. For each `action` type, a different set of options is displayed. Table 29-2 explains the options for each `<cffile>` type; optional arguments are marked with an asterisk.

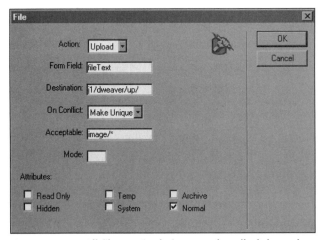

Figure 29-10: All file manipulations are handled through the Cold Fusion File object.

Table 29-2
Cold Fusion File Object Types

Action	Parameters	Description
Upload	Form Field	The name of the field in the form that was used to select the file. Do not use hash marks (#) to denote the field.
	Destination	The directory in which the file is to be stored
	On Conflict*	The action taken if a name conflict occurs (the uploaded file has the same name as a file already on the server). The options are as follows: **Error.** File not saved and an error is reported **Skip.** File not saved, but no error is reported **Overwrite.** The existing file is replaced **Make Unique.** A new unique name is created for the uploaded file
	Acceptable*	Limits uploadable files to MIME types, specified in a comma-delimited list (for example, "image/gif, image/jpg, image/png")
	Mode*	Sets file permissions for uploaded file with `chmod` values such as `666` or `777`. Valid only on Solaris servers.
	Attributes*: Read Only, Hidden, Temp, System, Archive, Normal	Set attributes for uploaded files. All attributes must be explicitly selected.
Move, Rename, or Copy	Source	The path name of the file to be moved
	Destination	The directory to which the file is moved
	Attributes	As above
Delete	File	The path name of the file to be removed
Read	File	The path name of the file to be read
	Variable	The variable designated to hold the contents of the file after it is read

Continued

		Table 29-2 *(continued)*	
Action	**Parameters**	**Description**
Write or Append	File	The name of the file to be created or added on to
	Mode	As above
	Output	The content to be included in the new or modified file
	Attributes	As above

*Optional

For more about file permissions as noted in the Mode parameter, see Chapter 15, "Accessing External Programs."

The Directory object

When new files are continually being added to a server, directory management becomes a necessity—otherwise, all the files could potentially end up in one enormous folder. Moreover, it usually takes someone with administrator-level access to even list the contents of a directory. With the Cold Fusion `<cfdirectory>` tag, access can be granted on a page-by-page basis.

The Cold Fusion Directory object has four different functions:

✦ **List** details the contents of the specified folder in a sorted or nonsorted table.

✦ **Create** makes the specified folder on the server.

✦ **Rename** changes the name of the folder.

✦ **Delete** removes the folder and all of its contents from the server.

To set up any of the `<cfdirectory>` options, first choose the Directory object from the Cold Fusion panel of the Objects Palette. In the Cold Fusion Directory dialog box, shown in Figure 29-11, first enter the name of the directory to be affected. Then, select the Action drop-down box. For each `action` type, a different set of options is displayed. Table 29-3 explains the options for each `<cfdirectory>` type; optional arguments are marked with an asterisk.

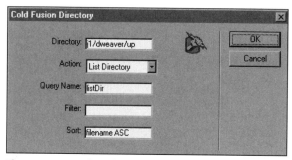

Figure 29-11: The Directory object gives you easy access to any folder on the server.

Table 29-3
Cold Fusion Directory Object Types

Action	Parameter	Description
List Directory	Query Name	Name of the output query to be used for listing.
	Filter*	File extension filter used to mask out all other file types, such as $*.cfm$.
	Sort*	Comma-delimited list of query columns to sort results by. The ASC (ascending) or DESC (descending) qualifier can be added for any specified column. For example: $dirname\ ASC$, $filename2$, $size\ DESC$.
Create Directory	Mode	Sets the file permission for the new directory. Entry is given in octal values, as in 666 or 777. Valid for Solaris servers only.
Rename Directory	New Name	The name to be applied to the specified directory.
Delete Directory	n/a	

Integrating Tango

After you've been immersed in Web development for a while, it's easy to forget that HTML is not necessarily the best environment in which to build an application. The most universal, yes, but certainly not the fastest or the most scalable. Tango has a slightly different solution — why not use a compiled program to generate the HTML as needed? Tango Application Files, recognizable by their .taf file extension, are compiled files that are quickly run by the Tango Server. The Tango Server can connect to any ODBC-compliant database, as well as Oracle-specific ones; there's even a special version of Tango for Filemaker databases.

Tango's parent company, Pervasive Software, partnered with Macromedia to deliver a dynamic page solution to Dreamweaver that fits the Tango environment well. Tango Application Files are built in the Tango Editor, which includes various rapid development tools for automating the process. A number of these tools, such as the Search Builder and New Record Builder, automatically generate HTML forms integrated with the requested database information. These HTML forms can then be easily customized in Dreamweaver for inclusion in your Web site.

Tango uses a series of what it calls *meta tags,* which are embedded in the HTML it generates. These meta tags (not to be confused with the HTML <meta> tags) always begin with an @ sign, as in <@if>. When the Tango Server processes a meta tag, the resulting information is integrated with the HTML and returned to the Web server to be sent back to the browser.

Tango has broken down Web interactivity into its key component parts. In Tango vernacular, any server request — whether to access a database or send out e-mail — is referred to as an *action.* Each action has a limited number of responses and each response corresponds to an HTML page. As an example, let's see how Tango handles a search query:

1. In the Tango Editor, shown in Figure 29-12, you specify which data source you'd like to work with and choose from which fields of that data source the user can query.

The form also contains a Submit button and, optionally, a Reset button.

2. You choose which fields from the data source are to be displayed in the record list, as well as any grouping or sorting required.

   Tango builds three different HTML files:

   • The **Results** HTML page, which contains a table of the matches from the specified criteria, and links to additional pages of records, if necessary

   • The **No Results** HTML page, which displays a message indicating that no matching records were found; and a link enabling the user to search again

   • The **Error** HTML page, which informs the user of an error encountered when processing the search

3. The Tango Application File can now be saved and run.

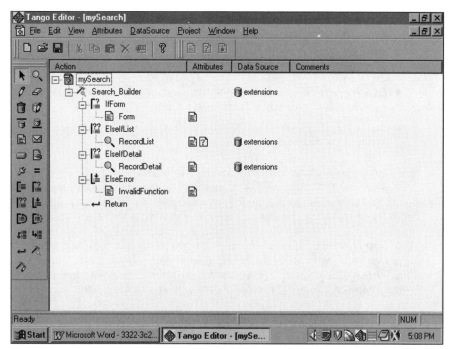

Figure 29-12: Database back-ends are developed in the Tango Editor, shown here. The front-end, seen by the user, is modified in Dreamweaver.

Tango builds an HTML page that includes a form to accept the query input. As you might expect, the HTML pages automatically built by Tango are pretty plain — very much "just the facts." Naturally, this is where Dreamweaver comes in. Each of these HTML files can be brought into Dreamweaver, and you can modify their look and feel to integrate completely into your Web site. Then, the enhanced HTML files are linked back in Tango and saved as part of the Tango Application File. Now, when the .taf files are run, you get the power of Tango and the style of Dreamweaver.

Note   As of this writing, the Tango extensions have not been officially released for Dreamweaver 2, and the following descriptions are based on a beta version. Although the general methodology and techniques are not expected to change, the dialog boxes, Property Inspectors, and Object icons have not been finalized. You may notice some discrepancies between the final version and the screen shots used here.

Working with Tango and Dreamweaver

Tango has implemented a very robust integration with Dreamweaver. Just how robust? Here's what you get when you install the Tango extension:

✦ Three different translators, including one that permits you to view sample data directly in Dreamweaver

✦ A third-party tag database file that describes 119 Tango meta tags with almost 20 different icons

✦ Two Property Inspectors — one for conditional tags, such as `<@if>`, and a generic one for all other Tango meta tags

✦ Seven Tango objects, capable of inserting virtually any Tango meta tag or configuration variable

The Tango extension is available on Macromedia's Dreamweaver Web site (`www.macromedia.com/...`). The installation is very straightforward. After downloading the Tango file, uncompress the file and double-click the executable to begin the installation. Follow the onscreen prompts and start Dreamweaver.

There are several methods for using the two programs together. One of the best ways I've found is to store the HTML files separately from the Tango Application Files. These files are then accessible for modification by Dreamweaver and inclusion in the Tango Editor. Follow these steps to set up this structure:

1. Use the Tango Editor to make the initial database connection and generate the basic HTML forms.

2. Double-click any HTML form to open its editing window in Tango.

3. From the Tango menus, first choose Edit ➪ Select All and then choose Edit ➪ Copy.

4. Switch to Dreamweaver and open a new document, if one is not already available.

5. Choose Edit ➪ Paste in Dreamweaver.

Caution

Tango inserts a `doctype` declaration before the opening `<html>` tag. This declaration is used by browsers to determine HTML compatibility at the top of the document. It looks like the following: `<!DOCTYPE HTML PUBLIC "-//W3C//DTD HTML 3.2//EN`. If you paste the Tango code in the Document Window, Dreamweaver inserts this declaration in the wrong location, right after the `<body>` tag. While this placement is generally ignored by browsers, you can avoid this potential problem by opening Dreamweaver's HTML Inspector, selecting all of the code and then pasting in the Tango HTML. This ensures that no code is improperly placed.

6. Save this file in Dreamweaver by choosing File ➪ Save.

Generally, HTML files should be stored in the same folder as or a subfolder of the Tango Application File.

7. Make any modifications in Dreamweaver desired and resave the file when you're done.

8. Return to the Tango Editor and replace all the HTML in the editor with a link to the file using Tango's `<@include>` and `<@appfilepath>` meta tags, as follows:

```
<@include file="<@appfilepath>myResults.htm">
```

Note that the `file` attribute is capable of mixing meta tags and literal text. The `<@appfilepath>` meta tag returns the file path for the current application file.

9. Repeat Steps 2–9 for any other HTML file generated by Tango that you want to modify in Dreamweaver.

Now, you — or another member of your team — can continue developing the database application while the front-end is being altered in Dreamweaver. Figure 29-13 shows two HTML files for a search page side-by-side; on the left is the original page as generated by Tango, with all the necessary database elements in place; and on the right is the same page after being modified in Dreamweaver. Because this modified page is now linked to the Tango Application File, it will be called when the application is run.

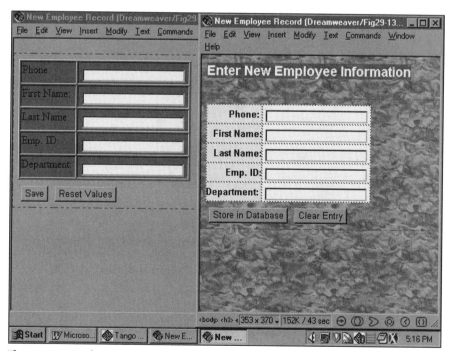

Figure 29-13: The Tango-generated code on the left was transformed into the page on the right in Dreamweaver.

Setting up the Tango Translators

To gain the full effects of the Dreamweaver-Tango integration, you have to make sure the translators are enabled. Translator control is handled through Preferences in the Translator panel. Generally, you want the translators to do their job every time there is any sort of modification on the page. This generalization is certainly true with two out of three of the Tango translators. However, with one of the translators — the Sample Data Translator — it's best to turn off automatic translation.

To set the Tango translators appropriately, follow these steps:

1. Choose Edit ➪ Preferences.

2. In the Preferences dialog box, choose the Translation category, shown in Figure 29-14.

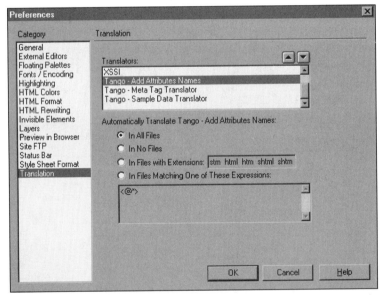

Figure 29-14: Adjust Tango translator settings in the Translation panel of the Preferences dialog box.

3. From the Translation panel, highlight Tango - Add Attributes Names in the Translators list.

4. Select In All Files as the Automatically Translate Tango - Add Attributes Names option.

5. Repeat Steps 3 and 4 for the Tango - Meta Tag Translator.

6. Make sure that the Automatically Translate option for Tango - Sample Data Translator is set to In No Files.

7. Click OK when you're done.

Applying the Tango Sample Data Translator

Normally, after you've modified your Tango-generated page in Dreamweaver, you'd view the .taf file through the Tango Server in a browser. After processing both the Tango meta tags and the HTML, the Tango Server sends the browser a completed HTML page with the requested data integrated. This is an obvious requirement for finalized pages. However, the Web designer only needs to see an *example* of the data embedded in the page to complete the job. The Tango - Sample Data Translator temporarily pulls in example data and populates the various fields implemented on the page. The command is invoked by choosing Modify ⇨ Translate ⇨ Tango - Sample Data Translator.

Aside from the translator, two other elements are necessary to make the example data appear in Dreamweaver: the Sample Data file and the Sample Data attributes. The Sample Data file is an XML file that lists the data to be presented in Dreamweaver. Three different data types can be specified: text, numeric, or date. These data types are later used to insert the proper kind of information in the example data showing in Dreamweaver.

The Sample Data file is named tangosampledata.xml and is stored in the Configuration\Tango folder. Regardless of the number of different Tango applications, there can only be one Sample Data file per system. However, the system is flexible enough to provide example data for a wide range of applications. The XML file follows the following format:

```
<tangosampledata>
  <sampledata type="typeData" value="valueData"/>
</tangosampledata>
```

where the possible values for *typeData* are "text", "numeric", and "date"; and *valueData* is any string. For example, let's say your Tango application returns a list of contacts and their phone numbers. Such information is always returned in tables, with each column holding a specific field — for this example, we'll presume a four-column table, like that depicted in Figure 29-15 — with column headings Record #, First Name, Last Name, and Telephone. The Tango Sample Data Translator reads the XML information sequentially, according to type, so our sampledatafile.xml would read as follows:

```
<tangosampledata>
  <sampledata type="text" value="John"/>
  <sampledata type="text" value="Smith"/>
  <sampledata type="numeric" value="234-3456"/>
  <sampledata type="text" value="Jack"/>
  <sampledata type="text" value="Omnitrade"/>
  <sampledata type="numeric" value="322-4576"/>
```

```
    <sampledata type="text" value="Sam"/>
    <sampledata type="text" value="Waters"/>
    <sampledata type="numeric" value="664-7532"/>
    <sampledata type="text" value="Art"/>
    <sampledata type="text" value="Vandelay"/>
    <sampledata type="numeric" value="664-7545"/>
  </tangosampledata>
```

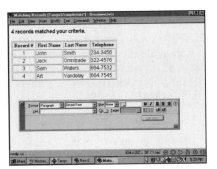

Figure 29-15: Tango's Sample Data feature simulates database output at the design stage.

Tip   If you don't mind repeating the same data over and over again, you could limit the number of `<sampledata>` tags to the number of fields being filled. The Tango Sample Data Translator loops through the data to fill the fields the required number of times.

In the example, you'll notice that while there are four fields, I've really only presented example data for three of them. The first field, Record #, is automatically generated by Tango through the `<@currow>` meta tag. Values are automatically generated for several other Tango meta tags, including `<@absrow>`, `<@curcol>`, `<@numrows>`, and `<@numcols>`.

The Sample Data attributes provide the link to the tags rendered in Dreamweaver. When the translator is run, the attributes establish the guidelines for Dreamweaver to integrate the sample data file information, essentially telling Dreamweaver where to put what kind of data and how much. The Sample Data attributes are as follows:

Attribute	Tag Used In	Description
samptype	`<@col>` or `<@column>`	Sets the sample data type to either `text`, `numeric`, or `date`
samplength	`<@col>` or `<@column>`	Determines the length of the sample data field
sampnumcols	`<@cols>`	Sets the number of columns of sample data to display
sampnumrows	`<@rows>`	Sets the number of rows of sample data to display

Attribute	Tag Used In	Description
samprownum	<@startrow>	Sets a value to represent the starting record number
samptotalrows	<@totalrows>	Sets a value representing the total number of rows to be displayed as part of the sample data

Currently, the Sample Data attributes must be coded by hand in the HTML Inspector or your favorite HTML editor. Following is the code used to generate the page seen previously in Figure 29-15, with the Sample Data attributes in bold:

```
<html>
<head>
<title>Matching Records</title>
</head>
<body bgcolor="#FFFFFF">
<b><font face="Arial, Helvetica, sans-serif"><@totalrows
samptotalrows=4> records
matched your criteria. </font></b>
<P>
<table border=0>
  <tr valign="top" align="left" bgcolor="#FFFFCC">
    <td><b>Record #</b></td>
    <td><b>First Name</b></td>
    <td><b>Last Name</b></td>
    <td><b>CustomerID</b></td>
  </tr>
  <@rows sampnumrows=4>
  <tr valign="top">
    <td>
      <div align="center"><font face="Arial, Helvetica, sans-
serif"><@currow></font></div>
    </td>
    <td><font face="Arial, Helvetica, sans-serif"><@col
name="Employees.FirstName" samptype="text"
samplength="15"></font></td>
    <td><font face="Arial, Helvetica, sans-serif"><@col
name="Employees.LastName" samptype="text"
samplength="15"></font></td>
    <td><font face="Arial, Helvetica, sans-serif"><@col
name="Employees.Phone" samptype="numeric"
samplength="11"></font></td>
  </tr>
  </@rows>
</table>
</body>
</html>
```

Understanding the Tango meta tags and Property Inspectors

At of this writing, 119 Tango meta tags are defined in the Third Party Tags XML file. In most cases, any tag created in the Tango Editor will be recognized by Dreamweaver and rendered either with an icon or with its contents displayed. In some cases, as with `<@ifshort>` and `<@scriptshort>`, a tag is only used in Dreamweaver and is automatically translated for the screen by the Tango translators.

When a particular Tango meta tag is selected, its custom Property Inspector is made available. There are four different custom Tango Property Inspectors:

✦ **Meta tag** is used to detail the attributes and values of most Tango meta tags. Selecting the parameter from the Attribute list displays the corresponding equivalence in the Value text box. Values can be modified in the Property Inspector.

✦ `@If` lists the components of an `<@if>` meta tag; the expression to evaluate and the statements to execute if the expression proves to be true.

✦ `@IfEmpty` describes the parts of an `<@ifempty>` tag; if a value is an empty string, the supplied string is inserted.

✦ `@IfEqual` details the sections of an `<@ifequal>` tag; if `Value1` is equal to `Value2`, the specified string is included.

The conditional Property Inspectors, `@if`, `@ifempty`, and `@IfEqual`, enable you to view included `@Else` and `@ElseIf` clauses as well. Choosing a different option from the drop-down list on the Property Inspector displays the appropriate interface.

Inserting Tango objects

All the Tango code applied in Dreamweaver doesn't have to come from the Tango Editor. The Tango extensions include nine objects that enable you to insert any Tango meta tag, as well as set variables or pull data from database results. After installation of the Tango extensions, all objects (described in Table 29-4) can be found on the Tango panel of the Objects Palette.

| Table 29-4 | |
| **Tango Objects** | |
Object	*Description*
Action Result Item	Used to reference data returned from an executed action, such as a search
Current Date or Time	Inserts the current date or time in one of 14 different formats

Object	Description
Form Field or URL Argument	Returns the name of a form field or URL argument sent to a Tango Application File
@IF	Sets up an If conditional statement; a series of statements are executed should a specified expression prove true
@IFEMPTY	Inserts an IfEmpty conditional statement. If the expression is true, one statement is inserted; otherwise, another one is included.
@IFEQUAL	Inserts an IfEqual conditional statement. If the given value is an empty string, one statement is inserted; otherwise, another one is included.
Request Parameter	Returns one of eight different environmental variables from the server, including Client Name, Client Domain, IP Address, Server Address, Server Port, Referer Page URL, and Method.
Variable	Sets a variable to a specified scope (Local, User, Cookie, Domain, System). If the variable is an array, the row and column can be specified.
Meta Tag	Enables you to insert any Tango meta tag

Summary

It's a pretty safe bet that active content is an issue in every Web designer's future. Not only can database-connected pages serve up simple data in an organized fashion, images, links, streaming video, and other media are also targetable content. Dreamweaver's extensibility makes it the ideal choice for a Web designer who needs to connect to the ever-expanding world of databases. When you're considering building an active content page, keep the following in mind:

✦ A database is a structured file for maintaining data. Databases are made up of tables, fields, and records. A database that can use two or more tables together is called a *relational database*.

✦ Web pages that link standard HTML and elements drawn from a database are referred to as *active content pages*. With an active content page, you change the data and the Web page is presented with the new information automatically.

✦ Allaire's Cold Fusion system works with many different types of servers and uses the Cold Fusion Markup Language (CFML) to create a rich server-side language. An array of Cold Fusions ship with Dreamweaver 2 and enable you to enter CFML tags in your Web pages without programming.

✦ Pervasive's Tango uses the Tango Editor to build the database-connected heart of an HTML page — which can then be enhanced and integrated into a Web site with Dreamweaver 2. The Tango extensions include a full array of Property Inspectors, objects, third-party tags, and translators to ease design chores.

In the next chapter, you learn how to use Dreamweaver to implement e-commerce solutions.

✦   ✦   ✦

E-Commerce Solutions

✦ ✦ ✦ ✦

In This Chapter

How e-commerce
works

Using cookies to
track customers

Building a shopping
cart

Working with iCat
e-commerce objects

✦ ✦ ✦ ✦

While the first age of the Internet was widely devoted to information — gathering, storing, archiving, and sharing it — the next era increasingly seems devoted to transactions and business. E-commerce (short for *electronic commerce*) is on the rise; online retail purchases are more than doubling each year as consumers feel more secure about shopping over the Web, and business-to-business sales are skyrocketing. You'll find numerous explanations for this explosive growth, but the bottom line is this: buying and selling online is here to stay.

More and more, Web designers are asked to build storefronts on the Web. Enabling a Web site for e-commerce is not a trivial task, as it requires a blend of Internet security, database connectivity, and marketing savvy. Macromedia has partnered with a leader in electronic commerce, iCat, to develop a series of commands and objects that simplify creating and hosting an online store, available on the Dreamweaver Web site. In this chapter, after an overview of e-commerce from a Web designer's point of view, you'll see how to implement these extensions and set up an Internet marketplace. Also, along the way, you'll see how Dreamweaver can help you with another e-commerce necessity: tracking customers with JavaScript cookies.

Understanding E-commerce

While there are almost as many variations to how shopping works as there are stores on the Web, many transactions take a similar path. Here's how a typical transaction makes its way around the Internet:

1. The user sees something desirable in the online store and clicks the "Buy" button to put the item in his or her shopping cart.

   The "Buy" triggers a cookie containing the item number and quantity to be written to the user's system.

2. After shopping for a bit more, the user decides to proceed to the check-out area of the site.

   The link on the Check-out Counter button is to a page on a secure server that employs Secure Server Layer (SSL) protocol. An icon on the user's browser — usually a locked padlock or a solid key — indicates the change. All communication between a user and secure server is coded or encrypted.

3. The user is given an opportunity to confirm the current contents of the shopping cart — and, if desired, change the quantity of any item.

   The cookie information (with the information about the selected products) that has been stored during the online shopping trip is read back into the browser.

4. If the customer has shopped at the online store before, a user ID and password are all that are required to retrieve all the pertinent account information: billing and shipping address, credit card numbers, e-mail address, and so forth.

   If the buyer is a first-time customer, forms with the applicable information are filled out and the data — along with a new user ID and password — is transferred to the store's system over the secure network.

5. The system at the online shop retrieves the order information and decodes it. The transactional information (credit card number, amount of purchase, etc.) is reencrypted and sent over secure phone lines to the credit-card clearinghouse with an authentication certificate from the store.

   The order information is entered into the database. Some systems deduct the order from inventory at this point, while others wait for the transaction to be confirmed by the bank.

6. The credit-card clearinghouse authenticates the merchant and forwards the transaction data to the bank.

7. The bank accepts or declines the charge and sends the results back to the clearinghouse, which then forwards it to the merchant.

8. The merchant sends two electronic confirmations to the customer: one to the browser as a thank-you and one via e-mail with full details of the order and shipping information. Any links from here, back to the main store, end the secure server connection.

As you can see, online selling requires a great deal of behind-the-scenes communication and coordination. However, it all boils down to two primary factors: security and connectivity.

Cross-Reference

Database connectivity is an expansive technology that Dreamweaver 2 is poised to handle. For more about using databases with Dreamweaver, see Chapter 29, "Dynamic Database Content."

Encryption

The facet of the Web that makes it so compelling — global access — is one of the factors that keeps consumers wary. The common fear is, "If anyone in the world can get online, can't they also get my credit card information?" Grabbing any data as it passes by on the Internet is certainly not a trivial task, and possible for only the most dedicated hackers. Even with the information in hand, however, cyberthieves still haven't made off with the loot — because whatever data they have is meaningless unless it is decoded.

Encryption is handled automatically, with all data passed through a *secure server*. A secure server is one that uses some form of coding, or *encryption*, technology. The most common form of Internet encryption comes from servers with a Secure Server Layer (SSL). To secure any information passed over the Web, the page with the form must access a secure server. Links for secure servers begin with `https://`, instead of the usual `http://` — the additional *s* stands, of course, for security.

Note   Depending on the user's browser settings, messages can appear when going from a secure server to a nonsecure server. As these alerts can be disconcerting to the novice user, it's a good idea to continue using the secure server for all Web pages accessed during the sales check-out procedure — even those pages that are purely informational and don't require the secure server to pass data.

Authentication

Encryption only solves half of the problem with online security — the other half is *authentication*. It does no good to receive an encrypted message from someone if you're not sure they are who they are supposed to be. Because online communication is largely anonymous — there's no visual or aural confirmation of identity — another method of identification is necessary.

The current basic method of authentication involves *digital certificates*. A digital certificate is a type of identity card for companies, Web sites, and online individuals. Digital certificates are issued by established certificate authorities, such as VeriSign, Inc. (`www.verisign.com`), and are generally automatically transferred by browsers. Companies (or individuals) applying for a digital certificate must prove their identity. With companies, the process is similar to applying for a merchant bank account; you must supply the business' articles of incorporation, tax id number, and so forth. With individuals, you need enter only an e-mail address. Higher classes of digital certificates include insured protection, which requires a more rigorous identification procedure. Digital certificates are typically offered when a user enters a secure server.

Passing Cookies

As noted earlier, cookies are used to track user information — such as what's in a shopping cart — from one Web page. A *cookie* is a small piece of information that can be passed along with the HTTP header that accompanies every Web page: The Web page is displayed by the browser and the cookie information is stored on the user's hard drive in a special file. Don't get the idea that cookies are just text files that can be used in any situation. Cookies have a very special format and definite limits.

Each domain is limited to 20 cookies and there is a 4-megabyte or 300-total cookie limit imposed by the browser. A cookie generally conveys four pieces of information:

✦ **Domain of Origin.** All cookies are domain-specific (sent from one particular Internet domain). Only the domain sending the cookie can retrieve it.

✦ **Expiration Date.** Many cookies are intended to be active for a single online session; when you leave the Web site, the cookie is no longer of any value. These cookies are maintained in memory only and never written to a file. Other cookies use specified expiration dates to keep the number of cookies down, so that new ones can be added.

✦ **Path of URL.** You can specify where a cookie is active on your site. Generally, it's best to keep the cookies available in the current directory

✦ **Name and Value Pairs.** The name and value pairs are the real content of a cookie. Each variable or name is set equal to a particular value, generally user-supplied either directly through a text box or by an action, such as selecting an Add to Shopping Cart button. The name and value pairs are later retrieved by a JavaScript or CGI program when the cookie is read.

Although Dreamweaver 2 doesn't come with any standard cookie behaviors, a number of them have been created by third-party developers. Generally, cookie behaviors come in a set — one behavior to set the cookie, another to read it, and yet another to remove it entirely. One of the better cookie behavior sets was built by Nadav Silvio of *Wired*'s Webmonkey Web site. With the Webmonkey Set and Read Cookie behaviors, you can even choose a form field on the Web page, such as a text box, to get the cookie from or set it to.

One of the drawbacks to cookies is that they're not universally accepted. Because of the possible security risk involved with any outside system writing and reading information to a local hard drive, browsers enable the user to choose whether they will accept cookies or be warned every time one is passed to their system. Using another third-party extension, the Check Cookie behavior by Jaro von Flocken, you can redirect to another page visitors whose browsers do not have cookies enabled.

Working with shopping carts

Whenever a customer selects an item online with the intent to buy it, the item goes into an online *shopping cart*. Although commonly thought of as a single object, a shopping cart is composed of several key components of a program or programs.

Basically, the shopping cart enables the potential customer to tag selected items for purchase and continue shopping. When the customer decides to finalize the purchase, the items are listed on the check-out screen and a total cost is calculated.

Generally, shopping cart functionality includes the ability to include any number of items and modify the quantity of the items — including changing the number to zero, thus removing it from the shopping cart. Most stores are set up so that items can be added to the shopping cart at any time in one session and check-out is always available.

Tip As well as the numerous high-end e-commerce products from such companies as Open Market (www.openmarket.com), Netscape (www.netscape.com), and ICVerify (www.icverify.com), you can also find several full-featured CGI online shopping solutions from such resources as Extropia (www.extropia.com) and The CGI Resource Index (www.cgi-resources.com) for free or a relatively low cost.

Because of the complexity of handling complete online shopping transactions and store management — and the inherent expense — several e-commerce solutions have separated the shopping cart component from the all-in-one store solution. Under a shopping cart–only arrangement, your Web pages include "Add to Shopping Cart" and "Proceed to Checkout" links that access the e-commerce solution's secure server instead of your own. This is an excellent route for a small business that wants to sell online, but whose business volume doesn't rate an in-house server. Such a solution from iCat is detailed in the following section.

Building an iCat storefront

There are many routes to creating an online store. Numerous server packages exist from top-rated vendors to assist with the design, building, and maintenance of any size e-commerce site. Surveying them all is beyond the scope of this book, but Dreamweaver 2 now offers an e-commerce solution developed in partnership with iCat, a leader in the field.

iCat Corporation is one of the pioneers in the electronic commerce field and was recently acquired by Intel. iCat was among the first to offer a turnkey e-commerce solution, involved in Web store development, creation, and hosting. iCat also made headlines by being the first to offer an entry-level e-commerce solution to small- and medium-sized businesses for free, with their iCat Commerce Online service.

iCat Commerce Online enables Web developers to create and maintain an online store, a shopping cart, or both. The costs for the service are on a sliding scale based on the number of products carried in the store. As of this writing, a shopping cart capable of working with ten or fewer items is available for $19.95 per month, while a store with 3,000 items is available for a monthly fee of $350. A Web Store option, unlike the shopping cart option, is free if your store has ten or fewer items — however, your design options are much more limited. Be sure to check the current pricing schedule for the iCat Commerce Online service at the iCat Web site (www.icat.com) when considering your e-commerce options.

When creating a store, iCat offers a series of professionally designed templates with several customizable features, such as a logo, from which to choose. The iCat Commerce Online store is explicitly designed to enable nontechnical business-people to create and administer fully functional Internet storefronts. No programming or graphic design experience is required.

Given that Dreamweaver is a program for Web designers who might prefer to incorporate a shopping cart into their own Web designs, the balance of this section details the use of iCat commands and objects available for such a setup. Many other online commerce solutions follow a similar but not identical pattern of development.

Note   To get the most current iCat objects, visit the Dreamweaver Web site at http://www.macromedia.com/software/dreamweaver/download/ extensions/ and select the iCat link.

Installing the iCat objects

Before you can start to build your iCat store, you have to install the iCat objects and commands. Once installed on your system, the iCat commands are used to register your shopping cart online, as well as to set up the individual store items. Begin the installation process by double-clicking the iCat Setup icon. Follow the onscreen prompts to complete the process and then restart Dreamweaver.

The iCat installation installs three commands and three objects. The commands, found under Commands ⇨ iCat E-commerce, are as follows:

✦ **Signup** opens a browser window and, if online, connects with the iCat Commerce Online registration site.

✦ **Edit Items** creates and modifies items for sale in your online store.

✦ **Update Commerce Cart** ensures that the items created on the local system and the iCat system are identical.

The three iCat objects, available on the iCat pane of the Objects Palette, are as follows:

✦ **Add to Cart** inserts a button that enables the user to add a particular store item to the current shopping cart.

✦ **View Cart** inserts a button that, when selected, displays the list of items currently in the user's shopping cart.

✦ **Checkout Cart** inserts a button that, when selected, enables the user to complete the order.

Setting up the store

Establishing your shopping cart on iCat is basically a two-part process. First, you need to fill out all the necessary electronic "paperwork" to complete your registration. Then, once your shopping cart is in the system, you can customize certain elements — to make sure that the external graphics mesh with your design and that the order options (such as confirmations, delivery charges, and taxes) are handled appropriately.

To register your shopping cart with the iCat Online Commerce system, follow these steps:

1. When you're connected to the Internet, choose Commands ➪ iCat E-commerce ➪ Signup from the Dreamweaver menu.

   Dreamweaver opens a new browser window and connects to the store/shopping cart registration area on the iCat Web site.

Caution When filling out the registration, always use the iCat navigation buttons (Next and Cancel), rather than the browser Back, Forward, and Refresh buttons. Using the browser buttons causes the form mechanism to lose your information. If you make a mistake, don't worry. You'll be given an opportunity at the end of the sign-up session to correct any errors.

2. After viewing the introductory screen, select the Build a Store Now link.

3. On the next screen, click Create New Store.

4. On the next screen, enter the user (creator/manager) and account (owner of store) information.

5. On the next screen (iCat's Step 2), select your service options:

   • Select whether you're opening a Web Store, Commerce Cart, or both by selecting from the drop-down lists.

   • Choose Monthly or Annual billing from the billing radio buttons.

   • Choose which level of service you'd prefer: Basic, Standard, Premium, Elite, Super, or Mega from the drop-down list. The different levels relate to the number of products your online store carries.

     After every choice, the screen redraws, depicting details about the selected service plan.

   • If you're building a Commerce Cart, select which HTML editor you'd prefer to use. Dreamweaver is the first option on the drop-down list.

Note As of this writing, all iCat stores and shopping carts are free for the first 30 days. If you decide iCat is not for you, you can delete the cart before the 30 days is over to avoid billing.

6. On the next screen (iCat Step 3), enter the credit card information.

   You must enter valid credit card information even if you choose one of the no-fee options.

7. On the next screen (iCat Step 4), specify the store name in the first text box, and a short directory name in the second.

   The store name can be up to 30 characters and is seen on all pages. The directory name identifies the folder in which your items are stored in the iCat system.

8. On the next screen (iCat Step 5), fill out the required survey about your organization.

9. The final screen is a confirmation screen, called the Summary. Review all information and if any changes are necessary on a particular page, select the link for that page. An additional confirmation is e-mailed to the administrator of the shopping cart and/or store.

Customizing your shopping cart

The only e-commerce method more flexible than hosting your own store—handling all the secure server access and database integration—is just using another organization's shopping cart system. In this manner, the Web designer controls the look and feel of the site and does not have to update pages through the host system. With iCat's shopping cart, you can use your own shopping cart graphics, or pick up one of iCat's images. But more important than the look of an e-commerce site is its content; details such as shipping options have to be clearly explained. With iCat, you can specify a wide variety of options for the customer to choose from at check-out. All of these customizations are available through the Edit Existing Store screen on the iCat Web site.

Note   On the Edit Existing Store screen, you'll see an Items button that enables you to enter new items for your online catalog. The iCat commands within Dreamweaver enable you to enter and modify your items offline and then synchronize them with iCat's server. This technique is described later in this section.

One of the most basic options for the merchant during check-out is whether the shopping cart is to use *online* or *offline credit-card processing*. With online processing, the credit card is authorized during the actual transaction on the Web, the merchant receives the confirmation (or denial), and the funds are credited into the merchant's account. With offline processing, iCat sends the merchant the credit-card information, which is authorized via telephone or credit-card reader. To qualify for online processing you must have an active merchant account with your bank. Some banks only permit offline processing, although as online shopping grows in popularity, many more banks are open to online processing as well. iCat also offers several options to help you sign up for a merchant account through their partners.

To customize your iCat shopping cart, follow these steps:

1. Go online and point your browser to the iCat Web site (`www.icat.com`). Enter your user name and password in the iCat Commerce Online section.

2. On the main iCat Commerce Online page, shown in Figure 30-1, select the Store Design button.

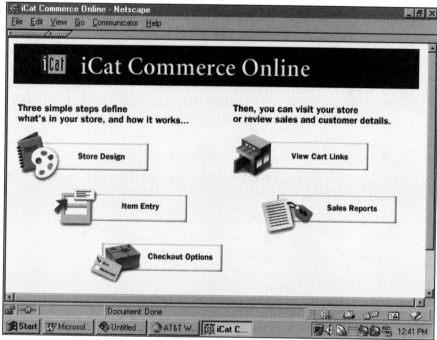

Figure 30-1: The iCat Commerce Online center is your launchpad for shopping cart customization.

3. With a shopping cart, the only graphic alteration you can make is to the background of the shopping cart pages. To alter the background, select the Next button.

4. To continue using the default, a neutral gray pattern, select the Default button.

   You can also upload a custom background by selecting the appropriate link and entering the filename of the image in the Upload dialog box. The custom background can be no more than 86 pixels square and must be in either GIF or JPEG format.

5. On the Edit Store Options screen, select the Checkout options button.

6. On the next screen, you can choose from the following options what you want to appear on the check-out page.

- Select which credit cards you'll accept: American Express, Optima, Discover, Visa, or MasterCard.

- Select whether you wish to use online processing or offline processing.

- Select your shipping options. You can decide which type of shipping your store is to offer — standard, two-day, or overnight — and what additional charges are to be applied.

- Select the applicable tax rates, if any, and whether they should be applied by state or zip code.

- Select what billing and shipping information is required, such as name, phone, e-mail, and so on.

- Choose whether to e-mail confirmations to the customer and/or merchant. You can also customize the confirmation message.

- Choose which gift wrapping options, if any, your store offers, as well as any surcharge for international orders.

- You can customize messages that appear on the shipping, check-out, and order form confirmation screens.

- Select whether your store enables fax and/or phone orders as well as online ordering and, if so, list the phone numbers to be printed.

7. When you're finished making your selections, log off of the iCat Web site.

After registering the store online, you're ready to begin setting up your store offline — by detailing the items for sale and all their particulars.

Stocking your virtual shelves

Just as a regular Web page is designed offline and then published to a Web server, the bulk of the store setup is accomplished on a local system and then uploaded to the iCat remote server. The iCat commands and objects in Dreamweaver 2 are designed to handle these tasks. The primary offline operation requires that all pertinent information about each item — item number, price, and any selectable options such as size or color — be available locally. Basically you're building a simple database of all items for sale, which will later be synchronized with the online store.

However, before you can begin entering items, you have to identify the store with which you're working. To do this, choose Commands ⇨ iCat E-commerce ⇨ Edit Items. The Edit Items dialog box appears, as shown in Figure 30-2. In the dialog box, you need to enter in the Directory text box the short directory name selected during the registration process.

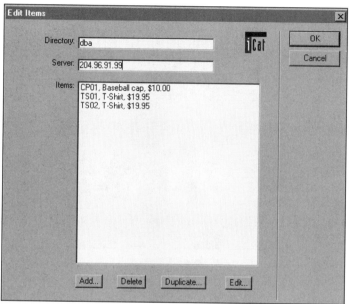

Figure 30-2: Manage your virtual store catalog through the Edit Items dialog box.

Now you're ready to begin adding items for your online store. After each one is entered, a summary of available items appears in the Items text area. To add, modify, or delete an item in your iCat online store, follow these steps:

1. If the Edit iCat Store dialog box is not already open, choose Commands ⇨ iCat E-commerce ⇨ Edit Items to display it.

2. Select the Add button.

   The iCat Item Properties dialog box is displayed, as shown in Figure 30-3.

3. Enter basic information about the item in the proper text field:

   • **Product No.** The unique catalog code or SKU number for the item. Do not use spaces or special characters in the Product No. field. Required.

   • **Item.** The name of the item, up to 79 characters. Required.

   • **Manufacturer.** The maker of the item. Optional.

   • **Description.** A brief description of the item as it is to appear in the catalog. Optional.

   • **Price.** The cost of the item, before shipping or taxes. Use only numbers and decimal points for your value, no dollar sign. Required. (You can also select the Taxable option, if desired.)

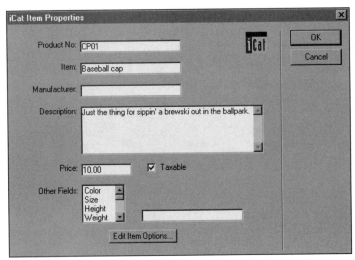

Figure 30-3: Details for each item are entered and modified through the iCat Item Properties dialog box.

Tip

If you don't like the way iCat labels these categories, you can adjust the label. For example, the product number field is initially labeled as SKU # — to change this to another name, such as Item #, change it online in the Item Entry section of the iCat Online Commerce site.

4. If desired, you can include additional information describing the item, such as Color: Silver. To do so, select one of the field names listed in the Other Fields menu list and enter the appropriate information in the accompanying text box. The available fields are Color, Size, Height, Weight, Text 1–5, and Numeric 1–8. The generic text and numeric fields are used to relate other information in text or number format; the labels can be altered online.

Note

The Size, Height, and Width fields require numeric entries. To enter text descriptions for size (such as Small, Medium, or Large), use one of the unspecified text fields.

5. To enter a user-selectable option for the item, choose the Edit Item Options button. Each item can have up to three different option selections. These options are displayed as a drop-down list item on the order page.

   The iCat Item Option Properties dialog box opens, as shown in Figure 30-4.

6. In the iCat Item Option Properties dialog box, enter the name for the options you wish to specify in the Option #1, #2, or #3 Label text box. If, for example, you want to enter a selection of sizes and color, enter Size as the Option #1 Label and Color as the Option #2 Label.

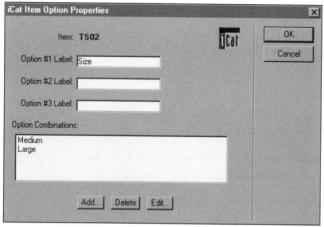

Figure 30-4: When you want to give your customers different options for the same item, enter the information in the iCat Item Option Properties dialog box.

7. Select the Add button to list the different possible options in the Option Combination text area. For example, the possibilities for a Size option could include Small, Medium, Large, and Extra Large.

8. Click OK to complete each item's specifications and return to the iCat Item Properties dialog box.

9. You can remove a highlighted item by selecting the Delete button.

10. To alter an existing item, select it and then choose the Edit button.

11. To create an item similar to an existing one, highlight it and choose the Duplicate button. Then edit the item in the Properties dialog box that appears.

12. When you're finished adding or modifying items, select the OK button.

Updating your shopping cart with iCat

Before the items you add to your online iCat store can be accessed by the customer, they must be entered onto the iCat server. This process is known as *updating* or *synchronization* because it is important that both the local and remote sites have identical information. When the iCat Edit Store command is run and items are added or modified, two files are written: items.tdv and itemoptions.tdv. Both files are stored in the Configuration\Ecommerce\iCat Data folder. In order for the local and remote system to be in sync, these two files must be the same in both locations.

Items can be altered on either the local system or the remote system. To synchronize changes made to items on a local system, follow these steps:

1. Go online and, in Dreamweaver, select Commands ⇨ iCat E-commerce ⇨ Update Commerce Cart.

2. In the Update Commerce Cart dialog box that appears, select the Launch Browser button.

   A new browser window opens and goes to the iCat Online Commerce site, where you need to enter your user name and password.

3. On the main iCat Online Commerce page, choose the Item Entry button.

4. On the External Application Help screen, click the Next button.

5. On the Item Entry screen, select the Import Items button.

   The Import Items screen displays the number of items currently in the store.

6. Click the Import Items button.

7. On the File Transfer window that opens, enter the path to the items.tdv file in the text box or use the Browse (Choose) button to locate the file and then click the Go button to upload the file.

8. Now, on the Item Entry screen, select the Import Options button.

9. On the File Transfer window that opens, enter the path to the itemoptions.tdv file in the text box or use the Browse (Choose) button to locate the file and then click the Go button to upload the file.

10. Log off when you're done.

 Tip

If you have a great number of items you'd like to include in your store, you might prefer to create a tab-delimited text file in a spreadsheet program like Excel. For more information about how to do this, see the section of the iCat Handbook entitled, "Importing Items and Item Options Using the Data Entry Spreadsheet." The iCat Handbook is available from the Help pages on the iCat Web site.

The other method of editing store items is to do so online at the iCat Online Commerce site. If you use this method, you'll need to export the items from the iCat Web site and save them on your local hard drive. To synchronize changes made on the remote system, follow these steps.

1. Follow the above procedure for logging onto the iCat Online Commerce site and your store.

2. On the main iCat Online Commerce page, choose the Item Entry button.

3. On the External Application Help screen, click the Next button.

4. On the Item Entry screen, select the Export Items button.

5. On the Export Items and Options screen, click the Export Items button.

6. Save the items.tdv file in the Configuration\Ecommerce\iCat Data, overwriting the existing file.

7. Now, on the Item Entry screen, select the Export Options button.

8. Save the itemoptions.tdv file in Configuration\Ecommerce\iCat Data, overwriting the existing file.

9. Log off when you're done.

Using the iCat objects

Now that your online store has been set up and the items listed in the catalog, it's time to incorporate the shopping cart into the Web pages. As noted earlier, three iCat objects can be inserted into your Web pages: an Add to Cart object used for each item in the catalog and both a View Cart and Checkout Cart object to include on every page. When any of these buttons are selected by a user, the link connects to the iCat Commerce Web site with specific information for your store. Here, for example, is a URL from one item on a site I'm building:

```
http://204.96.91.54/store/dba/index.icl?execute=plugins--
cart_addtoorder.icl&itmsku=CP01&srcquantity=1
```

The iCat Add to Cart object

Because these URLs are automatically generated for every item using an Add to Cart button, the iCat objects are real timesavers. All you have to do is select the item from a dynamic drop-down list that reads all the items in your catalog.

To insert an Add to Cart object in your Web page, follow these steps:

1. Position your cursor where you'd like the Add to Cart button to appear and select the Add to Cart object from the iCat panel of the Objects Palette. You can also drag the object to any existing location on the page.

The iCat Add to Cart dialog box appears, as shown in Figure 30-5.

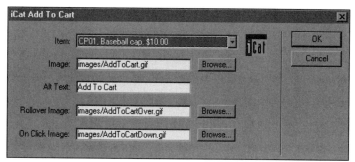

Figure 30-5: With iCat's Add to Cart object, a link to the proper item on the iCat commerce server is automatically set up.

2. Select the product code number for the desired item from the Item drop-down list.

3. Enter the path for the button image in the Image text box or use the Browse (Choose) button to locate the file.

4. Enter any text you want to use as the Alt Text, which appears as a tooltip on most browsers in the Alt Text text box.

5. If desired, enter the path to an image you want to appear when the user's pointer moves over the original image in the Rollover Image text box.

6. If desired, enter the path to an image you want to appear when the user clicks the original image in the On Click Image text box.

7. Click OK when you're done.

 Tip   iCat includes a series of shopping cart images to use in the `Configuration\ Ecommerce\ICat Data\Sample buttons` folder as well as on their Web site at `http://www.icat.com/products/icocartimages.htm`.

The first time a user clicks an Add a Cart button, a page on the iCat server is displayed confirming the choice. The user can then opt to not show the current page every time a new item is added to the shopping cart, to check out, or to just continue shopping.

View Cart

If your online store is a sizable one, you might want to consider adding a View Cart button to every page. You want the user to continue shopping without having to try to remember what's in the cart; the View Cart option displays all the items currently selected, but not paid for.

Inserting a View Cart button is very straightforward. Place your cursor where you would like the new button to appear and select the View Cart button from the iCat panel of the Objects Palette. In the View Cart dialog box, enter the source for the original image and, if desired, a rollover image and an `onMouseClick` image.

Check-out

One of the cardinal rules of all commerce, but especially Internet commerce, is Make it easy for the customer to pay. Check-out buttons indeed make it easy for the customer to pay, as they are used to initiate the final ordering procedure. It's a good idea to have a check-out button on every page on which a product is described or can be selected. The iCat Check-out buttons are very simple to insert and only require an image source.

A Check-out button is inserted like a View Cart button. Position your cursor wherever the new button should appear and select the Checkout Cart button from the iCat panel of the Objects Palette. In the Checkout Cart dialog box, enter the source for the original image and, if desired, a rollover image and an onMouseClick image.

When selected, a Check-out button takes you to a screen similar to the one shown in Figure 30-6. The iCat Check-out screen enables the customer to modify the quantity of items selected, as well as delete any unwanted items. Once the customer proceeds with the check-out procedure, billing, shipping, and credit card information is taken and an account established. The next time the customer visits your store, only a user name and password are required to retrieve the account information.

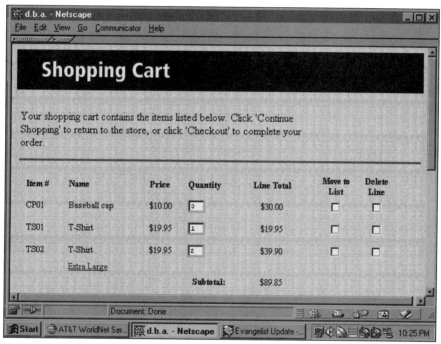

Figure 30-6: After the Check-out button is selected, the customer is taken to a secure server on iCat's system to complete the order.

Managing your storefront

Once you've inserted iCat objects into your Web page, all management of the e-commerce elements of the site take place online. Any previously set options can be changed, including the level of service — you can upgrade the level of service if you find you need to stock more items or downgrade it if you don't need as many. You can even cancel your iCat service by deleting the store online.

Perhaps one of the most important services an online store can offer is feedback. Any business needs an abundance of reports in order to gauge what is selling and who is buying it. The iCat Commerce Online site includes a large number of reports that can be generated for any timeframe desired, whether it's the last three days or the last month. Some of the reports capable of being generated include the following:

✦ **Customer Reports**, including a full customer list and a Best Customer list with account summaries or details.

✦ **Order Reports**, including reports organized by customer, item, or payment method; or a summary.

Reports can also be exported in a tab-delimited format for use in any database, spreadsheet, or word-processing program.

Summary

As more people find shopping online to be convenient, safe, and cost-effective, the prospect for e-commerce gets brighter and brighter. Establishing an e-commerce site, however, involves coordinating several diverse technologies. Dreamweaver, through its inherent extensibility, enables the Web designer to centralize these efforts, along with its e-commerce partner, iCat. When developing e-commerce sites, remember to keep the following points in mind:

✦ E-commerce requires access to a secure server that uses encryption and digital certificates to pass transactional information safely.

✦ Cookies are used to "follow" a customer through the online store, keeping track of all items in the user's shopping cart, until check-out time.

✦ Online stores can be set up entirely in-house or on a dedicated server linked to the rest of the Web site. Credit-card transactions can either be processed online in real time or offline. Companies need merchant accounts and cooperation with their banks to handle online processing.

✦ Macromedia has partnered with iCat, a leading e-commerce provider, to create a series of commands and objects for Dreamweaver 2 that enable easy setup, design, and management of an e-commerce site.

In the next chapter, you learn how to handle browser targeting, as well as cross-browser and backward-browser compatibility.

✦   ✦   ✦

Web Site Management Under Dreamweaver

Maximizing Browser Targeting

Each new release of a browser is a double-edged sword. On the one hand, an exciting new array of features is made possible. On the other, Web designers have to cope with yet another browser-compatibility issue. In today's market, you'll find in use all of the following:

✦ A host of 3.0 browsers, widely varying in their capabilities

✦ A growing number of fourth-generation (and, soon, fifth-generation) browsers

✦ A small group of 2.0 browsers in the machines of determined users who have never (and may never) upgrade

✦ A diverse assortment of browsers outside the mainstream, including Opera, WebTV, and Linux

✦ Various versions of America Online browsers, which range from being completely proprietary to a blend of current and special technologies

Browser compatibility is one of a Web designer's primary concerns (not to mention the source of major headaches); and many strategies are evolving to deal with this matter. Dreamweaver is in the forefront of cross-browser Web page design, both in terms of the type of code it routinely outputs and in its specialty functions. This chapter examines the browser-targeting techniques available in Dreamweaver. From multibrowser code to conversion innovations to browser validation capabilities, Dreamweaver helps you get your Web pages out to the widest audience, and with the most features.

Converting Pages in Dreamweaver

DHTML's gifts of layers and Cascading Style Sheets are extremely tempting to use because of their enhanced typographic-control and absolute-positioning capabilities. Many Web designers, however, have resisted using these features because only fourth-generation browsers can view them. Though Dreamweaver can't change the capabilities of 3.0 browsers, it can make it easy for you to create alternative content for them.

Dreamweaver makes it possible to convert Web pages designed with layers and CSS into pages that can be rendered by 3.0 browsers. Moreover, if you're looking to upgrade your site from nested tables to layers, you don't have to do it by hand. Dreamweaver also includes a command to convert tables to layers, preserving their location but enabling greater design flexibility and dynamic control. A Webmaster's life just got a tad easier.

Making 3.0-compatible pages

It's a slight misstatement that Dreamweaver converts 4.0 feature-laden pages into pages that can be read by 3.0 browsers. Actually, Dreamweaver creates a new 3.0-compatible page based on the 4.0 page — and does it in almost no time at all. Once you've converted your page, you can use Dreamweaver's Check Browser behavior to route users to the appropriate pages, based on their browser version.

Preparing your page for conversion

When Dreamweaver makes a new 3.0-compatible page, layers are converted to nested tables and Cascading Style Sheet references are converted to inline character styles. You have the option to convert either or both features. To accomplish this conversion of your 4.0 Web page, the document must meet the following conditions:

✦ **All content must be in layers.** Because Dreamweaver converts layers to tables, it must start with everything absolutely positioned.

✦ **Layers must not overlap.** During the conversion process, Dreamweaver warns you when it finds overlapping layers and even tells you which ones they are.

New Feature

A new feature in Dreamweaver 2 prevents you from encountering the problem of overlapping layers in the design stage. Enable the option by choosing View ➪ Prevent Layer Overlaps or clicking the Prevent Overlaps check-box on the Layer Palette. While this can't separate layers that are currently overlapping — you'll have to do that by hand — it does stop you from accidentally laying one layer on top of another, and makes 3.0 conversion a breeze.

✦ **Nesting layers are not allowed.** When one layer is inside another, the inner layer is placed relative to the outer layer. Dreamweaver cannot convert relatively positioned layers.

✦ **The <ilayer> tag cannot be used.** Because the <ilayer> tag is based on relative positioning, Dreamweaver cannot convert it. Use <layer>, <div>, or <span> instead.

New Feature

Some Web pages you'd like to convert — or devolve — from 4.0 to 3.0 applicability have content both in and out of layers. And, as noted, Dreamweaver needs to have all the Web page elements in a layer before proceeding with conversion. Previously, it was necessary to cut elements outside of a layer and paste them in to prepare the page for conversion. Now, Dreamweaver 2 does it for you — just choose Modify ⇨ Layout ⇨ Reposition Content Using Layers, or choose the keyboard shortcut, Ctrl-F6 (Command-F6). In the dialog box that appears, be sure to choose the Select Layer Overlap option to avoid that problem. Click OK and Dreamweaver places everything in a layer, automatically — without generating a new page. For more on using this new capability, see Chapter 25, "Working with Layers."

Running the conversion

Once your page is prepped, generating a 3.0-compatible Web page from a 4.0 version is straightforward. You only have a couple of options — whether to convert layers, CSS styles, or both — and once you make your choice and click OK, the rest of the process is almost instantaneous.

To create a 3.0-compatible version of a Web page with 4.0 features, follow these steps:

1. Choose File ⇨ Convert ⇨ 3.0 Browser.

   The Convert to 3.0 Browser Compatible dialog box opens, as shown in Figure 31-1.

Figure 31-1: Begin to build your cross-browser compatible site with Dreamweaver's Convert Layers to Table command.

2. From the Convert to 3.0 dialog box, select your options:

   • If you are converting layers to tables only, choose the Layers to Table radio button.

   • If you are converting Cascading Style Sheet styles to HTML tags only, choose the CSS Styles to HTML Markup radio button.

   • If you are making all conversions, select the Both radio button.

3. Click OK, and Dreamweaver starts the conversion. A dialog box informs you if a problem is encountered, such as a nested layer or overlapping layers. If the Web page has overlapping layers, another dialog box (shown in Figure 31-2) tells you which layers are overlapping. Dreamweaver cannot proceed until all conflicts are resolved.

If there are no problems, Dreamweaver creates the page in a new window.

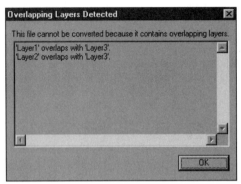

Figure 31-2: On a page with multiple layers, Dreamweaver spots the "illegal" overlapping ones when you try to convert the page to tables.

Note The CSS-to-HTML conversion disregards any CSS feature, such as line spacing, that is not implemented in regular HTML. In addition, the exact point size that can be specified in CSS is roughly translated to the relative size equivalents in HTML. Any font over 36 points is set to the largest HTML size, which is 7.

Evolving 3.0 pages to 4.0 standards

Web sites are constantly upgraded and modified. Eventually you'll need to enhance a more traditional site with new features, such as layers. Some of the older 3.0-oriented sites used elaborately nested tables on their pages to create a semblance of absolute positioning; normally, upgrading these Web pages would take hours and hours of tedious cutting and pasting. Now, however, Dreamweaver can bring these older pages up to speed with the Convert Tables to Layers command.

The Convert Tables to Layers command can also be used to make a version of a page created by another Web authoring program that uses nested tables for positioning (Net Objects Fusion, for example). Once tables have been transformed into layers, the layout of the entire page is much easier to modify. It's even possible to make the switch from 3.0 to 4.0 capabilities, modify your page and then, with the Convert to 3.0 Browser Compatible command, re-create your 3.0-compliant page.

The name of the Convert Tables to Layers command is another one that's a little misleading. Once you issue this command, every HTML element in the new page — not just the tables — is placed in a layer. Moreover, every cell with content in every table is converted into its own layer. In other words, if you are working with a 3 × 3 table in which one cell is left empty, Dreamweaver creates eight different layers for just the table. The only criterion for converting a page is that it contains at least one table.

Tip   If you want to convert a 3.0-compatible page to a page with layers but the page has no tables, you can add a dummy table with no data in it and choose File ➪ Convert ➪ Tables to Layers. Dreamweaver makes the conversion without the table, because the table was empty.

To convert a 3.0-browser-compatible Web page with tables to a 4.0-browser-compatible Web page with layers, choose File ➪ Convert ➪ Tables to Layers. If there are no tables in the page, Dreamweaver alerts you to this fact and aborts the process. If, on the other hand, one or more tables are found in the page, Dreamweaver creates a new page with your content in layers.

Ensuring Browser Compatibility

As more browsers and browser versions become available, a Web designer has two basic options to stay on the road to compatibility: *internal* and *external*.

✦ The **internal** method uses scripts on the same Web page that deliver the proper code depending on the browser detected. Many of Dreamweaver's own behavior functions manage the browser issue internally.

✦ The **external** approach examines each visitor's browser right off the bat and reroutes the user to the most appropriate Web page.

Both the internal and the external methods have their pluses and minuses, and both are better suited to particular situations. For example, it is impractical to use the external method of creating multiple versions of the same Web pages when you are working with a large site. Suddenly, you've gone from managing 300 pages of information to 900 or 1,200. Of course, you don't have to duplicate every page — but because of the open nature of the Web, where any page can be bookmarked and entered directly, you have to plan carefully and provide routing routines at the key locations. Conversely, sometimes you have no choice but to use multiple versions, especially if a page employs many browser-specific features.

Don't get the idea that the internal and external strategies are mutually exclusive. Several sites today are routing 3.0 browsers to one page, and using internal coding methods to differentiate between the various 4.0 browser versions on another page. This section examines techniques for implementing browser compatibility from both the internal and external perspective.

Internal coding for cross-browser compatibility

Imagine the shouts of joy when the Web development community learned that the 4.0 versions of Navigator and Internet Explorer both supported Cascading Style Sheet layers! Now imagine the grumbling when it became apparent that each browser uses a different JavaScript syntax for calling them. You get the picture: It all boils down to differences in each browser's Document Object Model.

Calling layers

When referring to a layer, Navigator uses this syntax:

```
document.layers["layerName"]
```

while Internet Explorer uses this:

```
document.all["layerName"]
```

The trick to internal code-switching is to assign the variations — the "layers" from Navigator and the "all" from Internet Explorer — to the same variable, depending on which browser is being used. Here's a sample function that does just that:

```
function init(){
if (navigator.appName == "Netscape") {
var layerRef="document.layers";
}else {
var layerRef="document.all";
}
}
```

In this function, if the visitor is using a Netscape browser, the variable `layerRef` is assigned the value `document.layers`; otherwise, `layerRef` is set to `document.all`.

Calling properties

If you're looking to assign or read a layer property, one variable is only half the battle. There is another difference: in the way properties are called. With Navigator, it's done like this:

```
document.layers["layerName"].top
```

while with Internet Explorer, it's as follows:

```
document.all["layerName"].style.top
```

Internet Explorer inserts another hierarchical division, called `style`, whereas Navigator doesn't use anything at all. The solution is another variable, `styleRef`, which for Internet Explorer would be set like this:

```
var styleRef="style"
```

And the Navigator `styleRef` is actually set to a *null string*, or nothing. You can combine the two variables into one initialization function, which is best called from an `onLoad` event in the `<body>` tag:

```
function init(){
if (navigator.appName == "Netscape") {
var layerRef="document.layers";
var styleRef = "";
}else {
var layerRef="document.all";
var styleRef="style";
}
}
```

Once these differences are accommodated, the variables are ready to be used in a script. To do this, you can use JavaScript's built-in `eval()` function to combine the variables and the object references. Here's an example that sets a new variable, `varLeft`, to whatever is the `left` value of a particular layer:

```
varLeft = eval(layerRef + '["myLayer"]' + styleRef + '.left');
```

Luckily, the variations between the Navigator and Internet Explorer DOM are consistent enough that a JavaScript function can assign the proper values with a minimum of effort.

Calling objects within layers

There's one other area where the two DOMs diverge. When you are attempting to address almost any entity inside a layer, Navigator uses an additional hierarchical layer to reference the object. Thus, a named image in a named layer in Navigator is referenced like this:

```
document.layers["layerName"].document.imageName
```

whereas the same object in Internet Explorer is called like this:

```
document.imageName
```

This is why the Show-Hide Layers behavior passes two arguments with the affected layers' name: one in the Navigator format and the other in the Internet Explorer syntax.

Designing Web pages for backward compatibility

The previous section describes a technique for dealing with the differences between 4.0 browsers, but how do you handle the much larger gap between third- and fourth- generation browsers? When this gap becomes a canyon, with DHTML-intensive pages on one side and incompatible browsers on the other, the ultimate answer is to use redirection to send a particular browser to an appropriate page. However, browsers can coexist in plenty of cases—with a little planning and a little help from Dreamweaver.

When designing backwardly compatible Web pages, browsers generally offer one major advantage: ignorance. If a browser doesn't recognize a tag or attribute, it just ignores it and renders the rest of the page. Because many of the newer features are built on new tags, or on tags such as <div> that previously were little-used, your Web pages can gracefully devolve from 4.0 to 3.0 behavior, without causing errors or grossly misrendering the page.

Take layers, for instance. One advantage offered by this DHTML feature is the capability to make something interactively appear and disappear. Although that's not possible in 3.0 browsers (without extensive image-swapping), it is possible to display the same material and even enable some degree of navigation. The key is proper placement of the layer code, and not the layer itself.

Browsers basically read and render the code for a Web page from top to bottom. You can, for example, make several layers appear one after another in a 3.0 browser, even if they appear to be stacked on top of one another in a 4.0 browser. All you have to do is make sure the code—not the position of the layers—appears in the document sequentially. You can see this effect in Figure 31-3, where all three layers have the same left coordinates. However, the layer symbols inserted by Dreamweaver to represent the actual code appear one after the other with a little whitespace in between. The navigational links in the upper-left have two roles: they are linked to the named anchor next to the layer's code and, through the Behavior Inspector, are set to show and hide the appropriate layers when selected (using the onClick event).

Because the code for the three layers is spaced one after the other, browsers that do not understand the style attribute in the <div> tags—which create the layers—simply render the information contained within all three tags, one after another.

The Dreamweaver Technique in the upcoming section is based on methods used by George Olsen, Design Director of 2-Lane Media (www.21m.com), and an article by Trevor Lohrbeer in the Dynamic HTML Zone (www.dhtmlzone.com).

Tip   It's even possible to animate your layers for the benefit of Dynamic HTML-enabled browsers and at the same time enable 3.0 browsers to just show the static images. The key is to make sure that your animations begin and end in the same locations.

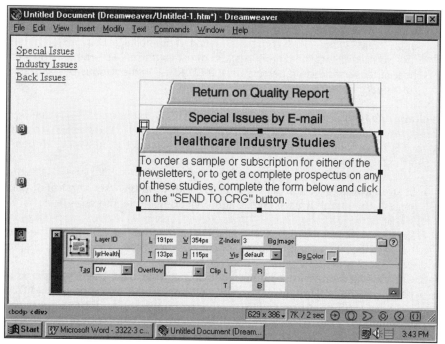

Figure 31-3: Careful placement of the code for layers can be an effective tool for backward compatibility.

Dreamweaver Technique: browser checking

Because of the major differences between third- and fourth-generation browsers, it is an increasingly popular practice to create a Web page geared to each browser and then use a *gateway* script to direct users to the proper page. A gateway script uses JavaScript to determine a visitor's browser version and route the page accordingly. Dreamweaver includes the Check Browser behavior (see Chapter 17, "Using Behaviors"), which makes this process relatively effortless.

For maximum efficiency, the best strategy is to use three pages: one page for 4.0 browsers, one page for 3.0 browsers, and a blank page that serves as your home page. Then, the Check Browser action can be assigned to the onLoad event of the blank page and can execute immediately. The other alternative is to use only two pages, one for each browser, and then run the Check Browser routine after the page is loaded and send the users of one browser version off to the other page. The disadvantage to this approach is that a good portion of your visitors have to sit through the loading process of one page, only to be whisked off to another to start again.

On the CD-ROM

Other variations besides those encountered in different browser versions may cause you to redirect a visitor to a different Web page. Screen resolution, color depth, MIME types — each come in a myriad of possibilities. Using different behaviors, you can detect the differences and direct your users accordingly. You'll find a host of these redirection helpers on the CD-ROM, in the various Behavior folders under each author's name.

The following technique takes you through the conversion of a layers-based page to a 3.0-compatible page; the creation of a new gateway page; and the incorporation of a Check Browser action that automatically directs users to a new page depending on their browser type:

1. In Dreamweaver, construct the fourth-generation browser version of your Web page — the one that uses layers and Cascading Style Sheets — first.

Note

Be sure no layers overlap and that the Web page otherwise meets the criteria noted in the "Preparing your page for conversion" section earlier in this chapter.

2. Choose File ➪ Convert ➪ 3.0 Browser Compatible. Save the new version of the page, created by Dreamweaver, with a name similar to the original (4.0) page, but with a different prefix or suffix. For example, you might call the page intended for 4.0 **browsers index40.html** and the 3.0 version **index30.html**.

3. Choose File ➪ New to create a new page. This page will serve as the gateway for the other two pages.

4. By default, Dreamweaver makes new pages with a white background. To make the gateway page as unobtrusive as possible, it's best to remove any background color options. To do this, choose Modify ➪ Page Properties. In the Page Properties dialog box, select the #FFFFFF value in the Background Color text box and press Delete. Click OK, and the Web page is seen without any background color selected.

5. In your blank gateway page, choose Window ➪ Behaviors to open the Behavior Inspector.

6. From the Tag Selector in the status bar of the Document Window, select the <body> tag.

7. In the Behavior Inspector, select the + (Add Behavior) button and choose the Check Browser action from the pop-up menu.

8. In the Check Browser parameter form:

   • Enter the URL for your 4.0 browser page in the URL text box or select the Browse (Choose) button to locate the file.

   • Enter the URL for your 3.0 browser page in the Alt URL text box or select the Browse (Choose) button to locate the file.

Click OK when you are done. If you haven't changed any of the other Check Browser default settings, both 4.0 browsers will go to the address in the URL text box, and all other browser versions will be directed to the address in the Alt URL text box (see Figure 31-4).

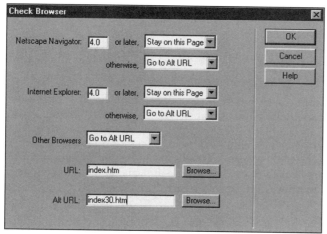

Figure 31-4: The Check Browser Behavior can build a gateway script for you with no coding.

9. Save your gateway page. If this page is to serve as the gateway for the home page(s) for your domain, save it as **index.html** or whatever name your server uses for default documents.

10. The gateway can now be preliminarily tested. However, because any Web page can be an entry point to a site, you also have to use the Check Browser action on each of the version-specific pages. Reopen the 4.0 browser page.

11. If necessary, open the Behavior Inspector by choosing Window ⇨ Behaviors or selecting the Show Behaviors button from the Launcher.

12. Repeat Steps 6–7 to get to the Check Browser parameter form.

13. This time, enter the URL for your 3.0 browser page in the Alt URL text box or select the Browse (Choose) button to locate the file.

14. In the sections for both Netscape and Internet Explorer 4.0 (or later), choose the Stay on this Page option from the drop-down list.

15. Select OK when you are finished and save the file.

16. Open the 3.0 browser page. Repeat Steps 12–15, but when you get to the Check Browser parameter form, enter the URL for the 4.0 browser page in the Alt URL text box.

Now visitors can come in through the front door of your home page, or through any side door, and be served the correct page. Generally, not all the pages in your site will use the high-end features available to the 4.0 browsers, so you only have to create gateways for those pages that do. If you plan your site with this strategy in mind — and avoid putting a moving layer on every page as a logo, for instance — you can manage your site more effectively.

Testing Your Page with a Targeted Browser

Testing is an absolute must when building a Web site. It's critical that you view your pages on as many browsers and systems as possible. Variations in color, gamma, page offset, and capabilities must be observed before they can be adjusted.

There is also a more basic, preliminary type of testing that can be done right from within Dreamweaver: code testing. Browsers usually ignore tags and attributes they do not understand. However, sometimes these tags can produce unexpected and undesirable results, such as exposing code to the viewer.

Dreamweaver's browser *targeting* feature, File ➪ Check Target Browsers, enables you to check a Web page — or an entire Web site — against any number of browser profiles. Currently, Dreamweaver comes with profiles for the following browsers:

Internet Explorer 2.0   Navigator 2.0

Internet Explorer 3.0   Navigator 3.0

Internet Explorer 4.0   Navigator 4.0

You can choose to check your page or site against a single browser profile, all of them, or anything in-between. Though not a substitute for real-world testing, browser targeting gives you an overview of potential errors and problematical code to look out for.

Testing browser compatibility for a Web page

To check a single Web page against specific browser targets, follow these steps:

Caution   With browser targeting, Dreamweaver checks the saved version of a Web page. So if you've made any modifications to your current page, save it *before* beginning the following process.

1. Choose File ➪ Check Target Browsers.

   The Check Target Browsers dialog box opens as shown in Figure 31-5.

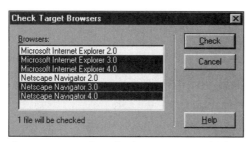

Figure 31-5: Select the browsers on which you'd like to check the code of your current page.

2. Select the browsers against which you want the current page to be checked. The usual selection techniques work in this list: To choose various browsers, press Ctrl (Command) while selecting. To specify a contiguous range of browsers, select the first one, press Shift, and then select the last one.

3. After you've chosen the target browsers, click the Check button. Dreamweaver opens your primary browser, if necessary, and outputs the report to the browser window (see Figure 31-6).

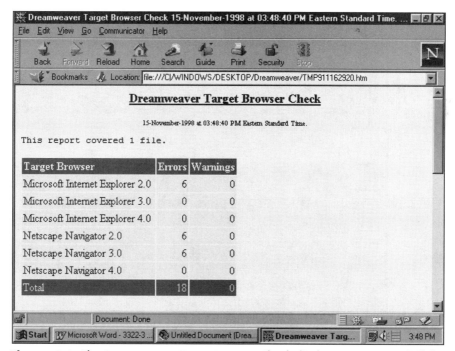

Figure 31-6: The Dreamweaver Target Browser Check displays a summary of all the errors it finds in your selected page. It's a good idea to print out the report or save it in a file.

4. Dreamweaver only stores the Target Browser Check temporarily and deletes the file after its use. To keep a record of the report, use your browser's File ⇨ Print or File ⇨ Save command.

The Dreamweaver Target Browser Check offers both a summary and a detail section. The summary, previously shown in Figure 31-6, lists the browser being tested and any errors or warnings. Totals for each category are listed beneath the columns.

The detail section of the browser check report, shown in Figure 31-7, lists the following:

✦ Each offending tag or attribute

✦ The browsers that do not support the tag or attribute

✦ An example HTML line

✦ Additional line numbers where the error occurred

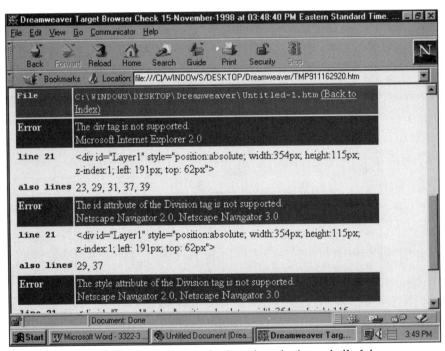

Figure 31-7: Detailed information can be found on the lower half of the Dreamweaver Target Browser Check report.

Testing browser compatibility for an entire site

With Dreamweaver, you can check browser compatibility for an entire Web site as easily as you can check a single page. Dreamweaver checks all the HTML files in a given folder, whether they are actually used in the site or not.

To check an entire site against specific browser targets, follow these steps:

1. Choose Window ⇨ Site Files (Site ⇨ Site Files View) or select the Show Site FTP button from the Launcher. The Site Window opens.

2. In the Site Window, select a folder from the Local Directory pane, or choose one of the listed sites from the Remote Site drop-down list.

3. Choose File ⇨ Check Target Browsers from the Site Window menu. The Check Target Browsers dialog box opens, shown earlier in Figure 31-5. Below the list of Browsers is a statement of how many pages are to be checked.

4. Select the browsers against which you want the current site checked.

5. When you're ready, select the Check button. Dreamweaver opens your primary browser, if necessary, and outputs the report to the browser window.

6. Dreamweaver only stores the Target Browser Check file temporarily and deletes the file after its use. To keep a record of the report, use your browser's File ⇨ Print or File ⇨ Save command.

When you're checking more than one page, the summary section of the Dreamweaver Target Browser Check gives you a list of the files containing errors as well as an error count. The summary section displays the errors for each file grouped together.

Using the results of the browser check

How you handle the flagged errors in Dreamweaver's Target Browser Check report is entirely dependent on the design goals you have established for your site. If your mission is to be totally accessible to every browser on the market, then you need to look at your page/site with the earliest browsers and pay special attention to those areas of possible trouble noted by the report. On the other hand, if your standards are a little more relaxed, then you can probably ignore the 2.0 browser warnings and concentrate on those appearing in the 3.0 and 4.0 categories.

Customizing a Browser Profile

In order for Dreamweaver's browser targeting feature to be effective, you must have access to profiles for all the browsers you need to check. You can create custom browser profiles to cover any new browser versions or browsers as they become available. The Browser Profile file is a text file and can be created or altered in any text editor.

This section examines the required structure and format for a Browser Profile file, and the steps for building one based on an existing file.

Understanding the browser profile structure

In order for Dreamweaver to properly process an HTML file using any browser profile, the profile must follow a precise format. Here's a sample taken from the Internet Explorer 3.0 browser profile:

```
<!ELEMENT H1 name="Heading 1" >
<!ATTLIST H1
        Align ( left | center | right )
        Class
        ID
        Style
>
```

As you can see, the HTML tag is listed in a very specific syntax. Here's how the syntax is formed:

```
<!ELEMENT htmlTag Name="tagName" >
<!ATTLIST htmlTag
unsupportedAttribute1 !Error !msg="The unsupportedAttribute1 of
the htmlTag is not supported. Try using thisAttribute for a
similar effect."
supportedAttribute1
supportedAttribute2    ( validValue1 | validValue2 | validValue3
)
unsupportedAttribute2 !Error !htmlmsg="<b>Don't ever use this
unsupportedAttribute2 of the  htmlTag !!</b>"
>
```

The variables in the syntax are as follows:

✦ htmlTag. The tag as it appears in an HTML document.

✦ tagName. Optional; how the tag is known. For example, the <applet> tag is called the "Java Applet." If it's noted in the file, the tagName is used in the error message; otherwise, htmlTag is used.

✦ unsupportedAttribute. Indicates invalid attributes so that a custom error message can be offered. Otherwise, all attributes not specifically listed are assumed to be unsupported.

✦ supportedAttribute. A valid attribute; all valid attributes must be listed. Only attributes listed without an !Error designation are supported.

✦ validValue. A value supported by the attribute.

Several other, not-so-obvious rules must be followed for Dreamweaver to correctly read the profile:

✦ The name of the profile must appear in the first line of the file, followed by a single carriage return. This is the profile name that appears in the Check Target Browser(s) dialog box and in the report.

✦ The key phrase PROFILE_TYPE=BROWSER_PROFILE must appear in the second line.

✦ On the !ELEMENT line, a single space must be used before the closing angle (>) bracket, after the opening parentheses, before the closing parentheses, and before and after each pipe (|) character in the list of values.

✦ There must be an exclamation point, without an intervening space, before the words ELEMENT, ATTLIST, Error, msg, and htmlmsg. For example:

!ELEMENT, !ATTLIST, !Error, !msg, and !htmlmsg.

✦ You can only use plain text in !msg messages, but a !htmlmsg message can use any valid HTML, including links.

✦ Don't use HTML comment tags, <!-- -->, because they interfere with the regular Dreamweaver processing of the file.

Creating a browser profile

As you can see, Dreamweaver browser profiles have a very specific structure. Consequently, it's far easier to modify an existing profile than to write one from scratch. The basic procedure takes three steps:

1. Choose an existing profile for a browser similar to the one for which you are creating a new profile. Open the profile in a text editor.

You'll find numerous custom browser profiles on the accompanying CD-ROM. You can copy them directly to your BrowserProfiles folder found in the Configuration folder or use them as models for modification.

2. Add any tags and attributes that are supported in the target browser but not in the existing profile.

3. Remove any tags or attributes not supported by your target browser. Or, you can add an !Error message after any attribute to flag it for Dreamweaver's Target Browser Check operation.

For example, take a look at the code fragment illustrated in Listing 31-1; it contains a portion of the browser profile I created for WebTV. Note the custom error messages after the <applet> tag and the rel attribute of the <a> tag.

When saving a new browser profile in Windows, there's a small trick to getting the version number to appear correctly at the end of the browser name, as in "Navigator 3.0." Choose File ➪ Save As from your text editor. Then, in the Filename text box enter your browser name with the filename extension (.txt), all enclosed in quotes. For example, to save the Web TV 1.0 file, I entered **WebTV_1.0.txt** in the Filename text box.

Listing 31-1: **Excerpt from Browser Profile file for WebTV**

```
WebTV 1.0
PROFILE_TYPE=BROWSER_PROFILE
-- Copyright 1997 Macromedia, Inc. All rights reserved.

<!ELEMENT A Name="Hyperlink Anchor" >
<!ATTLIST A
        Class           !Error
        HREF
        ID
        Name
        OnClick
        OnMouseOut
        OnMouseOver
        Rel             !Warning !msg "The rel attribute has
been modified by WebTV."
        Style           !Error
        Selected        !Error
        Target          !Error
>

<!ELEMENT Address >
<!ATTLIST Address
        Class           !Error
        ID              !Error
        Style           !Error
>

<!ELEMENT APPLET Name="Java Applet" > !Error !msg "WebTV does
not support Java Applets."
<!ATTLIST APPLET
        Align ( top | middle | bottom | left | right |
absmiddle | absbottom | baseline | texttop )
        Alt
        Archive         !Error
        Code
        Codebase
        Height
        HSpace
        Name
        VSpace
        Width
        Class
        ID
        Style
>
```

```
<!ELEMENT AREA Name="Client-side image map area" >
<!ATTLIST AREA
        Alt             !Error
        Class           !Error
        Coords
        HREF
        ID
        Name
        NoHREF
        NoTab
        OnMouseOut
        OnMouseOver
        Shape
        Style           !Error
        Target
>

<!ELEMENT AUDIOSCOPE Name="Audioscope" >
<!ATTLIST AUDIOSCOPE
        Align
        Border
        Gain
        Height
        LeftColor
        LeftOffset
        MaxLevel
        RightColor
        RightOffset
        Width
>

<!ELEMENT B Name="Bold" >
<!ATTLIST B
        Class           !Error
        ID              !Error
        Style           !Error
>

<!ELEMENT Base >
<!ATTLIST Base
        HREF
        Target
>

<!ELEMENT BaseFont >
<!ATTLIST BaseFont
        Size
>
```

Continued

Listing 31-1: *(continued)*

```
<!ELEMENT BGSOUND Name="Background sound" >
<!ATTLIST BGSOUND
        Loop
        Src
>

<!ELEMENT Big >
<!ATTLIST Big
        Class
        ID
        Style
>

<!ELEMENT Blackface >

<!ELEMENT Blink !Error >

<!ELEMENT Blockquote >

<!ELEMENT Body >
<!ATTLIST Body
        ALink                   !Error
        Background
        BGColor
        BGProperties
        Credits
        LeftMargin
        Link
        Logo
        OnBlur                  !Error
        OnFocus                 !Error
        OnLoad
        OnUnload
        Style                   !Error
        Text
        VLink
>

<!ELEMENT BQ Name="Block Quote" >

<!ELEMENT BR Name="Line break" >
<!ATTLIST BR
        Clear ( left | right | all )
>
```

Summary

Unless you're building a Web site for a strictly controlled intranet, in which case you know everyone is using the BrandX 4.03 browser, it's critical that you address the browser compatibility issues that your Web site is certain to face. Whether it's cross-browser or backward compatibility you're trying to achieve, Dreamweaver has features and techniques in place to help you get your Web pages viewed by the maximum number of users.

✦ Dreamweaver takes a Web page built with 4.0 features, including layers and CSS, and creates another Web page that is 3.0-compatible.

✦ Dreamweaver can take a Web page created with tables and create another Web page that uses layers instead. New tools in Dreamweaver 2, such as Reposition Content Using Layers, make it quick and straightforward.

✦ You can use JavaScript within a Web page to handle cross-browser compatibility problems with 4.0 browsers.

✦ Careful placement of your HTML objects can help with backward compatibility.

✦ Dreamweaver lets you check your Web page or Web site against a browser profile to look for tags and attributes that will not work in a particular browser version.

✦ Browser profiles can be customized or copied and modified for a new browser or browser version.

In the next chapter, you learn how to use Dreamweaver's Library feature to reuse repeating elements.

✦　　✦　　✦

Using the Repeating Elements Library

One of the challenges of designing a Web site is ensuring that buttons, copyright notices, and other cross-site features always remain consistent. Fortunately, Dreamweaver offers a useful feature called *Library items* that helps you insert repeating elements, such as a navigation bar or a company logo, into every Web page you create. With one command, you can update and maintain Library items efficiently and productively.

In this chapter you examine the nature and the importance of repeating elements, and learn how to effectively use the Dreamweaver Library feature for all of your sites.

Dreamweaver Libraries

Library items within Dreamweaver are another means for you, as a designer, to maintain consistency throughout your site. Suppose you have a navigation bar on every page that contains links to all of your site's other pages. It's highly likely that you'll eventually (and probably more than once) need to make changes to the navigation bar. In a traditional Web development environment, you must modify every single page. This creates lots of opportunities for making mistakes, missing pages, and adding code to the wrong place. Moreover, the whole process is tedious — ask anyone who has had to modify the copyright notice at the bottom of every Web page for a site with over 200 pages.

Another traditional method of updating repeating elements is using *server-side includes*. A server-side include causes the server to place a component, such as a copyright notice, in a specified area of a Web page when it's sent to the user. This arrangement, however, increases the strain on your already overworked Web server. Not to mention you have to know how to install server-side scripts. To add to the designer's frustrations, you can't lay out a Web page in a WYSIWYG format and simultaneously see the server-side scripts. So you either take the time to calculate that a server-side script will take up a specific space on the Web page, or you cross your fingers and guess.

There is a better way in Dreamweaver, using an important innovation called the Library. The Library is designed to make repetitive updating quick, easy, and as error-free as possible. The Library's key features include the following:

✦ Any item — whether text or graphic — that goes into the body of your Web page can be designated as a Library item.

✦ Once created, Library items can be placed instantly in any Web page in your site, without your having to retype, reinsert, or reformat text and graphics.

✦ Library items can be altered at any time. After the editing is complete, Dreamweaver gives you the option to update the Web site immediately or postpone the update until later.

✦ If you are making a number of alterations to your Library items, you can wait until you're finished with all the updates and then make the changes across the board in one operation.

✦ You can update one page at a time, or you can update the entire site all at once.

✦ A Library item can be converted back to a regular non-Library element of a Web page at any time.

✦ Library items can be copied from one site to another.

Using the Library Palette

Dreamweaver's Library control center is, of course, the Library Palette. There you find the tools for creating, modifying, updating, and managing your Library items. Shown in Figure 32-1, the Library Palette is as flexible and easy to use as all of Dreamweaver's primary palettes, with straightforward command buttons, an alphabetical listing of all available Library items, and a handy Preview pane.

As usual, you can open the Library Palette in several ways:

✦ Choose Window ➪ Library.

✦ Select the Library button from the Launcher.

✦ Press F6.

Inserted Library item   Library item list

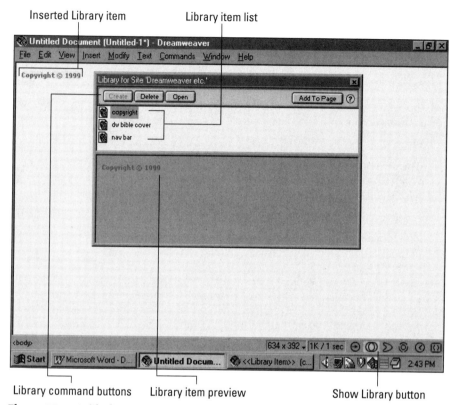

Library command buttons   Library item preview   Show Library button

Figure 32-1: With the Dreamweaver Library Palette, you can easily add and modify consistent objects to an entire Web site.

Caution   To use Library items, you must first create a site root folder for Dreamweaver, as explained in Chapter 5, "Setting Up Your First Site." A separate Library folder is created to hold the individual Library items and is used by Dreamweaver during the updating process.

Ideally, you could save the most time by creating all your Library items before you begin constructing your Web pages, but most Web designers don't work that way. Feel free to include, modify, and update your Library items as much as you need to as your Web site evolves — that's part of the power and flexibility you gain because of Dreamweaver's Library.

Adding a Library item

Before you can insert or update a Library item, that item must be designated as such within the Web page. To add an item to your site's Library, follow these steps:

1. Select any part of the Web page that you want to make into a Library item.

2. Open the Library Palette with any of the available methods: the Window ➪ Library command, the Library button in the Launcher, or F6.

3. From the Library Palette (see Figure 32-1), select the Create button.

   The selected page element is displayed in the lower pane of the Library Palette. In the upper pane — the Library item list — a new entry is highlighted with the default name "Untitled."

4. Enter a unique name for your new Library item, and press Enter (Return).

   The Library item list is resorted alphabetically, if necessary, and the new item is included.

When a portion of your Web page has been designated as a Library item, you'll notice a yellow highlight over the entire item within the Document Window. The highlight helps you to quickly recognize what is a Library item and what is not. If you find the yellow highlight distracting, you can disable it. Go to Edit ➪ Preferences and, from the Highlighting panel of the Preferences dialog box, deselect Show check box for Library Items. Alternately, deselecting View ➪ Invisibles will hide Library Item highlighting, along with any other invisible items on your page.

Caution   At this writing, Dreamweaver can include Library items only in the ⟨body⟩ section of an HTML document. You cannot, for instance, create a series of ⟨meta⟩ tags for your pages that must go in the ⟨head⟩ section.

Drag-and-Drop Creation of Library Items

A second option for creating Library items is the drag-and-drop method. Simply select an object or several objects on a page and drag them to the Library item list of the Library Palette; release the mouse button to drop them in.

You can drag any object into the Library Palette: text, tables, images, Java applets, plug-ins, and/or ActiveX controls. Essentially anything in the Document Window that can be HTML code can be dragged to the Library. And, as you might suspect, the reverse is true: library items can be placed in your Web page by dragging them from the Library Palette list and dropping them anywhere in the Document Window.

Moving Library items to a new site

Although Library items are specific to each site, they can be used in more than one site. When you make your first Library item, Dreamweaver creates a folder called Library in the local root folder for the current site. To use a particular Library item in another site, simply open the Library folder from your system's desktop and copy the item to the new site's Library folder.

Caution Be sure to also move any dependent files or other assets such as images and media files associated with the Library items.

Inserting a Library item in your Web page

When you create a Web site, you always need to incorporate certain features, including a standard set of link buttons along the top, a consistent banner on various pages, and a copyright notice along the bottom. Adding these items to a page with the Library Palette can be as easy as dragging and dropping them.

You must first create a Web site and then designate Library items (as explained in the preceding section). Once these items exist, you can add the items to any page created within your site.

To add Library items to a document, use the following steps:

1. Position the cursor where you want the Library item to appear.

2. From the Library Palette, select the item you wish to use.

3. Select the Add to Page button. The Library item appears on the Web page, highlighted in yellow.

Tip As noted earlier, you can also use the drag-and-drop method to place Library items in the Document Window.

When you add a Library item to a page, you notice a number of immediate changes. As mentioned, the added Library item will be highlighted in light yellow. If you click anywhere on the item, the entire Library item will be selected.

It's important to understand that Dreamweaver treats the entire Library item entry as an external object being linked to the current page. You cannot modify Library items directly on a page. For information on editing Library entries, see "Editing a Library Item" later in this chapter.

While the Library item is highlighted, you will also notice that the Property Inspector changes. Instead of displaying the properties for the HTML object that is selected, the item is identified as a Library item, as shown in Figure 32-2.

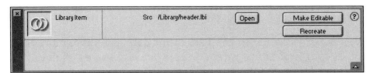

Figure 32-2: The Library item Property Inspector identifies the source file for any selected Library entry.

You can also see evidence of Library items in the HTML for the current page. Open the HTML Inspector, and you see that several lines of code have been added. The following code example indicates one Library item:

```
<!-- #BeginLibraryItem "/Library/title.lbi" -->
<font color="#FF6633" face="Verdana, Arial, Helvetica, sans-
serif" size="-4">
<b>Copyright &copy; 1999</b></font>
<!-- #EndLibraryItem -->
```

In this case, the Library item happens to be a phrase: "Copyright © 1999." (The character entity © is used to represent the c-in-a-circle copyright mark in HTML.) In addition to the code that specifies the font face, color, and size, notice the text before and after the HTML code. These are commands within the comments that tell Dreamweaver it is looking at a Library item. One line marks the beginning of the Library item:

```
<!--#BeginLibraryItem "/Library/title.lbi" -->
```

and another marks the end:

```
<!--#EndLibraryItem -->
```

Two items are of interest here. First, notice how the Library demarcation surrounds not just the text ("Copyright © 1999"), but all of its formatting attributes. Library items can do far more than just cut-and-paste raw text. The second thing to note is that the Library markers are placed discreetly within HTML comments. Web browsers ignore the Library markers and render the code in between them.

The value in the opening Library code, "/Library/title.lbi", is the source file for the Library entry. This file would be located in the Library folder, inside of the current site root folder. Library source (.lbi) files can be opened with a text editor or Dreamweaver; they consist of plain HTML code without the <html> and <body> tags.

The .lbi file for our title example would contain the following:

```
<font color="#FF6633" face="Verdana, Arial, Helvetica, sans-
serif" size="-4">
<b>Copyright &copy; 1999</b></font>
```

The power of repeating elements is that they are simply HTML. There is no need to learn proprietary languages to customize Library items. Anything, except for information found in the header of a Web page, can be included in a library file.

The importance of the `<!-- #BeginLibraryItem>` and `<!-- #EndLibraryItem>` tags becomes evident when you start to update Library items to a site. You examine how Dreamweaver can be used to automatically update your entire Web site in the later section "Updating your Web site with Libraries."

Deleting an item from the Library

Removing an entry from your site's Library is a two-step process. First, you must delete the item from the Library Palette. Then, if you want to keep the item on your page, you must make it editable again. Without completing the second step, Dreamweaver maintains the Library highlight and, more important, prevents you from modifying the element.

To delete an item from the Library, follow these steps:

1. Open the Web page containing the Library item you want to delete.

2. Open the Library Palette by choosing Window ⇨ Library or selecting the Library button from the Launcher.

3. Select the Library item in the Library Palette's list and click the Delete button.

4. Dreamweaver asks if you are sure you want to delete the item. Select Yes and the entry is removed from the Library item list. (Or select No to cancel.)

5. In the Document Window, select the element you are removing from the Library.

6. In the Property Inspector, click the Make Editable button.

7. As shown in Figure 32-3, Dreamweaver warns you that if you proceed, the item cannot be automatically updated (as a Library element). Select OK to proceed. The yellow Library highlighting vanishes and the element can now be modified individually.

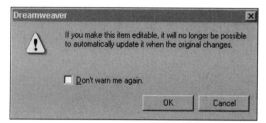

Figure 32-3: When removing an entry from the Library, Dreamweaver alerts you that, if you proceed, you won't be able to update the item automatically using the Library function.

Note Should you unintentionally delete a Library item in the Library Palette, you can restore it if you still have the entry included in a Web page. Select the element within the page and, in the Property Inspector, choose the Recreate [sic] button. Dreamweaver restores the item to the Library item list, with the original Library name.

Renaming a Library item

It's easy to rename a Library item, but you should exercise caution when doing so. Renaming a Library item only renames that item in the Library folder — it does not rename the item in any Web page where the item has already been inserted. Should you attempt to modify and update the renamed item, occurrences of the same item under the old name in existing pages will not be updated.

To give an existing Library entry a new name, open the Library Palette and click once on the name of the item. The name is highlighted and a small box appears around it. Enter the new name and press Enter (Return).

The best strategy to follow when renaming a Library item is to rename it before you insert the entry into any Web pages. If, however, you want to rename the item after it has been included in one or more Web pages, there are two approaches to the renaming task:

✦ If the renamed item is included in only a few Web pages, open every Web page containing the Library item that you've renamed. Delete the original entry from the Web page, and insert the renamed item.

✦ If the renamed item has been included on a number of pages in your Web site, use Dreamweaver's extended Find and Replace feature to change the item's name within the HTML code.

Let's look at an example of the second option. Suppose you've included a Library entry, originally called LibraryItem01, on six or seven Web pages within a site. Later you decide to change the name to something more descriptive, like CopyrightLine. After you've renamed the item in the Library, so all future uses of the entry will be correct, you need to correct the previously inserted entries. Because you have numerous entries to fix, you decide to use Dreamweaver's Replace command to change the name within the HTML. In your external editor, you would search for

```
<!-- #BeginLibraryItem "/Library/LibraryItem01.lbi" -->
```

and replace it with

```
<!-- #BeginLibraryItem "/Library/CopyrightLine.lbi" -->
```

Cross-Reference Dreamweaver 2 has added extremely powerful find-and-replace features that enable you to quickly change all the entries in all the pages of a Web site. You can find the details in Chapter 7, "Adding Text to Your Web Page."

Editing a Library Item

Rarely will you create a Library item that is perfect from the beginning and never needs to be changed. Whether it is due to site redesign or the addition of new sections to a site, you'll find yourself going back to Library items and modifying them, sometimes over and over again. You can use the full power of the Dreamweaver's design capabilities to alter your Library items, within the restraints of Library items in general. In other words, you can modify an image, reformat a body of text, add new material to a boilerplate paragraph, and have the resulting changes reflected across your Web site. However, you cannot add anything to a Library item that is not contained in the HTML <body> tags.

To modify Library items, Dreamweaver uses a special editing window that is identifiable by its neutral background. You access this editing window through the Library Palette. Follow these steps to modify an existing Library item:

1. In the Library Palette, select the item you wish to modify from the list of available entries.

2. Click the Open button. The Library editing window opens with the selected entry, as shown in Figure 32-4.

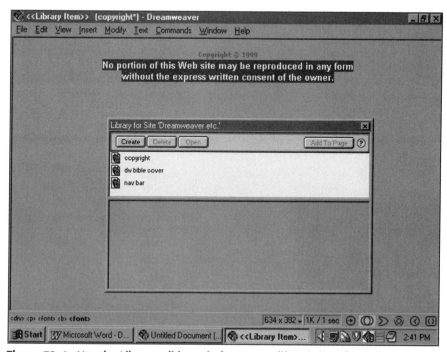

Figure 32-4: Use the Library editing window to modify existing Library items.

3. Make any necessary modifications to the Library entry.

4. When you are finished with your changes, choose File ➪ Save or press Ctrl-S (Command-S).

5. Dreamweaver notes that your Library item has been modified and asks if you would like to update all of the Web pages in your site that contain the item. Select Yes to update all of the Library items, including the one just modified, or select No to postpone the update. (See the next section, "Updating Your Web Site with Libraries.")

6. Close the editing window by selecting the Close button or choosing File ➪ Close.

Once you've completed the editing operation and closed the editing window, you can open any Web page containing the modified Library item to view the changes.

Caution You will not be able to use some features when editing Library items. These include timelines, behaviors, and styles. Each of these modifications requires a JavaScript function to be placed in the <head> tags of a page—a task that the Dreamweaver Library function cannot currently handle. As a workaround, you can use a Dreamweaver template to add entire pages with JavaScript functions included, as described in Chapter 34, "Using Dreamweaver Templates."

Updating Your Web Sites with Libraries

The effectiveness of the Dreamweaver Library feature becomes more significant when it comes time to update an entire multipage site. Dreamweaver offers two opportunities for you to update your site:

✦ Immediately after modifying a Library item, as explained in the preceding steps for editing a Library item

✦ At a time of your choosing, through the Modify ➪ Library command

An immediate update to every page on your site can be accomplished when you edit a Library item. After you save the alterations, Dreamweaver asks if you'd like to apply the update to Web pages in your site. If you click Yes, Dreamweaver not only applies the current modification to all pages in the site, but it also applies any other alterations that you have made previously in this Library.

The second way to modify a Library item is by using the Modify ➪ Library command, and when you use this method you can choose to update the current page or the entire site.

To update just the current page, choose Modify ➪ Library ➪ Update Current Page. Dreamweaver makes a quick check to see what Library items you are managing on the current page and then compares them to the site's Library items. If there are any differences, Dreamweaver modifies the page accordingly.

To update an entire Web site, follow these steps:

1. Choose Modify ➪ Library ➪ Update Pages. The Update Pages dialog box opens (see Figure 32-5).

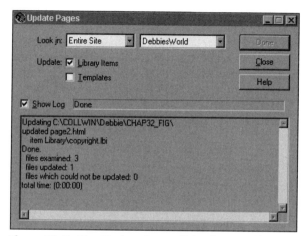

Figure 32-5: The Update Pages dialog box enables you to apply any changes to your Library items across an entire site, and informs you of the progress.

2. If you want Dreamweaver to update all of the Library items in all of the Web pages in your site, select Entire Site from the Look In drop-down list, and choose the name of your site in the drop-down list on the right. You can have Dreamweaver update only the pages in your site that contain a specific Library item by selecting the Files That Use option from the Look In drop-down list, and then select the Library item that you would like to have updated across your site from the drop-down list on the right.

3. If you want to see the results from the update process, leave the Show Log check-box selected. (Turning off the Log reduces the size of the Site Update dialog box.)

4. Choose the Start button. Dreamweaver processes the entire site for Library updates. Any Library items contained will be modified to reflect the changes.

Note
Although Dreamweaver does modify Library items on currently open pages during an Update Site operation, you will have to save the pages to accept the changes.

The Update Pages log displays any errors encountered in the update operation. A log containing the notation

```
item Library\Untitled2.lbi -- not updated, library item not
found
```

indicates that one Web page contains a reference to a Library item that has been removed. Though this is not a critical error, you might want to use Dreamweaver's Find and Replace feature to search your Web site for the code and remove it.

Applying Server-Side Includes

In some ways, the server-side include (SSI) is the predecessor of the Dreamweaver Library item. The difference is that with Library items, Dreamweaver updates the Web pages at design time, whereas with server-side includes, the server handles the updating at run time (when the files are actually served to the user). Server-side includes can also include server variables, such as the current date and time (both locally and Greenwich Mean Time) or the date the current file was last saved.

Because server-side includes are integrated in the standard HTML code, a special file extension is used to identify pages using them. Any page with server-side includes must be saved with either the .shtml or .shtm extension. When a server encounters such a file, the file is read and processed by the server.

Caution   Not all servers support server-side includes. Some Web hosting companies disable the function because of potential security risks and performance issues. Each .shtml page requires additional processing time and if a site uses many SSI pages, the server can slow down significantly. Be sure to check with your Web host as to their policy before including SSIs in your Web pages.

Server-side includes are often used to insert header or footer items into the `<body>` of an HTML page. Typically, the server-side include itself is just a file with HTML. To insert a file, the SSI code would look like the following:

```
<!-- #include file="footer.html" -->
```

Note how the HTML comment structure is used to wrap around the SSI directive. This ensures that browsers will ignore the code, but servers will not. The `file` attribute defines the path name of the file to be included, relative to the current page. To include a file relative to the current site root, use the `virtual` attribute, as follows:

```
<!-- #include virtual="/main/images/spaceman.jpg" -->
```

As evident in this example, you can use SSIs to include more than just HTML files — you can also include graphics.

New Feature   Prior to Dreamweaver 2, the only way to view your SSIs within the Web page was to upload them to a server and access the file. Now, with Dreamweaver 2's new translator mechanism, server-side includes can be visible in the Document Window during the design process. All you need to do is make sure that the Translation preferences are set correctly, as described in the "Modifying translators" section later in this chapter.

One of the major benefits of SSIs is inserting information from the server itself, such as the current file size or time. One tag, `<!-- #echo -->`, is used to define a custom variable that is returned when the SSI is called, as well as numerous *environmental variables*. An environmental variable is information available to the server, such as the date a file was last modified, or its URL.

Table 32-1 details the possible server tags and their attributes.

Table 32-1 Server-Side Include Variables		
Tag	**Attribute**	**Description**
`<!-- #config -->`	`errmsg`, `sizefmt`, or `timefmt`	Used to customize error messages, file size, or time and date displays
`<!-- #echo -->`	`var` or environmental variables such as `last_modified`, `document_name`, `document_url`, `date_local`, or `date_gmt`	Returns the specified variable
`<!-- #exec -->`	`cmd` or `cgi`	Executes a system command or CGI program
`<!-- #flastmod -->`	`file` or `virtual`	Displays the last modified date of a file other than the current one
`<!-- #fsize -->`	`file` or `virtual`	Displays the size of a file other than the current one
`<!-- #include -->`	`file` or `virtual`	Inserts the contents of the specified file to the current one

Modifying translators

When Dreamweaver 2 displays the contents of the file being called by a server-side include, it has the capability to function like a server — processing the instruction and inserting the file in your page. You can control whether this feature is turned on, or in which files such translation occurs. You can even opt to see the translation on a page-by-page basis. The translator controls are handled through the Preferences dialog box.

To change the translator options, follow these steps:

1. Choose Edit ⇨ Preferences and then select the Translation category.

   The Translation panel appears, as seen in Figure 32-6.

2. Select Server-Side Includes from the list of Translators.

   By default, Dreamweaver is set to automatically translate SSI content in all files.

3. To alter the conditions under which translation takes place, select one of the following options under the Automatically Translate heading:

   • **In All Files.** Translation occurs whenever there is a modification to the page.

   • **In No Files.** Translation must be specified manually.

   • **In Files with Extensions.** Only the files with the listed extension are automatically translated.

   • **In Files Matching One of These Expressions.** Only the files that include one or more of the listed tags are translated.

4. Click OK when you're done.

If you decide to handle all the SSI translations one page at a time by selecting the Automatically Translate Server-Side Includes In No Files option, to view a translated page, choose Modify ⇨ Translate — Server-Side Includes.

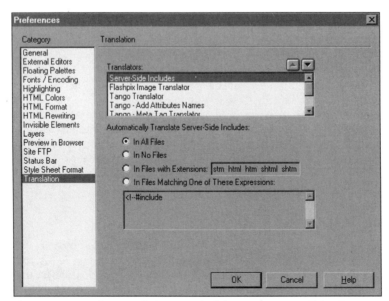

Figure 32-6: In the Translation panel of the Preferences dialog box, you can control Dreamweaver's processing of server-side includes.

Adding server-side includes

Dreamweaver 2 has made inserting a server-side include in your Web page very straightforward.

New Feature

Now, you can use a Dreamweaver object to easily select and bring in the files to be included. Any other type of SSI, such as declaring a variable, must be entered in by hand, but you can use the Comment object to do so without opening the HTML Inspector.

To use server-side includes to incorporate a file, follow these steps:

1. In the Document Window, place your cursor in the location where you would like to add the server-side include.

2. Select Insert ⇨ Server-Side Include or choose Insert Server-Side Include from the Invisibles panel of the Objects Palette.

   The standard Select File dialog box appears.

3. In the Select File dialog box, type in the URL of the HTML page you would like to include in the File Name text box, or use the Browse (Choose) button to locate the file. Click OK when you're done.

   Dreamweaver displays the contents of the HTML file at the desired location in your page, if the proper Translation option is enabled. Should the Property Inspector be available, the SSI Property Inspector is displayed (see Figure 32-7).

4. In the Property Inspector, if the server-side include calls a file relative document path, select the Type File option. Or, if the SSI calls a site root relative file, choose the Type Virtual option.

Tip

Because server-side includes can only be placed within the body of a Dreamweaver file, the contents of the HTML page that you wish to include should not have any tags that are not readable within the body section of a document, such as <head>, <title>, or <meta> — or the <body> tag itself. You can, however, design your HTML page in Dreamweaver, and then use the HTML editing panel to remove any such tags before inserting the page into your document with a server-side include.

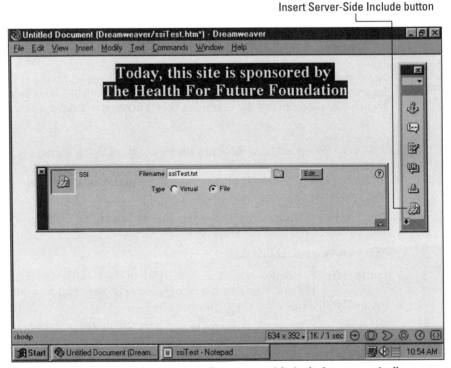

Figure 32-7: The selected text is actually a server-side include automatically translated by Dreamweaver 2, as evident from the SSI Property Inspector.

Editing server-side includes

Like Library items, it is not possible to directly edit files that have been inserted into a Web page using server-side includes. In fact, should you try, you'll notice that the entire text block highlights as one. The text for a server-side included file is not editable through Dreamweaver's HTML Inspector, although the SSI code is.

To edit the contents of the server-side included file, follow these steps:

1. Select the server-side include in the Document Window.

2. Select the Edit button from the SSI Property Inspector.

   The file opens in a new Dreamweaver window for editing.

3. When you've finished altering the file, select File ➪ Save or use the keyboard shortcut, Ctrl-S (Command-S).

4. Close the file editing window by choosing File ➪ Close.

   Dreamweaver automatically reflects the changes in your currently open document.

Unlike a Library item, Dreamweaver does not ask if any other linked files should be updated because all blending of regular HTML and SSIs happens at run time or when the file is open in Dreamweaver and the SSI translator is engaged.

Caution Currently, Dreamweaver does not properly display SSIs that insert graphic files. Instead of an image, you'll see the first part of the hexadecimal code for the file. In the case of a .gif file, `GIF89a-` is displayed and, with JPEGs, the rather cryptic ÿØÿà is shown.

Extending Dreamweaver with XSSI

Both Dreamweaver Library items and server-side includes are very useful for easily updating a range of pages by changing one item. But what if you have to change that one item several times a day—or based on which domain the user is coming from? To handle these tasks automatically, a system must support some form of conditional tags, like `If...Then` statements. Such a system is now available through Apache servers and XSSI, extended server-side includes. Most importantly, a full set of XSSI objects, translators, and Property Inspectors for Dreamweaver have been built by the wonderful programmers at Webmonkey (`www.wired.com/webmonkey`). The XSSI extensions can be found on the CD-ROM of this book.

In addition to handling standard server-side includes, the XSSI extensions offer a series of conditional statements: `if`, `elif` (else if), `else`, and `endif`. The beauty of the Webmonkey objects is that you can construct or edit these conditional statements through their graphical user interface. The basic syntax of the conditional statements is as follows:

```
<!--#if expr="text_expression" -->
If the above is true, perform this action
<!--#elif expr="text_expression" -->
Else if the above is true, do this
<!--#else -->
Otherwise, do this
<!--#endif -->
```

The XSSI extensions also have the capability of setting an environmental variable so that you can view your page under various conditions. For example, let's say you've written a script that, depending on which browser is being used, includes a particular file that greets the visitor in a proper way. Your conditional script would look to the `HTTP_USER_AGENT` variable to see which message to serve. With the XSSI Set Env Variables command, you could test out your script during the design phase without having to visit the server at different times of the day. The following figure displays the Set XSSI Environment Variables dialog box.

Continued

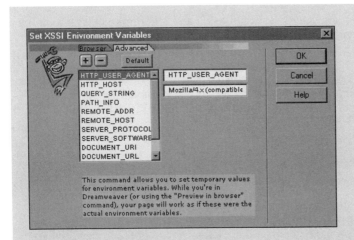

One note of caution: Due to a potential conflict between the two translators, installing the XSSI extensions disables the standard SSI translator. Make sure your system is XSSI-compatible (it uses an Apache server) before incorporating the XSSI extensions.

Summary

In this chapter, you learned how you can easily and effectively create Library items that can be repeated throughout an entire site to help maintain consistency.

✦ Library items can consist of any text, object, or HTML code contained in the `<body>` of a Web page.

✦ The quickest method to create a Library item is to drag the code from the Dreamweaver Document Window into the Library Palette's list area.

✦ Editing Library items is also very easy with the Library Palette. Just click the Edit button, and you can swiftly make all of your changes.

✦ The Modify ⇨ Library ⇨ Update the Entire Site command allows for easy maintenance of your Web site.

✦ Server-side includes enable files to be inserted into the final HTML at run time by the server. Dreamweaver 2's new translation feature enables you to preview these effects.

In the next chapter you learn how to publish your site to the Internet in Dreamweaver.

✦   ✦   ✦

Publishing Via Site FTP

Site management is an essential part of a Webmaster's job description. Far from static designs, the Web site is not like a magazine advertisement that you're done with as soon as you send the file to the printer. Publishing your Web site pages on the Internet is really just the first step in an ongoing, often day-to-day, management task.

Dreamweaver includes an integrated but separate process called Site FTP to handle all your Web management needs. With Site FTP, you can

- ✦ Transfer files to your remote site from your local development site and back again
- ✦ Issue system commands to enable CGI programs on the server
- ✦ Monitor your Web site for broken links and orphaned files
- ✦ Check a file in or out during team Web development

This chapter covers these site management functions and more. However, before you begin exploring the Site FTP features, it's helpful to know a little more about site management in Dreamweaver.

Site Management with Dreamweaver

At the simplest level, *site management* means transferring your files from the local drive to a publishing server. This is standard File Transfer Protocol (FTP), and many designers are accustomed to working with tools such as WS_FTP and Fetch. These utilities, however, only help you to move files back and forth — other issues must be addressed in a medium-to-large Web site. For instance:

✦ What happens when a large group is working on a single Web site? What prevents the graphics designer from altering the same file the JavaScript programmer is modifying?

✦ How can you tell which version of your logo is the final one among the 15 working versions in your local site root folder?

✦ Do you have to update all your files every time some change is made to a few? Or can you only update those that have changed? How can you tell which ones have changed?

To help the Dreamweaver developer cope with these issues and avoid the type of frustration they can produce, a useful site-management tool is included within Dreamweaver: Site FTP. Its key features include the following:

✦ A quick, visual view of the elements of your site, on your local and remote directories

✦ Fast drag-and-drop functionality for transferring files with dependent file support

✦ Site management check-in and check-out tools for groups working on files within the same Web site

✦ A Link Checker that helps you identify broken or unused objects being posted to your site

✦ A newly added Site Map that enables you to both visualize your Web site structure and alter it

On Windows systems, Site FTP runs as a connected but independent process, so that you can close your Document Window when you're finished designing and then publish your files to the Web through the Site FTP window.

Note   The Dreamweaver commands related to the Site Window features are in different places on the Windows and Macintosh systems. In Windows, the Site Window has it's own menu bar; all the Windows-oriented references in this chapter refer to this menu. Because Macintosh systems don't have a separate menu for a program's individual windows, Dreamweaver organizes the Site functions in a Site category of the main menu strip.

Setting Up a New Site

The first step in developing an effective site — one that links to other Web pages, uses images and library files, and offers other site-root-relative links — is, of course, to first establish a site. Dreamweaver has made this very easy to do.

For complete, detailed information on establishing your initial site, see Chapter 5, "Setting Up Your First Site."

You'll need to create a folder on your development system that contains all the HTML, as well as graphics, media, and other files, needed by the site. To create a new site, choose File ▷ New Site (Windows) or Site ▷ New Site (Macintosh). The Site Definition dialog box opens with the Local Info panel selected, as shown in Figure 33-1. Here you'll find the information and settings for the current site you are developing. Once you've entered this information, you'll seldom need to modify it.

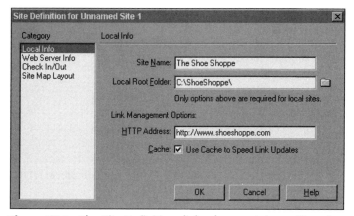

Figure 33-1: The Site Definition dialog box contains settings for the current site you are developing.

The data in the Site Definition dialog box is divided into four categories: Local Info, Web Server Info, Check In/Out, and Site Map Layout.

Local directory information

The local directory is in a folder on your development system, either on your own hard drive or on a network server.

Site Name

This is the name that appears in the File ▷ Open Site (Windows) or Site ▷ Open Site (Macintosh) drop-down list. The site name is a reference only you need to know, and it can be as fancy as you want. There are no hard and fast rules for creating a site name, except you should keep the name simple so you can easily reference it later. In a large Web design firm, you may need to develop more structured methods for naming various clients' Web sites.

Local Root Folder

The Local Root Folder is the location on your hard drive, or a network folder, where you will be placing your HTML pages, images, plug-in files, and Library items. Remember, the root folder is essential to an effective Dreamweaver site. As you add links to other Web pages and images, Dreamweaver needs to maintain the relative links between files. The benefit of this becomes very apparent when you upload your files to a Web server. By maintaining a root-relative relationship, you ensure that all of the files and associated images will transfer seamlessly together onto any Web site. You won't have to go back and replace the code for any broken images.

HTTP Address

The information entered in the HTTP Address field is used when you access the Link Checker. In this field you'll enter the remote URL that corresponds to the local root folder, as if it were a regular Web address.

For example, say you are developing a Web site for My Frozen Custard, Inc. For the HTTP Address field you would enter the URL for the Web site, like this:

```
http://www.myfrozencustard.com/
```

With this information, the Link Checker can compare absolute addresses embedded in your Web page to see whether those addresses refer to internal or external files.

Cache

Put a check mark in the Cache check-box to speed up Dreamweaver's links and site management tasks.

Web Server Info

The Web Server Info category contains all of the information required for you to post your files to a remote server. The setup allows for any type of host directory. Typically, though, you will be uploading your files to either a UNIX or NT Web server.

From the Web Server Info panel (see Figure 33-2), choose Local/Network from the Server Access drop-down menu to enter or select a folder on your hard drive or on the network from which your files will be served. Select FTP from the Server Access drop-down menu to be presented with a dialog box requesting information needed to access your remote site.

 Tip   If you don't know the name of your FTP host server or any of the other required host site information (directory, login ID, password, and firewall preferences), contact your ISP or system administrator.

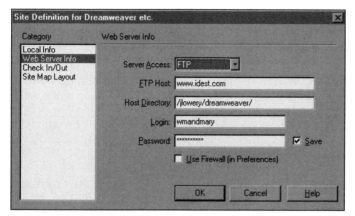

Figure 33-2: Information entered in the Web Server Info panel is essential for Dreamweaver to connect with your remote site.

FTP Host

The FTP Host is the name of the server on which you will be placing your files. The names for the host will be something like these:

```
www.yourdomain.com
ftp.yourdomain.com
```

Do not include the protocol information, such as `http://` or `ftp://`, in the FTP Host name.

Host Directory

The host directory is the one in which publicly accessible documents are stored on the server. Your remote site root folder will be a subfolder of the host directory. Here's an example of the host directory information:

```
/usr/www/htdocs/jlowery
```

Check with your Web server administrator for the proper directory path.

Login ID and Password

A login ID and password are required to transfer your files from your local root folder to the host. Your login ID is a unique name that tells the host who you are. Your password should be known only by you and the host. Every time you upload or download a file from the host server, you will be asked for your password. If you don't want to have to retype your password each time you log on, just select the Save check-box next to your password and Dreamweaver will remember it.

Caution   For security reasons, it is highly recommended that you do not allow anyone to know your password.

Use Firewall

Firewalls are security features used by many companies to prevent unwanted access to internal documents. There are many different types of firewalls, and all have a multitude of security settings. For instance, some firewalls allow people within a company to move documents back and forth through the firewall without any problems. Other companies will not allow Java or ActiveX controls to be moved through the firewall.

If you have a firewall that requires additional security to upload and download files, you will want to enable the Use Firewall check-box in the Site Definition window. Selecting this check-box requires that you go to the Dreamweaver Preferences and fill out additional information on proxy servers. A proxy server enables you to navigate files through a firewall.

To make the appropriate proxy server changes, go to Edit ➪ Preferences and choose the Site FTP category from the Preferences dialog box. This panel of settings contains selections for firewall information. Enter the firewall host name and port number, which will have been provided to you from your ISP or system administrator. By default, most firewalls use port 21.

Check In/Out

In this panel (see Figure 33-3), you can enable or disable Dreamweaver's Check In and Check Out. When you select Enable File Check In and Check Out, the two other fields become available. You then can select the Check Out Files While Opening option, which automates the check-out process to some degree.

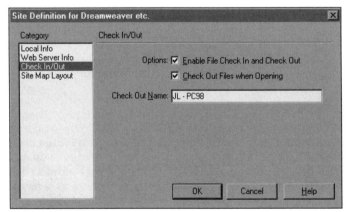

Figure 33-3: Turn on the file-locking feature of Dreamweaver in the Check In/Out panel of the Site Definition dialog box.

The name you enter in the Check Out Name field is used to let others in your group know when you have downloaded a file from the host server. Because the Check Out Name is one of several columns of information in the local and remote panes of the Site Window, it's a good idea to keep the name relatively short. (Your initials are an ideal choice for Check Out Name, if that is appropriate.)

Cross-Reference
For detailed information on the Site FTP preferences, see Chapter 3, "Setting Your Preferences."

Modifying the Site Map

You can control the way that Dreamweaver displays a Site Map in the Site Map Layout panel (see Figure 33-4). To do this, select File ➪ Open Site ➪ Define Sites (Site ➪ Define Sites). Select a site from the list in the Define Sites dialog box and click Edit to bring up the Site Definition dialog box. Then select Site Map Layout from the Category List to access the Site Map options.

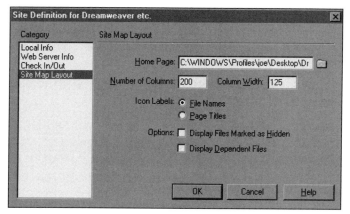

Figure 33-4: You can control what the Site Map shows as well as its overall appearance through the Site Map Layout panel.

Home Page

By default, Dreamweaver will look for a file called index.htm or index.html in your Local root folder from which to begin creating a Site Map. You can choose another page to appear at the top level of your Site Map by selecting a different file to serve as your home page.

Number of Columns/Column Width

This controls the way your Site Map is displayed on your screen. You can modify these values in order to make the Site Map fit more easily onto a single page for printing.

Tip   By default, the Site Map displays horizontally. You can switch the layout to vertical by changing the Number of Columns field to 1.

Icon Labels

The Icon Labels option enables you to select whether the icons in your Site Map should be displayed using their filenames or their page titles. Page titles are derived from the <title> tag in the <head> section of an HTML document. While this method can be more descriptive, you have to remember to insert the title, either through the Page Properties dialog box or by revealing the Head Content, selecting the Title icon, and entering the desired text in the Title Property Inspector. If you don't assign each page a title, you'll notice that Dreamweaver uses "Untitled Document" as the title.

Options

Checking Display Files Marked as Hidden will include hidden HTML files in your Site Map Layout; checking Display Dependent Files will include non-HTML files, such as graphic image files, in your Site Map Layout.

Using the Site Window

Dreamweaver's Site FTP utility runs in the Site Window. You can open the Site Window by any of the following methods:

✦ Choose File ➪ Open Site ➪ Your Site (Windows) or Site ➪ Open Site ➪ Your Site (Macintosh).

✦ Select the Show Site FTP button from either Launcher.

✦ Choose Window ➪ Site File.

✦ Press the keyboard shortcut, F5.

The Site Window is your vehicle for moving files back and forth between your local and remote folders. Figure 33-5 illustrates the various parts of the Site Window.

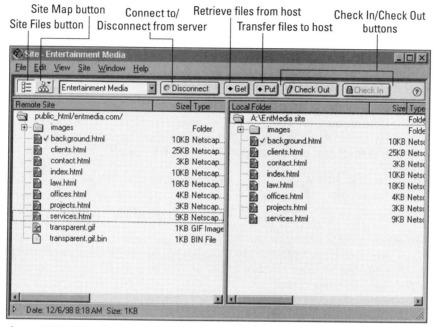

Site Map button   Connect to/   Retrieve files from host   Check In/Check Out
Site Files button | Disconnect from server | Transfer files to host   buttons

Figure 33-5: The Site Window is used for transferring files to and from your remote Web server.

Remote Site and Local Root Directory Windows

The Site Window is arranged in two main windows: the remote site is on the left and the local root directory is on the right. These two windows enable you to view all of the files contained within the two directories.

The View (Windows) or Site ➪ Site Files View (Macintosh) command also enables you to refresh the two windows. This can be useful when other people are working on the same site at the same time—refreshing your screen enables you to see if any additional files have been added or removed during your FTP session. You also need to refresh the site windows if you have modified a file during the FTP session. You can choose from two refresh commands: Refresh Local and Refresh Remote.

Another helpful view lets you see which files have been most recently added or modified since the last FTP transfer. Choose either Select Newer Local or Select Newer Remote in the View menu (or Site Files View ➪ Select Newer Local or Site Files View ➪ Select Newer Remote on a Macintosh). Dreamweaver compares the files within the two folders to see which ones have been saved since the last FTP session. The newer files are highlighted and can be easily transferred by selecting the Get or Put button (described in a later section).

Tip In large sites, the Select Newer Remote operation can take a fairly long time to complete. If possible, selecting individual folders to be checked, while leaving the others unscanned, can speed up the process.

Connect/Disconnect button

The Connect/Disconnect button lets you begin or end a live session with a remote host server. By clicking the Connect button, you start a new FTP session. You must have a way to connect to the Internet when you select Connect. You won't see any information in the Remote Site pane until you connect to it.

After Dreamweaver has made the connection to your Remote site — as identified in the Site Information dialog box — the Connect button becomes the Disconnect button. To end your FTP session with the host server, click the Disconnect button.

Tip You can monitor all of your site management transactions by looking at the FTP Log. Select Window ➪ Site FTP Log (Windows) or Site ➪ FTP Log (Macintosh) from within the Site Window. A new window pops up and shows you all your transactions as you perform them.

Get and Put buttons

Two of the most useful controls on the Site Window are the Get and Put buttons. The Get button retrieves selected files and folders from the host server. The Put button transfers selected files from your local root directory to the host server. Dreamweaver offers several ways to transfer files in the Site Window during an active FTP session.

To transfer one or more files from the local directory to the host server, use one of the following methods:

✦ Select the files from the Local Root Directory pane and drag them over to the Remote Directory pane.

✦ Use the keyboard shortcut — select the files and press Ctrl-Shift-U (Command-Shift-U).

✦ Highlight the files and choose File ➪ Put (Windows) or Site ➪ Put (Macintosh).

✦ Select the files in the Local Folder pane and click the Put button.

If the file you are transferring has any dependent files, such as inserted images or Java applets, the Dependent Files dialog box (see Figure 33-6) asks if you want to include dependent files. If you select Yes, all such files are transferred. Select No to move only the file you selected.

Tip

The Dependent Files dialog box includes a check-box that asks if you want to be reminded of this feature again. If you choose this option, but later want the reminder to reappear, you can select either of the Dependent Files options from the Site FTP panel of Preferences. To bring up the Dependent Files dialog box on a case-by-case basis, press Alt (Option) when selecting the Get, Put, Check In, or Check Out buttons.

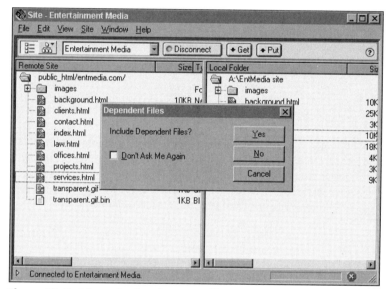

Figure 33-6: After selecting the HTML files, say Yes to the Dependent Files dialog box to transfer all the needed files.

To transfer one or more files from the host server to the local folder, use one of these techniques:

✦ Select the files you want from the Remote Site pane and drag them over to the Local Directory pane.

✦ Use the keyboard shortcut — select the files and press Ctrl-Shift-D (Command-Shift-D).

✦ Highlight the files and select File ➪ Get (Windows) or Site ➪ Get (Macintosh).

✦ Select the files in the remote directory and click the Get button.

Caution

If you select either File ➪ Get (Site ➪ Get) or the Get button without having selected any files in the Remote Site pane, all of the files from your host server will be moved.

Stop Current Task button

Use the Stop Current Task button to halt the current transfer of files in an active FTP session. The Stop Current Task button is the red X button located in the lower-right corner of the Site Window; it only appears while you are connected.

Checked Out check-box

The Check In/Check Out buttons, which are visible only if you've selected the Check In/Out category in the Site Definition Window (as previously shown in Figure 33-3), enable a user to officially check out an item from either the local or host server. The Checked Out check-box indicates that a file is currently in use by someone with access to the server. Details on how to use this feature are covered in the next section.

Checking a File In and Out

Your control over the files used for your Web site is very important if you are developing a site with a team. On larger sites, the various Webmaster chores — design, programming, management — are distributed among several people. Without proper check-in and check-out procedures, it's very easy for the same HTML page to get updated by more than person, and you can wind up with incompatible versions.

Dreamweaver's Check-In/Check-Out facility solves this file-control problem by permitting only one person at a time to modify a Web page or graphic. Once a file has been checked out — accessed by someone — the file must be checked in again before another person using Site FTP can download it and work on it.

Dreamweaver handles the functionality of Check-In/Check-Out very efficiently. Whenever you establish an active FTP session between your local root folder and the host server, any files you get or put are displayed with a green check mark. If other people in your group are also moving files back and forth, their transferred files are marked with a red check mark. This method provides a quickly recognized, visual representation of the status of files you and your teammates are handling. Files that do not have either a red or green check mark are not currently checked out by anyone and are available to work on.

If you want to see who is working on what, you can view user names in the Remote Site window. (You may have to scroll the window horizontally to see the column.) The name shown is the Check Out name that they use for logging on to the remote server. The Check Out name is entered through the Site Information dialog box.

Knowing who is working on what, and when, is a good control mechanism, but to really prevent duplication, site file control has to go one step further. Under Dreamweaver's Check In/Check Out system, when you transfer a file from your local root folder to the host server, the file on your local folder becomes read-only. Making the file read-only enables others to see the Web page, but prevents anyone else from overwriting the file. The file must be checked in again before others can modify it.

Dreamweaver accomplishes Check In/Check Out by using a set of special files. When a file is checked out, a text file of the same filename but with the extension .lck is placed on the server. The .lck file contains the name of the user who checked out the file, as well as the date and the time that the file was checked out. The .lck files cannot be viewed in the Site Window display, but can be seen when a third-party FTP program is used.

Caution   Unfortunately, Dreamweaver is not able to make checked-out files in the host server read-only. This means someone in your group using an FTP program other than Site FTP could very easily overwrite the checked-out file on the server.

To check out one or more files, use any of the following methods:

✦ Select the files you want to transfer and then click the Check Out button at the top of the Site Window. All of the files will be downloaded into your local folder, and checked out in your name (denoted by a green check mark).

✦ Select the files and choose File ⇨ Check Out (Windows) or Site ⇨ Check Out (Macintosh).

✦ Select the files and use the keyboard shortcut, Ctrl-Alt-Shift-D (Command-Option-Shift-D).

To check one or more files back in, do either of the following:

✦ Select the files you want to transfer and then click the Check In button at the top of the Site Window. All of the selected files will be uploaded from your local folder to the remote site, and the green check mark will be removed from their names.

✦ Select the checked-out files and choose File ⇨ Check In (Windows) or Site ⇨ Check In (Macintosh).

✦ Select the files and use the keyboard shortcut, Ctl-Alt-Shift-U (Command-Option-Shift-U).

To change the checked-out status of a file, use one of these methods:

✦ Select the file that's checked out, and then click the Check In button at the top of the Site Window.

✦ Select the file and choose File ⇨ Undo Check Out (Windows) or Site ⇨ Undo Check Out (Macintosh), or use the keyboard shortcut, Ctrl-Shift-L (Command-Shift-L).

Checking Links

During a Web site's development, hundreds of different files and links are often referenced from within the HTML code. Unfortunately, it's not uncommon for a user to enthusiastically follow a link on a site only to encounter the dreaded Web server error 404: File Not Found. *Broken links* are one of a Webmaster's most persistent headaches, because a Web page may have not only internal links pointing to other pages on the Web site, but external links as well—over which the Webmaster has no control.

Orphaned files constitute a parallel nightmare for the working Web developer. An *orphaned file* is one that is included in the local or remote site but is no longer actively referenced by any Web page. Orphaned files take up valuable disk space and can erroneously be transferred from an old site to a new one.

Dreamweaver includes for the Web designer a very useful feature to ease the labor in solving both of these problems: the Link Checker. The Link Checker command can be used to check a single page, selected pages, a subfolder, or an entire site. Once the Link Checker has completed its survey, you can view broken links, external files (links outside the site, such as absolute references and mailto's), and orphaned files. You can also repair broken links immediately or save the Link Checker results in a file for later viewing.

To check for links, follow these steps:

1. Make sure that the most current version of the files have been saved.

2. To check a single document from within Dreamweaver, open the file and then choose File ➪ Check Links ➪ This Document, or use the keyboard shortcut, Ctrl-F7 (Command-F7).

3. To check for links on an entire site from within Dreamweaver, choose File ➪ Check Links ➪ Entire Site or use the keyboard shortcut, Ctrl-F8 (Command-F8).

When Dreamweaver has finished checking for all of the links on your page or site, it opens the Link Checker dialog box. The Link Checker dialog box, shown in Figure 33-7, provides a summary report of the broken links, external links and, when an entire site is reviewed, orphaned files. You can also use the Save button to store a report, in a tab-delimited text file, of the problems that the Link Checker has found, for future reference.

When you list broken links, you'll be able to observe any file that is included as a link, inserted as an image, or embedded in the page, and which cannot be located. If you want to fix the broken link, you can do so by double-clicking on the highlighted broken-link file. This will bring up the file in Dreamweaver, where you can fix any problems with the Property Inspector.

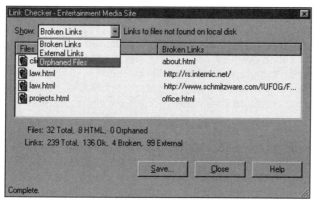

Figure 33-7: The Link Checker dialog box helps you determine which files have broken links and then fix the links directly.

You can also fix the link directly in the Link Checker window by following these steps:

1. Run the Link Checker command, either for the entire site or a single Web page.

2. In the Link Checker window, select the path and filename of the broken link you want to repair.

3. Enter the correct path for the missing file.

You can also open the page with the broken link and use the Property Inspector to locate the file in the Src attribute. To open the page from the Link Checker, double-click the Dreamweaver icon next to the broken link.

You can also access the Link Checker for both your local and remote folders. After you've selected your files or folders, choose File ➪ Check Links, from the main Dreamweaver menu, to check either the selected files or the entire Web site. Or, you can right-click (Shift-click) any of the selected files to display the shortcut menu and choose the Check Link options from there.

Working with the Site Map

A Web site consists primarily of pages linked to other pages, which in turn can be linked to more pages. The more complex the site, the more difficult it becomes to comprehend — or remember — the entire structure when looking at just a directory listing.

New Feature

Now, with Dreamweaver 2.0, you can easily view your entire Web site and all of its links as a hierarchical tree using the Site Map feature. Not only do problems like broken links jump out at you — after all, they're depicted in red — but the Site Map can give you a much needed overview of the entire site. Poor site design can lead to visitors getting "lost" in the site, or frustrated with the number of links it takes to get to an important page. Dreamweaver 2's Site Map not only gives you a visual reference, but also enables you to create the structure for entire sites in a point-and-click environment.

The Site Map is a graphical representation of your site, with all of its Web pages symbolized by icons, as shown in Figure 33-8. The Site Map resembles both an organizational chart and a flow chart. The Web site's home page is shown at the top of the chart. A link from one page to another is represented by a connecting line with an arrowhead. Any document, other than the home page, that is linked to additional pages, indicates these pages with a plus or minus symbol in Windows systems and a right or down arrow in Macintosh systems. By default, Dreamweaver displays your Site Map only two levels deep. Selecting the plus/minus (arrow) symbols shows and hides the view of the linked pages on deeper levels.

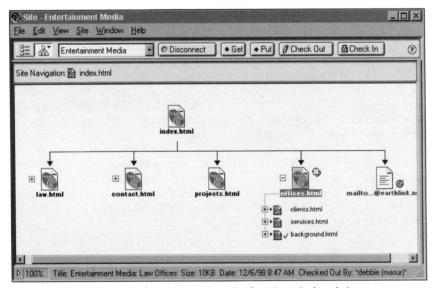

Figure 33-8: Clicking on the Site Map icon in the Site Window brings up a graphical representation of your site.

To open the Site Map from the Document Window, choose Window ➪ Site Map, or use the keyboard shortcut, Shift-F5. If the Site Window is open, you can select the Site Map button to bring up the Site Map. The Site Map button has two settings, which you can activate by clicking and holding down the corresponding button. The Map Only setting displays just the Site Map. The Map and Files setting shows the Site Map in one pane of the Site Window and the Local Files in the other.

The Site Map represents internal HTML pages with small Dreamweaver page icons. If the link is good, the name is in blue type; if the link is broken, it's red. External files — files on another site — and special links, such as a `mailto:` or `javascript:` link, are indicated with small globes. Initially, the Site Map only displays the HTML files in a site, and not any hidden or dependent files. (Hidden and dependent files are covered later in this section.)

If your site has enabled Dreamweaver's Check In/Out features, you'll see additional symbols on the site map. A file checked out by you is indicated by a green check mark. If the file has been checked out by someone else, the check mark is red. It's not uncommon for teams to prevent an important Web page from being altered by making it read-only (Windows) or locking it (Macintosh). Such files are noted with a lock symbol.

Note   To view a Site Map of your site, it must be in a local folder. To view a Site Map of a remote site, you must first download it to a local folder.

Storyboarding with the Site Map

Increasingly, Web designers lay out the structure of their sites before filling in the details with text, image, and media content. This approach is all but essential on larger sites where development is divided among many people. In many ways, laying out the site's structure ahead of the content makes the content phase much faster. You can, for example, pick an existing page from the Select File dialog box when building your links, rather than entering a nonexistent page's filename in the Link text box — and then trying to remember to create it later.

All you need to begin building your site with the Site Map is a single file, typically the site's home page. This home page is then defined as such in the Site Map Layout panel of the Site Definition dialog box.

To create a Web site structure from the Site Map, follow these steps:

1. Open the Site Map by choosing Window ⇨ Site Map or one of the other methods previously described.

2. Select the icon of the site's home page.

3. Choose Site ⇨ Link to a New File (Site ⇨ Site Map View ⇨ Link to a New File). You can also right-click (Shift-click) the page's icon and choose Link to New File from the shortcut menu.

   The Link to New File dialog box appears, as shown in Figure 33-9.

4. In the Link to New File dialog box, enter the filename with an .htm or .html extension in the File Name text box. Press Tab to move to the next text box.

5. Enter a title for the new page in the Title text box. Press Tab.

Figure 33-9: Use the Site Map to build the Web site's structure by creating new linked pages in one operation.

6. Enter the descriptive word or phrase to appear as a link on the original page in the Text of Link text box. Select OK or press Enter (Return) when you're done.

   The HTML page is created and an icon for the new page appears, with a line connecting it to the original page.

7. To add another link to the home page, select the home page icon again and repeat Steps 3–6.

8. To add a new link to the newly created page, select its icon and repeat Steps 3–6.

When text links are added to a page, they are placed at the bottom of an existing page, one after another in the same line, like a text-only navigation bar. If the page is new, the text links are naturally the only items on the page.

Connecting to existing pages

Adding existing files to the Site Map is even easier than adding a new file, especially if the file to which you're linking is already in the same site. Part of building a Web-like structure is connecting from one page to another. With the Site Map, this is literally a drag-and-drop affair.

When an HTML icon is selected in the Site Map, a small Point to File icon appears. The Point to File feature on the Site Map is basically used the same way it is on the Property Inspectors — just click on the symbol and drag your pointer to another file. You can point-and-link to files in the current site whether they're already in the Site Map or not.

To link to a file that's in the current site but not on the Site Map (in other words, a file that's not linked to the home page or any connected pages), it's best to have both the Site Map and the Local Files panels displayed. To show both panels, select and hold down the Site Map button, and then choose Map and Files from the drop-down list. Next, in the Site Map panel, select the file you want to link from — and a Point to File icon appears. Click and drag the Point to File icon from the Site Map to the Local Files panel to select the linking page. A line is drawn from the Point to File icon to the selected file, as shown in Figure 33-10. When your pointer is over the desired file, release the mouse button. The link is added, with a new icon appearing on the Site Map; and a text link is added to the originating page.

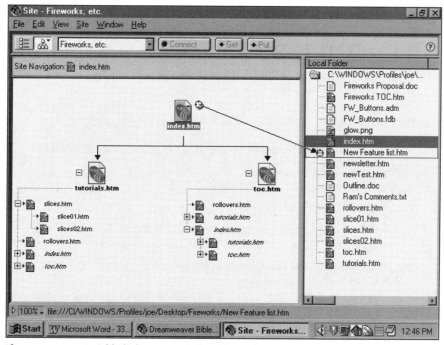

Figure 33-10: Quickly link to an existing file with Dreamweaver's Point to File feature.

If you're linking from one Site Map page to another, the Point to File icon is very handy. Just select the originating page's icon and drag its Point to File symbol to the page you want to link to. Rather than draw another line across the screen—which would quickly render the Site Map screen indecipherable with crisscrossing lines—links to existing Site Map files are shown in italics.

There are several other methods for linking to an existing file. First, you can open a Select File dialog box by selecting the originating file and then choosing Site ⇨ Link to Existing File (Site ⇨ Site Map View ⇨ Link to an Existing File). The keyboard shortcut for this command is Ctrl-Shift-K (Command-Shift-K). You can also invoke the command by choosing Link to an Existing File from the shortcut menu, brought up by right-clicking (Shift-clicking) the originating file's Site Map icon. Any of these techniques opens the Select File dialog box to enable you to browse for your file, which is very useful for selecting files not in the current site.

If you want to drag-and-drop external files to create a link, you can use the Site Map in combination with the Windows Explorer or Finder, depending on your operating system. Instead of pointing from the originating file to the linked file, you drag the name or icon representing the external file from Windows Explorer (Finder) and drop it on the Site Map icon of the originating page. To accomplish this, it's best to either have the Site Map and Windows Explorer (Finder) windows side-by-side or, if they are overlapping, have the Windows Explorer (Finder) window in front.

Modifying links

If you have spent any time in Web site design and management, you know nothing is written in stone. Luckily, Dreamweaver 2 makes changing a link from one page to another a breeze and handles the tedious task of updating changes in all linked pages. Moreover, if you have multiple pages linking to a single page, you can make all the pages in the Web site link to a different page.

To change a link from one page to another, follow these steps:

1. Select the icon of the linked page you want to alter in the Site Map.

2. Choose Site ⇨ Change Link (Site ⇨ Site Map View ⇨ Change Link) or use the keyboard shortcut, Ctrl-L (Command-L).

   The Select File dialog box opens.

3. Enter the path and filename in the File Name text box or select the Browse (Choose) button to locate the file. Click OK when you've selected your file.

   Dreamweaver displays the Update Files dialog box with all the connecting pages, as shown in Figure 33-11.

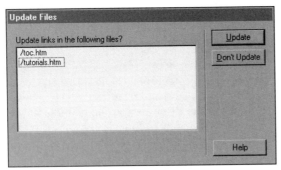

Figure 33-11: Changing a link in the Site Map brings up the Update Files dialog box.

4. To change the link in all the files, choose the Update button.

5. To change the link in some of the files, select the files first, using either the Shift-click or Ctrl-click (Control-click) methods, and then choose the Update button.

6. To cancel the link change, choose the Don't Update button.

If you have multiple pages linking to a single page that you want to alter, you can change a link sitewide. Simply select the icon for the linked page you want to modify and choose Site ⇨ Change Link Sitewide (Site ⇨ Site Map View ⇨ Change Link Sitewide). As with the Change Link command, the Update Files dialog box opens; the balance of the procedure remains the same.

Note After modifying numerous links on the Site Map, I've found it helpful to force Dreamweaver to redraw the screen by choosing View ⇨ Refresh (Site ⇨ Site Map View ⇨ Refresh) or using the keyboard shortcut, Ctrl-F5 (Command-F5). Be sure to click in the Site Map panel before executing this command; otherwise, Dreamweaver refreshes its reading of the local site folder, but doesn't redraw the screen.

Deleting links

You can delete a link from one page in several ways. First, select the icon and then do any of the following:

✦ Press the Delete key.

✦ Choose Site ⇨ Remove Link (Site ⇨ Site Map View ⇨ Remove Link).

✦ Press Ctrl-Shift-L (Command-Shift-L).

✦ Right-click (Shift-click) the icon and from the shortcut menu, choose Remove Link.

In all cases, the link is deleted without confirmation and the deletion cannot be undone.

Note Deleting a link does not delete the file itself, just the link. For the text link, the `href` attribute is eliminated, but the actual text remains.

Changing titles

Dreamweaver 2 gives you an easy way to change a Web page's title right in the Site Map. Before you can use this feature, however, you must be sure the titles are used to identify the icons, rather than the filenames. Choose View ⇨ Show Page Titles (Site ⇨ Site Map View ⇨ Show Page Titles) or use the keyboard shortcut, Ctrl-Shift-T (Command-Shift-T) to switch to a title view.

To retitle a Web page, click the title twice, slowly — make sure you don't double-click the title, which will open the file. Alternately, you can click the icon once and then the title. You can also choose File ⇨ Rename (Site ⇨ Rename) from the menus. All of these methods make the title an editable field that you can then modify.

Modifying pages through the Site Map

Once you've created and refined your site structure, you're ready to begin adding the content. The Site Map enables you to open a single page or a collection of pages. You can even quickly locate the text or graphic that serves as the source for the link in the connecting page.

Open a page in Dreamweaver's Document Window for editing by double-clicking the page's icon in the Site Map. To open more than one page, you must first select their icons. Multiple files can be selected by selecting one file and then Shift-clicking on the additional files. Another method of multiple selection is to click into an empty area in the Site Map and then drag a rectangle around the desired files. After all the needed files are selected, choose File ⇨ Open Selection (Site ⇨ Open Selection). Every file will open in a separate Dreamweaver Document Window.

Occasionally, you need to go right to the source of a link. Dreamweaver 2 enables you to open the connecting page and instantly select the actual link used to make the connection. To view the actual text or graphic used to make a link, first select the file's icon in the Site Map. Then, choose Site ⇨ Open Source of Link (Site ⇨ Open Source of Link). Dreamweaver loads the page containing the link, opens the Property Inspector, and selects the link.

Altering the home page

As noted earlier, the Site Map assigns a home page to use as the base for its organization. Like most items in Dreamweaver, this assignation can be changed. But why would you want to change a Web site's home page? One of the greatest purposes for the Site Map is to provide a visual representation of a site's structure — one that can easily be presented to a client for discussion. You can set up multiple views of a site, each with its own structure, by just switching the home page.

You can replace the home page with an existing page or a new one. To create a new page and make it the home page, select Site ⇨ New Home Page (Site ⇨ Site Map View ⇨ New Home Page). The New Home Page dialog box opens with two fields to fill out: File Name and Title. After you enter the needed information, the file is created and the icon appears by itself in the Site Map. Now you can use the Link to Existing File and Link to New features to build your new site organization.

To change the home page to an existing file, choose Site ⇨ Select Home Page (Site ⇨ Site Map View ⇨ Select Home Page). The Select File dialog box opens and enables you to choose a new file. Once you've selected a file, the Site Map is recreated using the new file as a base and displaying any existing links.

Viewing the Site Map

The more complex the site, the more important it is to be able to view the Site Map in different ways. To cut down on the number of pages showing, Dreamweaver 2 enables you to hide any pages you choose. For maximum detail, you can also display all the dependent files (such as a page's graphics) in the Site Map. You even have the option of temporarily limiting the view to a particular "branch" of the Site Map. Dreamweaver also lets you zoom out to get the big picture of a particularly large site or save the Site Map as a graphic.

Tip
If the Site Map columns are too narrow to see the full title or file name, use the Tool Tips feature. Enabling View ➪ Tool Tips (Site ➪ Site Map View ➪ Tool Tips) causes Dreamweaver to display the full text of the title or filename in a tooltip box when your pointer passes over the name.

Working with hidden and dependent files

Web sites are capable of containing several hundred, if not several thousand, pages. In these situations, the Site Map can become overcrowded. Dreamweaver can mark any file (and its associated linked files) as hidden with a single command, View ➪ Show/Hide Link (Site ➪ Site Map View ➪ Show/Hide Link). The Show/Hide Link command is a toggle — applying it a second time to a file removes the "hidden" designation.

To see previously hidden files, choose View ➪ Show Files Marked as Hidden Files (Site ➪ Site Map View ➪ Show Files Marked as Hidden). Hidden files made visible are displayed in italics.

Dependent files include any image, external style sheet, or media file (such as a Flash movie). By default, dependent files are not displayed in the Site Map; however, you can opt to view them by choosing View ➪ Show Dependent Files (Site ➪ Site Map View ➪ Show Dependent Files). Once visible on the Site Map, you can send any image to Dreamweaver's designated image editor by double-clicking its icon. You can also open the Styles Palette by double-clicking any external CSS file.

Focusing on part of a Site Map

Most of the time, the overall view, centered on the Web site's home page, is most useful. Sometimes, though, you want to examine a section of the site in greater detail. Dreamweaver lets you set any page to be treated like a temporary home page or *root*, ignoring all linking pages above it.

To view just a portion of your Web site, first select the page you wish to choose as the new root. Next, choose View ➪ View As Root (Site ➪ Site Map View ➪ View As Root) or use the keyboard shortcut, Ctrl-Shift-R (Command-Shift-R). The Site Map now depicts your selected file as if it were the home page. You'll also notice that the Site Navigation bar has changed, as shown in Figure 33-12. The Site Navigation bar shows the actual home page and any pages that have been chosen as roots, separated by right-pointing arrows. You can switch from one root to another, or to the actual home page, by clicking on its icon in the Site Navigation bar.

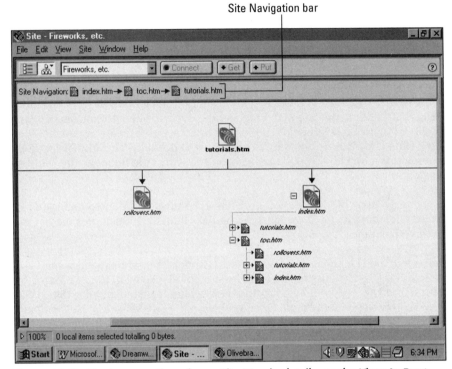

Figure 33-12: To view a section of your Site Map in detail, use the View As Root command.

Zooming out of your Site Map

What do you do when your site is so big that you can't see it all in one screen? Dreamweaver 2 provides a Zoom feature that enables you to pull back for a more encompassing view. The Site Map Zoom button is located on the far left of the Site Window's status bar. Selecting the Zoom button reveals the magnification options to choose from: 100%, 75%, 50%, 25%, and 12%.

Tip

If you find that Dreamweaver is displaying page icons only, with no filenames or titles, you can expand the column width in the layout. Choose View ⇨ Layout (Site ⇨ Site Map View ⇨ Layout) and change the value in the Column Width text box to a higher number. The default column width is 125 pixels.

Converting the Site Map into a graphic

Web designers like to believe that the whole world is wired and on the Web, but in truth, we're not there yet. Sometimes it's necessary to present a client or other interested party with a printout of a site design. Dreamweaver makes it possible to take a snapshot of the current Site Map and save it as a graphic file that can then be inserted into another program for printing—or, attached to an e-mail for easy transmission.

To convert the Site Map into a graphic, choose File ➪ Save Site Map As (Site ➪ Site Map View ➪ Save Site Map As PICT). On Windows systems, you can choose to save the file in either Bitmap or PING format by selecting one of the Save As Type options. All Macintosh images are saved in PICT format.

When you save a Site Map as a graphic, the image is saved at the size necessary to contain all the displayed icons. Figure 33-13 shows a 448 × 722 pixel-sized graphic, saved from a Site Map, in Fireworks.

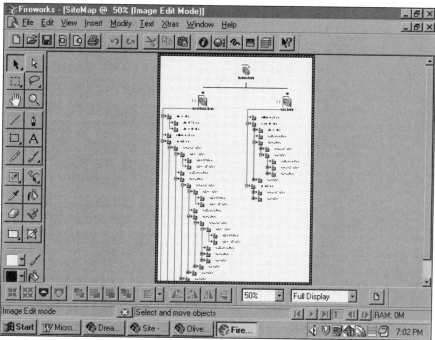

Figure 33-13: This Site Map image, ready for editing in Fireworks, was created in Dreamweaver.

Summary

With the Site Window and Dreamweaver's site management tools, a group or an individual Web designer can manage even large and diverse sites.

✦ Setting up a new site is an essential element in managing a Dreamweaver Web site. Without the root directory for the local files, Dreamweaver cannot properly manage the Web pages and associated links.

✦ The Site Window enables you to drag-and-drop files from the host server to the local root folder.

✦ All file check-in and check-out functions for teams can be handled through the Site Window.

✦ Broken links can be quickly found and fixed with the Link Checker. You can also find orphaned files and identify external links.

✦ Dreamweaver 2's new Site Map enables you to quickly visualize your overall site structure.

✦ The Site Map is also useful for creating new pages and their associated links. You can storyboard the entire site structure — links and all — before adding any content.

In the next chapter, you learn how to speed up your Web site production through the use of Dreamweaver templates.

✦   ✦   ✦

Using Dreamweaver Templates

Let's face it: Web design is a combination of glory and grunt work. Creating the initial design for a Web site can be fun and exciting, but when you have to implement your wonderful new design on 200 or more pages, the excitement fades as you try to figure out the quickest way to finish the work. Enter templates. Properly using templates can be a tremendous timesaver. Moreover, a template ensures that your Web site will have a consistent look and feel, which in turn generally means it's easier for users to navigate.

Dreamweaver 2 has completely revised its original concept of templates and produced what Macromedia refers to as *Dream Templates*. In Dreamweaver 2, new documents are produced from a standard design saved as a template, as in a word-processing program. Furthermore, you can alter a template and update all the files that were created from it earlier; this ability extends the power of the repeating element Libraries to overall page design. Templates also form the bridge to one of the hottest technologies shaping the Web — XML (Extensible Markup Language).

Dreamweaver makes it easy to access all kinds of templates — everything from your own creations to the default blank page. This chapter demonstrates the mechanism behind Dreamweaver templates and shows you the strategies for getting the most out of them.

Understanding Dream Templates

Templates exist in many forms. Furniture makers use molds as templates to create the same basic design over and over again, with new upholstery or stains used to differentiate the end results. A stencil, in which the inside of a letter, word, or design is filled-in, is a type of template as well. With computers, templates form the basic document into which specific details are added to create new, distinct documents.

New Feature Dreamweaver 2 has taken the concept of computer templates to new heights with the introduction of Dream Templates. Dream Templates, in terms of functionality, are a combination of traditional templates and updateable Library elements. With Dream Templates, a new page is created from a *mold*, or template. Once created, the new document remains attached to the original template unless specifically separated or detached. Because the new document maintains a connection, if the original template is altered, all the documents created from it can be automatically updated, as with Dreamweaver's repeating elements Library. In fact, templates can even include Library elements.

Dream Templates are composed of two types of regions: locked and editable. Every element on the Web page template falls into one category or the other. When a template is first created, all of the areas are locked. Part of the process of defining a template is to designate, and name, the editable regions. Then, when a document is created from that template, the editable regions are the only ones that can be modified.

Naturally, templates can be altered to mark additional editable areas or to relock editable areas. Moreover, you can detach a document created from a template at any point and edit anything in the document — you cannot, however, re-attach the document to the template without losing newly inserted content. On the other hand, a document based on one template can be changed to a completely different look but with the same content, if another template with identical editable regions is applied.

Dreamweaver 2 ships with a tutorial that illustrates the power of templates. The tutorial, found in the Dreamweaver/Tutorial folder, is based on an example Web site for a food company called Olivebranch. If you preview the site in a browser, you'll notice that in the catalog section, each of the sample pages for Wines, Cheeses, Mustards, and Oils are basically the same — only the product title, description, and images vary. The layout, background, and navigation controls are identical on every page. Each of these pages was created from the template page shown in Figure 34-1. Notice the highlighting surrounding certain areas — in a template, the editable regions are highlighted and the locked areas are not. When you create a new document based on the template, the reverse is true: the locked regions are highlighted (in a different color) and the editable regions are not.

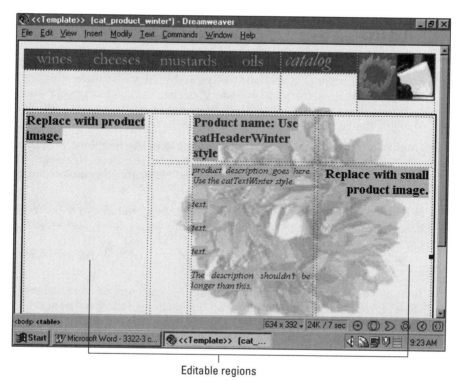

Figure 34-1: In this sample template from the Dreamweaver Tutorial, editable regions are highlighted.

Note   The term "template" can be a little confusing, especially because Dreamweaver uses the word to refer to very different types of documents. Earlier versions of Dreamweaver used "template" to refer to a kind of example document that could not be updated at all. This implementation still exists in the Configuration\ Templates folder with the Default.htm page — which serves as the "template" for any new, blank page created in Dreamweaver. Dream Templates are new to 2.0 and provide the most flexibility in design and maintenance. I've separated the two different types of templates and discuss the newer and far more powerful Dream Templates first.

Creating Your Own Templates

You can use any design you like for your own template. Perhaps the best course to take is to finalize a single page that has all the elements you want to include in your template. Then, convert that document to a template and proceed to mark all the changeable areas — whether text or image — as editable regions.

Before you save your file as a template, consider the following points when designing your basic page:

✦ **Use placeholders where you can.** Whether it's dummy text or a temporary graphic, placeholders give shape to your page. They also make it easier to remember which elements to include. If you are using an image placeholder, set a temporary height and width through the Property Inspector or by dragging the image placeholder's sizing handles.

✦ **Finalize and incorporate as much as possible in the template.** If you find yourself repeatedly adding the same information or objects to a page, add them to your template. The more structured elements you can include, the faster your pages can be produced.

✦ **Use sample objects on the template.** Many times you have to enter the same basic object, such as a plug-in for a digital movie, on every page — and only the filenames change. Enter your repeating object with all the preset parameters possible on your template page as an editable region, and you'll only have to select a new file for each page.

✦ **Include your `<meta>` information.** Search engines rely on `<meta>` tags to get the overview of a page, and then scan the balance of the page to get the details. You can enter a Keyword or Description object from the Head panel of the Objects palette so that all the Web pages in your site have the same basic information for cataloging.

✦ **Apply all needed behaviors and styles to the template.** When a document is saved as a template, all the code in the `<head>` section is locked. As most behaviors and CSS styles insert code here, this means that documents created from templates cannot apply new behaviors or create new styles.

You can create a template from a Web document with one command: File ⇨ Save As Template. Dreamweaver stores all templates in a Templates folder created for each defined site, with a special file extension, `.dwt`. After you've created your page and saved it as a template, you'll notice that Dreamweaver inserts `<<Template>` in the title bar to remind you of the page's status. Now you're ready to begin defining the template's editable regions.

Note   You can also create a template from an entirely blank page if you like. To do so, choose Window ⇨ Templates to open the Template palette. From the Template palette, click the New button. You'll find more information on how to use the Template palette later in this chapter.

Using Editable Regions

As noted earlier, when you convert an existing page into a template via the Save As Template command, the entire document is initially locked. If you attempt to create a document from a template at this stage, Dreamweaver alerts you that the template doesn't have any editable regions and you will not be able to change anything on the page. Editable regions are essential to any template.

Marking existing content as editable

There are two techniques for marking editable regions. First, you can designate any existing content as an editable region. Second, you can insert a new, editable region anywhere you can place your cursor. In both cases, you must give the region a unique name. Dreamweaver uses the unique name to identify the editable region when entering new content, applying the template, and exporting or importing XML.

Note   As noted, each editable region must have a unique name, but the names need only be different from any other editable region on the same page. The name could be used for objects or JavaScript functions, or for editable regions on a different template.

To mark an existing area as an editable region, follow these steps:

1. Select the text or object you wish to convert to an editable region.

Tip   The general rule of thumb with editable regions is that you need to select a complete tag pair, such as `<table>...</table>`. This has several implications. For instance, while you can mark an entire table or a single cell as editable, you can't select multiple cells, a row, or a column to be so marked. You have to select each cell at a time (`<td>...</td>`). Also, you can select the content of a layer to be editable and keep the layer itself locked (so that its position and other properties cannot be altered), but if you select the layer to be editable, you can't lock the content.

2. Choose Modify ➪ Templates ➪ Mark Selection As Editable. You can also use the keyboard shortcut, Ctrl-Alt-W (Command-Option-W), or right-click (hold-click) the selection and choose Editable Regions ➪ Mark Selection As Editable from the shortcut menu.

Dreamweaver displays the New Editable Region dialog box.

3. Enter a unique name for the selected area. Click OK when you're done or Cancel to abort the operation.

Caution   While you can use spaces in editable region names, some characters are not permitted. The illegal characters are the question mark (?), double quote ("), single quote ('), and left and right angle brackets: (< and >).

Dreamweaver highlights the selection with the color picked in Preferences on the Highlighting panel, if the Show option has been selected. You'll also find the name for your newly designated region listed alphabetically in the Modify ➪ Templates submenu. If still selected, the region name will have a check mark next to it. You can jump to any other editable region by selecting its name from the dynamic list.

Tip Make sure you apply any formatting to your text—either through HTML codes, such as `<font>`, or CSS styles before you select it to be an editable region. Generally, you want to keep the defined look of the content while altering just the text, so make just the text an editable region and exclude the formatting tags. It's helpful to have the HTML Inspector open for this detailed work.

Inserting a new editable region

Sometimes it's helpful to create a new editable region where no content currently exists. In these situations, the editable region name doubles as a label identifying the type of content expected, such as {CatalogPrice}. Dreamweaver always puts new region names in curly braces as shown here, and highlights the entry in the template.

To insert a new editable region, follow these steps:

1. Place your cursor anywhere on the template page.

2. Choose Modify ⇨ Templates ⇨ New Editable Region. You can also use the keyboard shortcut, Ctrl-Alt-V (Command-Option-V); or right-click (hold-click) the selection and choose Editable Regions ⇨ New from the shortcut menu.

   Dreamweaver displays the New Editable Region dialog box.

3. Enter a unique name for the new region. Click OK when you're done or Cancel to abort the operation.

   Dreamweaver inserts the new region name in the document, surrounded by curly braces, and adds the name to the dynamic region list (which you can display by choosing Modify ⇨ Templates).

Tip One editable region is automatically created when you save a document as a template: the Web page's title. The title is stored in a special editable region called `doctitle`. To change the title (which initially takes the same title as the template), choose Modify ⇨ Page Properties and enter the new text in the Title text box. You can also use the keyboard shortcut, Ctrl-J (Command-J). Finally, you can select View ⇨ Head Elements and choose the Title icon to enter the new text in the Property Inspector.

Locking an editable region

Inevitably, you'll mark a region as editable that you'd prefer to keep locked, or discover that every page constructed to date has required inputting the same content, so it should be entered on the template and locked. In either event, converting an editable region to an uneditable one is a simple operation.

To lock an editable region, follow these steps:

1. Place your cursor in the editable region you want to lock.

2. Choose Modify ➪ Templates ➪ Unmark Editable Region.

The Unmark Editable Region dialog box, shown in Figure 34-2, appears with the selected region highlighted.

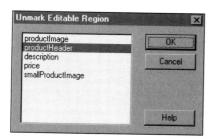

Figure 34-2: Convert an editable region to a locked one with the Unmark Editable Region command.

Note
You don't have to preselect the editable region to unmark it. If you don't, the Unmark Editable Region dialog box opens but doesn't highlight any selection; and you'll have to choose it by name.

3. Click OK in the Unmark Editable Region dialog box to confirm your choice.

The editable region highlight is removed and the area is now a locked region of the template.

Caution
Note two concerns when unmarking editable regions. If you are unmarking a newly inserted editable region that is labeled with the region name in curly braces, the label is not removed and must be deleted by hand on the template. Otherwise, it will appear as part of the document created from a template and won't be accessible. Also, be careful locking editable regions where pages have already been generated from the Dream Templates. On the next update, your page content will be replaced by the new locked region.

Adding Content to Template Documents

Constructing a template is only half the job — using it to create new pages is the other half. Because your basic layout is complete and you're only dropping in new images and entering new text, pages based on templates take a fraction of the time needed to create regular Web pages. Dreamweaver 2 makes it easy to enter new content as well — you can even move from one editable region to the next, much like filling out a form (which, of course, is exactly what you're doing).

To create a new document based on a template, follow these steps:

1. Choose File ➪ New from Template.

The Select Template dialog box, shown in Figure 34-3, appears.

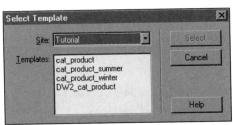

Figure 34-3: Create a new document based on any template in the Select Template dialog box.

2. If you wish to create a template from a local site other than the current one, select it from the Site drop-down list.

3. Select the desired template from those in the Templates list box.

4. Click OK when you're done.

When your new page opens, you'll notice that the highlighting is now reversed: the locked content is highlighted and the editable regions are not. You can see this clearly in Figure 34-4, where the template is on the left and the document created from the template is on the right. The highlighting makes is easy to differentiate the two types of regions.

Generally, it is easiest to select the editable region name or placeholder first and then enter the new content. Selecting the editable regions can be handled in several ways:

✦ Highlight each editable region name or placeholder with the mouse.

✦ Position your cursor inside any editable region and then select the `<mm:editable>` tag in the Tag Selector.

✦ Choose Modify ⇨ Templates and then select the name of your editable region from the dynamic list.

Note   If all of your editable regions are separate cells in a table, you can Tab forward and Shift-Tab in reverse through the cells. With each Tab, all the content in the cell is selected, whether it is an editable region name or a placeholder.

Naturally, you should save your document to retain all the new content that's been added.

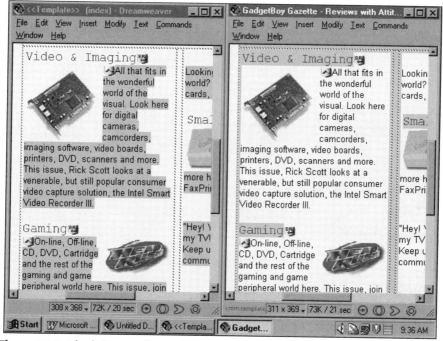

Figure 34-4: The left pane shows the template with the editable regions highlighted; the right pane has the document created from the same template, with the locked regions highlighted.

Working with the Template Palette

As a site grows, so do the number of templates it employs. Overall management of your template is conducted through the Template Palette. You can open the Template by choosing Windows ➪ Templates or by pressing the keyboard shortcut, Ctrl-F11 (Command-F11). Like the Library Palette, the Template Palette, shown in Figure 34-5, displays a list of the current site's available templates in the upper pane and a preview of the selected template in the lower pane.

The Template Palette has four buttons across the top:

✦ **New** creates a new, blank template.

✦ **Delete** removes the selected template.

✦ **Open** loads the selected template for editing.

✦ **Apply to Page** changes the locked region of one document created from a template to a different template.

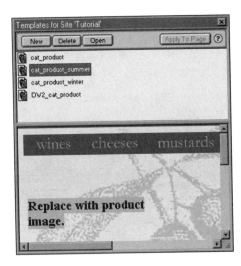

Figure 34-5: Use the Template Palette to preview, delete, open, create, or apply your current site's templates.

Creating a blank template

Not all templates are created from existing documents. Some Web designers prefer to create their templates from scratch. To create a blank template, follow these steps:

1. Open the Template Palette by choosing Window ➪ Templates.

2. From the Template Palette, select New.

    A new, untitled template is created.

3. Enter a title for your new template and press Enter (Return).

4. While the new template is selected, press the Open button.

    The blank template opens in a new Dreamweaver window.

5. Insert your page elements.

6. Mark any elements or areas as editable regions using one of the methods previously described.

7. Save your template.

Deleting and opening templates

As with any set of files, there comes a time to clean house and remove files that are no longer in use. To remove a template, first open the Template Palette. Next, select the file you want to remove and choose the Delete button.

Caution Be forewarned: Dreamweaver does not attempt to stop you or even warn you if there are files created from the template you're about to delete. Deleting the template, in effect, "orphans" those documents, and they can no longer be updated via a template.

You can edit a template — to change the locked or editable regions — in any one of several ways. To use the first method, choose File ⇨ Open and in the Select File dialog box, change the Files of Type to Template Files (*.dwt). Then, locate the Templates folder in your defined site to select the template to open.

The second method of opening a template for modification uses the Template Palette. Open the Template Palette by choosing Window ⇨ Templates. Then, select a template to edit and choose the Open button. You can also double-click your template to open it for editing.

Finally, if you're working in the Site Window, open a template by selecting the Templates folder for your site and open any of the files found there.

Tip After you've made your modifications to the template, you don't have to use the Save As Template command to store the file — you can use the regular File ⇨ Save command, or the keyboard shortcut, Ctrl-S (Command-S). Likewise, if you want to save your template under another name, use the Save As command.

Applying templates

Dreamweaver 2 makes it easy to try a variety of different looks for your document while maintaining the same content. Once you've created a document from a template, you can apply any other template to it. The only requirement is that the two templates have editable regions with the same names. When might this feature come in handy? In one scenario, you might develop a number of possible Web site designs for a client and create templates for each different approach, which are then applied to the identical content. Or, in an ongoing site, you could completely change the look of a catalog seasonally, but retain all the content. Figure 34-6 shows two radically different schemes for a Web site with the same content.

To apply a template to a document, follow these steps:

1. Open the Template Palette by choosing Window ⇨ Templates.

2. Make sure the Web page you want to apply the style to is the active document.

3. From the Template Palette, select the template you want to apply and click the Apply to Page button.

Tip You can also drag onto the current page the template you'd like to apply or choose Modify ⇨ Templates ⇨ Apply Template to Page from the menus.

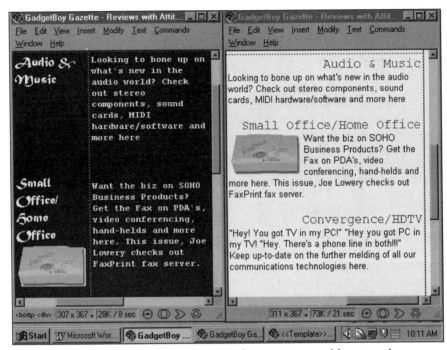

Figure 34-6: You can apply a template to a document created from another template to achieve different designs with identical content.

4. If there is no content in a matching editable region, Dreamweaver displays the Choose Editable Region for Orphaned Content dialog box. To receive the content, select one of the listed editable regions from the template being applied and click OK.

   The new template is applied to the document and all the new locked areas replace all the old locked areas.

Updating Templates

Anytime you save a change to an existing template — whether any documents have been created from it or not — Dreamweaver asks if you'd like to update all the documents in the local site attached to the template. As with Library elements, you can also update the current page or the entire site at any time. Updating documents based on a template can save you an enormous amount of time — especially when numerous changes are involved.

To update a single page, open the page and choose Modify ➪ Templates ➪ Update Current Page. The update is instantly applied.

To update a series of pages or an entire site, follow these steps:

1. Choose Modify ⇨ Templates ⇨ Update Pages.

   The Update Pages dialog box, shown in Figure 34-7, appears.

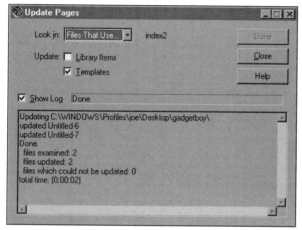

Figure 34-7: Any changes to a template can be automatically applied to its associated files with the Update Pages command.

2. To update all the documents using all the templates for an entire site, choose Entire Site from the Look In option and then select the name of the site from the accompanying drop-down list.

3. To update pages using a particular template, choose Pages Using from the Look In option and then select the name of the template.

4. To view a report of the progress of the update, make sure that the Show Log option is enabled.

5. Click Start to begin the update process.

   The log window displays a list of the files examined and updated, the total number of files that could not be updated, and the elapsed time.

Changing the Default Document

Each time you open a new document in Dreamweaver — or even just start Dreamweaver — a blank page is created. This blank page is based on an HTML file called Default.html that is stored in the Configuration\Templates folder. The default page works in a similar fashion to the Dream Templates in that you can create new documents from it, but there are no editable or locked regions — everything in the page can always be altered.

The basic blank-page document is an HTML structure with only a few properties specified: a document type, a character set, and a white background for the body:

```
<html>
<head>
<title>Untitled Document</title>
<meta http-equiv="Content-Type" content="text/html;
charset=iso-8859-1">
</head>

<body bgcolor="#FFFFFF">

</body>
</html>
```

Naturally, you can change any of these elements — and add many, many more — once you've opened a page. But what if you want to have a `<meta>` tag with creator information in every page that comes out of your Web design company? You can do it in Dreamweaver 2 manually, but it's a bother; and chances are, sooner or later, you'll forget. Luckily, with Dreamweaver, you have a more efficient solution.

Learning by Example

If you're just starting out in Web design, example pages are a good way to get a fast start. Aside from the Default.html template, Dreamweaver includes four different basic examples, each intended to offer a simple structure for you to build upon. You get the following examples with Dreamweaver, stored in the Configuration\Templates folder:

✦ Basic Tables

✦ Company Profiles

✦ Story Column

✦ Basic Frames

All the examples include descriptive text describing how each area of the template can be used or modified.

Caution: Unlike the Default.html blank page or any other new Dream Templates, when you open one of the other working examples in the Configuration\Templates folder, Dreamweaver does not create a new file based on that page. Instead, you must use the Save As command to save your new page under a different name before you do anything else. If you make any modifications to the examples and then save them in a normal fashion, the example is altered and the original will be lost. Otherwise, you could choose File ⇨ Save As Template to convert it to a Dream Template for your site.

In keeping with its overall design philosophy of extensibility, Dreamweaver enables you to modify the Default.html file as you would any other file. Just choose File ⇨ Open and select the Configuration\Templates\Default.htm file. As you've made your changes, save the file as you would normally. Now, to test your modifications, choose File ⇨ New — your modifications should appear in your new document.

Summary

Much of a Web designer's responsibility is related to document production, and Dreamweaver 2 offers a comprehensive template solution to reduce the workload. When planning your strategy for building an entire Web site, remember the following advantages provided by templates:

✦ Dream Templates can be created from any Web page.

✦ Dreamweaver templates combine locked and editable regions. Editable regions must be defined individually.

✦ Once a template is declared, new documents can be created from it.

✦ If a template is altered, pages built from that template can be automatically updated.

✦ You can modify the default template that Dreamweaver uses, so that every time you select File ⇨ New a new version of your customized template will be created.

✦   ✦   ✦

What's on the CD-ROM?

The CD-ROM that accompanies the *Dreamweaver 2 Bible* contains the following:

◆ Fully functioning trial versions of Dreamweaver 2, Fireworks, and Flash 3

◆ The Beatnik plug-in from Headspace

◆ All the code examples used in the book

Also included are over 300 Dreamweaver extensions from the leaders in the Dreamweaver community, designed to make your work more productive:

◆ Behaviors

◆ Objects

◆ Commands

◆ Inspectors

◆ Queries

◆ Browser profiles

Using the CD-ROM

The CD-ROM is what is known as a hybrid CD-ROM, which means it contains files that run on more than one computer platform—in this case, both Windows and Macintosh computers.

Several files, primarily the Macromedia trial programs and the Beatnik player, are compressed. Double-click these files to begin the installation procedure. Most other files on the CD-ROM are uncompressed and can be simply copied from the CD-ROM to your system by using your file manager. A few of the Dreamweaver extensions with files that must be placed in different folders are also compressed.

For the most part, the file structure of the CD-ROM replicates the structure that Dreamweaver sets up when it is installed. For example, objects found in the Dreamweaver\Configuration\Objects folder are located on both the CD-ROM and the installed program. One slight variation: In the Additional Extensions folder, you'll find the various behaviors, objects, and so on, filed under their author's name.

Files and Programs on the CD-ROM

The *Dreamweaver 2 Bible* contains a host of programs and auxiliary files to assist your exploration of Dreamweaver, as well as your Web page design work in general. Following is a description of the files and programs on the CD-ROM.

Dreamweaver 2, Fireworks, and Flash 3 demos

If you haven't had a chance to work with Dreamweaver (or Fireworks or Flash), the CD-ROM offers fully functioning trial versions of three key Macromedia programs for both Macintosh and Windows systems. The demo can be used for 30 days; it cannot be reinstalled for additional use time.

To install the demo, simply double-click the program icon in the main folder of the CD-ROM, and follow the installation instructions on your screen.

Note   The trial versions of Macromedia programs are very sensitive to system date changes. If you alter your computer's date, the programs will "time-out" and no longer be functional.

Trial versions of BBEdit and HomeSite, the external text editors supplied with the commercial version of Dreamweaver, are not included on the CD-ROM. You can download demos of both programs at the Web sites for these products, however.

✦ Bare Bones Software for BBEdit: http://www.bbedit.com/

✦ Allaire Software for HomeSite: http://www.allaire.com

Additional Extensions

Dreamweaver is amazingly extendible, and the Dreamweaver community has built some amazing extensions. In the Additional Extensions folder of the CD-ROM, you'll find over 300 behaviors, objects, commands, Inspectors, and more. The extensions are grouped according to author; and within each author's folder by function. Extensions that contain files that must be placed in different folders, such as the Commands and Inspectors directories, are compressed in a ZIP format.

Note Within the Additional Extensions folder, all behaviors are stored in the Behaviors folder to make it easy to access them. When installing, make sure to put them in the Configuration\Behaviors\Action folder on your system and not just the Behaviors folder.

You'll find a ReadMe.htm file in each of the author's folders, with links to their Web sites and more information about their creations.

Andrew Wooldridge

Andrew was one of the first Dreamweaver extensions authors and continues to push the envelope with his creations today. In addition to his collection of behaviors, objects, and commands, Andrew has also begun to explore the world of Dreamweaver queries — and you'll find some of those efforts here, as well.

Behaviors

AW_changeBGColor	Document Write
AW_javaConsole	DW_shakescreen
AW_loadframe	Execute Custom Code
AW_searchquery	Focus Remote
AW_writeframe	Focus Window
AWcomposer	Get Cookie
AWredirect	Kill Window
AWsearchentry	Move Layer
AWviewsource	Move Remote By
Back to my frame	Move Remote To
Bust Frames	MoveBy Window
Center Layers	MoveTo Window
Check Browser Version	Multi-Frame Control Layers
Check Browser	Open Fullscreen Window
ColorDepth Redirect	Persist Layer Stop
Conditional	Persist Layer
Create Layer	Popup Confirm
Delaylink	Popup Prompt
	Print Cross Browser

Behaviors (*continued*)

Quickwindow

Resize Layer

Resize Remote By

Resize Remote To

ResizeBy Window

ResizeTo Window

Screen based Move Layer

Screen based Resize Layer

Scroll Layer Stop

Scroll Layer

Set Cookie

Slide Layer Stop

Slide Layer

Spawn Window

Watch Property

Commands

Add Log Entry

All of Them

ASCIIToTable

Build Custom Tag

Changetag

Clear Page Content

Command Menu Manager

Create 3DML Spot

Create Site Log

Create Threadlist

Inherit Properties

Invert Table Axes

Name All Elements

Quick Site

Scheduled Behavior

Scratch Pad

Scratchdata

Style To Top

Tag Properties

Threads

Tweak Head

View Site Log

Web Bookmarks

Webbookdata

Wrap UnWrap Element

Zero Page Borders

Objects

3DML

AW_iframe

AW_mailto

AWactionmaker

AWbannerad

AWcalc

AWImgPreload

AWlinkoverride

AWobjmaker

AWrollover

Browselayer

Clickbar

Draglayer

Frames

Insertbff

Insertnbsp

Jsjumpmenu   Player

Jumpmenu   Randomimage

Jumpmenu2   ResizeBrowser

Marquee   Showobjects

Mycopyright   Stoperrors

Myrollbar   Ticker

Queries

Change_meta_description   Mailtos

Change_meta_keywords   Set_all_targets

Brendan Dawes

Without a doubt, Brendan's got the heppest Dreamweaver site going — it's guaranteed to be the only one you'll encounter that subtitles itself, "Dreamweaver Objects with Cheez!" As well as being extremely useful, Brendan's extensions are also quite tasty.

Behaviors   **Objects**

Control Beatnik   Beatnik

Create slideshow   Flash_movie

Flash 3 Detector   Guestbook-o-matic

Multiple Re-directl   Quicktime

Navigate slideshow   Realvideo

Hava Edelstein

Hava is a Macromedia Dreamweaver engineer, specializing in JavaScript, who has graciously donated several commands to help others create Dreamweaver extensions. Be sure to read her well-commented code to get the insider's viewpoint.

Eval

Set All Checkboxes

Show Browser References

Show Document Tree

Show Table Properties

Jaro von Flocken

Take a ride on the Web to the Yaromat to pick up some choice morsels — or you can just stop by Jaro's folder on this CD-ROM to sample his wares. Jaro has created some truly breathtaking extensions designed to sharpen the cutting-edge of any Web site.

Behaviors

Animate Image

Calendar

Check Cookie

Fly In Letters

Image Gauge

Layer Fx

Mouse Trace

RandomImage

RandomURL

Show-Hide Layer Group

Stop Layer Fx

Switch

Toggle Layer

ZoomIn

Commands

Anti Layer Bug NS4

Auto alt

Layer2Style

Inspectors

Body

Style

Objects

Fireworks

Machak FX

One of the newest — and busiest — Dreamweaver extension authors is Marijan Milicevic, better known by his e-mail name in the newsgroup "jjooee." Joe, as he likes to be called, is originally from Croatia and is currently living and working in the Netherlands. You'll find several new commands and behaviors under his company name, Machak FX. Machak, by the way, means "tomcat" in Croatian.

Behaviors

Machak Call Slide FX

Machak Top FX

Commands

Machak FX

Machak FX Vertical

Machak Slide FX

Machak Error

Massimo Foti — The Fantastic Corporation

The Dreamweaver community owes a debt of thanks to the Fantastic Corporation. First, for allowing Massimo Foti to build this wonderful collection of Dreamweaver extensions and, second, for permitting them to appear on this CD-ROM.

Behaviours

Back to my frame

Basic move layer

Centre window

Clip layer

Colordepth redirect

History go remote

History go

IE scrollbar

IE set layer background

Iechange background image

Layer clip bottom on percentage

Layer clip right on percentage

Layer position on percentage

Layer resize on percentage

Maximize window

Open fullscreen window

Opener location

Print cross browser

Resize layer

Screen based clip layer

Screen based move layer

Screen based resize layer

Scroll layer by

Scroll layer stop

Scroll layer

Set layer z-index

Window commander

Window crusher

Window launcher

Commands

Always on top

Back to my frame

Bordless frame

Browser 4 redirect

Close onblur

Colordepth redirect

CSS on browser

CSS on platform

CSS on resolution

Font tag killer

Fullscreen opener

Frame buster

JS on browser

NN resize fix

Onebyone

Onebyone_help

Page borders

Screen redirect

Set global var

Stop errors

Tag killer

Commands (*continued*)

Title for maps

Window maximizer

Zero frame scrollbars

Zero page scrollbars

Objects

Audioembed

Back to my frame

Background that fit

Base target

CSS depending on browser

CSS depending on platform

CSS depending on resolution

External CSS file

External JS file

Firestream

Frame buster

Fullscreen opener

JS depending on browser

NN resize fix

Videoembed

Window maximizer

Simon White — MediaFear

Somehow, in addition to heading MediaFear (Haight-Ashbury's premier Web design shop), answering a zillion queries in the Dreamweaver newsgroup as a Macromedia evangelist, and serving as the technical editor for this book, Simon White has had time to create several extremely useful Dreamweaver extensions. In addition to the commands and objects, you'll find new icons for Window users, complete with installation instructions.

Commands

Link TrueDoc Dynamic Fonts

Shop for Extensions

Objects

Page Transitions

Standard Ads

Icons

dw.ico

dwfolder.ico

dwq.ico

dwr.ico

dwt.ico

Queries

Change Meta Description

Change Meta Keywords

Set All Targets

Spooky and the Bandit

If it seems curious to include the single object provided by Spooky and the Bandit, an English Web design house, amidst all of these collections—that just means you haven't seen the object. Their Flash 3 object uses a Flash movie for the user interface and is a superb example of what's possible. Naturally, you must have the Flash plug-in installed on your system in order to use this object.

Webmonkey

Webmonkey is an excellent online resource sponsored by the folks who brought you *Wired* magazine. Wired uses Dreamweaver for all their in-house site designing and has developed several extensions to smooth their workflow—and, luckily, made them available to the public. Of special note is their XSSI extension with numerous objects, Inspectors, and translators—just double-click the XSSI installer to bring it onto your system.

Behaviors

Change Links

Position Layer

Special Extension

XSSI Extension

Dreamweaver 2 Bible Extensions

The majority of the following extensions were built specifically for this book. These extensions can be found in the Configuration folder on the CD-ROM.

Note One extension, AutoFixLayer, is stored as a ZIP file because it contains files that must go into different directories. This extension automatically inserts code to patch the Netscape layer resize bug.

Behaviors

Dreamweaver behaviors automate many functions that previously required extensive JavaScript programming. The behaviors included on the CD-ROM are in addition to the standard set of behaviors included with Dreamweaver and discussed in Chapter 17, "Using Behaviors." The behaviors on the CD-ROM are stored in the Dreamweaver\Configuration\Behaviors\Actions folder. Copy the behaviors to a similarly named folder in your system installation of Dreamweaver, and restart Dreamweaver to access the new behaviors.

Table A-1 lists the Dreamweaver behaviors available on the CD-ROM.

Table A-1
Behaviors on the CD-ROM

Behavior	Description
Add A Groovoid	Adds a Groovoid sound effect, playable with the Beatnik plug-in
Center Layers	Enables layers to be centered automatically at any screen resolution
Check Mime	Looks for a specific MIME type and redirects the user to a different URL if it is not found
Watch	Implements a watch command that triggers programmable JavaScript if a particular property is changed

Extending Dreamweaver: The Behaviors folder on the CD-ROM contains a copy of Macromedia's Extending Dreamweaver PDF file. The Extending Dreamweaver file contains detailed instructions on how to create your own Dreamweaver extensions. The Adobe Acrobat Reader, freely available from the Adobe Web site (www.adobe.com), is required to view the file.

Objects

Much of Dreamweaver's power derives from its extensibility. Each of the standard Dreamweaver objects is based on an HTML file. The CD-ROM contains various Dreamweaver objects designed to help you create your Web pages faster and more efficiently.

Each Dreamweaver object consists of two files: an HTML file, and a GIF file with the same name that is used to create the button on the Objects Palette. For example, the Character Entities object comprises the two files char_entities.htm and char_entities.gif.

Table A-2 lists the Dreamweaver objects available on the CD-ROM.

Table A-2
Dreamweaver Objects on the CD-ROM

Object	Filenames	Folder	Description
ActiveMovie	amovie.htm, amovie.gif	Media	Inserts an ActiveMovie/Audio file
Beatnik	beatnik.htm, beatnik.gif	Media	Inserts a Beatnik audio file
Character Entities	char_entities.htm, char_entities.gif	New	Inserts any Upper ASCII character

Object	Filenames	Folder	Description
DynSrc	dynsrc.htm, dynsrc.gif	Media	Inserts a DynSrc tag and attributes for an Internet Explorer movie
Enhanced Table	e_table.htm, e_table.gif	Common	Enables additional table attributes (including attributes specific to Internet Explorer) to be inserted
NewBreak	new_break.htm, new_break.gif	Invisibles	Enhanced line-break object
QuickTime	qtime.htm, qtime.gif	Media	Inserts QuickTime and QuickTimeVR movies
Sub	sub.htm, sub.gif	Invisibles	Inserts the $\langle sub \rangle$ tag for subscripted text
Sup	sup.htm, sup.gif	Invisibles	Inserts the $\langle sup \rangle$ tag for superscripted text

To install the Dreamweaver objects, go to Dreamweaver\Configuration\Objects and copy any pair of files from the subfolders Common, Forms, Invisibles, Media, and New to similarly named folders in your system installation of Dreamweaver. (The Media and New folders are not included in the standard release of Dreamweaver and must be created on your system.) Restart Dreamweaver to access the new objects.

Commands

Commands are proving to be the real workhorses of Dreamweaver 2 extensibility. Not only can they do pretty much everything that behaviors and objects can, but they have their own capabilities as well. Command files come in many shapes and sizes — from a single file to five or more files split across multiple folders. The commands found in the CD-ROM's Configuration\Commands folder go into the equivalent Dreamweaver folder on your system. The commands are as follows:

✦ **Replicator** duplicates any selected object, any number of times. Be sure to copy both Replicator.htm and Replicator.js into the Commands folder.

✦ **Install Shockwave HTML** reads an HTML file generated by Director to insert a Shockwave object, complete with proper dimensions and other needed parameters.

✦ **Change Case** converts the case of the selected text to uppercase or lowercase.

Browser profiles

Dreamweaver recognizes the proliferation of browsers on the market today and makes it easy for you to check your Web page creations against specific browser types. The browser targeting capability is available through the use of Browser profiles, covered in Chapter 31, "Maximizing Browser Targeting." In addition to the standard profiles that come with Dreamweaver, the CD-ROM contains several Browser profiles for checking various implementations of HTML, including the following:

+ HTML 2.0
+ HTML 3.2
+ HTML 4.0
+ Opera 3.2
+ Pocket Internet Explorer 1.0 (for Windows CE 1.0)
+ Pocket Internet Explorer 1.1 (for Windows CE 1.0)
+ Pocket Internet Explorer 2.0 (for Windows CE 2.0)

Each additional Browser Profile is contained in the Dreamweaver\Configuration\ BrowserProfiles folder of the CD-ROM. To install the Browser profiles, the files must be copied to a similarly named folder in your system installation of Dreamweaver. Restart Dreamweaver to access the new Browser profiles.

Dreamweaver 2 Bible code examples

Example code used in the *Dreamweaver 2 Bible* can be found in the Code folder of the CD-ROM. Also included and of particular note are the Dreamweaver Techniques from various chapters throughout the book. Each technique contains all the requisite example HTML files and graphics files within its own folder. You can easily view the files through Dreamweaver or your browser without transferring the files to your system. If you do wish to transfer the files, copy the entire folder over to your system.

Dreamweaver style sheets

Dreamweaver makes using Cascading Style Sheets (CSS) a point-and-click operation. One of the great features of CSS is the ability to link your Web site to external style sheets. The CD-ROM contains several external style sheets that you can customize for your Web sites. Each external style sheet comes with an example HTML file that you can view in your browser.

To incorporate the external style sheets in your Web sites, copy the file with the .css extension into your local site root folder. Then follow the instructions in the "Linking to an External Style Sheet" section found in Chapter 24.

Dreamweaver examples

One of the best ways to begin working in Web design is to customize another's designs. The CD-ROM includes several Web page examples aimed at giving you a running start in creating your own pages. Each example is found in its own subfolder in the Dreamweaver Bible Code\Examples folder.

You can use these examples in two ways from within Dreamweaver:

✦ Open them directly from the CD-ROM by using the File ➪ Open command.

✦ Transfer the files to your system and open them from there.

External programs

To extend their multimedia functionality, browsers use a fair number of plug-ins and external programs. The CD-ROM contains Beatnik Player, the plug-in from Headspace, Inc. To install Beatnik Player, just double-click the icon in the External Programs folder and follow the instructions on your screen. The Beatnik Player is © 1998 Headspace, Inc.

Web resource directory

The World Wide Web is a vital resource for any Web designer, whether you're a seasoned professional or a beginner. The CD-ROM contains an HTML page with a series of links to resources on the Web; the series contains general as well as Dreamweaver-specific references.

✦   ✦   ✦

BBEdit 5.0 Primer (For Macintosh Users)

reating great-looking Web sites is easy thanks to Dreamweaver's visual layout interface. Even so, sometimes it's helpful to switch from Dreamweaver's visual editor mode and edit the underlying HTML (Hypertext Markup Language) source code — particularly when you're troubleshooting HTML documents.

Dreamweaver has a basic built-in HTML editor: the HTML Inspector. When a more advanced code editor is needed, Macintosh users can use the BBEdit application from Bare Bones Software (http://www.bbedit.com/). This stand-alone editor is included on the CD-ROM that accompanies the full version of Dreamweaver.

BBEdit 5.0 is the most recent version of this popular, pre-Web, Macintosh programmer's text editor. In recent years, the program has evolved into a feature-packed text-based HTML editor that elegantly exploits the ease-of-use capabilities of the Macintosh OS. BBEdit is the choice of many Web professionals.

This appendix is written as a basic beginner's guide to BBEdit. The software has a myriad of features and capabilities; some of BBEdit's more advanced features are not covered here.

Getting Started

You can easily switch between Dreamweaver and BBEdit. A simple click on an icon toggles you from one application to the other. Elements selected in one application are automatically highlighted in the other. This capability makes it easy to find your place in the code, and modifications can be made quickly.

Key features

BBEdit is wonderfully full-featured and adaptable to your style of working. Just a few of BBEdit's many advantages follow:

- ✦ HTML syntax checking
- ✦ Multiple layers of Undo and Redo
- ✦ Spell-checking
- ✦ Multiple-file find and replace
- ✦ Support for files up to 2GB
- ✦ A file comparison feature for locating differences among files
- ✦ HTML syntax coloring
- ✦ "Open from" and "Save to" FTP servers from the File menu
- ✦ Table builder
- ✦ Web-safe color palette
- ✦ One-click preview in any browser

BBEdit installation

BBEdit 5.0, like Dreamweaver, runs on Power Macintoshes and compatible computers. Install BBEdit by launching the Install BBEdit 5.0 application on the CD-ROM supplied with the full version of Dreamweaver.

BBEdit installs several special folders during the installation process that provide additional functionality. These folders can be removed if you don't need their features. The following items are installed within the BBEdit 5.0 folder.

Folder	Contents
BBEdit Plug-ins	Modules that offer additional BBEdit features written and contributed by BBEdit users

Folder	Contents
BBEdit Scripts	AppleScripts ready for execution through the Scripts menu located on the right side of the main pull-down menu
BBEdit Glossary	Text files that can be inserted into an active editing window. Simply add text files to the folder and then use the Glossary command in the Windows menu to insert the contents of a text file.
BBEdit Dictionaries	Dictionaries used by BBEdit's spell-checker. The User Dictionary stores words you add to this personal dictionary. See the "Spell-checking" section later in this appendix for more information.

Working with Dreamweaver and BBEdit

Although Dreamweaver 2.0 enables you to assign any HTML editor as your external editor, Dreamweaver integrates optimally with BBEdit. Once you set up BBEdit as your default editor, switching between the two editors is just a button click or keyboard shortcut away.

Setting up BBEdit as your default editor

Before Dreamweaver can access BBEdit, you must make BBEdit your default HTML editor. Dreamweaver for the Macintosh ships with this feature enabled. A quick way to check is to look for a Launch BBEdit option under your Edit menu. If the option is not there, you can make this assignment through the Dreamweaver Preferences by following these steps:

1. In Dreamweaver, choose Edit ➪ Preferences to open the Preferences dialog box.

2. From the Category list on the left, choose External Editors to display that panel.

3. In the External Editors panel, click in the box that says Enable BBEdit Integration and click OK. The Edit menu option that used to read Launch Text Editor should now be Launch BBEdit.

If this sequence doesn't work, Dreamweaver can't find where you've installed BBEdit. Go back to the External Editors preferences and use the Browse (Choose) button to find BBEdit.

Cross-Reference The External Editor options that control file synchronization between Dreamweaver and BBEdit are explained in Chapter 3, "Setting Your Preferences."

Switching between Dreamweaver and BBEdit

You have several ways to switch to BBEdit while in Dreamweaver:

 ✦ Click the BBEdit button in the top-left corner of the HTML Inspector.

 ✦ Use the Finder.

 ✦ Choose Edit ⇨ Launch BBEdit.

 ✦ Use the keyboard shortcut, Command-E.

Caution

Depending on the file reloading options chosen in the External Editors prefer-ences, Dreamweaver may ask if you want to save the file first before you switch to BBEdit. If you do not save your Dreamweaver file, your modifications do not appear in BBEdit, and vice versa. For this reason, you should set your Reload Modified File option to Always.

After you've made your code modifications in BBEdit and you're ready to return to Dreamweaver, just click the Dreamweaver button near the center of BBEdit's HTML Tools Palette (see Figure B-1). The "HTML Tools Palette" section later in this appendix provides more information about this window.

Disabling BBEdit integration

You may disable BBEdit integration if you prefer working with an older version of BBEdit or if you use a different HTML text editor. Follow these steps:

1. Choose Edit ⇨ Preferences.

2. Select External Editors from the category list on the left.

3. Deselect the Enable BBEdit Integration option and click OK.

Note

Text selections are not tracked if integration is turned off.

BBEdit menus

Dynamic Menus: BBEdit uses an advanced menu system called *dynamic menus*. This system uses the Shift or Option keys to alter menu options while a menu is open.

Keyboard Shortcuts: Many of BBEdit's commands have keyboard equivalents. Pull-down menus show keyboard shortcuts. To see the keyboard equivalents for options in a dialog box, hold down the Command key. After a brief delay, the keyboard equivalents appear next to the buttons in the dialog box.

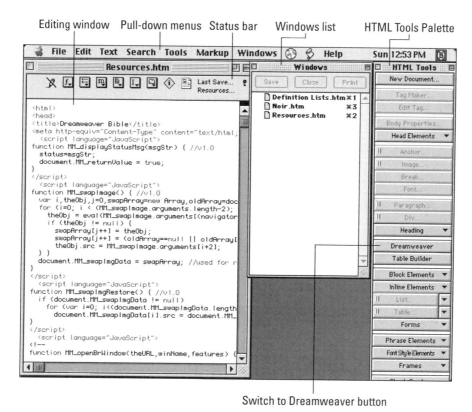

Figure B-1: The BBEdit 5.0 workspace.

BBEdit preferences

BBEdit offers a wealth of options for customizing the application to meet your needs. Use the Edit pull-down menu to select Preferences. A dialog box appears with several categories of options listed on the left side. When you select a category, a short description of the category is displayed at the top of the dialog box. Figure B-2 displays BBEdit's options for text-editing preferences.

Getting Help

BBEdit provides assistance with its functions with the Help pull-down menu. You can choose the BBEdit Guide to show a window that offers Help by topic, through an index, or via searching. This choice activates the Apple Guide-style interactive Help in BBEdit. Use the Show Balloons option to display the functions of many buttons and features as you move your mouse over various parts of BBEdit windows. To open the manuals in the BBEdit Documentation folder, you need to have the Adobe Acrobat Reader installed on your machine.

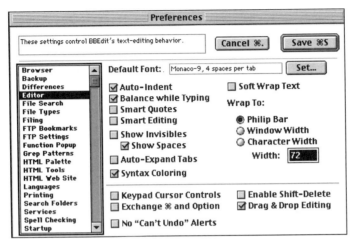

Figure B-2: BBEdit's Preferences dialog box showing Editor options.

HTML Document Basics

Once the BBEdit software is installed, you're ready to author HTML documents destined to become great-looking Web pages. This section explains the basics of creating, saving, and opening BBEdit documents.

Creating and saving new documents

Use the File menu to select New; then follow the pointer to the submenu. The most common options are Text Document and HTML Document.

Text document

This command opens an empty text file with two sub-options:

+ **With Selection** creates a new document containing text selected in another currently open BBEdit document. This is handy for quickly producing multiple pages that have common elements, such as a sitewide menu or background image.

+ **With Clipboard** creates a new document containing text copied into the Macintosh OS clipboard. The text could originate from any application.

HTML document

Choose HTML Document and you'll get a dialog box with options for creating a new HTML-formatted document. This option automatically places the HTML tags you need to begin building a page. This is the best option if you're starting a document from scratch.

Saving your work

When you're ready to save your newly created document, choose File ➪ Save. Give the document a name and choose the location where you wish to save the document.

The Save As command opens a standard Macintosh OS dialog box. The Option button within this dialog box gives you control over how file attributes are saved. You have two choices:

✦ **Save As Stationery** saves the document as a Macintosh OS stationery document. Later, when you open this document, BBEdit uses it as a template for a new untitled document. This option is useful if you will be creating multiple Web pages with common elements, such as a sitewide menu or background image.

✦ **Save Selection Only** instructs BBEdit to save only the selected text.

Opening existing BBEdit files

You have three ways to open existing BBEdit documents:

✦ Drag a file's icon to the BBEdit application icon, or to an alias of the icon. You can place the alias on your desktop for easy access. This option takes advantage of the Macintosh OS drag-and-drop feature.

✦ Simply double-click a BBEdit file. You can identify BBEdit documents by the associated BBEdit icon.

✦ With BBEdit launched, use the Open, Open Several, or Open Recent commands from the File menu.

Let's take a look at these File ➪ Open commands.

File ➪ Open

When you select Open from the File pull-down menu, a dialog box gives you the following options:

✦ **Open Read-Only.** This command opens the file so it can be viewed but not edited. To make a file editable, simply click the pencil icon in the status bar located at the top of each BBEdit document. (For a description of the status bar, see the "Editing Documents" section later in this appendix.)

✦ **Projector-Aware.** Use this option if collaboration on the document is ongoing with other users. This option is a safety feature; it assigns to the file a special notation indicating that the file is in use and should not be edited by another user. This is similar to Dreamweaver's Check-in/Check-out feature in the Site Window.

✦ **LF Translation.** Translates DOS or UNIX line breaks when you open a file. If this option is not selected, BBEdit leaves the original line breaks untranslated.

◆ **File Types.** A pop-up menu lets you select types of files to open. The default file type, All Available, lets BBEdit use its built-in translation system to open any files it can translate.

File ⇨ Open Recent

The Open Recent menu contains a list of files recently opened. To open one of these files, simply choose it from the submenu.

File ⇨ Open Several

This command lets you open multiple files simultaneously. This is particularly useful if you wish to open all the files in a folder — maybe all the HTML documents that make up your Web site. Here are the steps to open several files at once:

1. As you open the File menu, hold down the Option key to enable BBEdit's dynamic menu feature. You will see the Open Several command; select it and a dialog box appears (see Figure B-3).

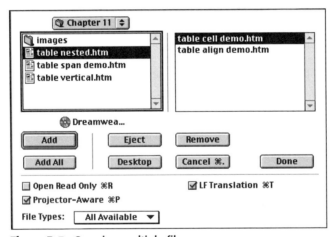

Figure B-3: Opening multiple files.

2. Choose a file you wish to open from the list on the left side of the dialog box.

3. Use Add to move the selected file to the list of files to be opened, on the right.

4. Use Add All to add all the files in the folder to the list of files to be opened.

5. Use the Add button to add any other files to the list on the right. Use Remove to eliminate unwanted files.

6. Choose any of the Open options you need (see File ⇨ Open, described in the preceding section).

7. Press Done to have BBEdit open the files.

Using file groups

BBEdit enables you to group files in a way that makes managing your Web site easier. You may want to group all the files that make up your Web site, or divide them into logical subsections that make sense to you.

A *file group* is a special BBEdit file that references other files in the file group. Any type of file can be included in a file group.

To start a file group:

1. Select File ➪ New ➪ File Group.

2. The resulting dialog box will ask you for a file group name (see Figure B-4).

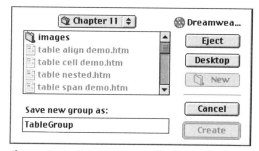

Figure B-4: Creating a new file group.

3. Click Create, and BBEdit opens a new empty file group.

To add files to a file group, simply drag any file from the Finder into the file group window (see Figure B-5). Or you can click the Add button to open a dialog box that enables you to choose files.

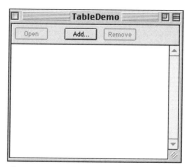

Figure B-5: An empty file group window.

To open a file within a file group, double-click the file. Or you can select the file and click the Open button.

Note   If the file is a BBEdit document, then BBEdit will open it. If the file is not a BBEdit document, then the application that created the file will be launched.

Editing Documents

This section guides you through BBEdit's menus, windows, and functions.

Basic text manipulation

BBEdit handles text in a way similar to many Macintosh text editors and word processors. Characters typed in BBEdit appear at the blinking vertical insertion point. The insertion point is controlled by placing the mouse in the desired location and clicking.

Click and drag the mouse to select several characters or words. If you select some text and then type, the new entry replaces the selected text. Use the Delete key to remove selected text.

Moving text

To easily move text from one location to another, follow these steps:

1. With the mouse, select the text you want to move.

Tip   If you wish to select all the text within a document choose Edit ⇨ Select All (keyboard shortcut: Command-A).

2. Choose Edit ⇨ Cut (Command-X) to remove the text from the window and store it in the Macintosh OS clipboard.

3. Find the new place where you wish to move the text, and click your mouse at the insertion point.

4. Choose Edit ⇨ Paste (Command-V) to place your text.

To copy text into the clipboard without deleting it from its original location, select Copy from the Edit pull-down menu (Command-C).

Dragging and dropping text

A fast and simple method to move text from one place to another takes advantage of the Macintosh OS drag-and-drop feature. Follow these steps:

1. Select the desired text.

2. Place the mouse pointer within the selected area.

3. Click and hold down the mouse button.

4. Drag the mouse pointer to the new position for the text.

5. Release the mouse button to drop in the text.

You can also use drag-and-drop to copy text to any other open BBEdit window.

Tip BBEdit enables you to drag-and-drop a text file from the Finder onto an editing window. Doing so inserts the file's contents where it's dropped.

Undo/Redo

The Edit ➭ Undo command (Command-Z) reverses changes — in chronological order — made to your file. The amount of available memory is the only limit to the number of edits that can be undone.

BBEdit also enables multiple Redos. Choose the Edit ➭ Redo command or use the keyboard shortcut, Command-Shift-Z.

Text wrapping

BBEdit wraps text in two ways: *soft wrapping* and *hard wrapping*. You can choose the option that works best for you, and have it take effect globally or for just one document.

✦ **Soft Wrapping.** Soft wrapping handles text like most word-processing software. As the insertion point reaches the limit of the right margin, it automatically moves to the next line. You never need to type a "return" at the end of a line unless you are beginning a new paragraph.

✦ **Hard Wrapping.** Hard wrapping enables you to type as far as you wish on a single line. You have to enter a "return" to end each line in order to begin a new line of text.

To change the text wrapping option in BBEdit, select Soft Wrap Text from the Window Options pop-up menu in the status bar (see "The Status bar" section coming up). Or you can choose Window Options via the Edit menu and select (or deselect) the Soft Wrap Text option from the Window Options dialog box.

What's in the BBEdit windows

Basic operation of BBEdit windows follows the standard Macintosh OS format. BBEdit offers two extra features: the status bar and the split bar.

The Status bar

The status bar (see Figure B-6) resides at the top of each editing window. This bar contains buttons and pop-up menus that help you work with the text in the window. Using the status bar you can save your work, show line numbers, display document information, and more.

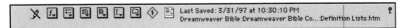

Figure B-6: BBEdit's status bar.

Tip   Use the Show Balloons option under the Help pull-down menu to show the function of the icons in the status bar. Hide the status bar by clicking the Key icon on the right side of the status bar.

The Split bar

Each editing window contains a *split bar*—it's a small black bar located just above the vertical scroll bar. The split bar divides the window into two panes, which is particularly helpful when you're editing a document in two places. Figure B-7 shows an editing window split into two panes.

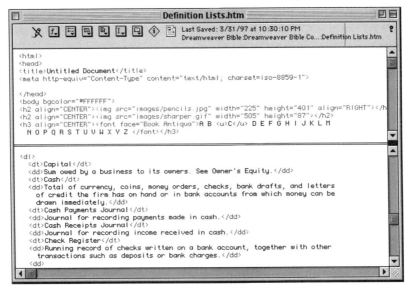

Figure B-7: Use the split bar to divide a window for editing a document in two places.

To split the window, drag the split bar from the top of the vertical scroll bar into the main window area. You can scroll both windows independently. Return to a full window by dragging the split bar to its original location.

 Tip Double-clicking the split bar divides a window into two equal panes, or removes the division from a split window.

Markup menu

The Markup pull-down menu and associated HTML Tools Palette together offer powerful assistance in designing the layout of your Web pages. In most respects the Markup menu and the HTML Tools Palette function similarly. Following are descriptions of some of the basic Markup menu functions.

Tag Maker command

The Tag Maker command brings up a list of HTML tags or HTML tag attributes that are available for insertion in your file. The command is context-sensitive — that is, the list of tags displayed is specific to the location in your document where your cursor is positioned when you choose this command. Select the desired tag or tag attribute from the list and click Insert to add the tag to your file.

Edit Tag command

To use the Edit Tag command, your cursor must be located inside an HTML tag in your document. Selecting the Edit Tag command brings up a context-sensitive dialog box that allows you to edit the attributes of that specific tag.

Head Elements menu

The Head Elements menu contains a variety of commands that allow you to set the properties of an entire HTML page. Examples of head elements are `<meta>` and `<title>` tags.

Body Properties command

The Body Properties command lets you specify a document's background image, background color, and default text and link colors as follows:

✦ Select a background graphic by typing the file's name into the Background field, or by pressing the File button to bring up a standard Macintosh dialog box.

✦ Assign a color for the background, default text, and links by checking the box next to the desired attribute and then selecting a color from the pop-up window of 216 Web-safe colors. Hold down the Option key while clicking a color to access the Apple color picker.

Block Elements menu

Insert HTML block elements, such as `<blockquote>`, `<address>` and `<pre>`, into your page by accessing this menu.

Heading menu

Use this menu to insert the HTML tags appropriate for heading levels 1 through 6, to distinguish the various titles and subheadings within a page.

Lists menu

This menu lets you organize lists of textual items, with optional indentation and a choice of bullets. BBEdit supports five list types: Unordered, Ordered, Definition, Menu, and Directory.

Tables menu

Tables are a great way to organize your Web page layout. The Tables menu provides you with the following table-creation tools:

✦ **Table Builder** displays the Table Builder utility. If the cursor is currently positioned within a table, the table is first selected.

✦ **Table** opens a dialog box that allows for a variety of table attributes to be specified, including Border, Width, Spacing, Padding, Frame, Rules, Align, Background color, the number of columns, and the number of rows. Inserts a `<table>...</table>` tag pair with the selected attributes, or encloses selected text with the same tag pair.

✦ **Row** opens a dialog box that allows for a variety of row attributes to be specified, including Align, Valign, and Background color. Inserts a `<tr>...</tr>` tag pair with the selected attributes, or encloses selected text with the same tag pair.

✦ **TD** opens a dialog box that allows for a variety of table cell attributes to be specified, including Rowspan, Colspan, Width, Height, Align, Valign, and Background color; and whether text wrapping is to be turned on or off. Inserts a `<td>...</td>` tag pair with the selected attributes, or encloses selected text with the same tag pair.

✦ **TH** opens a dialog box that allows for a variety of table header cell attributes to be specified, including Rowspan, Colspan, Width, Height, Align, Valign, and Background color; and whether text wrapping is to be turned on or off. Inserts a `<th>...</th>` tag pair with the selected attributes, or encloses selected text with the same tag pair.

✦ **Caption** inserts a `<caption>...</caption>` tag pair or encloses selected text with the same tag pair.

✦ **Convert to Table** converts the currently selected text to a table format using the parameters set by the displayed dialog box.

Inline Elements menu

An inline element is one that can be inserted next to another element without requiring a paragraph break. Following are some of the most commonly used tags:

✦ **Anchor** inserts an anchor tag with the associated attributes for creating a link or a base anchor.

✦ **Image** places a graphic image at the current insertion point. Size attributes are handled automatically for GIF, JPEG, and PNG files.

✦ **Font** opens a dialog box that allows for the specification of a font face, size, and color for the selected text. Click and hold the color chip to bring up a pull-down menu of Web-safe colors, or hold down the Option key while clicking on the color to open the Apple color picker.

Font Style Elements menu

Set the size and style of your font through the Font Style Elements menu. You can also open a separate Font Style palette, which contains all of the Font Style Elements commands, by selecting Font Palette from the Font Style Elements drop-down menu on the HTML Tools Palette.

The following font style options are available on this menu:

✦ **Big** sets the current text to use the `<big>...</big>` tag pair.

✦ **Small** sets the current text to use the `<small>...<.small>` tag pair.

✦ **Bold** sets the current text to use the `<b>...</b>` tag pair.

✦ **Italic** sets the current text to use the `<i>...</i>` tag pair.

✦ **Strike-Through** sets the current text to use the `<strike>...</strike>` tag pair.

✦ **Teletype Text** sets the current text to use the `<tt>...</tt>` tag pair.

✦ **Underline** sets the current text to use the `<ul>...</ul>` tag pair.

Check menu

This set of commands helps you to find problems such as bad links and HTML coding errors in your Web documents. Errors are shown in a new window, complete with the line number of the offending HTML code. The Check menu contains the following commands:

✦ **Document Syntax** checks the current document for HTML syntax errors. Faulty HTML may work fine when viewed in one browser but display incorrectly when viewed by another, and this command helps you avoid that problem.

Tip

One HTML error can result in the report of multiple subsequent errors. It's best to correct errors from the top of the document and then recheck the document after you correct each error.

✦ **Document Links** verifies that documents linked to a file actually exist, to help you identify bad links in your Web site. The command does not verify that these documents exist on your Web server, but rather that the documents exist in your site root folder (as defined in the HTML Preferences section of BBEdit's Preferences). See the "Internet Menu" section later in this appendix for information on checking external Web links.

✦ **Site Syntax** is similar to the Document Syntax command, but checks the syntax of every HTML file in the site root folder.

✦ **Site Links** operates like the Document Links command, but checks the validity of link references in every HTML file in the site root folder. No attempt is made to validate external links (such as sites on a remote Web server, for example). See the "Internet Menu" section later in this appendix for information on checking external Web links.

✦ **Balance Tags** selects the pair of container tags nearest the cursor, highlighting the tags and all the HTML text in between. If you select Balance Tags again, the next pair of tags is selected.

Update menu

This menu replaces all placeholders and includes in the current document (or the current site). See the BBEdit Help system for detailed information on using placeholders and includes.

Utilities menu

The Utilities menu offers a variety of page-oriented tools especially useful for prepping a regular text document for publication on the Web. You can open a separate palette that contains all of the Utilities commands by selecting Utilities Palette from the Utilities pull-down menu in the HTML Palette.

The Utilities commands are as follows:

✦ **Format.** Reformats the structure and display of the HTML text. Choose from the following:

- **Hierarchical** — Each set of tags is indented, and tag pairs appear on separate lines.

- **Gentle Hierarchical** — Similar to Hierarchical, but anchors within other tags are not indented.

- **Document Skeleton** — Hierarchical style but with everything removed that is not a tag or tag specification (such as all the text). Use this format to create a template.

- **Plain** — Each tag appears on a separate line.

- **Compact** — Deletes any unnecessary whitespace, including tabs, spaces, and carriage returns.

✦ **Optimize.** The Optimize command is similar to the Compact option under the Format command in that it deletes any unnecessary whitespace, but it also removes empty `<font>`...`</font>` tags, `naturalsizeflag` attributes, as well as quotes from around tag attributes that don't need them.

✦ **Translate.** Enables a variety of translation options, including conversions between the ISO Latin-1 and Macintosh character set, conversion of 8-bit characters to ASCII equivalents, and conversion of HTML standard characters such as < and > to character entities (and back). Adds or deletes <p> tags to or from paragraphs.

✦ **Remove Comments.** Deletes all commented material from the current page.

✦ **Remove Markup.** Deletes all HTML code from the file, yielding a clean text file.

✦ **Comment.** Surrounds selected text with HTML comment tags.

✦ **Uncomment.** Deletes comment tags from selected text.

✦ **Make Tags Upper Case.** Uppercases all HTML tags. Attribute values, such as filenames and functions, remain the same case.

✦ **Make Tags Lower Case.** Lowercases all HTML tags. Attribute values, such as filenames and functions, remain the same case.

Misc menu

The Misc menu holds a hodgepodge of special-purpose tools, including the following:

✦ **Document Size** returns the size of the current document and estimated download times over a variety of modems.

✦ **Index Document** creates an unordered list of all the links and images in every HTML page in the current page. The list appears at the current cursor position.

✦ **Index Site** creates an unordered list of all the links and images in every HTML page in the current site. Aside from the unordered list, there are four other predefined index styles available.

✦ **CyberStudio Cleaner** fixes problems associated with Web pages created or edited in GoLive CyberStudio.

✦ **PageMill Cleaner** fixes problems associated with Web pages created or edited in Adobe PageMill, including replacing multiple instances of the <br> tag with a single <p> tag. Removes the NATURALSIZE attribute from image tags and removes empty anchor tags.

Preview menu

This menu loads the active document into the default Web browser defined in the Web Browser section of BBEdit's Preferences.

Preview With menu

This menu allows the selection, from a drop-down menu, of a browser in which to preview the active document. Available browsers can be specified in the Web Browser section of BBEdit's Preferences.

HTML Tools Palette

The HTML Tools Palette (see Figure B-8) gives you a quick path to the most frequently used functions of BBEdit. You can place this floating palette anywhere on your desktop for easy access.

Figure B-8: The HTML Tools Palette.

Several buttons have submenus that appear when you click the button, presenting additional related options. Submenus are indicated by the right-pointing arrows on the right side of the button. For example, the Heading button enables the user to select the desired heading level.

A double vertical bar on the left side of some buttons (the grip strip) indicates that the button supports drag-and-drop. For example, you can drag the Table button into a document window to place a table at the insertion point. This action brings up the Table dialog box.

Windows menu

It can get confusing when you have many BBEdit windows open simultaneously. The Windows menu helps you manage the clutter.

The Windows List

BBEdit's Windows List helps you gain quick access to the files that make up your Web site. A special floating window (see Figure B-9) lists the names of all the open files.

Figure B-9: BBEdit's Windows List.

To make a window active, simply double-click its name within the Windows List. In addition, you can open a file by dragging the file's icon into the Windows List. Buttons at the top of the window offer Save, Close, and Print options.

Use the Option key to make the action of any button at the top of the window apply to all the files in the Windows List.

HTML Entities

This command displays the HTML Entities dialog box that enables easy entry of HTML character entities.

Web-Safe Colors

This command displays a palette of 216 browser-safe colors. Drag any color swatch from the palette to the document to insert a color value.

Arrange

BBEdit's Arrange command is a tool for organizing multiple windows in the editor. This is particularly helpful if you're using a small monitor to create your Web pages. When you select Window ⇨ Arrange, you get a dialog box from which to choose an arrangement for the windows.

Get Info

This command displays a dialog box that lists the number of characters, words, lines, and pages in any selected text (as well as the document). This same information is available by clicking the Info button on the status bar.

Reveal in Finder

Reveal in Finder is a handy feature with which you can quickly find a particular file without leaving the BBEdit application. This command opens the Macintosh OS Finder window that contains the active file.

Tip   Select the text of a filename (for example, index.html) within a document and hold down the Option key while opening the File pull-down menu. Choose the Reveal Selection command to open the Finder folder that contains that file.

Send to Back

This command places the front window behind all other windows.

Exchange with Next

This command lets you switch your screen between the front two windows.

Synchro Scrolling

Synchro Scrolling enables multiple files to scroll in unison — the files in all open windows scroll when you scroll just one. This feature is great for comparing two versions of the same file.

Window Names

All the open windows are listed at the bottom of the Windows pull-down menu. Simply select one to make it active.

Internet menu

If your computer is connected to the Internet — and it undoubtedly is — BBEdit offers additional valuable features. In order to use these features, you must you have the application Internet Config installed and configured. To make the Internet menu available from your menu bar, do the following:

1. Choose Edit ⇨ Preferences to open the Preferences dialog box.

2. From the Category list on the left, choose Services to display that panel.

3. Click in the box that says Internet Config and click OK. You must restart BBEdit for the Internet menu to appear.

The Internet menu is identified by a globe icon in the menu bar. An especially helpful feature of the Internet menu is Resolve URL.

Follow these steps to check the validity of an URL:

1. Make sure you have an active connection to the Internet.

2. Place the insertion point anywhere within the URL.

3. Open the Internet menu and choose the Resolve URL command. BBEdit launches your default Web browser. (If the Web browser can't be found, an alert beep sounds.)

Note that you can Command-click anywhere in an URL to resolve it.

4. If the URL is invalid, an alert beep sounds.

If the URL is valid, you'll be able to view the site in your browser.

Printing

To print a document, select the Print command from the File menu. A standard Macintosh OS Print dialog box appears, with a few special BBEdit printing options. Each printer type presents its own options, of course; Figure B-10 shows the printer options associated with an HP LaserJet 4ML.

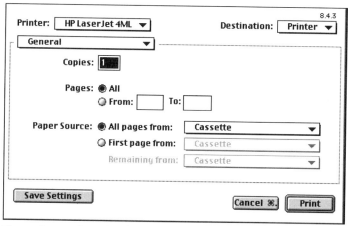

Figure B-10: The Print dialog box for an HP LaserJet 4ML.

Click the Options button to see which options are available for your printer (or, on the HP LaserJet 4ML printer shown in the figure, select General and then choose the options you want to view and/or change). Some of the commonly used options are outlined in the following table.

Print Option	Description
Print Page Headers	Prints the page number, filename, time, and date from the header of each page
Print Line Numbers	Displays line numbers along the left margin of the document. This is very useful when debugging a file because error reports point to actual line numbers within a file.
Print Two-Up	Use this option to save resources by printing two BBEdit pages on one sheet of paper.
1-Inch Gutter	Leaves a one-inch margin along the left side of the paper. Allows space for notes in the margin, for instance, or to accommodate placement in three-ring binders.
Print Full Pathname	Prints the full path name of the file, from the header
Time Stamp: Date Last Saved Date of Printing	This option lets you decide whether the header date is the date the file was last modified or the date the file was printed.
Print Rubber Stamp	You can specify a message to be printed diagonally across the page in gray (or outline). This feature may not work on all printers.

Other Useful BBEdit Features

This section takes a look at some selected BBEdit features that you may find useful.

Spell-checking

The Check Spelling command on the Text menu launches BBEdit's built-in spelling checker. The Spell Checker compares each word in the document with words in the Spell Checker's dictionaries. If a word can't be found in a dictionary, BBEdit attempts to offer a possible correction.

If the questioned word is actually spelled correctly, you can add the word to the User Dictionary or simply skip the word. BBEdit ignores HTML code and checks only the text that will actually appear in your Web page.

If you've used any spell-checkers at all, these steps will be familiar to you:

1. Select Text ➪ Check Spelling.

2. To limit spell-checking to only selected text, choose the Selection Only option.

3. Click Start to begin spell-checking.

4. If a Questioned Word is misspelled, choose the correct word from the Guesses list, or type a replacement word in the Replace With box.

If a Questioned Word is not misspelled, choose the Skip command or use the Add command to enter the word into your personal User Dictionary.

Altering the User Dictionary

BBEdit's User Dictionary is a simple editable text file that you can alter yourself. You can add and delete words quickly and easily.

Open the User Dictionary by double-clicking the file located inside the BBEdit Dictionaries folder within the main BBEdit 5.0. folder. Each dictionary word must be entered on a separate line. Edit the file just as you would any other BBEdit text file.

Caution

Do not alter the coded number that appears at the top of the file. This code lets BBEdit recognize the file as the User Dictionary.

Comparing files

BBEdit's Search menu contains a Find Differences command for comparing two files. For example, you may want to compare a file you have been working on locally to a file you just retrieved from a server, to find differences between the two. Figure B-11 demonstrates this feature at work.

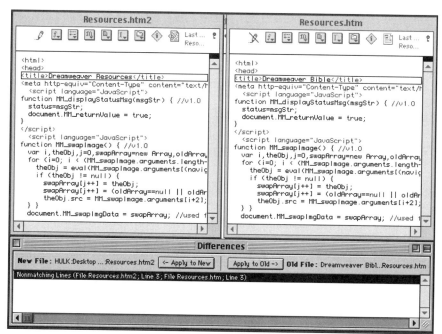

Figure B-11: Comparing differences in BBEdit files.

Follow these steps to use the comparison features of the Find Differences command:

1. Choose Search ⇨ Find Differences. The Find Differences dialog box appears.

2. Use the New and Old pop-up menus to choose the files you wish to compare. You can also drag file icons from the Finder into the New and Old portions of the dialog box.

3. Select the appropriate options — Case Insensitive or Ignore Leading Space — for your situation.

4. Click Compare to start the file-comparison operation.

If BBEdit finds differences, the two files will appear side by side. In addition, a Differences pane detailing the found differences appears at the bottom of the screen (as previously shown in Figure B-11). You can copy a line from one file to another by selecting the line and choosing either Copy to Old or Copy to New. BBEdit italicizes the line in the Differences pane to indicate the change has been applied.

Search menu

BBEdit's search and search-and-replace features work on a single file or multiple files. Follow these steps to search and/or replace text in the active window:

1. Select Search ⇨ Find.

2. Enter the text you wish to locate in the Search For box.

3. To enter a replacement string, do so in the Replace With box. Otherwise, leave this box empty.

4. Choose any options you wish to apply to the search, including the direction of the search (Start at Top, Wrap Around, or Backwards), the selection, and case sensitivity.

5. Click any of the buttons along the right side of the dialog box to begin the search operation: Find, Find All, Replace, Replace All, Don't Find, or Cancel. Don't Find saves the settings of your search without actually performing the search.

One of the options in the Search command's dialog box lets you search and/or replace text in multiple files. A handy use for this feature is updating each occurrence of a revised filename in several related HTML documents.

Follow these steps to perform multifile searches:

1. Select Search ⇨ Find.

2. Enter the text you wish to locate in the Search For box.

3. To enter a replacement string, do so in the Replace With box. Otherwise, leave this box empty.

4. Find the Multi-File Search option and click the triangle to reveal the Multi-File Search options. (This portion of the dialog box may already be visible.)

5. Choose the files you wish to search, using the buttons and pop-up menus in the bottom part of the dialog box.

6. Select any other options you wish to apply to the search, as you would in a single-file search.

7. Click the appropriate button along the right side of the dialog box to begin the operation.

Go To Line command

It's easy to move the insertion point instantly to a specific line in your document. Use the Go To Line command under the Search menu. Enter the line number in the dialog box and click Go To (see Figure B-12).

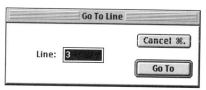

Figure B-12: The Go To Line dialog box.

Markers icon

BBEdit's *markers* enable you to quickly and easily move to a particular section of your file. You can give the marker a unique name that makes sense to you and helps you find it later. This feature helps you stay on track in a large HTML file.

To set markers:

1. First select the section of your document you wish to mark.

2. Click the Markers icon in the status bar, and select Set Marker from the pop-up menu.

3. In the Set Marker dialog box, enter a name for the marker and click the Set button.

   Once markers are established, the marker names appear at the bottom of the Mark pull-down menu. Simply select the marker name to take you to that location in your document.

4. When you want to clear markers you don't need anymore, click the Markers icon and select Clear Markers from the pop-up menu. In the Clear Markers dialog box, choose the marker you want to delete, and click the Clear button.

Syntax coloring

To make editing easier, BBEdit displays HTML tags in colored text. Be sure to save your HTML documents with the .html or .htm extensions to enable this feature. If you want to change the colors BBEdit uses for syntax coloring, you can do so in the Text Colors portion of the Preferences dialog box.

Working with servers

You will be placing your completed Web files on a public server that enables people to view your masterpiece worldwide. The public server uses the file transfer protocol (FTP) to send and receive files. Dreamweaver has built-in FTP capabilities that enable you to connect to a remote server to save (upload) and open (download) files; see Chapter 33 for more information on FTP publishing. In addition, BBEdit offers the following FTP capabilities.

Saving to a server (uploading)

Follow these steps to upload to a server:

1. With a document open in BBEdit, select File ⇨ Save to FTP Server.
2. To connect to a server, enter the name of the server. You can choose from previously used servers in the pop-up Server menu.
3. Enter your user name and password.
4. Click the Connect button to begin an FTP session.
5. Choose the destination directory on the server by using the standard Macintosh OS directory pop-up menu.

Tip   BBEdit will remember your password if you desire. Auto-Connect instructs BBEdit to automatically connect to a server using your saved password the next time you begin an FTP session.

Opening from a server (downloading)

If you wish to retrieve files from a server, use the File ⇨ Open From FTP Server command. The steps are similar to those for saving to an FTP server in the preceding section.

Once the connection is made, you'll use a standard Macintosh OS directory pop-up menu to navigate through the directories — just as you would if the files were stored locally on your Mac. Once you have located the file you desire, choose Save to begin the downloading process. After the file is completely downloaded, BBEdit displays the file in a new text-editing window.

✦   ✦   ✦

HomeSite 4.0 Primer (For Windows Users)

Designing and creating Web sites is intuitive and easy with Dreamweaver's visual interface. Yet there may be times when you'll want to leave the visual editor and get your hands on the underlying HTML code. In some cases, the Dreamweaver's built-in HTML editor will be all you need. Whenever you need a more advanced HTML editor to add features or troubleshoot your page, the Windows 95 version of Dreamweaver includes a complete registered version of HomeSite 4.0. This stand-alone HTML editor package for Windows works with Dreamweaver. HomeSite is one of the most popular HTML editors available today and enables you to produce HTML files without actually memorizing HTML tag commands.

This appendix provides instructions about how to access HomeSite's basic features. You can also access an Online User Manual and other invaluable Help resources by clicking the Help tab in the Resources area of the HomeSite screen. (Remember that you can resize this frame by clicking and dragging the borders to make reading the Help resources easier.) Also, you can visit Allaire's HomeSite 4.0 Web site at http://www.allaire.com.

Getting Started

It's easy to switch between Dreamweaver and HomeSite. A simple click on an icon toggles you from one application to the other. Elements selected in one application are automatically highlighted in the other, making it easy to keep your project organized.

Key features

"Full-featured" just scratches the surface when it comes to describing HomeSite. Many of the tools are the perfect complement to Dreamweaver's visual editor; others serve to make straight coding as efficient as possible. Here are just a few of the HomeSite highlights:

◆ Multiple layers of Undo

◆ Spelling checker

◆ Site link validation

◆ Automatic color coding of HTML, CFML, and other scripts

◆ Extended find-and-replace capabilities for making global edits

◆ Tag Insight, offering a list of attributes and attribute values as you enter tag code

◆ Customization of main and tag toolbars

◆ Wizards for complex tasks, including incorporating dynamic HTML, RealAudio, and RealVideo

◆ Toggle capability between multiple documents

◆ Drag-and-drop from image libraries into the page

◆ Access to remote sites via built-in FTP

◆ Estimates of document sizes and download times

◆ Management for Cascading Style Sheets, CFML server-side tags, Netscape and Internet Explorer HTML extensions, embedded multimedia and plug-ins, and ActiveX and Java controls

◆ Web-safe color palette

◆ HTML syntax checking

◆ One-click preview in any browser

◆ Design View WYSIWY Need Editing

◆ Style Editor for applying CSS styles

◆ SMIL support, with tags for multimedia applications

The HomeSite 4.0 interface

The HomeSite interface is simple and logical, making even the most demanding programming projects easier to accomplish. The workspace (see Figure C-1) has three primary areas: the Editor/Browser and Resource windows, and the command bars.

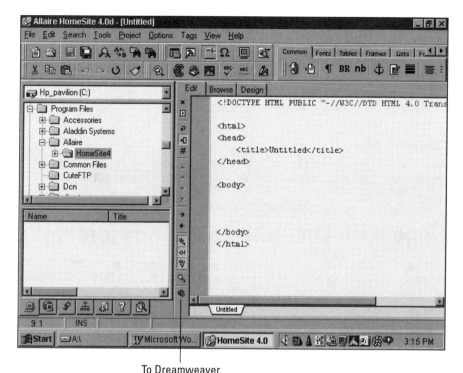

To Dreamweaver

Figure C-1: The HomeSite 4.0 workspace.

Editor/Browser window

Toggle between these two screens with F12. The Editor screen is where you enter HTML tags and place page content. The Browser screen is where you render the current document in the browser you choose.

Resource window

Click the tab buttons at the bottom of the Resource window to access areas where you manage files, custom tags, and online Help areas. From left to right, the tabs represent the following groups of resources:

✦ **Local.** Use the Directory and File panes to access local and network drives.

✦ **Remote.** Access remote servers with FTP.

✦ **Projects.** Create and manage HomeSite projects.

✦ **Site View.** Provides a graphic view of the links in a document.

◆ **Tag Snippets.** Store code for later use; see the section "Inserting tags in a document" later in this appendix.

◆ **Help.** Access Help files, including User Manual, FAQ, HTML reference files, and more.

◆ **Tag Inspector.** Displays all the tags in your document in a hierarchical tree, along with a list of properties for editing them.

Command bars

You'll find a rich supply of menus and toolbars throughout the HomeSite workspace, which you'll read about as you work through this appendix.

Working with Dreamweaver and HomeSite

Although Dreamweaver lets you assign any HTML editor as your external editor, it integrates best with HomeSite. Once you've set up HomeSite as your default editor, switching between Dreamweaver and HomeSite is just a button click or keyboard shortcut away.

Caution   Make sure you have the correct version of HomeSite 4.0 to work with Dreamweaver 2. If you don't have version 4.0d — as visible on the opening splash screen or by choosing Help ➪ About — you need to download this version from Allaire's Web site.

Setting up HomeSite as your default editor

Before Dreamweaver can access HomeSite, you must make HomeSite your default HTML editor. You can make this assignment through the Dreamweaver Preferences by following these steps:

1. In Dreamweaver, choose Edit ➪ Preferences to open the Preferences dialog box.

2. From the Category list on the left, choose External Editors to display that panel.

3. In the External Editor panel, enter the path to the HomeSite executable. The easiest way to do this is to select the Browse button and locate the file. If you installed HomeSite according to the defaults, this path should read c:\Program Files\Allaire\HomeSite4\homesite4.exe.

4. Click OK when you've finished.

Cross-Reference   The External Editor options that control file synchronization between Dreamweaver and HomeSite are explained in detail in Chapter 3, "Setting Your Preferences."

Switching between Dreamweaver and HomeSite

When you're in Dreamweaver, you have three ways to switch to HomeSite:

✦ Click the External Editor button in the top-left corner of the HTML Inspector.

✦ Choose Edit ⇨ Launch External Editor.

✦ Use the keyboard shortcut, Ctrl-E.

You can also select the other program's button on the taskbar or use the Alt-Tab method to switch between applications, but the file integration will not work under these circumstances.

Caution   Depending on the synchronization options chosen in the External Editor preferences, Dreamweaver may ask if you want to save the files first before you switch to HomeSite. If you do not save your Dreamweaver file first, your modifications will not appear in HomeSite (and vice versa). For this reason, I recommend setting your synchronization options to Always.

After you've made your code modifications in HomeSite and you're ready to return to Dreamweaver, you have three methods for switching back:

✦ Select the Dreamweaver button on HomeSite's Editor toolbar.

✦ Choose View ⇨ Open in Macromedia Dreamweaver.

✦ Use the keyboard shortcut, Ctrl-D.

Caution   If HomeSite doesn't switch to Dreamweaver using any of the methods just given, check your HomeSite settings. Choose Options ⇨ Settings (or press F8) to open the HomeSite Settings dialog box and select the HomeSite reload options from the Dreamweaver and File Settings tabs.

Disabling HomeSite integration

You can disable HomeSite integration if you prefer working with an older version of HomeSite or if you use a different HTML text editor. Here's how:

1. Choose Options ⇨ Settings.

2. Select the Dreamweaver tab.

3. Turn off Enable Dreamweaver Integration and click OK.

Creating Pages: Making HTML Files

You have a couple of ways to work with HTML files. You can either create a new file or open an existing one and edit it. This section shows you how to create, open, apply tags to, and save Web pages in HomeSite. Remember: Even if you create a Web page in another application, you can still edit the page with HomeSite.

If you're starting from scratch to create a new file, HomeSite offers the following ways to create a new document:

+ Select File ➪ New to open the New HTML Document dialog box. Select a blank document, one of the templates, or use any HTML file as a template. Template files are stored separately from the source documents, so you can modify the template files without worrying about changing the originals.

+ Click the New button on the main toolbar to open a new document based on your default template. Change the default template by choosing Options ➪ Settings (F8) and selecting the Locations tab. Then enter the address of the file you would like to use as a template in the Default Template field.

+ Use the Document wizard. Click the Quick Start button on the Common tab of the Tag Chooser (see Figure C-2), and follow the steps to design a new page or build your own template.

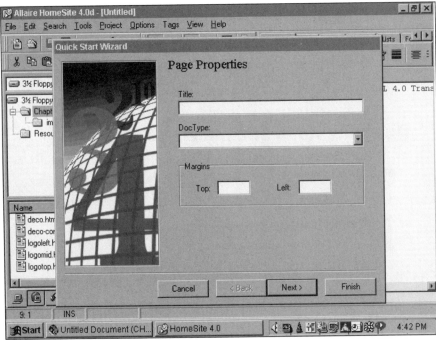

Figure C-2: Use the Quick Start wizard to build a new page or template.

✦ Select File ⇨ Convert Text File to convert an ASCII text file to an HTML file.

Opening an existing Web page

Another way to create a new HTML document is to start with an existing Web page. Use any of the following methods to open files:

✦ Select File ⇨ Open (Ctrl-O).

✦ Click the Open button on the main toolbar.

✦ In the Open HTML Document dialog box, double-click a file listed in the Local Files view of the Resource tab.

✦ To open Web files directly, select File ⇨ Open from the Web. Type in a URL or select a URL from your Favorites or Bookmarks list.

✦ Select File ⇨ Recent Files to see a list of recently used files.

Note

HomeSite treats read-only files differently from other files. These files are marked with a small red dot in the Resource window file list, and a warning message pops up if you try to open one. You cannot edit read-only files, but you can change the attribute on the file by right-clicking it, selecting Properties in the shortcut menu, and then deselecting the read-only attribute.

Inserting tags in a document

Of course, you can type codes directly into the document in the Edit screen, but the following methods are usually more efficient. To have HomeSite add tags for you, choose among these commands:

✦ Select ToolsTag ⇨ Chooser (Ctrl-E). Select from the Chooser list (see Figure C-3), which contains the complete HTML tag set as well as CFML, HDML, SMIL, VTML, and Custom tag sets. Double-click a tag to insert or to display a dialog box in which you can add tag-specific attributes, and then click Apply to add the tag to your document.

✦ From the Tags menu, choose from a basic set of formatting tags.

✦ Select Options ⇨ Settings (F8), and select the Tag Help tab to enable the display of options for Tag Insight and Tag Completion. The following sections describe these three tools and their benefits.

✦ Select Options ⇨ Settings (F8), and open the HTML tab to set alignment and centering tags and to toggle the case of inserted tags.

✦ To repeat the previous tag, select Edit ⇨ Repeat Last Tag (Ctrl-Q).

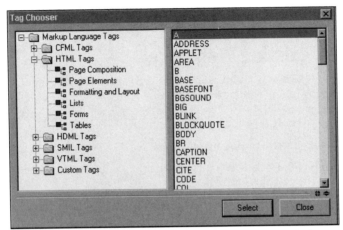

Figure C-3: Access any HTML tag — and many other varieties — through the Tag Chooser.

Using Tag Insight

The Tag Insight tool is a valuable aid to all Web designers, even beginners. It's a quick way to develop a tag as you type it by displaying a drop-down list of attributes and values for each tag. Click the Tag Insight button on the Editor toolbar to enable this feature. Or you can turn off Tag Insight in the Tag Help tab of the Settings dialog box (Options ➪ Settings, or F8). Finally, you can use it only when needed by pressing Shift-F2 when your cursor is in the first tag of a tag pair.

When Tag Insight is turned on, follow these steps to use this helpful feature:

1. Place the cursor in front of the start tag's end bracket (>). Press the spacebar to open the attribute list.

2. To add an attribute to the tag, double-click the attribute in the list. The cursor then moves between the double quotes of the attribute's value.

3. A list of values appears if the attribute has a fixed set of allowed values. To select a value from the list, press the spacebar. Once the value is inserted, the cursor moves in front of the closing bracket.

    If no allowed values appear, the attribute accepts programmer-specified values.

4. Continue selecting attributes until the tag code is complete.

Using Tag Completion

The Tag Completion feature automatically inserts the end tag after you type the start tag. Here are the steps to use this feature:

1. To enable Tag Completion, choose Options ➪ Settings (F8), and in the Tag Help tab check the Tag Completion box.

2. In the Tag Completion section of the Tag Help tab, select Edit to change the syntax of a selected tag.

3. You can use the Add and Delete buttons in the Tag Completion section to manage the list.

Tag Snippets

You can save portions of HTML code for easy recall in other files, using the valuable Tag Snippets feature. It's a lot easier than copying and pasting blocks of code from various files.

To save HTML code as a Tag Snippet, follow these steps:

1. Click the Tag Snippets tab at the bottom of the Resources panel to open the Tag Snippets window.

2. Right-click in the empty pane and select Create Folder from the drop-down menu.

3. Name the folder from which you want to save code, and press Enter.

4. From the Tag Snippets window, right-click the folder and select Add Snippet from the shortcut menu to open the Custom Tag dialog box.

5. Type the start and end tags or paste them from another file. Click OK to save the tag in the folder created in Step 2.

To add more snippets to a folder, right-click the snippet folder in the Tag Snippets window and select Add Snippet from the shortcut menu. You can delete or rename folders as well, from the right-click shortcut menu.

To insert a Tag Snippet you've saved, follow these steps:

1. In the Editing window, place the cursor where you want to insert the tag.

2. Open the Tag Snippet window using one of the methods described previously.

3. Double-click the folder that holds the snippet you'd like to enter.

4. Double-click the snippet you wish to insert into your document.

Entering text in a document

In HomeSite's Editor window, you can type in page content and tags directly, or use the numerous shortcuts to speed up the process. To check your work, toggle to the Browse mode by pressing F12, or click the Browse tab button on the Editor toolbar. Here are some examples of entering text in a document:

◆ To change the defaults for paragraph tags and filename cases, access the HTML tab by selecting Options ⇨ Settings (F8).

◆ To create a link, drag-and-drop a document file into the Editor window.

◆ To insert an image or other media file, drag-and-drop it into the Editor window to insert it.

◆ To insert an HTML, ASCII text, or Cascading Style Sheet file into a document, select File ⇨ Insert File.

◆ To display a menu of special and extended characters, select View ⇨ Special Characters (Ctrl-Shift-X). In the Special dialog box (see Figure C-4), click a character to insert it into your document.

◆ To insert text from any application to your document, use the standard Windows Copy, Cut, and Paste commands.

Figure C-4: Insert extended ASCII characters through the Special dialog box.

Saving files

When you view an unsaved document in either the internal or external browser, HomeSite saves a temporary copy of the file in memory. Thus, you should always save documents with new links in them *before* viewing them in a browser, to ensure that the file paths are identified.

To set the default file format:

1. Select Options ⇨ Settings and open the File Settings tab, shown in Figure C-5.

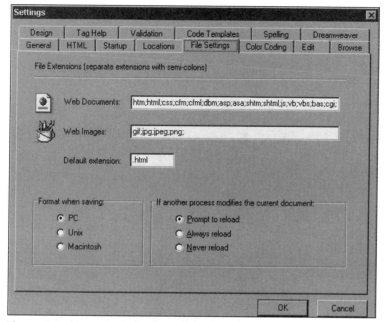

Figure C-5: HomeSite's Settings dialog box features many different options for customizing your work environment.

2. Check a format box among the Format When Saving options.

3. Now select one of the four Save commands from the File pull-down menu:

- **Save (Ctrl-S)** — Saves the current document.

- **Save As (Ctrl-Shift-S)** — Select a filename and click the Local tab to save the document locally, or click Remote to save the document to a server.

- **Save All** — Saves all open documents.

- **Save As Template** — Saves the HTML file as a template. Template files have the .hst extension and are stored separately. Later changes to the source document do not affect the corresponding template file in any way.

Browsing pages

It's imperative that you view your HTML pages in more than just one browser. HomeSite provides many browser options so you can test your pages against the array of available browsers.

Internal browser

If HomeSite 4.0 detects Microsoft Internet Explorer on your system during installation, you have the option of selecting it as the default HTML browser (see Figure C-6). Netscape Navigator cannot be used as the internal browser in HomeSite.

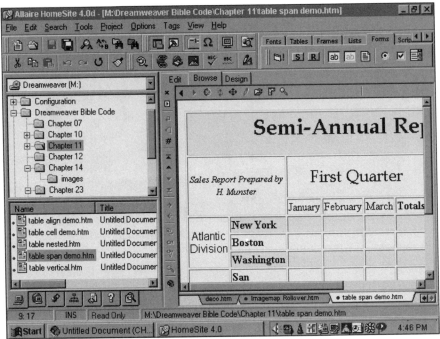

Figure C-6: Use HomeSite's internal browser to preview your Web pages.

If you don't want to have to toggle between the Editor and Browser windows, you can view both at once by clicking the Show Browser Below Editor button in the editing panel (the magnifying glass icon above the Dreamweaver button). You must be in the Editing pane for this button to be available. When you have HomeSite set up this way, you can see the changes you make to your code reflected in the Browser window instantly—without having to toggle the display. Remember that you can resize the Browser view by clicking and dragging the borders.

Mapping Your Web Site

HomeSite's Default Mapping feature sends a document through the specified Web server. If you don't run your own Web server, leave the mappings settings blank. If you do run your own server, here's how to set a default mapping for your Web server:

1. Access the Browser tab by selecting Options ➪ Settings.

2. Check the Use Microsoft Internet Explorer box.

3. Select the Enable Server Mappings option.

4. Select the Add button to open the Mapping dialog box.

5. In the Mapping dialog box, enter the path of the folder to be mapped in the Map From text box.

6. Enter the URL of the server in the Map To text box. Click OK when you're done.

7. To add additional mappings, select the Add button again and repeat Steps 5 and 6.

You also have the option to map any particular path to a file with a specific URL. This mapping capability enables you to use your remote server to preview server-side includes and other types of files. To define a separate mapping for a project:

1. In the Projects panel of the Resources window, right-click a project and select Properties.

2. In the Project Properties dialog box, access the Server Mapping tab. Enter the local path in the first text box, and the URL you want to use for that project in the second text box. Click OK.

Now, if you open this file from the project tree, the project mapping will override the default mapping.

External browser

HomeSite makes it easy to add browsers — and browser versions — to the External Browser list. To add, delete, or reconfigure an external browser, access the External Browsers panel by selecting Options ➪ Configure External Browsers. When you add a new browser to your list, you have the following options in the External Browsers panel (shown in Figure C-7), which affect your current document when you launch an external browser:

✦ Prompt to save changes to current document.

✦ Automatically save changes to the current document.

✦ Browse using a temporary copy (no need to save). This is the default setting; it enables you to view your current document without having to save the document itself. Thus, you can get a quick look at your current code without saving over the previous version of the file, in case you don't like what you see.

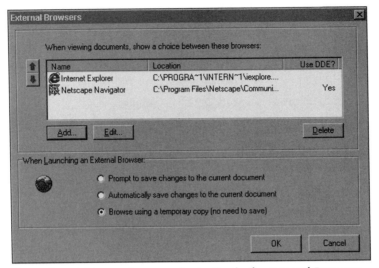

Figure C-7: Add more browsers for testing in the External Browsers dialog box.

Once you add at least one external browser to HomeSite, you can then choose a browser from the list when you click the Launch External Browser button on the main toolbar. Alternately, pressing F11 loads the current document in the first listed browser. To place your preferred browser at the top of the list, open the External Browsers panel, click the browser, and click the blue arrow buttons to move it to the top. Then click OK to save the change.

Setting up an FTP server

To establish an FTP server, follow these steps:

1. Open the Remote tab in the Resources area.

2. Right-click in the top pane of the Remote tab panel, and select Add FTP Server to open the Configure FTP Server panel (see Figure C-8).

3. At a minimum, complete the following fields:

   - **Description** — The name of the server
   - **Host Name** — The FTP address
   - **Username** — Your login name
   - **Password** — Your password, if any

4. Change the default Remote Port entry as needed.

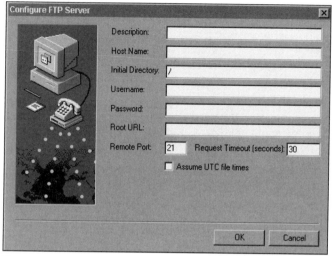

Figure C-8: Set up your FTP server so that you can publish directly to the Web from within HomeSite.

5. Click OK to close the dialog box. Right-click and select Refresh to update the server list.

6. Once you've established an FTP server, right-click the server name, and then select Connect. You'll see the server directory tree if you've connected correctly to the server.

To open a file on a server, you access the remote server's files directly. (To change server settings, right-click a server name, and then select Properties to open the Properties panel.) Here are the steps for opening a file:

1. Click the Remote tab in the Resources window, and double-click the Remote Servers icon in the top panel to display the server's directory tree.

2. Double-click an FTP icon to open a connection to the server.

3. Double-click a file to open it in the Editor window.

Remote files have a small dot on their filename tab at the bottom of the Editor window. To save changes to a remote file, click the Save button on the main toolbar.

Editing and Enhancing Your Pages

HomeSite makes it easy to customize your working space, modify HTML code, and add bells and whistles to your pages.

Changing how the Editor window looks and works

You can customize the Editor window's appearance as well as its operation to your liking.

✦ To remove any of the three toolbars from the screen, toggle them off from the View menu.

✦ To switch between open documents, click the tabs at the bottom of the window. If you've made changes to a document since the last time it was saved, the filename will be blue.

✦ To adjust the size of the text line in the Editor window, click the Toggle Word Wrap button on the Editor toolbar, or select Options ➪ Word Wrap.

✦ To view your document with an internal browser, press F12, or click the Browser button on the Editor toolbar. To enable the internal browser to Microsoft Internet Explorer, select Options ➪ Settings and open the Browse tab.

✦ To view your document with an external browser, press F11 to open the current document in the first browser in your External Browser list. Or click View External Browser List on the main toolbar and select a browser from the list.

✦ To have HomeSite insert ending tags automatically after you type in a start tag, toggle the Tag Completion button on the Editor toolbar.

Tag attribute values

Many HTML tags have attribute values that may enable you to define the tag's appearance or its usefulness. You can set attribute values as you create a tag, or later after you've previewed the page in a browser and you need to adjust the display. You can edit a tag with the Tag Inspector using any of the following methods:

✦ Right-click any start tag and select Edit Tag.

✦ Place the cursor in a start tag and press F4.

✦ Select Tags ➪ Inspect Current Tag.

To set or change attribute values with the Tag Editor, follow these steps:

1. Select a start tag or place the cursor inside it and then right-click and select the Edit Tag option or choose Tags ➪ Edit Current Tag.

2. Enter new values or edit the existing values in the Tag Editor panel; the options for `<body>` are shown in Figure C-9.

3. Complex tags may have multiple tabs in their Tag Editor windows. Click the tab names at the top of the Tag Editor panel to access the other attributes.

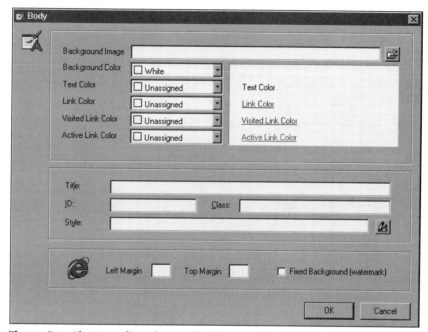

Figure C-9: The Tag Editor shows all of the options for any selected HTML tag.

4. Click the OK button to close the Tag Editor and have the attribute changes appear in the document.

Using bookmarks

You can set up to ten bookmarks in a document — very handy for finding a given spot in a large HTML file. To set and use bookmarks, follow these steps:

1. Select Edit ➪ Set Bookmark (Ctrl- K) to add a bookmark.

2. To go to the next bookmark, select Edit ➪ Go to Next Bookmark (Ctrl-Shift-K).

Using search

HomeSite has two levels of search and replace. *Basic searches* scan only the currently open document. *Extended searches* scan more than just the open document. Thus, it's easy to make global changes.

Performing basic searches

To search for a string in the currently open document, select Search ➪ Find (Ctrl-F). Then, if you want to replace a matching string in the currently open document, select Search ➪ Replace (Ctrl-R).

If the search panel is closed and you want to resume the previous search, select Search ⇨ Find Again (F3).

Performing extended searches

To search for a string among all open documents (or all HTML files in a particular directory, folder, or project), follow these steps:

1. Select Search ⇨ Extended Replace (Ctrl-Shift-R).

2. Enter your selections in the Extended Replace dialog box, shown in Figure C-10.

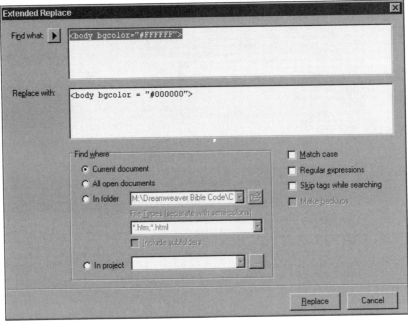

Figure C-10: HomeSite's Extended Find and Replace feature is extremely powerful and flexible.

3. Click the corresponding radio button to search all open documents or to specify a folder or project in which to search.

4. Select the Replace button.

5. You can see all of the matches in the Search Results tab. Double-click any match in the list to go directly to that file. Note that read-only files are not searched, and that you will not be prompted to confirm each replacement.

Spell check

HomeSite takes the normal spell-checking operation to the next level by providing a multilanguage Spell Check feature. When you install HomeSite, you can select additional language dictionaries to use. To run Spell Check, use any of the following methods:

✦ Select Tools ⇨ Spell Check (F7) to scan your current document for spelling errors.

✦ To configure the spell checker to skip all text within HTML tags, select Options ⇨ Settings and open the Spelling tab. In this tab you can also select the dictionaries you want the spell checker to use.

Using color-coded tags

To facilitate the quick scanning of documents, HomeSite displays tags in distinct colors. This includes all HTML tags, quoted attributes, and script and object tags. You can change the default colors used, and create custom colors as well.

Changing colors

To change color coding, access the Color Coding panel (see Figure C-11). Click on HTML in the scheme panel and select Edit Scheme.

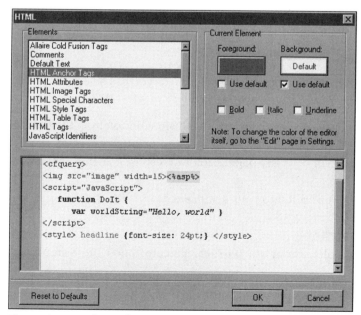

Figure C-11: Color-code your HTML to easily find specific or different kinds of tags.

You can also assign a color from the Basic Palette to any tag. Open the drop-down list for the tag you want to color and choose Custom. This opens the color palette. Pick a basic color and click OK.

Creating new colors

To create a custom color for a tag, follow these steps:

1. Open the Color Coding panel in the Settings dialog box. Select HTML from the list and click the Edit Scheme button.

2. Open the color palette by clicking the Foreground button.

3. Drag the arrow on the brightness scale to set a level.

4. Drag the color pointer to define a color. The color values display as you move the pointer, and the color displays in the Preview box.

5. Click Add to Custom Colors; then click OK to enter the color for the tag.

Adding colors

Wise use of color can make the difference between uninspired and exciting Web pages. HomeSite provides some easy ways to add and change colors in your pages. To insert a color value using Tag Insight:

1. Open Tag Insight by placing the cursor in front of the start tag's closing bracket and pressing the spacebar.

2. Double-click Color from the pop-up list.

3. Double-click a color from the drop-down menu.

HomeSite provides a list of colors to choose from, or you can select a specific color from a variety of color palettes. To insert a color from a palette:

1. To open a color palette, double-click the Custom button from the Colors drop-down list. This opens the Palette pane.

2. Position the cursor over any palette color to display its name or hexadecimal value.

3. Click a color to insert it into your document.

Working with palettes

To open a different palette from which to select colors, follow these steps:

1. Access the Palette drop-down menu, shown in Figure C-12, by clicking the Open Palette button on the left side of the Palette pane.

Figure C-12: Switch among any number of color sets through the Palette drop-down menu.

2. Click a palette to open it in the Palette pane.

You can edit and delete existing palettes from the Open Palette dialog box. You can create a new palette, too. Follow these steps:

1. From the Open Palette drop-down menu, select Edit Palette.

2. In the Palette dialog box, click the New Palette button.

3. Select RGB values, or click the Eyedropper button and drag the dropper over the color spectrum to create a color.

4. Once you create a color you want to add to your palette, click the Add button.

5. When you are done creating a new palette, click the Save button and enter a name for the palette. The new file is saved with a default .pal extension in the Palettes subdirectory.

Adding a palette from Paint Shop Pro

Paint Shop Pro is an excellent graphic editor that comes free with HomeSite and is available to Dreamweaver users who register HomeSite online. Follow these steps to bring a Paint Shop Pro palette into HomeSite:

1. In Paint Shop Pro, select Colors ➪ Save Palette to open the Save Palette panel.

2. Enter a name for the palette.

3. Set the Save As type to PAL-JASC Palette.

4. Save the file in the HomeSite\Palettes directory.

Adding images

HomeSite supports the standard Web graphics formats: GIF, JPG, PNG graphics files, and BMP (Internet Explorer only). To see all of your image files, right-click in one of the file list resource tabs, select Filter, and then select Web Images to limit the file display to images only. If you want to view thumbnails of the image files, click the Thumbnail button in the Resources menu bar.

To add an image to the current document, follow these steps:

1. Select an image in the file list and drag it directly into your document. The default image width and height will appear in the tag code.

2. Place the cursor anywhere in the image tag, right-click, and select Edit Tag.

3. Change the image settings in the editor as needed. You can click the Clear button to delete the current entries.

Testing Your Pages

Before you launch your Web site, you should test your code. HomeSite has several key features — HTML Validation, Link Checking, and Document Weighting — to put your Web page through its paces.

HTML validation

Before you FTP your files up to the remote server, it's a good idea to verify that your HTML code is sound. HomeSite includes a powerful tool for checking and reporting on HTML syntax errors. Although it won't automatically correct errors, it will identify them and give you a list of errors and comments. Double-click an error message to highlight the offending code in your document.

To set the HTML Validator options:

1. Select Options ⇨ Settings and choose the Validation tab. Click the Validator Settings button to open the dialog box shown in Figure C-13.

2. Complete the settings for Options, and then do the same for the Tags, Versions, and Values tabs.

3. Click OK to save your changes.

When you have the validation set up as desired, you're ready to use it to test code in your current document. Click the Validate Document button on the main toolbar, or select Tools ⇨ Validate Current Document. The results from the validation test appear in a new window below the current document. To find the code that corresponds to any error message, double-click it in the list.

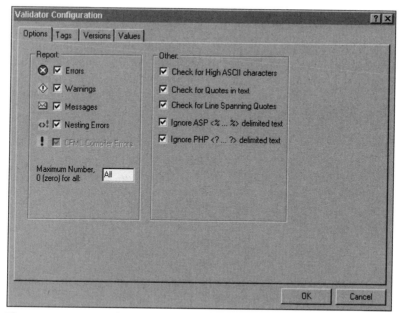

Figure C-13: Set up the HTML Validator to your specific parameters with the Validator options.

Testing your links

Links change often, so it's important to do regular testing of your documents' links. HomeSite makes the task easier with its built-in Link Checker. Besides testing URLs, it also will check directory paths of images and other Web page elements specified in the current HTML document.

Note that the Link Checker can't verify links to secure pages, FTP links, and mailto links. You need an active Internet connection to check remote URLs.

Follow these steps to use the Link Checker:

1. To start the Link Checker working on your current document, click the Verify Links button on the main toolbar, or select Tools ➪ Verify Links. A list is generated with each link's URL or path.

2. If you need to change the URL or the local directory, do this by first selecting the Set Root URL button next to the list of links. Next enter the new root URL in the Set Root URL text box that is displayed, or select the Folder icon to set the root directory and drive against which local links should be tested.

3. Click the Start Link Verification button, the right-pointing triangle found next to the list of links, to begin the verification. The status of each link is updated as it is processed.

4. A check mark tells you that the link works. An X indicates that it's a failed link, which means that the document or file couldn't be located. Double-click an item in the Verifier List to find the code that corresponds to the failed link.

Document weight

This handy feature estimates the upload time of your current page. To find out how long it'll take you to upload a page, select Tools ⇨ Document Weight. The Root URL setting in your FTP configuration is used to determine the relative path to files, and the results are displayed in the Document Weight dialog box (see Figure C-14).

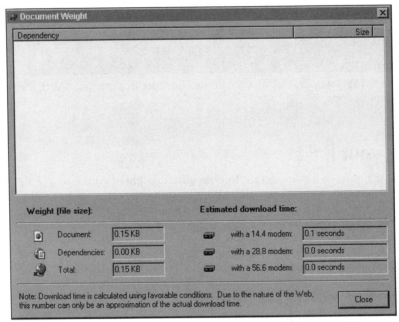

Figure C-14: It's a good idea to check on the probable download time for your Web page.

Creating Projects

If your Web site contains multiple files, you'll probably benefit by grouping the files as projects. HomeSite contains powerful project management features that help you organize your site or a collection of sites.

To create a new project, start by clicking the Projects tab at the bottom of the Resources window. From there, you have several alternatives. You can create a new project or import a project from an existing directory folder. To open the New Project dialog box shown in Figure C-15, right-click anywhere in the Project folder area, or select Project ➪ New Project.

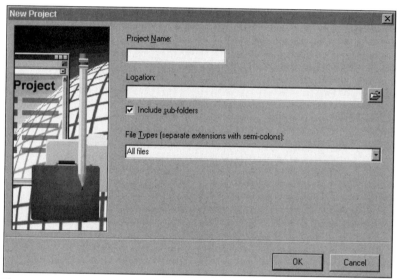

Figure C-15: Use the New Project dialog box to start your new Web site.

The project workspace gives you easy and organized access to related documents and files. The files in the project folders are pointers to your HTML documents. The documents are not physically moved or modified in any way.

Projects toolbar

When the Projects tab is open in the Resources window, you'll have access to the following tools:

- ✦ **Open Project** opens up a project from a local or remote folder.
- ✦ **New Project** brings up the New Project dialog box.
- ✦ **Upload Project** opens the Upload Project dialog box.

Uploading a project to a server

Use the Upload Project icon to select and upload project files to a server. You can select from the list of server connections you have established in the Remote tab.

To upload a project, follow these steps:

1. First, open the Upload Project dialog box by clicking the Upload Project button in the Project tab.

2. In the Upload Project dialog box, select whether you want to upload the entire site or upload only new or modified pages. Click Next.

3. Select the target server from the list in the Upload locations. (If the server you want is not on the list, close the dialog box and set up a protocol for an FTP connection as described earlier.)

4. Click OK to start the upload. The uploaded files are displayed in the file list.

Keyboard Shortcuts

As an alternative to using the pull-down menus, HomeSite 4.0 provides a full complement of keyboard commands, listed in Tables C-1 through C-4.

Table C-1 **File Menu Keyboard Shortcuts**	
File Command	*Keyboard Shortcut*
Open an HTML document	Ctrl-O
Save current document	Ctrl-S
Save As	Ctrl-Shift-S
Print current document	Ctrl-P
Close current document	Ctrl-W
Close All	Ctrl-Shift-W

Table C-2 **Tag Selector Keyboard Shortcuts**	
Tag	*Keyboard Shortcut*
Open the Tag Chooser	Ctrl-E
Open the Editor for the selected tag	Ctrl-F4
Open the Quick Anchor dialog box	Ctrl-Shift-A
Open the Image dialog box	Ctrl-Shift-I
Insert a paragraph tag	Ctrl-Shift-P

Tag	Keyboard Shortcut
Insert a break tag	Ctrl-Shift-B
Insert a nonbreaking space	Ctrl-Shift-Spacebar
Insert a bold tag	Ctrl-B
Insert an italic tag	Ctrl-I
Insert a center tag (`div align="center"`) by default	Ctrl-Shift-C
Insert a comment tag	Ctrl-Shift-M
Find matching tag	Ctrl-M
Repeat last tag	Ctrl-Q

Table C-3
Edit and Search Menu Keyboard Shortcuts

Edit Command	Keyboard Shortcut
Select all text in the current document	Ctrl-A
Copy selected text to the clipboard	Ctrl-C
Cut the selection to the clipboard	Ctrl-X
Paste selection from the clipboard	Ctrl-V
Insert bookmark at the current line	Ctrl-K
Go to the next bookmark	Ctrl-Shift-K
Open the Find dialog box	Ctrl-F
Run the Find command again	F3
Open the Replace dialog box	Ctrl-R
Open the Extended Find and Replace dialog box	Ctrl-Shift-R
Open the Go To line number dialog box	Ctrl-G
Undo the previous edit	Ctrl-Z
Validate HTML in the current document	Shift-F6
Spell-check the current document	F7
Open the special/extended character list	Ctrl-Shift-X
Indent the selected text block	Ctrl-Shift-. (period)
Unindent the selected text block	Ctrl-Shift-, (comma)

Table C-4
General Workspace Keyboard Shortcuts

Workspace Command	Keyboard Shortcut
Toggle the Quick toolbar	Ctrl-H
Display Help for current tag	F1
Open the Options ⇨ Settings menu	F8
Toggle the Resources tab	F9
Toggle Full Screen view	Ctrl-F12
Toggle Editor/Browser views	F12

✦   ✦   ✦

Dreamweaver 2 Attain

Web-based training is an explosive field. With the rise of the intranet, a potential learning delivery system is on every desktop: the browser. To meet the growing needs of corporate trainers, remote educators, and Internet instructors, Macromedia developed a special version of Dreamweaver called Dreamweaver Attain. Dreamweaver Attain extends the standard HTML authoring interface with a Knowledge Object Wizard designed to simplify the task of creating and testing instructional Web pages.

Dreamweaver 2 Attain allows the Web educator to take advantage of the enhancements in Dreamweaver 2 and greatly eases the creation and editing chores. The program now employs Property Inspectors and special Knowledge Object menu commands to facilitate the instructional design. Moreover, any modifications to Knowledge Object parameters are reflected in real time in the Document Window, which helps to cut development time significantly.

The intent of this appendix is twofold. First, I'd like to offer an overview of the product for the Web designer unfamiliar with the distance learning market; the need for designers with Web-training savvy is growing by leaps and bounds. Second, this appendix is intended to bridge the gap for educators beginning to explore the Internet as a delivery medium who may be completely at home with the testing concepts, but unfamiliar with Web design possibilities. This appendix is definitely not intended as a Dreamweaver 2 Attain instruction manual — a task beyond the scope of this book.

Understanding the Attain Interface

At the heart of Dreamweaver 2 Attain is the Knowledge Object Wizard. The Knowledge Object Wizard enables the Web designer to easily insert seven different types of testing objects, ranging from simple multiple-choice questions to complex drag-and-drop representations. The Knowledge Object Wizard also serves as the command center for interactions between testing conditions, and allows the answer to one question to affect how another is posed. You can also enable tracking with a Computer Managed Instruction (CMI) system such as Macromedia's Pathware or another database setup. Most important, the Knowledge Object Wizard handles all this complex interactivity through its point-and-click interface without the need for hand-coding the HTML or JavaScript.

Although the Knowledge Object Wizard is seen as a single object on Dreamweaver's Objects Palette, it acts as the gateway for inserting all the different types of Knowledge Objects, such as multiple-choice questions, timers, and text entry boxes. Most of the individual Knowledge Objects have a variety of options associated with them — and as you would expect given Dreamweaver's extensibility, new templates can be custom built and called from within the overall Knowledge Object Wizard.

With Dreamweaver 2 Attain, the Knowledge Object Wizard and the test question structures it generates are far more integrated into Dreamweaver. Special menu options have been added that allow inserted questions to be moved or deleted — without losing the associated code. You can even move any Knowledge Object into a layer to gain the benefits of absolute positions and visibility control.

Using the Knowledge Object Wizard: an overview

The Knowledge Object Wizard is a very sophisticated tool that interactively assists your Web instructional design. To give you some measure of its complexity, the Knowledge Object Wizard consists of over 80 layers — most of which are populated at run time — and utilizes over 20 separate HTML and JavaScript scripts. However, for all its behind-the-scenes intricacy, using the Knowledge Object Wizard is very straightforward.

After you've installed Dreamweaver 2 Attain, you'll find a new object added to the Common panel of the Objects Palette, the Knowledge Object. Selecting this object opens the Knowledge Object Wizard, shown in Figure D-1. The actual interface of the Knowledge Object Wizard varies depending on which implementation of the eight different Knowledge Objects you choose to insert; however, you'll always make your selections from a series of tabbed panels.

 Caution   Be sure to save your document before opening the Knowledge Object Wizard; Dreamweaver won't let you proceed until you do.

To give you a better idea of how the Knowledge Object Wizard works, here are the steps for inserting a relatively simple multiple-choice question that offers visual cues:

1. Position your cursor wherever you'd like the multiple choice question to appear.

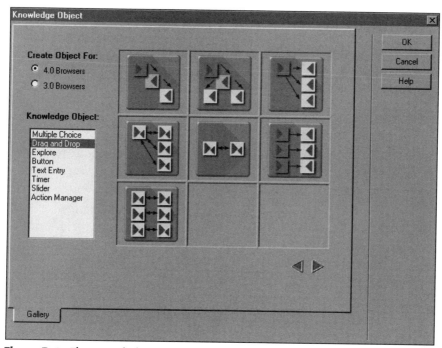

Figure D-1: The Knowledge Object Wizard is the control panel for almost all of Dreamweaver 2 Attain's power.

2. From the Objects Palette, choose the Knowledge Object.

   The Knowledge Object Wizard opens, displaying the Gallery tab.

3. Select the version of browser your Web learning project is targeting by choosing either 4.0 Browsers or 3.0 Browsers under the Create Object For option.

Note   While choosing the 3.0 Browsers option offers the greatest compatibility, none of the 4.0 capabilities, such as layers or CSS, are available to your design.

4. Choose Multiple Choice from the list of Knowledge Objects on the left.

   The available templates appear in the grid on the right of the Knowledge Object Wizard.

5. Select the first template with the three graphic symbols.

   The other tabs of the Knowledge Object Wizard appear, created in response to your selection. Also, the initial design for the multiple-choice question is displayed in the Document Window, as shown in Figure D-2.

6. Select the Interaction tab.

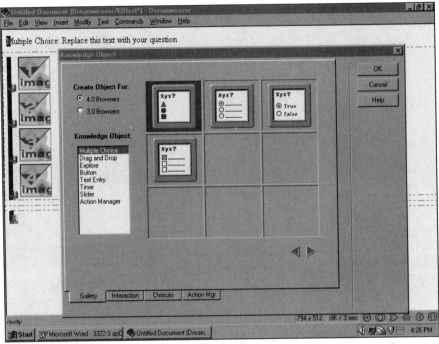

Figure D-2: As you build your Knowledge Object, the elements appear in the Document Window.

7. Enter the particular options that identify this test item, including the following:

- A unique name, used to identify this particular Knowledge Object

- The actual multiple-choice question

- The circumstances that determine when the question is judged correct or incorrect. Questions can be judged each time a selection is made or after an entire page of questions is submitted.

- Whether the results of the question are to be tracked by a test management program

- The number of attempts allowed for answering the question

- A time limit for answering the question

- Whether a Reset button is to be made available for this question

- Whether the question should be placed within a layer

8. If you've opted to send the results of the test question to a management system, select the Tracking tab and enter the necessary identifiers, as well as the relative weight of the question.

9. Select the Choices tab.

10. For each of the placeholders in the Choices list, enter its name, any optional text, the path to the image you want used, and whether the choice is correct or not. If the choice is correct, you can also enter the number of points to add to the user's score.

    Additional choices can be added, or the number of preset choices reduced, by using the Add and Delete buttons at the top of the panel, respectively.

11. Select the Action Mgr (Manager) tab.

    The Action Manager tab lists what actions are taken when the user interacts with the question. Actions can generally be thought of as a series of *If...then* statements. *If* a certain condition is met, *then* a defined action is taken. Actions are separated into different *segments*, such as when a particular option is selected. Figure D-3 shows the Action Manager listing for a four-option multiple-choice question.

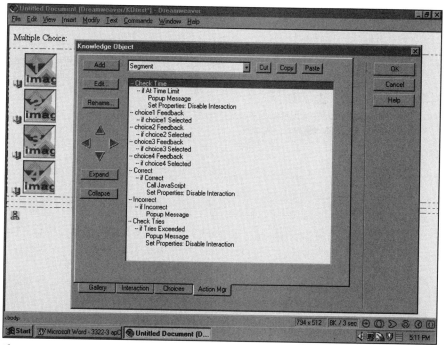

Figure D-3: The Action Manager tab provides an overview of how each question is evaluated at run time.

12. Segments can be added, deleted, renamed, or repositioned in the Action Manager panel. By accessing the drop-down list at the top of the panel, you can also insert special Attain behaviors, as well as any standard Dreamweaver behaviors.

13. Click OK when you're done.

Identifying tags and icons

Now that your multiple-choice question has been inserted into your Web page, you can modify its appearance using any of the standard Dreamweaver methods, such as selecting the text of the question and applying a new font face or size. You can also construct an entire page of questions and then use the Style Sheet Inspector to apply a uniform style. Dreamweaver 2 Attain makes it easy to identify and select individual Knowledge Objects through unique icons and a special tag.

Note   The Knowledge Object icon has one special property: it can never be hidden on your Document Window, even if the Invisible Elements option is deselected.

Any inserted Knowledge Object can be chosen by selecting the icon or the tag shown in Figure D-4. The Knowledge Object icon is similar to a layer or form in that when it is selected, all of the content that comprises the object — the text, images, form elements, and so on — are selected as well. This ensures that any editing includes the whole object. Dreamweaver 2 Attain also inserts a special tag, <attain ko>, which can be chosen from the Tag Selector to achieve the same effect.

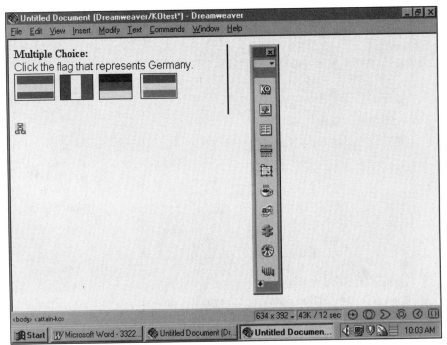

Figure D-4: Select the Knowledge Objects by choosing the icon in your Document Window or the <attain ko> tag in the Tag Selector on the status bar.

Caution You can't edit the inserted Knowledge Objects in any standard Dreamweaver fashion, such as drag-and-drop or regular cut-and-paste. Instead, you have to use the special Knowledge Object commands installed in the Edit menu, or their keyboard shortcuts. These commands are covered later in this chapter.

Working with the Knowledge Object Property Inspectors

When a Knowledge Object is selected, a special Attain Property Inspector is displayed. The Knowledge Object Property Inspector, shown in Figure D-5, has three basic functions:

✦ Editing the current Knowledge Object

✦ Selecting other Knowledge Objects in the page

✦ Moving the selected Knowledge Object into or out of a positionable layer

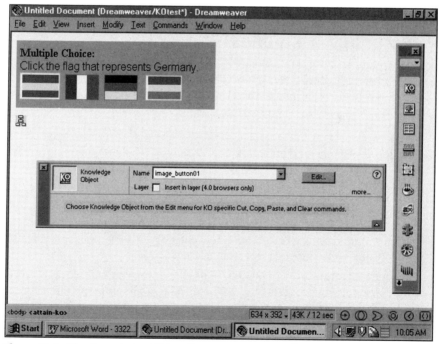

Figure D-5: The Knowledge Object Property Inspector allows you to quickly move from one Knowledge Object to another or to edit the current selection.

To modify an inserted Knowledge Object, select its icon or tag; then, from the Property Inspector, choose the Edit button. A dialog box similar to the Knowledge Object Wizard opens. The particular options displayed depend on the configuration of the Knowledge Object, but are generally a subset of the options offered when the object was constructed. The initial Knowledge Object Gallery and its accompanying template variations are not available.

If you have a fair number of Knowledge Objects on the current page, you can use the Property Inspector as a navigator of sorts between them. Select the Knowledge Object Property Inspector's drop-down list to reveal a dynamically generated list of the current Knowledge Objects. Select any one and the Document Window scrolls to its location, if necessary, and highlights the object.

Finally, the Knowledge Object Property Inspector is useful for moving the individual Knowledge Objects into — or out of — layers. In Dreamweaver 2 Attain, all Knowledge Objects offer you the option of placing the object in a layer at design time. The Property Inspector allows you to change your mind if you so choose by selecting or deselecting the Layer option. Once in a layer, the Knowledge Object can be positioned anywhere on the page; but, of course, layers can only be used in conjunction with 4.0 or later browsers.

Accessing the menus

Dreamweaver 2 Attain takes advantage of the new Command feature's facility for inserting menus wherever appropriate. After installing Dreamweaver 2 Attain, you'll find new menu additions in the File, Edit, and Insert menus. While the Insert menu option simply calls the Knowledge Object Wizard, the other new menu options are more extensive.

Under the File menu, you'll find a new Knowledge Object menu option with four submenu offerings:

✦ **Save to Gallery.** One of the easiest ways to add new options to the Knowledge Object Wizard is to customize an existing object and then use this command. Custom Knowledge Objects can be stored under an existing category (such as Multiple Choice) or under a new category. It's even possible to select and store an entire page as a Gallery item.

✦ **Create Pathware Frameset.** Pathware is Macromedia's Computer Managed Instruction program and can be used in conjunction with Dreamweaver 2 Attain to track user results. Pathware uses a two-frame frameset structure to display content in one frame and test results in another. The Create Pathware Frameset automatically builds this frameset and loads the current page in the content frame.

✦ **Copy Support Files.** If you're moving Dreamweaver 2 Attain files from one site to another, all you have to do is save the HTML page and then execute this command. All of your dependent files, such as graphics and scripts, are copied to the current folder. This command is also used with the next command for updating previous versions of Dreamweaver Attain files.

✦ **Convert to DW2 Attain.** Files created in the earlier version of Dreamweaver Attain cannot be edited in the current version without conversion. After you've loaded the Web page with the Knowledge Objects to convert and invoke this command, Dreamweaver stores your old files with a .bak file extension and the converted file under the original name. According to Macromedia, it's best to copy old scripts to a new folder and delete the Scripts folder before beginning the conversion.

Because of the structure of Knowledge Objects on the page, you can't use ordinary Cut, Copy, or Paste commands to move or delete them. Therefore, Dreamweaver 2 Attain includes five new commands under the Edit ⇨ Knowledge Object menu: Edit, Cut, Copy, Paste, and Clear. Like selecting the Edit button, choosing Edit ⇨ Knowledge Object ⇨ Edit opens the Wizard dialog box. The Knowledge Object–specific Cut, Copy, and Paste commands work exactly like the standard Dreamweaver ones, except the information is stored in a special temporary buffer instead of the usual clipboard. More importantly, the Knowledge Object edit commands are designed to gather all the required code so you can safely move any object. If you select Edit ⇨ Knowledge Object ⇨ Clear, all traces of the object's md source code is deleted. Be careful with this command: No confirmation is requested before the action is carried out.

Macromedia provides keyboard shortcuts for the Knowledge Object editing commands, which you'll find listed in Table D-1.

Table D-1
Knowledge Object Editing Shortcuts

Command	Windows	Macintosh
Edit	Ctrl-Alt-J	Command-Option-J
Cut	Ctrl-Alt-B	Command-Option-B
Copy	Ctrl-Alt-N	Command-Option-N
Paste	Ctrl-Alt-M	Command-Option-M
Clear	Ctrl-Alt-Q	Command-Option-Q

Surveying the Knowledge Objects

To better understand the capabilities of Dreamweaver 2 Attain, you need to know how the various Knowledge Objects are used. In all, there are eight different Knowledge Objects: Multiple Choice, Drag and Drop, Text Entry, Explore, Button, Timer, Slider, and Action Manager. All but the Action Manager insert an actual object or series of objects in your Web page — the Action Manager controls the interactions between Knowledge Objects on the same Web page.

Most of the Knowledge Objects have multiple templates to choose from and all vary in terms of which parameters are available. You'll find that some of the objects, such as the Timer and the Slider, are far more useful when working in conjunction with another object. By combining a variety of Knowledge Objects, your Web training pages can encompass a wide variety of models and simulations.

Multiple Choice Knowledge Object

The Multiple Choice Knowledge Object encompasses all types of choice questions, not just the traditional pop-quiz type of text questions. There are four templates for this object:

+ **Graphic** — Displays images for choices with an optional text line.

+ **Radio buttons** — Allows one answer to be chosen from a group of possibilities.

+ **True/False** — Permits an answer to be one of two possibilities.

+ **Check boxes** — Lets the user select any number of answers from a group of possibilities.

All the options allow the designer to specify the text of the question during object setup. You can alter the font face, size, and color — or specify a style — from the Document Window.

Drag and Drop Knowledge Object

Computer-based training can be used to simulate the assembly of components or to demonstrate knowledge of the relationship of one object to another. The Drag and Drop Knowledge Object (shown in Figure D-6) allows the user to move one on-screen item and drop it on another. The graphics specified can appear to fit together or lay on top of one another.

Dreamweaver 2 Attain ships with a variety of Drag and Drop Knowledge Object templates:

+ **One object to two targets, in two steps.** Used to demonstrate two-phased operations.

+ **One object to target, with two steps and one distracter.** Similar to the previous template, except the second step has one correct and one incorrect target.

+ **One object to multiple targets.** Used to demonstrate that the object can be associated with any of the on-screen targets.

+ **One object to many, many to one matching.** Uses four draggable items on-screen; the first object can be dropped on any of the other three items, each of which can in turn be dropped on the first object.

+ **One object to one, two ways.** Provides two draggable objects, each of which can be a target for the other.

✦ **One to one matching.** Establishes a series of objects on the left and targets on the right, which must be correctly paired.

✦ **One to one both ways.** Places objects in pairs, and allows either object to be dropped on its pair.

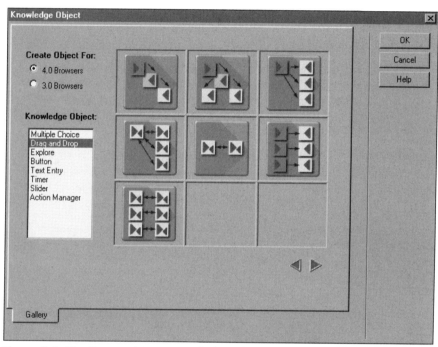

Figure D-6: The Drag and Drop Knowledge Object uses draggable layers that can snap to their targets.

The Drag and Drop Knowledge Object is accomplished using layers and, like Dreamweaver's standard Drag Layer behavior, the layer being dragged can be made to "snap" to specific coordinates when the correct target is approached. Moreover, if the wrong target is chosen, the dragged layer can snap back to its original position.

Explore Knowledge Object

The Explore Knowledge Object uses an image map and a series of hotspots to permit the user to "explore" the on-screen graphic. A click in a particular area — or on a certain part — generates a specific response, which could take the form of a pop-up message or a jump to another URL. Any of the available Dreamweaver behaviors can be attached to a defined hotspot by using the Action Manager tab of the Explore Knowledge Object.

Two templates are available for the Explore Knowledge Object:

✦ **Hotspots at various locations.** Five different hotspots are initially identified, although these can be customized to represent any graphic.

✦ **Hotspots in quadrants.** Use this template when you want to divide an image into four equal areas that cover the entire graphic.

Button Knowledge Object

The Button Knowledge Object is generally used in conjunction with other Knowledge Objects on the page to represent selections or choices. One button, when selected, could initiate a series of actions with another button; clicking a button, for example, could start or stop a timer. One bank of buttons could activate another bank of buttons as well.

Although there is only one template for the Button Knowledge Object — an on/off type switch — Dreamweaver 2 Attain includes nine different appearances from which to choose, as shown in Figure D-7. The buttons can be set to highlight like a rollover and/or be initially deactivated, if desired.

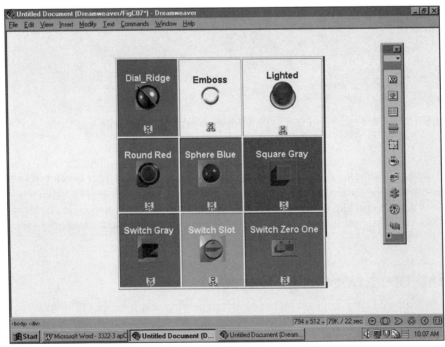

Figure D-7: Choose from any of the nine different types of buttons included with the Button Knowledge Object.

Text Entry Knowledge Object

While multiple-choice and true/false questions are often used to handle text-based questions, sometimes you want to test a user's retention. The Text Entry Knowledge Object allows you to request information to be keyed in by the user, which can then be judged as correct by comparing the input to a specified list of possible answers. You can also use the Text Entry Knowledge Object to request a user ID and password.

The three templates for the Text Entry Knowledge Object are as follows:

✦ Single line of text

✦ Multiple lines of text

✦ Single line of hidden (password) text

Timer Knowledge Object

With the Timer Knowledge Object, questions can be judged incorrect if the answer is not chosen within the time limit. An on-screen timer — such as an hourglass, a clap board, or a set of rising bars — can visually mark off seconds or be used as a countdown. Specific triggers can be set at any point in the timeline to activate behaviors such as a pop-up message or a custom function. The two templates for the Timer Knowledge Object allow you to easily choose a count up or count down scenario.

Slider Knowledge Object

The Slider Knowledge Object is similar to the Button Knowledge Object in that it is generally used with other Knowledge Objects on the page. However, whereas a Button is used to represent a binary set of values, a Slider is used to show a linear range of values. Dreamweaver 2 Attain includes almost 20 different slider appearances from which to choose; generally, one type of slider is offered in both a horizontal and vertical format. Like the Timer, the Slider Knowledge Object can trigger behaviors at specified points.

You have two Slider Knowledge Object templates to choose from:

✦ **Range of values.** Actions are triggered when the slider is moved anywhere within a set range of values.

✦ **Specific values.** Actions are triggered when the slider is moved to specific values within a specified range.

Action Manager Knowledge Object

The Action Manager Knowledge Object is used to coordinate information from the various Knowledge Objects on a given page, whether it is to send all the answers to a database or to switch the interactions from a tutorial to a test. Bear in mind that the Action Manager Knowledge Object is different from the Action Manager panel found in the wizard, which is used to control a single Knowledge Object.

Generally, the Action Manager Object is placed first on the HTML page so that it is set up to interact with all Knowledge Objects that follow. Because all customization occurs within the Action Manager Object, it has only one template.

✦   ✦   ✦

Index

Continued

Continued

Continued

Continued

Continued

Continued

Continued

Continued

Continued

Continued

IDG Books Worldwide, Inc.
End-User License Agreement

<u>READ THIS.</u> You should carefully read these terms and conditions before opening the software packet(s) included with this book ("Book"). This is a license agreement ("Agreement") between you and IDG Books Worldwide, Inc. ("IDGB"). By opening the accompanying software packet(s), you acknowledge that you have read and accept the following terms and conditions. If you do not agree and do not want to be bound by such terms and conditions, promptly return the Book and the unopened software packet(s) to the place you obtained them for a full refund.

1. **<u>License Grant.</u>** IDGB grants to you (either an individual or entity) a nonexclusive license to use one copy of the enclosed software program(s) (collectively, the "Software") solely for your own personal or business purposes on a single computer (whether a standard computer or a workstation component of a multiuser network). The Software is in use on a computer when it is loaded into temporary memory (RAM) or installed into permanent memory (hard disk, CD-ROM, or other storage device). IDGB reserves all rights not expressly granted herein.

2. **<u>Ownership.</u>** IDGB is the owner of all right, title, and interest, including copyright, in and to the compilation of the Software recorded on the disk(s) or CD-ROM ("Software Media"). Copyright to the individual programs recorded on the Software Media is owned by the author or other authorized copyright owner of each program. Ownership of the Software and all proprietary rights relating thereto remain with IDGB and its licensers.

3. **<u>Restrictions On Use and Transfer.</u>**

   (a) You may only (i) make one copy of the Software for backup or archival purposes, or (ii) transfer the Software to a single hard disk, provided that you keep the original for backup or archival purposes. You may not (i) rent or lease the Software, (ii) copy or reproduce the Software through a LAN or other network system or through any computer subscriber system or bulletin-board system, or (iii) modify, adapt, or create derivative works based on the Software.

   (b) You may not reverse engineer, decompile, or disassemble the Software. You may transfer the Software and user documentation on a permanent basis, provided that the transferee agrees to accept the terms and conditions of this Agreement and you retain no copies. If the Software is an update or has been updated, any transfer must include the most recent update and all prior versions.

4. **<u>Restrictions On Use of Individual Programs.</u>** You must follow the individual requirements and restrictions detailed for each individual program in Appendix D of this Book. These limitations are also contained in the individual

license agreements recorded on the Software Media. These limitations may include a requirement that after using the program for a specified period of time, the user must pay a registration fee or discontinue use. By opening the Software packet(s), you will be agreeing to abide by the licenses and restrictions for these individual programs that are detailed in Appendix D and on the Software Media. None of the material on this Software Media or listed in this Book may ever be redistributed, in original or modified form, for commercial purposes.

5. <u>**Limited Warranty**</u>.

    (a) IDGB warrants that the Software and Software Media are free from defects in materials and workmanship under normal use for a period of sixty (60) days from the date of purchase of this Book. If IDGB receives notification within the warranty period of defects in materials or workmanship, IDGB will replace the defective Software Media.

    (b) IDGB AND THE AUTHOR OF THE BOOK DISCLAIM ALL OTHER WARRANTIES, EXPRESS OR IMPLIED, INCLUDING WITHOUT LIMITATION IMPLIED WARRANTIES OF MERCHANTABILITY AND FITNESS FOR A PARTICULAR PURPOSE, WITH RESPECT TO THE SOFTWARE, THE PROGRAMS, THE SOURCE CODE CONTAINED THEREIN, AND/OR THE TECHNIQUES DESCRIBED IN THIS BOOK. IDGB DOES NOT WARRANT THAT THE FUNCTIONS CONTAINED IN THE SOFTWARE WILL MEET YOUR REQUIREMENTS OR THAT THE OPERATION OF THE SOFTWARE WILL BE ERROR FREE.

    (c) This limited warranty gives you specific legal rights, and you may have other rights that vary from jurisdiction to jurisdiction.

6. <u>**Remedies**</u>.

    (a) IDGB's entire liability and your exclusive remedy for defects in materials and workmanship shall be limited to replacement of the Software Media, which may be returned to IDGB with a copy of your receipt at the following address: Software Media Fulfillment Department, Attn.: *Dreamweaver 2 Bible*, IDG Books Worldwide, Inc., 7260 Shadeland Station, Ste. 100, Indianapolis, IN 46256, or call 1-800-762-2974. Please allow three to four weeks for delivery. This Limited Warranty is void if failure of the Software Media has resulted from accident, abuse, or misapplication. Any replacement Software Media will be warranted for the remainder of the original warranty period or thirty (30) days, whichever is longer.

    (b) In no event shall IDGB or the author be liable for any damages whatsoever (including without limitation damages for loss of business profits, business interruption, loss of business information, or any other pecuniary loss) arising from the use of or inability to use the Book or the Software, even if IDGB has been advised of the possibility of such damages.

(c) Because some jurisdictions do not allow the exclusion or limitation of liability for consequential or incidental damages, the above limitation or exclusion may not apply to you.

7. **U.S. Government Restricted Rights.** Use, duplication, or disclosure of the Software by the U.S. Government is subject to restrictions stated in paragraph (c)(1)(ii) of the Rights in Technical Data and Computer Software clause of DFARS 252.227-7013, and in subparagraphs (a) through (d) of the Commercial Computer — Restricted Rights clause at FAR 52.227-19, and in similar clauses in the NASA FAR supplement, when applicable.

8. **General.** This Agreement constitutes the entire understanding of the parties and revokes and supersedes all prior agreements, oral or written, between them and may not be modified or amended except in a writing signed by both parties hereto that specifically refers to this Agreement. This Agreement shall take precedence over any other documents that may be in conflict herewith. If any one or more provisions contained in this Agreement are held by any court or tribunal to be invalid, illegal, or otherwise unenforceable, each and every other provision shall remain in full force and effect.

Add Flash
To Your Website!

macromedia
FLASH 3
The Web Standard
for Vector Graphics
and Animation

Create beautiful, compact Web pages with shape morphing and transparency. Design fast vector graphics and animations—no programming required! Create interactive, animated interfaces,

navigation buttons, text, ad banners, logos, technical illustrations, and cartoons for every page of your Web site. Or integrate existing graphics from your favorite illustration program, like Macromedia FreeHand.

Flash files stream, or play as they download, so your content appears immediately, even over 28.8 modems. Deliver the content your audience wants the way they want it through

an ActiveX control, Shockwave Flash plug-in, GIF animation, or Java. Flash 3 gives you worry-free playback in any browser!

For more information, visit **www.macromedia.com/flash.** To upgrade or order in the U.S. and Canada, call **800 457 1774.** For the name of a reseller near you, call **800 326 2128.**

macromedia®
add life to the web

The Solution for Professional Web Graphics Design and Production

Fireworks is the first graphics production tool to overcome the specific challenges facing Web graphic designers and producers. With just one application, you can now design, optimize, and integrate fully-editable Web graphics, animations, and comps. And, since Fireworks exports clean, compact HTML code, you can use it in conjunction with your favorite HTML editor to create dynamic Web sites.

Design editable Web graphics, animations, and Web comps in an instant.

Optimize the Web graphics workflow to meet the demands of constant edits, updates, and changes.

Create interactive rollovers and buttons that integrate with your HTML editor.

For more information, visit **http://www.macromedia.com/software/fireworks**.
To purchase Fireworks, please visit **http://www.macromedia.com/software/fireworks/buy/**.
Or call your favorite Macromedia reseller or Macromedia directly at **800 457 1774**.

macromedia®
add life to the web

my2cents.idgbooks.com

Register This Book — And Win!

Visit **http://my2cents.idgbooks.com** to register this book and we'll automatically enter you in our fantastic monthly prize giveaway. It's also your opportunity to give us feedback: let us know what you thought of this book and how you would like to see other topics covered.

Discover IDG Books Online!

The IDG Books Online Web site is your online resource for tackling technology — at home and at the office. Frequently updated, the IDG Books Online Web site features exclusive software, insider information, online books, and live events!

10 Productive & Career-Enhancing Things You Can Do at www.idgbooks.com

- Nab source code for your own programming projects.
- Download software.
- Read Web exclusives: special articles and book excerpts by IDG Books Worldwide authors.
- Take advantage of resources to help you advance your career as a Novell or Microsoft professional.
- Buy IDG Books Worldwide titles or find a convenient bookstore that carries them.
- Register your book and win a prize.
- Chat live online with authors.
- Sign up for regular e-mail updates about our latest books.
- Suggest a book you'd like to read or write.
- Give us your 2¢ about our books and about our Web site.

You say you're not on the Web yet? It's easy to get started with IDG Books' *Discover the Internet*, available at local retailers everywhere.

CD-ROM Installation Instructions

The *Dreamweaver 2 Bible* CD-ROM contains a trial version of Dreamweaver as well as a full complement of auxiliary files such as Dreamweaver Objects and Behaviors.

Accessing the Programs on the CD-ROM

Only two files, the Dreamweaver trial program and the Beatnik player, are compressed. Double-click these files to begin the installation procedure (Dreamweaver installation instructions are listed below). All other files on the CD-ROM are uncompressed and can simply be copied from the CD-ROM to your system by using your file manager.

The file structure of the CD-ROM replicates the structure that Dreamweaver sets up when it is installed. For example, objects found in the Dreamweaver\Configuration\ Objects folder are located in both the CD-ROM and the installed program.

For a detailed synopsis of the CD-ROM contents, see Appendix D, "What's on the CD-ROM."

Installing Dreamweaver

To install Dreamweaver on your Windows system, follow these steps:

1. Insert the Dreamweaver Bible CD-ROM into your CD-ROM drive.
2. Double-click the Dreamweaver.exe file to unpack it and begin the installation process.
3. Follow the onscreen instructions. Accept the default options for program location.

Changing the Windows Read-Only Attribute

You may not be able to access files on the CD-ROM after you copy the files to your computer. After you copy or move the entire contents of the CD-ROM to your hard disk or another storage medium (such as a Zip disk), you may get the following error message when you attempt to open a file with its associated application:

```
[Application] is unable to open the [file]. Please make sure
the drive and file are writable.
```

Windows sees all files on a CD-ROM drive as *read-only*. This normally makes sense because a CD-ROM is a read-only medium — that is, you can't write data back to the CD-ROM.

However, when you copy a file from a CD-ROM to your hard disk or to a Zip disk, Windows doesn't automatically change the file attribute from read-only to writable.

Installation software normally takes care of this chore for you, but in this case, since the files are intended to be manually copied to your disk, you have to change the file attribute yourself. Luckily, it's easy — just follow these steps:

1. Click the Start menu button.
2. Select Programs.
3. Choose Windows Explorer.
4. Highlight the file name(s) on the hard disk or Zip disk.
5. Right-click the highlighted file name(s) to display a pop-up menu.
6. Select Properties to display the Properties dialog.
7. Click the Read-only option so that it is no longer checked.
8. Click the OK button.

You should now be able to use the file(s) with the specific application without getting the annoying error message.